The **Contemporary** Reader

EIGHTH EDITION

Gary Goshgarian

NORTHEASTERN UNIVERSITY

PEARSON
Longman

New York Boston San Francisco
London Toronto Sydney Tokyo Singapore Madrid
Mexico City Munich Paris Cape Town Hong Kong Montreal

Senior Vice President and Publisher: Joseph Opiela
Senior Acquisitions Editor: Lynn M. Huddon
Development Manager: Janet Lanphier
Development Editor: Katharine Glynn
Marketing Manager: Deborah Murphy
Senior Supplements Editor: Donna Campion
Media Supplements Editor: Nancy Garcia
Production Manager: Charles Annis
Project Coordination, Text Design, and Electronic Page Makeup: Nesbitt Graphics, Inc.
Cover Design Manager: Wendy Ann Fredericks
Cover Designer: Maria Ilardi
Cover Photos: Clockwise from top, left: Scott Gries/Getty Images; Jeff Gross/Getty Images;
    Stephanie Rausser/Taxi/Getty Images; David McNew/Getty Images; Evan Agostini/Getty
    Images; and Michael Shay/Taxi/Getty Images.
Photo Researcher: Photosearch, Inc.
Manufacturing Buyer: Lucy Hebard
Printer and Binder: R.R. Donnelley & Sons Co.
Cover Printer: Coral Graphic Services

For permission to use copyrighted material, grateful acknowledgement is made to the copyright holders on pages 539–542, which are hereby made part of this copyright page.

Library of Congress Cataloging-in-Publication Data
The contemporary reader / [edited by] Gary Goshgarian.—8th ed.
      p. cm.
    Includes bibliographical references and index.
    ISBN 0-321-20782-3 (student copy)—ISBN 0-321-24508-3 (p-copy)
    1. College readers. 2. English language—Rhetoric—Problems, exercises, etc.
3. Report writing—Problems, exercises, etc. I. Goshgarian, Gary.
PE1417.C6523 2005
808'.0427—dc22
                                                                          2004014218

Please visit us at http://www.ablongman.com/goshgarian.

ISBN 0-321-20782-3

6 7 8 9 10—DOC—07 06

Contents

Introduction: How to Read and Write Critically   1

---

1   Fashion and Flesh: The Images We Project   43

Never Too Buff   45
John Cloud

"New studies reveal that something awful has happened to American men over the past few decades. They have become obsessed with their bodies."

What I Think About the Fashion World   50
Liz Jones

"We decided to publish two covers for the same edition [of *Marie Claire*]—one featuring Sophie Dahl, a size 12; the other, Pamela Anderson, a minute size 6—and we asked readers to chose . . . You would think that we had declared war."

I'm So Fat (NEDA advertisement)   56

Weighing In   58
Sandra Hurtes

"After watching the Academy Awards I decided to go off my diet. Looking at actresses who earn enough money to feed entire nations, yet appear emaciated and in desperate need of a good meal, sent me charging to the fridge."

My Hips, My Caderas   61
Alisa Valdes

"In Spanish, the word for hips is *caderas*—a broad term used to denote everything a real woman carries from her waist to her thighs, and the bigger, the better. In English, hips are something women try to be rid of."

Scar   64
Cythia Audet

"The mark on my face made me who I am."

The Skinny on Small   67
Diane Sepanski

"By the tender age of thirteen, I was already hoofing high heels. I already knew I was short. And I knew I didn't like it."

The Bald Individualist   71
Ptolemy Tompkins

"As a teenager, I shaved my head to find myself. But with nose rings and tattoos routine, what's left for today's teenagers?"

RESEARCH ISSUE

6 Making the Grade: Education Today   319

in class, show that women are still losing. The problem is not others, the problem is us."

The New Sexual Stone Age   386
Andre Mayer

"Outmoded notions about the roles of men and women are relaxing; except, that is, in pop music, where quite the opposite is true. . . . We've returned to an age of rampant chauvinism, where men swagger about in a testosterone rage and women are reduced to sexual ornaments."

Three Cheers for Patriarchy!   390
Christine Rosen

Can patriarchy be as bad as some would have us believe?

VIEWPOINTS   ▶ **Revisionist Feminism: A Dialogue   395**
Susan Faludi and Karen Lehrman

"Dear Karen, I enter into this conversation with you about feminism with some misgivings. Not because I don't want to talk to you. It is just that I suspect it will be like a phone conversation where the connection's so bad neither party can hear the other through the static."

RESEARCH ISSUE   **An Identity Reduced to a Burka   403**
Semeen Issa and Laila Al-Marayati

"Like the differences in our clothing from one region to another, Muslim women are diverse. Stereotypical assumptions about Muslim women are as inaccurate as the assumption that all American women are personified by the bikini-clad cast of *Baywatch*."

---

8   Sports Culture: Not Just a Game   407

Unpaid Professionals   409
Andrew Zimbalist

The stakes are high: the TV money pumping up college basketball just keeps getting bigger. But is it shortchanging the athletes?

A Whole New Ball Game?   417
Skip Rozin, with Susan Zegel

"A glorious autumn day. School colors flying. Bands blaring fight songs. Cheerleaders in skimpy skirts kicking up their heels. Stands vibrating from the stomping feet of fans. Isn't this what college is all about? Er . . . not according to a killjoy named Gordon Gee."

Sports Centered   424
Jay Weiner

Our obsession has ruined the game. How can we save it?

Rhetorical Contents

PERSUASION AND ARGUMENT
Appealing to Reason and Emotion

HUMOR AND SATIRE
Making Us Laugh While We Think

Preface

Like its predecessors, the eighth edition of *The Contemporary Reader* is almost an entirely new book. The nature of the subject matter covered necessitates constant updating to keep abreast of trends in popular culture, media, and society. However, despite such change, the book's foundation remains the same: It continues to provide a collection of well-written, thought-provoking readings that students can relate to—readings that stimulate classroom discussion, critical thinking, and writing. The new edition includes five completely new chapter topics. The other five topics that were kept, as a result of overwhelming approval from instructors using the last edition, contain many new readings and visuals. We have reshaped several of the chapters, repeated from the seventh edition, to provide a stronger focus on contemporary issues, again in response to reviewer feedback.

The Contemporary Reader, eighth edition, is contemporary in more than just the selections. The introduction includes strategies for critical writing. Continuing this theme throughout the book, the apparatus includes the latest and most effective rhetorical theory and practice. Preceding each reading is a **Critical Thinking** question that helps orient the student to the topic and the reading. Directly following each reading is a **Freewriting Assignment**, designed to promote the flow of impressions and ideas about the article. Where appropriate, we have included a directional cue in italics before certain writing questions, such as "personal narrative," or "research and analysis" to help students focus their critical writing. **Viewpoints** articles continue to be a feature of this edition, in which authors explore different aspects of the same issue.

New Chapter Topics

Due to popular response to the last edition, we have repeated several of the chapter topics featured in the preceding volume. However, while some topics are featured again, we have selected new readings to accompany these popular themes. We have also introduced a few entirely new chapter themes (featured in boldface below).

1. Fashion and Flesh: The Images We Project
2. Advertising: Wanting It, Selling It
3. Television: For Better or for Worse
4. The Family in Flux: Love and Marriage

5. Humans Inc.: Cloning and Our Genetic Future
6. **Making the Grade: Education Today**
7. **Gender Perceptions: Has Anything Changed?**
8. Sports Culture: Not Just a Game
9. **Stereotyping and Profiling: Looking Beyond Race**
10. **The American Experience: One Nation, Many Faces**

These themes were chosen to reflect a wide spectrum of issues that affect all of us. Most importantly, they capture some of the conflicts and paradoxes that make our culture unique. From fashion and advertising to television and sports, ours is a culture caught in conflicts. We are a people who crave the modern, yet long for nostalgia. We are as much a society steeped in traditional values and identities as we are one that redefines itself in response to trends and subcultures.

A Closer Look at Chapter Themes

The ten thematic chapters are organized to progress from the world of popular culture to the individual's place in it, ending with a look at the issues that face the next generation.

The first three chapters focus on the visual forces in our popular culture that help forge our behavior—areas that influence us the most. Chapter 1, for instance, examines how caught up we can be in finding the right look to define ourselves and the role of body image in our social and personal consciousness. Chapter 2 explores how advertising so craftily capitalizes on our fantasies—including those previewed in Chapter 1. Chapter 3 considers the positive and negative aspects of television, its role in our lives, and its influence on how we think and how its power can sway young minds. Chapter 4 examines the redefinition of the American family unit, especially the role of marriage in contemporary society.

The next four chapters focus on very disparate, but timely issues. Chapter 5 considers the ways in which new technology is forcing us to rethink what it means to be human. Chapter 6 takes a close look at the state of education today and some issues facing America's schools. And Chapter 7 explores how we perceive gender in our society—from how men are portrayed on television to how women are referred to in music lyrics. Chapter 8 takes a hard look at college sports and some of the controversial issues connected with collegiate athletics.

The last two chapters address multicultural subjects. Chapter 9 discusses the controversial issues of racial profiling and stereotyping. Finally, Chapter 10 revisits the concept of the great American melting pot as we struggle to collaborate as one nation comprised of many different peoples.

Variety of Readings

In addition to extensively revising the chapter themes, we include many different types of readings. Expository communication comes in all shapes and models. This book includes newspaper stories, editorials, political cartoons, advertisements, academic essays, magazine articles, television interviews, Internet articles from "e-zines," student essays, humor columns, and a lot more. Students will read academic articles, personal narratives, objective essays, position papers, political arguments, and research reports.

New Advertisements

The chapter on advertising, one of the most popular in previous editions, has been updated with new advertisements. Each ad is accompanied by specific questions to help students closely analyze how advertising—and the particular ad at issue—affects us. The questions should spark lively class discussion about the art and craft of advertising. Beyond that, they encourage students to increase their "visual literacy" and critical thinking powers by closely focusing on particular print ads and making new associations and discoveries.

Viewpoints

The new **Viewpoints** articles bring the traditional "pro/con" debates to a more focused level. Viewpoints articles aim to help students explore the different sides of a focused issue, such as body stereotyping, human cloning, or a particular aspect of advertising. The questions following these readings aim to help students consider multiple sides of an issue and move toward a collaborative discussion rather than a heated debate.

Research Issues

New to this edition is the **Research Issue** reading included at the end of each chapter. Each Research Issue encourages students to explore new avenues of thinking or to pursue a topic in greater depth outside the text. The apparatus features critical thinking questions designed to help students analyze the topic. Many include Web sites to help students begin their research on the issue online. The book's Companion Website provides additional resources for students to continue their research efforts.

New Rhetorical Features

New Introduction to Critical Reading *and* Writing

The premise of the new edition of *The Contemporary Reader* is that effective writing grows out of effective thinking, and effective thinking grows out of thoughtful reading. We intertwine these three concepts in the new introduction featuring sections that discuss both critical reading *and* critical writing. The introductionary chapter illustrates the process in a detailed sample analysis of John Leo's essay, "Now Cut That Out!" The sample analysis demonstrates systematic approaches to critical reading and then continues this exploration into the critical writing section.

Critical Thinking Considerations

Following the introduction of each essay is a **Critical Thinking** question that helps guide the student before and during the actual reading process. These questions also connect to the chapter's overall theme.

Freewriting Assignment

The **Freewriting Assignment** is designed to promote the free-flow of thoughts, ideas, and impressions students may have immediately upon finishing the essay. Freewriting assignments may direct students to write about a particular issue or concept raised by the article or ask students to write about their impressions of it. These assignments can be part of a journal-keeping project throughout the course, or a private exercise by the student.

Group Projects

Active communities work together—accepting multiple points of view and interacting with different identities, values, ideas, races, social outlooks, ethnicities, and educational backgrounds. In an effort to develop students' skill for working and learning together and to expose them to different points of view, **Group Projects** accompany each reading. These exercises emphasize collaborative research, topic exploration, group writing and problem solving. They also may encourage students to incorporate resources outside the classroom—to search the Internet, explore pop-culture sources, interview people, and conduct observations—to explore further what they have read.

Supplements

Companion Website

The updated Companion Website (http://www.ablongman.com/goshgarian) prepared by Kathryn Goodfellow, includes links to additional online readings for each chapter, thematic questions, a guide to researching popular culture issues, and much more.

Instructor's Manual

The Instructor's Manual includes suggested responses to the critical reading questions in the text as well as offers ideas for directing class discussion and eliciting student response.

Acknowledgments

Many people behind the scenes deserve much acknowledgment and gratitude. It would be impossible to thank all of them, but there are some for whose help I am particularly grateful. First, I would like to thank all the instructors and students who used the first seven editions of *The Contemporary Reader.* Their continued support has made this latest edition possible. Also, I would like to thank those instructors who spent hours answering lengthy questionnaires on the effectiveness of the essays and who supplied many helpful comments and suggestions in the preparation of this new edition. They are Cathy Gorvine, Delgado Community College; Erin Herberg, Rowan University; Robert Honeman, West Virginia Northern Community College; Debra Matier, College of Southern Idaho; Kate Maurer, University of Minnesota–Duluth; and Diane S. Thompson, Harrisburg Area Community College.

A very special thanks goes to Kathryn Goodfellow for her assistance in locating articles and writing the study apparatus, as well as all her work on the Companion Website. I would also like to thank Danise Cavallaro for her help in securing per-missions for the readings featured in this volume. I am also grateful to Charles O'Neill for updating his popular essay "The Language of Advertising" especially for this edition.

Finally, my thanks to the people of Longman Publishers, especially Lynn Hud-don and Katharine Glynn, who helped conceptualize this edition as its editors, and Stacy Dorgan, for her work on the Companion Website.

Gary Goshgarian

Introduction
How to Read and Write Critically

What Is Critical Thinking?

Whenever you read a magazine article, newspaper editorial, or a piece of advertising and find yourself questioning the author's claims, you are exercising the basics of critical reading. You are looking beneath the surface of words and thinking about their meaning and significance. And, subconsciously, you are asking the authors some of the following questions:

- What did you mean by that?
- Can you back up that statement?
- How do you define that term?
- How did you draw that conclusion?
- Do all the experts agree?
- Is this evidence dated?
- What is your point?
- Why do I need to know this?
- Where did you get your data?

You are also making some internal statements:

- That isn't true.
- You are contradicting yourself.
- I see your point, but I don't agree because. . . .
- That's a poor choice of words.
- You are jumping to conclusions.
- Good point. I never thought of that.
- That was nicely stated.
- This is an extreme view.

Whether conscious or unconscious, such responses indicate that you are thinking critically about what you read. You are weighing claims, asking for definitions, evaluating information, looking for proof, questioning assumptions, and making judgments. In short, you are processing another person's words, rather than just accepting them at face value.

Why Read Critically?

When you read critically, you think critically. Instead of blindly accepting what is written on a page, you begin to separate yourself from the text and decide for yourself what is or is not important, logical, or right. And you do so because you bring to your reading your own perspective, experience, education, and personal values, as well as your powers of comprehension and analysis.

Critical reading is an active process of discovery. You discover an author's view on a subject, you enter into a dialogue with the author, you discover the strengths and weaknesses of the author's thesis or argument, and you decide if you agree or disagree with the author's views. The result is that you have a better understanding of the issue and the author. By questioning and analyzing what the author says with respect to other experiences or views of the issue—including your own—you actively enter into a dialogue or a debate and seek the truth on your own.

In reality, we understand truth and meaning through interplay. Experience teaches us that knowledge and truth are not static entities but the by-products of struggle and dialogue—of asking tough questions. We witness this phenomenon all the time, recreated in the media through dialogue and conflict. And we recognize it as a force of social change. Consider, for example, how, since the 1950s, our culture has changed its attitudes concerning race, and its concepts of success, kinship, social groups, and class. Perhaps the most obvious example regards gender: Were it not for the fact that rigid old conventions have been questioned, most women would still be bound to the laundry and the kitchen stove.

The point is that critical reading is an active and reactive process that sharpens your focus on a subject and your ability to absorb information and ideas and at the same time encourages you to question accepted norms, views, and myths. And that is both healthy and laudable, for it is the basis of social evolution.

Critical reading also helps you become a better writer, because critical reading is the first step to critical writing. Good writers look at one another's writing the way architects look at a house: They study the fine details and how those details connect and create the whole. Likewise, they consider the particular slants and strategies of appeal. Good writers always have a clear sense of their audience—their reader's racial makeup, gender, and educational background; their political and/or religious persuasions; their values, prejudices, and assumptions about life; and so forth. Knowing your audience helps you to determine nearly every aspect of the writing process: the kind of language to use, the writing style (casual or formal, humorous or serious, technical or philosophical), the particular slant to take (appealing to the reader's reason, emotions, or ethics, or a combination of these), what emphasis to give the essay, the type of evidence to offer, and the kinds of authorities to cite.

The better you become at analyzing and reacting to another's written work, the better you will analyze and react to your own. You will ask yourself questions such as the following: Is it logical? Do my points come across clearly? Are my examples solid enough? Is this the best wording? Is my conclusion persuasive? Do I have a clear sense of my audience? What strategy did I take—an appeal to logic, emotions, or ethics? In short, critical reading will help you to evaluate your own writing, thereby making you both a better reader and a better writer. Although you may already employ many strategies of critical reading, the following text presents some techniques to make you an even better critical reader.

How to Read Critically

To help you improve your critical reading, use these six proven basic steps:

- Keep a journal on what you read.
- Annotate what you read.
- Outline what you read.
- Summarize what you read.
- Question what you read.
- Analyze what you read.

To demonstrate just how these techniques work, we will apply each of them to a sample essay: "Now Cut That Out!" by John Leo, appearing in the June 30, 2003, issue of *U.S. News and World Report*. This piece works well because, like all of the pieces in this book, it addresses a contemporary issue and presents opportunities for debate.

Sample Essay for Analysis

Now Cut That Out!
John Leo

1   Which of the following stories would be too biased for schools to allow on tests? (1) Overcoming daunting obstacles, a blind man climbs Mount McKinley; (2) Dinosaurs roam the Earth in prehistoric times; (3) An Asian-American girl, whose mother is a professor, plays checkers with her grandfather and brings him pizza.

2   As you probably guessed, all three stories are deeply biased. (1) Emphasis on a "daunting" climb implies that blindness is some sort of disability, when it should be viewed as just another personal attribute, like hair color. Besides, mountain-climbing stories are examples of "regional bias," unfair to readers who live in deserts, cities, and rural areas. (2) Dinosaurs are a no-no—they imply acceptance of evolutionary theory. (3) Making the girl's mother a professor perpetuates the "model minority" myth that stereotypes Asian-Americans. Older people must not be shown playing checkers. They should be up on the roof fixing shingles or doing something vigorous. And pizza is a junk food. Kids may eat it—but not in a school story.

3   That's what's going on in schools these days. Diane Ravitch's new book, *The Language Police*, documents "an intricate set of rules" applied to test questions as well as textbooks. A historian of education who served as an assistant secretary of education for the first President Bush, Ravitch offers many eye-catching cases of subjects vetoed: peanuts as a good snack (some children are allergic), owls (taboo in Navajo culture), and the palaces of ancient Egypt (elitist).

4   Back in the 1980s and 1990s, lots of us chuckled at the spread of the "sensitivity" industry in schools. Words were removed from tests and books lest they hurt someone's feelings, harm the classroom effort, or impair morals. Most of us assumed that this was a fad that would soon disappear as grown-ups in education exerted the rule of reason.

5   But ridicule had little effect, and grown-ups either converted to the sensitivity ethic or looked the other way. Textbook publishers, with millions of dollars at stake, learned to insulate themselves from criticism by caving in to all objections and writing craven "guidelines" to make sure authors would cave, too.

6   No, no, no! Ravitch warns that these guidelines amount to a full-blown form of "censorship at the source" in schools and "something important and dangerous" that few people know about. She blames both the religious right and the multicultural-feminist left. The right objects to evolution, magic and witchcraft, gambling, nudity, suicide, drug use, and stories about disobedient children. The left objects to "sexist" fairy tales, Huckleberry Finn, religion, smoking, junk food, guns and knives, and what some guidelines call "activities stereotyping" (blacks as athletes, men playing sports or working with tools, women cooking or caring for children).

7   What started out as a sensible suggestion—don't always show women as homemakers or minorities in low-level jobs—developed into hard reverse stereotypes (women must not be shown in the home, maids can't be black). "In the ideal world of education-think," Ravitch writes, "women would be breadwinners, African-Americans would be academics, Asian-Americans would be athletes and no one would be a wife or a mother."

8   Whites are a group, perhaps the only group, not protected by smothering sensitivity. This follows multicultural dogma. One set of guidelines (McGraw-Hill) "express[es] barely concealed rage against people of European ancestry" as "uniquely responsible for bigotry and exploitation," Ravitch notes.

9   What can be done? Ravitch recommends eliminating the current system in which 22 states adopt textbooks for all their schools. She says it results in cartel-like behavior that allows extremists to manipulate textbook requirements, particularly in the two big states that matter most—California and Texas. Opening up the market, she thinks, would free teachers to choose biographies, histories, or anthologies, rather than sensitivity-laden textbooks.

10   Panels that analyze tests and texts should include teachers of the subjects, not just diversity specialists, Ravitch says. She insists we need better-educated teachers and an end to secrecy about sensitivity: State education officials must put bias and sensitivity reviews on the Internet, listing the reasons that passages and test items were rejected.

11   Unsurprisingly, *The Language Police* has gotten the cold shoulder from our education establishment, which usually limits discussion to three topics: promoting di-

versity, reducing classroom size, and increasing funding. Ravitch speaks for parents more concerned about something else: substituting censorship and propaganda for actual learning.

Keep a Journal on What You Read

Unlike writing an essay or a paper, journal writing is a personal exploration in which you develop your own ideas without set rules. It is a process of recording impressions and exploring feelings and ideas. Journal writing is a freewriting exercise in which you express yourself without restrictions and without judgment. You do not have to worry about breaking any rules—because in a journal, anything goes.

Reserve a special notebook just for your journal—not one you use for class notes or homework. Also, date your entries and include the titles of the articles to which you are responding. Eventually, by the end of the semester, you should have a substantial number of pages to review, enabling you to see how your ideas and writing style have developed over time.

What do you include in your journal? Although it may serve as a means to understanding an essay, you are not required to write only about the essay itself. Perhaps the article reminds you of a personal experience. Maybe it triggered an opinion you did not know you had. Or perhaps you wish to explore a particular phrase or idea presented by the author.

Some students may find keeping a journal difficult because it is so personal. They may feel as if they are exposing their feelings too much. Or they may feel uncomfortable thinking that someone else—a teacher or another student—may read their writing. Such apprehensions should not prevent you from exploring your impressions and feelings. If you must turn in your journal to your teacher, do not include anything you do not want others to read. Consider keeping a more private journal for your own benefit.

Reprinted below is one student's journal entry on our sample essay:

John Leo's essay on Diane Ravitch's book helps support his personal opinion that "language police" are controlling the content of texts and tests in American schools and hurting students. Apparently, Ravitch feels that multicultural-feminists AND the religious right have distorted what material is presented in the classroom. The feminists and the religious right are demanding that the language used in textbooks and tests be "sensitive" and "unbiased."

Ravitch and Leo seem to think that the revisions made in the '80s and '90s have gone too far. At first, it seems as if Leo agrees that the original desire to be sensitive was a good idea, but he then agrees with Ravitch's opinion that the panels that decide what language to use on standardized tests have a cartel-like hold on our educational system. Leo often quotes Ravitch, and it is clear that he agrees with her. His fourth paragraph particularly reveals his position.

I think that both Ravitch and Leo are missing a very important point. Language can hurt. And it can influence how we think. They don't seem to acknowledge this. Maybe they have never experienced biased writing? I know from personal experience that it can affect students. I even remember stopping to think about how a question seemed biased on the SAT. I probably didn't need to waste my time thinking about that.

If language policing has gone to an extreme, like Leo says, there must be a happy middle, right?

Annotate What You Read

It's a good idea to underline (or highlight) key passages and make marginal notes when reading an essay. (If you do not own the publication in which the essay appears, or choose not to mark it up, make a photocopy of the piece and annotate that.) You should annotate on the second or third reading, once you have an understanding of the essay's general ideas.

There are no specific guidelines for annotation. Use whatever technique suits you best, but keep in mind that in annotating a piece of writing, you are engaging in a dialogue with the author. As in any meaningful dialogue, you hear things you may not have known—things that may be interesting and exciting to you, things with which you may agree or disagree, or things that give you cause to ponder. The other side of the dialogue, of course, is your response. In annotating a piece of writing, that response takes the form of underlining (or highlighting) key passages and jotting down comments in the margin. Such comments can take the form of full sentences or some shorthand codes. Sometimes "Why?" or "True" or "NO!" will be enough to help you respond to a writer's position or claim. If you come across a word or reference that is unfamiliar to you, underline or circle it. Once you have located the main thesis statement or claim, highlight or underline it and jot down "CLAIM" or "THESIS" in the margin.

On the following page is the Leo essay reproduced in its entirety with sample annotations.

Now Cut That Out!

John Leo

1 Which of the following stories would be too biased for schools to allow on tests? (1) Overcoming daunting obstacles, a blind man climbs Mount McKinley; (2) dinosaurs roam the Earth in prehistoric times; (3) an Asian-American girl, whose mother is a professor, plays checkers with her grandfather and brings him pizza.

Are these examples from a real test, or did Leo make them up?

2 As you probably guessed, all three stories are deeply biased. (1) Emphasis on a "daunting" climb implies that blindness is some sort of disability, when it should be viewed as just another personal attribute, like hair color. Besides, mountain-climbing stories are examples of "regional bias," unfair to readers who live in deserts, cities, and rural areas. (2) Dinosaurs are a no-no—they imply acceptance of evolutionary theory. (3) Making the girl's mother a professor perpetuates the "model minority" myth that stereotypes Asian-Americans. Older people must not be shown playing checkers. They should be up on the roof fixing shingles or doing something vigorous. And pizza is a junk food. Kids may eat it—but not in a school story.

Oh, come on!

Loose interpretation of evolutionary theory. Isn't evolutionary theory related to human's connection to apes? Look up this issue.

3 That's what's going on in schools these days. Diane Ravitch's new book, *The Language Police*, documents "an intricate set of rules" applied to test questions as well as textbooks. A historian of education who served as an assistant secretary of education for the first President Bush, Ravitch offers many eye-catching cases of subjects vetoed: peanuts as a good snack (some children are allergic), owls (taboo in Navajo culture), and the palaces of ancient Egypt (elitist).

Check out this book in university library.

Whose rules?

Who "vetoed"?

Why is this word in quotes?

4 Back in the 1980s and 1990s, lots of us chuckled at the spread of the "sensitivity" industry in schools. Words were removed from tests and books lest they hurt someone's feelings, harm the classroom effort, or impair morals. Most of us assumed that this was a fad that would

Well, many words did hurt—especially ones that were racist or sexist.

soon disappear as grown-ups in education exerted the rule of reason.

5   But ridicule had little effect, and grown-ups either converted to the sensitivity ethic or looked the other way. Textbook publishers, with millions of dollars at stake, learned to insulate themselves from criticism by caving in to all objections and writing craven "guidelines" to make sure authors would cave, too.

This is a sweeping generalization as to motivation of teachers and publishers.

look up

6   No, no, no! Ravitch warns that these guidelines amount to a full-blown form of "censorship at the source" in schools and "something important and dangerous" that few people know about. She blames both the religious right and the multicultural-feminist left. The right objects to evolution, magic and witchcraft, gambling, nudity, suicide, drug use, and stories about disobedient children. The left objects to "sexist" fairy tales, Huckleberry Finn, religion, smoking, junk food, guns and knives, and what some guidelines call "activities stereotyping" (blacks as athletes, men playing sports or working with tools, women cooking or caring for children).

Check source for context.

look up

Says who?

7   What started out as a sensible suggestion—don't always show women as homemakers or minorities in low-level jobs—developed into hard reverse stereotypes (women must not be shown in the home, maids can't be black). "In the ideal world of education-think," Ravitch writes, "women would be breadwinners, African-Americans would be academics, Asian-Americans would be athletes and no one would be a wife or a mother."

So author approves that changes were made?

What about white women?

8   Whites are a group, perhaps the only group, not protected by smothering sensitivity. This follows multicultural dogma. One set of guidelines (McGraw-Hill) "express[es] barely concealed rage against people of European ancestry" as "uniquely responsible for bigotry and exploitation," Ravitch notes.

What exactly is "multicultural dogma"?

Ravitch's interpretation of the guideline's tone?

9   What can be done? Ravitch recommends eliminating the current system in which 22 states adopt textbooks for all their schools. She says it results in cartel-like behavior that allows extremists to manipulate textbook requirements, particularly in the two big states that matter most—California and Texas. Opening up the market, she

She wants to overhaul the way 22 states choose their textbooks. Doesn't that go against what seems to be an approved consensus? What about the other 28 states that don't use such guidelines?

thinks, would free teachers to choose biographies, histories, or anthologies, rather than sensitivity-laden textbooks.

examples?

10   Panels that analyze tests and texts should include
teachers of the subjects, not just diversity specialists,
Ravitch says. She insists we need better-educated teachers and an end to secrecy about sensitivity: State education officials must put bias and sensitivity reviews on the
Internet, listing the reasons that passages and test items
were rejected.

They should be!
They aren't now?
Is this really true?

This is another
issue entirely.

11   Unsurprisingly, *The Language Police* has gotten the
cold shoulder from our education establishment, which
usually limits discussion to three topics: promoting diversity, reducing classroom size, and increasing funding.
Ravitch speaks for parents more concerned about something else: substituting censorship and propaganda for
actual learning.

Censorship, maybe.
But is Leo concerned
that presenting
blacks as academics
or women Asians
as athletes is
actually propaganda?

Outline What You Read

Briefly outlining an essay is a good way to see how writers structure their ideas.
When you physically diagram the thesis statement, claims, and supporting evidence,
you can better assess the quality of the writing and decide how convincing it is. You
may already be familiar with detailed, formal essay outlines in which structure is
broken down into main ideas and subsections. However, for our purposes, a brief
and concise breakdown of an essay's components will suffice. This is done by simply jotting down a one-sentence summary of each paragraph. Sometimes brief paragraphs elaborating the same point can be lumped together:

- Point 1
- Point 2
- Point 3
- Point 4
- Point 5
- Point 6, etc.

Such outlines may seem rather primitive, but they demonstrate how the various
parts of an essay are connected—that is, the organization and sequence of ideas.

Below is a sentence outline of "Now Cut That Out." It identifies the point(s) of
each paragraph in an unbiased way. The purpose of summarizing is to better understand the author's point and how this point is constructed.

POINT 1: The author provides three examples of stories that
would not appear on a standardized test because they may use insensitive or biased language.

POINT 2: Diane Ravitch has written a book titled The Language Police, in which she discusses the language used in school textbooks and tests.

POINT 3: The author notes that some people may have viewed the language "sensitivity" movement in schools during the 1980s and 1990s as a passing "fad." He states that instead of passing, the movement became entrenched in schools, and publishers followed suit in order to please their buyers.

POINT 4: Ravitch feels that the guidelines developed to encourage language sensitivity in textbooks and tests is a form of censorship. She claims that people who hold extreme viewpoints are controlling the content of school materials.

POINT 5: The author concedes that language sensitivity was based on a good idea, but that it has reached extremes.

POINT 6: Ravitch advocates eliminating the current system used by 22 states to adopt textbooks in order to loosen the "cartel-like" hold extremists have on the educational system.

POINT 7: Ravitch also supports the idea that textbook selection panels include teachers who use the adopted texts and test, and that the panel should publicly explain its reasons for using certain questions on tests while rejecting others.

POINT 8: The author concludes that Ravitch's observation "speaks for parents," while the education establishment focuses on other issues, including diversity, class size, and educational funding.

At this point, you should have a fairly solid grasp of the points expressed in the essay, and the author's position on the issue. This exercise prepares you to critically evaluate the essay.

Summarize What You Read

Summarizing is perhaps the most important technique to develop for understanding and evaluating what you read. This means reducing the essay to its main points. In your journal or notebook try to write a brief (about 100 words) synopsis of the reading in your own words. Note the claim or thesis of the discussion (or argument) and the chief supporting points. It is important to write these points down (rather than passively highlighting them with a pen or pencil), because the act of jotting down a summary helps you absorb the argument.

Now let us return to the sample essay. In the following paragraph we offer a summary of Leo's essay, mindful of using our own words rather than those of the author to avoid plagiarism. Again, you should approach this aspect of critical reading impartially—summary is not your opinion, that will come later. At times, it may be impossible to avoid using the author's own words in a summary; but if you do, remember to use quotation marks.

> In this essay, John Leo discusses a book by Diane Ravitch, The Language Police, in which she asserts that language sensitivity in textbooks and tests is controlled by extreme groups such as the "religious right" and the "multicultural-feminist left." These groups have, in turn, influenced the language publishers use in order to better appeal to the panels that select the textbooks. Leo and Ravitch are in agreement that this control is a form of censorship and must stop. Panels that choose textbooks and test questions should include teachers and should also explain the reasons behind language choices.

Although this paragraph seems to do a fairly good job of summarizing Leo's essay, it took us a few tries to get it down to under 100 words. So, do not be too discouraged when trying to summarize a reading on your own.

Question What You Read

Although we break down critical reading into discrete steps, these steps will naturally overlap in the actual process of reading and writing critically. In reading this essay you were simultaneously summarizing and evaluating Leo's points, perhaps adding your own ideas or even arguing with him. If something strikes you as particularly interesting or insightful, make a mental note of it. Likewise, if something strikes you the wrong way, argue back. For beginning writers, a good strategy is to convert that automatic mental response into actual note taking.

In your journal (or, as suggested below, in the margins of the text), question and challenge the writer. Jot down any points in the essay that do not measure up to your expectations or personal views. Note anything about which you are skeptical. Write down any questions you have about the claims, views, or evidence. If some point or conclusion seems forced or unfounded, record it and briefly explain why. The more skeptical and questioning you are, the better reader you are. Likewise, note what features of the essay impressed you—outstanding points, interesting wording, clever or amusing phrases or allusions, particular references, the general structure of the piece. Record what you learn from the reading and the aspects of the issue you would like to explore.

Of course, you may not feel qualified to pass judgment on an author's views, particularly if the author is a professional writer or expert on a particular subject. Sometimes the issue discussed might be too technical, or you may not feel informed enough to make critical evaluations. Sometimes a personal narrative may focus on experiences completely alien to you. Nonetheless, you are an intelligent person with the instincts to determine if the writing impresses you or if an argument is sound, logical, and convincing. What you can do in such instances—and another good habit to get into—is to think of other views on the issue. If you have read or heard of experiences different from those of the author, or arguments with the opposing views, jot them down. Similarly, if you agree with the author's view, highlight the parts of the essay with which you particularly identify.

Let us return to Leo's essay, which is, technically, an argument. Although it is theoretically possible to question or comment on every sentence in the piece, let us select a few key points that may have struck you, made you question, or made you want to respond. Refer to your point-by-point outline to assist you in this exercise.

PARAGRAPHS 1&2: While I understand Leo's point here with these examples, are they real examples from actual tests or ones Leo just made up to support his argument? If they are real, it would greatly support his position. However, these examples probably represent extreme illustrations of test questions. Furthermore, I wonder why certain adjectives are used at all. The stories could stand up on their own without the story being about a blind man, or an Asian American professor. Couldn't the story just be about a girl whose mother is a professor and who also plays a <u>game</u> with her grandfather? Why is omitting the adjectives so controversial anyway?

PARAGRAPH 3: Leo states that there is "an intricate set of rules" that Ravitch cites in her book. His essay would be strengthened if he cited these rules and their source. That way, we would have more hard evidence, rather than what seems to be opinion.

PARAGRAPH 4: In this paragraph, Leo states his own position on language sensitivity by admitting he is one of "us" who "chuckled" at the "sensitivity industry" in schools during the '80s and '90s. As such, he admits that he thought that the movement was frivolous (he calls it a "fad"). However, he seems to admit in paragraph 7 that it wasn't entirely a bad idea.

PARAGRAPH 6: Leo takes quotations from Ravitch's book to support his assertion that the language police are out of control. While it is good to quote sources, Ravitch herself seems questionable as a reliable source.

PARAGRAPHS 7 & 8: It seems as if Leo admits that at one time unbiased language was a good idea—"a sensible suggestion." And he may have a point if things have really swung to an extreme. But why is he so against the idea that blacks not be portrayed as maids, etc.? Who does it hurt? Maybe more importantly, who does it help? Leo's comment on whites being the only group not "protected" by the language police is revealing. Elsewhere in his essay, he comments on the "rule" that women cannot be shown in the home or as mothers. Well, what about women who are white? What Leo really meant to say here was "white males." Another point about paragraph 8 relates to the last sentence. Is this Ravitch's interpretation? Can she really interpret "barely concealed rage" in a set of guidelines prepared by a textbook company? Quoting this material would help the readers decide for themselves.

PARAGRAPHS 9 & 10: Leo relays Ravitch's suggestions for change, and he clearly endorses these changes. This helps his essay because it isn't just a long complaint; the essay actually advocates something. Whether these solutions are possible, or even necessary, is up to his reader.

PARAGRAPH 11: Most of Leo's concluding paragraph could be read in a neutral way. Educators aren't really reacting to Ravitch's book. Rather, they are responding to more pressing issues. Leo's final sentence might make the reader pause—while influencing language may seem like a form of censorship, does he really feel that depicting women as professionals, blacks as academics, and Asians as athletes are equal to propaganda?

Analyze What You Read

To analyze something means breaking it down into its components, examining those components closely while evaluating their significance, and determining how they relate as a whole. In part, you already did this by briefly outlining the essay. However, there is more. Analyzing what you read involves interpreting and evaluating the points of a discussion or argument as well as its presentation—that is, its language and structure. Ultimately, analyzing an essay after establishing its key points will help you understand what may not be evident at first. A close examination of the author's words takes you beneath the surface and sharpens your understanding of the issues at hand.

Although there is no set procedure for analyzing a piece of prose, there are some specific questions you should raise when reading an essay, particularly one that is trying to sway you to its view.

- What kind of audience is the author addressing?
- What are the author's assumptions?
- What are the author's purpose and intentions?
- How well does the author accomplish those purposes?
- How convincing is the evidence presented? Is it sufficient and specific? Relevant? Reliable and not dated? Slanted?
- What types of sources were used—personal experience, outside authorities, factual references, or statistical data?
- Did the author address opposing views on the issue?
- Is the perspective of the author persuasive?

Using the essay by Leo once more, let us apply these questions to his article.

What Kind of Audience Is the Author Addressing?

Before the first word is written, a good writer considers his or her audience—that is, their age group, gender, ethnic and racial makeup, educational background, and socioeconomic status. Writers also take into account the values, prejudices, and assumptions of their readers, as well as their readers' political and religious persuasions. Some writers, including several in this book, write for a "target" audience—readers who share the same interests, opinions, and prejudices. Other authors write for a "general" audience. Although general audiences consist of very different people with diversified backgrounds, expectations, and standards, think of them as the people who read *Time, Newsweek,* and your local newspaper. You can assume general audiences are relatively well informed about what is going on in the country, that they have a good comprehension of language and a sense of humor, and that they are willing to listen to new ideas.

Because Leo's essay appeared in his column in *U.S. News and World Report,* he is clearly writing for a "general" audience—an audience with an average age of

35, possessing a high school education and some college, politically middle of the road, and comprised of a vast racial and ethnic makeup. A close look tells us more about Leo's audience:

1. The language level suggests at least a high school education.

2. The references to attitudes in the 1980s and the concerns of parents suggest an older audience—certainly at least 30 years old.

3. The references to politics, academic and political movements, and panel policies for textbook selection imply that the readers are culturally informed.

4. The slant of Leo's remarks assumes a more conservative view toward educational trends, perhaps one opposed to the "new" trend of multiculturalism.

5. The language level addresses an audience which will see the absurdity of the language situation, and which does not presumably belong to the groups criticized by Leo.

What Are the Author's Assumptions?

Having a sense of the audience leads writers to certain assumptions. If a writer is addressing a general audience as is Leo, then he or she can assume certain levels of awareness about language and current events, certain values about education and morality, and certain nuances of an argument. After going through Leo's essay, the following conclusions might be drawn about the author:

1. Leo assumes that his readers have a basic understanding of the concept of political "right" and "left."

2. He assumes that his audience is as exasperated as he is that extreme groups are controlling the content of textbooks and test questions in public schools.

3. He assumes that his readers believe that the claims of these groups (the religious right and the multicultural-feminist left) are questionable.

4. He assumes that his readers have a basic understanding of multiculturalism, and suspect that these principles have gone too far.

5. He assumes his readers will agree that the issues the educational establishment are most concerned with—diversity, class size, and school funding—are not as important as stopping "censorship and propaganda" in schools.

What Are the Author's Purpose and Intentions?

A writer has a purpose in writing beyond wanting to show up in print. Sometimes it is simply the expression of how the writer feels about something; sometimes the intention is to convince others to see things in a different light; sometimes the purpose is to persuade readers to change their views or behavior. We might infer the following about Leo's intentions:

1. To alert people that extreme interest groups are controlling the content of textbooks and tests in American schools.

2. To urge people to demand changes in their schools and in the way books and material are selected, especially in the 22 states that currently use this system.

3. To raise public awareness that apathy toward this trend is detrimental to education and harmful to students.

4. To urge people to stop "turning a blind eye" to the "language police" and say "enough is enough."

5. To encourage people to demand reform from the education establishment to focus on issues that matter most.

How Well Does the Author Accomplish Those Purposes?

Determining how well an author accomplishes such purposes may seem subjective, but in reality it comes down to how well the case is presented. Is the thesis clear? Is it organized and well-presented? Are the examples sharp and convincing? Is the author's conclusion a logical result of what came before? Returning to Leo's essay, let us apply these questions:

1. Leo keeps to the point for most of his essay, although he sometimes blurs his opinion with that of Diane Ravitch's.

2. He offers many examples of the situation, presents his view clearly, and cites Ravitch's book.

3. Because Leo focuses on a book expressing the opinions of one person, the examples he uses to express his point need more support, perhaps from the original sources Ravitch uses.

4. Leo's essay is well-constructed and entertaining. He holds his

reader's attention through his strong writing style.

How Convincing Is the Evidence Presented? Is It Sufficient and Specific? Relevant? Reliable and Not Dated? Slanted?

Convincing writing depends on convincing evidence—that is, sufficient and relevant facts along with proper interpretations of facts. Facts are pieces of information that can be verified—such as statistics, examples, personal experience, expert testimony, and historical details. Proper interpretations of such facts must be logical and supported by relevant data. For instance, it is a fact that SAT verbal scores went up in 2003, and that students from Massachusetts had the highest national scores. One reason might be that students are spending more time reading and less time watching TV than in the past. Or that Massachusetts has many colleges and universities available, prompting students to study harder for the test in that state. But without hard statistics documenting the viewing habits of a sample of students, such interpretations are shaky, the result of a writer jumping to conclusions.

Is the Evidence Sufficient and Specific? Writers routinely use evidence, but sometimes it may not be sufficient. Sometimes the conclusions reached have too little evidence to be justified. Sometimes writers make hasty generalizations based solely on personal experience as evidence. How much evidence is enough? It is hard to say, but the more specific the details, the more convincing the argument. Instead of generalizations, good writers cite figures, dates, and facts. Instead of paraphrasing information, they quote the experts verbatim.

Is the Evidence Relevant? Good writers select evidence based on how well it supports their thesis, not on how interesting, novel, or humorous it is. For instance, if you are claiming that Barry Bonds is the greatest living baseball player, you should not mention that he was born in California, had a father who played for the San Francisco Giants, or that his godfather is Willie Mays. Those are facts, and they are very interesting, but they have nothing to do with Bonds' athletic abilities. Irrelevant evidence distracts readers and weakens an argument.

Is the Evidence Reliable and Current? Evidence should not be so dated or vague that it fails to support your claim. For instance, it is not accurate to say that candidate Jones fails to support the American worker because 15 years ago she purchased a foreign car. Her current actions are more important. Readers expect the information writers provide to be current and to be specific enough to be verifiable. A writer supporting animal rights may cite cases of rabbits blinded in drug research, but such tests have been outlawed in the United States for many years. Another may point to medical research that appears to abuse human subjects, but not name the researchers, the place, or the year of such testing. Because readers may have no way of verifying the evidence, the claims become suspicious and will weaken your points.

Is the Evidence Slanted? Sometimes writers select evidence that supports their case and ignore evidence that does not. Often referred to as "stacking the deck," this practice is unfair and potentially self-defeating for a writer. Although some evidence presented may have merit, an argument will be dismissed if readers discover that evidence was slanted or suppressed. For example, suppose you heard a classmate state that he would never take a course with Professor Sanchez because she gives surprise quizzes, assigns 50 pages of reading a night, and does not grade on a curve. Even if these statements are true, that may not be the whole truth. You might discover that Professor Sanchez is a dynamic and talented teacher whose classes are stimulating. Withholding that information may make an argument suspect. A better strategy is to acknowledge counterevidence and to confront it—that is, to strive for a balanced presentation by raising views and evidence that may not be supportive of your own.

Let us take a look at the evidence in Leo's essay, applying some of the points we have just covered.

1. Leo quotes information from Ravitch's book without documenting her sources. This may make the reader wonder if the information is fact or opinion.

2. His use of quotes from Ravitch's book without verifying his own position may make it appear that he is hiding behind her words, rather than supporting his argument on his own.

3. He makes many assumptions about how the general public feels about the language sensitivity movement in schools.

4. Leo assumes that the reason the "fad" of language sensitivity didn't "go away" was because people looked the other way. He doesn't allow for alternative reasons, such as the possibility that people thought the idea was a good one.

5. His argument is emotional rather than logical. Likewise, his presentation of the facts is clearly one-sided.

6. He makes statements without qualifying them, such as "Ravitch speaks for parents more concerned about something else: substituting censorship and propaganda for actual learning." He does not prove that the language sensitivity movement has harmed education, or that parents are indeed concerned that it is hindering the learning process.

What Types of Sources Were Used—Personal Experience, Outside Authorities, Factual References, or Statistical Data?

Writers enlist four basic kinds of evidence to support their views or arguments: personal experience (theirs and others'), outside authorities, factual references and examples, and statistics. In your own writing, you should aim to use combinations of these.

Personal Testimony cannot be underestimated. Think of the books you have read or movies you have seen based on word-of-mouth recommendations. (Maybe you learned of the school you are attending through word of mouth!) Personal testimony—which provides eyewitness accounts not available to you or to other readers—is sometimes the most persuasive kind of evidence. Suppose you are writing about the rising abuse of alcohol on college campuses. In addition to statistics and hard facts, quoting the experience of a first-year student who nearly died one night from alcohol poisoning would add dramatic impact. Although personal observations are useful and valuable, writers must not draw hasty conclusions based only on such evidence. The fact that you and a few friends are in favor of replacing letter grades with a pass-fail system does not provide support for the claim that the student body at your school is in favor of the conversion.

Outside Authorities are people recognized as experts in a given field. Appealing to such authorities is a powerful tool in writing, particularly for writers wanting to persuade readers of their views. We hear it all the time: "Scientists have found. . . ." "Scholars inform us that. . . ." "According to his biographer, Abraham Lincoln. . . ." Although experts try to be objective and fair-minded, their testimony may be biased. You would not expect scientists working for tobacco companies to provide unbiased opinions on lung cancer. And remember to cite who the authorities behind the statements are. It is not enough to simply state "scientists conducted a study"; you must say *who* they were and *where* the study was conducted.

Factual References and examples do as much to inform as to persuade. If somebody wants to sell you something, they will pour on the details. Think of the television commercials that show a sports utility vehicle climbing rocky mountain roads as a narrator lists all its great standard features—four-wheel drive, alloy wheels, second-generation airbags, power brakes, cruise control, etc. Or cereal "infomercials" in which manufacturers explain that new Yummy-Os have 15 percent more fiber to help prevent cancer. Although readers may not have the expertise to determine which data are useful, they are often convinced by the sheer weight of the evidence—like courtroom juries judging a case.

Statistics impress people. Saying that 77 percent of your school's student body approves of women in military combat roles is much more persuasive than saying "a lot of people" do. Why? Because statistics have a no-nonsense authority. Batting averages, polling results, economic indicators, medical and FBI statistics, and demographic percentages are all reported in numbers. If accurate, they are persuasive, although they can be used to mislead. The claim that 139 people on campus protested the appearance of a certain controversial speaker may be accurate; however, it would be a distortion of the truth not to mention that another 1,500 people attended the talk and gave the speaker a standing ovation. Likewise, the manufacturer who claims that its potato chips are fried in 100 percent cholesterol-free vegetable oil misleads the public, because vegetable oil doesn't contain cholesterol—which is found only in animal fats. That is known as the "bandwagon" use of statistics— appealing to what people want to hear.

Now let us briefly examine Leo's sources of evidence:

1. Leo draws much of his support from one source, Diane Ravitch.

   Although her qualifications as a former assistant secretary of education may elevate her authority, she still represents only one opinion. His argument might be stronger if he had quoted some of the groups that held "extreme" views.

2. He provides examples of biased stories deemed unacceptable for tests without explaining whether these are real examples, and who rejected them.

3. Leo's citing of Ravitch's examples of vetoed subjects (peanuts, owls, and palaces in Egypt) may support his point to his target audience; but some readers may agree that these subjects were indeed unacceptable.

4. His statement that "women must not be shown in the home, maids can't be black" fails to support his premise that this "control" of language is harmful to students. He also fails to show the other side of the issue, such as the idea that some students may be hurt by certain stereotypes.

Did the Author Address Opposing Views on the Issue?

Many of the essays in this book will in varying degrees try to persuade you to agree with the author's position. But, of course, any slant on a topic can have multiple points of view. In developing their ideas, good writers will anticipate different and opposing views. They will cite alternative opinions, maybe even evidence that does not support their own position. By treating alternative points of view fairly, writers strengthen their own position. Failing to present or admit other views could leave their perspective open to scrutiny, as well as claims of naïveté and ignorance. This is particularly damaging when discussing a controversial issue.

Let us see how Leo's essay addresses alternative points of view:

1. Leo does not introduce alternative points of view into his editorial. However, it is, after all, an editorial, and, thus, is based on his opinion as he can best support it.

2. Although it is an editorial, and therefore his own point of view, his discussion would have been made stronger if he had approached the issue more fairly. For example, if he had admitted the possibility that biased language can be harmful, or that some sensitivity is desirable, he may have reached a wider audience.

Is the Perspective of the Author Persuasive?

Style and content make for persuasive writing. Important points are how well a paper is composed—the organization, the logic, the quality of thought, the presentation of evidence, the use of language, the tone of discussion—and the details and evidence.

Turning to Leo's essay, we might make the following observations:

1. On the surface, Leo presents his argument well. A closer reading, however, raises more questions about the author's presentation of the material. He bases his argument primarily on generalizations and personal opinion.

2. He appears to be "pushing buttons" rather than presenting a well-formed, logical argument. He taps into his assumption of his audience's common view that the influence of multicultural feminists and the religious right on language is ridiculous and should be curtailed.

3. He makes many statements without qualifying them, and presents his own assumptions about the opinions of parents and teachers rather than providing proof of these assumptions.

By now, you should have a fairly clear idea of how critical reading can help your comprehension of a work, and make you a better writer in the process. Make critical reading part of your daily life, not just something you do in the classroom or while studying. As you wait for the bus, look at some billboards and consider how they try to hook their audience. While watching TV, think about the techniques advertisers use to convince you to buy their products. And try to apply some of the elements of critical reading while perusing the articles and editorials in your favorite magazine or newspaper. The more you approach writing with a critical eye, the more natural it will become, and the better writer you will be.

What Is Critical Writing?

Critical writing is a systematic process. When following a recipe, you would not begin mixing ingredients together haphazardly. Instead, you would first gather your ingredients and equipment, and then combine the ingredients according to the recipe outlined. Similarly, in writing, you could not plan, write, edit, and proofread all at the same time. Rather, writing occurs one thoughtful step at a time.

Some writing assignments may require more steps than others. An in-class freewriting exercise may allow for only one or two steps—light planning and writing. An essay question on a midterm examination may permit enough time for only three steps—planning, writing, and proofreading. A simple plan for such an assignment need answer only two questions: "What am I going to say?" and "How am I going to develop my idea convincingly?" For example, you have to answer the following question: "Do you agree with Leo's assertion in 'Now Cut That Out!' that the 'language police' are controlling language in schools to the detriment of students?" You might decide to answer with the statement, "The words we use in textbooks and tests should reflect reality while also being sensitive to student's feelings." Or you could decide to answer, "Leo makes an interesting point in his essay that language sensitivity has gone too far. When textbooks no longer reflect reality because words are so controlled, education suffers." You would then develop your idea by comparing or contrasting your own experiences in school with the examples Leo gives in his essay, or presenting data or information that challenges or supports his argument.

A longer, out-of-class paper allows you to plan and organize your material, and to develop more than one draft. In this extended version of the writing process you will need to do the following to write a strong, critical paper:

- Develop your ideas into a focused thesis that is appropriate for your audience.
- Research pertinent sources.
- Organize your material and draft your paper.
- Proofread your paper thoroughly.

Those are the general steps that every writer goes through when writing a paper. In the following sections the use of these strategies will be discussed so that you can write most effectively.

Developing Ideas

Even the most experienced writers sometimes have trouble getting started. Common problems you may encounter include focusing your ideas, knowing where to begin, having too much or too little to say, and determining your position on an issue. There are developmental strategies that can help promote the free expression of your ideas and make you more comfortable with writing.

Although your finished product should be a tightly focused and well-written essay, you can begin the writing process by being free and sloppy. This approach allows your ideas to develop and flow unblocked onto your paper. Writing techniques such as brainstorming, freewriting, and ballooning can all help you through the process of development. As with all writing strategies, you should try all of them at first, to discover which ones work best for you.

Brainstorming

The goal of brainstorming is to generate and focus ideas. Brainstorming can be a personal exercise or a group project. You begin with a blank sheet of paper (or a blackboard) and, without paying attention to spelling, order, or grammar, simply list ideas about the topic as they come to you. You should spend at least 10 minutes brainstorming, building on the ideas you write down. There are no "dumb" ideas in brainstorming—the smallest detail may turn into a great essay.

Let us assume, for example, that you decide to write a paper supporting Leo's assertion in "Now Cut That Out!" Brainstorming for a few minutes may provide something like this:

> language sensitivity may be getting out of hand when NO women are
>
> allowed to be depicted as mothers and NO blacks may be presented
>
> as athletes—it could imply that there is something wrong with
>
> these choices
>
> get a bunch of textbooks written after 1995 to see if such language
>
> bias is prevalent, get real examples
>
> read Ravitch's book—how does it connect to this essay? what
>
> sources does she cite?
>
> explore other multicultural issues
>
> get other people's opinions (especially parents of school-age kids) on
>
> this issue
>
> try and locate the textbook adoption system in place in the 22 states
>
> that Leo/Ravitch cite
>
> check out the McGraw-Hill guidelines (see Ravitch book?) Leo cites
>
> in paragraph 8

You may notice that this brainstorming example has little structure, no apparent order, and even spelling errors. Its purpose is to elicit all the ideas you have about a subject so you can read your ideas and identify an interesting topic to develop.

Freewriting

Freewriting, just as brainstorming, is a free expression of ideas. It helps you jump-start the writing process and get things flowing on paper. Freewriting is unencumbered by rules—you can write about your impressions, ideas, and reactions to the article or essay. You should devote about 10 minutes to freewriting, keeping in mind that the goal is to write about the topic as ideas occur to you. If you are writing on a particular topic or idea you may wish to note it at the top of your paper as a visual reminder of your focus. Structure, grammar, and spelling are not important—just focus on the free flow of ideas. And above all, do not stop writing—even if you feel that what you are writing is silly or irrelevant. Any one, or a combination of the ideas expressed in a freewrite can be developed into a thoughtful essay.

Here is an example of a freewriting exercise:

In this essay Leo is presenting his opinion, and the opinion of Diane Ravitch. In my opinion, I think Leo could actually make a good point, if his information wasn't so skewed and his bias so apparent. I guess it doesn't help matters much that he is a white male, and so may be viewed as less likely to suffer from language insensitivity. In one place in his essay, he begins to admit that language sensitivity started out as a "sensible suggestion," but he never elaborates, and that could be where his essay could be most helped, because it is at this point he could balance out his viewpoint. For example, he could have admitted that presenting women as mothers, maybe at the expense of presenting men as caregivers, was insensitive to women and girls, as well as to men and boys. He could have advocated for balance—sometimes women could be shown as both. The same could hold true for athletes and academics—when nationality has to be expressed at all. I sort of wonder about that—why do you need to say that someone is blind or that a girl's mother is Asian American and a professor at all? Just say a guy climbed a mountain or a girl's mother went to work (this actually allows the woman to be a mother AND a working woman . . .). I guess the other issue I wonder about is if this language policing is hurting anyone. Maybe it sort of upsets white guys like Leo, who are left out in the cold, but everyone else seems to be ok. I mean, it isn't as if there are no texts or tests anymore? Why all the fuss?

Ballooning

There are many names for ballooning, including "mind mapping," "clustering," or "grouping." These techniques all provide a more graphic presentation of ideas, allowing writers to visualize ideas and connections stemming from these ideas. Ballooning is particularly effective if you already have a fairly clear idea about your topic and wish to develop it more fully.

Write your main topic in the center of a large sheet of paper or a blackboard and circle it. Using the circled idea as your focus, think of subtopics and place them in circles around the center circle, connecting them to each other with lines (see figure). Remember to keep the subtopics short. Continue doing this until you feel you

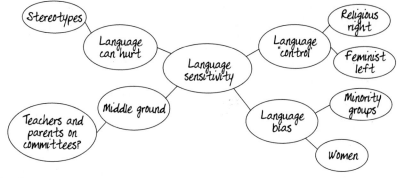

Ballooning

have developed all the subtopics more fully. When you have finished this exercise, you should be able to visualize the connections between your main topic and its sub-points, and have a starting point for your essay.

Narrowing the Topic

Although brainstorming, freewriting, and ballooning help list and develop general ideas, you still need to narrow one idea down to something more manageable. Narrowing a topic can be quite a challenge—you might like more than one idea, or you may be afraid of limiting yourself to only one concept. Nevertheless, you must identify one idea and focus on developing it into an essay. Choose an idea that will interest you and your audience. Remember that if you do not like the way one idea begins to develop, you can always go back and develop another one instead. Once you identify your topic, you are ready to develop the thesis statement for your essay.

Based on the freewriting exercise described earlier—and additional idea development using ballooning techniques—we will follow a student who has decided to write his paper on the idea that language sensitivity is a good idea, and it helps more students than it harms. The idea stems from a response to Leo's essay, but it will develop into a thesis that uniquely belongs to the student.

Identifying Your Audience

Identifying your audience is one of the most important steps in organizing your essay. Knowing what your audience needs and expects from your essay will help you compose a convincing, effective paper. The following questions can help you identify the expectations of your audience:

- Who is my audience?
- What do they already know about my topic?
- What questions do they have about my topic?
- What do they need to know to understand my point?

- What is the best order to present the information they need to know?
- How do they feel about this topic?
- Why would they want to read my essay?

Based on these questions, our student determined that her audience would be her teacher and fellow expository writing classmates. All of them would be familiar with Leo's article and would have discussed it to some extent in class. As members of an academic institution, they should be familiar with the basics of multicultural theory, feminism, and politics, but may need some background on it. They may have different opinions on the issue, so supporting evidence (from both Leo's article and some outside research) would be necessary to effectively make her point. Because the essay would be about an issue directly concerning both teachers and students, it should generate some level of personal interest, and thus engage her readers.

Developing a Thesis

The **thesis** is a form of contract between the writer and reader. It makes a claim or declaration—telling your audience exactly what you are going to discuss. It should be stated in the opening paragraph, with the rest of the paper developing and supporting it.

As you write and develop your paper, your thesis should guide you as clearer and more precise thoughts evolve. Don't be constrained by your first thesis. If your paper is changing as you write, your thesis may change. Remember to go back and revise the thesis so that it matches the points made in your essay.

Although the thesis represents the last step in developing the topic for your essay, it is only the beginning of the actual writing process. For her paper, our student worked out the following sentence to help develop her thesis:

> The language sensitivity movement of the 1980s and 1990s grew out of a belief that stereotyping and racial or cultural bias could offend or negatively influence students' self-esteem. As a result, publishers and test panels began to carefully consider the language they used. While language sensitivity may sometimes seem extreme, it ultimately benefits students, and the society of which they will later become a part.

Understanding Your Paper's Objective

Before determining how to research or organize your paper, consider what you are trying to achieve by writing it. Your objective may be to inform, to describe, or to persuade. To define your purpose, you should first determine your objective, and then identify what you need to do to accomplish this objective. This helps you determine what you need to put into the body of your paper.

Writing to inform involves anticipating the questions your audience may have regarding the topic, and how much background your audience will need to understand it. Once you have developed a list of questions, you can determine what order will best present the information that will answer these questions.

Writing to describe also involves answering some questions. First, you must identify what is important or relevant about the topic you intend to describe. Then you should determine what information is vital to conveying this importance. List these elements and order them in a way that presents a clear view of the experience to the reader.

Writing to persuade presents a perspective on an issue and attempts to convince readers to agree with it. You must provide reasons and supporting evidence to persuade your audience that your perspective makes sense. Although you might not sway all readers to your point of view, you should make enough of a case to allow them to understand your argument, even if they might not agree with it.

The first step in persuasive writing is to determine your position and to identify the objections others might have to it. Remember that there are many different reasons readers may not agree with you. By identifying the arguments against your position, you are better able to address them and thus support your own argument in the process. Three primary kinds of arguments are used in persuasive writing:

- *Arguments based on disputed facts or consequences,* such as the claim that the building of a gambling casino generated revenue for a bankrupt town, created jobs, and improved the quality of life there.
- *Arguments that advocate change*, such as arguing for a lower drinking age or changing the ways the penal system punishes juvenile offenders.
- *Arguments based on evaluative personal claims*, as right or wrong, ethical or immoral, or favoring one thing or idea over another—such as arguing that physician-assisted suicide is wrong or that supermodels contribute to the development of anorexia nervosa in young women.

The key to effective persuasive writing is to support your perspective with statistics, factual data, and examples. Although your opinions drive the essay, your supporting evidence is what convinces your audience of the validity of your main point.

Researching

Research can involve a few, or many, steps, depending on the type and length of the paper you are writing. In many cases, simply reviewing the article and applying the steps of critical reading will be the final step you take before organizing your paper. For longer research papers that require outside sources, you will probably need to tap into library resources or even find information online.

Researching may even involve taking surveys and conducting interviews. For her paper on language sensitivity in education, our student decided to speak to schoolchildren and teachers to determine their opinions on "language policing" and Leo and Ravitch's claims.

Selecting Sources for Your Paper

The best place to start is the library, either physically or online. Most libraries have their holdings archived on electronic cataloging systems that let you look up books by author, title, and subject. Although books are a rich source of information, they can be dated, and are sometimes inappropriate for essays addressing contemporary issues. For such papers, journals and periodicals are better. With all the different ways of researching, gathering useful and appropriate information can be overwhelming. Do not be afraid to ask the librarian for help.

For many people, the Internet has become the first avenue of research on a topic, and it can be an extremely useful way to locate information on contemporary issues. In addition to web sites, newsgroups and bulletin boards can aid your research process. Remember that the Internet is largely unregulated, so you should surf the web with the careful eye of a critic. Simply because something is posted online does not mean it is accurate or truthful. Whenever possible, take steps to verify your sources. When you do find a good source, write it down immediately. Many students lament the loss of a valuable resource because they forgot to write down the title of the book or Internet address. A good technique is to write down your sources on 3 × 5 cards. For example:

> Steel, Jon. *Truth, Lies and Advertising.* New York: John Wiley & Sons, 1998. 150–178.

> Kohner-Zuckerman, David. "Brokering Beauty." BRN TWD Magazine Jan/Feb 2000. http://www.brntwdmagazine.com/jan-feb/tech/tech-2.html.

These cards allow you to add sources and arrange them alphabetically without having to rewrite as you would with a list. You can write down quotes for your paper on these cards for quick retrieval, and use them to help write your "Works Cited" section at the end of your essay.

Documenting Sources

Sources help support your ideas and emphasize your points. It is very important to cite these sources when you use them in your essay. Whether you quote, paraphrase, or use an idea from another source, you must identify the source from which your information came. Documenting sources gives credit to the person who did the work, and helps locate information on your topic. Even if you rewrite information in your own words, you must still document the source because it is borrowed information. Failure to document your sources is called plagiarism—presenting someone else's work as your own—and it is considered by most academic institutions a form of theft. The following checklist should help you determine when to document your sources:

- Using someone's exact words
- Presenting someone else's opinion
- Paraphrasing or summarizing someone else's ideas
- Using information gathered from a study
- Citing statistics or reporting the results of research not your own.

It is not necessary to cite dates, facts, or ideas considered common knowledge.

Organizing Your Paper

There are many ways to organize your paper. Some students prefer to use the standard outline technique, complete with roman numerals and indented subpoints. Other students prefer more flexible flowcharts. The key to organizing is to define your focus and plan how to support your thesis statement from point to point in a logical order.

Drafting Your Essay

When writing your essay, think of your draft as a work in progress. Your objective should be to present your ideas in a logical order. You can address spelling, grammar, and sentence structure later. If you get stuck writing one paragraph or section, go on and work on another. Depending on how you write, you may choose to write your draft sequentially; or you may choose to move from your thesis to your body paragraphs, leaving your introduction and conclusion for last. Feel free to leave gaps or write notes to yourself in brackets to indicate areas to develop later when revising. Do not make the mistake of thinking that your first draft has to be your final draft. Remember that writing is a process of refinement—you can always go back and fix things later.

Writing Your Introduction

For many students, the hardest part of writing an essay is drafting the first paragraph. Humorist James Thurber once said "Don't get it right, get it written." What Thurber means is just start writing, even if you do not think it sounds very good. Use your thesis statement as a starting point and build around it. Explain what your essay will do, or provide interesting background information that serves to frame your points for your audience. After you have written the first paragraph, take a break before you revise it. Return to it later with a fresh outlook. Likewise, review your first paragraph as you develop the other sections of your essay to make sure that you are meeting your objectives.

Turning back to our student paper, an introduction might look like this. Note that the introduction works with the thesis statement developed earlier, and builds in a few more ideas.

> The language sensitivity movement of the 1980s and 1990s grew out of a belief that stereotyping and racial or cultural bias could offend or negatively influence students' self-esteem. As a result, publishers and test panels began to carefully consider the language they used. Some people fear that language sensitivity has gone too far and no longer reflects reality. Others are concerned that panels are focusing too much on not offending anyone, at the expense of education. While language sensitivity may sometimes seem extreme, it ultimately benefits students, and the society of which they will later become a part.

Developing Paragraphs and Making Transitions

A paragraph is a group of sentences that supports and develops a central idea. The central idea serves as the core point of the paragraph, and the surrounding sentences support it.

There are three primary types of sentences that comprise a paragraph: the topic sentence, supporting sentences, and transitional sentences.

The core point, or the **topic sentence,** is usually the first or second sentence in the paragraph. It is the controlling idea of the paragraph. Placing the topic sentence first lets the reader immediately know what the paragraph is about. However, sometimes a transition sentence or some supporting material needs to precede the topic sentence, in which case the topic sentence may appear as the second or third sentence in the paragraph. Think of the topic sentence as a mini-thesis statement; it should connect logically to the topic sentences in the paragraphs before and after it.

Supporting sentences do just that, support the topic sentence. This support may be from outside sources in the form of quotes or paraphrased material, or it may be from your own ideas. Think of the support sentences as "proving" the validity of your topic sentence.

Transitional sentences link paragraphs together, making the paper a cohesive unit and promoting its "readability." Transitional sentences are usually the first and last sentences of the paragraph. When they appear at the end of the paragraph, they foreshadow the topic to come. Words such as *in addition, yet, moreover, furthermore, meanwhile, likewise, also, since, before, hence, on the other hand, as well,* and *thus* are often used in transitional sentences. These words can also be used within the body of the paragraph to clarify and smooth the progression from idea to idea. For example, the last sentence in our student's introductory paragraph sets up the reader's expectations that the paragraphs that follow will explain why language sensitivity in educational materials is a good idea. It forecasts what will come next.

Paragraphs have no required length. Remember, however, that an essay comprised of long, detailed paragraphs might prove tiresome and confusing to the reader. Likewise, short, choppy paragraphs may sacrifice clarity and leave the reader with unanswered questions. Remember that a paragraph presents a single unified idea. It should be just long enough to effectively support its subject. Begin a new paragraph when your subject changes.

Use this list to help keep your paragraphs organized and coherent:

- Organize material logically—present your core idea early in the paragraph.
- Include a topic sentence that expresses the core point of the paragraph.
- Support and explain the core point.
- Use transitional sentences to indicate where you are going and where you have been.

Let us see how our student applies these ideas to the second paragraph of her essay.

To better approach this issue, we must first understand a little bit more about the "language sensitivity" movement. For much of the twentieth century, textbooks taught primarily from a white, Anglo-Saxon, Protestant-Christian, and male-centered perspective. Stereotyping was common, with girls playing with dolls, boys participating in sports, and mothers and fathers depicted in traditional roles as homemakers and wage-earners, respectively. By the 1980s, however, publishers began to listen to the concerns expressed by academics and outside interest groups that educational material be more inclusive, more sensitive, and include the perspectives of women, racial, ethnic, and religious groups [*topic sentence*]. The goal was that through such language awareness, students would learn to avoid stereotyping, to be more tolerant of others, and to feel pride in their own social and cultural backgrounds [*supporting sentence*]. Considering the fact that America is often called the "great melting pot," it is surprising that it took so long to institute this inclusionary approach to language. Not everyone, however, has embraced this new academic approach [*transitional, "forecasting" sentence*].

Concluding Well

Your conclusion should bring together the points made in your paper and reiterate your final point. You may also use your conclusion as an opportunity to provoke a final thought you wish your audience to consider. Try to frame your conclusion to mirror your introduction—in other words, be consistent in your style. You may wish to repeat the point of the paper, revisit its key points, and then leave your reader with a final idea or thought on your topic.

Conclusions are your opportunity to explain to your reader how all your material adds up. In a short essay of about three to four pages, your conclusion should begin around the penultimate paragraph, "winding down" the discussion. Avoid the temptation to simply summarize your material; try to give your conclusions a little punch. However, it is equally important not to be overly dramatic, because you can undercut your essay. Rather, conclusions should sound confident and reflective.

Notice how our student concludes her essay, making references to her final point as well as to the paper against which she is arguing, the essay by John Leo. Based on her conclusion, we may infer that she has supported all of her final points within the actual body of her essay.

The key to language sensitivity is creating a balance between maintaining the principles of tolerance while maintaining reasonable expectations. Simply because the language sensitivity ethic is relatively new does not make it a "fad" or passing fancy. It means we are progressing as a culture. There is a saying "you can't please all of the people, all of the time," which holds particularly true for this issue. Understanding, and tolerating, alternative cultural, religious, and social points of view through language sensitivity does not mean that students are missing out on a good education. Moreover, language sensitivity ensures that children are not alienated by what they read. Rather than arguing that Asian American athletes are not a realistic norm, or questioning why panels avoid casting black women in the role of maids, we should instead consider how language sensitivity affords children more possibility, hope, and acceptance. It will help nurture future generations of children to be more tolerant and accepting of different viewpoints and ways of life.

Editing and Revising

Once you have drafted a paper and, if possible, spent several hours or even a day away from it, you should begin editing and revising it. To edit your paper, read it closely, marking the words, phrases, and sections you want to change. Have a grammar handbook nearby to quickly reference any grammatical questions that may arise. Look for things that seem out of place or sound awkward, passages that lack adequate support and detail, and sentences that seem wordy or unclear. Many students find that reading the essay aloud helps them to recognize awkward sentences and ambiguous wording. This technique may also reveal missing words.

As you read, you should always ask if what you have written refers back to your thesis:

- Does this paragraph support my thesis?
- What does my reader need to know?
- Do my paragraphs flow in a logical order?
- Have I deviated from my point?

As you revise your paper, think about the voice and style you are using to present your material. Is your style smooth and confident? How much of yourself is in the essay, and is this level appropriate for the type of paper you are writing? Some writers, for example, overuse the pronoun "I." If you find that this is the case try to rework your sentences to decrease the use of this pronoun.

Using Active Voice

Although grammatically correct, the use of the passive voice can slow down the flow of a paper or distance the reader from your material. Many students are befuddled by the active versus the passive voice, confusing it with past, present, and future tense. The active voice can be used in any tense, and, in most situations, it is the better choice. In the active voice, you make your agent "actively" perform an action. Consider the following examples:

PASSIVE: In "Now Cut That Out!" in order to describe how extremist groups are controlling language, examples of rejected subjects are provided by John Leo.

ACTIVE: In his essay, "Now Cut That Out," John Leo provides examples of subjects language extremist groups have vetoed.

PASSIVE: The control of textbook content by the "language po-

lice" is feared by Ravitch.

ACTIVE: Ravitch fears that the "language police" are controlling

textbook content.

In both of these examples, using the active voice makes the sentences cleaner, stronger, and more engaging.

Grammar and Punctuation

You probably already have a grammar handbook; most first-year composition courses require students to purchase these invaluable little books. If you do not have a grammar handbook, get one. You will use it throughout your college—and probably your professional—career. Grammar handbooks can help you identify problems with phrases and clauses, parallel structure, verb tense agreement, commas, colons and semicolons, and punctuation. Most have useful sections on common usage mistakes, such as when to use "further" and "farther," and "effect" and "affect." Try not to rely on grammar checking software available on most word processing programs. You are the best checker of grammar for your essay.

Proofreading Effectively

The final step in preparing a paper is proofreading, the process of reading your paper to correct errors. You will probably be more successful if you wait until you are fresh to do it: Proofreading a paper at 3:00 A.M. immediately after finishing it is not a good idea. With the use of word-processing programs, proofreading usually involves three steps: spell-checking, reading, and correcting.

If you are writing your paper using a word-processing system, you probably have been using the spellchecker throughout the composition process. Most word-processing systems highlight misspelled words as you type them into the computer. Remember to run the spellchecker every time you change or revise your paper. Many students make last minute changes to their papers and neglect to run the spellchecker one last time before printing it, only to discover a misspelled word as they turn in their paper or when it is returned to them. Keep in mind that spellcheckers can fix only words that are misspelled—not words that are mistyped but are still real words. Common typing errors in which letters are transposed such as "from" and "form," and "won" and "own," will not be caught by a spellchecker because they all are real words. Other common errors not caught by spellcheckers include words incompletely typed, such as leaving off the "t" in "the" or the "e" in "here." Reading your paper carefully will catch these errors.

To proofread correctly, you must read slowly and critically. Try to distance yourself from the material. One careful, slow, attentive proofreading is better than six careless reads. Look for and mark the following: errors in spelling and usage, sentence fragments and comma splices, inconsistencies in number between nouns and pronouns and between subjects and verbs, faulty parallelism, other grammar errors, unintentional repetitions, and omissions.

After you have proofread and identified the errors, go back and correct them. When you have finished, proofread the paper again to make sure you caught everything. As you proofread for grammar and style, ask yourself the questions listed above and make corrections on your paper. Be prepared to read your essay through multiple times. Having only one or two small grammatical corrections is a good indication that you are done revising.

If your schedule permits, you might want to show your paper to a friend or instructor for review. Obtaining feedback from your audience is another way you can test the effectiveness of your paper. An outside reviewer will probably think of questions you have not thought of, and if you revise to answer those questions, you will make your paper stronger.

In the chapters that follow, you will discover over a hundred different selections, both written and visual, ranging widely across contemporary matters, that we hope you will find exciting and thought provoking. Arranged thematically into 10 chapters, the writings represent widely diverse topics—from the ways we construct beauty, to what makes us want to buy something, to the way the Internet is changing our lives, to the ethical issues surrounding human reproduction and gene technology. Some of the topics will be familiar; others you may be encountering for the first time. Regardless of how these language issues touch your experience, critical thinking, critical reading, and critical writing will open you up to a deeper understanding of our culture as we begin the twenty-first century.

Approaching Visuals Critically

We have all heard the old saying, "a picture is worth a thousand words." Our daily lives are filled with the images of pop culture, influencing us about what to buy, how to look, even how to think. Symbols, images, gestures, and graphics all communicate instant information about our culture.

Now more than ever before, ours is a visual world. Everywhere we look there are images vying for our attention—magazine ads, T-shirt logos, movie billboards, artwork, traffic signs, political cartoons, statues, and store-front windows. Glanced at only briefly, visuals communicate information and ideas. They may project commonly held values, ideals, and fantasies. They can relay opinion, inspire reaction, and influence emotion. And because the competition for our attention today is so great, and the time for communication is so short, visuals compete to make an instant impression or risk being lost.

Consider the instant messages projected by brand names, company logos, or even the American flag. Or the emotional appeal of a photo of a lost kitten or dog attached to a reward notice on a telephone pole. Without the skills of visual literacy, we are at the mercy of a highly persuasive visual universe. Just as we approach writing with the tools of critical analysis, we should carefully consider the many ways visuals influence us.

Understanding the persuasive power of visuals requires a close examination and interpretation of the premise, claims, details, supporting evidence, and stylistic touches embedded in any visual piece. Just as when we examine written arguments, we should ask ourselves the following four questions when examining visual arguments:

- Who is the target *audience*?
- What are the *claims* made in the images?
- What shared history or cultural *assumptions*—or warrants—does the image make?
- What is the supporting *evidence*?

Like works of art, visuals employ color, shape, line, texture, depth, and point of view to create their effect. Therefore, to understand how visuals work and to analyze the way visuals persuade, we must also ask questions about specific aspects of form and design. For example, some questions to ask about print images, such as those in newspaper and magazine ads, include:

- What in the frame catches your attention immediately?
- What is the central image? What is the background image? Foreground images? What are the surrounding images? What is significant in the placement of these images? Their relationship to one another?
- What verbal information is included? How is it made prominent? How does it relate to the other graphics or images?
- What specific details (people, objects, locale) are emphasized? Which are exaggerated or idealized?
- What is the effect of color and lighting?
- What emotional effect is created by the images—pleasure? longing? anxiety? nostalgia?
- Do the graphics and images make you want to know more about the subject or product?
- What special significance might objects in the image have?
- Is there any symbolism imbedded in the images?

Because the goal of a calculated visual is to persuade, coax, intimidate, or otherwise subliminally influence its viewer, it is important that its audience can discern the strategies or technique it employs. To get you started, we will critically analyze two types of visuals—advertisements and editorial cartoons.

Images and Advertising

Images have clout, and none so obvious or so craftily designed as those that come from the world of advertising. Advertising images are everywhere—television, newspapers, the Internet, magazines, the sides of buses, and on highway billboards. Each year, companies collectively spend more than $150 billion worth of print ads and television commercials (more than the gross national product of many countries). Advertisements comprise at least a quarter of each television hour and form the bulk of most newspapers and magazines. Tapping into our most basic emotions, their appeal goes right to the quick of our fantasies: happiness, material wealth, eternal youth, social acceptance, sexual fulfillment, and power.

Yet, most of us are so accustomed to the onslaught of such images that we see them without looking and hear them without listening. But if we stopped to examine how the images work, we might be amazed at their powerful and complex psychological force. And we might be surprised at how much effort goes into the crafting of such images—an effort solely intended to separate us from our money.

Like a written argument, every print ad or commercial has an audience, claims, assumptions and evidence. Sometimes these elements are obvious, sometimes understated, sometimes implied. They may boast testimonials by average folk or celebrities, or cite hard scientific evidence. And sometimes they simply manipulate our desire to be happy or socially accepted. But common to every ad and commercial, no matter what the medium, is the claim that you should buy this product.

Print ads are potentially complex mixtures of images, graphics, and text. So in analyzing an ad, you should be aware of the use of photography, the placement of the images, the use of text, company logos, and other graphics (such as illustrations, drawings, side bar boxes, logos, etc.). And you should keep in mind that every aspect of the image has been thought about and designed carefully even in those ads where the guiding principle was minimalism. Let's take a look at a recent magazine ad for Altoids (see page 38).

Altoids Ad

When analyzing a print ad, we should try to determine what first catches our attention. In the accompanying Altoids ad, the image of the soldier, featured floating on a pale green solid background, pops from the page. This is a calculated move on the part of the ad's designers. The soldier fills the center of the page, and the image is arresting—we stop and look. Ad images are staged and manipulated for maximum attention and effect. The uncluttered nature of this advertisement forces us to look at the soldier and the little tin he is holding in his hand.

The person featured in the ad is almost comic. He is wearing an ill-fitted uniform, he sports thick glasses, and he lacks the chiseled quality of many male models commonly used in advertising. This comic quality, coupled with the text under the ad, appeals to the viewer's sense of humor.

What Is the Claim?

Because advertisers are fighting for our attention, they must project their claim as efficiently as possible in order to discourage us from turning the page. The Altoids ad states its "claim" simply and boldly in white letters against a pale green background below the central photograph. In large typeface, the slogan and "claim" come in two parts. The first two sentences presumably come from the soldier: "Thank you sir! May I have another!" The second statement tells us more specifically what the soldier wants: "The curiously strong mints." It is interesting to note

©2000 Callard & Bowser-Suchard Inc.   www.altoids.com

that the actual name of the product, Altoids, only appears on the little tin held in the soldier's right hand.

But let's take a closer look at the intention of framing the claim in two sentences and at how the layout subtly directs us. The first statement is intended to tap into our shared cultural expectations of what we know about military service. Soldiers must shout responses to their superiors and thank them even for punishments. For example, after being assigned 20 pushups as disciplinary action, a soldier is expected to not only thank his sergeant for the punishment, but to actually ask for more. The ad twists this expectation by having Altoids be the "punishment." In this ad, the soldier is actually getting a treat.

The indirect claim is that the reader should also want these "curiously strong mints." The word "curiously" is designed to set the product apart from its competitors. Curiously" is more commonly used in British English; and the parent company for Altoids—Callard & Bowser-Suchard Inc.—has its roots in England. Viewers familiar with the mint will enjoy the ad for its comic appeal. Those readers who are unfamiliar with the product may wonder just what makes these mints "curiously strong." And curiosity is an effective hook.

Another possible claim could be connected to the scenario leading to the soldier's receiving the first mint. We know that soldiers are supposed to shout back responses to their commanding officer, often face to face. Perhaps his commanding officer was appalled at his recruit's bad breath and "punished" him with the directive to have a mint. The claim is that even at extremely close range, Altoids fixes bad breath.

What Is the Evidence?

Altoid's tag line, "The curiously strong mints," implies that other mints are simply ordinary and unremarkable. Altoids are different—they are "curiously strong" and thus, presumably, superior to their bland competition. And referring back to the possible scenario that led to the soldier's first mint, viewers might presume that if a commanding officer would "treat" his company's bad breath with this mint, it must be good.

Around the language of advertising, we should tread cautiously. As William Lutz warns us about in his essay, "With These Words I Can Sell You Anything" (page 134), we hear promises that aren't really being made. The Altoids text does not say that it is, indeed, *better* than other mints, just that they are "curiously strong." What does the word "curiously" really mean? And stronger than what? According to Lutz, such words sound enticing, but are really telling readers nothing meaningful about the product.

What Are the Assumptions?

The creators of this ad make several assumptions about the audience: (1) that they are familiar with the phrase "Thank you sir, may I have another;" (2) they understand who is depicted in the ad—a soldier at boot camp; and (3) we want to have fresh breath.

Altoids Questions

1. What cultural conventions does this ad use to promote the product? What does it assume about the viewer? Would it work in another country, such as France or China? Explain.
2. This ad lists a web site. Visit the Altoids web site at www.altoids.com. How does the web site compliment the print ad? Who would visit this site? Evaluate the effectiveness of having companion web sites in addition to printed advertisements.
3. Would you try Altoids based on this advertisement? Why or why not?

4. How does this photograph capture your attention? Can you tell at a glance what it is selling? Where is your eye directed?

Deciphering Editorial Cartoons

Editorial cartoons have been a part of American life for over a century. They are a mainstay feature on the editorial pages in most newspapers—those pages reserved for columnists, contributing editors, and illustrators to present their views in words and pen and ink. As in the nineteenth century when they first started to appear, such editorial cartoons are political in nature, holding political and social issues up for public scrutiny and sometimes ridicule.

A stand-alone editorial cartoon—as opposed to a strip of multiple frames—is a powerful and terse form of communication that combines pen-and-ink drawings with dialogue balloons and captions. They're not just visual jokes, but visual humor that comments on social/political issues while drawing on viewers' experience and knowledge.

The editorial cartoon is the story of a moment in the flow of familiar current events. And the key words here are moment and familiar. Although a cartoon captures a split instant in time, it also infers what came before and, perhaps, what may happen next—either in the next moment or in some indefinite future. And usually the cartoon depicts a moment after which things will never be the same. One of the most famous cartoons of the last 40 years is the late Bill Mauldin's Pulitzer-Prize-winning drawing of the figure of Abraham Lincoln with his head in his hands. It appeared the morning after the assassination of President John Kennedy in 1963. There was no caption nor was there a need for one. The image represented the profound grief of a nation that had lost its leader to an assassin's bullet. But to capture the enormity of the event, Mauldin brilliantly chose to represent a woeful America by using the figure of Abraham Lincoln as depicted in the sculpture of the Lincoln Memorial in Washington, D.C. In so doing, the message implied that so profound was the loss that it even reduced to tears the marble figure of a man considered to be our greatest president, himself assassinated a century before.

For a cartoon to be effective, it must make the issue clear at a glance and it must establish where it stands on the argument. As in the Mauldin illustration, we instantly recognize Lincoln and identify with the emotions. We need not be told the circumstances, since by the time the cartoon appeared the next day, all the world knew the horrible news that the President had been assassinated. To convey less obvious issues and figures in a glance, cartoonists resort to images that are instantly recognizable, that we don't have to work at to grasp. Locales are determined by give-away props: airports will have an airplane out the window, the desert is identified by a cactus and cattle skull; an overstuffed arm chair and TV for the standard living room. Likewise, human emotions are instantly conveyed: pleasure is a huge toothy grin; fury is steam blowing out of a figure's ears; love is two figures making goo-goo eyes with floating hearts. People themselves may have exaggerated features to emphasize a point or emotion.

In his essay "What Is a Cartoon?", Mort Gerberg (*The Arbor House Book of Cartooning*, HarperCollins, 1989) says that editorial cartoons rely on such visual clichés to instantly convey their messages. That is, they employ stock figures for their representation—images instantly recognizable from cultural stereotypes. The fat-cat tycoon, the mobster thug, the sexy female movie star. And these come to us in familiar outfits and props that give away their identities and profession. The cartoon judge has a black robe and gavel; the prisoner wears striped overalls and a ball and chain; the physician dons a smock and forehead light; the doomsayer is a scrawny long-haired guy carrying a sign saying "The end is near." These are visual clichés known by the culture at large, and we get them.

The visual cliché may be what catches our eye in the editorial cartoon, but the message lies in what the cartoonist does with it. As Gerberg observes, "the message is in twisting it, in turning the cliché around."

Cloning Cartoon

Consider the Jack Ohman cartoon that follows. The cliché is a woman shopping in a supermarket. We know that from the familiar props: the shopping cart, the meat display unit, the department banner, and the hint of shelving in the background. Even the shopper is a familiar figure, an elderly woman in her overcoat pushing her cart. The twist, of course, is that instead of a refrigeration unit displaying lamb, beef, and poultry, we see trays of neatly arranged embryo clones with their genetic specialties in stickup signs. The issue, of course, is the debate on human cloning. The cartoon was published on December 10, 2001, shortly after the announcement by the genetics firm Advanced Cell Technology in Worcester, Massachusetts, that they had

cloned the first human embryo. (The embryos only survived a few cell divisions before they ceased.) Although the lab claimed that the intentions of cloning was not to create human beings but to treat particular human ailments, such as Parkinson's disease, cancer, and strokes, the publicity fanned the flames of debate over the ethics and morality of cloning. Some people view such breakthroughs as medically promising; others fear crossing the line of playing God.

The cartoon's joke is in the twist—the gap between the familiar and the unexpected. The familiar is the supermarket cliché; the unexpected is the casual display of embryo flagged for desirable traits in a Cloned Embryo Department. Of course the scene depicts some indefinite future time when cloning is permitted by law and widely practiced.

What Is the Claim?

The claim in this cartoon is that natural birth is better than genetic engineering. That is implicit in the satirical image of the human talents and traits quantified and commercialized in the meat section of the supermarket. And it is explicit in the woman's thoughts, "I miss the stork. . . "

What Are the Assumptions?

This cartoon makes the assumptions that people see human beings as more complex and elusive than particular traits and talents, and that purchasing babies according to desired traits is perverse and unnatural.

What Is the Evidence?

The evidence is in the darkly satirical notion that instead of natural procreation we would someday shop for scientifically perfected babies in a supermarket. Next to more "serious" preferences, such as embryos cloned from donors with "1600 SAT" scores and "20/20 vision," are the embryos cloned from people good at juggling and ear-wiggling. It is in these juxtapositions where the cartoonist gives away where he stands on the issue. He is mocking our society by reducing the aspiration of would-be parents to have kids with narrowly specific talents. To clinch Ohman's stand is the woman's thought bubble—"I miss the stork. . . " The message is that in the imagined new world where we can shop for our ideal babies, there are those who yearn for the good old days. Of course, "the stork" is a polite metaphorical reference to sexual reproduction—a term appropriate for the customer in the drawing—an elderly woman conservatively dressed. However, the term is another cliché, and in a curious twist it plays off the supermarket meat department display—as if stork were another kind of poultry option.

As you review the various visuals throughout the text, approach what you see with the critical eye of a skeptic. Many of the techniques used in reading critically can be applied to visuals. Consider the ways symbolism, brand recognition, stereotyping, and cultural expectations contribute to how such illustrations communicate their ideas. Try to think abstractly, taking into account the many different levels of consciousness that visuals use to communicate. Consider also the way shading, lighting, and subject placement in the photos all converge to make a point. "Read" them as you would any text.

Fashion

and Flesh

The Images We Project

1

Pick up a magazine. Turn on the television. View a film. Every day we are bombarded with images and messages telling us that slim is sexy and beauty means happiness. The right labels mean success and respect. The right look means acceptance. And overwhelmingly, our culture buys into these messages.

We live in a society caught up in images of itself—a society seemingly more driven by the cultivation of the body and how we clothe it than in personal achievement. In fact, so powerful is the influence of image that other terms of self-definition are difficult to identify. In this chapter, several writers grapple with questions raised by our cultural preoccupation with flesh and fashion. Are we our bodies? Can our inner selves transcend the flesh? Do the clothes we wear express the self we want to be? From where does all the body-consciousness pressure come? Some essays in this chapter recount people at war with their bodies due to cultural pressure. Other essays are accounts of people rising above the din of fashion's dictates to create a sense of self that is authentic and rooted in personal happiness. And some explore the cultural trends that help direct contemporary fashion.

Many women feel that men are free from the social pressures associated with body image. It may come as a surprise to some people that many men, like women, are concerned with body image. The first selection, "Never Too Buff" by John Cloud, reports the disturbing trend that many men, and even young boys, are struggling with the cultural pressure to achieve physical perfection with which women often must deal. Former fashion editor Liz Jones questions the influence of the fashion industry on women's feelings about their bodies. Why does the fashion industry continue to promote tall, emaciated models on runways and magazine covers when the average woman is five foot four inches tall and about 160 pounds?

The next cluster of essays deals with how we, as individuals, feel about our bodies. In a society in which beauty seems to be precisely defined, there is little room for variations from the prescribed parameters of beauty. Sandra Hurtes discusses how watching the perfect bodies of actresses on the Academy Awards made her go off her diet in frustration. In "My Hips, My Caderas," Alisa Valdes examines the cultural differences that define beauty as she tries to balance her sense of body image between her Hispanic and white roots. Cynthia Audet reflects on how a scar on her face, which family and friends pressured her to have removed, helped shape her sense of who she was. And Diane Sepanski gives us the "Skinny on Small," as she describes her struggle to fit into a world where beautiful equaled tall and thin when her genes dictated that she be short and plump.

Although many people equate social acceptability with standard definitions of beauty, others strive to exhibit their individuality by setting their own styles. Such expressions are most common among teenagers and young adults, who strive to define themselves as distinct from their mainstream parents. The next three essays describe a few of the different ways youth culture asserts its independence through fashion. Ptolemy Tompkins explains how shaving his head marked him as both "weird" and independent. In "The Bald Individualist," he also questions what unique modes of expression are left for today's teenagers. We follow with a humorous essay by columnist Dave Barry, "The Ugly Truth About Beauty," which discusses the differences between how men and women feel about their looks.

Finally, the Viewpoints section ends the chapter with a bit of humor, and, at the same time, raises some poignant questions. First, *Ottawa Citizen* reporter Scott Mc-Keen provides a list of ways for men to hide a pot belly in "A Man's Guide to Slimming Couture." Following this light and witty advice, Catherine Lawson, the fashion editor for the *Ottawa Citizen*, raises the question, "Why Do We Get to Laugh at Fat Guys?" Her article zeroes in on some of the inequities in our society concerning obesity, which, considering current trends in how our culture connects body image and body size, are unlikely to change.

The final reading, and this chapter's Research Issue, addresses the concept of beauty. Elizabeth Snead's report, "The Beauty of Symmetry," explains that we instinctually prefer symmetrical faces, and why. Is beauty really skin deep?

Never Too Buff
John Cloud

While men with lean and muscular bodies have always been admired, the idea that men obsess about their body image as much as women may seem ludicrous to some people. We tend to assume that most men simply do not care about their appearance the way women do. Not so, according to psychiatrists Harrison Pope, Katharine Phillips, and psychologist Roberto Olivardia. Their research reveals a disturbing trend: just as many young women aspire to be supermodel thin, an increasing number of young men yearn for the steroid-boosted and buff bodies typical of today's action heroes and weightlifters. In the following article, John Cloud reports on this groundbreaking research, and what it might mean for boys and men in the years ahead.

Harrison Pope, a professor of psychiatry at Harvard Medical School, and Katharine Phillips, a professor of psychiatry at Brown University, in conjunction with Roberto Olivardia, a clinical psychologist at McLean Hospital in Massachusetts, have researched male body image for the past fifteen years. Their book, *The Adonis Complex*, published in 2000, concludes that "something awful has happened to American men over the past few decades"—they have become obsessed with their bodies. Journalist John Cloud discusses some of the key highlights of their research in this article, which first appeared in *Time* magazine on April 24, 2000, one week before their book was published.

CRITICAL THINKING   Try to imagine the "perfect" male body. What does it look like? Is your image influenced by outside forces, such as the media, your gender, or your age? How do real men you know compare to the image in your mind?

1 Pop quiz. Who is more likely to be dissatisfied with the appearance of their chests, men or women? Who is more likely to be concerned about acne, your teenage son or his sister? And who is more likely to binge eat, your nephew or your niece?

2   If you chose the women and girls in your life, you are right only for the last question—and even then, not by the margin you might expect. About 40 percent of Americans who go on compulsive-eating sprees are men. Thirty-eight percent of men want bigger pecs, while only 34 percent of women want bigger breasts. And more boys have fretted about zits than girls, going all the way back to a 1972 study.

3   A groundbreaking new book declares that these numbers, along with hundreds of other statistics and interviews the authors have compiled, mean something awful has happened to American men over the past few decades. They have become obsessed with their bodies. Authors Harrison Pope and Katharine Phillips, professors of psychiatry at Harvard and Brown, respectively, and Roberto Olivardia, a clinical psychologist at McLean Hospital in Belmont, Mass., have a catchy name to describe this obsession—a term that will soon be doing many reps on chat shows: the Adonis Complex.

4   The name, which refers to the gorgeous half man, half god of mythology, may be a little too ready for Oprah, but the theory behind it will start a wonderful debate. Based on original research involving more than 1,000 men over the past 15 years, the book argues that many men desperately want to look like Adonis because they constantly see the "ideal," steroid-boosted bodies of actors and models and because their muscles are all they have over women today. In an age when women fly combat missions, the authors ask, "What can a modern boy or man do to distinguish himself as being 'masculine'?"

5   For years, of course, some men—ice skaters, body builders, George Hamilton—have fretted over aspects of their appearance. But the numbers suggest that body-image concerns have gone mainstream: nearly half of men don't like their overall appearance, in contrast to just 1 in 6 in 1972. True, men typically are fatter now, but another study found that 46 percent of men of normal weight think about their appearance "all the time" or "frequently." And some men—probably hundreds of thousands, if you extrapolate from small surveys—say they have passed up job and even romantic opportunities because they refuse to disrupt workouts or dine on restaurant food. In other words, an increasing number of men would rather look brawny for their girlfriends than have sex with them.

6   Consider what they're spending. Last year American men forked over $2 billion for gym memberships—and another $2 billion for home exercise equipment. *Men's Health* ("Rock-hard abs in six weeks!" it screams every other issue) had 250,000 subscribers in 1990; now it has 1.6 million. In 1996 alone, men underwent some 700,000 cosmetic procedures.

7   At least those profits are legal. Anabolic steroids—the common name for synthetic testosterone—have led to the most dramatic changes in the male form in modern history, and more and more average men want those changes for themselves. Since steroids became widely available on the black market in the 1960s, perhaps 3 million American men have swallowed or injected them—mostly in the past 15 years. A 1993 survey found that 1 Georgia high school boy in every 15 admitted having used steroids without a prescription. And the Drug Enforcement Administration reports that the percentage of all high school students who have used steroids has increased 50 percent in the past four years, from 1.8 percent to 2.8 percent. The abuse of steroids has so alarmed the National Institute on Drug Abuse that on Friday

it launched a campaign in gyms, malls, bookstores, clubs and on the Internet to warn teenagers about the dangers. Meanwhile, teenagers in even larger numbers are buying legal but lightly regulated food supplements, some with dangerous side effects, that purport to make you bigger or leaner or stronger.

8   As they infiltrated the body-building world in the '70s and Hollywood a decade later, steroids created bodies for mass consumption that the world had literally never seen before. Pope likes to chart the changes by looking at Mr. America winners, which he called up on the Internet in his office last week. "Look at this guy," Pope exclaims when he clicks on the 1943 winner, Jules Bacon. "He couldn't even win a county body-building contest today." Indeed, there are 16-year-olds working out at your gym who are as big as Bacon. Does that necessarily mean that today's body builders—including those 16-year-olds—are 'roided? Pope is careful. "The possibility exists that rare or exceptional people, those with an unusual genetic makeup or a hormonal imbalance," could achieve the muscularity and leanness of today's big body builders, he says.

9   But it's not likely. And Pope isn't lobbing dumbbells from an ivory tower: the professor lifts weights six days a week, from 11 A.M. to 1 P.M. (He can even mark historical occasions by his workouts: "I remember when the Challenger went down; I was doing a set of squats.") "We are being assaulted by images virtually impossible to attain without the use of drugs," says Pope. "So what happens when you change a million-year-old equilibrium of nature?"

10   A historical loop forms: steroids beget pro wrestlers—Hulk Hogan, for one, has admitted taking steroids—who inspire boys to be just like them. Steroids have changed even boys' toys. Feminists have long derided Barbie for her tiny waist and big bosom. The authors of *The Adonis Complex* see a similar problem for boys in the growth of G.I. Joe. The grunt of 1982 looks scrawny compared with G.I. Joe Extreme, introduced in the mid-'90s. The latter would have a 55-in. chest and 27-in. biceps if he were real, which simply can't be replicated in nature. Pope also points out a stunning little feature of the three-year-old video game Duke Nukem: Total Meltdown, developed by GT Interactive Software. When Duke gets tired, he can find a bottle of steroids to get him going. "Steroids give Duke a super adrenaline rush," the game manual notes.

11   To bolster their argument, the Adonis authors developed a computerized test that allows subjects to "add" muscle to a typical male body. They estimate their own size and then pick the size they would like to be and the size they think women want. Pope and his colleagues gave the test to college students and found that on average, the men wanted 28 lbs. more muscle—and thought women wanted them to have 30 lbs. more. In fact, the women who took the test picked an ideal man only slightly more muscular than average. Which goes a long way toward explaining why Leonardo DiCaprio can be a megastar in a nation that also idealizes "Stone Cold" Steve Austin.

12   But when younger boys took Pope's test, they revealed an even deeper sense of inadequacy about their bodies. More than half of boys ages 11 to 17 chose as their physical ideal an image possible to attain only by using steroids. So they do. Boys are a big part of the clientele at Muscle Mania (not its real name), a weight-lifting store that *Time* visited last week at a strip mall in a Boston suburb. A couple of

teenagers came in to ask about tribulus, one of the many over-the-counter drugs and body-building supplements the store sells, all legally.

13   "A friend of mine," one boy begins, fooling no one, "just came off a cycle of juice, and he heard that tribulus can help you produce testosterone naturally." Patrick, 28, who runs the store and who stopped using steroids four years ago because of chest pain, tells the kid, "The s__ shuts off your nuts," meaning steroids can reduce sperm production, shrink the testicles and cause impotence. Tribulus, Patrick says, can help restart natural testosterone production. The teen hands over $12 for 100 Tribulus Fuel pills. (Every day, Muscle Mania does $4,000 in sales of such products, with protein supplements and so-called fat burners leading the pack.)

14   Patrick says many of his teen customers, because they're short on cash, won't pay for a gym membership "until they've saved up for a cycle [of steroids]. They don't see the point without them." The saddest customers, he says, are the little boys, 12 and 13, brought in by young fathers. "The dad will say, 'How do we put some weight on this kid?' with the boy just staring at the floor. Dad is going to turn him into Hulk Hogan, even if it's against his will."

15   What would motivate someone to take steroids? Pope, Phillips and Olivardia say the Adonis Complex works in different ways for different men. "Michael," 32, one of their research subjects, told *Time* he had always been a short kid who got picked on. He started working out at about 14, and he bought muscle magazines for advice. The pictures taunted him: he sweated, but he wasn't getting as big as the men in the pictures. Other men in his gym also made him feel bad. When he found out they were on steroids, he did two cycles himself, even though he knew they could be dangerous.

16   But not all men with body-image problems take steroids. Jim Davis, 29, a human-services manager, told *Time* he never took them, even when training for bodybuilding competitions. But Davis says he developed a form of obsessive-compulsive disorder around his workouts. He lifted weights six days a week for at least six years. He worked out even when injured. He adhered to a rigid regimen for every session, and if he changed it, he felt anxious all day. He began to be worried about clothes, and eventually could wear only three shirts, ones that make him look big. He still felt small. "I would sit in class at college with a coat on," he says. You may have heard this condition called bigorexia—thinking your muscles are puny when they aren't. Pope and his colleagues call it muscle dysmorphia and estimate that hundreds of thousands of men suffer from it.

17   Even though most boys and men never approach the compulsion of Davis or Michael (both eventually conquered it), they undoubtedly face more pressure now than in the past to conform to an impossible ideal. Ripped male bodies are used today to advertise everything that shapely female bodies advertise: not just fitness products but also dessert liqueurs, microwave ovens and luxury hotels. The authors of *The Adonis Complex* want guys to rebel against those images, or at least see them for what they are: a goal unattainable without drug use.

18   Feminists raised these issues for women years ago, and more recent books such as *The Beauty Myth* were part of a backlash against the hourglass ideal. Now, says Phillips, "I actually think it may be harder for men than women to talk about these problems because it's not considered masculine to worry about such things." But

maybe there is a masculine alternative: Next time WWE comes on, guys, throw the TV out the window. And order a large pizza. ◆

FREEWRITING ASSIGNMENT

Pope, Phillips, and Olivardia report that, in general, men would like to add 28 pounds more muscle to their frames but believe women would prefer even more—at least 30 pounds more muscle. What, in your opinion, accounts for this perception? Does it seem reasonable?

CRITICAL READING

1. Evaluate the comment made by Pope, Phillips, and Olivardia that young men are increasingly obsessed with body image because they feel that muscle is all men have "over women today." Do you agree or disagree with this statement? Explain.
2. Analyze the author's use of statistics to support his points. Do their conclusions seem reasonable based on the data they cite? Why or why not?
3. Visit the Muscle Memory web site and look at the photographs of some of the Mr. America winners over the past 50 years at www.musclememory .com/articles/MrAmerica.html. How do they compare to today's body builders? Explain.
4. According to the author, what cultural messages tell children that steroid use is okay? Describe some of the ways children receive these messages.
5. In paragraph 16, Cloud tells the story of Jim Davis. Compare Jim to Diane Sepanski, the author of the article "The Skinny on Small." How are they similar and different? Can you find any irony in their situations? Explain.

CRITICAL WRITING

6. *Analytical Writing*: Write a detailed description of your ideal male image (what you desire in a male or what you would most want to look like as a male). How does your description compare with the conclusions drawn by the psychiatrists and psychologist in the article? Did outside cultural influences direct your description? Explain.
7. *Personal Narrative:* Looking back at your experience in high school, write a narrative about the males who were considered the most "buff." What qualities made these particular males more desirable and more enviable than their peers? How much of their appeal was based on their physical appearance? How much on something else?
8. *Persuasive Writing*: Pope, Phillips, and Olivardia comment that media pressure is connected to the emergence of men's new obsession with body image. Write an essay discussing whether this is true or not true. Support your perspective using examples from Cloud's article and your own experience.

GROUP PROJECTS

9. Create and administer your own survey regarding the ideal male appearance. As a group, come up with a list of qualities—such as intelligence, body build, facial features, sense of humor, and physical strength—that can be ranked in order of importance. Try to come up with 8–12 qualities or characteristics. Distribute your poll among men and women on your campus (indicate whether the poll is given to a man or a woman). Tabulate the results and present your findings to the class. (For an interesting comparison, groups may also want to distribute a similar list of female characteristics and qualities.)

10. Have everyone in the group bring a copy of a men's magazine (*Details*, *GQ*, *Esquire*). Different group members may want to focus on different aspects of the magazines—such as advertising, articles, fashion, or advice columns. Do the models in the magazine fit the description in Cloud's article? What do the articles suggest men should aspire to look like? How many articles on improving appearance are featured? After reviewing the magazines, discuss your findings and collaborate on an essay about how men's fashion magazines help define the "ideal" male.

11. Working in small groups, arrange to visit your campus gym or local health club. Split up and take notes about what kinds of men you see working out there. What patterns of behavior do you see—for example, are there more men working with weights than doing aerobics? Write brief descriptions of the men's workout attire. Do they seem concerned with how they look? Why or why not? After your visit, get together and compare notes. Write a report on your findings and present your conclusions to the class.

What I Think About the Fashion World
Liz Jones

For many young women, perfect beauty is defined by the supermodels. Tall, thin, long limbed, and with sculpted features, supermodels and popular actresses embody what it means to be beautiful in our society. Images in magazines further promote this often unattainable ideal. In a culture in which women are often measured by how they look, the pressure to be thin can be great. But such women represent a very small minority of body type. In this article, Liz Jones gives her perspective on the way women are treated by the fashion industry. Are thin models part of a fashion conspiracy, or are they merely reflective of what the public wants to see?

Liz Jones is the former editor of the British edition of *Marie Claire*, a women's fashion magazine. In June 2000, while still editor of *Marie Claire*, she shocked the fashion world by featuring two covers, one featuring Pamela Anderson and one with voluptuous Sophie Dahl, then a size 12. The Dahl cover prevailed, but many critics spoke out against Jones for using the magazine as a forum to "forward her own agenda." Jones, a recovering anorexic, admitted she used her position as editor to highlight the issue, claiming it was an issue that needed to be addressed. Jones is now editor of the Life and Style section of the *London Evening Standard*. This article was first published in *You* magazine, a supplement of the *Mail on Sunday*, in the April 15, 2001 edition of the *London Daily Mail*.

CRITICAL THINKING   Try to picture your version of the perfect female body. What does it look like? Is your image influenced by outside forces, such as the media, your gender, or your age? How do real women you know compare to the image in your mind?

1   For four weeks last month I sat in the front row of catwalk shows in London, Milan, Paris and New York watching painfully thin models walking up and down inches from my nose.

2   Kate Moss, the original 'superwaif', was looking positively curvaceous compared to the current bunch of underweight teenagers.

3   For those used to the fashion industry there was nothing unusual about the shows at all. But for me it was the end; it was then that I decided to resign as editor of *Marie Claire* magazine.

4   I had reached the point where I had simply had enough of working in an industry that pretends to support women while it bombards them with impossible images of perfection day after day, undermining their self-confidence, their health and hard-earned cash.

5   My decision to quit was partly precipitated by the failure of a campaign I started a year ago to encourage magazines, designers and advertisers to use models with more realistic, representative body images. Then I could not have anticipated the extraordinarily hostile reaction to my fairly innocuous suggestions from fellow editors and designers. A year later I have come to realize the sheer terrorism of the fashion industry and accept that, alone, I cannot change things.

6   But in the spring last year I was full of optimism that we could change. I believed wholeheartedly that we could stop magazines and advertisers using underweight girls as fashion icons. I had already banned diets and slimming advice from our pages but after meeting Gisele, the Brazilian supermodel credited with bringing 'curves to the catwalk', and discovering that she is a tiny size 8, I decided to challenge the status quo.

7   We decided to publish two covers for the same edition—one featuring Sophie Dahl, a size 12; the other, Pamela Anderson, a minute size 6—and we asked readers to choose between the skinny, cosmetically enhanced 'perfection', or a more attainable, but still very beautiful curvy woman. Sophie Dahl won by an overwhelming majority.

8   But you would think that we had declared war. The reaction was staggering. Newspapers, radio and TV stations were largely behind us. They welcomed the opportunity to demystify the closed and cliquey world of fashion. Our covers were in the national press for weeks—even making headlines in the *New York Post*. I had re-

quests from universities here and abroad wanting to include our experiment in their college courses. Documentaries were made in the US and Germany. The response from readers was unprecedented. We received 4,000 letters in two weeks.

9   However, the very people from whom I had expected the most support—my fellow female editors—were unanimous in their disapproval.

10   I was invited to speak at the Body Image Summit set up by Tessa Jowell, Minister for Women, in June 2000 to debate the influence of media images on rising problems of anorexia and bulimia among women. One suggestion was that a group—consisting of editors, designers, young women readers and professionals who treat women with eating disorders—should get together on a regular basis to monitor the industry, bring in guidelines on using girls under a certain body size and weight and discuss ways the industry could evolve. My job was to gather these people: not one single other editor agreed to take part.

11   Instead most of them were hostile and aggressive. Jo Elvin, then editor of *New Woman*, accused *Marie Claire* of 'discriminating against thin women'. (As if there aren't enough role models in the media for thinness, from Jennifer Aniston to Gwyneth Paltrow to American supermodel Maggie Rizer.) Another fashion editor made the point that there had always been skinny women—look at Twiggy, for example. Jasper Conran absurdly suggested we should be looking at obesity as a serious health problem instead of anorexia and bulimia. I didn't bother to point out that people with obesity were not usually put on magazine covers as fashion icons.

12   The next day, after the summit, I received a fax, signed by nearly all the other editors of women's magazines and some model agencies, stating that they would not be following any initiative to expand the types of women featured in their magazines—one of the topics up for discussion at the summit was how to introduce more black and Asian women onto the pages of Britain's glossies.

13   When I read the list of names, I felt like giving up the fight there and then. I was isolated, sickened to my stomach that something so positive had been turned into a petty catfight by women I respected and admired. They were my peers, friends and colleagues I sat next to in the front row of the fashion shows. They were also the most important, influential group of women in the business, the only people who could change the fashion and beauty industry. Why were they so reluctant to even think about change?

14   Like me, they had sat at the summit while a group of teenage girls, black, Asian and white, some fat, some thin, had berated us all for what we were doing to their lives. I had found it moving to listen to these young women, brave enough to come and talk in front of all these scary high profile people. Anyway, to me, it made good business sense to listen to them and address their concerns: why alienate your readers? I could see those teenagers turning away from magazines because we seemed hopelessly outmoded, old fashioned, unattainable. But I was clearly alone.

15   The other editors seemed to revel in the chance to counter attack. Alexandra Shulman, editor of *Vogue*, denounced the whole campaign as a promotional tool for *Marie Claire* and said that suggestions of an agreement to set up a self-regulatory body within the industry was 'totally out of order'. Debbie Bee, then editor of *Nova*—a supposedly cutting edge fashion magazine for young women—asserted in

her editorial the following month that magazines didn't cause anorexia as readers were intelligent enough to differentiate between an idealized model and real life.

16   Fiona McIntosh, editor of *Elle*, published a cover picture of Calista Flockhart with the caption, 'I'm thin, so what?' She accused me of 'betraying the editors' code'. Frankly, I didn't even know there was a code; only one, surely, to put your readers first.

17   Some model agencies blacklisted the magazine. Storm, who represents Sophie Dahl and who you would have thought would have been happy that one of their models was being held up as an example of healthy gorgeousness, told us that we could no longer book any of their girls. Several publicists from Hollywood, reacting both to the cover and a feature called 'Lollipop ladies' about women in Hollywood whose heads are too big for their tiny bodies, wrote to me saying their stars would not be gracing our covers—ever.

18   I had clearly put my head too far above the parapet. I realized that far from being the influential trendsetters I had thought, magazine editors are more often ruled by fear—and advertisers. No one feels that they can afford to be different. They are happy to settle, instead, for free handbags and relentless glamour.

19   To be honest, it would have been very easy to give up then. Every time the contacts of a fashion shoot landed on my desk with a model whose ribs showed, whose bony shoulders and collar bone could have cut glass, whose legs were like sticks, we could have published them anyway and said, 'oh well, we tried'. But we didn't. We threw them out, set up a reshoot, and eventually, slowly, agencies started to take us seriously and would only send girls with curves in all the right places.

20   I cannot deny the campaign got the magazine talked and written about. The choice of covers got the readers involved and made them have a little bit of power for a change; they got to choose who they wanted on the cover. The Sophie Dahl cover started to sell out, and readers would phone me, frantic, saying, 'I could only buy the Pamela Anderson cover, but I want you to register my vote for Sophie.' It could never have been a scientific exercise—subscribers to the magazine had to take pot luck; but still they would phone up saying, 'No, I wanted Sophie!'

21   But I was dismayed by accusations that this was just another way to boost sales. I suffered from anorexia from the age of 11 until my late twenties and understand first hand the damaging effect of a daily diet of unrealistically tiny role models gracing the pages of the magazines that I was addicted to. Although it did not cause my illness, the images definitely perpetuated the hatred I had for my own body.

22   I agree with Debbie Bee of *Nova* that young women are intelligent enough to be able to tell the difference between a model and real life but the effects are often subliminal. One piece of research we did at *Marie Claire* was to ask a group of intelligent professional women about their bodies then let them browse a selection of magazines for an hour, before asking them again. Their self-esteem had plummeted.

23   Never before have we been bombarded with so many images of perfection: more and more glossies on the shelves, web sites, digital satellite channels, more and more channels showing music videos 24 hours a day. New technology is also removing the images we see of women even further from reality. Just try finding a cover on the shelves this month where the star has not had her spots removed, the

dark circles under her eyes eradicated, the wrinkles smoothed and her waist trimmed.

24   It is common practice nowadays to 'stretch' women whose legs aren't long enough. One men's magazine currently on the shelves, so the industry gossip has it, has put one star's head on another woman's body—apparently, her original breasts weren't 'spherical enough'.

25   So women have been conditioned to go to the gym and diet, or if they don't, to feel guilty about it, but that still won't achieve 'cover girl' perfection because you can't be airbrushed in real life. I've seen the models close up: believe me, lots of them have varicose veins, spots, appendectomy scars and, yes, cellulite. Only the 16 year olds don't have fine lines.

26   The pressure on actresses in Hollywood to be a certain size is enormous. You would think we would have been on pretty safe ground shooting Renee Zellweger, the star of *Bridget Jones*, for our April cover. I had seen the movie; she was, well, Bridget: curvy, busty, with cellulite and a healthy appetite. On the shoot? She was an American size two (UK six). All the outfits, which were samples—clothes made for the catwalk and fitted on size 8 models—swamped her.

27   She turned down the Bridget sequel because it would mean piling on the pounds all over again. Jennifer Aniston admits in the current issue of *Vanity Fair* that she lost 30 pounds to get the role of Rachel in *Friends*. On the rare occasion a star is a 'normal' size, it is very hard getting hold of clothes that will be big enough. None of the samples will fit, so fashion editors have to trawl the stores borrowing off the rails. One of the most beautiful women in the world, Liv Tyler, is a healthy size 12; none of the designers are able to dress her directly from clothes that are on the catwalk.

28   So did I achieve anything with my campaign? I believe so. One newspaper conducted a survey of high street and designer shops and proved how women over size 12 were not being catered for. Stores are now providing a broader range of sizes.

29   In the May issue, we published naked pictures of eight ordinary women, and asked readers to fill in a questionnaire telling us honestly how they feel about the women in the photographs, and about their own bodies. Interestingly, of the respondents so far, all the women say their boyfriends find the size 16 woman the most attractive. The results will be made into a Channel 4 documentary in the autumn.

30   In the next issue, my final edition as editor, we have on our cover three young women, all a size 12, curvy, imperfect, but very beautiful all the same. On the shoot, it was apparent that Suzanne, Myleene and Kym from Hear'Say were all happy in their own skin. For now. On the Popstars program, Nasty Nigel had told the girls they should go on a diet. 'Christmas is over,' he said to Kym, 'but the goose is still fat.' How long before the girls start feeling paranoid about their bodies, under the constant pressure of fame, is anybody's guess.

31   In Britain an estimated 60,000 people, most of them young women, suffer from eating disorders while far greater numbers have an unhealthy relationship with food. Many of them take up smoking or eat diet pills to keep their weight below a certain level. Of all psychiatric disorders, anorexia has the most fatalities—it is very hard to recover from. I refuse to conform to an industry that could, literally, kill.

32   It's time for the industry—the photographers, the editors, the casting directors, designers and the advertisers—to wake up and allow women to just be themselves. From the phone calls and letters I received at *Marie Claire*, I know that women are fed up with feeling needlessly bad about their wobbly bits.

33   I only hope that my successor listens to them. ◆

FREEWRITING ASSIGNMENT ——————————————

Is the fashion industry exerting pressure on women to be thin? Consider the women featured on the covers of popular magazines for men and women, including *Marie Claire*, *Cosmopolitan*, *Vogue*, *Maxim*, and *Vibe*. Do you think such magazine covers influence how we define beauty and desirability?

CRITICAL READING

1. In your opinion, is the fashion industry's use of extremely thin models harmful? In your opinion, has mass media created unrealistic expectations of beauty? Explain.

2. By running the two covers, Jones sought to discover whether women wanted perfection and aspiration or something more realistic and attainable. What did sales of the June 2000 cover reveal? Based on your own observations, how do you think American women would have reacted to the same experiment?

3. How did other fashion magazine editors react to Jones's *Marie Claire* covers? What do you think their reaction reveals about the fashion industry?

4. Debbie Bee of *Nova*, another British fashion magazine, argues that young women are "intelligent enough to be able to tell the difference between a model and real life." How does Jones test this theory? What does she discover?

5. Evaluate how well Jones supports her viewpoint in this essay. Does she provide supporting evidence? Is she biased? Does she provide a balanced perspective, or does she slant her data? Explain.

6. Jones is a former editor for a major fashion magazine. Does the fact that she held this position and was willing to risk her career for this issue influence your opinion of her essay or her points? Why or why not?

CRITICAL WRITING

7. *Exploratory Writing*: Do you know someone who seems obsessed with his or her weight or who suffers from an eating disorder? Discuss what you feel are the causes of the problem. Do you agree with Jones that many eating disorders are influenced by the cult of thinness perpetuated by the fashion industry? Why or why not?

8. *Exploratory Writing*: Write an essay exploring the connections among the fashion industry, body image, and self-esteem. Does the fashion industry have a direct role in our feelings of self-worth and acceptance? Support your viewpoint with examples from the text and your own personal experience.

9. *Personal Narrative*: Write an essay in which you analyze your own feelings about your self-image. What factors do you think shaped your feelings? What elements of our culture, if any, influenced your development of body consciousness? Explain.

GROUP PROJECTS

10. With your group, gather magazine photographs of several models and analyze their body types. What common elements do you notice? How are they similar or different? How do they compare to "real" people? Based on the photographs, can you reach any conclusions about fashion models in today's culture?

11. Discuss in your group the following question: If you could be either very beautiful or very wealthy, which would you choose? Explain the motivation behind your choice. Based on your group's multiple responses, can you reach any conclusions about the influence of beauty on men and women in today's society?

I'm So Fat (NEDA advertisement)

Most people—often young women—who suffer from eating disorders such as anorexia nervosa or bulimia also experience distorted self-perception. The person they see in the mirror differs drastically from their physical reality. In 2004, the National Eating Disorders Association (NEDA) launched the "Get Real" awareness campaign to portray how distorted the self-image of someone suffering from an eating disorder can be. The campaign ran ads in several magazines including *People* and *InStyle* and also aired television spots on major stations. The goal of the campaign was to increase awareness while encouraging people with eating disorders to seek assistance through its free hotline. This print ad was created for NEDA by Porter Novelli, a public relations firm known for health promotion campaigns.

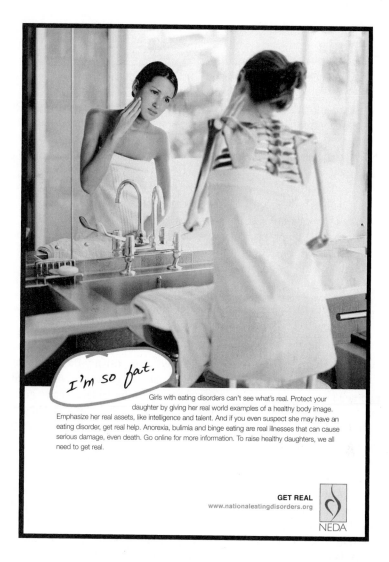

1. If you were leafing through a magazine and saw this ad, would you stop to read it? Why or why not? What catches your eye? How long would you spend looking at the ad? Explain.
2. Visit the NEDA website at www.nationaleatingdisorders.org and read about eating disorders in men and women (look at the "eating disorder info" pages). Who is at risk for an eating disorder? What role does social and cultural pressure play in exacerbating eating disorders? Explain.
3. What is happening in the photo? What is the woman thinking? What does she see? What do we see? What message does the photo convey?
4. Who is the target audience for this ad? Do you think someone with an eating disorder will be persuaded to follow the advice in the ad? If not, who is likely to respond to it? Explain.

Weighing In

Sandra Hurtes

American popular culture is strongly influenced by the images projected by Hollywood. In the next essay, Sandra Hurtes describes how watching actresses on the Academy Awards made her want to go off of her diet. How much of our own personal identity becomes blurred by media images of beauty? Is Hollywood promoting an unrealistic, and even unhealthy, ideal?

Sandra Hurtes teaches creative nonfiction at Hunter College in New York. Her essays and articles have appeared in many publications, including *The New York Times*, *New Age*, *The Washington Post*, and *The Forward*. She has been nominated for the Jackauer Award for excellence in Jewish Journalism for her essay on 9/11. She is currently working on a family memoir about the Holocaust. This essay was first posted on *Feminist.com*.

CRITICAL THINKING Does the size of your clothing influence how you feel about your body? Do you think women think more about clothing size than men do?

1   After watching the Academy Awards I decided to go off my diet. Looking at actresses who earn enough money to feed entire nations, yet appear emaciated and in desperate need of a good meal, sent me charging to the fridge. That's not to say I wouldn't like to be a size two and wear a clingy dress like Uma or Hilary. I have been as thin as they are, and the truth is, once the novelty wore off, I wasn't any happier than I am right now.

2   I've spent over one-half of my life concerned about my weight. The eternal ten pounds that I mull over in my mind, for a minute here, a minute there, add up to a nice chunk of time that I could be thinking about far meatier issues—raising money for AIDS research, housing the homeless, even my next article. But with the self-centeredness of the body-obsessed, the scale in my mind never sleeps. While waiting for a train, attending a business meeting, or sitting at my computer, a voice inside my head comes out of nowhere, and tells me, "I'm so fat."

3   In the movie "Sex, Lies and Videotape," Andie MacDowell's character tells her therapist that women would be fat and happy if there were no men in the world. Although all the women in the audience laughed in acknowledgment, I don't believe it's as simple as a female/male issue. I've never been with a man who thought I needed to lose ten pounds. Still, I wage a daily war with myself, equating sexuality with being thin and I dole out self acceptance with how closely I weigh in.

4   When the television program "Melrose Place" was on the air, I wanted to send the show's female stars a care package. They were scarily skinny. Was I jealous? Yes. But I was angry too. Although I knew better than to let the media define me, the messages fed into what I've been taught ever since I began to care about how I look. If Heather Locklear, a size 2, had a different man every week begging her for

sex, somewhere inside me I believed that if I was ever to have sex again, I had to look, at least from the back, like a pubescent girl. So during commercials, instead of writing a letter to producer Aaron Spelling, I was on the floor doing sit ups.

5   Don't get me wrong. I'm not opposed to healthful living. It's just that often the true meaning of the terms get blurred. Especially by me. Several years ago I went to a health spa for a vacation. Comfortable with my weight, I didn't go there for the dieting but to relax and spend a week of healthy living.

6   After three days I got caught up in the low calorie meals and strenuous exercise and the effect they were having on my body. I loved it, believing I was only in it for the week. But when I got home, something strange happened to me. I couldn't start my day without a bowl of shredded wheat, couldn't even look at 'fattening' food, and the early morning hikes I enjoyed so much, translated in city terms to walking everywhere, forget about subways or buses. After a month of continuous diet and exercise the pounds began to fall off. I was in awe of the process and loved getting skinny. Three months later I was two sizes smaller, and my hip bones stuck out prominently enough that I could see them through my clothes. What a rush.

7   I looked good, although some friends thought I was too thin. I felt fit and was eating healthfully. Sounds great. The problem was that all I thought about was food. What I would eat for my next meal. What I wasn't eating. What other people were eating that they shouldn't be. How many miles I would walk the next day to work off the extra bites of something I wished I hadn't eaten. I wasn't aware of the treadmill I was on until I ran into a friend I hadn't seen in a long time, and she asked me how my summer was. I realized that the only pleasure I had during those leisurely months was showing off my new body in skimpy clothes. A day at the beach was less about fun and more about saying no to food and comparing myself to other women. It felt a little crazy and dangerously close to anorexia.

8   I loosened my grip on myself, and my weight went up a bit. I've gained a few pounds, an indicator that I love to eat and get great pleasure from food. I'm not skinny anymore, but I'm not overweight. Can I leave myself alone?

9   I'm trying. I went shopping for clothes the other day. Browsing through the store I caught a glimpse of myself in the mirror, and what I saw upset me. It wasn't my body, but the way I was dressed. Long flannel shirt, baggy pants—a woman in hiding. I rummaged through the racks and found something black, sexy, with a little cling. I bought it.

10   Still, this body acceptance thing is going to take time, and I can't do it alone. You see, when I was shopping I noticed an interesting phenomenon. Women's clothes now start at size zero. How low can we possibly go? Before starving into non-existence, it's time to stop and think about something. Is this the change that we've been fighting for—to be heard but not seen? ◆

FREEWRITING ASSIGNMENT ────────────────

Is body size a part of who you are? Do we try to pretend body size doesn't matter, while feeling that it really does? Explain.

CRITICAL READING

1. Why does watching thin women featured on the Academy Awards actually make Hurtes go off of her diet? Why is this ironic?
2. Sandra Hurtes notes that she has been very thin before, but it didn't make her any happier. What is the connection between thinness and happiness? Explain.
3. Analyze Hurtes's tone. How does her tone influence the message of her article? Explain.
4. Who is Hurtes's audience and what assumptions does she make about this audience?
5. Although Hurtes says that she no longer obsesses about her weight, she notes, in her first paragraph, that she is dieting. How does this information influence the rest of her essay? Explain.

CRITICAL WRITING

6. *Exploratory Writing*: Vanity and obsessive preoccupation with self-image have historically been connected to women more than men. In your opinion, do men and women approach the issue of fashion and body image differently? If so, in what ways?
7. *Exploratory Writing*: Social scientists conjecture that physical appearance may indeed affect our chances of securing higher paying jobs and achieving greater social acceptance. In this essay, Sandra Hurtes discusses that her thinness was a source of pride to her, but soon became an obsession. She enjoyed comparing herself to others. Write an essay in which you address how we strive to look a certain way to conform to social expectations that imply success and confidence. Drawing from this article and others in the chapter, write an essay in which you explore the connection between our personal sense of success and our physical appearance.
8. *Exploratory Writing*: In paragraph three, Hurtes quotes Andie MacDowell's character in "Sex, Lies and Videotape," in which she tells her therapist that women would be fat and happy if there were no men in the world. Write an essay responding to this idea. On what social and cultural assumptions is it based? Does it have a kernel of truth? Explain.

GROUP PROJECT

9. Make a list of the most popular prime-time shows on television. After compiling the list, identify the body size of the characters on each program. How many male and female characters could be considered overweight? What is the male-to-female ratio of these characters? Discuss your findings with the rest of the class in a discussion about how actors on television promote (or do not promote) certain body types as more desirable than others.

My Hips, My Caderas
Alisa Valdes

The saying "beauty is in the eye of the beholder" may be better expressed as "beauty is in the eye of the culture." A feature or characteristic that one culture finds unappealing may be considered beautiful in another. Physical beauty seems to be largely a subjective thing—some cultures artificially elongate the neck, others put plates in their lips, and others prefer tiny feet or high foreheads. As a Latina woman with a white mother and a Cuban father, Alisa Valdes finds herself straddling the beauty preferences of two cultures. In the next essay, Valdes explores how she learned to love her body despite receiving conflicting messages from two cultural traditions.

After receiving her bachelor's degree from Berklee College of Music, Alisa Valdes earned her master's degree in journalism from Columbia University. She has won several awards in writing and has been nominated for a Pulitzer Prize. Valdes now reports on the Latin music scene for the *Los Angeles Times*. The following article was published online by MSN's *UnderWire* e-zine in April 2000.

CRITICAL THINKING
Is beauty a cultural construction? Why are some physical characteristics admired in some cultures and not in others? Can you think of any physical traits that Americans esteem that other cultures do not?

1   My father is Cuban, with dark hair, a cleft in his chin and feet that can dance the Guaguanco. My mother is white and American, as blue-eyed as they come.

2   My voluptuous/big hips are both Cuban and American. And neither. Just like me. As I shift different halves of my soul daily to match whichever cultural backdrop I happen to face, I also carefully prepare myself for how differently my womanly/fat hips will be treated in my two realities.

3   It all started 15 years ago, when my hips bloomed in Albuquerque, New Mexico, where I was born. I went from being a track club twig—mistaken more than once for a boy—to being a splendidly curving thing that Chicano men with their bandanas down low whistled at as they drove by in their low-riders. White boys in my middle school thought I suddenly had a fat ass, and had no problem saying so.

4   But the cholos loved me. San Mateo Boulevard . . . I remember it well. Jack in the Box on one corner, me on a splintered wooden bench with a Three Musketeers bar, tight shorts, a hot summer sun, and those catcalls and woof-woofs like slaps. I was 12.

5   My best friend Stacy and I set out dieting right away that summer, to lose our new hips so boys from the heights, like the nearly albino Tim Fairfield with the orange soccer socks, would like us. In those days, I was too naive to know that dismissing the Chicano guys from the valley and taking French instead of Spanish in middle school were leftovers of colonialism. Taking Spanish still had the stigma of

shame, like it would make you a dirty wetback. So Stacy and I pushed through hundreds of leg lifts on her bedroom floor, an open *Seventeen* magazine as a tiny table for our lemon water, and the sound of cicadas grinding away in the tree outside.

6   In Spanish, the word for hips is caderas—a broad term used to denote everything a real woman carries from her waist to her thighs, all the way around. Belly, butt, it's all part of your caderas. And caderas are a magical sphere of womanhood. In the lyrics of Merengue and Salsa, caderas are to be shaken, caressed, admired and exalted. The bigger, the better. In Spanish, you eat your rice and beans and sometimes your chicharrones because you fear your caderas will disappear.

7   In my work as a Latin music critic for a Boston newspaper, I frequent nightclubs with wood-paneled walls and Christmas lights flashing all year long. I wear short rubber skirts and tall shoes. There, I swing my round hips like a metronome. I become fierce. I strut. In the red disco lights, my hips absolutely torture men. I can see it on their faces.

8   "Mujeron!" they exclaim as I shimmy past. Much woman. They click their tongues, buy me drinks. They ask me to dance, and I often say "no," because I can. And these men suffer. Ironically, this makes the feminist in me very happy. In these places, my mujeron's hips get more nods than they might at a pony farm.

9   In English, your hips are those pesky things on the sides of your hipbones. They don't "menear," as they do in Spanish; they "jiggle." In English, hips are something women try to be rid of. Hips are why women bruise themselves in the name of liposuction.

10   My mother's people hate my hips. They diet. My aunt smokes so she won't eat. And in the gym where I teach step aerobics—a habit I took up in the days when I identified more with my mother's than my father's people—I sometimes hear the suburban anorexics whisper in the front row: "My God, would you look at those hips." Sometimes they walk out of the room even before I have begun teaching, as if hips were contagious. In these situations, I am sad. I drive home and examine my hips in the mirror, hit them for being so imprudent, like great big ears on the side of my body. Sometimes I fast for days. Sometimes I make myself puke up rice and beans. Usually I get over it, but it always comes back.

11   Sociologists will tell you that in cultures where women are valued for traditional roles of mother and caregiver, hips are in, and that in cultures where those roles have broken down and women try to be like men were in traditional societies—i.e., have jobs—hips are out.

12   So when I want to be loved for my body, I am a Latina. But most Latino men will not love my mind as they do my body, because I am an Americanized professional. Indeed, they will feel threatened, and will soon lose interest in hips that want to "andar por la calle come un hombre" (carry themselves like a man).

13   When I want to be loved for my mind, I flock to liberal intellectuals, usually whites. They listen to my writings and nod . . . and then suggest I use skim milk instead of cream. These men love my fire and passion—words they *always* use to describe a Latina—but they are embarrassed by my hips. They want me to wear looser pants.

14   In some ways I am lucky to be able to move between two worlds. At least my hips get acknowledged as beautiful. I can't say the same for a lot of my bulimic

friends, who don't have a second set of standards to turn to. But still, I dream of the day when bicultural Latinas will set the standards for beauty and success, when our voluptuous caderas won't bar us from getting through those narrow American doors. ◆

FREEWRITING ASSIGNMENT

Write about a time in your life when you realized that other people noticed your body. How did it make you feel? How did you react?

CRITICAL READING

1. Valdes notes that sociologists conjecture that in cultures in which women adhere to the more "traditional" roles of housewife and mother, hips and voluptuous forms are considered beautiful. Evaluate this theory and its implied inversion—that in societies in which women hold jobs outside the home, small waists and hips are culturally preferred by both sexes.
2. Does the author view the transformation of her hips from her "track club twig" physique to her more womanly shape as a positive or negative change? How does her writing reveal her feelings?
3. In paragraph 5, Valdes describes how she and her best friend Stacy worked out to reduce their hips. How does she connect these efforts to other practices of her youth, such as taking French in middle school? Explain.
4. Valdes writes, "My mother's people hate my hips." Who are her "mother's people"? Does it seem strange that she would refer to her relatives this way? Compare her description of her mother's side of the family to that of her father's side of the family.
5. How can driving men wild with her hips make "the feminist in [Valdes] very happy"? Why does she consider this "ironic"?
6. How does Valdes's mixed background create conflict in her life? How does she deal with this conflict?
7. Valdes uses striking, vivid language in her essay to describe the two cultures she straddles. What particular words and phrases work especially well in conveying her message?

CRITICAL WRITING

8. *Exploratory Writing*: Valdes writes, "in cultures where women are valued for traditional roles of mother and caregiver hips are in." If beauty is a cultural creation, how is it constructed? Write an essay exploring the idea that social politics influence our cultural sense of beauty.
9. *Narrative and Analysis*: Write a short essay describing the parts of your body you find especially appealing and why. Does your culture influence your perception of your body? What outside forces influence your sense of physical identity? What changes would you make if you could? Explain.

10. *Research and Analysis*: In your library, newsstand, or bookstore, locate at least two fashion magazines from cultures or ethnicities different from yours. Compare how beauty differs between the two, as well as your own. How are the models similar and different? Is beauty based on universal principles with a few deviations, or is it a social construction based on individual cultural factors? Write an essay detailing your conclusions, using your magazine research and personal perspective as support.

GROUP PROJECTS

11. In her article, Alisa Valdes implies that white women feel more pressure to be thin than Latino women do because Latin culture holds women to a different standard of beauty. In small groups, explore the idea that beauty is culturally determined—that is, what one group may find beautiful, another may not. Can you find any evidence that the all-American image of beauty is changing?

12. Have each member of your group interview a man or woman from another country to ask the following question: "What characteristics are considered physically beautiful in your culture?" Descriptions may be of both men and women, or of only one sex. Compare your notes with the group. What traits are universally admired and what ones are different? Report your findings to the class.

Scar
Cynthia Audet

We are a culture that prizes physical perfection. Millions of dollars are spent annually in creams, skin medications, and lotions promising to erase wrinkles, cure acne, and mask imperfections. Plastic surgery can fix what the makeup counter can't. In the next short essay, Cynthia Audet describes how a scar on her face, from an injury when she was three years old, influenced how she felt about herself and helped shape her sense of identity.

Cynthia Audet is a writer in Oakland, California. Her work has appeared in *UTNE* magazine and *Dermanities*, an open-access electronic journal. This essay first appeared in the essay section of the January 2003 issue of the *Sun*.

CRITICAL THINKING   In the next editorial, Cynthia Audet describes how her father insisted that she have the scar on her face removed. Consider the ways our parents influence how we feel about our physical appearance. Can you think of an instance where a parent was critical of how you looked? How did it make you feel? How did you react?

Growing up, I had a scar on my face—a perfect arrow in the center of my cheek, pointing at my left eye. I got it when I was three, long before I knew that scars were a bad thing, especially for a girl. I knew only that my scar brought me attention and tenderness and candy.

As I got older I began to take pride in my scar, in part to stop bullies from taunting me, but mainly as a reaction to the assumption that I should feel embarrassed. It's true, I was embarrassed the first couple of times someone pointed at my cheek and asked, "What's that?" or called me "Scarface." But the more I heard how unfortunate my scar was, the more I found myself liking it.

My friends liked it, too. They made up elaborate tales about how I'd gotten it in a fight or from a dog attack. They laughed at their stories and thought I was all the more interesting because I could laugh with them.

When I turned fifteen, my parents—on the advice of a plastic surgeon—decided it was time to operate on what was now a thick, shiny red scar. As my father drove me home from the local mall, he explained that I would have the surgery during my summer vacation, to allow time for it to heal.

"But I don't mind the scar, really," I told him. "I don't need surgery." It had been years since I had been teased. And my friends, along with my boyfriend at the time, felt as I did, that my scar was unique and almost pretty in its own way. After so many years, it was a part of me.

"You do need surgery," my father said, his eyes on the road, his lips tight.

"But I like it," I told him. "I don't want to get rid of it."

"You need surgery," he said again, and he lowered his voice. "It's a deformity." I don't know what hurt more that day: hearing my father call my scar a deformity, or realizing that it didn't matter to him how I felt about it.

I did have plastic surgery that summer. They cut out the left side of the arrow, leaving a thinner, zigzag scar that blended into the lines of my face when I smiled. The following summer they did the same to the right side of the arrow. Finally, when I was eighteen, the surgeon sanded my cheek smooth.

In my late twenties, I took a long look at my scar, something I hadn't done in years. It was still visible in the right light, but no one asked me about it anymore. I examined the small steplike pattern and the way it made my cheek dimple when I smiled. As I leaned in awkwardly toward the mirror, I felt a sudden sadness.

There was something powerful about my scar and the defiant, proud person I became because of it. I have never been quite so strong since they cut it out. ◆

FREEWRITING ASSIGNMENT

Have you ever considered having plastic surgery to change a body feature you don't like? If money were no object, would you have plastic surgery? If so, what would you change, and if not, why?

CRITICAL READING

1. Audet writes her essay as a personal narrative. How does she use her personal experience to present her perspective?

2. How does Audet feel about her scar? What do her feelings about it tell you about her personality? Her friends? How does she feel about the removal of her scar? Explain.
3. In her opening paragraph, Audet notes that she got her scar when she was only three, before she understood that scars "were a bad thing, especially for a girl." Evaluate this comment in your own words.
4. How did Audet's scar help shape her identity? In your opinion, do you think she should have fought harder to not have the surgery? Did she really have a choice?

CRITICAL WRITING

5. *Personal Narrative and Exploratory Writing*: Audet writes a personal narrative describing her memory of her scar and different reactions to it, including her own. Write a short essay exploring how you feel about your own personal appearance. You could explore how certain "ethnic" features influenced your identity, or how your physical appearance made you feel included or excluded in certain social situations. Connect your narrative to some of the ideas expressed by Audet in her editorial.
6. *Personal Narrative*: Audet relates that her father coerced her into having her scar removed, at the expense of her own feelings about it. Write an essay in which you explore how a parent or relative pressured you into doing something you did not want to do. What do you think motivated them to exert this pressure? If you gave in, are you glad that you did? If you resisted, do you think you made the right choice, and why?
7. *Personal Narrative*: Write an essay about a time when you think your looks made you stand out or feel different. It could be because of the way you were dressed, the way you styled your hair or the color of your skin, your sex or size—anything that made you feel different from the rest of the group. What made you more distinctive, and how did it make you feel? Did you wish you could blend in, or were you proud that you stood out? Explain.

GROUP PROJECT

8. With your group, access the American Society of Plastic Surgeons' web site at www.plasticsurgery.org. Review the statistics, types of procedures, and patient testimonials (under their public awareness campaign) concerning plastic surgery. Who is having plastic surgery? What procedures are the most common? Is plastic surgery becoming more or less common? Based on your research at the web site, present your findings to the class for discussion.

The Skinny on Small
Diane Sepanski

The desire to fit in is particularly compelling during adolescence, when teens feel like they are constantly being judged on how they look. While clothing and hairstyles can be copied, body size and shape are often determined by genetics. In the next essay, Diane Sepanski describes her personal struggle to fit in as a short girl in a society where height was an essential component of beauty and, thus, popularity. Says Sepanski, "at thirteen, I knew I was short. And I knew I didn't like it." In a culture where the synonyms used to describe "petite" include "petty" and "trifling," Sepanski found that even language was against her.

Diane Sepanski is a freelance writer from Seattle. This essay was first published in *Body Outlaws*, 2002.

CRITICAL THINKING | Think about how you felt about your body when you were a child. Can you recall a time when you began to grow dissatisfied with your body, and the reason for this change in self-perception? Explain.

1 I was eleven years old in 1978 when Randy Newman's song "Short People" became a hit. I measured exactly four feet, nine inches; I know this because every year on my birthday my father marked my height on the cold grey pillar that supported his basement workroom. Every year I looked forward to the moment when, after Carvel ice cream cake and presents, Dad would chart my physical journey toward adulthood in black Magic Marker. These longitudinal readings are faint now, and the last of them remains the clearest: By 1980 I had sprouted up to a full five-foot-one.

2 I don't know why my dad and I stopped our ritual. Perhaps my impending entrance into high school signaled a symbolic denouement: Now I was to put aside childish ways, put on makeup and slowly prepare to enter the world, standing tall on high heels. Or maybe it was because, by the tender age of thirteen, I was already hoofing high heels, making precise proportions, if not beside the point, then at least a lot less imperative. I already knew I was short. And I knew I didn't like it.

3 I'm short and I'm skinny and I'm small-boned. *Petite* is the euphemism. *Little, small, dainty, dinky, elfin, diminutive, miniature, pygmy, Lilliputian, wee, tiny, teeny, teeny-weeny* and *itsy-bitsy* are some of the synonyms. Notice the list degenerating into "baby talk"; the next word in Roget's catalogue is *baby*, and it just gets worse from there: *toy, portable, compact, poky, cramped, no room to breathe, narrow, runty, puny, weak, petty, trifling, inconsiderable, one-horse* . . . until finally we get to the crux of the matter. The last synonym on the list is *unimportant.*

4 Girls learn early what's important. When I was six I thought it was the height of hilarity that when I tried to make my Barbie walk, her impossibly long and coltish legs inevitably caused her to topple backwards. At thirty, I can joke that the only way I'd ever look like Barbie is if I shrunk her in the dryer and then amputated those coltish legs at the knee. But in 1978, before the concept of *grrrls* was invented, it

was desperately important to me to fit in with all the bigger, more developed girls who seemed like Barbies to my Midge. I wasn't the smallest girl in my class—but it was close, and the distance between who was popular and who was distinctly, absolutely and positively *not* could be—and was—precisely measured. Bigger was better (as long as it wasn't too big, but I did say *precisely*, didn't I?); bigger, in short, was power.

5 Now power in 1978 in my coed Catholic grammar school in my small Long Island town was a lot of things, and most of them spelled *boys*. For those of you who may not know Long Island, it's a place where kids grow up fast. The race was on, and the track back then looked something like this: If you fit in, you were popular, and if you were popular, you got a boy, and the sooner you got a boy, the sooner you became a woman. You can understand, then, why I couldn't wait to grow up. Pun intended. I waited while Megan and Kathleen and Doreen and Suzanne got their training bras and their periods. I waited while they pushed five-five, then five-six, then five-seven. I waited and watched while they played Seven Minutes in Heaven with the cool boys, the boys we all wanted, the boys who sniffed out the scent of approaching womanhood the way a police dog sniffs out drugs.

6 Still, I played the same game of adolescent dress-up we all did: feathered Farrah Fawcett hair, earth shoes, Bonne Bell Lip Smacker, ears pierced, eyelashes curled. But my velour top drooped on my slight shoulders like a flimsy excuse; when I looked in the mirror, all I saw was a girl looking back at me. This girl felt ethereal, insubstantial, unlikely. This girl got pelted with snowballs and didn't fight back. This girl didn't take up much room. She just looked at her shoes.

7 I want to tell you about Megan. She and I became best friends in about fourth or fifth grade. Megan was descended from what is probably a long line of raw-boned, chestnut-maned, strong Irish belles. By the time we reached eighth grade, Megan was five-seven, wide-shouldered yet slim-hipped, a couple of bra sizes ahead of me. She looked great in a bikini. Which is why, to the tune of endless cicadas invisibly whirring in a perfect blue sky, I was walking the two blocks to her house on Saturday morning. We would butter ourselves thoroughly with tanning oil and wait to see who "dropped by." Summer on Long Island was all about the perfect body, the perfect tan—and, of course, the perfect boy.

8 Megan was already stretched out on a deck chair when I arrived. I would say she looked like Xena, Warrior Princess, except that goddess didn't yet exist. So let me settle for an angel: one of Charlie's. I was wearing my favorite sky-blue-trimmed-with-white terry cloth matching shorts and top set over my bathing suit. For some reason I went inside their house, into the kitchen, and Megan followed. Megan's mom was sitting at the table; she looked me up and down and burst out laughing. "You're wearing a diaper," she said, and then Megan started laughing too. "Your shorts look like a diaper!" They snickered for a long time. I don't remember what I said, although I'm pretty sure I said nothing. I went back outside, my eyes squinting against the sunlight's stare, and fastidiously removed my ugly clothes in slow, deliberate motion, as if my body would somehow shatter with any sudden movement, as if I were made of glass.

9 How can I tell you what the space around Megan felt like? If I close my eyes, the feeling is still palpable—the way she moved through space; acted on it; occupied

it; owned it; made molecules of air dance through her fingers. More than boy-attention, what Megan—and Doreen and Suzanne—possessed was a physical power I felt I would never have, no matter how much swimming, bike-riding, running, walking or playing I did. They took their bodies for granted, felt at home in them. What I perceived from those girls, the only word for it, is presence.

10   Whereas what I felt was a sort of absence: a hyperbolic diminishment conferred on me solely by virtue of my physical being, threatening to converge me to the vanishing point; to lead me, as does my dictionary, from smallness to scarcity to invisibility to—ultimately—disappearance.

11   Although this absence had always been viscerally defined for me by the visual juxtaposition between my body and those of other girls, and in truth, had begun way before puberty—begun, in fact, in another girl's kitchen, with another girl's mother commenting on my "birdlike" six-year-old appetite—it wasn't until adolescence that it took on a political dimension. I saw clearly society's equation between size and power, and I knew I fell on the wrong side of that equation: Mattel didn't manufacture petite Barbies. I could be Midge, or goofy Thelma from *Scooby Doo*, or Nancy Drew's best friend Bess, but I would always be the sidekick, the buddy, the second banana whose dumb name signaled her unattractive and inferior status. I wasn't just different, I was deficient. I would never be the star of my own show.

12   How did I know? Randy Newman told me: "Short people got/no reason/short people got/no reason/to live." So did the salesclerk at Macy's who, when I asked her if she carried that beautiful satin skirt in size two, replied, "I'm sure you can find something you like in the Juniors department." Even strangers felt the need to comment: "Just wait dear, you'll hit a growth spurt in your twenties, I'm sure." It wasn't big of me—maybe it was even a shortcoming—but I hated them, and I sure didn't like myself.

13   I could easily have disappeared. I had packed my small self in a box marked "fragile," the glass house of my body translucent and easily broken, but soon, without quite realizing why, I decided to throw stones and break out of my prison. My weapon of choice was the only thing big about me: my voice. Naturally loud, an alto by sixth grade, and a smart-ass by nature, I had always been a talker, had already been thrown out of class many times for my gabbing, but somewhere between sixth and eighth grades, the quality of this talk changed, became charged, vital and underscored with meaning in a way I only now understand. Suddenly, I became known for my "big mouth." I was talking, quite simply, to exist.

14   There were problems. It seems that some people, many of whom were boys, didn't like the fact that when they teased me about my size, I now had something to say about it. I had run into a new obstacle: machismo. We live in a world where anything "big" is seen as the province of men, including a big mouth. As a *small* woman I was twice removed from that most elemental of powers—brute strength—which men have conveniently defined as the basis of *all* power. Nonetheless, I posed a big threat. My existence, embodied in a new way, broke all the old rules of the schoolyard. I wasn't exactly running with the big boys, but I had claimed their swagger as my own, and it felt wild—like flying—like laughing out loud.

15   What I know now is how perilously close I came to letting others define my existence for me. I *became* small to measure up to society's limited vision of who I

am. By opening up my big mouth, I grew into myself, filled myself, in a way I would not have thought possible back in those difficult adolescent years. I no longer wear high heels: At five feet, three-and-one-half inches, I am a large person with an absolutely huge appetite for life. Being born petite taught me to claim a different kind of power. But I'm lucky. I've chosen to work with words, to pursue a profession that doesn't emphasize brawn. For thousands of other women, women whose dreams are to become firefighters, to work in construction or to attend a military academy, size still matters. We need to open our big mouths for those women, to rewrite the definitions.

16   Big: *grand, substantial, considerable, respectable, weighty, ample, generous, voluminous, capacious, spacious, profound, deep, great in stature, tall, lofty, high, strong, mighty, powerful, influential, intense, superior, of consequence, of consideration, of importance, of concern, crucial, essential, pivotal, central, meaningful, worthwhile, to be taken seriously, not to be despised, not to be overlooked, valuable, significant, necessary, vital, indispensable, irreplaceable, key,*

17   *world-shaking, earthshaking*

18   *noisy, loud*

19   *soaring, climbing, ascending.* ◆

FREEWRITING ASSIGNMENT

Sepanski notes that in her school, bigger (taller) was better, because bigger was power. Write about the relationship between body size and power. What shapes are more "powerful" and why?

CRITICAL READING

1. How did Sepanski feel about her height when she was a teenager? How does she feel about her height now? What influenced her self-image and how did she react? Explain.

2. Sepanski connects body size and height with presence or invisibility. In what ways does the dictionary seem to collaborate her assessment?

3. In paragraph 11, Sepanski discusses the relationship between height/size and political power. Small people are side-kicks, or "buddies," but are rarely given leadership roles in popular culture. Is this true? If so, how does this cultural trend influence our self-perception?

4. Sepanski comments in paragraph 15 that many young women are faced with inequalities in professions because "size matters." What solution does she propose to help these women? Is her solution realistic? Why or why not?

5. Analyze Sepanski's argument. Are there areas in which she seems particularly effective? Are there weak areas of her essay? Identify any parts of her essay with which you could identify and why.

CRITICAL WRITING

6. *Personal Narrative*: Using Sepanski's essay as a model, write a narrative about your own feelings about your weight. Have you ever been on a diet? If so, what motivated you to go on one in the first place? Do you think the media influences how we perceive how attractive we believe ourselves to be? If you have never considered your weight to be an issue, write about why it has not been a concern for you.

7. *Research and Analysis*: This essay originally appeared in a collection of essays called *Adios Barbie*. The book's cover featured a pair of pink Barbie shoes. Mattel sued the editors for using the pumps on the cover of the book. Research the controversy over the title and cover of *Adios Barbie* (including Sepanski's commentary on the lawsuit) at *http://www. seattleweekly.com/features/0009/books-sepanski.shtml*. Do you think Mattel was justified in suing the publication? Or was the issue, as Sepanski implies, more about a political "struggle for control of women's bodies"? Explain.

8. *Persuasive Writing*: You have probably heard the expressions "don't judge a book by its cover" and "the clothes don't make the man." Write an essay in which you agree or disagree with these statements. Be sure to support your position with logical examples.

GROUP PROJECTS

9. Investigate the connection between popularity and teen fashion. Group member evidence can be drawn from television, sporting events, advertising, and magazines. Discuss what trends you find and write a collaborative essay detailing your conclusions.

10. Select two characters from a novel, film, or television program. Write a description of each character's body type and attire. Discuss with your group the connection (if any) between the physical appearance of the characters you selected and the temperment, personality, or nature of the character.

The Bald Individualist
Ptolemy Tompkins

The authors of the preceding essays discussed how physical deviations made them feel different from their peers. Most of these writers, however, grew to appreciate their distinctive features as part of their personal identity. For many teens, having an identity separate from their parents is a key part of growing up and establishing independence. In the next article, Ptolemy Tompkins relates his experiment with personal self-expression. As a teenager, he shaved his head to find himself. But considering the current fascination with nose rings and tattoos, he wonders what is left for today's teenagers?

Ptolemy Tompkins is a writer for the New York Times. He is also the author of Paradise Fever: Growing Up in the Shadow of the New Age. The following article first appeared in the New York Times on June 21, 1998.

CRITICAL THINKING

Why is personal style considered important? Is it more meaningful to have your own look? How important is it to have a look that is different from the previous generation?

1   One afternoon in the fall of 1978, when I was in the first week of my junior year of high school, I asked my mother to drop me off in front of the Italian barbershop I had been visiting since boyhood. Once stationed in the chair and staring at myself in the big, wall-size mirror, I surprised Enzo, the barber on duty that day, with a fresh request.

2   "Take it all off, please."

3   Enzo raised his glasses. "All of it?"

4   "Yup. All of it."

5   There were no other bald students walking around my high school that fall, and as a result of my stop at Enzo's, I changed overnight from just another overtall, un-dercoordinated blur on the periphery to someone with a bona fide image. I had officially become "weird." People who before had paid no attention to me now visibly shied away when I passed them in the corridors; others boldly approached and asked me about my appearance. Did I have cancer? Head lice? Was I receiving shock treatment?

6   I had none of these things. What I had was a stepbrother named Nicky, eight years older than I. He was a Buddhist. In the service of his new calling, Nicky had recently shaved his head, and I found the fact that he had done so strangely fascinating.

7   As Enzo reluctantly ran his razor over my head, I watched the "me" that everybody thought they knew so well fall away in clump after clump onto the linoleum. The sensation was pleasurable and refreshing on an almost physical level.

8   "He must be copying Nicky," the adults around me would often remark—an explanation that, to my mind, missed the point entirely. Sure I was copying him, but only insofar as someone who is lost in a desert "copies" someone else who has found a spring and is drinking from it. By committing this simple action, I felt as if I was becoming myself in a way that I never had before—and the fact that I didn't know why this was so did very little to take away from the strength of the feeling.

9   The results of this one-step attempt at self-transformation were as immediate, and as oddly gratifying, beyond school as they were within it. From anguished concern (my mother), to flat-out irritation (my father), to the countless fleeting looks of puzzlement, amusement or general discomfort that I saw in the eyes of all the shop-keepers, bus drivers and neighbors I passed in the course of a day, I found myself registering in the consciousness of just about everyone I came into contact with. Which, of course, was the point. Among all the other separate selves out there in the world, I was now a force in my own right: a genuine and irreducible "me" in a sea of indefinite and unknowable others. And with each raised eyebrow, I was given a fresh reminder of this.

10   Today I live in New York, and I pass bald 16-year-olds, both male and female, all the time. The ostensible reasons for their baldness are many, and not always easy to differentiate at a glance. Are they punks? Post-punks? Neo-feminists? Quasi-Buddhists? Perhaps just members of a tightly knit sports team? Whatever their ideological leanings, I suspect that when the clippers were running over their heads, many of these young men and women experienced the same triumphant feeling of leaving the beaten track behind and entering into the bright, surprising wilderness of their secret personhood that I did back in suburban Virginia some 20 years ago.

11   Yet something appears to be missing from the experience now. Shaving your head no doubt still feels good, but the look is so widespread that achieving it is no longer, I suspect, as richly collaborative an event as it was for me in 1978. Nor does this just go for haircuts. The physical modifications that a teenager can make in order to enlist the outside world's help in discovering the contours of their true individuality are becoming ever fewer, even while they seem, on the surface, to be growing. Cartilage studs, nose rings, lip plugs, South Pacific tribal war tattoos: the whole warehouse of initiatory paraphernalia, ransacked from cultures that long ago and far away knew how to make such alterations actually count for something, is being raided so fast and so desperately these days that soon the shelves will be completely bare.

12   What will happen then? If an experience is valuable enough, new ways of getting it tend to appear when the old ones wear out. Perhaps the solution to this sudden, drastic shortage in the symbolism of transformation is being cooked up right now, by some disgruntled, as-yet-unknown adolescent visionary. Whatever that solution turns out to be, when it at last appears, one thing is certain. We adults won't like the look of it. ◆

FREEWRITING ASSIGNMENT

Did you try to distinguish yourself physically when you were in high school? If so, what did you do and what motivated this form of expression?

CRITICAL READING

1. Why does Tompkins say that his parents' explanation that he was copying his brother "missed the point entirely"?
2. Tompkins comments that after shaving his head, he had "officially become 'weird.' " How does he feel about this label?
3. In paragraph 8, Tompkins notes that the simple action of shaving his head made him feel like he was "becoming myself in a way that I never had before—and the fact that I didn't know why this was so did very little to take away from the strength of the feeling." In your opinion, do you think teens make a reasoned choice to be different, or are teens motivated on a more subconscious level? Explain.
4. How did reactions to Tompkins's new look affect his self-image?
5. Why does Tompkins feel that expressions of individuality, such as shaving one's head, no longer have the impact they once had? Do you agree or disagree with his conclusion?
6. Tompkins ends his essay with the comment that no matter what new trend teens come up with next, "We adults won't like the look of it." Is adult disapproval a fundamental element of teen fashion? Explain.

CRITICAL WRITING

7. *Exploratory Writing*: Consider and list some fashion trends embraced by different generations in an effort to look different from the generation before it. How does the style of your generation differ from the style of your parents' generation? Your grandparents'? Write an essay examining the different styles of at least three generations, including your own.
8. *Critical Analysis*: Tompkins fears that every physical modification that can shock and deviate from mainstream trends has been done. Do you agree with him? Why or why not? Based on current trends in the teen culture scene, write an essay in which you evaluate Tompkins's comment.
9. *Personal Narrative*: Write an essay describing a time when you discovered a deeper sense of self-awareness by changing something about yourself. Perhaps you wore different clothes or makeup, dyed or cut your hair, wore peculiar jewelry, painted your nails an unusual color, or even got a tattoo. Did people react or treat you differently because of your new look? Did you act differently? Did you find the experience empowering? Explain.

GROUP PROJECTS

10. Each member of your group should arrange to interview a teenager between the ages of 14 and 18 years. Elicit their opinions regarding self-

expression and individuality. How do they distinguish themselves from other generations? What do they think of the ways older generations expressed themselves? Discuss the results of your interviews to see if there are any common ideas. How do you think the older generation would have responded if you could go back in time and ask them the same questions when they were teens?

11. Research teen fashion trends from two different decades. Consult popular media such as MTV, teen fashion magazines, popular television programs, and movies aimed at the age group. For example, evaluate trends from the 1960s and the 1990s. What common themes can you find in both groups? What differences seem distinct to each group? Share your evaluation with the class to promote discussion on similarities and differences in teen self-expression.

The Ugly Truth About Beauty
Dave Barry

It is a common belief that American women are deeply concerned about their looks, and a billion-dollar beauty industry would seem to support this view. In the next essay, columnist Dave Barry takes a humorous look at the difference between how men and women feel about their appearance. As you read, consider how Barry uses humor to discuss more serious issues.

Dave Barry is a syndicated humor columnist. He has been called "America's most preposterous newspaper columnist," a man "incapable of not being funny." The winner of a Pulitzer Prize, he is the author of many books, most recently, *Dave Barry Hits Below the Beltway* (2002) and *Dave Barry's Homes and Other Black Holes* (2003). This column first appeared in the February 1, 1998 edition of the *Miami Herald*.

CRITICAL THINKING   The next essay pokes fun of the way women ask "How do I look?" Why do we ask others to judge our appearance? Whose opinion matters most to you?

1   If you're a man, at some point a woman will ask you how she looks.

2   "How do I look?" she'll ask.

3   You must be careful how you answer this question. The best technique is to form an honest yet sensitive opinion, then collapse on the floor with some kind of fatal seizure. Trust me, this is the easiest way out. Because you will never come up with the right answer.

4   The problem is that women generally do not think of their looks in the same way that men do. Most men form an opinion of how they look in the seventh grade, and they stick to it for the rest of their lives. Some men form the opinion that they are irresistible stud muffins, and they do not change this opinion even when their

faces sag and their noses bloat to the size of eggplants and their eyebrows grow together to form what appears to be a giant forehead-dwelling tropical caterpillar.

5   Most men, I believe, think of themselves as average-looking. Men will think this even if their faces cause heart failure in cattle at a range of 300 yards. Being average does not bother them; average is fine for men. This is why men never ask anybody how they look. Their primary form of beauty care is to shave themselves, which is essentially the same form of beauty care that they give to their lawns. If, at the end of his four-minute daily beauty regimen, a man has managed to wipe most of the shaving cream out of his hair and is not bleeding too badly, he feels that he has done all he can, so he stops thinking about his appearance and devotes his mind to more critical issues, such as the Super Bowl.

6   Women do not look at themselves this way. If I had to express, in three words, what I believe most women think about their appearance, those words would be: "not good enough." No matter how attractive a woman may appear to others, when she looks at herself in the mirror, she thinks: woof. She thinks that at any moment a municipal animal-control officer is going to throw a net over her and haul her off to the shelter.

7   Why do women have such low self-esteem? There are many complex psychological and societal reasons, by which I mean Barbie. Girls grow up playing with a doll proportioned such that, if it were human, it would be seven feet tall and weigh 81 pounds, of which 53 pounds would be bosoms. This is a difficult appearance standard to live up to, especially when you contrast it with the standard set for little boys by their dolls . . . excuse me, by their action figures. Most of the action figures that my son played with when he was little were hideous-looking. For example, he was fond of an action figure (part of the He-Man series) called "Buzz-Off," who was part human, part flying insect. Buzz-Off was not a looker. But he was extremely self-confident. You could not imagine Buzz-Off saying to the other action figures: "Do you think these wings make my hips look big?"

8   But women grow up thinking they need to look like Barbie, which for most women is impossible, although there is a multibillion-dollar beauty industry devoted to convincing women that they must try. I once saw an Oprah show wherein supermodel Cindy Crawford dispensed makeup tips to the studio audience. Cindy had all these middle-aged women applying beauty products to their faces; she stressed how important it was to apply them in a certain way, using the tips of their fingers. All the women dutifully did this, even though it was obvious to any sane observer that, no matter how carefully they applied these products, they would never look remotely like Cindy Crawford, who is some kind of genetic mutation.

9   I'm not saying that men are superior. I'm just saying that you're not going to get a group of middle-aged men to sit in a room and apply cosmetics to themselves under the instruction of Brad Pitt, in hopes of looking more like him. Men would realize that this task was pointless and demeaning. They would find some way to bolster their self-esteem that did not require looking like Brad Pitt. They would say to Brad: "Oh YEAH? Well what do you know about LAWN CARE, pretty boy?"

10   Of course many women will argue that the reason they become obsessed with trying to look like Cindy Crawford is that men, being as shallow as a drop of spit, WANT women to look that way. To which I have two responses:

11   1. Hey, just because WE'RE idiots, that does not mean YOU have to be; and

12   2. Men don't even notice 97 percent of the beauty efforts you make anyways. Take fingernails. The average woman spends 5,000 hours per year worrying about her fingernails; I have never once, in more than 40 years of listening to men talk about women, heard a man say, "She has a nice set of fingernails!" Many men would not notice if a woman had upward of four hands.

13   Anyway, to get back to my original point: If you're a man, and a woman asks you how she looks, you're in big trouble. Obviously, you can't say she looks bad. But you also can't say that she looks great, because she'll think you're lying, because she has spent countless hours, with the help of the multibillion-dollar beauty industry, obsessing about the differences between herself and Cindy Crawford. Also, she suspects that you're not qualified to judge anybody's appearance. This is because you have shaving cream in your hair. ◆

FREEWRITING ASSIGNMENT

Barry jokes that men and women think about their appearances very differently: most men think that they are average looking, while women are far more critical. How would you rate your appearance, and why? Does appearance matter to you? Why or why not?

CRITICAL READING

1. How would you characterize Barry's tone? What assumptions does he make about his audience? Identify areas of his essay where his assumptions are apparent. Why is it important that Barry know his audience? Explain.
2. Barry states that men are essentially trapped when women ask, "How do I look"? Why does he believe this is so? How does popular culture support his viewpoint? Explain.
3. Humor is often a device used to mask more serious issues. What serious issues could Barry be addressing in this essay? Explain.
4. In paragraphs eight and nine, Barry relates an episode on "Oprah" in which women received beauty tips from Cindy Crawford. Why does he think this situation is funny? Do you agree with him? Why or why not?

CRITICAL WRITING

5. *Research and Analysis*: In this essay, Barry says that the reason women are so concerned with their looks is due to the influence of the Barbie doll. Although he says this with humor, other writers in this chapter, such as Diane Sepanski, have commented that Barbie indeed does shape young girls' opinions of beauty and self-image. Write an essay exploring the effect the Barbie doll has had on girls. Interview women and girls for their opinions of the doll, and research Barbie online (try http://www.barbie

.com/ and http://www.mattel.com/our_toys/ot_barb.asp to start). What cultural influence, if any, has the doll exerted on women? Is it simply a toy, or an icon that has indeed influenced generations of women? Explain.

6. Imagine that you are a newspaper critic. Write a critique of Barry's column, focusing on how effective you find his humor. Support your critique with examples from the text.

7. Using Barry's first line as the lead-in, write your own column on this topic expressing your own point of view.

GROUP PROJECT

8. In this essay, Barry identifies Barbie as a major cultural influence on women. As a group, try to identify as many toys as possible that were popular when you were growing up. Did these toys exert any influence on how you felt about yourself? For example, did a toy make you feel powerful or strong? Pretty? Inadequate? Discuss the connection between popular toys and children's self-image.

▶ **A Man's Guide to Slimming Couture**
Scott McKeen

▶ **Why Do We Get to Laugh at Fat Guys?**
Catherine Lawson

The next two readings explore different views of the same issue. Although obesity is a sensitive issue for many people, it is also a common theme in humor. And culturally, we seem to like fat guys. They play funny sidekicks in movies, goofy fathers and husbands in sitcoms, and everybody's pal at the bar. In "A Man's Guide to Slimming Couture," Scott McKeen treats the issue of a pot belly with humor and cunning as he details eight ways to hide one's middle region.

Although popular media seem to welcome the comedic outlet provided by fat men, the same does not seem to hold true for women. Socially, we simply do not find fat women as funny, or as acceptable, as fat men. Catherine Lawson, responding to McKeen's article, asks "Why Do We Get to Laugh at Fat Guys?" After laughing at McKeen's list, Lawson suddenly realizes that she would not be laughing if the article gave advice to fat women. Is this lack of sensitivity to male obesity fair to men? And why is it more acceptable for men to be fat than for women? But why do we feel it is permissible to lampoon fat people in general?

Scott McKeen and Catherine Lawson are both reporters for the *Ottawa Citizen*, in which their articles appeared on December 9, 1999.

CRITICAL
THINKING Think of the number of popular movies and television programs featuring fat men as the focal point for humor. Now think of the number of programs that feature fat women. How do the two compare?

A Man's Guide to Slimming Couture
Scott McKeen

1 Trick No. 1: Never, ever wear horizontal stripes. Vertical stripes, in shirts and in suits, are good because they lengthen one's silhouette, which is slimming, don't you know?

2 Trick No. 2: Always wear a jacket or suit, unless you work near dangerous industrial machinery. Jackets are good because they hide that stuff spilling over your belt.

3 Trick No. 2A: A double-breasted jacket, with its large lapels, can create a slimming V-shape and is always buttoned, putting a curtain between your gut and the world.

4 Trick No. 2B: Warning: if a double-breasted jacket is too long it will shorten your legs, visually, and you'll be a fat troll in a blazer. On some men, blazers look tent-like. Ask your wife or girlfriend: "Do I look fat in this?"

5 Trick No. 2C: A three-button single-breasted jacket is often better than a two-button because the lapels are shorter, making the body of the suit—and you—appear longer and slimmer.

6 Trick No. 3: Never, ever, tie your necktie too short. It will sit over your belly like a neon motel sign, pointing directly to your straining waistline, screaming "NO VACANCY."

7 Trick No. 4: The fat man's paradox: a big man squeezed into small clothes will look bigger, what with all the tell-tale strains, wrinkles, rolls, button gaps and— yeesh—underwear lines.

8 Trick No. 4A: Buy one size too big and you'll look relaxed; your collar won't create an unsightly skin turtleneck and your clothes will drape properly, hiding those rolls or bulges.

9 Trick No. 4B: When shopping, don't even look at the suit or waist size. If it fits, it fits. Just because you're now wearing a 42 waist doesn't mean you're not still a great big loveable guy. Honest.

10 Trick No. 4C: If you scrutinize waist size, pride will take over. You'll walk out with a size 34 waist and in those pants, you'll look stressed, fat, and your vitals will go numb. Hence the stress.

11 Trick No. 5: Stick with dark, classic, and solid colors—black, blue and grey. Anything else, especially on a shirt, will draw the eye to your stomach. You don't want eyes on your stomach.

12   Trick No. 5A: Be mostly monochromatic in your entire ensemble. A dark shirt and trousers create one, long, slimming silhouette. A light shirt with dark trousers draws the eye to the border between the two, your belt line, which, to the observer, looks like the equator.

13   Trick No. 5B: The same rules apply to a jacket and shirt. Wear an unbuttoned dark jacket with a white shirt and it will be like opening the curtain on an off-Broadway production of Porky's.

14   Trick No. 5C: Same goes for dark suspenders over a white shirt. The suspenders will frame the bulk like a photo of fat. A dark vest with dark trousers is good, though.

15   Trick No. 6: Damn the fashions, pleats on pants are good for pot bellies. Straight, slim-profile pants contrast with a larger upper half, creating "chicken legs," as one well-known local sartor put it.

16   Trick No. 7: To tuck or not to tuck? Unless you're in the cast of Friends, skinny, or under 25, tuck your shirt into your pants. Anything else screams: FAT GUY HIDING HIS FAT.

17   Trick No. 8: Don't fret over The Big Question About Pot Bellies, which is: where should my belt ride—below the gut, on the gut, or above the gut? Let comfort decide. . . .

18   Trick No. 8A: But be warned: a belt riding below the gut can cause an unsightly case of cascading corpulence. On the other hand, chest-high pants makes it appear as if your shoulders are riding directly atop your butt.

19   Trick No. 8B: Suspenders can work, especially on bigger pots. They allow for large pants to cross just below the navel—and stay there. No problems then with butt crack, shirt-tail escape or that cinched look you get with a too-tight belt across the stomach.

20   Trick No. 8C: Owners of difficult-to-fit potbellies might want to try a pair of tailored slacks, especially if the proper waist size creates other problems, like an unwieldy crotch. (Don't even go there.) Handmade slacks will cost you so much money, though, that you might actually prefer numb vitals. Ask your wife. ◆

Why Do We Get to Laugh at Fat Guys?
Catherine Lawson

1 The first time I read Scott McKeen's article on eight tricks to hide a pot belly [above], I laughed all the way through it. I loved its hectoring tone, and the way he didn't mince words on the best way to disguise fat wrinkles, rolls, button gaps and underwear lines.

2   Then it hit me. Would I be laughing if these were fashion tips for women? I thought of all the fashion advice for overweight women that I have ever read. The

tone is usually deadly serious, and there are terms like "empowerment," "self-acceptance" and "body image" sprinkled liberally throughout.

3   Mr. McKeen, on the other hand, although he dispenses some excellent advice, is playing it for laughs.

4   So why is it still OK to make jokes about fat men, but completely taboo to laugh at fat women? (Heck, I'm not even comfortable putting the words "fat" and "women" together.)

5   Would I have accepted a story for publication that described portly women in double-breasted blazers as looking like fat trolls? Definitely not. Would I have chosen to illustrate a story on fashion for plus-size women with a close-up photo of a stomach encased in a too-tight top? Unthinkable.

6   It's conventional wisdom that men and women have vastly different body images. Kellogg's Special K has spun an entire ad campaign on this. Remember the TV commercial with the men sitting around a bar, whining about their figures? We laughed because it was ludicrous to think of men obsessing that way. The current ad shows a very flabby, but very happy, man at a beach. "You accept his imperfections. Why not your own?" the ad asks.

7   The subtext is that overweight women should lighten up, so to speak, and be more like those jolly, chubby men, who can still enjoy a day at the beach, despite the fact their flesh has all the pretense, but none of the cuteness, of a baby beluga.

8   There is truth in the Special K campaign, or it would not resonate as it does. However, it would be a simplification to say that overweight men are happy and overweight women are not. It's been reported that aspiring comic Flip Schultz, the star of the Special K commercial, has lost 20 pounds since he saw himself in that Speedo. The late John Candy was known to be extremely sensitive about his weight, and never wanted his comedy to be focused on it.

9   And we all know women who are comfortable in their own skins. Remember actress Camryn Manheim when she accepted her Emmy award exclaiming, "This is for all the fat girls!"

10   But there's only one funny fat girl on TV these days—Mimi on The Drew Carey Show. And the writers and producers have gone out of their way to stress that Mimi is not funny because she is fat. It's because she wears neon blue eyeshadow, her clothes look like they came from a circus, and she has the personality of a piranha.

11   Drew Carey has to put up with jokes about his weight, but he is also held to be loveable. He's part of a long tradition of loveable fat guys. In *Only the Lonely,* John Candy's cuddly character didn't have to lose an ounce to win the heart of a young, slim woman. Neither did John Belushi in *Continental Divide.* Even Mr. Special K guy has someone to call honey. But no one has cast Ms. Manheim as a romantic lead.

12   Women pick up on that kind of inequity.

13   And it leads us to the stark truth that, in our society, a woman's appearance is still far more important than a man's. We can laugh at fat guys because they are also inherently loveable, well-dressed or not. A woman who fails to dress in a way that disguises those extra pounds is out of the game. If you make a joke about a man's gut, all you've done is make fun of his stomach. Insult a woman's body, and you wound her soul.

14   I called Scott McKeen to ask if there had been any complaints about his article when it ran in the *Edmonton Journal.*

15   "Not a one," he said.

16   Many people did ask if the pot belly in the photo is his. He stresses that it definitely is not.

17   You see, fat guys may be funny, but no one aspires to be one. ◆

FREEWRITING ASSIGNMENT

Answer Lawson's question in your own words: "Why do we get to laugh at fat guys?"

CRITICAL READING

1. Analyze McKeen's tone. How does his tone influence the message of his article? Explain.
2. Who is McKeen's audience, and what assumptions does he make about this audience? Refer to examples from his article to support your response.
3. Did you find McKeen's article funny? Why or why not?
4. Why is Lawson uncomfortable even "putting the words 'fat' and 'women' together"? What is the source of her discomfort?
5. According to Lawson, what are some of the disparities between fat men and fat women? Do you agree or disagree with her assessment? Explain.
6. Evaluate Lawson's conclusion. How does her conclusion support the points she makes in her essay?
7. How do people learn prejudice against fat people in the first place? Why do we think it is okay to make fun of obese people? How do you think Larson and McKeen would respond to this question? Explain.

CRITICAL WRITING

8. *Research and Analysis*: Write an essay in which you trace the development of the "fat funny guy" in cinema and/or television. Try to identify several overweight male comedians from previous decades and discuss whether their size was part of their comedy, or merely incidental. Can you draw any conclusions from your research?
9. *Exploratory Writing*: Lawson comments that if you joke about a man's gut, all you have done is made fun of his stomach. But if you "insult a woman's body, you wound her soul." Write an essay in which you explore this idea.
10. *Persuasive Writing*: Lawson notes that overall, it is more socially acceptable for us to laugh at fat men than at fat women. Write a response to Lawson in which you agree or disagree with her conclusion.

GROUP PROJECTS

11. Make a list of the prime-time comedy shows on television. After compiling the list, identify the overweight characters on each program. What is the male-to-female ratio of these characters? Compare your findings with some of the points made in Lawson's essay, and formulate a response in which you support or question her conclusions.

12. With your group, consider the parts of the body we consider funny and why. Adopting McKeen's format, compile a list of tricks to hide a physical flaw. Share your list with the rest of the class. As a class, discuss whether gender is an important part of the comedy. Is it easier to make fun of men's body parts? Why or why not?

RESEARCH ISSUE **The Beauty of Symmetry**
Elizabeth Snead

Can your looks be measured by a mathematical ratio? Studies show that "beautiful" people actually are just "more proportional" people. *USA Today* reporter Elizabeth Snead explains that beauty may simply be a numbers game.

1   Everyone knows the adage "Don't judge a book by its cover." But we can't help it; we do just that, day in and day out, consciously and subconsciously. We rate others on the basis of their appearance and compare our own looks with the enhanced images of beautiful women and handsome men in movies and magazines and on TV and billboards.

2   Beauty not only sells—it pays off. Beautiful babies get more attention from parents and teachers. Good-looking guys get more dates than average ones. Pretty women get out of traffic tickets and into exclusive clubs. The list of pluses for being one of the "beautiful people" goes on and on.

3   So what makes a person attractive? Don't bother looking in the mirror; just get out a measuring tape. Widespread studies, such as those conducted by Randy Thornhill (University of New Mexico) and Karl Grammer (University of Vienna), confirm that beauty is simply balance: The more symmetrical a face, the more appealing it appears. The concept applies to bodies, too. Physical symmetry is subconsciously perceived as a reflection of a person's youth, fertility, health and strength. And although bilateral (left-right) symmetry might not be a bona fide health certificate these days, it has been a marker of good health and genes throughout human evolution.

4   "Our sensitivity to beauty is hard-wired—that is, governed by circuits in the brain shaped by natural selection," says Nancy Etcoff, author of *Survival of the Prettiest: The Science of Beauty*. "We love to look at smooth skin, shiny hair, curved waists and symmetrical bodies because, over the course of evolution, people who noticed these signals and desired their possessors had more reproductive success. We're their descendants."

5   Symmetry also is sexy. In a study by biology professor Thornhill and University of New Mexico psychology professor Steven Gangestad, hundreds of college-age women and men were measured (including their ears, feet, ankles, hands and elbows). Questionnaires revealed that men who were more symmetrical started having sex three to four years earlier and had more sex partners than their asymmetrical counterparts.

6   Symmetrical people smell better, too. Thornhill and Gangestad found that women prefer the scent of symmetrical men, and vice versa. So much for Old Spice and Chanel No. 5.

7   If you weren't born symmetrical, don't despair. Plastic surgeons are skilled at creating and restoring symmetry through popular procedures such as face-lifts, nasal refinements, eyelid lifts, collagen injections, liposuction and cheek and breast implants. Once reserved for the wealthy, plastic surgery now is fairly common for middle-class folks seeking to gain confidence and improve their career and romance prospects.

8   Stephen Marquardt, a retired California plastic surgeon who researches attractiveness, has moved from beauty's medical side to its mathematical side. He notes that a certain ratio has been found to recur in beautiful things both natural (flowers, pine cones, seashells) and man-made (the Parthenon, Mozart's music, da Vinci's paintings). This "golden ratio" is 1:1.618, with the number rounded to 1.618 known as "phi."

9   Using phi as his guide, Marquardt designed a mask that applies the golden ratio to the face. For example, the ideal ratio between the width of the nose and the width of the mouth is—you guessed it—1:1.618. The closer a face fits the mask, he finds, the more attractive the face is perceived to be. "Even average-looking people fit the mask, just not as closely as really attractive people," he says. "A lot of this is biology. It's necessary for us to recognize our species. Humans are visually oriented, and the mask screams, 'Human!' "

10   Marquardt's Web site shows the mask on timeless beauties from Queen Nefertiti to Marilyn Monroe (it works on all ethnicities, with slight variations). There's also a mask for men—a close fit on Pierce Brosnan, but not quite right on Tom Cruise.

11   Not everyone seeking symmetry goes under the knife. Although makeup artists don't slap Marquardt's mask on their clients, they do emulate its template, making eyes appear larger, cheeks higher, noses narrower and lips fuller using the magic of light-reflective foundations, powders and lip glosses. (Sorry, guys: Women have a slight edge on achieving symmetry.) Anyone can create the illusion of a symmetrical face, says Hollywood makeup artist Jeanine Lobell, founder of Stila cosmetics. "Creating symmetry is all about using light, dark and reflection," says Lobell, whose clients include actresses Heather Graham, Liv Tyler, Michelle Pfeiffer, Kate Hudson and Mena Suvari.

12   Sure, when you look good, you feel better. But don't get carried away in search of symmetry. Nobody's perfect, and that's just fine, Lobell says. "When you look at a beautiful face, embrace the unique qualities, including the unevenness." Individuality—now that's beautiful. ◆

CRITICAL THINKING

1. Snead reports that the "golden ratio" of phi fits closely on faces that are considered the most beautiful because these faces are also the most symmetrical. Think about the actors and models you consider the most beautiful. What accounts for their appeal? Is it, indeed, simply the symmetry of their parts?
2. In paragraph 3, Snead asks, "So what makes a person attractive?" Answer this question from your own personal perspective. In your response, consider the information Snead provides in her article, and explain why you agree or disagree, in whole or in part, with them.

RESEARCH PROJECTS

3. Plastic surgeon Stephen Marquardt created a mask that applied the "golden ratio" of 1:1.618 (1.618) known as "phi." Learn more about phi and the mask Marquardt developed at *www.beautyanalysis.com.* Apply the mask to some faces you consider beautiful, and see how they measure up. (You can even apply the mask to your own face by uploading a digital photo.) Discuss your experiments, as well as Marquardt's explanation of phi, in a short essay.
4. In paragraph 7, Snead tells readers that if they wish for more symmetrical faces, plastic surgery could be a solution. Visit the web site of the American Society of Plastic Surgeons (ASPS) at *www.plasticsurgery.org.* Read about some of the procedures and review the statistics on plastic surgery (you can directly access the statistics by typing in *http://www.plasticsurgery.org/public_education/Statistical-Trends.cfm* into the web address line). Who is having plastic surgery and why? What procedures are the most common? What conclusions might you infer from the statistics? Is plastic surgery becoming more or less common? Based on your research, write an essay about the role of plastic surgery in modern American life. If you wish, you may include personal perspectives on this topic, including whether you were likely to consider plastic surgery yourself after reading about it on the ASPS web site.

Additional essay topics, writing assignments, research guidelines, and readings for this chapter can be found online at **www.ablongman.com/goshgarian**.

Advertising

2

Wanting It,
Selling It

Advertising is everywhere—television, newspapers, magazines, the Internet, the sides of buses and trains, highway billboards, T-shirts, sports arenas, and even license plates. It is the driving force of our consumptive economy, accounting for 150 billion dollars worth of commercials and print ads each year (more than the gross national product of many countries in the world), and filling a quarter of each television hour and the bulk of most newspapers and magazines. It is everywhere people are, and its appeal goes to the quick of our fantasies: happiness, material wealth, eternal youth, social acceptance, sexual fulfillment, and power. Through carefully selected images and words, it is the most pervasive form of persuasion in America, and, perhaps, the single most significant manufacturer of meaning in our consumer society. And many of us are not aware of its astounding influence on our lives.

Most of us are so accustomed to advertising that we hear it without listening and see it without looking. However, if we stop to examine how it works on our subconscious, we would be amazed at how powerful and complex a psychological force it is. This chapter examines how words compel us to buy, how images feed our fantasies, and how the advertising industry tempts us to part with our money.

We begin by taking a closer look at the connections among advertisements, media, and our consumer culture. In "Targeting a New World," Joseph Turow discusses the ways in which advertisers exploit rips in the American social fabric to target particular products to specific audiences. Although it may seem obvious that advertisers wish to target their ads to the people who will want to use their products most, Turow questions the long-term social impact of this marketing strategy and what it might mean to American culture in general.

Following this examination of advertising language, Ken Sanes takes a close look at how television commercials create a simulated life—a life better than we could possibly hope to attain, because it isn't real. This construction of "postmodernity," says Sanes, inspires in the consumer a desire to achieve the utopian world depicted on the television set.

The next two articles, "Lunchbox Hegemony," by Dan Cook, and "A Brand by Any Other Name," by Douglas Rushkoff, confirm what parents have long suspected—that Madison Avenue is after their children. Television and the Internet make it easier to target the child market. Advertisers have declared an all-out market assault on today's kids, surrounding them with logos, labels, and ads literally from the day they are born. Are we simply giving children more choices, or are we controlling childhood itself?

Countering all this criticism of advertising and the consumer market, James Twitchell, in "A (Mild) Defense of Luxury," argues that while academics like to wring their hands over the materialistic excesses of society, the truth is, humans have always loved nice things. He contends that even academics would have to admit that the things they think are essential are considered luxuries to another segment of society. It is all in how you look at it.

This chapter's Viewpoints focuses on advertising language. By its nature, the language of advertising is a very special one, combining words cleverly and methodically to get us to spend our money. In "With These Words, I Can Sell You Anything," "word-watcher" William Lutz explores how advertisers twist simple words so that these words appear to promise what the consumer wants to hear. In the second piece, "The Language of Advertising," advertising executive Charles A. O'Neill concedes that the language of ads can be very appealing, but that's the point. However, unless consumers are willing, no ad can force them to part with their money.

"A Portfolio of Advertisements," featuring twelve recently published magazine ads, is followed by a set of questions to help you analyze how ads work their appeal. Apply a critical eye to all the advertisements, and consider the universal and individual ways they appeal to us.

The chapter ends with a piece by Damien Cave, "On Sale at Old Navy: Cool Clothes for Identical Zombies!" in which he questions the trend of mass-market stores that essentially sell the same bland things. This chapter's Research Issue explores how such stores encourage conformity in the name of convenience.

Targeting a New World
Joseph Turow

Advertisers do not target their campaigns to universal audiences. Rather, they target specific audiences to market specific products. In this article, communications professor Joseph Turow explores how the techniques of "target marketing" by advertising agencies widen divisions in American society. To advertisers, the catch phrase is "divide and conquer," and the American consumer public is what they aim to divide.

Joseph Turow is a professor in the Annenberg School for Communication at the University of Pennsylvania. He is the author of many books, including *Media Systems in Society: Understanding Industries, Strategies, and Power*, and *Playing Doctor: Television, Storytelling and Medical Power*. The next essay is excerpted from his book, *Breaking Up America: Advertisers and the New Media World* (1997).

CRITICAL THINKING

How can exploiting Americans' social and cultural divisions actually help advertisers market products to consumers?

"Advertisers will have their choice of horizontal demographic groups and vertical psychographic program types."

"Our judgment as to the enhanced quality of our subscriber base has been confirmed by the advertisers."

"Unfortunately, most media plans are based on exposure opportunities. This is particularly true for television because G.R.P. analysis is usually based on television ratings and ratings do not measure actual exposure."

1   Most Americans would likely have a hard time conceiving the meaning of these quotations. The words would clearly be understood as English, but the jargon would seem quite mysterious. They might be surprised to learn that they have heard a specialized language that advertisers use about them. Rooted in various kinds of research, the language has a straightforward purpose. The aim is to package individuals, or groups of people, in ways that make them useful targets for the advertisers of certain products through certain types of media.

2   Clearly, the way the advertising industry talks about us is not the way we talk about ourselves. Yet when we look at the advertisements that emerge from the cauldron of marketing strategies and strange terminology, we see pictures of our surroundings that we can understand, even recognize. The pictures remind us that the advertising industry does far more than sell goods and services through the mass media. With budgets that add up to hundreds of billions of dollars, the industry exceeds the church and the school in its ability to promote images about our place in society—where we belong, why, and how we should act toward others.

3   A revolutionary shift is taking place in the way advertisers talk about America and the way they create ads and shape media to reflect that talk. The shift has been influenced by, and has been influencing, major changes in the audiovisual options available to the home. But it most importantly has been driven by, and has been driving, a profound sense of division in American society.

4   The era we are entering is one in which advertisers will work with media firms to create the electronic equivalents of gated communities. Marketers are aware that the U.S. population sees itself marked by enormous economic and cultural tensions. Marketers don't feel, though, that it benefits them to encourage Americans to deal with these tensions head-on through a media brew of discussion, entertainment, and argumentation aimed at broadly diverse audiences. Rather, new approaches to marketing make it increasingly worthwhile for even the largest media companies to separate audiences into different worlds according to distinctions that ad people feel make the audiences feel secure and comfortable. The impact of these activities on Americans' views of themselves and others will be profound, enduring, and often disturbing.

5   The changes have begun only recently. The hallmark is the way marketers and media practitioners have been approaching the development of new audiovisual technology. Before the late 1970s, most people in the United States could view without charge three commercial broadcast stations, a public (noncommercial) TV station, and possibly an independent commercial station (one not affiliated with a network). By the mid-1990s, several independent broadcast TV stations, scores of cable and satellite television channels, videocassettes, video games, home computer programs, online computer services, and the beginnings of two-way ("interactive") television had become available to major segments of the population with an interest and a budget to match.

6   People in the advertising industry are working to integrate the new media channels into the broader world of print and electronic media to maximize the entire system's potential for selling. They see these developments as signifying not just the breakup of the traditional broadcast network domain, but as indicating a breakdown in social cohesion, as well. Advertisers' most public talk about America—in trade

magazine interviews, trade magazine ads, convention speeches, and interviews for this book—consistently features a nation that is breaking up. Their vision is of a fractured population of self-indulgent, frenetic, and suspicious individuals who increasingly reach out only to people like themselves.

7   Advertising practitioners do not view these distinctions along primarily racial or ethnic lines, though race and ethnicity certainly play a part, provoking turf battles among marketers. Rather, the new portraits of society that advertisers and media personnel invoke involve the blending of income, generation, marital status, and gender into a soup of geographical and psychological profiles they call "lifestyles."

8   At the business level, what is driving all this is a major shift in the balance between targeting and mass marketing in U.S. media. Mass marketing involves aiming a home-based medium or outdoor event at people irrespective of their background or patterns of activities (their lifestyles). Targeting, by contrast, involves the intentional pursuit of specific segments of society—groups and even individuals. The Underground [radio] Network, the Comedy Central cable channel, and *Details* magazine are far more targeted than the ABC Television Network, the Sony Jumbotron Screen on Times Square, and the Super Bowl. Yet even these examples of targeting are far from close to the pinpointing of audiences that many ad people expect is possible.

9   The ultimate aim of this new wave of marketing is to reach different groups with specific messages about how certain products tie into their lifestyles. Target-minded media firms are helping advertisers do that by building *primary media communities.* These are formed when viewers or readers feel that a magazine, TV channel, newspaper, radio station, or other medium reaches people like them, resonates with their personal beliefs, and helps them chart their position in the larger world. For advertisers, tying into those communities means gaining consumer loyalties that are nearly impossible to establish in today's mass market.

10   Nickelodeon and MTV were pioneer attempts to establish this sort of ad-sponsored communion on cable television. While they started as cable channels, they have become something more. Owned by media giant Viacom, they are lifestyle parades that invite their target audiences (relatively upscale children and young adults, respectively) into a sense of belonging that goes far beyond the coaxial wire into books, magazines, videotapes, and outdoor events that Viacom controls or licenses.

11   The idea of these sorts of "programming services" is to cultivate a must-see, must-read, must-share mentality that makes the audience feel part of a family, attached to the program hosts, other viewers, and sponsors. It is a strategy that extends across a wide spectrum of marketing vehicles, from cable TV to catalogs, from direct mailings to online computer services, from outdoor events to in-store clubs. In all these areas, national advertisers make it clear that they prefer to conduct their targeting with the huge media firms they had gotten to know in earlier years. But the giants don't always let their offspring operate on huge production budgets. To keep costs low enough to satisfy advertisers' demands for efficient targeting, much of ad-supported cable television is based on recycled materials created or distributed by media conglomerates. What makes MTV, ESPN, Nickelodeon, A&E, and other such "program services" distinctive is not the uniqueness of the programs but the special character created by their *formats:* the flow of their programs, packaged to attract the right audience at a price that will draw advertisers.

12   But media firms have come to believe that simply attracting groups to special-ized formats is often not enough. Urging people who do not fit the desired lifestyle profile *not* to be part of the audience is sometimes also an aim, since it makes the community more pure and thereby more efficient for advertisers. So in the highly competitive media environment of the 1980s and early 1990s, cable companies aim-ing to lure desirable types to specialized formats have felt the need to create "signa-ture" materials that both drew the "right" people and signaled the "wrong" people that they ought to go away. It is no accident that the producers of certain signature programs on Nickelodeon (for example, *Ren and Stimpy*) and MTV (such as *Beavis and Butt-head*) in the early 1990s acknowledge that they chase away irrelevant viewers as much as they attract desirable ones.

13   An even more effective form of targeting, ad people believe, is a type that goes beyond chasing undesirables away. It simply excludes them in the first place. Using computer models based on zip codes and a variety of databases, it is economically feasible to tailor materials for small groups, even individuals. That is already taking place in the direct mail, telemarketing, and magazine industries. With certain forms of interactive television, it is technologically quite possible to send some TV pro-grams and commercials only to neighborhoods, census blocks, and households that advertisers want to reach. Media firms are working toward a time when people will be able to choose the news, information, and entertainment they want when they want it. Advertisers who back these developments will be able to offer different product messages—and variable discounts—to individuals based on what they know about them.

14   Clearly, not all these technologies are widespread. Clearly, too, there is a lot of hype around them. Many companies that stand to benefit from the spread of target marketing have doubtless exaggerated the short time it will take to get there and the low costs that will confront advertisers once they do. Moreover, as will be seen, some marketers have been slower than others to buy into the usefulness of a media system that encourages the partitioning of people with different lifestyles.

Nevertheless, the trajectory is clear. A desire to label people so that they may be separated into primary media communities is transforming the way television is pro-grammed, the way newspapers are "zoned," the way magazines are printed, and the way cultural events are produced and promoted. Most critically, advertisers' interest in exploiting lifestyle differences is woven into the basic assumptions about media models for the next century—the so-called 500 Channel Environment or the future Information Superhighway.

15   For me and you—individual readers and viewers—this segmentation and tar-geting can portend terrific things. If we can afford to pay, or if we're important to sponsors who will pick up the tab, we will be able to receive immediately the news, information, and entertainment we order. In a world pressing us with high-speed concerns, we will surely welcome media and sponsors that offer to surround us with exactly what we want when we want it.

16   As an entirety, though, society in the United States will lose out.

17   One of the consequences of turning the U.S. into a pastiche of market-driven la-bels is that such a multitude of categories makes it impossible for a person to di-rectly overlap with more than a tiny portion of them. If primary media communities

continue to take hold, their large numbers will diminish the chance that individuals who identify with certain social categories will even have an opportunity to learn about others. Off-putting signature programs such as *Beavis and Butt-head* may make the situation worse, causing individuals annoyed by the shows or what they read about them to feel alienated from groups that appear to enjoy them. If you are told over and over again that different kinds of people are not part of your world, you will be less and less likely to want to deal with those people.

18   The creation of customized media materials will likely take this lifestyle segregation further. It will allow, even encourage, individuals to live in their own personally constructed worlds, separated from people and issues they don't care about or don't want to be bothered with. The desire to do that may accelerate when, as is the case in the late-twentieth-century United States, seemingly intractable antagonisms based on age, income, ethnicity, geography, and more result from competition over jobs and political muscle. In these circumstances, market segmentation and targeting may accelerate an erosion of the tolerance and mutual dependence between diverse groups that enable a society to work. Ironically, the one common message across media will be that a common center for sharing ideas and feelings is more and more difficult to find—or even to care about. ◆

FREEWRITING ASSIGNMENT

Turow comments that the ways advertisers exploit fissures in American society is "often disturbing." Why is it disturbing? Alternatively, other critics argue that we should not be concerned with this advertising dynamic. React to that viewpoint.

CRITICAL READING

1. Turow uses three quotations to begin his essay. How do these quotations contribute to the points he makes in his article? Are they an effective way to reach his audience? Explain.
2. How does packaging individuals, or groups of people, make them "useful targets" for advertisers? Can you think of any examples of ways advertisers "package" people or groups of people?
3. According to Turow, what social impact does "target marketing" have on America? Do you agree with his perspective? Explain.
4. Evaluate Turow's tone in this essay. What phrases or words reveal his tone? Who is his audience? How does this tone connect to his intended audience?
5. What are primary media communities? How do they help advertisers market a product?
6. Why would producers of certain programs actually want to chase away certain viewers? How can audience exclusion actually help improve a market or sell a product?

CRITICAL WRITING

7. *Research and Exploratory Writing*: Locate a few advertisements or write down the details of a few commercials for some popular products. Write about each ad's intended audience. Applying some of the information you learned from Turow's article, discuss the ways your ads are targeted to specific audiences. Do they exploit cultural fissures? Do you think they help contribute to the fragmenting of American culture? Explain your viewpoint.

8. *Persuasive Writing*: Turow comments that "new approaches to marketing make it increasingly worthwhile for . . . media companies to separate audiences into different worlds according to distinctions that ad people feel make the audiences feel secure and comfortable" (paragraph 4). What types of ads appeal to you and why? Do you feel that advertisements that actively target you as part of a particular segment of society work more effectively on you as a consumer? Explain your perspective in a well-considered essay. Cite specific ads in your response to support your view.

9. *Exploratory Writing*: Write an essay in which you explore the connection between product targeting, audience packaging, and social diversification.

GROUP PROJECTS

10. Turow describes some of the ways advertisers target audiences by exploiting cultural divisions in American society. You and the members of your group are members of an advertising agency developing a campaign for a new cologne. First, determine to whom you will market this new product, and then create an advertising strategy for the product. What will your ads look like? If you use commercials, when will they air and during what programs? Explain the rationale for your campaign to the class, referring to some of the points Turow makes in his article about product targeting.

11. Select several advertisements from a diversified collection of magazines (news, fashion, business, music, etc.). With your group, try to determine the ways in which each ad uses product targeting. Based on your results, present the advertisements to a few people that you feel fit the audience profile you linked to the ad. Ask them for their impressions of the advertisement and its overall effectiveness. Discuss the results with your group.

Advertising and the Invention of Postmodernity

Ken Sanes

Advertising is based on implied promises. Whether products follow through with their promises is beside the point—the goal is to get us to first want, and then buy the merchandise. In the next essay, Ken Sanes explores the simulated world of television commercials, in which everyone and everything is better than the mundane world that we inhabit. The message is if we want to be like the beautiful, blissfully happy people in the ad, we must buy the product. The problem is that products don't come with soundtracks, and utopia can't be found in a bottle of shampoo, an allergy medication, or a fruity candy.

Ken Sanes is a former newspaper writer and columnist. His articles have been published in the *Boston Globe*, the *San Diego Union-Tribune*, the *Nation,* and *Newsday.* He is the creator of the acclaimed media literacy web site *Transparency,* from which this essay was taken.

CRITICAL THINKING

How does the world depicted in television commercials compare to the "real" world in which we live? How do the people look? What landscapes do they inhabit? How do they interact with their environment? Consider how commercials create a simulated reality to sell a product.

---

1 When we examine television advertising we once again find art and technology being used to create simulations that tell stories in an effort to evoke desired reactions from audiences. But in advertising we see a strange new cultural creation: the 30-second "cinematic" production full of dancing, singing and joke-telling characters playing physicians, housewives, and used car salesmen, with ultra-abbreviated plots and quick resolutions of conflict in which the characters overcome obstacles and fulfill their desires in record time with the help of the product. Unlike movies, which will evoke the wrath of the audience if the unfolding of the story is interrupted, in commercials there is virtually no story to interrupt. The entire commercial is a dynamic, graphic field composed of images, music, theatrical performances, superimposed illustrations, narration, and other elements, which reinforce each other to achieve their effect.

2 Like other complex simulations, these inventions of sound-bite television are typically made up of a great many individual forms of fakery and illusion. For example, they display products that are cosmetically altered to seem more appealing to viewers. Raw turkeys are made to look baked and delicious with food coloring, while the sizzle of cooking food turns out to be a sound effect that has been added to the scene. These sensory deceptions are supplemented by exaggerated claims, to create a false identity for the product.

3 Commercials also include another kind of simulation in the form of digitally manipulated images, which are used to portray another realm of fantasy in which the limits imposed by the physical world no longer seem to be in effect. As a result, they are full of talking dogs, children who grow to giant size, products that zoom into space, dancing credit cards and scenes that suddenly become two-dimensional screens, which spin out of existence, creating a virtual world that surpasses anything produced by Imax or Nintendo.

4 Commercials take these elements—visual fantasy, deceptive images of the products, and false claims—and weave them into their various approaches. There are, perhaps, a half dozen kinds of approaches that they rely on and put together in different ways, just as the theme parks, video games, television and news fall into a few basic categories. Some present trivial product information as if it is of momen-

tous importance. Others use glamour or sex, or they try to evoke a sense of empathy and sincerity in an effort to melt viewers emotionally into buying the product. A great many use humor to win over viewers and reduce the pretentiousness of the message, since pretending to be absurd is the best camouflage for something that really is absurd.

5   But what may be most common, are commercials that convey a sense of life as celebration, full of enraptured people who can't help but sing out because they love their Skittles, or who emerge from swimming pools, all luminescent, with magnificent hair and wonderful lives, surrounded by bright colors, upbeat music and dancing friends, in which everything is in motion to convey a sense of what life can be if we buy the product. These kaleidoscope-like images of endlessly festive situations, which are the same as we saw in Disney, are a constant presence, conveying the ultimate image that consumer culture can offer of the good life as an endless party.

6   Whatever form they take, commercials are, ultimately, about what the product will allow consumers to achieve. If politics is about the transformation of the nation to an ideal state, then commercial advertising is about the transformation of you, the viewer, offering the promise of prestige and self-esteem, control over your life, luxury and good times, and a work-free existence. In effect, commercials try to inspire in viewers a sense that they can escape from the flawed and mundane state of everyday existence. They appeal to the same desires for freedom and perfection that Disney appeals to, turning the yearning for a better life into a tool of manipulation.

7   Many television commercials thus give us another variation on Umberto Eco's absolute fakes; they are false promises that make everything seem better than it is. Like theme parks, they make mundane realities look like transcendent utopias. One might say that if Disney is a permanent world's fair that creates fictions intended to reveal the way technology will one day free us from the constraints of life, then television advertising is a virtual world's fair that creates fictions about how the products of technology can free us now.

8   Like Disney, all of these 30-second spots end up inventing a postmodern world for us. It isn't that we live in anything that deserves to be called postmodern; it is just that the fictionalizers of American culture keep pretending we do, and inviting us to pretend along. A truly postmodern society (although I doubt it would call itself that) would be one that is able to use technology to significantly transcend the limits imposed by the physical world. We aren't a postmodern society. We merely play one on television.

* * *

9   Some commercials create invented "worlds" based on fantasy and desire. To achieve their effects, they engage in the new production process of high-tech capitalism, which is to turn everything into an image.

10   This process is very evident in what happens to the actors—they are turned into simplified human images. Their role is to become characters in false utopias so they can act as living sales pitches for products.

11   Like Charlie Chaplin in *Modern Times*, and the workers in the movie *Metropolis*, they become cogs in the machine of technology. But now that machine

is about etherealizing—using the appearance of actual people, objects, places and situations to create images and stories that can be sold and/or used to sell other things that are, themselves, increasingly made up of images or simulations.

12   I don't mean to make all that much of this—I'd rather be an actor than a factory worker; and I'd rather live in a society that has the luxury of devoting many of its resources to creating images, than one stuck trying to figure out how to get coal out of the ground. And many kinds of work are repetitive and alienating. Even being an actor in a Shakespearean drama involves repetition and can involve a feeling of being lost in one's character.

13   But most of today's human images aren't doing Shakespeare. They are doing sales-entertainment, of which commercials are an extreme version that casts light on the rest.

14   Audiences suffer forms of alienation, as well, as they feel increasingly trapped in a culture of con artistry in which they are surrounded by sensory images, stories, rhetoric and presentations that are intended to get them to buy something or buy into something. This culture fakes the appearance of places and people and situations, as the window dressing for fake promises and false claims. It offers sales pitches disguised to look like a new and better "postmodern" reality.

15   All cultures place people inside invented worlds; so that, in itself, isn't what is new about all this. The human world is by nature full of fictionalization and metaphor and drenched in stories and metaphysical assumptions, much of it contrived by conscious and unconscious design to support the claims of those in power. But never before has a culture been scientifically invented in this way, using the tools of rationalization—including marketing studies and computers—to sell products and a way of life. These tools of rationality extract the essence of our own irrationality—our fantasies, imbued with fears and desires—and give them back to us in the form of their invented worlds.

16   Most viewers know it is all a manipulation, even if they don't always reflect on what they know. But many still respond by buying the product, voting for the candidate and admiring the celebrity, as if they have been taken in by the message. It is as if the radio audience in 1938 had realized it was listening to a performance by Orson Welles but decided to panic anyway because the play was so convincing and so much fun to believe. ◆

FREEWRITING ASSIGNMENT

How much attention do you give to television commercials? What makes you stop and watch a commercial? Beauty? Humor? Spectacle? What holds your attention?

CRITICAL READING

1. Sanes notes that commercials employ multiple tools to create tightly woven mini "cinematic" productions to promote their product. How does he feel about this approach to advertising? Explain.

2. How does the simulated world of television commercials influence our general perceptions of the real world? Do we create unrealistic expecta-

tions based upon these commercials, or do we see through the spectacle? Explain.

3. Sanes notes that many products are cosmetically altered to make them more appealing to viewers (paragraph 2). Do advertisers have a right to do this? Is such modification unethical? Is it lying? Or do viewers simply expect advertisers to skew the truth?

4. What elements does Sanes identify used by commercials to weave their productions of simulated reality? How do these elements work together? Can you think of any others?

5. Sanes notes that the most popular tactic employed by commercials today is "life as a celebration." Why is this form of commercial so popular? Identify a few commercials that follow this format.

6. What assumptions does Sanes make concerning his audience? What do his language choices and his cultural references tell you about this audience? Explain.

7. What does Sanes mean when he says "We aren't a postmodern society? We merely play one on television"? What is the connection between the invented worlds presented in television commercials and our "postmodern" society?

CRITICAL WRITING

8. Sanes's essay addresses the way images manipulate viewers of television commercials in much the same way language can sway consumers to buy a product. How do you think William Lutz or Charles O'Neill would respond to Sanes's observations? Write a response to Sanes's essay from the perspective of either Lutz or O'Neill.

9. *Exploratory Writing*: Sanes postulates that the utopian world created by television commercials creates unrealistic social expectations of our real world. Write an essay exploring the psychological aspects of desire. Why are we so vulnerable to the implicit promises made by commercials?

10. Sanes makes references to the movies *Modern Times* and *Metropolis*. Watch one of these movies and write a summary of it, connecting its theme to points expressed by Sanes in his essay. What parallels can you make between the movie and the world of television commercials?

11. Write an essay evaluating advertising techniques in the twenty-first century. Have ads changed over the last 20 years or so? What accounts for similarities or differences? Has advertising become more or less ethical? Creative? Focused? Be sure to explain your position and support it with examples from real advertisements.

GROUP PROJECTS

12. As a group, watch several commercials (you may wish to record them to reference later) and analyze them applying some of the points made by Sanes in his essay. How do they use color, music, graphics, narration, and

celebrity to promote the product? What cultural assumptions do they make? What promises do they imply? Finally, how do they contribute to the simulated utopia Sanes discusses?

13. Adbusters.org is committed to exposing the unethical ways advertisers manipulate consumers to "need" products. However, if we consider ads long enough we can determine for ourselves the ways we may be manipulated. Visit their web site and select a campaign to discuss as a group. Summarize the points made by Adbusters against the campaign you selected and add some observations of your own. Share your summary with the class.

Lunchbox Hegemony
Dan Cook

There was a time when pitches for children's products were aimed at mothers, not kids. But that's all changed, as marketers have discovered this eager and impressionable segment of the population, turning kids into consumers of brand-name products practically after birth. Children today have more money to spend and more products to choose from, making them very attractive targets for advertising pitches. Today, entire television programs promote toys and games for children. Internet web sites lure youngsters in with promises of games, e-mail, and free stuff, while subtly selling a product to them. In this article, Dan Cook takes a closer look at "kiddie capitalism" and the history of the child consumer.

Dan Cook is an assistant professor of advertising and sociology at the University of Illinois at Urbana Champaign. This essay was first published in the August 20, 2001, issue of *LiP Magazine*, an online "not-for-profit print and electronic media project dedicated to the building of a sustainable society that values diversity."

| **CRITICAL THINKING** | Think about your consumer habits as a child. What did you want to buy and how did you learn about the product? What made you want the product? |

1 If you want to catch a glimpse of the gears of capitalism grinding away in America today, you don't need to go to a factory or a business office.

2 Instead, observe a child and parent in a store. That high-pitched whining you'll hear coming from the cereal aisle is more than just the pleadings of a single kid bent on getting a box of Fruit Loops into the shopping cart. It is the sound of thousands of hours of market research, of an immense coordination of people, ideas and resources, of decades of social and economic change all rolled into a single, "Mommy, pleeease!"

3 "If it's within [kids'] reach, they will touch it, and if they touch it, there's at least a chance that Mom or Dad will relent and buy it," writes retail anthropologist Paco Underhill. The ideal placement of popular books and videos, he continues, should be on the lower shelves "so the little ones can grab Barney or Teletubbies

unimpeded by Mom or Dad, who possibly take a dim view of hyper-commercialized critters."

4   Any child market specialist worth their consulting fee knows that the parental "dim view" of a product most often gives way to relentless pestering by a kid on a quest to procure the booty of popular culture. Officially, marketers refer to the annoyance as children's "influence" on purchases; unofficially, it is the "nag factor." The distinction is important because businesses are discouraged from explicitly inciting children to nag their parents into buying something, according to advertising guidelines from the Better Business Bureau.

Do Kids Use Products, or Vice Versa?

5   One strain of academic thought asserts that media and consumer products are just cultural materials, and children are free to make use of them as they will, imparting their own meanings to cartoons, toys, games, etc.

6   There's little doubt that children creatively interpret their surroundings, including consumer goods. They color outside the lines, make up rules to games, invent their own stories and make imaginary cars fly. If we lose sight of children's ability to exercise personal agency and to transform the meanings imposed on them by advertising (as well as those imparted by parents), we will forever be stuck in the belief structure which grants near-omnipotence to the corporate realm.

7   Granting children magical transformative powers of the imagination, however, only further romanticizes an already oversentimentalized view of childhood. Children are human. Imaginations can be colonized. The materials they use to create their own meanings are pre-programmed with brand identification, gender, race and class clichés, and standard good-bad dichotomies. And, as any marketer will tell you, exposure to target market is nine-tenths of the brand battle.

It's Not Just the Corporations

8   How has this kid consumer world come to be? Easy explanations abound, from spoiled children to over-indulgent or unengaged parents. Easiest of all is to accuse corporations of turning kids into blank-faced, videogame-playing, violence-saturated, sugar-mongering, overweight, docile citizens of the future. Pundits and politicians from far-left to far-right have found ideologically comfortable soapboxes from which to voice their opposition to the corporate incursion into childhood.

9   Soulless advertisers and rapacious marketers alone, however, cannot account for the explosion of the kids' 4 to 12 market, which has just about tripled since 1990, now raking in around $30 billion annually, according to latest estimates.

10   Don't get me wrong, the target of the critique is on track. What is troubling, though, is not just that kids demand goods by brand name as early as 2 years old. It's the habit of thought which conveniently separates children from economic processes, placing these spheres in opposition to one another, and thereby allowing anyone—including corporations—to position themselves on the side of "innocent" children and against "bad" companies or products.

11   Marketers and advertisers tell themselves—and will tell you if you ask—that they are giving kids what they "want," or providing educational devices or opportunities for "self-expression."

12   The thing of it is, on some level, they are right. What is most troubling is that children's culture has become virtually indistinguishable from consumer culture over the course of the last century. The cultural marketplace is now a key arena for the formation of the sense of self and of peer relationships, so much so that parents often are stuck between giving into a kid's purchase demands or risking their child becoming an outcast on the playground.

13   The relationship is reciprocal. Childhood and consumer capitalism inform and co-create each other. It is not just that the children's market is the Happy Meal version of a grown-up one. It stands apart from others because childhood is a generative cultural site unlike any other.

14   Children consumers grow up to be more than just adult consumers. They become mothers and fathers, administrative assistants and bus drivers, nurses and realtors, online magazine editors and assistant professors—in short, they become us who, in turn, make more of them. Childhood makes capitalism hum over the long haul.

15   Kids' consumer culture takes a most intimate thing—the realization and expression of self—and fuses it with a most distant system—the production of goods, services and media in an impersonal market.

16   Cumulatively, this fusion has been forged cohort by cohort and generation by generation over the 20th century, making each of us a small conspirator in its reproduction. The process is so insidious that by the time a child gains the language and capacity to grasp what is occurring, his or her attention patterns, preferences, memories and aspirations cannot be neatly separated from the images and poetics of corporate strategy.

The History We Are

17   Adults are the living legacies of commodified childhoods gone by. Our memories, our sense of personal history are, to some extent, tied to the commercial culture of our youth: an old lunchbox with television characters on it; a doll, a comic book or a brand of cereal; a sports hero, perhaps; certainly music of one sort or another.

18   These may seem like benign artifacts of a fading past, harmless enough, slated to wind up as pieces of nostalgia at junk shops and yard sales. They might seem particularly benign when viewed against the backdrop of today's hyper-aggressive children's marketing strategies, which target children who eat branded foods and play in branded spaces, who are exposed to television in school courtesy of Channel One and who, to take one infamous example, learn geometry by measuring the circumference of Oreo cookies.

19   The "hegemonic power" of that Starsky and Hutch lunchbox of yesteryear seems almost laughable by comparison.

20   But the joke unfortunately is on us, in part, because the Teletubbies and Pokemon of the '90s would not have been possible without the Starsky and Hutch of the '70s; and those crime-fighting hunks would not have been possible in some measure

without the Mouseketeers of the '50s, whose apple-pie smiles would not have been possible without the Lone Ranger of the radio days of the '30s. If we are to intervene in the rampant commodification of childhood, we need to balance the impulse to place exclusive blame on corporations for polluting children's minds and bodies with a larger, historical perspective.

Creating the Child's Point of View

21   At the opening of the 20th century, working-class children still toiled in the factories or worked the streets of the rising industrial city as bootblacks, newsies and helpers. They (mostly boys) spent their money on food and candy, in the new nickelodeon theaters, pool halls and restaurants. Aside from these amusements, there was no children's consumer market to speak of.

22   Enter the "bourgeois child" at the end of the 19th century, whose value was no longer economic, but sentimental. Liberated from direct, industrial labor and placed into school, this child was trained in the technical skills and social posture appropriate for a new bureaucratic order. His (again, usually his) childhood was to be full of fancy, not preoccupied with factory or farm work; his first school, a "children's garden," as close to Eden as possible.

23   The image of the bourgeois child would spread beyond the confines of a rising urban, white middle class to become the model for virtually all childhoods in industrialized nations by the millennium.

24   During the second decade of the 20th century, department stores began to recognize and welcome the bourgeois child, providing separate, modest toy departments with play spaces where mothers could "check" their children while they shopped. Prior to about 1915, there were also no separate infants' and children's clothing departments in department stores—clothes tended to be stocked by item, not size. One could find children's socks in hosiery, children's shirts in the men's or women's department, etc.

25   A Chicago manufacturer of baby garments, George Earnshaw, hit upon something when he began to convince department store management to devote separate space to children's clothing and furnishings. Mothers and expectant mothers were to be served by this new arrangement, which would have "everything they needed" in one place.

26   Much ink was spilled in the trade and consumer journals throughout the '20s, '30s and '40s in the attempt to discern the tastes, priorities and foibles of "Mrs. Consumer," a caricature which continues today as something of an icon of consumer society. (How else would we know that "Choosy mothers choose Jif"?) The first children's retail spaces were built, located, staffed and stocked with the consuming mother, not the child, in mind.

27   By the 1930s, however, individualized clothing and toy departments in department stores gave way to entire "floors for youth," complete with child-size fixtures, mirrors, and eye-level views of the merchandise. Merchants hoped to provide children with a sense of proprietorship over the shop or area by visually, acoustically and commercially demonstrating that it was a space designed with them in mind.

28   The basic arrangement was to display older children's clothing and related furnishings at the entrance to a floor or department. As kids moved through the department, they encountered progressively younger styles until reaching the baby shop in the back. A designer of one such floor explained in a 1939 issue of the Bulletin of the National Retail Dry Goods Association:

29   Older children . . . are often reluctant to shop on a floor where "all those babies" are shopping. The younger children are delighted to see the older children shopping as they go through these departments, for all children want to be older than they are. The little boy and little girl seeing the big boys and big girls buying will long for the day when he (sic) too can come to these departments and buy. . . . In this way a valuable shopping habit is created.

30   Note here how the child's viewpoint, agency and emergent autonomy are transformed into exchangeable, marketable values. What's new is the way that the child's perspective is invoked as legitimate authority within the context of commercial enterprise.

31   This was the beginning of a fundamental shift in the social status of children from seen-and-not-heard, wait-till-you-grow-up dependency to having retail spaces, shelving in stores and media messages tailored to their viewpoint, making it the basis of economic action. Today, we expect to see video monitors flashing images of Britney Spears, oversized replicas of teddy bears, and primary-colored display fixtures every time we walk into a Kids 'R' Us.

And Now a Word from Our Sponsored Kids

32 Over a number of generations, children and younger adults became key arbiters of kid-taste in the U.S.

33   Children moved to the front-and-center of popular culture with the early successes of Shirley Temple and others like Mickey Rooney in the '30s. Their images provided a foundation for the publicly shared persona of the bourgeois child as one who moves in a world virtually independent from adult concerns and preoccupations—one that makes sense only in reference to its own child-logic. Think of the Peanuts characters whose world is totally devoid of adults of any consequence: All framing is child-eye level, only the legs of adults are shown, and when adults speak, their voices are non-linguistic trombone-like notes.

34   Meanwhile, back in the marketplace, children were also acquiring status as spokespersons for goods throughout the 20th century—from fictional icons like Buster Brown (1910s) and the Campbell's Soup Kids (1920s), to actors like Cowboy Bobby Benson (1950s), to voice-overs for commercials during the Saturday morning "children's" television time (1960s). By the '60s, the child spokesperson had become such a fixture that market researchers felt comfortable enough to query children directly for their product preferences, giving them a "voice" in the market sphere.

35   Children—or to be precise, media-massaged images of children—now routinely and aggressively hawk almost any kind of product, from car tires to vacations to refrigerators to grape juice, as advertisers make use of both "cute appeal" and safety fears.

36   Kids frequently serve as peer arbiters in newspapers, magazines and web sites, reviewing movies, videogames, toys and television shows—as it is assumed, often correctly, that they have more intimate knowledge about the detail and appeal of these things than adults do. This is a world under continuous construction and it is theirs: oriented around their "desires," retrofitted to their physical size and tweaked in just the right way to produce that all-important feeling of inadequacy if this or that product is not in their possession.

Factoring in the Nag

37 Kids not only want things, but have acquired the socially sanctioned right to want— a right which parents are loath to violate. Layered onto direct child enticement and the supposed autonomy of the child-consumer are the day-to-day circumstances of overworked parents: a daily barrage of requests, tricky financial negotiations and that nagging, unspoken desire to build the life/style they have learned to want during their childhoods.

38   Sometimes the balancing act is overwhelming. "Moms have loosened nutritional controls," enthuses Denise Fedewa, a vice president and planning director at Leo Burnett in Chicago. "They now believe there are so many battles to fight, is fighting over food really worth it?"

39   Unsurprisingly, mainstream media provides few correctives. A recent *Time* cover story on kids' influence on parents gushes over the excesses of the upper-middle-class in typical fashion, successfully detracting from the larger, more generalized problem of struggling parents.

Slipping the Parent Trap

40 If kid marketing tactics were merely blatant, their power would not be so great, but consumption enfolded into daily existence. Places like zoos and museums are promoted as "educational," toys are supposed to "teach," clothing allows for "individuality" and who can suggest that there is something wrong with "good ol' family fun" at, say, Dollywood?

41   The children's market works because it lives off of deeply-held beliefs about self-expression and freedom of choice—originally applied to the political sphere, and now almost inseparable from the culture of consumption. Children's commercial culture has quite successfully usurped kids' boundless creativity and personal agency, selling these back to them—and us—as "empowerment," a term that appeases parents while shielding marketers.

42   Linking one's sense of self to the choices offered by the marketplace confuses personal autonomy with consumer behavior. But, try telling that to a kid who only sees you standing in the way of the Chuck-E-Cheese-ified version of fun and happiness. Kids are keen to the adult-child power imbalance and to adult hypocrisy, especially when they are told to hold their desires in check by a parent who is blind to her or his own materialistic impulses.

43   We have to incite children to adopt a critical posture toward media and consumption. A key step in combating the forces eating away at childhood is to recog-

nize our own place as heirs of the bourgeois child and thus as largely unwitting vehicles of consumer culture. The mere autocratic vetoing of children's requests will only result in anti-adult rebellion.

44   The challenge facing us all—as relatives, teachers, friends or even not-so-innocent bystanders—is to find ways to affirm children's personal agency and their membership in a community of peers, while insisting that they make the distinction between self-worth and owning a Barbie or a Pokemon card. Or anything, for that matter. ◆

FREEWRITING ASSIGNMENT

What is your perception of how children are targeted by advertisers today? Have brand-awareness and demand for branded products increased since when you were a child? Explain your point of view.

CRITICAL READING

1. How do advertisers "pre-program" products to have particular meanings for children? Why do they do this? How does pre-programming influence the child consumer? Childhood itself?
2. According to Cook, what are the most troubling elements of children's consumer culture? What is the relationship between children's culture and consumer culture? Explain.
3. What proof does Cook offer to support his argument? How effective is his evidence? Does Cook's recounting of the history of the children's market help support his conclusions? Is it helpful to the reader? Explain.
4. How do advertisers "create" a child's point of view? Is this practice unethical? Why or why not?
5. What is the "nag factor"? How do marketers of children's products use the nag factor to sell merchandise?
6. In your opinion, what limits, if any, should be imposed on advertising for the children's market? Explain.
7. What are the author's conclusions about the trend toward marketing to children? Do you feel this trend is inevitable? Should it be controlled? If so, how?

CRITICAL WRITING

8. *Research and Analysis*: Write an essay evaluating advertising techniques used on children as demonstrated by print and/or media advertisements. Has advertising become more or less ethical? Creative? Focused? Has the way advertisers target children changed? Be sure to explain your position and support it with examples from real advertisements.
9. *Persuasive Writing*: Cook suggests that changes in family structure—that is, overworked two-income households in which parents "pick their battles"—has contributed to kids having more money and parents succumb-

ing to the "nag factor" more readily. Write an essay discussing the role you feel parents should play in shaping their children's behavior as consumers. What steps should they take (or not take)? On the other hand, can parents influence their children at all in today's media driven society?

10. *Exploratory Writing*: Cook states, "The children's market works because it lives off of deeply-held beliefs about self-expression and free choice." Write an essay exploring the connection between the democratic values Cook cites above and the children's market. Are advertisers twisting these noble principles? Is children's consumer culture really about empowering children, or manipulating them? Explain.

GROUP PROJECTS

11. In small groups, do some research on how the Internet is used as a marketing tool to sell to children. Locate web sites for toys and games, and evaluate how they market to children. What do these sites offer? How do they contribute to the desirability and sale of the product? Report your findings to the class.

12. In the past, toys were created after a particular television program proved popular and marketable. Today, toys are created first, then the television program helps market the product. Each member of your group should select two different cartoons to watch and research. After viewing each cartoon, research the products that are associated with the cartoon. In class discussion, contrast how today's cartoons promote products as compared to cartoons when you were a child.

A Brand by Any Other Name
Douglas Rushkoff

Brand-name products target groups of consumers—sometimes large, diverse populations, such as Pepsi or Coke, or very elite ones, such as Fendi or Gucci. Brands depend on image—the image they promote, and the image the consumer believes they will project by using the product. For teens, brands can announce membership in a particular group, value systems, and personality type. Douglas Rushkoff explains in this article that the youth generation is more consumer-savvy, forcing retailers to rethink how they brand and market goods. Brands are still very important to them, but they like to think they are hip to the advertising game. As Rushkoff explains, it is a game they cannot win.

Douglas Rushkoff is a writer and columnist who analyzes, writes and speaks about the way people, cultures, and institutions create, share, and influence each other's values. He is the author of many books on new media and popular culture, including *Media Virus* and *Coercion: Why We Listen to What "They" Say*, and the novels *Ecstasy Club* and *Exit Strategy*. His commentaries have aired on *CBS Sunday Morning* and NPR's *All Things Considered*, and he has appeared on *NBC Nightly News, Frontline,* and *Larry King.* The author of a monthly column on cyberculture for the *New York Times,* his articles have been published in *Time,* the *Guardian, Esquire,* and *GQ.* This essay appeared in the April 30, 2000, edition of the *London Times.*

CRITICAL THINKING   When you were a teenager, did you have particular brands to which you were most loyal? Did this loyalty change as you got older? Why did you prefer certain brands over others? What cultural and social influences contributed to your desire for that brand?

---

1   I was in one of those sports "superstores" the other day, hoping to find a pair of trainers for myself. As I faced the giant wall of shoes, each model categorized by either sports affiliation, basketball star, economic class, racial heritage or consumer niche, I noticed a young boy standing next to me, maybe 13 years old, in even greater awe of the towering selection of footwear.

2   His jaw was dropped and his eyes were glazed over—a psycho-physical response to the overwhelming sensory data in a self-contained consumer environment. It's a phenomenon known to retail architects as "Gruen Transfer," named for the gentleman who invented the shopping mall, where this mental paralysis is most commonly observed.

3   Having finished several years of research on this exact mind state, I knew to proceed with caution. I slowly made my way to the boy's side and gently asked him, "What is going through your mind right now?"

4   He responded without hesitation, "I don't know which of these trainers is 'me.'" The boy proceeded to explain his dilemma. He thought of Nike as the most utilitarian and scientifically advanced shoe, but had heard something about third world laborers and was afraid that wearing this brand might label him as too anti-Green. He then considered a skateboard shoe, Airwalk, by an "indie" manufacturer (the trainer equivalent of a micro-brewery), but had recently learned that this company was almost as big as Nike. The truly hip brands of skate shoe were too esoteric for his current profile at school—he'd look like he was "trying." This left the "retro" brands, like Puma, Converse and Adidas, none of which he felt any real affinity, since he wasn't even alive in the 70's when they were truly and non-ironically popular.

5   With no clear choice and, more importantly, no other way to conceive of his own identity, the boy stood there, paralyzed in the modern youth equivalent of an existential crisis. Which brand am I, anyway?

6   Believe it or not, there are dozens, perhaps hundreds of youth culture marketers who have already begun clipping out this article. They work for hip, new advertising agencies and cultural research firms who trade in the psychology of our children and the anthropology of their culture. The object of their labors is to create precisely the state of confusion and vulnerability experienced by the young shopper at the shoe wall—and then turn this state to their advantage. It is a science, though not a pretty one.

7   Yes, our children are the prey and their consumer loyalty is the prize in an escalating arms race. Marketers spend millions developing strategies to identify chil-

dren's predilections and then capitalize on their vulnerabilities. Young people are fooled for a while, but then develop defense mechanisms, such as media-savvy attitudes or ironic dispositions. Then marketers research these defenses, develop new countermeasures, and on it goes. The revolutionary impact of a new musical genre is co-opted and packaged by a major label before it reaches the airwaves. The ability of young people to deconstruct and neutralize the effects of one advertising technique are thwarted when they are confounded by yet another. The liberation children experience when they discover the Internet is quickly counteracted by the lure of e-commerce web sites, which are customized to each individual user's psychological profile in order to maximize their effectiveness.

8   The battle in which our children are engaged seems to pass beneath our radar screens, in a language we don't understand. But we see the confusion and despair that results—not to mention the ever-increasing desperation with which even three-year-olds yearn for the next Pokemon trading card. How did we get in this predicament, and is there a way out? Is it your imagination, you wonder, or have things really gotten worse?

9   Alas, things seem to have gotten worse. Ironically, this is because things had gotten so much better.

10   In olden times—back when those of us who read the newspaper grew up—media was a one-way affair. Advertisers enjoyed a captive audience, and could quite authoritatively provoke our angst and stoke our aspirations. Interactivity changed all this. The remote control gave viewers the ability to break the captive spell of television programming whenever they wished, without having to get up and go all the way up to the set. Young people proved particularly adept at "channel surfing," both because they grew up using the new tool, and because they felt little compunction to endure the tension-provoking narratives of storytellers who did not have their best interests at heart. It was as if young people knew that the stuff on television was called "programming" for a reason, and developed shortened attention spans for the purpose of keeping themselves from falling into the spell of advertisers. The remote control allowed young people to deconstruct TV.

11   The next weapon in the child's arsenal was the video game joystick. For the first time, viewers had control over the very pixels on their monitors. The television image was demystified.

12   Lastly, the computer mouse and keyboard transformed the TV receiver into a portal. Today's young people grew up in a world where a screen could as easily be used for expressing oneself as consuming the media of others. Now the media was up-for-grabs, and the ethic, from hackers to camcorder owners, was "do it yourself."

13   Of course, this revolution had to be undone. Television and Internet programmers, responding to the unpredictable viewing habits of the newly liberated, began to call our mediaspace an "attention economy." No matter how many channels they had for their programming, the number of "eyeball hours" that human beings were willing to dedicate to that programming was fixed. Not coincidentally, the channel surfing habits of our children became known as "attention deficit disorder"—a real disease now used as an umbrella term for anyone who clicks away from programming before the marketer wants him to. We quite literally drug our children into compliance. Likewise, as computer interfaces were made more complex and opaque—think Windows—the do-it-yourself ethic of the Internet was undone. The

original Internet was a place to share ideas and converse with others. Children actually had to use the keyboard! Now, the World Wide Web encourages them to click numbly through packaged content. Web sites are designed to keep young people from using the keyboard, except to enter in their parents' credit card information.

14 But young people had been changed by their exposure to new media. They constituted a new "psychographic," as advertisers like to call it, so new kinds of messaging had to be developed that appealed to their new sensibility.

15 Anthropologists—the same breed of scientists that used to scope out enemy populations before military conquests—engaged in focus groups, conducted "trend-watching" on the streets, in order to study the emotional needs and subtle behaviors of young people. They came to understand, for example, how children had abandoned narrative structures for fear of the way stories were used to coerce them. Children tended to construct narratives for themselves by collecting things instead, like cards, bottlecaps called "pogs," or keychains and plush toys. They also came to understand how young people despised advertising—especially when it did not acknowledge their media-savvy intelligence.

16 Thus, Pokemon was born—a TV show, video game, and product line where the object is to collect as many trading cards as possible. The innovation here, among many, is the marketer's conflation of TV show and advertisement into one piece of media. The show is an advertisement. The story, such as it is, concerns a boy who must collect little monsters in order to develop his own character. Likewise, the Pokemon video game engages the player in a quest for those monsters. Finally, the card game itself (for the few children who actually play it) involves collecting better monsters—not by playing, but by buying more cards. The more cards you buy, the better you can play.

17 Kids feel the tug, but in a way they can't quite identify as advertising. Their compulsion to create a story for themselves—in a world where stories are dangerous—makes them vulnerable to this sort of attack. In marketers' terms, Pokemon is "leveraged" media, with "cross-promotion" on "complementary platforms." This is ad-speak for an assault on multiple fronts.

18 Moreover, the time a child spends in the Pokemon craze amounts to a remedial lesson in how to consume. Pokemon teaches them how to want things that they can't or won't actually play with. In fact, it teaches them how to buy things they don't even want. While a child might want one particular card, he needs to purchase them in packages whose contents are not revealed. He must buy blind and repeatedly until he gets the object of his desire.

19 Worse yet, the card itself has no value—certainly not as a play-thing. It is a functionless purchase, slipped into a display case, whose value lies purely in its possession. It is analogous to those children who buy action figures from their favorite TV shows and movies, with no intention of ever removing them from their packaging! They are purchased for their collectible value alone. Thus, the imagination game is reduced to some fictional moment in the future where they will, presumably, be resold to another collector. Children are no longer playing. They are investing.

20 Meanwhile, older kids have attempted to opt out of aspiration, altogether. The "15-24" demographic, considered by marketers the most difficult to wrangle into submission, have adopted a series of postures they hoped would make them impervious to marketing techniques. They take pride in their ability to recognize when

they are being pandered to, and watch TV for the sole purpose of calling out when they are being manipulated. They are armchair media theorists, who take pleasure in deconstructing and defusing the messages of their enemies.

21   But now advertisers are making commercials just for them. Soft drink advertisements satirize one another before rewarding the cynical viewer: "image is nothing," they say. The technique might best be called "wink" advertising, for its ability to engender a young person's loyalty by pretending to disarm itself. "Get it?" the ad means to ask. If you're cool, you do.

22   New magazine advertisements for jeans, such as those created by Diesel, take this even one step further. The ads juxtapose imagery that actually makes no sense—ice cream billboards in North Korea, for example. The strategy is brilliant. For a media-savvy young person to feel good about himself, he needs to feel he "gets" the joke. But what does he do with an ad where there's obviously something to get that he can't figure out? He has no choice but to admit that the brand is even cooler than he is. An ad's ability to confound its audience is the new credential for a brand's authenticity.

23   Like the boy at the wall of shoes, kids today analyze each purchase they make, painstakingly aware of how much effort has gone into seducing them. As a result, they see their choices of what to watch and what to buy as exerting some influence over the world around them. After all, their buying patterns have become the center of so much attention!

24   But however media-savvy kids get, they will always lose this particular game. For they have accepted the language of brands as their cultural currency, and the stakes in their purchasing decisions as something real. For no matter how much control kids get over the media they watch, they are still utterly powerless when it comes to the manufacturing of brands. Even a consumer revolt merely reinforces one's role as a consumer, not an autonomous or creative being.

25   The more they interact with brands, the more they brand themselves. ◆

FREEWRITING ASSIGNMENT

What can a brand tell you about the person who uses it? Explain.

CRITICAL READING

1. Look up the phrase "Gruen transfer" on the Internet. Were you aware of this angle of marketing practice? Does it change the way you think about how products are sold to you?
2. While the boy's dilemma in Rushkoff's introduction is humorous on the surface, it is a serious situation for the teen. Why is his choice of sneaker so important to him? What expectations does he seem to connect with his choice? What could happen if he picks the wrong shoe?
3. In order to stay in business, marketers have had to rethink how they sell products to the youth market. How is the youth market changing the way marketers do business? Explain.
4. How does Rushkoff support his essay? Evaluate his use of supporting sources. Are there any gaps in his article? If so, identify areas where his

essay could be stronger. If not, highlight some of the essay's particular strengths.

5. In paragraph 9, Rushkoff notes that things have gotten worse because they have gotten better. What does he mean? What is the irony of the youth consumer market?

6. Rushkoff notes in paragraph 14 that the youth generation "constitutes a new psychographic." What makes this generation different from previous generations of consumers? If you are a part of this generation (ages 12-21), explain why you think you, indeed, represent a "new psychographic" or not.

7. In his conclusion, Rushkoff predicts that even media-savvy kids will still "lose" the game. Why will they fail? Explain.

CRITICAL WRITING

8. *Exploratory Writing*: Teens and young adults covet certain brand name clothing because they believe it promotes a particular image. What defines brand image? Is it something created by the company, or by the people who use the product? How does advertising influence the social view we have of ourselves and the brands we use? Write an essay on the connections between advertising and our cultural values of what is "in" or popular and what is not.

9. *Exploratory Writing:* What makes you want to buy a product? Is it peer influence, cultural pressure, or social status? Do generational marketing techniques, like the ones described by Rushkoff, influence you? Write an essay exploring the way advertising targets specific age groups. Support your essay with information from this article, as well as from your own consumer experience.

10. *Interview:* Interview several young people between the ages of 12 to 17 about the products they like and why. Inquire what they like about a brand, and the reasons why they would not buy a particular brand. Evaluate the results in a short essay on the purchasing habits of young consumers.

GROUP PROJECTS

11. In small groups, do some research on how the Internet is used as a marketing tool to sell to children. Locate web sites for toys and games and evaluate how they market to children. What do these sites offer? How do they contribute to the desirability and sale of the product? Report your findings to the class.

12. In the past, toys were created after a particular television program proved popular and marketable. As Rushkoff describes in the case of Pokemon, now toys are created first, and the television program and Internet web site helps market the product. Each member of your group should select a different popular cartoon to watch and research. After viewing each cartoon for a few days, research the products that are associated with the cartoon. In class, discuss how today's cartoons promote products.

13. Each member of your group should watch an hour of television aimed at children—Saturday morning programs, after-school features, Nickelodeon, or the Cartoon Network. Jot down the shows you watch and all the commercials that run during the programs. Include how much time is spent airing commercials. As a group, analyze the data. How many commercials ran during a 15-minute segment of programming? Was there a pattern to the commercials? Did any seem manipulative or compelling—and if so, how? (As an additional writing project, watch these programs with a child. Note his or her responses to the commercials. Did the child seem influenced by the ads? Explain.)

14. Develop a marketing plan to the youth market for a long-established product, such as Levi's jeans, Adidas sneakers, or Dr. Pepper cola. Refer to points made by Rushkoff in his essay as you develop your plan. After creating your marketing plan, explain why you chose this strategy, and why it is likely to appeal to the youth market.

Trademarks and Brand Logos

In the last essay, a teenager is faced with a daunting challenge—choosing a sneaker brand that was "him." Sneakers are well-known for their use of logos to distinguish brands from each other. The young man worries that choosing the wrong brand will make him look like he is "trying" or is a member of the wrong group. Clearly, he believes the expression "the clothes make the man." To him, a logo is a reflection of his identity, and of the image he wishes to project.

Logos are graphic designs that represent and help market a particular brand or company. Some logos are instantly recognizable, needing no words to explain what they represent. A good example of a logo with international recognition is the image of the Olympic rings. Other logos may be more obscure—specific to particular countries or demographic groups. Chances are most senior citizens wouldn't recognize the Lugz logo, or know what product was associated with it. Sometimes a logo can simply be the initial or name of the brand. Chanel is famous for its interlocking C design, and Kate Spade's name serves as her logo. Spade's logo is distinctive because of the font face used to spell her name, written in lowercase letters.

Most logos have meaning behind their design. For example, the Olympic ring logo was designed by Pierre de Coubertain for the 1914 Paris Congress of the Olympic Movement, celebrating its twentieth anniversary. The Olympic ring logo itself was probably designed by him, despite some references to using a stone unearthed in Delphi, Greece, as his inspiration. A Frenchman, de Coubertain was president of the USFSA French sports federation (Union des Sociétés Françaises des Sports Athlétiques), which used an emblem consisting of two interlocking rings. The symbol of the USFSA probably served as his model. For the colors,

de Coubertain decided to use the colors from the flags of all countries that were part of the Olympic Movement; white for the cloth and red, yellow, green, blue, and black for the rings. The Olympic Charter identifies the five rings as representing the union of the five continents and the convergence of athletes from throughout the world at the Olympic Games. No continent is represented by any specific ring. The choice of a circle is also deliberate: circles represent wholeness, and interlocking them "joins" the continents they represent.

As you look at these logos, consider the brands they represent and what they say about the people who use or purchase that brand.

1. Identify the brands represented by the logos above. What do the logos stand for? Who buys the products they represent? What does the logo tell you about the person who uses that brand?
2. What brands do you tend to purchase, and why? Are there particular logos that are associated with the brands you prefer? Explain.
3. Are you more likely to purchase a product with a prominent or prestigious logo than a "no name" brand? Why or why not?
4. Examine the clothing you are wearing and the personal items within ten feet of you right now. How many items bear a logo? What are they?
5. What is your college or university's "logo"? Is it a shield? A phrase? A mascot? How does the symbol chosen by your school reflect its values and identity. Explain.

A Portfolio of Advertisements

The following section features 12 recently published magazine advertisements. Diverse in content and style, some ads use words to promote the product, while others depend on emotion, name recognition, visual appeal, or association. They present a variety of sales pitches and marketing techniques.

Following the ads are a list of questions to help you analyze how the ads work their appeal to promote their products. When studying them, consider how they target our social perception and basic desires for happiness, beauty, and success. Approach each as a consumer, an artist, a social scientist and a critic with an eye for detail.

where the beach >>>>>>>>> meets the street >>>>>>>>> where the beach >>>>>>>>> meets the street >>

QUINCY™/ grey/confetti
also in black/white and seal brown suede

available at Vans / vans.com

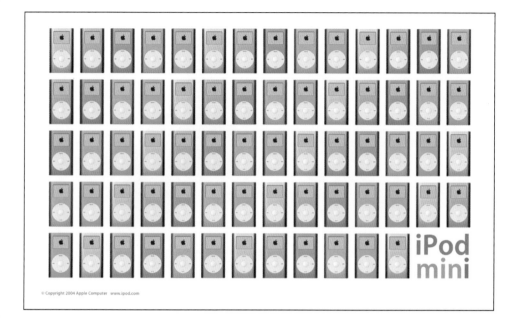

iPod
mini

The new sound system

NOKIA
MUSIC STAND

TECHNOLOGY IN ACTION

It's nice to know your loved ones are safe at home. Wherever you are, you can monitor your home – even remotely control home appliances, temperatures and security devices. And in the ubiquitous networked society of the near future, you'll be connected to everyone and everything, anytime and anyplace. Even your cat. From broadband access networks, data storage solutions and hard disk drive technologies, to information devices like plasma displays and PDAs, Hitachi's technological expertise and services are making this a reality. Just one more example of technology not for its own sake but for the benefit of all. As an innovative global solutions company, Hitachi touches your life in many ways. Visit us on the Web and see technology in action.

"There's not much we can do about our dependence on foreign oil. We only have so many reserves."
▲ Laron Johnson and Rima Koka/Medical Professionals

Though we do have some options. As we continue to invest in alternative energy sources like solar, the immediate need for oil and gas still remains. Over the next 10 years, we're investing $15 billion in the Gulf of Mexico to find and produce new energy supplies. Today, nearly 70% of the oil we use to make fuels in the U.S. comes from North America.

It's a start.

bp

beyond petroleum™

bp.com

SITTING PRETTY

This spokescandy for "M&M's" Chocolate Candies, photographed in the factory, surrounds himself with thousands of the little chocolate guys that made him famous.

"I know people undress me in their minds. Chocolate... peanut...that's what they see."

www.m-ms.com

©Mars, Incorporated 2000

M&M's and the M&M's Blue Character are the registered trademarks of Mars, Incorporated and its affiliates. They are used with permission. Mars, Incorporated is not associated with Gary Goshgarian or Longman Publishers. Copyright Mars, Incorporated 2005.

ABSOLUTE ON ICE.

NEARLY 50% OF AUTOMOBILE FATALITIES ARE LINKED TO ALCOHOL • 10% OF NORTH AMERICANS ARE ALCOHOLICS
A TEENAGER SEES 100,000 ALCOHOL ADS BEFORE REACHING LEGAL DRINKING AGE

GM Certified Vehicles

1. What is happening in this ad? How long does it take you to figure out the point? Does this work in the ad's favor? Explain.
2. How is humor and surprise used to promote the product in this advertisement? Is humor important to the product? The success of the ad? Explain.
3. After viewing this ad, are you more likely to follow its "advice"? Why or why not?
4. What catches your attention in this ad? What do you read first? Do you look at the car, the woman, or the cart? Would the ad be as effective if it featured a man eating? A different setting such as a beach or shopping mall? Is setting important? Explain.

Vans

1. Analyze the different images featured in the ad. What do they depict? How do the different photos contribute to the tone the ad wishes to set?
2. Do you know who the woman is in the ad? What sort of person do you imagine her to be? What is she wearing? Is her clothing important in promoting the product—sneakers? How does her location promote the product's image?
3. What is this woman known for? Why do you think she is pictured without the equipment she uses as part of her profession?
4. Who would you say is the target audience for this ad? Why? Consider age, gender, lifestyle, etc. in your response.
5. Consider the different angles at which photographs included in this ad were taken. How would its impact be different if it were shot from above? What if the woman in the photo was looking away from the camera? Explain.

Apple iPod Mini

1. If you did not know what an iPod was, could you determine anything about it from this ad? Explain.
2. How important is brand/name recognition to the success of this ad? Who would know what this brand was, and what it was selling?
3. Who is the target audience for this brand? How does this ad appeal to that audience?
4. How does this ad use color and graphics to catch your eye? If you were looking through a magazine and saw this ad, would you stop and look at it? Why or why not?

Nokia

1. What is this ad selling? Can you tell? If you had never heard of the company, Nokia, what might you guess this ad was selling? Explain.
2. How does the woman next to the guitar visually contribute to the advertisement? Would the image work as well with a man? Why or why not?
3. Who is the target audience for this ad? How does the ad appeal to this target audience?

Hitachi

1. What makes you stop and look at this ad? After looking at the picture, are you motivated to read the ad copy? Why or why not?
2. What is this ad selling? After viewing this ad, are you likely to remember the brand? Explain.
3. Apply the Fog Index described in Charles O'Neill's essay "The Language of Advertising" to the blurb at the bottom of the page. What is the grade level of the language? What does the language level reveal about the target audience for the ad?
4. In what type of magazines would you expect to see this ad?
5. Would this ad be as effective if the cat were further away from the camera? If another animal were featured? Explain.

BP/Beyond Petroleum

1. At first glance, who do you look at first in the ad? Why?
2. Who are the people in the ad? What do they do? Why do you think BP mentions their profession in the ad? Explain.
3. What is the woman in the ad doing? Why do you think she is there? Would the ad be any different if it were just the man featured in the ad? Explain.
4. What do you think is happening in this ad? What situation does it aim to convey? Where are the subjects located?
5. After reading this ad, have you learned something that you did not know about foreign and domestic energy sources? Did it serve to educate you? Do you think that is the purpose of the ad?

M & M's

1. Evaluate this advertisement's use of color and texture. How does it promote the product? Would the effectiveness of this ad be the same if it were printed in black and white, such as in a newspaper? Explain.
2. What is this ad mimicking? Explain.
3. None of the text in this advertisement is "serious"; that is, the advertisers do not "speak" to the audience about the product. Evaluate the use of text in this ad. How does it complement the picture? Is anything lost by not telling the audience about the product? Why or why not?
4. Would you stop and look at this ad? Why or why not?
5. Evaluate the personification of the candy in this ad. Does this seem like an effective vehicle to promote the product? Explain.

Absolute on Ice

1. What is the purpose of this ad? What is it "selling?"
2. How does this ad rely on our previously established expectations regarding the product it satirizes, and how it has been marketed?
3. Visit the Absolut Vodka web site at *www.absolutvodka.com* to see real ads produced by this company. How does the spoof ad incorporate elements of the real ads? Explain.
4. What are your gut reactions to this ad? Do you find it disturbing? Offensive? Effective? Enlightening? Explain.
5. Evaluate the effectiveness of photographic decisions in this ad. Would it be as effective if the ad featured an entire body? A face? Explain.

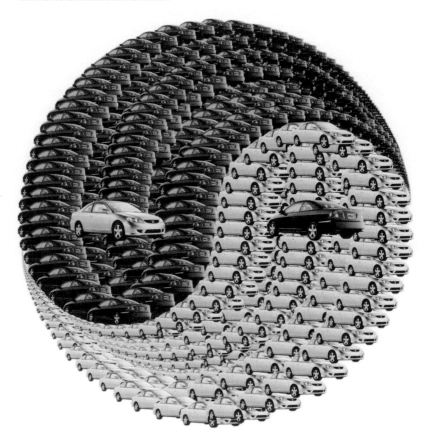

YOUR RIGHT BRAIN AND YOUR LEFT BRAIN WILL FINALLY BE OF THE SAME MIND. A car that can quench your emotional side and satiate your rational side. The stylish and 5-star-crash-test-rated* Civic Coupe.

HONDA

Honda

1. How does this photograph capture your attention? Can you tell at a glance what this ad is selling? How long does it take to figure out what the product is? Is this a positive or negative aspect of the ad?
2. What visual conventions does this ad employ? What symbolism does it use? How much does this ad rely on symbol recognition? What are the implications of this symbolism toward the product? If you didn't know what the symbolism was in this ad, would it fail to effectively sell the product? Explain.
3. Consider the text at the bottom of the ad. What does it say about the product? About the person who buys the product?
4. Rate this advertisement on a scale of 1–10 in terms of appeal, with 10 being a perfect score. What score would you give it, and why does it deserve such a ranking?

Phoenix Wealth Management

1. Who is depicted in this picture? What do their clothing, hairstyle, and demeanor imply about them? Why is how they look important to the product and its message? Would it be different if the same women were photographed in sweatshirts and jeans? Jogging suits? Explain.
2. What is the setting for this ad? How does the setting contribute to the mood? Explain.
3. What do the statements next to each woman tell the viewer about her? About the product?
4. How does the slogan "Money. It's just not what it used to be." connect to the people in the ad? To the product the ad is promoting? Explain.
5. If you were perusing a magazine and saw this ad, would you stop to read it? Why or why not? In what types of magazines would you expect to see this ad, and why?

Maybe I was supposed to get Parkinson's.

Maybe the last 20 years were just a warm-up for this moment. After all, my career has given me a certain stature (even for a short guy). And people seem to pay attention when I speak. So listen to this: Of all the brain disorders, Parkinson's is the one that scientists truly believe may be closest to a cure. Yet it remains severely underfunded. In fact, with enough funding, they feel they can crack it within 10 years. And if they can cure Parkinson's, then similar diseases like Alzheimer's, Huntington's, and ALS (Lou Gehrig's Disease) may not be far behind. You can help make that happen. Go to my Web site. Or call to make a donation. You have the power to wipe out this disease. To affect millions of lives. Okay, okay. I'll get off my soapbox now.

Make a donation today. Visit www.michaeljfox.org or call 1-800-708-7644.

Parkinson's Foundation

1. Do you find this ad particularly compelling? Why or why not? What kind of an impact does the spokesman's statement have on his audience? Explain.
2. What is the man standing on? Why?
3. Who is the man in the advertisement? What is his connection to the "product"? How is he dressed and posed? Do these photographic elements make the ad more effective? If so, why?
4. How does the text featured at the bottom of the ad work to complement the overall ad, including the quote at the top. What tense and voice does it use? To whom is it addressed?

Eduardo:
Trabaja 14 horas al día
6 días a la semana
Tiene 4 hijos

Lunes: noche de matemáticas con los niños

Encontrar tiempo para ayudar a sus hijos con las matemáticas no es fácil ni conveniente para una persona como Eduardo. Pero es importante. Él lo considera una inversión en el futuro de sus hijos. Porque con educación, ellos tendrán más oportunidades cuando sean mayores.

 ÉXITO EN LA ESCUELA = ÉXITO EN LA VIDA
1-800-281-1313   www.exitoescuela.org

Una Asociacion del NAACP y la Fundacion People For the American Way.

Ad Council ad on Education (in Spanish)

[*Translation:*
Eduardo:
Works 14 hours a day
6 days a week
Has 4 children

Monday: Math night with the kids

Finding time to help his children with math is not easy or convenient for a person like Eduardo. But it is important. He considers it an investment in his children's future. Because with education, they will have more opportunities when they grow up.

Success in school = Success in life]

1. Who is the person in the picture? What is he doing? What does this picture tell you about Eduardo? How does the text help promote our understanding of him? Explain.
2. What is the purpose of this advertisement, and who is it trying to reach? What can you determine about the intended audience based on the picture, language and message?
3. If there were no text in this ad, what other things could it promote? Explain.
4. Visit the web site (*www.successinschool.org* or *www.exitoescuela.org*). Would the ad lead you to look up the web site? How useful is this web site to the intended audience? Explain.

A (Mild) Defense of Luxury

James Twitchell

While media and academic critics question the methods of advertising agencies and lament the sacrifice of values in the name of consumerism, professor James Twitchell openly embraces the media-driven world of advertising. In the next piece, Twitchell explores the joys of luxury and challenges the academic criticism that condemns our material instincts as shallow and self-centered. He realizes that his viewpoint may not be popular, but it is honest. Because the truth is, we love nice stuff. Is that so wrong?

James Twitchell is a professor of English and advertising at the University of Florida. He switched from teaching poetry to the study of mass culture and advertising after discovering that his students could recite more ad jingles than they could lines of poetry. Since then, he has written many books on the subject, including *Twenty Ads that Shook the World* (1998) and *Lead Us into Temptation: The Triumph of American Materialism* (1999). This essay is an excerpt from his 2002 book, *Living It Up: America's Love Affair with Luxury.*

CRITICAL THINKING   Why is materialism so criticized, yet obviously so wholeheartedly embraced by American society? If we are basically lovers of luxury, why are we so quick to condemn advertising and consumerism?

1   Who but fools, toadies, and hacks have ever come to the defense of modern American luxury? No one, not even bulk consumers of the stuff, will ever really defend it. And why should they? The very idea that what we have defines who we are is repulsive to many of us. The irrationality of overvaluing certain rocks, fabrics, logos, textures, wines, bottles, appliances, nameplates, tassels, zip codes, T-shirts, monograms, hotel rooms, purses, and the like is insulting to our intellect. At one level this kind of luxury is indefensible. The "good life" seems so blatantly unnecessary, even evil, especially when millions of people around the globe are living without the bare necessities. Plus, after all, it's just cake, a sugar high. Empty calories.

2   And few of us truly admire those who have amassed vast quantities of this stuff. If Donald Trump has his defenders, it is primarily those who are entertained, not edified, by his obstreperousness. Imelda Marcos is a pathetic character. Ditto Leona Helmsley. It's hard to be on Rodeo Drive and see a man wearing a pinkie ring, a flashy Rolex, decked out like Regis Philbin, getting into a Lincoln Navigator, and not feel a kind of smug self-satisfaction with one's own life. And let's face it, the Vegas Strip is an exciting place to visit, but most of us wouldn't want to live there.

3   Generations ago the market for luxury goods consisted of a few people who lived in majestic houses with a full complement of servants, in some time-honored enclave of the privileged. As Holly Brubach (1998) has wittily observed, they ordered their trunks from Louis Vuitton, their trousseaus from Christian Dior, their Dom Perignon by the case, and spent lots of time looking out over water. Their taste, like their politics, was determined largely by considerations of safeguarding

wealth and perpetuating the social conventions that affirmed their sense of superiority. They stayed put. We watched them from afar. We stayed put. Maybe they had money to burn. We had to buy coal.

4   The very unassailability of old luxe made it safe, like old name, old blood, old land, old pew, old coat of arms, or old service to the crown. Primogeniture, the cautious passage and consolidation of wealth to the first-born male, made the anxiety of exclusion somehow bearable. After all, you knew your place from the moment of birth and had plenty of time to make your peace. If you drew a short straw, not to worry. A comfortable life as a vicar would await you. Or the officer corps. For females marriage became the defining act of social place.

5   The application of steam, and then electricity, to the engines of production brought a new market of status, an industrial market, one made up of people who essentially bought their way into having a blood line. From them this new generation of consumer has descended. First the industrial rich, then the inherited rich, and now the incidentally rich, the accidentally rich. Call them yuppies, yippies, bobos, nobrows, or whatever; although they can't afford a house in Paris's Sixteenth Arrondissement or an apartment on Park Avenue, they have enough disposable income to buy a Vuitton handbag (if not a trunk), a bottle of Dior perfume (if not a flagon), a Bombay martini (if not quite a few), and a timeshare vacation on the water (if not a second home). The consumers of the new luxury have a sense of entitlement that transcends social class, a conviction that the finer things are their birthright—never mind that they were born into a family whose ancestral home is a tract house in the suburbs, near the mall, not paid for, and the family crest comes downloaded from the Internet.

6   These new *customers* for luxury are younger than *clients* of the old luxe used to be, they are far more numerous, they make their money far sooner, and they are far more flexible in financing and fickle in choice. They do not stay put. They now have money to burn. The competition for their attention is intense, and their consumption patterns—if you haven't noticed—is changing life for the rest of us. How concerned should we be? I say, not very. Let them eat cake.

The Economic Defense of Opuluxe

7   While making status distinctions on the basis of luxury consumption seems silly, even incompatible with common sense, contemporary economists and sociologists aren't so sure. Economists like Martin Feldstein at Harvard and Paul David at Stanford have been arguing that certain acts of consumption mimic a kind of equitable savings, a kind of universal investment in a mythic bank of communal value (Lewis 1998:B7). After all, it may be more efficient—not to mention, more fun—to spend your money buying a badge good like a fancy car or an Armani wardrobe to announce your social place than to do it the old-fashioned way and join the country club. Plus, you don't have to play golf.

8   Although it is not pictured this way in popular culture, the consumption of high-end goods is rarely impulsive, emotional, or extravagant. Instead it may more often be thoughtful, clever, and sensible. *Pretty Woman* makes a point worth considering.

In a sense modern luxury is insurance against misunderstanding, a momentary stay against panic and confusion. If you can't tell where you are in life by consulting the Social Register; then check your car nameplate, your zip code, the amount of stainless steel wrapped around your barbecue.

9   That such "peace of mind" can be bought may seem shallow until you realize that the transformation is dependent only on money, and the color of money is always the same. This is a far more equitable currency than the capriciousness of ancestry and the whimsy of gender and birth order. Well into the nineteenth century the placement of your family pew was a marker of status. The higher your birth and the larger your bank account, the closer you were to the front—the closer, by implication, to God. Given a choice between a lucky-sperm culture in which birth decides social place or a lucky-stock-option culture in which market whimsy decides social place, I think I prefer the latter.

Why Academics Criticize the New Luxury

10   Remember in *King Lear* when the two nasty daughters want to strip Lear of his last remaining trappings of majesty? He has moved in with them, and they don't think he needs so many expensive guards. They convince themselves by saying that their dad, who is used to having everything he has ever wanted, doesn't need a hundred or even a dozen soldiers around him. They whittle away at his retinue until only one is left. "What needs one?" they say. Rather like governments attempting to redistribute wealth or like academics criticizing the consumption habits of others, they include that his needs are excessive. They are false needs: sumptuous, wasteful, luxurious. Lear, however, knows otherwise. Terrified and suddenly bereft of purpose, he bellows from his innermost soul, "Reason not the need."

11   True, Lear doesn't need these soldiers any more than Scrooge needed silver, Midas needed gold, the characters on *Friends* need stuff from Crate & Barrel, those shoppers on Rodeo/Worth/Madison Avenues need handbags, or I need to spend the night at the Luxor. But not needing doesn't stop the desiring. Lear knows that possessions are definitions—superficial meanings, perhaps, but meanings nonetheless. Without soldiers he is no king. Without a BMW there can be no yuppie, without tattoos no adolescent rebel, without big hair no southwestern glamourpuss, without Volvos no academic intellectuals, without cake no Marie Antoinette.

12   Professor Robert Frank tells a revealing story in his *Luxury Fever: Why Money Fails to Satisfy in an Era of Excess.* It seems a relative of his bought a red Porsche in France. When the relative returned to California, he found that the German car couldn't be retrofitted to meet the state's rigorous pollution regulations. He offered it to the professor at a fraction of its market value. Now, in Professor Frank's words,

> I was sorely tempted. Yet my small upstate college town has a strong, if usually unstated, social norm against conspicuous consumption. People here are far more likely to drive Volvos than Jaguars, and although ours is a cold climate, we almost never see anyone wearing a fur coat. At that time, a red Porsche convertible really would have been seen, as an in-your-face car in a community like ours. Although I have never thought of myself as someone

> unusually sensitive to social pressure, I realized that unless I could put a sign
> on the car that explained how I happened to acquire it, I would never really
> feel comfortable driving it. (168)

Professor Frank knows exactly what goods to buy and exactly what goods *not* to
buy. He doesn't want to keep up with the Joneses or ditch the Joneses. He wants to
fit in with the Joneses. He knows who the Joneses are. It's pretty much bow ties,
Volvos, and horn-rimmed glasses, thank you very much.

13   My point is simple: This is a social decision, not a moral one or even an economic one. He has decided not to define himself in terms of a red Porsche convert-
ible. He wants what his consumption community wants. But this opens up such an
interesting question, at least to me. Why have academics proved such myopic observers of the consumerist world? Why so universally dour and critical? And why
can't they see that their own buying habits are more a matter of taste than degree?

14   Here, for instance, is Frank talking in *Luxury Fever* not about consumption per
se but about the anxieties of relative position. He is using his sons' behavior to illustrate the childish nature of competitive consumption. Read just a bit between the
lines:

> Having been raised as an only child, I have always observed the sibling rival-
> ries among my own children with great interest. On returning from a friend's
> house, my 8-year-old son immediately asks, "Where's Chris?" if his 11-year-
> old brother is not in sight. When Chris is at his violin lesson, or at the ortho-
> dontist's office, we have no problem. But let him be at a movie, or just visit-
> ing a friend, the next thing we'll hear is Hayden's angry shout of "That's not
> fair!"—the inevitable prelude to an anguished outburst about the injustice of
> life. (1999:109–10)

Now, I don't know either Professor Frank or his sons, but I'll make a prediction.
Here's what the boys can look forward to: straight teeth, plenty of soccer (not football) equipment, music lessons galore (preferably piano and violin), summer camp
at Duke, magnet school or maybe a year or two at Deerfield, trips to Europe, four
years at a private college or university or at one of the public Ivys (celebrated on the
rear windscreen of the professor's BMW—not Volvo; remember he's in the
B-school, not arts and sciences), and then postgraduate polishing. Nothing extraordinary about this expenditure of—what?—about $400,000 a kid.

15   What's extraordinary is that rarely, if ever, will Frank roll over at night and
think he is spending foolishly. Never will he see himself as a luxury consumer,
deeply embedded in a consumption community. No, to bobos like the professor (and
me, I hasten to add), these choices have nothing to do with taste. They are needs,
goddammit! Educational affiliations for academic offspring have nothing to do with
the lawyer next door who drives an S-class Mercedes or the software designer I play
tennis with who sports a Patek Philippe wristwatch. Nothing! We're talking education here, not tail fins!

16   I think one reason we academics have been so unappreciative of the material
world, often so downright snotty about it, is that we don't need it. Academics say
they don't need it because they have the life of the mind, they have art, they contem-
plate the best that has been thought and said. (Plus, not a whole lot of disposable in-

come.) But that's not the entire story. I think that another reason most academics don't need store-bought affiliation is because the school world, like the church world it mimics, is a cosseted world, a world in which rank and order are well-known and trusted and stable. In fact, buying stuff is more likely to confuse status than illuminate it.

17   Let me tell you who I am in this context. I am a professor in the English department at the University of Florida; I teach romanticism. Here's what that sentence looks like when I explode it to show how each part marks me on the academic totem pole.

I am a	named professor *professor* associate professor assistant professor instructor teaching assistant	in the	philosophy mathematics *English* department history sociology
at the	Ivy League public Ivy good big school *University of Florida* not so good big school community college	I teach	medieval lit Renaissance lit postmodern litcrit eighteenth-century lit *romanticism* modern lit American lit film popcrit

18   Now of course, if you are an academic, you will immediately disagree with how I have arranged the hierarchies. But you can't disagree with the depth of the description, nor, when you think about it, how deep the academic system is relative to others. If you are an academic, I instantly know about you from just a few words. Just say something like "I am a visiting assistant professor of sociology at Podunk U" and I can pretty accurately spin a description of what your life has been like. Give me a bit more, like a publication cite (not the subject, but where it appears), and you are flying right into my radar. This system of social place is so stable that you wear it like a pair of Gucci sunglasses or an old school tie. Little wonder academics are so perplexed by an outside world that seems preoccupied with social place via consumption. Little wonder we misunderstand it. I can't imagine what it would be like to tell someone I was a DFO of a pre-IPO dot-com. I'd much rather just have them check out my nifty chunky loafers from Prada and my Coach edition of Lexus out in the driveway.

Was It Worth It?

19 The question then becomes: Are we better off for living in a culture in which luxuries are turned into necessities, in which mild addictions are made into expected tastes, in which elegancies are made niceties, expectancies are made into entitlements, in which opulence is made into populence?

20 And the answer, from the point of view of those historically excluded, is yes. Absolutely, yes. Ironically, just as the very stuff that I often find unaesthetic and others may find contemptible has ameliorated the condition of life for many, many millions of people, the very act of getting to this stuff promises a better life for others. I don't mean to belittle the value of religion, politics, law, education, and all the other patterns of meaning making in the modern world but only to state the obvious. Forget happiness; if decreasing pain and discomfort is a goal, consumption of the "finer things" has indeed done what governments, churches, schools, and even laws have promised. Far more than these other systems, betterment through consumption has delivered the goods. Paul Krugman is certainly correct when he writes, "On sheer material grounds one would almost surely prefer to be poor today than upper middle class a century ago" (2000:A15).

21 But is it fair? Do some of us suffer inordinately for the excesses of others? What are we going to do when all this stuff we have shopped for becomes junk? What about the environment? How close is the connection between the accumulation of the new luxury and the fact that the United States also leads the industrialized world in rates of murder, violent crime, juvenile violent crime, imprisonment, divorce, abortion, single-parent households, obesity, teen suicide, cocaine consumption, per-capita consumption of all drugs, pornography production, and pornography consumption? What are we going to do about the lower sixth of our population that seems mired in transgenerational poverty?

22 These are important questions I will leave to others. Entire academic, governmental, and commercial industries are dedicated to each of them. One of the most redemptive aspects of cultures that produce the concept of luxury is that they also produce the real luxury of having time and energy to discuss it. Who knows? Perhaps the luxury of reflection will help resolve at least some of the shortcomings of consumption. ◆

FREEWRITING ASSIGNMENT

Write about how you feel about luxury. What is luxury to you? Is there a point when it seems excessive? If so, what is your luxury threshold, and why?

CRITICAL READING

1. In his opening paragraph, Twitchell comments, "who but fools, toddies, and hacks have ever come to the defense of modern American luxury," right before he proceeds to do precisely that. How does this approach set

the tone for his essay? What can you surmise from his tone and use of language? Does it make him more or less credible? Explain.

2. How does Twitchell's opinion expressed in this essay differ from others in this section in his attitude toward advertising? Are they likely to be swayed by his argument? Why or why not?

3. What, according to Twitchell, is the general attitude of academia toward consumerism? How does Twitchell feel about this attitude? Why does he say this viewpoint is fundamentally flawed?

4. According to Twitchell, why is luxury so important to Americans? What is the connection between desire and social status? Self-image? Explain.

5. How well does Twitchell support his argument? Evaluate his use of supporting evidence. How well does he convince his readers that his position is reasonable and correct? Explain.

6. Evaluate Twitchell's analysis of excerpts from Professor Frank's book. What does he determine about Frank? Do you think he is probably right? Explain.

7. In his conclusion, Twitchell asserts that while consuming luxury goods may seem wasteful, it really isn't all that bad when you consider how much better off society is as a whole. Do you agree with this conclusion? Why or why not?

CRITICAL WRITING

8. *Exploratory Writing*: Twitchell wonders in his conclusion whether luxury consumption is fair. "Is it fair? Do some of us suffer inordinately for the excesses of others?" Respond to his question, addressing one or more of the issues he raises (crime, environment, etc.).

9. *Personal Narrative*: Write a brief narrative about a time you experienced a decadent spending situation—either for yourself or with someone else. What motivated your spending? How did you feel after it? Can you relate your experience to any of the motivations Twitchell describes in his essay?

10. *Exploratory Writing*: Twitchell outlines his personal "context" as an academic at the University of Florida. Our context, he explains, influences our consumer habits. Prepare a similar outline for yourself. What does your "explosion" tell you about yourself? If someone constructed a sentence based on your diagram, what might they assume about your consumer habits?

GROUP PROJECTS

11. With your group, make a list of standard appliances, equipment, and possessions that people have in their homes—refrigerators, microwave ovens, pocketbooks, personal planners, fans, coffeemakers, DVD players, computers, VCRs, televisions, stereos (include components), ipods, blowdryers, scooters, etc. Make a list of at least 25–30 items. After the group has

created a list, separately rank each item as a necessary, a desirable, or a luxury item. For example, you may decide a refrigerator is a necessary item, but list an air conditioner as a luxury item. Do not look at how other members of your group rank the items until you are all finished. Compare your list with others in your group. Do the lists match, or are there some surprising discrepancies? Discuss the similarities and differences between your lists.

12. Examine the collection of ads on the preceding pages. Select one of the ads and identify the consumer group it targets. Develop a profile of a typical consumer of the product it promotes; and, like Twitchell does with Professor Frank in his essay, try to create a likely summary of their lives or the lives of their children.

VIEWPOINTS

▶ **With These Words, I Can Sell You Anything**
William Lutz

▶ **The Language of Advertising**
Charles A. O'Neill

Words such as "help" and "virtually" and phrases such as "new and improved" and "acts fast" seem like innocuous weaponry in the arsenal of advertising. But not to William Lutz, who analyzes how such words are used in ads—how they misrepresent, mislead, and deceive consumers. In this essay, he alerts us to the special power of "weasel words"—those familiar and sneaky little critters that "appear to say one thing when in fact they say the opposite, or nothing at all." The real danger, Lutz argues, is how such language debases reality and the values of the consumer. Marketing executive Charles A. O'Neill, however, disputes Lutz's criticism of advertising doublespeak. Although admitting to some of the craftiness of his profession, O'Neill defends the huckster's language—both verbal and visual—against claims that it distorts reality. Examining some familiar television commercials and magazine ads, he explains why the language may be charming and seductive, but it is far from brainwashing.

William Lutz teaches English at Rutgers University and is the author of several books, including *The New Doublespeak: Why No One Knows What Anyone's Saying Anymore* (1997) and *Doublespeak Defined* (1999). The following essay is an excerpt from Lutz's book, *Doublespeak* (1990). Charles O'Neill is senior vice president of marketing for Colonial Investment Services in Boston. His essay first appeared in the textbook *Exploring Language*.

CRITICAL THINKING   Consider the phrases used in advertising such as "new and improved" and "cleans like a dream." Do we think about such advertising phrases? How much do such phrases influence you as a consumer? Explain.

With These Words, I Can Sell You Anything

William Lutz

1　One problem advertisers have when they try to convince you that the product they are pushing is really different from other, similar products is that their claims are subject to some laws. Not a lot of laws, but there are some designed to prevent fraudulent or untruthful claims in advertising. Even during the happy years of non-regulation under President Ronald Reagan, the FTC did crack down on the more blatant abuses in advertising claims. Generally speaking, advertisers have to be careful in what they say in their ads, in the claims they make for the products they advertise. Parity claims are safe because they are legal and supported by a number of court decisions. But beyond parity claims there are weasel words.

2　Advertisers use weasel words to appear to be making a claim for a product when in fact they are making no claim at all. Weasel words get their name from the way weasels eat the eggs they find in the nests of other animals. A weasel will make a small hole in the egg, suck out the insides, then place the egg back in the nest. Only when the egg is examined closely is it found to be hollow. That's the way it is with weasel words in advertising: Examine weasel words closely and you'll find that they're as hollow as any egg sucked by a weasel. Weasel words appear to say one thing when in fact they say the opposite, or nothing at all.

"Help"—The Number One Weasel Word

3　The biggest weasel word used in advertising doublespeak is "help." Now "help" only means to aid or assist, nothing more. It does not mean to conquer, stop, eliminate, end, solve, heal, cure, or anything else. But once the ad says "help," it can say just about anything after that because "help" qualifies everything coming after it. The trick is that the claim that comes after the weasel word is usually so strong and so dramatic that you forget the word "help" and concentrate only on the dramatic claim. You read into the ad a message that the ad does not contain. More importantly, the advertiser is not responsible for the claim that you read into the ad, even though the advertiser wrote the ad so you would read that claim into it.

4　The next time you see an ad for a cold medicine that promises that it "helps relieve cold symptoms fast," don't rush out to buy it. Ask yourself what this claim is really saying. Remember, "helps" means only that the medicine will aid or assist. What will it aid or assist in doing? Why, "relieve" your cold "symptoms." "Relieve" only means to ease, alleviate, or mitigate, not to stop, end, or cure. Nor does the claim say how much relieving this medicine will do. Nowhere does this ad claim it will cure anything. In fact, the ad doesn't even claim it will *do* anything at all. The ad only claims that it will aid in relieving (not curing) your cold symptoms, which are probably a runny nose, watery eyes, and a headache. In other words, this medicine probably contains a standard decongestant and some aspirin. By the way, what does "fast" mean? Ten minutes, one hour, one day? What is fast to one person can be very slow to another. Fast is another weasel word.

5   Ad claims using "help" are among the most popular ads. One says, "Helps keep you young looking," but then a lot of things will help keep you young looking, including exercise, rest, good nutrition, and a facelift. More importantly, this ad doesn't say the product will keep you young, only "young *looking*." Someone may look young to one person and old to another.

6   A toothpaste ad says, "Helps prevent cavities," but it doesn't say it will actually prevent cavities. Brushing your teeth regularly, avoiding sugars in foods, and flossing daily will also help prevent cavities. A liquid cleaner ad says, "Helps keep your home germ free," but it doesn't say it actually kills germs, nor does it even specify which germs it might kill.

7   "Help" is such a useful weasel word that it is often combined with other action-verb weasel words such as "fight" and "control." Consider the claim, "Helps control dandruff symptoms with regular use." What does it really say? It will assist in controlling (not eliminating, stopping, ending, or curing) the *symptoms* of dandruff, not the cause of dandruff nor the dandruff itself. What are the symptoms of dandruff? The ad deliberately leaves that undefined, but assume that the symptoms referred to in the ad are the flaking and itching commonly associated with dandruff. But just shampooing with *any* shampoo will temporarily eliminate these symptoms, so this shampoo isn't any different from any other. Finally, in order to benefit from this product, you must use it regularly. What is "regular use"—daily, weekly, hourly? Using another shampoo "regularly" will have the same effect. Nowhere does this advertising claim say this particular shampoo stops, eliminates, or cures dandruff. In fact, this claim says nothing at all, thanks to all the weasel words.

8   Look at ads in magazines and newspapers, listen to ads on radio and television, and you'll find the word "help" in ads for all kinds of products. How often do you read or hear such phrases as "helps stop . . . ," "helps overcome . . . ," "helps eliminate . . . ," "helps you feel . . . ," or "helps you look . . ."? If you start looking for this weasel word in advertising, you'll be amazed at how often it occurs. Analyze the claims in the ads using "help," and you will discover that these ads are really saying nothing.

9   There are plenty of other weasel words used in advertising. In fact, there are so many that to list them all would fill the rest of this book. But, in order to identify the doublespeak of advertising and understand the real meaning of an ad, you have to be aware of the most popular weasel words in advertising today.

Virtually Spotless

10   One of the most powerful weasel words is "virtually," a word so innocent that most people don't pay any attention to it when it is used in an advertising claim. But watch out. "Virtually" is used in advertising claims that appear to make specific, definite promises when there is no promise. After all, what does "virtually" mean? It means "in essence of effect, although not in fact." Look at that definition again. "Virtually" means *not in fact.* It does *not* mean "almost" or "just about the same as," or anything else. And before you dismiss all this concern over such a small word, remember that small words can have big consequences.

11   In 1971 a federal court rendered its decision on a case brought by a woman who became pregnant while taking birth control pills. She sued the manufacturer, Eli

Lilly and Company, for breach of warranty. The woman lost her case. Basing its ruling on a statement in the pamphlet accompanying the pills, which stated that, "When taken as directed, the tablets offer virtually 100% protection," the court ruled that there was no warranty, expressed or implied, that the pills were absolutely effective. In its ruling, the court pointed out that, according to *Webster's Third New International Dictionary,* "virtually" means "almost entirely" and clearly does not mean "absolute" (*Whittington* v. *Eli Lilly and Company,* 333 F. Supp. 98). In other words, the Eli Lilly company was really saying that its birth control pill, even when taken as directed, *did not in fact* provide 100 percent protection against pregnancy. But Eli Lilly didn't want to put it that way because then many women might not have bought Lilly's birth control pills.

12   The next time you see the ad that says that this dishwasher detergent "leaves dishes virtually spotless," just remember how advertisers twist the meaning of the weasel word "virtually." You can have lots of spots on your dishes after using this detergent and the ad claim will still be true, because what this claim really means is that this detergent does not *in fact* leave your dishes spotless. Whenever you see or hear an ad claim that uses the word "virtually," just translate that claim into its real meaning. So the television set that is "virtually trouble free" becomes the television set that is not in fact trouble free, the "virtually foolproof operation" of any appliance becomes an operation that is in fact not foolproof, and the product that "virtually never needs service" becomes the product that is not in fact service free.

New and Improved

13 If "new" is the most frequently used word on a product package, "improved" is the second most frequent. In fact, the two words are almost always used together. It seems just about everything sold these days is "new and improved." The next time you're in the supermarket, try counting the number of times you see these words on products. But you'd better do it while you're walking down just one aisle, otherwise you'll need a calculator to keep track of your counting.

14   Just what do these words mean? The use of the word "new" is restricted by regulations, so an advertiser can't just use the word on a product or in an ad without meeting certain requirements. For example, a product is considered new for about six months during a national advertising campaign. If the product is being advertised only in a limited test market area, the word can be used longer, and in some instances has been used for as long as two years.

15   What makes a product "new"? Some products have been around for a long time, yet every once in a while you discover that they are being advertised as "new." Well, an advertiser can call a product new if there has been "a material functional change" in the product. What is "a material functional change," you ask? Good question. In fact it's such a good question it's being asked all the time. It's up to the manufacturer to prove that the product has undergone such a change. And if the manufacturer isn't challenged on the claim, then there's no one to stop it. Moreover, the change does not have to be an improvement in the product. One manufacturer added an artificial lemon scent to a cleaning product and called it "new and im-

proved," even though the product did not clean any better than without the lemon scent. The manufacturer defended the use of the word "new" on the grounds that the artificial scent changed the chemical formula of the product and therefore constituted "a material functional change."

16   Which brings up the word "improved." When used in advertising, "improved" does not mean "made better." It only means "changed" or "different from before." So, if the detergent maker puts a plastic pour spout on the box of detergent, the product has been "improved," and away we go with a whole new advertising campaign. Or, if the cereal maker adds more fruit or a different kind of fruit to the cereal, there's an improved product. Now you know why manufacturers are constantly making little changes in their products. Whole new advertising campaigns, designed to convince you that the product has been changed for the better, are based on small changes in superficial aspects of a product. The next time you see an ad for an "improved" product, ask yourself what was wrong with the old one. Ask yourself just how "improved" the product is. Finally, you might check to see whether the "improved" version costs more than the unimproved one. After all, someone has to pay for the millions of dollars spent advertising the improved product.

17   Of course, advertisers really like to run ads that claim a product is "new and improved." While what constitutes a "new" product may be subject to some regulation, "improved" is a subjective judgment. A manufacturer changes the shape of its stick deodorant, but the shape doesn't improve the function of the deodorant. That is, changing the shape doesn't affect the deodorizing ability of the deodorant, so the manufacturer calls it "improved." Another manufacturer adds ammonia to its liquid cleaner and calls it "new and improved." Since adding ammonia does affect the cleaning ability of the product, there has been a "material functional change" in the product, and the manufacturer can now call its cleaner "new," and "improved" as well. Now the weasel words "new and improved" are plastered all over the package and are the basis for a multimillion-dollar ad campaign. But after six months the word "new" will have to go, until someone can dream up another change in the product. Perhaps it will be adding color to the liquid, or changing the shape of the package, or maybe adding a new dripless pour spout, or perhaps a _____. The "improvements" are endless, and so are the new advertising claims and campaigns.

18   "New" is just too useful and powerful a word in advertising for advertisers to pass it up easily. So they use weasel words that say "new" without really saying it. One of their favorites is "introducing," as in, "Introducing improved Tide," or "Introducing the stain remover." The first is simply saying, here's our improved soap; the second, here's our new advertising campaign for our detergent. Another favorite is "now," as in, "Now there's Sinex," which simply means that Sinex is available. Then there are phrases like "Today's Chevrolet," "Presenting Dristan," and "A fresh way to start the day." The list is really endless because advertisers are always finding new ways to say "new" without really saying it. If there is a second edition of this book, I'll just call it the "new and improved" edition. Wouldn't you really rather have a "new and improved" edition of this book rather than a "second" edition?

Acts Fast

19 "Acts" and "works" are two popular weasel words in advertising because they bring action to the product and to the advertising claim. When you see the ad for the cough syrup that "Acts on the cough control center," ask yourself what this cough syrup is claiming to do. Well, it's just claiming to "act," to do something, to perform an action. What is it that the cough syrup does? The ad doesn't say. It only claims to perform an action or do something on your "cough control center." By the way, what and where is your "cough control center"? I don't remember learning about that part of the body in human biology class.

20 Ads that use such phrases as "acts fast," "acts against," "acts to prevent," and the like, are saying essentially nothing, because "act" is a word empty of any specific meaning. The ads are always careful not to specify exactly what "act" the product performs. Just because a brand of aspirin claims to "act fast" for headache relief doesn't mean this aspirin is any better than any other aspirin. What is the "act" that this aspirin performs? You're never told. Maybe it just dissolves quickly. Since aspirin is a parity product, all aspirin is the same and therefore functions the same.

Works Like Anything Else

21 If you don't find the word "acts" in an ad, you will probably find the weasel word "works." In fact, the two words are almost interchangeable in advertising. Watch out for ads that say a product "works against," "works like," "works for," or "works longer." As with "acts," "works" is the same meaningless verb used to make you think that this product really does something, and maybe even something special or unique. But "works," like "acts," is basically a word empty of any specific meaning.

Like Magic

22 Whenever advertisers want you to stop thinking about the product and to start thinking about something bigger, better, or more attractive than the product, they use that very popular weasel word, "like." The word "like" is the advertiser's equivalent of a magician's use of misdirection. "Like" gets you to ignore the product and concentrate on the claim the advertiser is making about it. "For skin like peaches and cream" claims the ad for a skin cream. What is this ad really claiming? It doesn't say this cream will give you peaches-and-cream skin. There is no verb in this claim, so it doesn't even mention using the product. How is skin ever like "peaches and cream"? Remember, ads must be read literally and exactly, according to the dictionary definition of words. (Remember "virtually" in the Eli Lilly case.) The ad is making absolutely no promise or claim whatsoever for this skin cream. If you think this cream will give you soft, smooth, youthful-looking skin, you are the one who has read that meaning into the ad.

23 The wine that claims "It's like taking a trip to France" wants you to think about a romantic evening in Paris as you walk along the boulevard after a wonderful meal in an intimate little bistro. Of course, you don't really believe that a wine can take you to France, but the goal of the ad is to get you to think pleasant, romantic thoughts about

France and not about how the wine tastes or how expensive it may be. That little word "like" has taken you away from crushed grapes into a world of your own imaginative making. Who knows, maybe the next time you buy wine, you'll think those pleasant thoughts when you see this brand of wine, and you'll buy it. Or, maybe you weren't even thinking about buying wine at all, but now you just might pick up a bottle the next time you're shopping. Ah, the power of "like" in advertising.

24   How about the most famous "like" claim of all, "Winston tastes good like a cigarette should"? Ignoring the grammatical error here, you might want to know what this claim is saying. Whether a cigarette tastes good or bad is a subjective judgment because what tastes good to one person may well taste horrible to another. Not everyone likes fried snails, even if they are called escargot. (*De gustibus non est disputandum,* which was probably the Roman rule for advertising as well as for defending the games in the Colosseum.) There are many people who say all cigarettes taste terrible, other people who say only some cigarettes taste all right, and still others who say all cigarettes taste good. Who's right? Everyone, because taste is a matter of personal judgment.

25   Moreover, note the use of the conditional, "should." The complete claim is, "Winston tastes good like a cigarette should taste." But should cigarettes taste good? Again, this is a matter of personal judgment and probably depends most on one's experiences with smoking. So, the Winston ad is simply saying that Winston cigarettes are just like any other cigarette: Some people like them and some people don't. On that statement, R. J. Reynolds conducted a very successful multimillion-dollar advertising campaign that helped keep Winston the number-two-selling cigarette in the United States, close behind number one, Marlboro.

Can't It Be Up to the Claim?

26   Analyzing ads for doublespeak requires that you pay attention to every word in the ad and determine what each word really means. Advertisers try to wrap their claims in language that sounds concrete, specific, and objective, when in fact the language of advertising is anything but. Your job is to read carefully and listen critically so that when the announcer says that "Crest can be of significant value . . ." you know immediately that this claim says absolutely nothing. Where is the doublespeak in this ad? Start with the second word.

27   Once again, you have to look at what words really mean, not what you think they mean or what the advertiser wants you to think they mean. The ad for Crest only says that using Crest "can be" of "significant value." What really throws you off in this ad is the brilliant use of "significant." It draws your attention to the word "value" and makes you forget that the ad only claims that Crest "can be." The ad doesn't say that Crest *is* of value, only that it is "able" or "possible" to be of value, because that's all that "can" means.

28   It's so easy to miss the importance of those little words, "can be." Almost as easy as missing the importance of the words "up to" in an ad. These words are very popular in sale ads. You know, the ones that say, "Up to 50 percent Off!" Now, what does that claim mean? Not much, because the store or manufacturer has to reduce the price of only a few items by 50 percent. Everything else can be reduced a lot

less, or not even reduced. Moreover, don't you want to know 50 percent off of what? Is it 50 percent off the "manufacturer's suggested list price," which is the highest possible price? Was the price artificially inflated and then reduced? In other ads, "up to" expresses an ideal situation. The medicine that works "up to ten times faster," the battery that lasts "up to twice as long," and the soap that gets you "up to twice as clean"—all are based on ideal situations for using those products, situations in which you can be sure you will never find yourself.

Unfinished Words

29 Unfinished words are a kind of "up to" claim in advertising. The claim that a battery lasts "up to twice as long" usually doesn't finish the comparison—twice as long as what? A birthday candle? A tank of gas? A cheap battery made in a country not noted for its technological achievements? The implication is that the battery lasts twice as long as batteries made by other battery makers, or twice as long as earlier model batteries made by the advertiser, but the ad doesn't really make these claims. You read these claims into the ad, aided by the visual images the advertiser so carefully provides.

30 Unfinished words depend on you to finish them, to provide the words the advertisers so thoughtfully left out of the ad. Pall Mall cigarettes were once advertised as "A longer finer and milder smoke." The question is, longer, finer, and milder than what? The aspirin that claims it contains "Twice as much of the pain reliever doctors recommend most" doesn't tell you what pain reliever it contains twice as much of. (By the way, it's aspirin. That's right; it just contains twice the amount of aspirin. And how much is twice the amount? Twice of what amount?) Panadol boasts that "nobody reduces fever faster," but, since Panadol is a parity product, this claim simply means that Panadol isn't any better than any other product in its parity class. "You can be sure if it's Westinghouse," you're told, but just exactly what it is you can be sure of is never mentioned. "Magnavox gives you more" doesn't tell you what you get more of. More value? More television? More than they gave you before? It sounds nice, but it means nothing, until you fill in the claim with your own words, the words the advertisers didn't use. Since each of us fills in the claim differently, the ad and the product can become all things to all people, and not promise a single thing.

31 Unfinished words abound in advertising because they appear to promise so much. More importantly, they can be joined with powerful visual images on television to appear to be making significant promises about a product's effectiveness without really making any promises. In a television ad, the aspirin product that claims fast relief can show a person with a headache taking the product and then, in what appears to be a matter of minutes, claiming complete relief. This visual image is far more powerful than any claim made in unfinished words. Indeed, the visual image completes the unfinished words for you, filling in with pictures what the words leave out. And you thought that ads didn't affect you. What brand of aspirin do you use?

32 Some years ago, Ford's advertisements proclaimed "Ford LTD—700 percent quieter." Now, what do you think Ford was claiming with these unfinished words?

What was the Ford LTD quieter than? A Cadillac? A Mercedes Benz? A BMW? Well, when the FTC asked Ford to substantiate this unfinished claim, Ford replied that it meant that the inside of the LTD was 700 percent quieter than the outside. How did you finish those unfinished words when you first read them? Did you even come close to Ford's meaning?

Combining Weasel Words

33 A lot of ads don't fall neatly into one category or another because they use a variety of different devices and words. Different weasel words are often combined to make an ad claim. The claim, "Coffee-Mate gives coffee more body, more flavor," uses Unfinished Words ("more" than what?) and also uses words that have no specific meaning ("body" and "flavor"). Along with "taste" (remember the Winston ad and its claim to taste good), "body" and "flavor" mean nothing because their meaning is entirely subjective. To you, "body" in coffee might mean thick, black, almost bitter coffee, while I might take it to mean a light brown, delicate coffee. Now, if you think you understood that last sentence, read it again, because it said nothing of objective value; it was filled with weasel words of no specific meaning: "thick," "black," "bitter," "light brown," and "delicate." Each of those words has no specific, objective meaning, because each of us can interpret them differently.

34 Try this slogan: "Looks, smells, tastes like ground-roast coffee." So, are you now going to buy Taster's Choice instant coffee because of this ad? "Looks," "smells," and "tastes" are all words with no specific meaning and depend on your interpretation of them for any meaning. Then there's that great weasel word "like," which simply suggests a comparison but does not make the actual connection between the product and the quality. Besides, do you know what "ground-roast" coffee is? I don't, but it sure sounds good. So, out of seven words in this ad, four are definite weasel words, two are quite meaningless, and only one has any clear meaning.

35 Remember the Anacin ad—"Twice as much of the pain reliever doctors recommend most"? There's a whole lot of weaseling going on in this ad. First, what's the pain reliever they're talking about in this ad? Aspirin, of course. In fact, any time you see or hear an ad using those words "pain reliever," you can automatically substitute the word "aspirin" for them. (Makers of acetaminophen and ibuprofen pain relievers are careful in their advertising to identify their products as nonaspirin products.) So, now we know that Anacin has aspirin in it. Moreover, we know that Anacin has twice as much aspirin in it, but we don't know twice as much as what. Does it have twice as much aspirin as an ordinary aspirin tablet? If so, what is an ordinary aspirin tablet, and how much aspirin does it contain? Twice as much as Excedrin or Bufferin? Twice as much as a chocolate chip cookie? Remember those Unfinished Words and how they lead you on without saying anything.

36 Finally, what about those doctors who are doing all that recommending? Who are they? How many of them are there? What kind of doctors are they? What are their qualifications? Who asked them about recommending pain relievers? What other pain relievers did they recommend? And there are a whole lot more questions about this "poll" of doctors to which I'd like to know the answers, but you get the point. Sometimes, when I call my doctor, she tells me to take two aspirin and call her office in the morning. Is that where Anacin got this ad?

Read the Label, or the Brochure

37 Weasel words aren't just found on television, on the radio, or in newspaper and magazine ads. Just about any language associated with a product will contain the doublespeak of advertising. Remember the Eli Lilly case and the doublespeak on the information sheet that came with the birth control pills. Here's another example.

38   In 1983, the Estée Lauder cosmetics company announced a new product called "Night Repair." A small brochure distributed with the product stated that "Night Repair was scientifically formulated in Estée Lauder's U.S. laboratories as part of the Swiss Age-Controlling Skincare Program. Although only nature controls the aging process, this program helps control the signs of aging and encourages skin to look and feel younger." You might want to read these two sentences again, because they sound great but say nothing.

39   First, note that the product was "scientifically formulated" in the company's laboratories. What does that mean? What constitutes a scientific formulation? You wouldn't expect the company to say that the product was casually, mechanically, or carelessly formulated, or just thrown together one day when the people in the white coats didn't have anything better to do. But the word "scientifically" lends an air of precision and promise that just isn't there.

40   It is the second sentence, however, that's really weasely, both syntactically and semantically. The only factual part of this sentence is the introductory dependent clause—"only nature controls the aging process." Thus, the only fact in the ad is relegated to a dependent clause, a clause dependent on the main clause, which contains no factual or definite information at all and indeed purports to contradict the independent clause. The new "skincare program" (notice it's not a skin cream but a "program") does not claim to stop or even retard the aging process. What, then, does Night Repair, at a price of over $35 (in 1983 dollars) for a .87-ounce bottle do? According to this brochure, nothing. It only "helps," and the brochure does not say how much it helps. Moreover, it only "helps control," and then it only helps control the "*signs* of aging," not the aging itself. Also, it "encourages" skin not to *be* younger but only to "look and feel" younger. The brochure does not say younger than what. Of the sixteen words in the main clause of this second sentence, nine are weasel words. So, before you spend all that money for Night Repair, or any other cosmetic product, read the words carefully, and then decide if you're getting what you think you're paying for.

Other Tricks of the Trade

41 Advertisers' use of doublespeak is endless. The best way advertisers can make something out of nothing is through words. Although there are a lot of visual images used on television and in magazines and newspapers, every advertiser wants to create that memorable line that will stick in the public consciousness. I am sure pure joy reigned in one advertising agency when a study found that children who were asked to spell the word "relief" promptly and proudly responded "r-o-l-a-i-d-s."

42   The variations, combinations, and permutations of doublespeak used in advertising go on and on, running from the use of rhetorical questions ("Wouldn't you re-

ally rather have a Buick?" "If you can't trust Prestone, who can you trust?") to flattering you with compliments ("The lady has taste." "We think a cigar smoker is someone special." "You've come a long way baby."). You know, of course, how you're *supposed* to answer those questions, and you know that those compliments are just leading up to the sales pitches for the products. Before you dismiss such tricks of the trade as obvious, however, just remember that all of these statements and questions were part of very successful advertising campaigns.

43   A more subtle approach is the ad that proclaims a supposedly unique quality for a product, a quality that really isn't unique. "If it doesn't say Goodyear, it can't be polyglas." Sounds good, doesn't it? Polyglas is available only from Goodyear because Goodyear copyrighted that trade name. Any other tire manufacturer could make exactly the same tire but could not call it "polyglas," because that would be copyright infringement. "Polyglas" is simply Goodyear's name for its fiberglass-reinforced tire.

44   Since we like to think of ourselves as living in a technologically advanced country, science and technology have a great appeal in selling products. Advertisers are quick to use scientific doublespeak to push their products. There are all kinds of elixirs, additives, scientific potions, and mysterious mixtures added to all kinds of products. Gasoline contains "HTA," "F–130," "Platformate," and other chemical-sounding additives, but nowhere does an advertisement give any real information about the additive.

45   Shampoo, deodorant, mouthwash, cold medicine, sleeping pills, and any number of other products all seem to contain some special chemical ingredient that allows them to work wonders. "Certs contains a sparkling drop of Retsyn." So what? What's "Retsyn"? What's it do? What's so special about it? When they don't have a secret ingredient in their product, advertisers still find a way to claim scientific validity. There's "Sinarest. Created by a research scientist who actually gets sinus headaches." Sounds nice, but what kind of research does this scientist do? How do you know if she is any kind of expert on sinus medicine? Besides, this ad doesn't tell you a thing about the medicine itself and what it does.

Advertising Doublespeak Quick Quiz

46 Now it's time to test your awareness of advertising doublespeak. (You didn't think I would just let you read this and forget it, did you?) The following is a list of statements from some recent ads. Your job is to figure out what each of these ads really says:

> DOMINO'S PIZZA: "Because nobody delivers better."
> SINUTAB: "It can stop the pain."
> TUMS: "The stronger acid neutralizer."
> MAXIMUM STRENGTH DRISTAN: "Strong medicine for tough sinus colds."
> LISTERMINT: "Making your mouth a cleaner place."
> CASCADE: "For virtually spotless dishes nothing beats Cascade."
> NUPRIN: "Little. Yellow. Different. Better."
> ANACIN: "Better relief."

SUDAFED: "Fast sinus relief that won't put you fast asleep."

ADVIL: "Advanced medicine for pain."

PONDS COLD CREAM: "Ponds cleans like no soap can."

MILLER LITE BEER: "Tastes great. Less filling."

PHILIPS MILK OF MAGNESIA: "Nobody treats you better than MOM (Philips Milk of Magnesia)."

BAYER: "The wonder drug that works wonders."

CRACKER BARREL: "Judged to be the best."

KNORR: "Where taste is everything."

ANUSOL: "Anusol is the word to remember for relief."

DIMETAPP: "It relieves kids as well as colds."

LIQUID DRANO: "The liquid strong enough to be called Drano."

JOHNSON & JOHNSON BABY POWDER: "Like magic for your skin."

PURITAN: "Make it your oil for life."

PAM: "Pam, because how you cook is as important as what you cook."

IVORY SHAMPOO AND CONDITIONER: "Leave your hair feeling Ivory clean."

TYLENOL GEL-CAPS: "It's not a capsule. It's better."

ALKA-SELTZER PLUS: "Fast, effective relief for winter colds."

The World of Advertising

47 In the world of advertising, people wear "dentures," not false teeth; they suffer from "occasional irregularity," not constipation; they need deodorants for their "nervous wetness," not for sweat; they use "bathroom tissue," not toilet paper; and they don't dye their hair, they "tint" or "rinse" it. Advertisements offer "real counterfeit diamonds" without the slightest hint of embarrassment, or boast of goods made out of "genuine imitation leather" or "virgin vinyl."

48   In the world of advertising, the girdle becomes a "body shaper," "form persuader," "control garment," "controller," "outerwear enhancer," "body garment," or "anti-gravity panties," and is sold with such trade names as "The Instead," "The Free Spirit," and "The Body Briefer."

49   A study some years ago found the following words to be among the most popular used in U.S. television advertisements: "new," "improved," "better," "extra," "fresh," "clean," "beautiful," "free," "good," "great," and "light." At the same time, the following words were found to be among the most frequent on British television: "new," "good-better-best," "free," "fresh," "delicious," "full," "sure," "clean," "wonderful," and "special." While these words may occur most frequently in ads, and while ads may be filled with weasel words, you have to watch out for all the words used in advertising, not just the words mentioned here.

50   Every word in an ad is there for a reason; no word is wasted. Your job is to figure out exactly what each word is doing in an ad—what each word really means, not what the advertiser wants you to think it means. Remember, the ad is trying to get you to buy a product, so it will put the product in the best possible light, using any device, trick, or means legally allowed. Your only defense against advertising (besides taking up permanent residence on the moon) is to develop and use a strong critical reading, listening, and looking ability. Always ask yourself what the ad is

really saying. When you see ads on television, don't be misled by the pictures, the visual images. What does the ad say about the product? What does the ad *not* say? What information is missing from the ad? Only by becoming an active, critical consumer of the doublespeak of advertising will you ever be able to cut through the doublespeak and discover what the ad is really saying. ◆

The Language of Advertising
Charles A. O'Neill

1 His name is Joe. But he's not just your ordinary Joe. You've probably seen him; he's Joe Camel. On the billboards and in the magazine ads, he looked vaguely like a cartoonist's composite sketch of the Rolling Stones, lounging around in a celebrity waiting area at MTV headquarters in New York. He was poised, confident, leaning against a railing or playing pool with his friends. His personal geometry was always just right. He often wore a white suit, dark shirt, sunglasses. Cigarette in hand, wry smile on his lips, his attitude was distinctly confident, urbane.

2 Joe was very cool and very powerful. So cool and powerful that more than 90% of six-year-olds matched Joe Camel with a picture of a cigarette, making him as well-known as Mickey Mouse.[1]

3 Good advertising, but bad public relations.

4 Finally, in 1997, after extended sparring with the tobacco company about whether in fact Joe promoted smoking, and whether cartoons were most likely to be noticed by children or adults, the FTC brought the ads to an end. President Clinton spoke for the regulators when he said, "Let's stop pretending that a cartoon camel in a funny costume is trying to sell to adults, not children."

5 Joe's 23-year-old advertising campaign was stopped because it was obvious that his mission was to turn kids into lung cancer patients. That's bad enough. But beneath the surface, the debate about Joe typifies something more interesting and broad based: the rather uncomfortable, tentative acceptance of advertising in our society. We recognize the legitimacy—even the value—of advertising but on some level we can't quite fully embrace it as a "normal" part of our experience.

6 At best, we view advertising as distracting. At worst, we view it as dangerous to our health and a pernicious threat to our social values. One notable report acknowledged the positive contribution of advertising (e.g., provides information, supports worthy causes, and encourages competition and innovation), then added, "In the competition to attract even larger audiences . . . communicators can find themselves pressured . . . to set aside high artistic and moral standards and lapse into superficiality, tawdriness and moral squalor."[2]

7 How does advertising work? Why is it so powerful? Why does it raise such concern? What case can be made for and against the advertising business?

8 In order to understand advertising, you must accept that it is not about truth, virtue, love, or positive societal values. It is about money. It is about moving customers through the sales process. Sometimes the words and images are concrete;

sometimes they are merely suggestive. Sometimes ads provide useful information; sometimes they convince us that we need to spend money to solve a problem we never knew we had. Ads are designed to be intrusive. We're not always pleased about the way they clutter our environment and violate our sense of private space. We're not always happy with the tactics they use to impose themselves upon us.

9   Whatever the product or creative strategy, advertisements derive their power from a purposeful, directed combination of images. These can take the form of words, sounds, or visuals, used individually or together. The combination of images is the language of advertising, a language unlike any other.

10   Everyone who grows up in the civilized world soon learns that advertising language is different from other languages. Read this aloud: "With Nice 'n Easy, it's color so natural, the closer he gets the better you look" Many children would be unable to explain how this classic ad for Clairol's Nice 'n Easy hair coloring differs from "ordinary language," but they would say, "It sounds like an ad." Whether printed on a page, blended with music on the radio, or whispered on the sound track of a television commercial, advertising language is *different*.

11   The language of advertising changes with the times. Styles and creative concepts come and go. But there are at least four distinct, general characteristics of the language of advertising that make it different from other languages. They lend advertising its persuasive power:

1. The language of advertising is edited and purposeful.
2. The language of advertising is rich and arresting; it is specifically intended to attract and hold our attention.
3. The language of advertising involves us; in effect, *we* complete the message.
4. The language of advertising is simple and direct. It holds no secrets from us.

Edited and Purposeful

12   In his book, *Future Shock*, Alvin Toffler described various types of messages we receive from the world around us each day. He observed that there is a difference between normal "coded" messages and "engineered" messages. Much of normal, human experience is "uncoded." When a man walks down a street, for example, he sees where he is going and hears random sounds. These are mental images, but they are not messages "designed by anyone to communicate anything and the man's understanding of it does not depend directly on a social code—a set of agreed-upon signs and definitions." [3] In contrast, Toffler describes a talk show conversation as "coded"; the speaker's ability to exchange information with the host depends upon societal conventions.

13   The language of advertising is coded. It exists in the context of our society. It is also carefully engineered, and ruthlessly purposeful. When he wrote in the 1960s, he estimated that the average adult was exposed to 560 advertising messages each day. That was back in the 1960s. Now, our homes are equipped with 400-channel, direct-broadcast satellite television, the Internet, video streaming mobile devices, video games and other new forms of mass media. We're literally swimming in a sea of information. We're totally wired and wireless. We're overwhelmed by countless bill-

boards in subway stations, stickers on light poles, 15-second spots on television, and an endless stream of spam and pop up messages online.

Demanding Attention

14 Among the hundreds of advertising messages in stores for us each day, very few will actually command our conscious attention. The rest are screened out. The people who design and write ads know about this screening process; they anticipate and accept it as a premise of their business.

15 The classic, all-time favorite device used to breach the barrier is sex. There was a time, many years ago, when advertisers used some measure of subtlety and discretion in their application of sexual themes to their mass media work. No more. Sensuality has been replaced by in-your-face, unrestrained sexuality. One is about romance and connection; the other, physical connection and emotional distance.

16 A poster promotes clothing sold by the apparel company, French Connection group, United Kingdom: (FCUK). Large type tells us, "Apparently there are more important things in life than fashion. Yeah, right." This text is accompanied by a photo of two young people in what has become a standard set up: A boy. A girl. She is pretty, in a detached, offhand sort of way. He has not shaved for 48 hours. Behind them there is a vague impression of a waterfront. They are sharing physical space, but there is no sense of human contact or emotion. The company name appears on the lower right hand side of the poster. The headline is intended to be ironic: "Of course there are things that are more important than fashion, but right now, who cares?" The company maintains that they are "not trying to shock people." As absurd as it may seem, this is actually the truth. This company is not in the business of selling shock. They are selling clothes. They are making a lot of money selling clothes because they know what motivates their teenaged customers—a desire to separate from their parents and declare their membership in the tribe of their peers.

17 Fortunately, advertisers use many other techniques to attract and hold the attention of the targeted consumer audience. The strategy may include strong creative execution or a plain, straightforward presentation of product features and customer benefits. Consider this random cross-section of advertisements from popular media.

- An ad for SalesForce.com used a photo of the Dalai Lama beneath the headline, "There is no software on the path to enlightenment." (What does this mean? "SalesForce.com provides computer services, so I won't have to buy software myself.")
- An ad for two products—the Volkswagen Beetle, and the Apple iPod—used only one word: "Duh." Above it, moving from left to right, we see a photo of the car, a plus sign and to the right, the iPod. (What makes this work? Fast Company (10/03) described this as "a marriage of two classic 'underdog' brands . . . a psychographic match made in heaven. VW and Apple both appeal to young, high-income, adventure-seeking customers. . . .")
- "Can a security blanket be made of sheet metal?" (GM) In the background, there is a photo of a tot asleep in a car seat (Who doesn't like cute little kids? What parent doesn't think about safety these days?)

- Some ads entertain us and are effective, even though they don't really focus on the product. They work because we remember them. Geico is an automobile insurance company, but they use a cute little lizard as a character in their ads. (What does a lizard have to do with an insurance company? More than meet the eye. A *gecko* is a type of lizard.)
- Some ads tell us we have problems—real or imagined—that we'd better solve right away. Do you have dry skin or "unsightly eyebrow hairs?" ("I never really noticed, but now that you mention it. . . .")

  "Give your car the pink slip." (A short term car rental company lets us know that we don't need to own a car—we can pick one up whenever and wherever we need it.)

18   Soft drink companies are in an advertising category of their own. In the archetypical version of a soft drink TV spot, babies frolic with puppies in the sunlit foreground while their youthful parents play touch football. On the porch, Grandma and Pops quietly smile as they wait for all of this affection to transform the world into a place of warmth, harmony, and joy.

19   Dr. Pepper ads say "Be you!" and feature dancers prancing around singing songs about "Individuality." In Coke's ads, the singer Maya tells us this can of syrupy fizz is "Real." And Pepsi has Britney Spears singing "Pepsi: for those who think young!" The message: If you are among the millions of people who see the commercial and buy the product, you will become 'different'. You will find yourself transformed into a unique ("Be you", "Individuality", "Real"), hip ("young") person. [4]

20   These "slice of life" ads seduce us into feeling—somewhere in the back of our heads—that if we drink the right combination of sugar, preservatives, caramel coloring, and a few secret ingredients, we'll fulfill our yearning for a world where folks from all nations, creeds and sexual orientations live together in a state of perfect bliss. At least for the five minutes it takes us to pour the stuff down our parched, fast-food-filled throats.

21   If you don't buy this version of the American Dream, look around. You are sure to find a product that promises to help you gain prestige in whatever posse you do happen to run with.

22   When the connection is made, the results can be very powerful. Even a commodity product like coffee can be artfully changed from a mere beverage into an emotional experience. *The Wall Street Journal* (7/14/03) summarized the challenge the marketers at Starbucks faced in promoting their stores in China: "Selling an upscale, Western lifestyle that is both in demand in China yet meets resistance among those unfamiliar with the taste of coffee." The article goes on to describe a customer in Shanghai, who drinks tea at home but coffee in public. He said he prefers the taste of tea, but he likes the image that drinking Starbucks coffee conjures up: relaxed affluence. "It's an attitude." A medium size latte costs the equivalent of $2.65. In Shanghai, the monthly disposable income of an average three-person household is $143.00. One cup of coffee costs nearly 2% of the average household's monthly income.

23   What Starbucks has accomplished is not far short of astonishing. They have been successful in taking a purely commodity product that their prospective customers do not particularly enjoy and turning it into not just another drink, but a hip,

groovy and chic "attitude"; and they've done this in a Communist country, where the rules according to Mao would have us believe that there are no class distinctions. What's more, they have created primary demand for a product category; a difficult, if not nearly impossible, feat.

24   Ad campaigns and branding strategies do not often emerge like Botticelli's Venus from the sea, flawless and fully grown. Most often, the creative strategy is developed only after extensive research. "Who will be interested in our product? How old are they? Where do they live? How much money do they earn? What problem will our product solve?" The people at Starbucks did not decide to go to China on a whim. The people at French Connection did not create their brand name just to offend everyone who is old-fashioned enough to think that some words don't belong on billboards, T-shirts and store fronts.

Involving

25 We have seen that the language of advertising is carefully engineered; we have discovered a few of the devices it uses to get our attention. Coke and Pepsi have entranced us with visions of peace and love. An actress offers a winsome smile. Now that they have our attention, advertisers present information intended to show us that their product fills a need and differs from the competition. Advertisers exploit and intensify product differences when they find them, and invent them when they do not.

26   As soon as we see or hear an advertisement, our imagination is set in motion, and our individual fears, aspirations, quirks and insecurities come out to play.

27   It was common not long ago for advertisers in the fashion industry to make use of gaunt, languid models. To some observers, these ads promoted "heroin chic." Perhaps they were not substance abusers, but something was most certainly unusual about the models appearing in ads for Prada and Calvin Klein Products. A young woman in a Prada ad projects no emotion whatsoever. Her posture suggests that she is in a trance or drug-induced stupor. In a Calvin Klein ad, a young man, like the woman from Prada, is gaunt beyond reason. He is shirtless. As if to draw more attention to his peculiar posture and "zero body fat" status, he is shown pinching the skin next to his navel. To some, this also suggests that he is preparing to insert a needle.

28   The fashion industry backed away from the heroin theme. Now the models look generally better fed. But they are, nonetheless, still lost in a world of ennui and isolation. In an ad by Andrew Mark NY, we see a young woman wearing little leather shorts. Her boyfriend's arm is wrapped around her, his thumb pushing ever-so-slightly below the waistband of her pants. What does he look like? He appears to be dazed. He is wearing jeans, an unzipped leather jacket. He hasn't shaved for a couple of days. We are left with the impression that either something has just happened here, or is about to. It probably has something to do with sex.

29   Do these depictions of a decadent lifestyle exploit certain elements of our society—the young, insecure or clueless? Or did these ads, and others of their ilk, simply reflect profound bad taste? Most advertising is about exploitation—the systematic, deliberate identification of our needs and wants, followed by the delivery of a carefully constructed promise that the product will satisfy them.

30   Advertisers make use of a great variety of techniques and devices to engage us in the delivery of their messages. Some are subtle, making use of warm, entertaining or comforting images or symbols. Others, as we've seen, are about as subtle as an action sequence from Quentin Tarantino's latest movie. Although it may seem hard to believe, advertising writers did not invent sex. They did not invent our tendency to admire and seek to identify ourselves with famous people. Once we have seen a famous person in an ad, we associate the product with the person. When we buy Coke, we're becoming a member of the Friends of Maya Club. The logic is faulty, but we fall for it just the same. Advertising works, not because Maya and Britney have discriminating taste, or the nameless waif in the clothing ad is a fashion diva, but because we participate in it.

Keeping It Simple

31   Advertising language differs from other types of language in another important respect, it is a simple language. To measure the simplicity of an ad, calculate its Fog Index. Robert Gunning[5] developed this formula to determine the comparative ease with which any given piece of written communication can be read.

- Calculate the number of words in an average sentence.
- Count the number of words of three or more syllables in a typical 100-word passage, omitting words that are capitalized, combinations of two simple words, or verb forms made into three-syllable words by the addition of -*ed* or -*es*.
- Add the two figures (the average number of words per sentence and the number of three-syllable words per 100 words), then multiply the result by 4.

32   In an advertisement for Harry Potter books, the visual is a photo of a slightly menacing fellow standing next to his bike in an alley. Here is the text:

Flying cars. Fire Whiskey. Death Eaters.

There's some pretty tough stuff in Harry Potter—bad guys so bad they're called Death Eaters. That's only one of the wicked reasons even bikers think Harry Potter is cool enough to ride with them.

33   *Reader's Digest* has a Fog Index of 8. *US News & World Report* and *Time Magazine* are about 9. There are 8.5 words—none three syllables—in the average "sentence."

1. Words per sentence: 8.5
2. Three syllable words/100:   0
3. Subtotal: 8.5
4. Multiply by .4:   3.4

34   According to Gunning's scale, you should be able to comprehend this ad if you are about half way through the third grade. Comic books weigh in at 6; *Reader's Digest* at 9; *Atlantic Monthly* is 12.

35   Why do advertisers generally favor simple language? The answer lies with the consumer. As a practical matter, we would not notice many of these messages if length or eloquence was counted among their virtues. Today's consumer cannot

take the time to focus on anything for long, much less blatant advertising messages. Every aspect of modern life runs at an accelerated pace. Voice mail, pagers, cellular phones, e-mail, the Internet—the world is always awake, always switched on, and hungry for information. Time generally, and TV-commercial time in particular, is dissected into increasingly smaller segments.

36   Toffler views the evolution toward shorter language as a natural progression: three-syllable words are simply harder to read than one- or two-syllable words. Simple ideas are more readily transferred from one person to another than complex ideas. Therefore, advertising copy uses increasingly simple language, as does society at large. In *Future Shock,* Toffler speculates:

> If the [English] language had the same number of words in Shakespeare's time as it does today, at least 200,000 words—perhaps several times that many—have dropped out and been replaced in the intervening four centuries. The high turnover rate reflects changes in things, processes, and qualities in the environment from the world of consumer products and technology.

37   It is no accident that the first terms Toffler uses to illustrate his point ("fastback," "wash-and-wear," and "flashcube") were invented not by engineers, or journalists, but by advertising copywriters.

38   Advertising language is simple language; difficult words are deleted and replaced by simple words or images not open to misinterpretation.

Who Is Responsible?

39 Some critics view the advertising industry as a cranky, unwelcomed child of the free enterprise system—a noisy, whining, brash kid who must somehow be kept in line, but can't just yet be thrown out of the house. In reality, advertising mirrors the fears, quirks, and aspirations of the society that creates it (and is, in turn, sold by it). This alone exposes advertising to parody and ridicule. The overall level of acceptance and respect for advertising is also influenced by the varied quality of the ads themselves. Some ads, including a few of the examples cited here, are deliberately designed to provoke controversy. Critics have declared Advertising guilty of other failings as well:

1. Advertising encourages unhealthy habits.
2. Advertising feeds on human weaknesses and exaggerates the importance of material things, encouraging "impure" emotions and vanities.
3. Advertising sells daydreams—distracting, purposeless visions of lifestyles beyond the reach of the majority of the people who are most exposed to advertising.
4. Advertising warps our vision of reality, implanting in us groundless fears and insecurities.
5. Advertising downgrades the intelligence of the public.
6. Advertising debases English.
7. Advertising perpetuates racial and sexual stereotypes.

40   What can be said in advertising's defense? Does it encourage free-market competition and product innovation? Sure. But the real answer is simply this: Advertising is, at heart, only a reflection of society.

41   What can we say about the charge that advertising debases the intelligence of the public? Exactly how intelligent is "the public?" Sadly, evidence abounds that the public at large is not particularly intelligent, after all. Americans now get 31 percent of their calories from junk food and alcoholic beverages. [6] Michael can't read. Jessica can't write. And the entire family spends the night in front of the television, watching idiots eat living insects in the latest installment for a 'reality' show.

42   Ads are effective because they sell products. They would not succeed if they did not reflect the values and motivations of the real world. Advertising both reflects and shapes our perception of reality. Ivory Snow is pure. Federal Express won't let you down. Absolut is cool. Sasson is sexy. Mercedes represents quality. Our sense of what these brand names stand for may have as much to do with advertising as with the objective "truth."

43   Good, responsible advertising can serve as a positive influence for change, while fueling commerce. But the obverse is also true: Advertising, like any form of mass communication, can be a force for both "good" and "bad." It can just as readily reinforce or encourage irresponsible behavior, ageism, sexism, ethnocentrism, racism, homophobia, heterophobia—you name it—as it can encourage support for diversity and social progress.

44   As Pogo once famously said, "We have met the enemy, and he is us." [7] ◆

Notes

1. Internet: *http://www.joechemo.org.*
2. Pontifical Council for Social Communications, "Ethics in Advertising," published 2/22/97.
3. Alvin Toffler, *Future Shock* (New York Random House, 1970), p. 146.
4. Shannon O'Neill, a student at the University of New Hampshire, contributed this example and others cited here.
5. Curtis D. MacDougall, *Interpretive Reporting* (New York: Macmillan, 1968), p. 94.
6. 2000 study by the American Society for Clinical Nutrition (Boston Globe, 7/29/93).
7. Walt Kelly, "Pogo" cartoon (1960s); referring to the Vietnam War.

FREEWRITING ASSIGNMENT

Describe an experience in which you purchased a product because you were influenced by its advertising language. For example, did you buy a hair, beauty, or electronic product because of the promises made by its ad? Explain.

CRITICAL READING

1. Consider Lutz's argument that advertisers are trying to "trick" consumers with their false promises and claims. How much are our expectations of product performance influenced by the claims and slogans of advertising? How do you think O'Neill would respond to Lutz's accusation?

2. Does the fact that O'Neill is a professional advertiser influence your reception of his essay? Does it make his argument more or less persuasive?
3. Review the rules and regulations concerning the words "new" and "improved." How do advertisers address the problem of product regulations? Do such rules really protect consumers? Explain.
4. O'Neill is an advertising professional. Does his writing style reflect the advertising techniques he describes? Cite examples to support your answer.
5. How does O'Neill address any objections his audience may have to his argument? Are the objections he anticipates indeed the ones you had as a reader? Does his "answer" make his essay stronger? Explain.
6. O'Neill notes that symbols have become important elements in the language of advertising. Can you think of some specific symbols from advertising that you associate with your lifestyle? How important are these symbols to you? How do they work as wordless advertising? Explain.
7. A "weasel word" is a word so hollow it has no meaning. Consider your own reaction to weasel words when you hear them. Try to identify as many weasel words as you can. What are the words and what do consumers think they mean?
8. Do you think it is ethical for advertisers to create a sense of product difference when there really isn't any? Consider advertisements for products such as gasoline, beer, or coffee.

CRITICAL WRITING

9. *Exploratory Writing*: O'Neill, in his essay, makes several generalizations that characterize the language of advertising. Think about ads that you have recently seen or read and make a list of your own generalizations about the language of advertising. Refer to some specific advertisements in your response.
10. *Persuasive Writing*: O'Neill believes that advertising language mirrors the fears, quirks, and aspirations of the society that creates it. Do you agree or disagree with this statement? Explain your perspective in a brief essay supporting your response with examples.
11. *Analytical Writing*: Choose a brand-name product that you use regularly or to which you have particular loyalty, and identify one or more of its competitors. Examine some advertisements for each brand. Write a short paper explaining what makes you prefer your brand to the others.

GROUP PROJECTS

12. Review Lutz's "Doublespeak Quick Quiz." Choose five items and analyze them, using dictionary meanings to explain what the ads are really saying.
13. With your group, think of some recent advertising campaigns that created controversy (Abercrombie and Fitch, Calvin Klein, Benetton, etc.) What made them controversial? How did this impact sales?

14. O'Neill (paragraph 30) notes that sometimes advertisers use symbols to engage their audience. With your group, create a list of brand symbols or logos, their corresponding products, and what lifestyle we associate with the logo or symbol. Are some logos more popular or prestigious? Explain.

15. Working in a group, develop a slogan and advertising campaign for one of the following products: sneakers, soda, a candy bar, or jeans. How would you apply the principles of advertising language to market your product? After completing your marketing plan, "sell" your product to the class. If time permits, explain the reasoning behind your selling technique.

RESEARCH ISSUE ## On Sale at Old Navy: Cool Clothes for Identical Zombies!

Damien Cave

Mass-market retail stores like Old Navy, Gap, Pottery Barn, and Ikea have enjoyed enormous popularity in recent years. Part of their appeal is that they market the concept of "cool." But are these stores just marketing conformity under the guise of "cool"? Are they crushing our individuality? Are we moving rapidly to the day where we will all dress the same way, own the same furniture, and want the same things? Writer and Phillips Foundation fellow Damien Cave thinks so. This article first appeared in the November 22, 2000, issue of the e-zine *Salon.*

1   Thomas Frank walks by the candy-cane-adorned displays of Old Navy, passing the sign exclaiming "priced so low, you can't say no," and into the chain's San Francisco flagship store. The all-devouring Christmas rush hasn't started yet, but it's clear from the frown on Frank's face that he's not being seduced by the cheap but stylish clothes, the swirling neon and the bass-heavy hip-hop pounding in his ears.

2   "Oh God, this is disgusting," Frank says. This reaction isn't surprising. The bespectacled Midwesterner is a pioneering social critic—one of the first writers to document how, starting in the '60s, American businesses have co-opted cool anticorporate culture and used it to seduce the masses. His arguments in the *Baffler,* a pugnacious review Frank founded in 1988, and in 1997's "The Conquest of Cool" read like sermons, angry wake-up calls for consumers who hungrily ingest hipperthan-thou ("Think Different") marketing campaigns without ever questioning their intent.

3   Old Navy and other cheap but tasteful retailers provide perfect fodder for Frank's critique. Their low prices and hip-but-wholesome branding strategy are supposed to present a healthy alternative to the conspicuous consumption of a Calvin Klein. But critics like Frank and Naomi Klein, author of "No Logo," argue that the

formula is really nothing more than the wolf of materialism wrapped in cheaper sheep's clothing.

4   Consumers are being scammed, says Klein, arguing that stores like Old Navy and Ikea are duping millions, inspiring mass conformity while pretending to deliver high culture to the masses. "It's this whole idea of creating a carnival for the most homogeneous fashions and furniture," says Klein. "It's mass cloning that's being masked in a carnival of diversity. You don't notice that you're conforming because everything is so colorful."

5   Klein and Frank say that few consumers recognize just how conformist their consumption habits have become. And certainly, it's hard to argue that Ikea's and Old Navy's items haven't become icons of urbanite and suburbanite imagination. Watch MTV, or rent "Fight Club," to see Ikea's candy-colored décor, then truck down to your local Old Navy flagship store. When you arrive, what you'll find is that hordes of people have beaten you there. At virtually every opening of Old Navy's and Ikea's stores—in the New York, Chicago and San Francisco areas, for example—tens of thousands of people appeared in the first few days. Even now, long after the stores first opened, lines remain long.

6   What's wrong with these people? Nothing, say defenders of the companies. The popularity of brands like Ikea and Old Navy, they argue, derives from the retailers' ability to offer good stuff cheap. "They provide remarkable value," says Joel Reichart, a professor at the Fordham School of Business who has written case studies on Ikea. "They're truly satisfying people's needs."

7   Despite his irritation with the way companies like Old Navy market themselves, Frank acknowledges that businesses have always sought to offer cheap, relatively high-quality merchandise and concedes that there is some value in their attempts. He even admits that consumerism is good for the economy.

8   But he and other critics argue that in the end we're only being conned into thinking that our needs are being satisfied. What's really happening, they argue, is that clever marketers are turning us into automatons who equate being cool with buying cheap stuff that everyone else has. Under the stores' guise of delivering good taste to the general public, any chance we have at experiencing or creating authenticity is being undermined. Ultimately, our brave new shopping world is one in which we are spending more time in the checkout line than reading books, watching movies or otherwise challenging ourselves with real culture.

9   "Shopping is a way of putting together your identity," laments "Nobrow" author John Seabrook. And the "homogenized taste" of today's Old Navy and Ikea shoppers proves, he says, that Americans either are consciously choosing to look and live alike or are determined not to notice that that is what they're doing.

10   According to Christine Rosen, a professor in the Haas School of Business at UC-Berkeley, people who fill their closets, homes and lives with Old Navy and Ikea—or Pottery Barn or a host of other slick stores—are simply new examples of the trend toward conformity that started when the first "brands" appeared in the 1910s and '20s, "We're Pavlovianly trained to respond to this," she says.

11   And we're also just too damn lazy. That's the theory floated by Packard Jennings, an anti-consumerism activist who says that stores like Old Navy are designed

to numb the brain and remove all semblance of creativity from the purchasing process. "Ikea pre-arranges sets of furniture in its stores, thereby lessening individual thought," he says. Once people are in the store, they can't resist. "Entire households are purchased at Ikea," he says.

12   Indeed, Janice Simonsen, an Ikea spokeswoman, confirmed that a large part of the chain's demographic consists of "people who come in and say, 'I need everything.'" Meanwhile, those who don't want everything usually end up with more than they need, says Fordham's Reichart. "The way they design their stores"—with an up escalator to the showroom and no exit until the checkout—"you end up going through the entire store," he says.

13   Old Navy plays by the same sneaky rules. When Frank and I entered the San Francisco store, clerks offered us giant mesh bags. Ostensibly, this is just good service, but since the bags are capable of holding at least half a dozen pairs of jeans and a few shirts, it's obvious that they're also meant to encourage overconsumption.

14   Frank called the bags "gross" but not out of line with other state-of-the-art retailing practices. But according to Klein, the sacks, in conjunction with Old Navy's penchant for displaying T-shirts in mock-1950s supermarket coolers, prove that the company is aiming to do something more. The idea behind this "theater for the brand" architecture is to commodify the products, to make them "as easy to buy as a gallon of milk," Klein says. "The idea is to create a Mecca where people make pilgrimages to their brand," Klein says. "You experience the identity of the brand and not the product."

15   Disney, which opened its first store in 1987, was the first to employ this strategy. And since then others have appeared. Niketown, the Body Shop, the Discovery Store—they all aim to sell products by selling a destination.

16   Old Navy and Ikea, however, are far more popular than those predecessors—and, if you believe the more pessimistic of their critics, more dangerous. Not only are the two chains remaking many closets and homes into one designer showcase, says Klein, but they are also lulling consumers to sleep and encouraging them to overlook some important issues.

17   Such as quality. People think they're getting "authenticity on the cheap," says David Lewis, author of "The Soul of the New Consumer." But the truth may be that they're simply purchasing the perception of quality and authenticity. "Because [Ikea and Old Navy] create these self-enclosed lifestyles," Klein explains, "you overlook the fact that the products are pretty crappy and fall apart." Adds Jennings, "Things may be cheaper, but you keep going back to replace the faulty merchandise."

18   Then there is the trap of materialism. Survey after survey suggests that people who place a high value on material goods are less happy than those who do not, says Eric Rindfleisch, a marketing professor at the University of Arizona. The focus on bargains, incremental purchases and commodification plays to a uniquely American blind spot.

19   "We operate with a duality," explains Rindfleisch, who has conducted studies linking materialism with depression. "Americans know that money doesn't buy happiness, but most people somehow believe that increments in pay or goods will improve our lives. It's a human weakness—particularly in America."

20   The most insidious danger may be more abstract. The anti-consumerism critics argue that by elevating shopping to cultural status, we are losing our grip on real culture. We live in a time where college kids think nothing of decorating their rooms with Absolut vodka ads and fail to realize that they're essentially turning their rooms into billboards. Meanwhile, museum stores keep getting larger, Starbucks sells branded CDs to go with your coffee and because Ikea and other stores now look like movie theaters or theme parks, we don't just shop, "we make a day of it," as Klein puts it.

21   This only helps steer us away from other endeavors. When people spend so much time buying, thinking and talking about products, they don't have time for anything else, for real conversations about politics or culture or for real interaction with people.

22   Ultimately, the popularity of Old Navy, Ikea and their ilk proves that we're stuck in what Harvard professor Juliet Schor calls "the cycle of work and spend." Breaking that cycle may not be easy, but if one believes critics like Frank, it's essential if we are to control our own culture, instead of allowing it to be defined by corporations.

23   The cycle may not be possible to break. Frank, for one, is extremely pessimistic about our chances for turning back the tide of conformity and co-opted cool. Maybe that's one reason why he wanted to get out of Old Navy as fast as he could.

24   But I'm not so sure. When "Ikea boy," Edward Norton's character in "Fight Club," watched his apartment and his Swedish furniture explode in a blaze of glory, I wasn't the only one in the theater who cheered. ◆

CRITICAL THINKING

1. In paragraph 2, Cave notes that American businesses have "co-opted cool anti-corporate culture." What does he mean? What is "anti-corporate" culture, and why is it "cool"? What started it, and how are businesses using it to their advantage? In what ways is this ironic? Explain.

2. In paragraph 20, Cave observes that "college kids think nothing of decorating their rooms with Absolut vodka ads and fail to realize that they're essentially turning their rooms into billboards." What decorating choices have you made to your personal space? In what ways has your decorating style been influenced by outside forms of advertising? Explain.

3. What techniques do mass-market stores employ to squeeze the maximum profit from consumers who enter them? Were you aware of these techniques? Have you fallen victim to them yourself? Explain.

RESEARCH PROJECTS

4. In paragraph 9, author John Seabrook comments, "Shopping is a way of putting together your identity." Consider the ways your shopping habits put together your identity. Arrange to go shopping with a few friends at several popular stores. As you shop, consider whether you or your com-

panions seem to be influenced by some of the techniques described in this essay. Consider not just what you buy, but where you shop, why you shop, and with whom. Note whether your companions criticize certain products, and why. How do your shopping companions influence each other's choices? Finally, how does branding appeal to their desire to buy particular things as part of presenting a personal identity? Write an essay describing the experience, and what you learned about marketing culture from your observations.

5. Visit the websites of the stores that Cave cites in his essay (*www. potterybarn.com*, *www.ikea.com*, *www.oldnavy.com*, etc.) and review their merchandise from the perspective of a cultural analyst. Acting like a social anthropologist, write an essay describing what American consumers are like—for example, what they buy, their personal style preferences, and what they desire based on what you see on the websites you analyzed. Can you determine any common themes? Does anything seem surprising? What might a person from another country, such as China or El Salvador determine about American consumers based on the offerings at these stores? Explain.

Additional essay topics, writing assignments,
research guidelines, and readings for this chapter can
be found online at **www.ablongman.com/goshgarian**.

Television

For Better or for Worse?

3

Television is the prime mover of modern culture. In five decades, it has become the country's foremost source of entertainment and news. More than any other medium, television regulates commerce, lifestyles, and social values. But the medium is also the object of considerable scorn. For years, television has been blamed for nearly all of our social ills—the rise in crime, increased divorce rates, lower voter turnouts, racism, falling SAT scores, increased sexual promiscuity, drug addiction, and the collapse of the family. In short, it has been cited as the cause of the decline of Western civilization.

Certainly, television can be blamed for piping into America's homes hours of brain-numbing, excessively violent, exploitative trash. And given the fact that the average 20-year-old viewer will have spent nearly three years of his or her life in front of the television set, it plays a significant and influential role in our daily lives. But to categorically condemn the medium is to be blind to some of the quality programming television is capable of producing—and not just those produced by PBS and educational channels such as TLC, Discovery, and the History Channel. The essays in this chapter will explore some of the ways television is a part of our lives—for better or worse—and will examine the areas in which television appears to have failed, and where it shines.

The chapter opens with an essay exploring the powerful influence television exerts on our culture. Despite the criticism, says writer Jane Rosenzweig, television's influence is not always a bad one—television can serve as an effective vehicle to promote social awareness and moral values. In "Can TV Improve Us?," Rosenzweig describes some of the positive ways television serves society.

Not everyone, however, agrees with Rosenzweig that television can improve us. Just as television can promote positive values, it may advance stereotypes and violence. Teaching children how to critically evaluate what they see on television may be more important than ever in this era of media violence. According to George Gerbner of the Cultural Indicators project, the average American child will have witnessed 8,000 murders on television by the age of twelve. In "The Man Who Counts the Killings," Scott Stossel reports some of the findings resulting from Gerbner's 30 years of research into media violence and its effects on society.

While television programming can be quite violent, television talk shows seem to follow similar patterns, reaching audiences through conflict and aggression. In "TV's War of Words," linguist Deborah Tannen explains how "Scream TV" reduces all discussions to oversimplified, polarized arguments. Shades of gray are scorned as weak and distracting, because the goal is not to understand an issue, but to win an argument. And, sometimes, winning does not mean that your argument was the best, but that your argument was the *loudest.*

Jason Kelly continues the discussion of television and children in "The Great TV Debate," in which he confesses that he finds it difficult to restrict his son's television time when he himself enjoys television so much. He wonders why television is stigmatized—do we all lie about how much we watch? Then, Elaine Showalter discusses the merits of reality programs in "Window on Reality: *American Idol* and the Search for Identity."

Many of us rely on the evening news to inform us of local, national, and international events. Television's unique ability to combine print, voice, and televised images makes its news programming distinctly different from newspapers or radio journalism. Neil Postman and Steve Powers argue that television's primary function as an entertainment medium conflicts with its role as an objective source of information. In "TV News: All the World in Pictures," they explain that television news is essentially entertainment disguised as objective journalism.

The chapter's two Viewpoints discuss television programming, parental responsibilities, and young children. First, we present a press release by the American Academy of Pediatrics warning against television viewing for very young children. "AAP Discourages Television for Very Young Children" explains that children need personal interaction that television cannot provide, and are, because of their age, unable to be "media educated persons." In "TV Can Be a Good Parent," Ariel Gore disagrees with the AAP policy, arguing that there is a time and place for television for young viewers. She questions the timing of the AAP policy and the logic behind its decision.

A short history of African American television programs is this chapter's Research Issue. "Television and African Americans," by Kate Tuttle, describes how African American programs have emerged from humble, often racist, origins to a medium only now coming into its own.

Can TV Improve Us?
Jane Rosenzweig

Although television is often cited as the source of many social ills—from teen violence to the decline of the family—many people point out that it also teaches, informs, and entertains us. The next article takes the debate one step further by postulating that TV can actually improve us. Jane Rosenzweig describes some of the ways in which television has forced us to think about social issues and has promoted moral values. And although television may not be the ideal vehicle to advocate values, it may be the best one we have.

A former staff editor for the *Atlantic Monthly*, Jane Rosenzweig now teaches writing at Yale University. This article was first published in the July/August 1999 issue of the *American Prospect*.

CRITICAL THINKING   Think about how television can increase awareness about a particular issue or promote certain values in audiences. What social or moral themes can you recall that were recently featured in popular television programs?

1   It's eight o'clock Wednesday evening and a rumor is circulating at a small-town high school in Massachusetts that a student named Jack is gay. Jack's friends—one of whom is a 15-year-old girl who has been sexually active since she was 13, and another of whom has a mother who has recently committed adultery—assure him it would be okay with them if he were, but admit their relief when he says he isn't. An

hour later, in San Francisco, a woman named Julia is being beaten by her boyfriend. Meanwhile, in Los Angeles, a young stripper who has given birth out of wedlock learns that her own mother locked her in a basement when she was three years old, an experience that she thinks may explain her inability to love her own child.

2   A typical evening in America? If a visitor from another planet had turned on the television (specifically the WB and Fox networks) on the evening of Wednesday, February 10, 1999, with the aim of learning about our society, he would likely have concluded that it is made up pretty exclusively of photogenic young people with disintegrating nuclear families and liberal attitudes about sex. It's obviously not an accurate picture, but what might our visitor have learned from the programs he watched? Would all the sex, violence, and pathology he saw teach him antisocial behavior? Or might he glean from prime-time dramas and sitcoms the behavior and attitudes that he would do well to adopt if he intended to go native in America?

3   This is not an idle question—not because aliens might be watching American television, but because people are, particularly impressionable children and teenagers. In a time when 98 percent of U.S. households own at least one television set—a set which is turned on for an average of nearly seven hours a day—the degree to which people learn from and emulate the behavior of the characters they see on TV is an academic cottage industry. Some evidence does support the widespread belief that children and teenagers are affected by violence and other antisocial behavior in the media. When Dan Quayle made his infamous comments in 1992 about Murphy Brown having a baby out of wedlock, he was merely doing what numerous concerned parents, ethnic groups, religious organizations, gun-control advocates, and others were already doing—blaming television for encouraging certain types of behavior.

4   But if television contributes to poor behavior, might it also be a vehicle for encouraging good behavior? In 1988, Jay Winsten, a professor at the Harvard School of Public Health and the director of the school's Center for Health Communication, conceived a plan to use television to introduce a new social concept—the "designated driver"—to North America. Shows were already dealing with the topic of drinking, Winsten reasoned, so why not add a line of dialogue here and there about not driving drunk? With the assistance of then-NBC chairman Grant Tinker, Winsten met with more than 250 writers, producers, and executives over six months, trying to sell them on his designated driver idea.

5   Winsten's idea worked; the "designated driver" is now common parlance across all segments of American society and in 1991 won entry into a Webster's dictionary for the first time. An evaluation of the campaign in 1994 revealed that the designated driver "message" had aired on 160 prime-time shows in four seasons and had been the main topic of twenty-five 30-minute or 60-minute episodes. More important, these airings appear to have generated tangible results. In 1989, the year after the "designated driver" was invented, a Gallup poll found that 67 percent of adults had noted its appearance on network television. What's more, the campaign seems to have influenced adult behavior: polls conducted by the Roper Organization in 1989 and 1991 found significantly increasing awareness and use of designated drivers. By 1991, 37 percent of all U.S. adults claimed to have refrained from drinking at least once in order to serve as a designated driver, up from 29 percent in 1989. In

1991, 52 percent of adults younger than 30 had served as designated drivers, suggesting that the campaign was having greatest success with its target audience.

6   In 1988 there were 23,626 drunk driving fatalities. By 1997 the number was 16,189. While the Harvard Alcohol Project acknowledges that some of this decline is due to new laws, stricter anti-drunk driving enforcement, and other factors, it claims that many of the 50,000 lives saved by the end of 1998 were saved because of the designated driver campaign. (The television campaign was only a part of the overall campaign; there were strong community-level and public service components as well.) As evidence, the project cites statistics showing the rapid decline in traffic fatalities per 100 million vehicle miles traveled in the years during and immediately following the most intensive period of the designated driver campaign. Officials at the National Highway Traffic and Safety Administration have stated that the only way to explain the size of the decline in drinking-related traffic fatalities is the designated driver campaign.

7   Following the success of the Harvard Alcohol Project's campaign, various other advocacy groups—the majority of them with progressive leanings—have begun to work within the existing structures of the television industry in a similar fashion, attempting to influence programming in a positive direction. In truth, there are limits to the effect any public interest group can have on what gets broadcast. Commercial television's ultimate concerns are Nielsen ratings and advertisers. Thus there will always be a hefty quantity of sex and violence on network television. As Alfred Schneider, the former vice president of policy and standards for ABC, asserts in his contribution to the forthcoming anthology *Advocacy Groups and the Television Industry,* "While [television] can raise the consciousness of the nation, it should not be considered as the major vehicle for social relief or altering behavior." But why not?

8   Other groups remain optimistic, emulating Winsten's method of treating television as a potential ally rather than an adversary and approaching writers and producers likely to be receptive to particular ideas. When writers and producers for the WB network's critically acclaimed new drama *Felicity* were working on the script for a two-part story about date rape, they wanted to make sure they got the details right. They sought the advice of experts from the Kaiser Family Foundation, a nonprofit that focuses on education about health issues; its Program on Entertainment Media and Public Health offers briefings, research services, and a hotline for script writers with health-related questions. "We were really aware of the message we were sending out," the show's executive producer Ed Redlich told me recently. "Given that our audience is teenage girls, we wanted to be correct. At the same time we didn't want it to be an extended public service announcement." As the scripts went through revisions, the show's writers sat down to discuss date rape with representatives from Kaiser, who had previously offered their services to the WB. In whom might a young woman confide after being raped? What kind of advice might a rape counselor provide? What physical tests would the woman undergo? What kind of message would the show be sending if the rapist didn't use a condom?

9   Meanwhile, WB network executive Susanne Daniels sought input on the *Felicity* scripts from Marisa Nightingale at the National Campaign to Prevent Teen Pregnancy, an advocacy group formed in 1995 with the goal of reducing teen preg-

nancies by one-third by the year 2005. Nightingale, the manager of media programs, spends her days meeting with writers and producers to offer statistics, information on birth control methods, and suggestions for how to incorporate pregnancy prevention into storylines. "I can't knock on every door in the country and discuss safe sex with teenagers," she says, "but if Bailey and Sarah on [the Fox network's] *Party of Five* discuss it, that's the next best thing."

10   According to a recent Kaiser Foundation survey, 23 percent of teens say they learn about pregnancy and birth control from television and movies. Clearly, we should be mindful of what exactly teenagers are watching. On a recent episode of *Dawson's Creek* two 16-year-olds contemplating sex ran into each other at a drugstore only to discover they were standing in front of a condom display, which led to a frank discussion about safe sex. An episode of *Felicity* featured the title character researching birth control methods and learning the proper way of putting on a condom. Once prepared, Felicity then decided in the heat of the moment she wasn't quite ready to have sex. A young woman's decision to put off having sex is rarely portrayed in prime time, but Felicity is a strong character and her reasoning is probably convincing to a teenage audience. She may well have more influence on teenage girls than a public service announcement.

11   Of course, making television an explicit vehicle for manipulating behavior has its dangers. My idea of the good may not be yours; if my ideas have access to the airwaves but yours don't, what I'm doing will seem to you like unwanted social engineering. We can all agree that minimizing drunk driving is a good thing—but not everyone agrees on the messages we want to be sending to, say, teenage girls about abstinence versus condoms, about having an abortion, or about whether interfaith marriages are okay. Television's power to mold viewers' understanding of the world is strong enough that we need to be aware that embedding messages about moral values or social behavior can have potent effects—for good or for ill.

12   For the moment, Hollywood's liberal tilt (yes, it really has one) makes it likely that the messages and values it chooses to incorporate into its television programs will be agreeable to progressives. But how active a role do we want television to play in the socialization of our youth? If advocacy groups can gain access to Hollywood with messages that seem like positive additions to existing fare, then they may someday be able to do the opposite—to instill, say, values of a particular religion or an intolerant political group through television.

13   Consider the popularity of CBS's *Touched by an Angel,* which has just completed its fifth season and has secured a regular place among the top ten Nielsen-rated programs. The show, which features angels—not winged creatures, but messengers of God who arrive to help mortals in times of crisis—has sparked a mini-trend in prime time. Along with its spin-off *Promised Land* and the WB's *7th Heaven, Touched by an Angel* has carved out a new niche in family hour entertainment: fare that's endorsed by many groups on the religious right (as well as, to be fair, by people not of the Christian right who are seeking wholesome television entertainment).

14   *7th Heaven's* producer Brenda Hampton, who created the show for Aaron Spelling's production company (the creative force behind such racier fare as *Beverly Hills 90210* and *Melrose Place*), emphasizes in interviews that she is not influenced by religious groups and that her goal is simply to create entertaining television. But

Martha Williamson, the producer of *Touched by an Angel,* is very outspoken about her Christianity. While Williamson, too, emphasizes that she aims primarily to entertain, the program's religious message is unmistakably in the foreground. Williamson says she is regularly contacted by viewers who say the show helped them make a decision—to get in touch with a long-estranged relative or to stop smoking.

15   On its face there's nothing objectionable about this; in fact, it's probably good. And there's no evidence that *Touched by an Angel* is actively converting people, or making unwilling Jews or atheists into Christians. Still, the show does proselytize for a set of values that some viewers might find alienating or offensive. A more extreme version could become Big Brotherish propaganda, beamed into the homes and receptive minds of the seven-hour-a-day TV watchers. At this point, the most offensive thing about *Touched by an Angel* is its saccharine writing (even some religious groups have criticized it on these grounds). But it is perhaps telling that a Republican Congress has awarded Williamson a "Freedom Works Award" for "individuals and groups who seek the personal reward of accepting and promoting responsibility without reliance on or funding from the federal government."

16   Given that writers have to create 22 episodes each season, it's not surprising that they are receptive to outside groups pitching socially redeeming story ideas. *Dawson's Creek* producer Paul Stupin estimates he sits down with three to five advocacy groups at the beginning of each season and always finds the meetings useful. The fact that large numbers of writers and producers attend briefings sponsored by Kaiser, the National Campaign to Prevent Teen Pregnancy, or Population Communications International (which recently sponsored a "Soap Summit") suggests that others feel the same way.

17   The strongest evidence that advocates can effect change through partnerships with the television industry comes from the success of the designated driver campaign. While there are as of yet no large-scale studies exploring the effects of public health advocacy through television, a survey conducted by the Kaiser Foundation is enlightening. On April 10, 1997, NBC aired an episode of *ER* focusing on morning-after contraception, put together with the help of Kaiser Foundation research. Before the show aired, independent researchers interviewed 400 of the show's regular viewers about their knowledge of options for preventing unwanted pregnancy even after unprotected sex. In the week after the show aired, 305 more viewers were interviewed. The number of *ER* viewers who said they knew about morning-after contraception went up by 17 percent after the episode aired. The study concluded that up to six million of the episode's 34 million viewers learned about emergency contraception for the first time from the show (and 53 percent of *ER* viewers say they learn important health care information from the show).

18   Even the limited evidence provided by the *ER* study suggests the scope of television's power to educate and influence. And additional Kaiser studies suggest that the lobbying of public health groups advocating safe sex and birth control is not yet having nearly enough of a beneficial effect. While 25 percent of teenagers say they have learned "a lot" about pregnancy and birth control from TV shows and movies, and 40 percent say they have gotten ideas about how to talk to their boyfriend or girlfriend about sex from TV and movies, 76 percent say that one reason teens feel

comfortable having sex at young ages is that TV shows and movies "make it seem normal" to do so.

19   Another problem: According to Kaiser, while 67 percent of *ER* viewers knew about morning-after contraception when questioned immediately following the show, only 50 percent knew about it when questioned two-and-a-half months later. This suggests that the 17 percent who gained new information about contraception from the episode may not have retained it. Jay Winsten says that because new information fades without repetition, for a single message to take hold the way the designated driver campaign did will require a barrage of appearances on a wide range of TV shows, over an extended period of time.

20   The role of advocacy groups as a resource for Hollywood writers and producers is growing, and it's worth taking seriously. Their approach—presenting ideas to a creative community that is constantly in need of ideas—is proving effective. Yes, the messages are diluted to fit sitcom or drama formats. Yes, for every "good value" that makes its way onto the small screen, a flurry of gunshots on another network will partly counteract it. And yes, when *Time* cites Ally McBeal as a factor in the demise of feminism, it is placing absurdly disproportionate responsibility on a television character, and on the creative community that invented her. Yet if the college women on *Felicity* practice safe sex, or if a prime-time parent talks about drugs—or adoption, or eating disorders, or the Holocaust—with a child, the message is likely to resonate with an audience comprised of people who relate to their favorite television characters as if they knew them.

21   Is television the ideal forum for a culture to define its values? No. As long as television remains a profit-driven industry, the best we can hope to do—especially those of us who have views in common with those who create television content (and fortunately for liberals, we tend to)—is to work within the existing system to make it better. We do need to be realistic about the limits of television in packaging messages to fit this format. To turn *Friends* into a show about capital punishment would be ineffective as well as dramatically unconvincing; but to encourage the producers of *Dawson's Creek* to portray young people facing the realistic consequences of adult decisions just might work. ◆

FREEWRITING ASSIGNMENT

In paragraph 11, Rosenzweig states that "manipulating behavior has its dangers." In what ways can using television as a vehicle for public service announcements be dangerous?

CRITICAL READING

1. Assess Rosenzweig's question in paragraph 4, "if television contributes to poor behavior, might it also be a vehicle for encouraging good behavior?" What assumptions does Rosenzweig make about her audience by phrasing the question this way?
2. Based on your overall impression of Rosenzweig's article, what conclusions can you make about the author's social and political leanings? Cite some examples from the text to support your answer.

RDG 101:BA   **Week 3**   **Assignment Sheet #1**   **Prof. Okomba**   **Fall 2007**

September 24: "Can TV Improve Us?"

    -Read

    -Annotate/highlight

    -Respond to questions 1, 2 & 3, pg. 166-167

September 26: Written Assignment- Journal Entry

    In paragraph 11, Rosenzweig states that "manipulating behavior has its dangers." In what ways can using television as a vehicle for public service announcements be dangerous? Discuss. Cite specific examples.

        -Must be typed

        -No **less** than one page, double spaced

3. Evaluate the author's use of supporting evidence and examples in this arti-cle. Is her evidence fair and balanced? Does it seem credible? Is it accessi-ble to her audience? Explain.

4. Rosenzweig notes that although it was easy for Hollywood to incorporate the issue of drunk driving into its programming, other issues have met with less success. What makes a social issue interesting, and why?

5. Rosenzweig states in a side comment that Hollywood "really has" a lib-eral tilt (paragraph 12). On what evidence does she base this statement? Do you agree or disagree with her view?

CRITICAL WRITING

6. *Creative Analysis*: In her introduction, Rosenzweig questions what visi-tors from another planet would think about our society based on what they learned from watching television on one specific evening. Pretend you are such a visitor, and you know nothing about American culture or social values. Based on an evening's television viewing (you may hop between several programs), what conclusions would you make about our culture? Cite specific examples in your analysis.

7. *Personal Narrative*: Has a television program ever made you think about a social or moral issue that you would not otherwise have thought about had you not watched the program? Write a personal narrative about a tele-vision program that influenced, or even changed, how you felt about a so-cial or moral issue.

8. *Exploratory Writing*: Rosenzweig comments that television programs may attempt to promote social agendas with which some viewers may not agree. Watch one, or several, of the programs she cites in her article to which people may object. What concerns may some audiences have with these programs? What social agendas do they promote? Write an essay in which you support or argue against the use of television to promote social, political, or religious perspectives.

GROUP PROJECTS

9. Rosenzweig notes that although the issue of drunk driving was easy for Hollywood to incorporate into its programming, other issues have met with less success. With your group, make a list of the issues that television programming has addressed in your viewing experience. After reviewing the list, expand it to include other important, but less "exciting" issues, such as the hole in the ozone layer or recycling. Develop a story line to-gether for a popular program dealing with one of these less stimulating is-sues and present it to the class.

10. Using a television weekly programming guide for reference, try to iden-tify the political "tilt" of prime-time programs with the members of your group. In your analysis, include television dramas, news programs, and sitcoms. Based on your results, personal experience, and the information

provided by Rosenzweig, participate in a class discussion on the social and political influences of television programming.

The Man Who Counts the Killings
Scott Stossel

In 1968, as a result of President Lyndon Johnson's National Commission on the Causes and Prevention of Violence, George Gerbner, the former dean of the Annenberg School of Communication at the University of Pennsylvania, founded the Cultural Indicators project. For over 30 years, Gerbner and his team of researchers have studied the role of media violence in American society. One of the most disturbing estimates made by the Cultural Indicators project is that the average American child will have watched over 8,000 murders on television by the time he or she reaches 12 years of age. The next article discusses some of Gerbner's findings, how television violence influences the social perception of violence, and what this might mean to American culture in the future.

A former staff editor at the *Atlantic*, Scott Stossel is now the associate editor of the *American Prospect*. This article first appeared in the May 1997 issue of the *Atlantic*.

CRITICAL THINKING	Think about the level of violence in the programs you watch on television. Is violence a common theme? Does it make an impression on you? Why or why not?

1 In 1977 Ronny Zamora, a fifteen-year-old, shot and killed the eighty-two-year-old woman who lived next door to him in Florida. Not guilty, pleaded his lawyer, Ellis Rubin, by reason of the boy's having watched too much television. From watching television Ronny had become dangerously inured to violence. Suffering from what Rubin called "television intoxication," he could no longer tell right from wrong. "If you judge Ronny Zamora guilty," Rubin argued, "television will be an accessory." The jury demurred: Ronny was convicted of first-degree murder.

2 Although few anti-television activists would agree that excessive television viewing can exculpate a murderer, a huge body of evidence—including 3,000 studies before 1971 alone—suggests a strong connection between television watching and aggression. "There is no longer any serious debate about whether violence in the media is a legitimate problem," Reed Hundt, the chairman of the Federal Communications Commission, said in a speech in 1996. "Science and commonsense judgments of parents agree. As stated in a year-long effort, funded by the cable-TV industry . . . 'there are substantial risks of harmful effects from viewing violence throughout the television environment.'"

3 The study cited by Hundt reveals nothing new. Researchers have been churning out studies indicating links between television violence and real-life violence for as

long as television has been a prominent feature of American culture. Just a few examples demonstrate the range of the investigations.

4   In 1960 Leonard Eron, a professor of psychology at the University of Michigan's Institute for Social Research, studied third-graders in Columbia County in semi-rural New York. He observed that the more violent television these eight-year-olds watched at home, the more aggressive they were in school. Eron returned to Columbia County in 1971, when the children from his sample were nineteen. He found that the boys who had watched a lot of violent television when they were eight were more likely to get in trouble with the law when older. Eron returned to Columbia County a third time in 1982, when his subjects were thirty. He discovered that those who had watched the most television violence at age eight inflicted more violent punishments on their children, were convicted of more serious crimes, and were reported more aggressive by their spouses than those who had watched less violent television. In 1993, at a conference of the National Council for Families & Television, Eron estimated that 10 percent of the violence in the United States can be attributed to television.

5   Although Eron's study did not make a special effort to control for other potentially violence-inducing variables, other longitudinal studies have done so. For example, in 1971 Monroe Lefkowitz published "Television Violence and Child Aggression: A Follow-up Study," which confirmed that the more violence an eight-year-old boy watched, the more aggressive his behavior would be at age eighteen. Lefkowitz controlled for other possible variables, directly implicating media violence as an instigator of violent behavior.

6   Shouldn't the weight of thousands of such studies be sufficient to persuade broadcasters, required by law since the 1930s to serve the public interest, to change the content of television programming? Especially when polls—such as one conducted by *U.S. News & World Report*—indicate that 90 percent of Americans think that violent television shows hurt the country? We don't want to become a nation of Ronny Zamoras, do we?

7   In 1968 President Johnson's National Commission on the Causes and Prevention of Violence appointed George Gerbner, who had already been studying violence in the media at the Annenberg School, to analyze the content of television shows. Thus began the Cultural Indicators project, the longest-running continuous media-research undertaking in the world. Gerbner and his team presented findings about both the quantity of violence on prime-time television—that is, how many violent acts are committed each night—and the quality. In analyzing these acts Gerbner's team asked questions like: Was it serious or funny? Was it the only method of conflict resolution offered? Were realistic repercussions of violence shown? Who committed most of it? Who suffered the most because of it? The quantity of violence on television was stunning; no less significant to Gerbner, though, were the ways in which this violence was portrayed. But in the first instance of what has since become a frustrating pattern for him, the mainstream media seized on the quantity and ignored his findings about the quality of television violence.

8   The media continue to be fixated on the amount of violence the Cultural Indicators project finds, because the numbers are staggering. Today someone settling down to watch television is likely to witness a veritable carnival of violent behavior.

On average there are more than five violent scenes in an hour of prime time, and five murders a night. There are twenty-five violent acts an hour in Saturday-morning cartoons—the programs most watched by children, usually without any supervision. And that's only network television. A survey by the Center for Media and Public Affairs that looked at all programming—including cable—in Washington, D.C., on April 7, 1994, tallied 2,605 acts of violence that day, the majority occurring in the early morning, when kids were most likely to be watching. By the reckoning of the Cultural Indicators project, the average American child will have witnessed more than 8,000 murders and 100,000 other violent acts on television by the time he or she leaves elementary school. Another study, published in the *Journal of the American Medical Association* in 1992, found that the typical American child spends twenty-seven hours a week watching television and will witness 40,000 murders and 200,000 other violent acts by the age of eighteen. Ellis Rubin's defense of Ronny Zamora begins to sound plausible.

9   "Never was a culture so filled with full-color images of violence as ours is now," Gerbner wrote recently. This is an assertion he makes often, in his writings and speeches and interviews.

10   Of course, there is blood in fairy tales, gore in mythology, murder in Shakespeare, lurid crimes in tabloids, and battles and wars in textbooks. Such representations of violence are legitimate cultural expressions, even necessary to balance tragic consequences against deadly compulsions. But the historically defined, individually crafted, and selectively used symbolic violence of heroism, cruelty, or authentic tragedy has been replaced by the violence with happy endings produced on the dramatic assembly line.

11   The Cultural Indicators project has since 1968 amassed a database of reports on the recurring features of television programming. Today its archive contains observations on more than 3,000 programs and 35,000 characters. In looking at characters, coders record, among other characteristics, sex, race, height, level of aggressiveness, and drug, alcohol, or tobacco use. For every conflict the coder records how the character acts: Did he get angry? How did he resolve the conflict? If a character is part of a violent act, the coder records whether he suffered or committed it, and whether it was committed in self-defense. The results are then analyzed statistically to try to account for differences in the behavioral trends of the characters. Are there statistically significant differences in the percentage of, say, victimhood or alcohol abuse by sex? By level of education? By race? By social status?

12   In addition to this "message system analysis," Gerbner's researchers do "cultivation analysis," which tries to measure how much television contributes to viewers' conceptions of reality. Cultivation analysis asks, in other words, to what extent television "cultivates" our understanding of the world. Gerbner believes this to be the most important aspect of his research. It is also the part routinely ignored by the mainstream press and attacked by the broadcasting industry.

13   One of the basic premises of Gerbner's cultivation analysis is that television violence is not simple acts but rather "a complex social scenario of power and victimization." What matters is not so much the raw fact that a violent act is committed but who does what to whom. Gerbner is as insistent about this as he is about anything, repeating it in all his writings and speeches. "What is the message of violence?" he

asks me rhetorically over tea in his office at the University of Pennsylvania, a cozy, windowless rectangle filled with books, pictures, and objets d'art. "Who can get away with what against whom?" He leans forward intently, as though confiding something, although he has already said this to me several other times, during several other conversations. His eagerness to make me understand is palpable. "The media keep focusing on the amount of violence. But concentrating on that reinforces the message of violence. It concentrates on the law-and-order aspect of violence. Harping on this all the time makes people more fearful—which is the purpose of violence to begin with."

14   So what, exactly, has nearly thirty years of cultivation analysis shown? Among other things, the following:

15   Americans spend fully a third of their free time with television. This is more than the next ten highest-ranked leisure-time activities put together.

16   Women make up a third or less of the characters in all samples except daytime serials.

17   The "lower classes" are almost invisible on television. According to the U.S. Census, at least 13 percent of the population is "poor," with a significant additional percentage being classified as "low-income wage-earners." Yet the lower classes make up only 1.3 percent of prime-time characters.

18   For every white male victim of violence there are seventeen white female victims.

19   For every white male victim there are twenty-two minority female victims.

20   For every ten female aggressors there are sixteen female victims.

21   Minority women are twice as likely to be victims as they are to be aggressors.

22   Villains are disproportionately male, lower-class, young, and Latino or foreign.

23   What is the significance of all this? First, the sheer quantity of violence on television encourages the idea that aggressive behavior is normal. Viewers become desensitized. The mind, as Gerbner puts it, becomes "militarized." This leads to what Gerbner calls "the Mean World Syndrome." Because television depicts the world as worse than it is (at least for white suburbanites), we become fearful and anxious— and more willing to depend on authorities, strong measures, gated communities, and other proto-police-state accouterments. Discounting the dramatic increase in violent crime in the real world, Gerbner believes, for example, that the Mean World Syndrome is an important reason that the majority of Americans now support capital punishment, whereas they did not thirty years ago. "Growing up in a violence-laden culture breeds aggressiveness in some and desensitization, insecurity, mistrust, and anger in most," he writes. "Punitive and vindictive action against dark forces in a mean world is made to look appealing, especially when presented as quick, decisive, and enhancing our sense of control and security."

24   The more violence one sees on television, the more one feels threatened by violence. Studies have shown direct correlations between the quantity of television watched and general fearfulness about the world: heavy viewers believe the world to be much more dangerous than do light viewers. Thus heavy viewers tend to favor more law-and-order measures: capital punishment, three-strikes prison sentencing, the building of new prisons, and so forth. And the fact that most of the heavy viewers are in low-income, low-education families means that the most disenfranchised

in our society—and, it should be said, the people most exposed to real violence—are making themselves even more so by placing their fate in the hands of an increasingly martial state. Politicians exploit this violence-cultivated sensibility by couching their favored policies in militaristic terms: the War on Crime, for example, or the War on Drugs. "We are headed in the direction of an upsurge in neofascism in a very entertaining and very amusing disguise," Gerbner told a lecture audience in Toronto two years ago.

25   The first time I talked to Gerbner after reading his writings, I asked him if this wasn't all a bit Big Brotherish. "TV images are complex," he told me. "The disempowering effects of television lead to neofascism. That kind of thing is waiting in the wings. Nazi Germany came on the heels of a basic sense of insecurity and powerlessness like we have here now. I don't want to oversimplify, but that is the direction we might be heading."

26   Violence, Gerbner says, is all about power. The violence on television serves as a lesson of power that puts people in their place. Members of minority groups grow up feeling that they're more vulnerable than others. Television cultivates this view. But, I counter, minorities *are* more vulnerable. They are victims more often than middle-class white Americans are. Improving the depiction of minorities on television will not change this social fact. Gerbner strives to clarify:

27   Television doesn't 'cause' anything. We're wary of saying television 'causes' this or that. Instead we say television 'contributes' to this or that. The extent of contribution varies. But it's there.

28   Elsewhere Gerbner is less circumspect. "The violence we see on the screen and read about in our press bears little relationship either in volume or in type, especially in its consequences, to violence in real life," he has written. "This sleight of hand robs us of the tragic sense of life necessary for compassion." No doubt a victim of the Mean World Syndrome myself, I was surprised to learn that Gerbner is absolutely right, at least about the volume of violence. Scary and crime-ridden though the world is these days (violent crime has more than doubled over the past thirty years; an American is six times as likely to be the victim of assault with a weapon as he or she would have been in 1960), prime-time television presents a world in which crime rates are a hundred times worse. ◆

FREEWRITING ASSIGNMENT

What types of television programs do you prefer to watch and why? Do you prefer action, drama, comedy? Do you view television as a chance to escape reality, or connect to a larger community?

CRITICAL READING

1. Evaluate Stossel's use of examples to support his essay's points. How effective are his examples? Do they seem credible and/or appropriate? Are they balanced and fair? Explain.
2. Since 1930, broadcasters have been "required by law" to serve the public interest (paragraph 6). Do you think that they have successfully lived up

to this expectation? As you form your response, refer to information from the essay as well as from your personal experience.

3. What is the happy violence that Stossel describes (paragraph 10)? Can you think of any examples from your own television viewing experience?

4. Stossel explains that according to Gerbner, "What matters is not so much the raw fact that a violent act is committed, but who does what to whom" (paragraph 13). What does Gerbner mean? Explain.

5. Review the list of some of the results of Gerbner's cultivation analysis (paragraphs 15–22). Can you develop a "violence profile" based on his results? Is this profile an accurate or predominantly fabricated reflection of real social violence? Explain.

6. Stossel states that "the more violence one sees on television, the more one feels threatened by violence" (paragraph 24). What evidence does Stossel use to support this statement? Do you agree or disagree with him?

7. Why might Gerbner's studies seem "Big Brotherish" (paragraph 25)? How does he stand on this aspect of his research? What is your opinion of his research and results? Explain.

CRITICAL WRITING

8. *Exploratory Writing*: Stossel cites a report conducted by *U.S. News & World Report* that indicates that 90 percent of Americans think that violent television programs hurt the country (paragraph 6). Does this figure seem accurate? Where do you stand on this issue? Write an essay in which you describe your position on television violence and its overall impact on American society.

9. *Research and Analysis*: Visit the Media Awareness web site and read the interview between George Gerbner and media author/critic Todd Gitlin at *www.media-awareness.ca/eng/issues/violence/resource/articles/gerbner. htm*. Evaluate how each expert defends his views on media violence. Which authority do you agree with more, and why? Write an essay explaining your view using examples from the interview and other information from the Media Awareness web site.

10. *Critical Analysis*: Stossel states that "blood in fairy tales" is a legitimate cultural expression necessary to "balance tragic consequences against deadly compulsions" (paragraph 10). Read some traditional fairy tales in their original (not "Disneyfied") versions from authors such as the Brothers Grimm or Perrault. Select one or two of the tales and analyze the violence in them. Does the violence seem to be a justifiable "cultural expression"?

GROUP PROJECTS

11. *Class Project*: Stossel begins his essay with the story of 15-year-old Ronny Zamora, who claimed that television violence had caused the "media intoxication" that incited him to kill his next-door neighbor. Stage your own trial in the spirit of the Zamora case, and put on trial a fictitious

teenager tried for a violent act using the "media intoxication" defense. If you wish, you may use another high-profile case, such as the case of William and Joshua Buckner, who told police they were emulating the video game *Grand Theft Auto* on the night of June 25, 2003, when they opened fire on vehicles driving on Interstate 40 in Tennessee. The class should be split into two or four groups to help prepare one side of the case. From these groups, your teacher will select students to serve as defense and prosecuting attorneys, defendant, judge, and, if desired, experts. The rest of the class will act as jury to decide the case based on the arguments of the lawyers, experts, and defendant. Discuss as a group the verdict after it has been reached.

12. Stossel states that "today someone settling down to watch television is likely to witness a veritable carnival of violent behavior" (paragraph 8). With your group engage in a media study of your own. Track the number of violent acts in a specific period of time, such as prime time or during Saturday morning cartoons. Each member of the group should be responsible for counting and describing violent acts on a single network during the specified time period. Compare your findings with the statistics cited in Stossel's article, and discuss the implications of your results with the group.

13. The Cultural Indicators project tracks not only the number of violent acts, but their specific characteristics, such as race, sex, height, level of aggressiveness, substance abuse, and the reason for conflict of the people involved in the act. With your group, conduct a similar study of a few nights of programming and compare your results. Address some of Gerbner's questions. Are there statistically significant differences in the percentage of victimhood or alcohol abuse by sex, race, age, level of education, or social status? Share your results with the rest of the class.

TV's War of Words
Deborah Tannen

Since the 1980s, television talk shows have become part of almost every network's program offerings. More recently, however, some of these "talk shows" have changed into screaming matches between the program's participants, especially programs that profess to "debate" a particular issue. Instead of understanding the nuances of an issue or point of view, these programs promote conflict and argument. Although ratings may be part of the appeal of "scream TV," Deborah Tannen explains in this essay that it is simply another characteristic of our argument culture. Television is both promoting and supporting a growing attitude in the viewing public: watching people fight is fun.

Deborah Tannen is a professor of linguistics at Georgetown University. She is the author of many best-selling books on linguistics, including *I Only Say This Because I Love You* (2001), *The Argument Culture* (1999), and *You Just Don't Understand* (1997). She has been a guest on *20/20*, *48 Hours*, *CNN*, and *The NewsHour with Jim Lehrer*. This article first appeared in the September 1999 issue of *Brill's Content*.

CRITICAL THINKING   Think about some popular television debate programs. How many of them aim to resolve conflicts or promote understanding and how many of them thrive on dissent and discord? What programs enjoy higher ratings?

1   When my book *The Argument Culture* was published, I appeared on *Charles Grodin*. Returning home after the show, I found a message on my answering machine. "I tuned in at the time you told me," a friend's voice said, "but there were two men shouting over each other, and it set my teeth on edge. I switched it off."

2   I laughed at the irony. In introducing me, Grodin confessed that he had at times been guilty of the kind of interview I wrote about. He had an illustration for the viewers to see: himself and then Senator Alan Simpson shouting at each other. This is what drove my friend from her screen—proving a point I made in the book and on the show.

3   Why are more news and public-affairs shows turning into shouting matches between left and right, liberal and conservative, Democrat and Republican? For one thing, with round-the-clock news, the airwaves have to be filled, and these shows are easy and economical to assemble: Find a conservative and a liberal and you've got your show. Also, with the advent of cable has come increased competition, so producers need to make shows entertaining. But where do they get the idea that watching fights is fun? The answer is the argument culture.

4   The argument culture is a pervasive war-like atmosphere that makes us approach public dialogue, and just about anything else we need to accomplish, as if it were a fight. It rests on the assumption that opposition is the best way to get anything done: The best way to discuss an idea is to set up a debate; the best way to settle a dispute is litigation that pits one party against the other; the best way to begin an essay is to attack someone; the best way to show you're really thinking is to criticize; and—as we see in the scream TV shows—the best way to cover news is to find spokespeople who express the most extreme views and present them as "both sides." Conflict and opposition are as necessary as cooperation and agreement, but the scale is off balance, with conflict and opposition overweighted.

5   By turning everything into a left-right fight, the argument culture gives us trumped-up, showcase "debates" between two oversimplified sides, leaving no room for the real arguments. What's wrong with lively debate? Nothing, when debate is a synonym for open discussion. But in most televised debates, the goal is not to understand but to win. You can't explore nuances or complexities; that would weaken your position. And few issues fall neatly into just two sides. Most are a crystal of many sides—and some have just one. Perhaps most destructive, if the goal is a lively fight, the most polarized views are best, so the extremes get the most airtime and are allowed to define the issues. Viewers conclude that if the two sides are so far apart, the problem can't be solved, so why try?

6   If everything has to be squeezed into the procrustean bed of left and right, moderate views are drowned out. *The Boston Globe* columnist Ellen Goodman (perceived

as "the left") notes that if she's invited to appear on a show that she'd just as soon not do, all she needs to say is, "I can see both sides; it's complicated." Ann Coulter (a commentator on "the right") also finds that when she takes a position that doesn't fit producers' ideas of conservative, they don't want her.

7   The time crunch is a major factor in scream TV. A half-hour show (only 22 minutes of programming), is broken into three or four segments, each treating a different issue in progressively shorter chunks of time that are shared among four, five, even six, commentators. As if even these short segments aren't fast enough, each show presents instant pronouncements, such as McLaughlin's end-of-show round-the-table predictions, the mid-show highlights on *Hardball With Chris Matthews*, or *The Capital Gang*'s viewer-submitted "Outrage of the Week." (It's telling that it's the outrage of the week: in this format, provocative typically means "provoking to anger.")

8   The battle imagery starts with the names: *Crossfire* (hinting war), *Hardball* (hinting super-competitive sports), *The Capital Gang* (a whiff of brash street fighters). The very structure of these shows is based on underlying metaphors of war and sports: Two sides duke it out; one wins, the other loses. But it's all a game: See the warring parties jocularly sparring at the end of the show, as the camera pulls away? Those who take part in these pseudo-debates know that there is a display aspect to it.

9   The shout-down shows distort public discussion of vital issues. Their pacing corrupts the information viewers get. Eleanor Clift (as I quoted her in *The Argument Culture*) explains, "The nature of these shows is you're forced to speak more provocatively to make a point in the short time you have before you get interrupted. People know there's an entertainment factor, but the danger is, it turns us all into stereotypes, because you don't have time to express the ifs, ands, or buts."

10   When I talk about the argument culture, I am often asked about *Jerry Springer*. Springer's show is also scream TV. Phil Donahue, who pioneered the format, used it to convey information provided by experts with the audience interaction added. Oprah Winfrey saw the potential of the format to create a sense of connection among her guests, the studio audience, viewers, and herself by focusing less on the expert guests and more on the average people who come on to talk about their lives. Springer dispenses with experts entirely and exploits only one kind of drama: getting average people to come on his show to fight. But I worry less about Springer because no one is watching his show to form opinions about current events, as they are with news and information shows.

11   The argument culture also encompasses an ethic of aggression—praising those in power would be boring, rolling over. Those who take positions against the president, for example, don't just criticize—they sneer, ridicule, and heap scorn. By setting that tone, scream TV encourages viewers to approach others in an adversarial spirit, creating an atmosphere of animosity that spreads like a fever. As the Egyptian author Leila Ahmed wrote, describing the effect of the terms and tone in which Gamal Abdel Nasser habitually denounced his enemies, "once you make hatred and derision . . . normal and acceptable in one area, they become generalized to everything else."

12   [. . .] *Larry King Live* is also a talking-heads cable show that airs weeknights, but one that gives viewers an extended conversation with one guest at a time. Though King is often ridiculed by his peers for asking only "softball" questions of

his guests, far more viewers prefer his approach, giving him, according to Nielsen, 0.5 percent (or 538,000) of households. That's far larger than the audience of *Cross-fire* and *Hardball* [0.3 percent].

13   What do audiences like about these shows? Part of their appeal, I think, lies in their hosts. John McLaughlin's booming voice sounds like an old newsreel voice-over. Introducing a topic, he uses strategic pauses and sudden loudness to add drama: "The AMA," he tells viewers, "has voted to allow doctors [pause] TO UNIONIZE!!" American bombing of the Chinese Embassy in Belgrade "was . . . CRIMINAL NEGLIGENCE!!" (though he adds, sotto voce, "many believe"). McLaughlin's manner comes across as good-natured bluster.

14   Chris Matthews of *Hardball* does not shout or pronounce in dramatic highs and lows, stops and starts. He charms with his blond, boyish good looks and ready smile. The drama comes from the fast pace at which the words roll off his tongue, like a sportscaster rushing to keep up with the plays—in keeping with the metaphor of the show's name and his nightly call to arms: "Let's play hardball."

15   Why has talk on radio and TV become more a matter of having arguments than of making arguments? As I explain in *The Argument Culture*, part of the cause is the medium itself. Television (like radio) returns, in some ways, to the past. It was the advent of print that made Western society less disputatious, according to cultural linguist Walter Ong: In the absence of audiences before which to stage debates, attention gradually focused on the internal argumentation of published tracts rather than debaters' performance. The rise of contentiousness today is fueled in part by the return of oral argument on TV and radio, where once again the ability to dispute publicly is valued—and judged—as a performance. ◆

FREEWRITING ASSIGNMENT

In this essay, Tannen ascribes the emergence of "scream TV" to our "argument culture." In your own words, what is "argument culture" and what is its current role in modern society?

CRITICAL READING

1. Why was the fact that Tannen's friend shut off the TV while watching *Charles Grodin* ironic? How does this gesture help frame the points Tannen makes in her essay?
2. According to Tannen, what is the "argument culture"? What is your opinion on her theory? Explain.
3. Define "debate." Is argument the same as debate?
4. What happens when guests invited to "debate" on scream TV shows express that they "can see both sides" of an issue? Why do producers often turn these individuals down?
5. How can "shout downs" on debate programs distort public discussion of vital issues? Do you think, as Tannen does, that they can actually work against public discussion of important issues? Explain.

6. What accounts, according to Tannen, for the appeal of television debate programs—especially ones that feature the attributes of "scream TV"? Do the ratings really reflect that this debate technique is popular?

CRITICAL WRITING

7. *Research and Analysis*: Watch a few of the programs Tannen mentions in her essay *(Crossfire, Hardball, Larry King Live, The Capital Gang, Charles Grodin*, etc.). Look up the definition of debate and argument in the dictionary. Based on your observation of the programs, write an essay on whether these programs are debate, argument, both, or neither. Support your points with examples from your viewing experience, Tannen's essay, and your personal perspective.

8. *Exploratory Writing*: Tannen comments that defenders of "scream TV" claim that "audiences love it. Ratings . . . are the pudding-proof." Is scream TV delivering what audiences want to see and hear? In a carefully considered essay, discuss and describe your own television viewing desires. What do you watch on television? What do you like to see, and what causes you to change the channel or turn off the set? How do your own viewing likes and dislikes compare to the points Tannen makes in her essay?

GROUP EXERCISES

9. Make a list of TV debate programs (use the programs Tannen cites as a starting point) and select four programs from the list. Group members should watch all four of the programs (try to synchronize so you are all watching the same debates on the same nights) and analyze each program for its effectiveness as a debate program. Note the topic discussed, the opinions of each guest, their backgrounds, and their debate styles. Rate each program on a 1–5 scale, with 5 indicating a highly effective and engaging debate. Compare your ratings with other members of the group. How are your impressions similar and how are they different?

10. Stage your own debate program. The teacher should propose a social or political question to the class and have students briefly write about where they stand on the issue. Based on student responses, the teacher should select four to five students to debate the issue in front of the class and select one student to serve as moderator. (Debate "guests" should all agree to "obey" the moderator.) The rest of the class will serve as the audience. After the debate, the audience can discuss the effectiveness of the debate and the "performance" of each of the participants. Here are some sample topics: We should reintroduce prayer in public schools; television promotes eating disorders; we need more strict gun laws; it should be harder for people to divorce; college athletes should be held accountable for their academic performances; and/or affirmative action laws are no longer necessary.

The National Television Violence Study
Summary of Findings

Content Analysis of Violence in Television Percentage of . . .	Year One (1994–1995)	Year Two (1995–1996)	Year Three (1996–1997)
Programs on television that contain violence	58%	61%	61%
Violent interactions that involve multiple acts of aggression	58%	58%	61%
Violent interactions that show no pain	58%	55%	51%
Violent programs that depict long-term negative consequences of violence	16%	13%	16%
Violent children's programs that show long-term negative consequences of violence	5%	2%	6%
"Good" characters who are punished for violence	15%	31%	18%
Violent programs that emphasize an antiviolence theme	4%	4%	3%
Violent interactions on television that involve the use of a handgun	25%	23%	26%
Violent interactions in children's programs that depict harm unrealistically	56%	66%	57%
Programs that portray violence in a humorous context	39%	43%	42%
Children's programs that portray violence in a humorous context	67%	76%	68%

National Television Violence Study. 1997. *Issue Briefs.* Studio City, CA.: Mediascope.

The National Television Violence Study is the most comprehensive scientific assessment of television violence ever undertaken. This three-year study, initiated and administered by Mediascope and conducted by more than 80 researchers and associates at the Universities of California at Santa Barbara, North Carolina at Chapel Hill, Texas at Austin, and Wisconsin at Madison, is divided into three research components: a content analysis of the amount, nature, and context of violence on television; an examination of how children respond to ratings and advisories; and research on the effectiveness of antiviolence messages.

Examined in each year of the study were about 2,700 programs from more than 2,000 hours of television. These were taken from a randomly selected composite week of television on 23 channels over a 20-week period. The study monitored programs between 6:00 AM and 11:00 PM, a total of 17 hours a day per channel.

The Great TV Debate

Jason Kelly

Many parents struggle with the question of how much television is too much. Is it fair to restrict our children's television time while we fail to curtail our own? Is television promoting illiteracy, as some critics warn? Or are we overreacting to hype? In the next essay, writer Jason Kelly worries about his son's viewing habits.

Jason Kelly is a writer based in Atlanta. His work has appeared in many magazines and newspapers, including *The Atlanta Journal-Constitution* and *Forbes*. He's the former editor of *digitalsouth,* an Atlanta-based magazine covering emerging technology companies. He prepared this essay for the "Kid Issue" of *PopPolitics*, December 2001.

CRITICAL THINKING   Do you think parents have a responsibility to teach their children how to watch television? If so, what skills do they need to teach and how should they go about teaching their children?

1   I worry about a lot of things related to my son. Sept. 11 brought almost more than I could bear. Today, for instance, I'm worried that he's pushing other kids at his day care center. Alas, there are a few constant worries, including this one: Am I already letting him turn his brain to mush?

2   When I got this assignment, I set out to try and understand the latest salvos in the great TV debate. I'd planned to do a sensibly journalistic, fully objective treatment of both sides. Then I realized that, especially as a dad, that's nearly, if not totally, impossible.

3   My wife and I have operated under the notion that I'd ascribe to most people— we allow our son, Owen, age 2, to watch some television, though we worry about him watching too much. We'll give into the pressure a little too often, pushing in a Teletubbies or Elmo video when we need a mental break, or need to actually get something done.

4   It's worth confessing here that I like TV, and maybe slightly more than the average bear. I watch enough shows regularly to have strong opinions about, and feelings for, fake people: Carrie on *Sex and the City*, Jack on *Will & Grace*, Donna on *West Wing*. I do feel like I know them. I, of course, hide behind my occupation as a "writer," tricking myself (but not others, I'm afraid) into thinking that watching these shows is really work, as if talking about them in important terms—"Sorkin's gift for writing that crisp, banter-y dialogue makes these shows feel more like plays than movies"—will make them important, will turn them into high art.

5   And so, actually, I feel slightly ashamed of my own viewing habits. Why not include my son in my neuroses ("Paging Dr. Frasier Crane")? These overlapping guilts lead to a creeping sense of hypocrisy, whereby I deprive my son of watching "Clifford: The Big Red Dog" but, when he leaves the room, quickly switch over to "Today," so I can see Katie banter with Matt about listening to the Shrek soundtrack in her minivan. At least Clifford's got a "big idea of the day"—usually something

like "respect" or "sharing"—on at the end of every show. Katie and Matt just have Willard and his jelly jars every few days.

6   In the great American spirit of rationalization, I've convinced myself that my son—who goes to daycare during the week—actually watches less TV than a kid who stays at home full-time with a parent or a nanny. I know that occasionally his teachers roll in the television and slip in a video, but it's certainly not every day. Owen has always been somewhat fickle about watching TV, and in this I see the tendencies that stay with you through adulthood. Sometimes, the dude just wants to chill out and watch the Teletubbies (or, in his lingo, simply "Tubbies"). Other times, he's far too busy, and actually walks over and turns it off in favor of reading a book, coloring or building Lego towers.

7   I spent hours on the Web sifting through searches on "Kids and TV," looking for guidance. While on the Cartoon Network site, I came across a link for "TV Parental Guidelines." That's the site for the classification system that puts the little box on the screen that says "TV-MA (mature audiences only)," for example. The guidelines, at least for me, have become more or less invisible; they're pretty broad and based on the quite-flawed Motion Picture Association of America guidelines, which say it's OK for 13-year-olds to both see and hear the F-bomb.

8   The Fox Kids TV site was suitably frightening to me, with its animation and teasers—"It's the stinkiest Ripping Friends ever!!" The site for the PBS shows (for better or worse, the only shows we let Owen watch) was similarly predictable in its "We're really about education here" language. Drilling through the Teletubbies, I noted the repeated use of carefully chosen words like "safe," "friendly" and "stimulating."

9   After wading through the positive messages from the purveyors themselves, I found the Washington, D.C.-based TV-Turnoff Network, which appears to have a reputable staff and advisory board. I gave them a call and they mailed me a packet of materials supporting a TV-free lifestyle, including the requisite bumper stickers. The one that made me chuckle was designed to mimic the warnings on cigarette boxes: "Surgoen Generel's Warnig: Telivison Promots Iliteracy." They also feature some startling statistics, like the fact that the average 2- to 17-year-old viewer watches nearly 20 hours of TV per week. And that 73 percent of American parents would like to limit their kids' TV-watching.

10   Writing this story forced the topic to the front of my mind, and as I chatted with friends and colleagues, even interview subjects for other stories, about various other topics, I often tried to sneak this one in. One friend told me that his kids watch about an hour of TV a month. It took me a full minute to stop saying "Wow." He and his wife both work, and have had a full-time nanny since their now-7- and 9-year-old children were born. The nanny knows that no TV is the rule. "And the nanny's a TV junkie" in her off-hours, my friend tells me.

11   In an odd turn of events, two days later we go with another family on a Sunday outing, loading three adults and three kids comfortably into their family minivan, one of the new, decked-out Honda Odysseys. The high-end versions of these verita-ble cruise ships on wheels have a VCR and video screen installed; the player sits in the middle console up front, and the screen flips down from the ceiling just behind the front seats. Our hour-plus trip was nearly silent. We could've ridden for days it seemed, despite the fact that we had three sub-6 year olds in the car.

12   Somewhere in the middle of these two extremes is where I fall, and, by the looks of it, so does a lot of America. Schools across the country embrace the idea of using TV as a learning tool and are aided by groups like Cable in the Classroom and Channel One, which provide special programming. The latter is the much-ballyhooed 11-year-old network that broadcasts to roughly 12,000 American middle, junior and high schools; the network claims those schools represent more than 8 million students and 400,000 educators. There is, however, a catch: Channel One also broadcasts commercials. So while the kids are learning more about, say, life in space, they're also being told to eat Mars bars.

13   More pointedly, many of the kids TV shows—led by the granddaddy of educational TV, Sesame Street—encourage kids to read. Clifford the Big Red Dog, we're told at the end of his PBS show, wants us to "be the best-read dog on the block." And in fact, Clifford was born as a book character himself, then migrated to PBS. Teletubbies and others took the reverse path. But they all stress the value of reading. My own son seems to have no problem reading and watching TV, often at the same time. It's a brand of multi-tasking I'm sure my wife and I have encouraged by example, as we talk on the phone, listen to the radio, cook dinner and read a magazine, all in one fluid, continuous motion.

14   I'm starting to come to grips with the idea that this is just how it is, that we live in an information and media drenched society. We can't stop it, as the wise man said, we can only hope to contain it. Then, as I'm putting all my thoughts together, I come across one more thing that makes me throw my hands up.

15   Neil Postman's *Amusing Ourselves to Death* is a book I read in college that paints a stark picture of what TV is doing to us, and our children. He spends 163 pages undermining just about every idea set forth by the Cable in the Classrooms and PBS's of the world, namely that "educational television" is a contradiction in terms. While his data is old—the book was published in 1985—his arguments likely have more, not less, relevance.

16   And his voice, while somewhat histrionic, does echo in my ears: "Like the alphabet or the printing press, television has by its power to control the time, attention and cognitive habits of our youth gained the power to control their education."

17   And so I end much like I began—pretty damn confused, with my finger poised uncertainly in front of the "play" button. ◆

FREEWRITING ASSIGNMENT

Kelly admits that he likes to watch television, "maybe slightly more than the average bear." What role does TV play in your daily life? Could you easily go without it, or would your quality of life be compromised, and why?

CRITICAL READING

1. Kelly's son is two years old. In your opinion, do you think two years old is too young to watch television? Why or why not? Can you tell how Kelly feels about his son's viewing habits? Explain.

2. Why is Kelly "ashamed" of his own television viewing habits? What is the social stigma of enjoying television? Have you ever lied about how much television you watch? If so, explain.

3. In paragraph 10, Kelly comments on his astonishment that his friends' children, ages 7 and 9, only watch about an hour of television a month. Do you think this is admirable, as Kelly seems to imply? Unrealistic? Harmful? What would your response be to this parent? Explain.

4. PBS children's programming has a reputation for being more acceptable than programs aired by other networks. What accounts for this reputation? Why do you think Kelly makes the side comment "for better or worse" these are the only programs he lets his child watch? Explain.

5. Kelly titled his essay "The Great TV Debate." From his article, can you determine exactly what the "great TV debate" is? Can you define it in your own words?

6. Kelly observes that Channel One, an educational channel frequently aired in schools, also broadcasts commercials. Why is this a "catch"? Do you think that educational television should also be commercial free? Why or why not?

CRITICAL WRITING

7. Kelly seems to be concerned that he is letting his child watch too much television. Write a response to Kelly, referring to the information he provides in his essay.

8. *Research and Analysis*: To prepare to write this essay, Kelly conducts an Internet keyword search on "kids and TV." Conduct your search, using a search engine such as Google.com. or Dogpile.com. Evaluate the information available, and write a short informational essay on the best websites for parents on this topic. Explain the reasoning behind your selections.

9. *Personal Narrative*: In an effort to discuss this issue, Kelly provides personal information about his own viewing habits. In a well-considered essay, using the Kelly piece as a model, write a narrative that is both reflective and critical of your own childhood experience with television.

10. Assume the role of a media critic. Visit the TV-Turnoff Network's web site at *http://www.tvturnoff.org/* and evaluate the web site and its message. Prepare an editorial in which you report on this organization.

GROUP PROJECTS

11. Kelly notes that the average child watches 20 hours of TV per week. Each group member should conduct a few interviews with some children and their parents on television viewing habits. How much television do kids watch? How involved are parents in what their children watch? How do the parents feel about their children's television viewing habits? Do they seem concerned? If so, do you think their concern is legitimate, or influenced by social pressure and opinion? After discussing your interviews as

a group, decide if the average child is indeed watching too much television and how much TV is too much. Share your viewpoint with the class.

12. With your group, compare the children's television programs aired on PBS to those aired on other channels, such as Nickelodeon, Fox Kids, and the major networks. With your group, develop a checklist of program elements that make a children's program superior, such as "teaches a lesson," "encourages reading," "fosters critical thinking," "teaches (math) (alphabet)," etc. Different group members should watch and critique several children's programs for discussion. Determine whether your group's observations support or refute Kelly's claim (or inference) that PBS programs are better than those of other channels.

Window on Reality: *American Idol* and the Search for Identity

Elaine Showalter

> While reality television programs are fodder for critics, there is no denying their popularity. Far from a passing fad, there are more reality television programs than ever before. Several programs have emerged as constant hits, including *Survivor, The Bachelor,* and *American Idol.* In this essay, sociologist Elaine Showalter explains how *American Idol,* isn't just entertainment—it is a fascinating and engaging look at teen popular culture. And critics aside, it presents a positive social message—that in America, you can be a star, regardless of your race or religion, as long as you have the talent and personality to make it to the top.
>
> Elaine Showalter is a professor of English at Princeton University. She is the author of several books, including *The Female Malady: Women, Madness, and English Culture, 1830–1980* (1986), and *Hystories* (1997). She is a frequent contributor to the *Times Literary Supplement,* the *London Review of Books*, and many other journals. This article first appeared in the July 3, 2003, issue of the *American Prospect.*

CRITICAL THINKING Do you watch reality TV programs? If so, which ones? What inspires you to watch these programs?

1 "Reality" television is generally scorned as mindless, vulgar, exploitative and contrived. So is it ever sociology, is it ever real? Yes, if it's *American Idol*, the FOX show that recently wrapped up its blockbuster second season. The program, for the uninitiated, pitted 12 young performers against one another for a chance at a $1 million recording contract. True, *American Idol* was adapted from a British series, *Pop Idol*, which had attracted a record 14 million voters and made an instant celebrity of a colorless boy singer. True, the program's producers were motivated by only the slickest of intentions: to manufacture a lucrative audience for a recording star before

even one CD had been released. True, the twice-weekly programs, with their drawn-out commercial breaks and clumsily staged group numbers, were not the material of art.

2   And yet, in its shape and timing, *American Idol* has provided a fascinating snapshot of American youth culture in the 21st century. At once a competition, a talent show, a soap opera, a makeover fest, a patriotic celebration and an election, *American Idol* showed how the postmillennial United States is changing with regard to race, class, national identity and politics. As its affiliate FOX News was cheering on the Iraq War, the FOX network's *American Idol*—one of the top-rated TV shows of the period leading up to, during and after the Iraq invasion—offered both a mirror image and a contradictory view of the nation's mind-set. Appealing simultaneously to Marines, Mormons, gays, blacks and Latinos, and to every region of the country, *American Idol* has a legitimate claim to its label of reality TV.

Playing the Race Chord

3 *American Idol* promoted multiculturalism with an ease missing from most network television, and quite distinct from its precursor. Although the British show began with a wide range of candidates, black and Indian aspirants were quickly eliminated; despite the influence of Asian styles from Bollywood and Bhangra, and black styles from the Caribbean, Africa and American hip-hop, the British pop scene is still white. In contrast, *American Idol* showed a youth culture and a young generation past the tipping point of racial harmony. Sociologically the program has been what one critic called "the Ellis Island of talent shows." In order to achieve this particular American dream of fame, 70,000 aspirants dressed in everything from yellow pimp suits to preppy khakis, then flew, drove and hitchhiked to grueling auditions in seven iconic American cities—New York, Detroit, Miami, Atlanta, Nashville, Austin and Los Angeles—for the second season.

4   Vying for only a dozen finalists' slots, an astonishing mix of blond Asians, yodeling twins, inner-city rappers, hopeful ex-convicts and desperate single mothers slept on the sidewalks and endured the blunt dismissals of multicultural judges Randy Jackson (a black music-company executive), Paula Abdul (a Brazilian/French-Canadian recording star and choreographer), and Simon Cowell (a white British music producer whose merciless insults and fearless observations as a *Pop Idol* judge had delighted U.K. audiences). The *American Idol* finalists included several black candidates plus two from biracial families. Despite the fears of some critics that no black candidate could win, Ruben Studdard, the soulful "velvet teddy bear" from Birmingham, Ala., who proudly displayed his 205 area code on his size XXXL T-shirt, took home the prize. Imagine a black singer as a Birmingham booster in the '60s! Ruben's distance from the racist history of the city where Martin Luther King, Jr., began the civil rights movement is a statement of how far this country has come.

5   In a vote so close that it recalled the 2000 presidential election, Clay Aiken, a white college student from North Carolina who worked with autistic teens and had become Ruben's best friend, came in second. At his audition, one reviewer recalled, Clay looked "like Alfred E. Neuman and Howdy Doody crashed head-on." Twenty weeks later, tanned, ironed and styled to rock-star perfection, Clay still retained his

down-home charm and modesty. Guest judges alternated between Motown gods (Lamont Dozier, Gladys Knight) and white songwriters (Diane Warren, Billy Joel). Jackson's slang epithets ("dawg," as a term of affectionate greeting, was a favorite) domesticated the outlaw rapper idiom of hip-hop culture and repackaged it for middle America.

6   But there was a subtext to this surface of racial harmony and equality. Three black or biracial finalists and semifinalists were disqualified for concealing criminal records or for behavior unfitting to American Idols, suggesting disparities of opportunity and continuing cultural differences. One ex-finalist, Corey Clark, accused the producers of exploiting him for ratings when a web site revealed that he was facing trial on assault charges, and he had to tape an on-air defense interview for *American Idol* that he claimed was misleadingly edited.

U.K. and U.S.A.: The Pop Coalition

7 The change of venue from England to the United States not only shifted racial meanings but highlighted national differences. To the British, "Pop Idol" means something specific: a mainstream, TV-packaged, youth-oriented, music-biz phenomenon. There was no conscious sense of national identity in the choice of *Pop Idol* winners Will Young and Gareth Gates. But *American Idol* had a different agenda, especially the second series, which coincided with the buildup to and climax of the Iraq War. For their charity single benefiting the American Red Cross, 10 of the finalists recorded a hokey Reaganesque anthem, "God Bless the USA," which zoomed to the top of the charts. Part of the patriotic message was the presence among the finalists of husky Marine Josh Gracin, whose commanding officers hinted that he could be sent to Iraq at any moment. (He wasn't.)

8   Yet in the midst of all this flag waving, the edgy presence of Cowell shocked the American judges into taking a tougher line, just as the critical, even whining, war coverage of the BBC balanced and challenged the excessive optimism of American news correspondents. Cowell's refusal to be kind, tactful, warm and fuzzy, or euphemistically upbeat, made him a bracing presence on the show. Unintimidated by the politically correct, he told biracial Kimberley Locke that her performance improved as soon as she had her bushy curls straightened and highlighted. "Now," he said approvingly, "you look cute." Unmoved by the tears of losers, he was also the only judge unsoftened by the shrill audition of a 5-year-old black child. "I didn't think it was any good," he said forthrightly. The studio audience regularly booed Cowell, but his candor and insistence on high standards made the pop coalition of *American Idol* work.

The Democratic Process: Elections and Parodies

9 In the show's finale on May 21, more than 24 million votes came in to *American Idol*. We can't compare the percentage of response to a real election because *Idol* participants were allowed to vote more than once. But the electoral structure of the program reflected American attitudes about the political process, and perhaps even served as a mass-culture referendum on the mood of the nation. Both professional

reviewers and fans chatting on the Web speculated on voting blocs, on campaigns and on whether the voting was rigged; Cowell told *People* magazine that some of the finalists "play the role like presidential candidates. If there was a baby in the audience, they'd be running over to kiss it." Local newspapers ran opinion polls on behalf of hometown candidates. In the end, some reviewers even wondered about having the votes audited, bringing back memories of counting chads.

10   With *American Idol* providing its own parody of elections, it's no wonder that satirists were also attracted to the format. The *Onion* proposed a new FOX reality show called *Appointed by America*, in which contestants would vie in "a democracy quiz, a talent competition, and nation-building activities" to lead postwar Iraq. Who would it be: Ahmed Chalabi, leader of the exiled Iraqi National Congress? A peshmurga fighter from Kurdistan? Or Kymbyrley Lake, a cashier from Garland, Texas, who has always dreamed of "doing something to help bring about a more peaceful world"?

11   A third series of *American Idol* is promised for next year, with Paul McCartney rumored to be a guest judge. I'd bet the Bush twins and some Democratic candidates will be in the audience, too. This reality show could be a better political photo-op than the USS Abraham Lincoln. ◆

FREEWRITING ASSIGNMENT

If you could be a contestant on a reality television program, which one would you go on, and why?

CRITICAL READING

1. In her introductory comments, Showalter asks of reality programming, "is it ever real?" *American Idol*, she explains, is indeed a *reality* program. Why does she feel this program, as opposed to many others of its genre, is more real than others? Explain.
2. Showalter comments that *American Idol* promotes multiculturalism and that Americans have positively responded to it. Explain the ways in which Americans have supported the multicultural aspects of the program?
3. In what ways is *American Idol* a "fascinating snapshot of American youth culture" in the twenty-first century? Explain.
4. Showalter is a renowned sociologist. What elements in her essay reveal her professional interests? Does the fact that she is a serious academic make her points seem more valid? Why or why not?
5. What made *American Idol* different from its British inspiration, *Pop Idol*?
6. Showalter notes that there is a "subtext to [the] surface of racial harmony and equality" on *American Idol* (paragraph 6). Explain what she means?
7. What strikes Showalter as particularly remarkable about Ruben Studdard's victory in the second season of *American Idol*? What are the sociological and cultural messages suggested by his victory? Explain.

CRITICAL WRITING

8. When Showalter wrote this essay in August 2003, *American Idol* had just completed its second season. By the end of August, the search for contestants for the third season, scheduled to air in January 2004, had already begun. Visit the *American Idol* web site and view the contestants, including the top runners-up at *http://www.idolonfox.com*. View their profiles and respond to Showalter's observation that *American Idol* presents a truly multicultural America. If you do not feel this is true, explain why, referring to her essay and from your research on the FOX web site.
9. *Research and Analysis*: Compare and contrast *American Idol* (at *http://www.idolonfox.com*) with its British progenitor, *Pop Idol* (*http://www.itv.com/popidol/index.stm*). In what ways are they similar? Based on Showalter's essay, do you notice any fundamental differences between the two programs? If so, would you have noticed these differences before you read her essay? Explain.
10. Visit the *NewsHour* web site on the popularity of reality programming featuring Robert Thompson, head of the Center for the Study of Popular Television at Syracuse University, and Frank Farley, a past president of the American Psychological Association, and professor at Temple University at *www.pbs.org/newshour/forum/july00/reality.html*. Read the ques-

tions and responses posted at the web site, and respond to them with your own viewpoint. Note that the web site was first posted in 2000. How has reality television changed since then?

GROUP PROJECTS

11. With your group, compile a list of reality programs and their contestant profiles. (You may have to look up these programs online to see the most recent contestant roster.) What programs were the most successful? Did they appeal to a broad, multicultural audience? Discuss your list and observations in class as part of a wider discussion on diversity and reality television programs.

12. Develop your own reality television program. Include the show's premise, its object and goal, why people would want to watch it, and who would be a typical contestant. Outline the program and present it to the class. The class should vote on which program it finds the most engaging.

TV News: All the World in Pictures
Neil Postman and Steve Powers

It's 6 P.M. and you turn on the local evening news. You depend on it to keep you informed of the day's events in your area, your nation, and worldwide. But how much do you really learn from that nightly news broadcast? According to Neil Postman and Steve Powers, the answer is not very much. The nightly news, they argue, is really visual entertainment that only creates the illusion of keeping the public informed.

A professor at New York University, the late Neil Postman founded the Steinhardt School of Education's program in media ecology at NYU in 1971. He was chair of the Department of Culture and Communication until 2002. During his career, he wrote 20 books on a wide variety of subjects ranging from education to television to technology's influence on modern life. His most recent books include *The End of Education: Redefining the Value of School* (1995) and *Building a Bridge to the 18th Century: How the Past Can Improve Our Future* (1999).

Steve Powers is an award-winning journalist with more than 30 years of experience in broadcast news. Postman and Powers are co-authors of *How to Watch TV News* (2000) from which this essay was taken.

CRITICAL THINKING   Think about your local television news broadcast. How much does it rely on video clips to tell the story? How are events narrated? How much information do you learn from each clip?

---

1   When a television news show distorts the truth by altering or manufacturing facts (through re-creations), a television viewer is defenseless even if a re-creation is

properly labeled. Viewers are still vulnerable to misinformation since they will not know (at least in the case of docudramas) what parts are fiction and what parts are not. But the problems of verisimilitude posed by re-creations pale to insignificance when compared to the problems viewers face when encountering a straight (no-monkey-business) show. All news shows, in a sense, are re-creations in that what we hear and see on them are attempts to represent actual events, and are not the events themselves. Perhaps, to avoid ambiguity, we might call all news shows "re-presentations" instead of "re-creations." These re-presentations come to us in two forms: language and pictures. The question then arises: what do viewers have to know about language and pictures in order to be properly armed to defend themselves against the seductions of eloquence (to use Bertrand Russell's apt phrase)? . . .

2   [Let us look at] the problem of pictures. It is often said that a picture is worth a thousand words. Maybe so. But it is probably equally true that one word is worth a thousand pictures, at least sometimes—for example, when it comes to understanding the world we live in. Indeed, the whole problem with news on television comes down to this: all the words uttered in an hour of news coverage could be printed on one page of a newspaper. And the world cannot be understood in one page. Of course, there is a compensation: television offers pictures, and the pictures move. Moving pictures are a kind of language in themselves, but the language of pictures differs radically from oral and written language, and the differences are crucial for understanding television news.

3   To begin with, pictures, especially single pictures, speak only in particularities. Their vocabulary is limited to concrete representation. Unlike words and sentences, a picture does not present to us an idea or concept about the world, except as we use language itself to convert the image to idea. By itself, a picture cannot deal with the unseen, the remote, the internal, the abstract. It does not speak of "man," only of a man; not of "tree," only of a tree. You cannot produce an image of "nature," any more than an image of "the sea." You can only show a particular fragment of the here-and-now—a cliff of a certain terrain, in a certain condition of light; a wave at a moment in time, from a particular point of view. And just as "nature" and "the sea" cannot be photographed, such larger abstractions as truth, honor, love, and falsehood cannot be talked about in the lexicon of individual pictures. For "showing of" and "talking about" are two very different kinds of processes: individual pictures give us the world as object; language, the world as idea.

4   There is no such thing in nature as "man" or "tree." The universe offers no such categories or simplifications; only flux and infinite variety. The picture documents and celebrates the particularities of the universe's infinite variety. Language makes them comprehensible.

5   Of course, moving pictures, video with sound, may bridge the gap by juxtaposing images, symbols, sound, and music. Such images can present emotions and rudimentary ideas. They can suggest the panorama of nature and the joys and miseries of humankind.

6   Picture—smoke pouring from the window, cut to people coughing, an ambulance racing to a hospital, a tombstone in a cemetery.

7   Picture—jet planes firing rockets, explosions, lines of foreign soldiers surrendering, the American flag waving in the wind.

8   Nonetheless, keep in mind that when terrorists want to prove to the world that their kidnap victims are still alive, they photograph them holding a copy of a recent newspaper. The dateline on the newspaper provides the proof that the photograph was taken on or after that date. Without the help of the written word, film and video-tape cannot portray temporal dimensions with any precision. Consider a film clip showing an aircraft carrier at sea. One might be able to identify the ship as Soviet or American, but there would be no way of telling where in the world the carrier was, where it was headed, or when the pictures were taken. It is only through language—words spoken over the pictures or reproduced in them—that the image of the aircraft carrier takes on specific meaning.

9   Still, it is possible to enjoy the image of the carrier for its own sake. One might find the hugeness of the vessel interesting; it signifies military power on the move. There is a certain drama in watching the planes come in at high speeds and skid to a stop on the deck. Suppose the ship were burning: that would be even more interest-ing. This leads to an important point about the language of pictures. Moving pictures favor images that change. That is why violence and dynamic destruction find their way onto television so often. When something is destroyed violently it is altered in a highly visible way; hence the entrancing power of fire. Fire gives visual form to the ideas of consumption, disappearance, death—the thing that burned is actually taken away by fire. It is at this very basic level that fires make a good subject for television news. Something was here, now it's gone, and the change is recorded on film.

10   Earthquakes and typhoons have the same power. Before the viewer's eyes the world is taken apart. If a television viewer has relatives in Mexico City and an earth-quake occurs there, then he or she may take a special interest in the images of de-struction as a report from a specific place and time; that is, one may look at televi-sion pictures for information about an important event. But film of an earthquake can be interesting even if the viewer cares nothing about the event itself. Which is only to say, as we noted earlier, that there is another way of participating in the news—as a spectator who desires to be entertained. Actually to see buildings topple is exciting, no matter where the buildings are. The world turns to dust before our eyes.

11   Those who produce television news in America know that their medium favors images that move. That is why they are wary of "talking heads," people who simply appear in front of a camera and speak. When talking heads appear on television, there is nothing to record or document, no change in process. In the cinema the situ-ation is somewhat different. On a movie screen, closeups of a good actor speaking dramatically can sometimes be interesting to watch. When Clint Eastwood narrows his eyes and challenges his rival to shoot first, the spectator sees the cool rage of the Eastwood character take visual form, and the narrowing of the eyes is dramatic. But much of the effect of this small movement depends on the size of the movie screen and the darkness of the theater, which make Eastwood and his every action "larger than life."

12   The television screen is smaller than life. It occupies about 15 percent of the viewer's visual field (compared to about 70 percent for the movie screen). It is not set in a darkened theater closed off from the world but in the viewer's ordinary liv-ing space. This means that visual changes must be more extreme and more dramatic

to be interesting on television. A narrowing of the eyes will not do. A car crash, an earthquake, a burning factory are much better.

13   With these principles in mind, let us examine more closely the structure of a typical newscast, and here we will include in the discussion not only the pictures but all the nonlinguistic symbols that make up a television news show. For example, in America, almost all news shows begin with music, the tone of which suggests important events about to unfold. The music is very important, for it equates the news with various forms of drama and ritual—the opera, for example, or a wedding procession—in which musical themes underscore the meaning of the event. Music takes us immediately into the realm of the symbolic, a world that is not to be taken literally. After all, when events unfold in the real world, they do so without musical accompaniment. More symbolism follows.

14   The sound of teletype machines can be heard in the studio, not because it is impossible to screen this noise out, but because the sound is a kind of music in itself. It tells us that data are pouring in from all corners of the globe, a sensation reinforced by the world map in the background (or clocks noting the time on different continents). The fact is that teletype machines are rarely used in TV news rooms, having been replaced by silent computer terminals. When seen, they have only a symbolic function.

15   Already, then, before a single news item is introduced, a great deal has been communicated. We know that we are in the presence of a symbolic event, a form of theater in which the day's events are to be dramatized. This theater takes the entire globe as its subject, although it may look at the world from the perspective of a single nation. A certain tension is present, like the atmosphere in a theater just before the curtain goes up. The tension is represented by the music, the staccato beat of the teletype machines, and often the sight of news workers scurrying around typing reports and answering phones. As a technical matter, it would be no problem to build a set in which the newsroom staff remained off camera, invisible to the viewer, but an important theatrical effect would be lost. By being busy on camera, the workers help communicate urgency about the events at hand, which suggests that situations are changing so rapidly that constant revision of the news is necessary.

16   The staff in the background also helps signal the importance of the person in the center, the anchor, "in command" of both the staff and the news. The anchor plays the role of host. He or she welcomes us to the newscast and welcomes us back from the different locations we visit during the filmed reports.

17   Many features of the newscast help the anchor to establish the impression of control. These are usually equated with production values in broadcasting. They include such things as graphics that tell the viewer what is being shown, or maps and charts that suddenly appear on the screen and disappear on cue, or the orderly progression from story to story. They also include the absence of gaps, or "dead time," during the broadcast, even the simple fact that the news starts and ends at a certain hour. These common features are thought of as pure technical matters, which a professional crew handles as a matter of course. But they are also symbols of a dominant theme of television news: the imposition of an orderly world—called "the news"—upon the disorderly flow of events.

18   While the form of a news broadcast emphasizes tidiness and control, its content can best be described as fragmented. Because time is so precious on television, be-

cause the nature of the medium favors dynamic visual images, and because the pressures of a commercial structure require the news to hold its audience above all else, there is rarely any attempt to explain issues in depth or place events in their proper context. The news moves nervously from a warehouse fire to a court decision, from a guerrilla war to a World Cup match, the quality of the film most often determining the length of the story. Certain stories show up only because they offer dramatic pictures. Bleachers collapse in South America: hundreds of people are crushed—a perfect television news story, for the cameras can record the face of disaster in all its anguish. Back in Washington, a new budget is approved by Congress. Here there is nothing to photograph because a budget is not a physical event; it is a document full of language and numbers. So the producers of the news will show a photo of the document itself, focusing on the cover where it says "Budget of the United States of America." Or sometimes they will send a camera crew to the government printing plant where copies of the budget are produced. That evening, while the contents of the budget are summarized by a voice-over, the viewer sees stacks of documents being loaded into boxes at the government printing plant. Then a few of the budget's more important provisions will be flashed on the screen in written form, but this is such a time-consuming process—using television as a printed page—that the producers keep it to a minimum. In short, the budget is not televisable, and for that reason its time on the news must be brief. The bleacher collapse will get more time that evening.

19   While appearing somewhat chaotic, these disparate stories are not just dropped in the news program helter-skelter. The appearance of a scattershot story order is really orchestrated to draw the audience from one story to the next—through the commercial breaks to the end of the show. The story order is constructed to hold and build the viewership rather than place events in context or explain issues in depth.

20   Of course, it is a tendency of journalism in general to concentrate on the surface of events rather than underlying conditions; this is as true for the newspaper as it is for the newscast. But several features of television undermine whatever efforts journalists may make to give sense to the world. One is that a television broadcast is a series of events that occur in sequence, and the sequence is the same for all viewers. This is not true for a newspaper page, which displays many items simultaneously, allowing readers to choose the order in which they read them. If newspaper readers want only a summary of the latest tax bill, they can read the headline and the first paragraph of an article, and if they want more, they can keep reading. In a sense, then, everyone reads a different newspaper, for no two readers will read (or ignore) the same items.

21   But all television viewers see the same broadcast. They have no choices. A report is either in the broadcast or out, which means that anything which is of narrow interest is unlikely to be included. As NBC News executive Reuven Frank once explained:

> A newspaper, for example, can easily afford to print an item of conceivable interest to only a fraction of its readers. A television news program must be put together with the assumption that each item will be of some interest to everyone that watches. Every time a newspaper includes a feature which will attract a specialized group it can assume it is adding at least a little bit to its circulation. To the degree a television news program includes an item of this sort . . . it must assume that its audience will diminish.

22   The need to "include everyone," an identifying feature of commercial television in all its forms, prevents journalists from offering lengthy or complex explanations, or from tracing the sequence of events leading up to today's headlines. One of the ironies of political life in modern democracies is that many problems which concern the "general welfare" are of interest only to specialized groups. Arms control, for example, is an issue that literally concerns everyone in the world, and yet the language of arms control and the complexity of the subject are so daunting that only a minority of people can actually follow the issue from week to week and month to month. If it wants to

23 act responsibly, a newspaper can at least make available more information about arms control than most people want. Commercial television cannot afford to do so.

But even if commercial television could afford to do so, it wouldn't. The fact that television news is principally made up of moving pictures prevents it from offering lengthy, coherent explanations of events. A television news show reveals the world as a series of unrelated, fragmentary moments. It does not—and cannot be expected to—offer a sense of coherence or meaning. What does this suggest to a TV viewer? That the viewer must come with a prepared mind—information, opinions, a sense of proportion, an articulate value system. To the TV viewer lacking such mental equipment, a news program is only a kind of rousing light show. Here a falling building, there a five-alarm fire, everywhere the world as an object, much without meaning, connections, or continuity. ◆

FREEWRITING ASSIGNMENT

Consider the phrase "a picture is worth a thousand words." Do you think it is true? How does it apply to television journalism?

CRITICAL READING

1. According to Postman and Powers, what is wrong with news programs recreating actual events? How does recreation affect the viewer? How does it affect the story?
2. Consider the "pictures" in paragraphs 6 and 7. Imagine you are seeing each of these pictures without any explanation accompanying them. How many different ways could these pictures be interpreted? How important are words to the contexts of these pictures?
3. What is the authors' position on news broadcasts? How can you tell?
4. How do you think a broadcast journalist from your local television network would respond to this essay? How argumentative is this essay? Explain.
5. What is the price viewers pay for fragmented video clips? Evaluate the pros and cons of this style of journalism.
6. How does the order in which news stories are presented during the news broadcast "control" the audience? Does the knowledge that you are being manipulated change your opinion of the nightly news? Explain.
7. Analyze the authors' last paragraph that television programs cannot offer a sense of coherence and meaning. Do you agree with this? Why might this be ironic when you consider the reasons why people watch the news?

CRITICAL WRITING

8. What is news? Many of us think we know the answer, but what might be newsworthy to one person may seem superfluous to another. Write a short essay on what you expect (or want) from a news program and what you actually get. How much does the tradition of news broadcasts influence your expectations?

9. You are a television news producer who must develop a new local television news program to compete against others in the early evening time slot. Conduct a survey on what people want to watch on local television news. After gathering your information, design your newscast and explain in detail the reasons for your design. How much does your new program resemble others already on the air? What assumptions do you make about your overall audience? Predict the success of your broadcast, based on your program's rationale.

GROUP PROJECTS

10. Evaluate television newscasts. Each member of your group should watch several television newscasts from major networks. What differences, if any, are notable between networks? Are there differences between local and national news broadcasts? What assumptions seem to be made about the audiences of the various newscasts? Consider the stories reported, their order, how newscasters are dressed, the set, and the advertisements appearing on each program. Write a group-informed essay in which you describe your discoveries and analyze their relevance.

11. Prepare a survey questionnaire that seeks to find out just what it is that people want to watch on television news. Do they watch it to be entertained, informed, or both? What expectations do they bring to the programs? Do they feel newscasts are reliable sources of information? Each member of the group should survey at least 10 people and be prepared to discuss the responses with the group. Based on the responses, do viewers think the purpose of television news programs is to inform or to entertain?

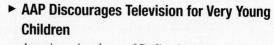

VIEWPOINTS

▶ **AAP Discourages Television for Very Young Children**
American Academy of Pediatrics

▶ **TV Can Be a Good Parent**
Ariel Gore

In August 1999, the American Academy of Pediatrics (AAP) issued a new policy statement urging parents to avoid exposing their children under the age of 2 years to television of any kind, and to carefully monitor viewing in children over that age. It further recommended that pediatricians incorporate questions about media exposure into routine child health visits. Although the policy seems to make some sense, some parents question the sweeping judgments it makes about the use of television in American homes. One such parent, Ariel Gore, argues that television can be a good co-parent, giving parents, especially working or single ones, needed relief from the demands of parenting. Although she agrees with the AAP's claim that young children need direct interaction with adults to grow mentally and socially, she questions how this assessment translates into a policy advocating no television exposure at all.

The American Academy of Pediatrics is a national organization of physicians specializing in children's health. The press release that follows was released on August 2, 1999. It summarizes some of the points made in AAP's new policy that appeared in the August 1999 issue of *Pediatrics*, the scientific journal of the AAP. Ariel Gore is the author of two books on parenting, *The Hip Mama's Survival Guide* (1998) and *The Mother Trip: Hip Mama's Guide to Staying Sane in the Chaos of Motherhood* (2000). Her most recent book is *Atlas of the Human Heart: A Memoir* (2003). This article appeared in the August 16, 1999, publication of *Salon*.

CRITICAL THINKING Think about some of the children's television programs popular today. Who is responsible for developing and distributing these programs?

AAP Discourages Television for Very Young Children
American Academy of Pediatrics

1 A new policy from the American Academy of Pediatrics (AAP) urges parents to avoid television for children under 2 years old.

2 "While certain television programs may be promoted to this age group, research on early brain development shows that babies and toddlers have a critical need for direct interactions with parents and other significant care givers for healthy brain growth and the development of appropriate social, emotional, and cognitive skills," the policy says. The new AAP statement on media education also suggests parents create an "electronic media-free" environment in children's rooms, and avoid using media as an electronic babysitter. In addition, it recommends pediatricians incorporate questions about media into routine child health visits, as education can reduce harmful media effects.

3 "With an educated understanding of media images and messages, users can recognize media's potential effects and make good choices about their and their children's media exposure," states the new policy.

4   According to the AAP, a media educated person understands that:

- all media messages are constructed;
- media messages shape our understanding of the world;
- individuals interpret media messages uniquely; and
- mass media has powerful economic implications.

5   Research strongly suggests that media education may result in young people becoming less vulnerable to negative aspects of media exposure, the AAP says. In some studies, heavy viewers of violent programming were less accepting of violence or showed decreased aggressive behavior after a media education intervention. Another study found a change in attitudes about wanting to drink alcohol after a media education program. Canada, Great Britain, Australia and some Latin American countries have successfully incorporated media education into school curricula, the statement says. "Common sense would suggest that increased media education in the United States could represent a simple, potentially effective approach to combating the myriad of harmful media messages seen or heard by children and adolescents."

6   In addition, the AAP emphasized that media education should not be used as a substitute for careful scrutiny of the media industry's responsibility for its programming. ◆

TV Can Be a Good Parent
Ariel Gore

1 Let me get this straight.

2   The corporations have shipped all the living-wage jobs off to the developing world, the federal government has "ended welfare" and sent poor women into subminimum wage "training programs" while offering virtually no child-care assistance, the rent on my one-bedroom apartment just went up to $850 a month, the newspapers have convinced us that our kids can't play outside by themselves until they're 21, and now the American Academy of Pediatrics wants my television?

3   I don't think so.

4   Earlier this month, the AAP released new guidelines for parents recommending that kids under the age of 2 not watch TV. They say the box is bad for babies' brains and not much better for older kids. Well, no duh.

5   When I was a young mom on welfare, sometimes I needed a break. I needed time to myself. I needed to mellow out to avoid killing my daughter for pouring bleach on the Salvation Army couch. And when I was at my wits' end, Barney the Dinosaur and Big Bird were better parents than I was. My daughter knows that I went to college when she was a baby and preschooler. She knows that I work. And, truth be told, our television set has been a helpful co-parent on rainy days when I've been on deadline. Because I'm the mother of a fourth-grader, Nickelodeon is my trusted friend.

6   There was no TV in our house when I was a kid. My mother called them "boob tubes." But that was in the 1970s. My mother and all of her friends were poor—they were artists—but the rent she paid for our house on the Monterey (Calif.) Peninsula was $175 a month and my mother and her friends helped each other with the kids. The child care was communal. So they could afford to be poor, to stay home, to kill their televisions. I, on the other hand, cannot.

7   Now the AAP is saying I'm doing my daughter an injustice every time I let her watch TV. The official policy states that "Although certain television programs may be promoted to [young children], research on early brain development shows that babies and toddlers have a critical need for direct interactions with parents and other significant caregivers for healthy brain growth and the development of appropriate social, emotional, and cognitive skills. Therefore, exposing such young children to television programs should be discouraged."

8   Maybe my brain has been warped by all my post-childhood TV watching, but I'm having a little trouble getting from point A to point B here. Babies and toddlers have a critical need for direct interactions with actual people. I'm with them on this. "Therefore, exposing such young children to television programs should be discouraged." This is where they lose me. I can see "Therefore, sticking them in front of the TV all day and all night should be discouraged." But the assumption that TV-watching kids don't interact with their parents or caregivers is silly. Watching TV and having one-on-one interactions with our kids aren't mutually exclusive.

9   I've been careful to teach my daughter critical thinking in my one-woman "mind over media" campaign. It started with fairytales: "What's make-believe?" and "How would you like to stay home and cook for all those dwarves?" Later we moved on to the news: "Why was it presented in this way?" and "What's a stereotype?" But if you think I was reading "Winnie the Pooh" to my toddler when I thought up these questions, think again. I was relaxing with a cup of coffee and a book on feminist theory while Maia was riveted to PBS.

10   I read to my daughter when she was little. We still read together. But even a thoughtful mama needs an electronic baby sitter every now and again. Maybe especially a thoughtful mama.

11   Not surprisingly, the television executives feel there's plenty of innocuous programming on television to entertain young kids without frying their brains. "It's a bunch of malarkey," said Kenn Viselman, president of the itsy bitsy Entertainment Co., about the new policy. Itsy bitsy distributes the British show *Teletubbies*, which is broadcast on PBS. While I prefer Big Bird to Tinky Winky, I have to agree with him when he says, "Instead of attacking shows that try to help children, the pediatricians should warn parents that they shouldn't watch the Jerry Springer show when kids are in the room."

12   The AAP's policy refers to all television, of course, but it's hard not to feel like they're picking on PBS. *Teletubbies* is the only program currently shown on non-cable television marketed toward babies and toddlers. Just two weeks ago, the station announced a $40 million investment to develop six animated programs for preschoolers. The timing of the AAP's report is unfortunate.

13   Cable stations offer a wider variety of kid programming. Take for example Nick Jr., an offshoot of the popular Nickelodeon channel. On weekdays from 9 a.m.

to 2 p.m., the programming is geared specifically toward the preschool set. "Our slogan for Nick Jr. is 'Play to Learn'," Nickelodeon's New York publicity manager, Karen Reynolds, told me. "A child is using cognitive skills in a fun setting. It's interactive. With something like *Blues Clues*, kids are talking back to the TV. They are not just sitting there."

14   Still, the station has no beef with the new AAP policy on toddlers. "Nick Jr. programs to preschool children ages 2 to 5, but we are aware that children younger than 2 may be watching television," said Brown Johnson, senior vice president of Nick Jr. "We welcome a study of this kind because it encourages parents to spend more time bonding and playing with their children."

15   In addition to telling parents that young children shouldn't watch television at all and that older kids shouldn't have sets in their bedrooms, the AAP is recommending that pediatricians ask questions about media consumption at annual check-ups. The difference between recommending less TV-watching and actually mandating that it be monitored by the medical community is where this could become a game of hardball with parents. What would this "media file" compiled by our doctors be used for? Maybe television placement in the home will become grounds for deciding child custody. ("I'm sorry, your honor, I'll move the set into the bathroom immediately.") Or maybe two decades from now Harvard will add TV abstention to their ideal candidate profile. ("*Teletubbies* viewers need not apply.") Better yet, Kaiser could just imprint "Poor White Trash" directly onto my family's medical ID cards. Not that those cards work at the moment. I'm a little behind on my bill.

16   I called around, but I was hard-pressed to find a pediatrician who disagreed with the academy's new policy. Instead, doctors seemed to want their kids to watch less TV, and they're glad to have the AAP's perhaps over-the-top guidelines behind them. "If all your kids did was an hour of *Barney* and *Sesame Street* a day, I don't think that the academy would have come out with that statement," said a pediatrician at La Clinica de la Raza in Oakland, Calif., who asked not to be named. "It's not the best learning tool." And he scoffs at the notion of "interactive" TV. "It's not a real human interaction. When you're dealing with babies and toddlers, this screen is an integral part of their reality. You want kids to be able to understand interaction as an interaction. It's like the Internet. We're getting to a place where all of your relationships are virtual relationships."

17   Fair enough.

18   I'm not going to say that TV is the greatest thing in the world for little kids—or for anyone. I'm not especially proud of the hours I spend watching *Xena: Warrior Princess*, *The Awful Truth* and *Ally McBeal*. Mostly I think American television is a string of insipid shows aired for the sole purpose of rounding up an audience to buy tennis shoes made in Indonesian sweatshops.

19   But it seems that there is a heavy middle-class assumption at work in the AAP's new policy—that all of us can be stay-at-home moms, or at least that we all have partners or other supportive people who will come in and nurture our kids when we can't.

20   I say that before we need a policy like this one, we need more—and better—educational programming on TV. We need to end the culture of war and the media's glorification of violence. We need living-wage jobs. We need government salaries

for stay-at-home moms so that all women have a real career choice. We do not need "media files" in our pediatricians' offices or more guilt about being bad parents. Give me a $175 a month house on the Monterey Peninsula and a commune of artists to share parenting responsibilities, and I'll kill my TV without any provocation from the AAP at all. Until then, long live Big Bird, *The Brady Bunch* and all their very special friends! ◆

FREEWRITING ASSIGNMENT

Do you think that television is harmful to babies and toddlers? Why or why not?

CRITICAL READING

1. On what criteria does the AAP base its new policy? Does the policy seem logical and sound? What is the basic point of the AAP's new policy?
2. Gore explains that when she called to ask pediatricians for their viewpoint on the new AAP policy, she was "hard-pressed" to find a pediatrician who disagreed with it. How does she respond to this reaction?
3. The AAP is an organization of medical doctors specializing in children's health. Gore is the author of two books on parenting. Which source seems more credible to you, and why?
4. Does Gore's response to the AAP's sweeping ban on television for toddlers seem reasonable and well-considered? Does it change or influence your view of the AAP's policy decision? Explain.
5. Gore questions the AAP's recommendation that pediatricians ask parents questions about media in the home in their routine child health examinations (paragraph 15). Do her fears of "media files" seem reasonable? Does the AAP policy allow for any flexibility in this type of questioning?

CRITICAL WRITING

6. *Analysis and Exploratory Writing*: In paragraphs 7–8, Gore analyzes and responds to the AAP's policy statement that young children should not watch television. In your own words, respond to the AAP's statement explaining your viewpoint on this issue. Like Gore, support your stance by analyzing the wording of the AAP's policy and your personal experience.
7. *Critical Analysis*: Visit the AAP's web site and review their policy on media and children at *www.aap.org/policy/re09911.html*. Imagine that you are a representative of the AAP. Write a thoughtful response to Gore's argument in which you carefully critique her logic and argue against her claims. Be sure to refer to specific statements from both her article and the AAP policy in your rebuttal.
8. *Research and Analysis:* Gore comments that it seems as if the AAP is specifically targeting programs such as *Teletubbies* and other PBS pro-

grams geared toward young children. Visit the Teletubbies web site at *www.pbs.org/teletubbies* and read about the show and its premise. You may also want to read "The Trouble with Teletubbies" by Susan E. Linn and Alvin F. Poussaint printed in the May–June 1999 issue of *The American Prospect* at *www.prospect.org*. Write an essay in which you analyze the program, its benefit to children, and the AAP's statement against television for young children.

GROUP PROJECTS

9. With your group, watch some of the children's programs Gore cites in her essay (*Sesame Street*, *Barney and Friends*, *Teletubbies*, and *Blues Clues*). Evaluate these programs for their content, style, interactivity, and audience age. With your group, discuss the following question: "If I had a toddler, would I let him or her watch these programs?" Explain your stance to the group, allowing for rebuttal or agreement.

10. Conduct a survey of young parents and their children's television viewing habits. In what ways, if any, do they use television (or other forms of media such as videos) to augment their childcare? How do they feel about physicians asking them about media use in the home? How do your results compare with the recommendations made by the AAP? Discuss your results with the class to facilitate class discussion on these issues.

11. Visit the PBS web site and access their children's programming web page at *www.pbs.org/kids*. With your group, review some of the programs for very young children (such as *Teletubbies*). Based on the program's descriptions and your assessment of the elements of the program, develop your own program for children. Create the characters, set, and the activities for a single 15-minute segment of programming. Present your program to the class and explain the rationale behind your characters, props, set, and plot.

RESEARCH ISSUE **Television and African Americans**
Kate Tuttle

From the negative stereotypes in *Beulah* and *Amos 'n' Andy* to the "white Negroes" in *Julia* and *I Spy* to the arguably too-perfect Huxtable family on *The Cosby Show*, the majority of portrayals of African Americans on television have been one dimensional, distorted, insulting, or sugarcoated. For many viewers, though, even unsatisfactory images seem preferable to the general absence of black television characters during television's early days. The history of the depiction of blacks on television has evolved from near invisibility broken by a parade of stereotypes to greater diversity and realism, but most critics agree that the medium has far to go. Kate Tuttle is senior editor of *Africana* magazine. This history appears on their web site, at *www.africana.com.*

The Early Years

1   Commercial television was born in 1948 as each of the three major networks, ABC, CBS, and NBC, began broadcasting. 1948 was also a significant year in African American history, with the desegregation of the United States armed forces and an endorsement of civil rights in the presidential platform of the Democratic Party, headed by President Harry S. Truman.

2   But black presence in the early years of television followed the pattern earlier set by radio. In fact, the first two series starring African Americans both came to television after decades of popularity on radio, and each replaced white radio actors with black actors. *Beulah*, which showcased a supporting character on the popular *Fibber McGee and Molly* show, debuted in 1950. As played by Ethel Waters, Hattie McDaniel, and Louise Beavers on television, Beulah was cast in the stereotypical mold of the happy, overweight, black female "mammy." Cheerfully caring for the white family who employed her as housekeeper, Beulah had little discernible life of her own (although the cultural critic Donald Bogle points out that the interaction between Beulah and her long-time boyfriend provided some of the show's best moments). Beulah ran until 1953, when protests by the National Association for the Advancement of Colored People (NAACP) and other groups forced the network to cancel the series.

3   *Amos 'n' Andy*, which ran from 1951 to 1953, was based on the most listened-to radio show of the 1930s and 1940s. Unlike *Beulah*, *Amos 'n' Andy* portrayed an all-black world in which the shiftless, joking Andy (played by Spencer Williams) and the passive, long-suffering Amos (Alvin Childress) interacted with characters depicting the entire range of stereotypical black images. Its roots in the tradition of minstrelsy caused the NAACP to launch lawsuits and boycott threats that were instrumental in causing the show's cancellation. Speaking in the documentary *Color Adjustment*, written and directed by Marlon Riggs, the actress Diahann Carroll remembers being forbidden to watch *Amos 'n' Andy*, which her parents felt was demeaning to blacks. But some modern critics have praised the show's intricate and sophisticated comedy and lauded the actors, many of whom came from the black vaudeville tradition. After the series was cancelled, it continued to appear in syndication until 1966.

4   Other black images in 1950s television included variety shows, which occasionally featured African American entertainers. Duke Ellington, Cab Calloway, Paul Robeson, Ella Fitzgerald, Sarah Vaughan, and others appeared on shows hosted by veteran white entertainers such as Ed Sullivan, Milton Berle, and Steve Allen. But no African American had his own national variety show until 1956, when The *Nat "King" Cole Show* premiered. Cole, who had hosted a radio program in the 1940s, was urbane, elegant, and considered non-threatening by white viewers. His show featured both white and black entertainers, including Pearl Bailey, Count Basie, and Mahalia Jackson, and was a great source of pride for black viewers starved for positive African American television images. But with the deepening

racial tensions of the 1950s, Cole had difficulty attracting corporate sponsors, especially after some white viewers became outraged when Cole touched the arm of a white female guest. The show was cancelled after one season.

Civil Rights and the "White Negro"

5 One arena in which African Americans appeared on television beginning in the 1950s, and reaching a peak in the 1960s, was in the serious documentaries about rural poverty, segregation, and the growing Civil Rights Movement. In addition, as the white segregationist backlash exploded into violence throughout the American South, "images of black people dominated the news," according to the writer and scholar Henry Louis Gates Jr. Seen as a noble, almost saintly figure, the Reverend Martin Luther King Jr., whose marches in Selma, Birmingham, and Montgomery, Alabama, heightened white America's awareness of the Civil Rights Movement, became black America's spokesperson on television in the eyes of many newly sympathetic white viewers. By contrast, some black leaders were treated harshly on television. Malcolm X was the subject of a documentary titled *The Hate that Hate Produced* (1959), which did little to dispel white fears of the Nation of Islam leader.

6 At the same time, as television news shows began to report seriously on racism and the fight for civil rights, television's entertainment programs became even more overwhelmingly white. Since its birth, the medium had avoided controversy, possibly offensive to viewers (and advertisers). During the 1960s, as protests rose against both racism and the Vietnam War, programming became less and less realistic. (For example, some of the most popular shows on television at that time featured witches, genies, and other escapist fantasy.) As the cultural critic J. Fred McDonald pointed out, comedies such as *Petticoat Junction* and *The Andy Griffith Show*, both set in the South, portrayed all-white worlds in which prejudice seemingly did not exist.

7 When black characters did appear, network executives crafted the most inoffensive, blandly perfect images possible. *I Spy* (1965–1968), which starred Bill Cosby and Robert Culp as an interracial team of secret agents, presented Cosby's character, Alexander Scott, as a Rhodes scholar, an elegant sophisticate whose education was superior not only to the vast majority of African Americans but also to nearly all whites. *Julia* (1968–1971) featured Diahann Carroll as a widowed nurse and single mother. Carroll's character was bland, bleached of all evidence of black culture. Derided as a "white Negro" by critics, and suspected of being played by a white actress in darkening makeup, Carroll's Julia never encountered poverty or racism. Still, *Julia* was, according to African American actress Esther Rolle, "a step above the grinning domestic."

8 Designed to overcome negative stereotypes, such series presented "fully assimilable black people," according to Gates. In an era that featured so few black representations in the mass media, even positive images were heavily scrutinized by African Americans and usually found wanting. Shows like *I Spy*, *Julia*, and the action series *Mod Squad* and *Mission Impossible* (each of which featured black costars) clashed with the reality of most African Americans' lives. But attempts to present a more balanced picture, such as the short-lived dramatic series *East Side,*

West Side (1963–1964), usually failed quickly. Starring James Earl Jones and Cicely Tyson, *East Side, West Side* featured sophisticated writing and provocative situations depicting both ghetto life and the pain of integration. The show lasted only one season.

Relevance and Roots

9   By the late 1960s television began to emerge from its fantasy world to present programming more in touch with the reality of the tumultuous times. The first comedy series to deal with race was *All in the Family* (1971–1979), a show with a mostly white cast. At its head was Archie Bunker (played by Carroll O'Connor), an unrepentant racist, bigot, and homophobe. While some felt that Archie's use of racial slurs amounted to condoning prejudice, most saw the series as an important move toward realism, particularly in terms of race relations, on television. In fact, the Bunkers' next door neighbors were a black family whose characters were later featured in a popular spinoff series, *The Jeffersons,* which aired from 1975 to 1985.

10   One of the most dramatic changes came in children's television, which had been a wasteland in terms of black images. Starting in 1969 the public television series *Sesame Street* showed children and adults of a variety of racial and ethnic backgrounds interacting and learning. *Fat Albert and the Cosby Kids* (1972–1989) was an animated version of children and events from producer Bill Cosby's own Philadelphia childhood. More shows followed, including cartoons based on the adventures of the *Jackson Five* and the *Harlem Globetrotters*.

11   Produced by the *All in the Family* team, *Good Times* (1974–1979) was the first television comedy to focus on a poor black family, one including both father and mother, living in the midst of a vibrant, diverse black community. But social relevance gave way to echoes of the minstrel character Stepin Fetchit, as the show increasingly revolved around the buffoonish character of JJ, the elder son. According to Esther Rolle, the actress who played JJ's mother, "negative images have been quietly slipped in on us" through the clowning, wide-eyed JJ.

12   Although the 1970s saw a dramatic rise in the number of television shows built around black characters, most made no pretense of seriousness or realism. *Sanford and Son* (1972–1977) starred the veteran comedian Redd Foxx as an irascible junk dealer and Demond Wilson as his long-suffering son. Despite the implied social relevance of its ghetto setting, the show was vintage 1970s escapism. Its wide popularity derived in part from its self-aware use of stereotypical aspects of black humor, elaborate insults, shrill women, scheming men, and it inspired a succession of inferior shows, including *Grady* (1975–1976), *Baby I'm Back* (1978), and *What's Happenin'* (1976–1979), which critics dubbed "the new minstrelsy."

13   No dramatic series starring a black actor aired until the 1980s. But it was in drama, made-for-television movies and miniseries, that some of the most significant television images of African Americans emerged in the 1970s. *The Autobiography of Miss Jane Pittman* (1974), starring Cicely Tyson, was hailed as "possibly the finest movie ever made for television." The movie, a series of flashbacks, is set in 1962 and traces Pittman's life from her childhood in slavery to the civil rights era

she lived to see (the character is 110 years old). Its climactic scene features Pittman bending to take a sip from a whites-only water fountain.

14   *Roots*, which aired over eight nights in 1977, was a television event not only for African Americans but for all Americans. The highest-rated miniseries ever, *Roots*, based on Alex Haley's book about his family's history from freedom in Africa to slavery in the American South, attracted an estimated 130 million viewers. According to the cultural critic Marlon Riggs, *Roots* was presented as an immigrant tale that white audiences could relate to, "transforming a national disgrace into an epic triumph of the family and the American dream." Although carefully crafted to appeal to the white audience (it was reported that the actor LeVar Burton, who played Kunta Kinte, was nearly dropped from the project because producers thought his lips were too large), *Roots* was nonetheless a stirring and powerful drama. It was also a showcase for many black actors, including Burton, Louis Gossett Jr., and Cicely Tyson.

Material Success

15 By the late 1970s no obvious color line remained in television. Black actors appeared in soap operas, as costars in dramatic series, and as the focus of comedies. In the wake of *Roots,* several television movies, including *King* (1978), *Roots: The Next Generations* (1979), and *Attica* (1980), featured African American historical themes. But most depictions of blacks in television continued to follow the pattern of either high-minded history lesson or low-rent stereotypic comedy. Rarely allowed to exist as fully realized human beings, some of the most popular black characters of the early 1980s were wisecracking black children adopted into white families, the situation in both *Different Strokes* (1978–1986) and *Webster* (1983–1987), or, as in earlier television history, loyal sidekicks to white heroes.

16   When *The Cosby Show* debuted in 1984, it won enthusiastic reviews and a loyal audience, both black and white. Focusing on a loving, intact, successful African American family, *The Cosby Show* starred Bill Cosby and Phylicia Rashad as the upper-middle class parents of five children. Like the white families in 1950s television, theirs was a caring, supportive unit that blended humor with wisdom. Cosby, who had long criticized the negative portrayals of African Americans in television, consulted psychiatrist Dr. Alvin Poussaint in writing and producing the program, resulting in a positive, almost educational tone. The top-rated series for many of its nine seasons, *Cosby*, according to critic Patricia Turner, reinforced "the notion that the Civil Rights Movement took care of all the racial inequities of society."

17   One series that attempted a more balanced depiction was the short-lived *Frank's Place* (1987–1988), about a black professor who inherits a New Orleans restaurant. Tim Reid, who had previously costarred in *WKRP in Cincinnati*, produced and starred in *Frank's Place*, which he said reflected his desire to see blacks portrayed not monolithically but with the full range of humanity. Although the well-written show won an Emmy Award, it was cancelled after one season.

18   Like Cosby and Reid, a rising number of African Americans began working behind the television camera in the late 1980s, resulting in a flowering of black-

themed shows. *A Different World*, which spun off from Cosby and was produced by Debbie Allen, depicted life at a historically black university. Others included Quincy Jones's *Fresh Prince of Bel Air*, starring Will Smith, and *In Living Color*, produced by Keenan Ivory Wayans. *In Living Color*, one of the then-new Fox network's first hits, brought freshness and irreverence to its humor, much of which was based on racial stereotypes (the show's outrageousness reminded some critics of *The Flip Wilson Show*, which ran from 1970 to 1974).

19   Fox, which also produced *Living Single, Martin*, and *South Central*, was the first network to focus so much energy on attracting black audiences with shows featuring African American actors. Some critics, among them Frank Reid, charged that the Fox shows merely perpetuated the old, negative stereotypes, this time in the lingo of the hip hop generation. (One Fox series, *Roc*, with a brilliant ensemble cast culled mostly from August Wilson's stage play *Fences*, escaped this criticism.) But with the increasing fragmentation of the television audience, caused in part by the growth of cable television, black viewers responded eagerly to the new black shows. Another venue for television geared exclusively to the African American community came of age in the early 1990s. Black Entertainment Television (BET) capitalized on music videos, sports, and reruns of black-focused series to attract a nationwide audience.

20   Black programming was lucrative because it appealed not only to the black audience but also to whites, especially white youth, increasingly enamored of black culture. Michael Jordan and other basketball stars became some of corporate America's favorite spokespersons, and white teenagers took their fashion and language cues from rap musicians. The success of African Americans *Arsenio Hall* and *Oprah Winfrey* in late-night and daytime talk shows led to dozens of imitators, both black and white. In addition, Winfrey produced and acted in *The Women of Brewster Place*, a 1988 miniseries based on Gloria Naylor's novel, and in 1998 produced the television adaptation of Dorothy West's *The Wedding*, among other made-for-television projects. A cultural phenomenon and one of the richest people in America, Winfrey's naturalness, warmth, and pride in her African American culture have found favor with both blacks and whites.

21   By the late 1990s more African Americans than ever were involved in the television industry, some in executive and production roles. Taboos against interracial sex and other forms of social equality had eroded. But there are still no prime-time dramatic series devoted to telling the stories of black Americans, and many of the images seen by black children (who are estimated to watch television at a rate 64 percent higher than the national average) continue to perpetuate limited stereotypes. ◆

CRITICAL THINKING

1. Tuttle notes that in the late 1980s and in the 1990s, "Black programming was lucrative because it appealed not only to the black audience but also to whites, especially white youth, increasingly enamored of black culture." What accounts for the appeal of black programming among young

white audiences? Could this appeal influence American culture in the next generation? Explain.

2. Tuttle's essay ends with a description of programming in the late 1990s. Write three or four additional paragraphs to her history describing television programs over the last four years that feature either a primarily African American cast or include African American roles of significance. Incorporate any observations you may have regarding the cultural significance of these programs. Then write a concluding paragraph projecting the future of this genre.

RESEARCH PROJECTS

3. Tuttle notes that many television programs featuring African American characters promoted stereotypes. During the 1970s and 1980s, some of these stereotypes were challenged and others were reinforced. Make a list of all the programs that feature primarily African American casts. Watch each program at least once, and write a summary of how the characters are portrayed, the themes the programs address, and the cultural images they promote. Write an essay in which you describe how African American television programs either continue to promote ethnic stereotypes or how these programs have transcended ethnic boundaries.

4. Visit the Neilson data website presenting data on African American viewing audiences at *http://www.nielsenmedia.com/ethnicmeasure/african-american/indexAA.html*. Then visit the BET web site at *http://www.bet.com/*. Write an essay discussing the current trends in African American television viewers and programs based on your research gathered at these two websites.

Additional essay topics, writing assignments, research guidelines, and readings for this chapter can be found online at **www.ablongman.com/goshgarian**.

The Family

in Flux

Love and Marriage

4

The American family is always in a state of change. How we perceive the very concept of family is based largely on where we come from and what values we share. We have a tendency to base our views on traditional constructs—models that are generations old and perpetuated by media archetypes. As a result, sociologists tell us, our vision of family is usually not based on realistic examples but on political ideals and media images. Yet the traditional family is obviously changing. Stepfamilies, same-sex relationships, single-parent households, and extended families with several generations living in one home all force us to redefine, or at least reexamine, our traditional definitions of family.

This chapter examines love and marriage in modern families. From traditional "nuclear family" models of husband, wife, children, to same-sex unions, this chapter takes a look at how our concept of marriage has changed. Divorce, for example, is a widely accepted reality of life, and is no longer viewed as a deviation from the norm. Single motherhood is no longer ascribed the social stigma it had 30 or 40 years ago. Some states are taking steps to legalize same-sex unions, and across the country, many companies already formally recognize these relationships in benefit programs. Our perspective of marriage is shifting, and so have our attitudes. And as attitudes change, so do our expectations and social collective consciousness.

We open the chapter with an examination of family from an academic perspective. In "Family: Idea, Institution, and Controversy," Betty G. Farrell discusses the social and political structures that influence our concept of family, and how the institution of family is firmly entrenched in our cultural consciousness. She also explores the concept of the family in transition and why we seem to fear change when it comes to family structures—structures that are based more on nostalgia than on reality.

The next essay further examines the American desire for nostalgia and how we often base our vision of the perfect marriage and family on a media-influenced ideal. In "The New Nostalgia," Rosalind C. Barnett and Caryl Rivers explain that old television models of marriage and family such as *Ozzie and Harriet* and *Leave It to Beaver* create complicated messages for modern couples. Politicians who lament the loss of the traditional family and people who long for "the way things used to be" are recalling an illusion rather than reality. Such nostalgia is not only misplaced, but it can also be dangerous, setting an unachievable standard.

When Alex Kotlowitz was asked by *Frontline* to prepare a piece on the "marriage movement," a conservative initiative encouraging marriage in urban communities, he thought the idea was ludicrous. However, after investigating the issue, he isn't so sure anymore. In "Are the Conservatives Right?" he wonders if promoting marriage could actually help urban communities escape poverty and crime.

Not everyone agrees that marriage is best, however. Sociologist Stephanie Coontz challenges the idea that marriage should be a goal. There is no way, she contends, that marriage can be reestablished as the main site of family and interpersonal relationships in our modern world, a view she defends in "Nostalgia as Ideology."

The instability of American marriage is often cited as the source of many childhood problems. Most of us have heard the troubling statistics—over half of all U.S.

marriages end in divorce. The next essay, by college student Lowell Putnam, argues that children of divorce are not as scarred by the experience as politicians and the media seem to think. Having lived most of his life as a "child of divorce" he wonders, "Did I Miss Something?"

In "Unmarried Bliss," Marshall Miller and Dorian Solot, an unmarried, but committed, couple who founded the Alternatives to Marriage Project, challenge the legal barriers that prevent couples like them from enjoying the rights granted to married people, such as health care coverage. They explain, times have changed, and so should the way we recognize committed relationships.

Anjula Razdan provides a different look at marriage—that of a young woman raised by traditional Indian parents who support the practice of arranged marriages. While her parents believe that arranged marriages are the most practical and logical way to unify young couples—and Razdan wonders if they are on to something—she would still prefer to hold out for love.

This chapter's *Viewpoints* section addresses the issue of gay marriage. The issue has been hotly argued for the past few years, as some states ban, and others begin to permit, same-sex marriage. In "Unveiled," Andrew Sullivan explains that marriage should be a bond between two loving adults who wish to make a lifelong commitment to each other, regardless of gender. Jeff Jacoby questions this stance in "The Danger in Same-Sex Marriage" The section also features a political cartoon from Dan Wasserman titled "Wasserman's View: Assault on Family Values."

The final reading, a Research Issue entitled "Cohabiting Is NOT the Same as Commitment" by Karen S. Peterson, presents the research issue of cohabitation before marriage. Peterson reports that men who cohabit with women are less bound to marry at all. The big question is, "Why?"

Family: Idea, Institution, and Controversy
Betty G. Farrell

Although the family has always been in a state of transition, many politicians will have us believe that the family is not just in a state of change; it is in a state of decline. And whether this is true or not, it seems that many people agree that most of society's ills are directly connected to the "decline" of the family. The truth is, family is more than an icon in our culture. It is an American institution, subject to intense scrutiny and criticism. Betty G. Farrell explores the importance of the institution of family in American culture, and how this importance is inextricably linked to our social and political consciousness.

Betty G. Farrell is a professor at Pitzer College in California and the author of several books on family, including *Elite Families: Class and Power in 19th Century Boston* (1993). This essay is excerpted from the introduction to her book, *Family: The Making of an Idea, an Institution, and a Controversy in American Culture* (1999).

Social scientists and family historians often comment that the American family is in a "state of transition." What do they mean? What is transition? Is it a positive or negative thing?

Q: What did Eve say to Adam on being expelled from the Garden of Eden?
A: "I think we're in a time of transition."

1   The irony of this joke is not lost as we begin a new century and anxieties about social change seem rife. The implication of this message, covering the first of many subsequent periods of transition, is that change is normal; there is, in fact, no era or society in which change is not a permanent feature of the social landscape. Yet, on the eve of the twenty-first century, the pace of change in the United States feels particularly intense, and a state of "permanent transition" hardly seems a contradiction in terms at all. To many, it is an apt description of the economic fluctuations, political uncertainties, social and cultural upheaval, and fluidity of personal relationships that characterize the times. For a large segment of the population, however, these transitions are tinged with an acute sense of loss and nostalgia. Moral values, communities, even the American way of life seem in decline. And at the core of that decline is the family.

2   In a nationwide poll conducted by the *Los Angeles Times*, May 26, 1996, 78 percent of respondents said they were dissatisfied with today's moral values, and nearly half of that group identified divorce, working parents, and undisciplined children as the key problems. Only 11 percent of the respondents believed that their own behavior had contributed to the moral problems in the United States, and a resounding 96 percent believed that they were personally doing an excellent or good job of teaching moral values to their children. Conversely, 93 percent thought that *other* parents were to blame for the inadequate moral upbringing of their children. The sense of loss and decline many Americans feel today is filled with such contradictions. Americans want their families to offer unconditional love yet also to enforce and uphold strict moral values. They want flexibility, mobility, and autonomy in their personal lives but yearn for traditional communities and permanently stable families. When the substance of the debate over families is this ambiguous and contradictory, it is important to look more closely at the underlying issues in this time of transition.

3   For most people in most eras, change seems anything but normal. Periods of social change can evoke much social anxiety, because the unknown is inherently unsettling and because many people are stakeholders in the status quo. Those who seek change generally want to effect a shift in the relations of power, either for themselves or for others. But such shifts are always unpredictable, and they can seem treacherous to those who hold the reins of power as well as to those who feel their social, economic, or political power eroding. The groups with eroding power are the ones most likely to resist, through active strategies and passive resistance, the ideas, values, symbols, and behavior associated with change. This describes such groups in the contemporary United States as militias who see minorities, foreigners, and new cultural values as a threat to the American way of life; whites who see blacks,

Latinos, and Asians as challenging their privileges and claim on limited resources in a zero-sum game; pro-life advocates who see pro-choice supporters as threatening traditionally defined family roles; and antigay proponents who see gays and lesbians as subverting the gendered social order. Although social structural forces are ultimately responsible for the realignment of prestige and power among social groups in any society, these forces are always complex, abstract, intangible, and invisible. So those who symbolize or represent the forces of the new—women, minorities, immigrants, the poor, and other marginalized groups—tend to be singled out and blamed for the disruptions and upheaval associated with change. Social psychologists identify this process as scapegoating, the act of displacing generalized anxiety onto a conveniently visible and available target. Scapegoats have been identified in every era; but in periods in which the pace of change is particularly fast and a sense of unsettling disruption is acute, those social newcomers who challenge established values and behavior can all too readily become the targets of the rage, fear, and ambivalence of people feeling the earthquake tremors of social change.

Popular Perspectives on the Family

4 The family values debate has been generated against just such a backdrop in the late-twentieth-century United States. Fundamental changes in the expectations, meanings, and practices defining American family life have characterized much of the twentieth century, but especially the final thirty years. Consequently, concern about the family has moved to the center of the political arena. Threats to the family, on the one hand, and salvation through the family, on the other, are the two most prominent themes in the recent family politics discourse. That the American family is broken and in need of repair is a common assumption of many social observers. Its complement is that families are worth fixing because making them strong (again) is the key to solving most of society's ills. Neither of these assumptions has been subject to much critical scrutiny, nor has the historical image of the strong, vital, central family institution of the past on which they rest. Longing for order is one of the impulses behind the current turn to family politics in the United States; and feminists, gays and lesbians, single-parent mothers, absent fathers, pregnant teenagers, and gang-oriented youth, among others, have all at one time or another been made the scapegoats for family decline in the United States.

5   Longing for a more orderly, mythic past is most commonly associated with the conservative position on the family politics spectrum, and it would be easy to caricature the nostalgia for a family modeled on the classic 1950s television sitcom as the sum total of this side of the family values debate. But if we assume that concerns about The Family, writ large, are only those of conservative politicians attempting to manipulate public sentiment, we would overlook the vast reservoir of social anxiety about contemporary family life that is also being tapped by many others from a variety of political and social perspectives: working mothers who are consumed with worry about childcare; white Christian men who, by the tens of thousands in the late 1990s, attended Promise Keepers revivals that focused on renewing their traditional roles as husbands and fathers; adolescents seeking the emotional attachment of family ties among peers and in gangs when it is found lacking in their own homes; com-

mitted gay and lesbian couples fighting for inclusion in the legal definition of family even as they retain a skeptical stance toward this fundamentally heterosexual institution. Why such concern about the family? One reason is that the metaphor evoked by family is a powerful one. A family is defined not so much by a particular set of people as by the quality of relationships that bind them together. What seems to many to be the constant feature of family life is not a specific form or structure but the meanings and the set of personal, intimate relationships families provide against the backdrop of the impersonal, bureaucratized world of modern society.

6   The core sentiments of family life that define the nature and meaning of this social institution for most Americans are unconditional love, attachment, nurturance, and dependability. The hope that these qualities are common to family relationships accounts for the shock with which we react to reports of violence, abuse, and neglect occurring inside the sanctuary of the private home. In popular culture, as in real life, stories of families beset by jealousy, envy, lust, and hatred rather than by the ideals of love, loyalty, and commitment provide an endless source of titillation and fascination. Family stories are not only the stuff of life we construct through our daily experience but the narrative form used to entice us as consumers into a marketplace adept at presenting all sorts of products as invested with emotional qualities and social relationships.

7   The widely promoted "Reach Out and Touch Someone" advertising campaign developed by AT&T in 1978 was a prototype of this genre. In this set of ads, a powerful multinational company hoped to pull at the heartstrings and the pocketbooks of the consuming public by promoting itself as the crucial communication link between family members separated by great global distances. The copy in the print advertisements told heartwarming personal tales of mothers and sons, uncles and nephews, and grandmothers and grandchildren reunited by AT&T's implied commitment to family values, albeit at long distance phone rates. The family metaphor works as an advertising ploy because there is widespread sentimentality in American society about family life. What makes families so compelling for those of us who actively choose to live in them, as well as for those of us who just as actively reject them as oppressively confining, is that families reside at the intersection of our most personal experience and of our social lives. They are institutions we make, yet they are in no small part also constructed by cultural myths and social forces beyond any individual's control.

8   A desire for the kind of care and connection provided by the ideal family cuts across class, race, and ethnic lines in the United States. A commitment to family seems to be so widely shared across groups of all kinds in the hybrid mix that makes up American culture as to be nearly universal. It therefore comes as some surprise that the qualities many accept as natural components of family ties today—unconditional love, warmth, enduring attachment—were not the same expectations most American families had until 150 years ago. The historical variations in family life challenge the claim that the family, even within the same culture, has had the same meaning or has offered the same timeless experiences to its members.

9   Assumptions about American family life in the past are widely shared. These include the beliefs that families were large and extended, with most people living in multigenerational households; that marriages occurred at an early age and were

based on permanent, unwavering commitment between spouses; that the ties between kin were stronger and closer than those experienced today; and that family
life in the past was more stable and predictable than it is currently. These assumptions about the family of the past have collectively produced an image that one sociologist has called "the Classical Family of Western Nostalgia." It is the image upon
which politicians and advertisers, among others, routinely draw as they explain contemporary social problems by reference to family breakdown or as they tap consumer desires by associating a product with positive family values and warm family
feeling. The family is a potent symbol in contemporary American society because it
touches our emotional needs for both intimate personal attachments and a sense of
embeddedness in a larger community.

10   Is there truth to the fears that family values are weaker today than in the past—
that children are more vulnerable, adolescents more intractable, adults less depend-
able, and the elderly more needy? In both popular culture and political discourse,
sentimentality and nostalgia about the family have often prevailed, and a social and
historical context for framing the issues has largely been missing. It is important to
challenge the popular understanding of the family as an institution that is biologically based, immutable, and predictable with a more culturally variable and historically grounded view. Because families are central to the way we talk about ourselves and about our social and political lives, they deserve to be studied in their
fullest scope, attached to a real past as well as a present and future.

Academic Perspectives on the Family

11 Assumptions about the nature of the family abound not only in popular culture but
in social science as well. The disciplines of anthropology, sociology, history, and
psychology all have particular orientations to the institution of the family that define
their theoretical positions and research agendas. Among sociologists and anthropologists, for example, a starting premise about the family has been that it is one of the
central organizing institutions of society. Its centrality comes from having the capacity to organize social life quite effectively by regulating sexuality, controlling reproduction, and ensuring the socialization of children who are born within the family unit. Many social science disciplines start with the question "How is society
possible,"? and they recognize that the organization of individuals into family units
is a very effective means of providing social regulation and continuity. Through the
institution of the family, individuals are joined together and given the social and legal sanction to perpetuate their name and traditions through their offspring. Whole
societies are replenished with future generations of leaders and workers.

12   In the early twentieth century, the anthropologist Bronislaw Malinowski made
the argument that the most universal characteristic of family life in all cultures and
all time periods was the "principle of legitimacy." He had noted that the rules for
sexual behavior varied widely across cultures but that control over reproduction was
a common feature of every social order. Every society made the distinction between
those children (legitimate) born to parents who had been culturally and legally sanctioned to reproduce and those children (illegitimate) whose parents were not accorded this sanction. The function of the principle of legitimacy, according to Mali-

nowski, was to ensure that a child born into a society had both an identifiable mother and father. The father might, in fact, not be biologically related to the child, but his recognized sociological status as father was the affiliation that gave the child a set of kin and a social placement in that social order.

13   In addition to being the only sanctioned setting for reproduction, families are important sources of social continuity because they are most often the setting in which children are cared for and raised. The power of social forces is such that parents normally can be counted on to provide long-term care for their dependent children because the emotional closeness of family bonds makes them *want* to do so. Families are therefore particularly effective institutions because they press people into service for their kin by the dual imperatives of love and obligation. Although it is possible that food, shelter, physical care, and emotional nurturance could be provided through alternative means by the state or other centrally administered bureaucratic agencies, it would require considerable societal resources and effort to ensure that these needs were effectively met for a majority of individuals in a society. What families seem to provide naturally, societies would otherwise have to coordinate and regulate at great cost.

14   To argue that families are effective or efficient as social institutions is not, however, to claim that they are necessary or inevitable. One common fallacy that some sociologists have promoted in studying the family at the societal level is the equation of its prevalence with the idea that it is functionally necessary. The assumption that societies "need" families in order to continue, based on the observation that some form of family exists in all known societies, ignores the range of variation in or the exceptions to this institution. Individuals and subgroups within all societies have constructed alternative arrangements to the traditional family of parents and their children. But the very fact that they are considered alternatives or experimental social organizations suggests how powerful the dominant family norm continues to be.

15   Another assumption that is shared across several social science disciplines is that family harmony and stability constitute the basis for order and control in the larger society. From this perspective, the family is a microcosm of the larger society, and social regulation in the domestic sphere helps promote order and control at all social levels. Individual social analysts might alternatively celebrate or lament the kind of control, regulation, and social order that was understood to begin in the family and radiate outward to the larger society; but the assumption that society was built on the foundation of the family was rarely challenged.

16   As a microcosm or a miniature society of the rulers and the ruled who are bound together by reciprocal rights and obligations, the family helps maintain social order first by its capacity to place people in the social system. It does so by providing them with identifiable kin and establishing the lines of legitimate succession and inheritance that mark their economic, political, and social position in society. Because individuals are located in an established social hierarchy by their birth or adoption into a particular family group, the nature of power and access to resources in a society remain largely intact from one generation to the next. Thus, one meaning of the family as a central institution of the social order is that it reinforces the political and economic status quo. Families ensure that the distribution of resources both to the advantaged and disadvantaged will remain relatively stable, since the

transmission of wealth, property, status, and opportunity is channeled along the lines of kinship.

17   In another important way, families help to regulate the social order. Family life, according to both law and custom, prescribes roles for men, women, and children. Although these roles are really the products of social and cultural forces rather than biological imperatives and are therefore highly fluid in times of change, they appear to most people to be prescribed by stable and immutable rules governing everyday life. The meaning of "traditional" family life is that people are conscripted into established roles. Everyone knows his or her place and tends to keep to it by the pressures of community norms and social sanctions. But such traditional family roles exact a toll, as well. What promotes social harmony and order to the advantage of some produces severe constraints on others. Women and children, whose roles in the family have traditionally been subordinate to those of men, have sometimes resisted such prescriptive expectations and have led the charge for social change in both overt and covert ways. It is not surprising that in times of rapid social change the family has been identified as an inherently conservative institution, one that not only helps to perpetuate the status quo but is perceived as being oppressively restrictive to many of its own members.

18   Although many changes have characterized American family life over time, we should be mindful of important continuities as well. The most striking continuity is the importance that the family holds for so many people. The reasons that the family is important have varied historically, but there is no doubt that it has been a central institution, one on which people have pinned all manner of beliefs, values, and prejudices, as well as fears about and hopes for the future. Families reside at the intersection of private and public experience. We are all experts, since most of us have lived within one or more families at some point in our lives. Families can house both our highest hopes and our greatest disappointments, and their fragility or resilience therefore carries great personal meaning, in addition to social significance. The novelist Amos Oz has called the family "the most mysterious, most secret institution in the world." Its mysteries and secrets are not fully revealed in the social and historical record, but in reconstructing some of the patterns of family life we can begin to understand why it has continued to play such a central role in American culture, as an organizing social institution, a lived experience, and a powerful metaphor. ◆

FREEWRITING ASSIGNMENT

Farrell notes that in a 1996 poll on moral values, 78 percent of respondents said that they were dissatisfied with today's moral values, but that only 11 percent believed that their own behavior had contributed to this moral decline. What is your own opinion about today's moral values, and how does your own behavior fit in with these values?

CRITICAL READING

1. Evaluate Farrell's opening joke about Adam and Eve. How does it connect to her material? Is it an effective means of drawing in readers and orienting them to her topic?

2. Farrell notes that Americans want their families to "offer unconditional love yet also to enforce and uphold strict moral values. They want flexibility, mobility, and autonomy . . . but yearn for traditional communities and permanently stable families" (paragraph 2). What, according to the author, is problematic with this yearning? Do you agree? Explain.

3. In her third paragraph, Farrell discusses our social fear of change. How does our fear of change connect to the practice of scapegoating? Identify some social scapegoats of the last century—for what were they blamed, and why? Who "represent the forces of the new" today?

4. Farrell comments that our social concern for "The Family" is rooted in the "metaphor evoked by family" (paragraph 5). What does she mean? How does she define family in this paragraph, and how does this definition connect to our social concerns about the decay of the family in general? Explain.

5. How do we construct the institution of the family? What cultural myths and social forces contribute to our construction of this institution? How does nostalgia influence our view as well? Explain.

6. According to Farrell, what assumptions about family span many academic disciplines, such as anthropology, sociology, history, and psychology? How do these assumptions form the basis for the theoretical approaches of these disciplines? Explain.

7. How do families "help to regulate the social order" (paragraph 17)? How can this regulation "exact a toll" on certain members of society? Do you agree or disagree with Farrell's assessment? Explain.

CRITICAL WRITING

8. *Exploratory Writing*: At the end of her essay, Farrell quotes novelist Amos Oz who calls the family "the most mysterious, most secret institution in the world." Write an essay in which you explore this idea. How is the family "secret"? If almost everyone has a family and understands what the term implies, how can it be "mysterious"? Support your position with information from Farrell's article as well as your own personal perspective.

9. *Research and Analysis*: If you are a practicing member of an organized religious faith, research your religion's beliefs on family. If you are not a member of an organized religion, select one to research. Be sure to include references from news sources, journals, theologians, religious texts, and spiritual leaders of the faith. If possible, interview a religious leader for a summary of beliefs. Write an essay in which you describe the position the religious faith has on family, and how these beliefs are "institutionalized" in the religion.

10. *Exploratory Writing*: In a letter to a politician or public figure of your choice, discuss the current state of the family as it applies to the concept of family as an institution in American culture. In your letter, you should make specific references to the politician's own stance on the state of the family.

GROUP PROJECTS

11. Design and administer a poll to people outside your class. Ask for opinions on the health of the American family versus its decline, the ideal role each family member should play in family structure, the desirability of day care, and so on. Also ask for anonymous information about each participant's age, economic status, education, political affiliation, religion, and race. After you have assembled the data you collected as a group, analyze the results. Do any groups seem more or less optimistic about the state of the American family? If so, in what ways? Are some groups more "traditional"? Explain.

12. Farrell notes that although politicians and social conservatives attribute social ills to failings within the institution of family, there are other forces that help formulate popular opinion about the family. Visit the American Family Association (AFA) web site at *www.afa.org* and evaluate its social and political stance on family. What conventions does it embrace, and how does it feel about "nontraditional" family structures? What outside forces, according to the AFA, threaten today's families? Explain.

The New Nostalgia
Rosalind C. Barnett and Caryl Rivers

As Betty G. Farrell explained in the preceding essay, most Americans today feel the family is in a state of decline. Underlying this feeling is the social sense that the decay of the family is linked to the loss of "traditional family" values held in the 1950s. However, in this article, Rosalind C. Barnett and Caryl Rivers tell us that we're actually in much better shape than we think we are. Rather than apologizing for the state of our families, Barnett and Rivers say we should start appreciating our amazing adaptability. In fact, the very "problems" that critics of new family structures want to fix may actually be creating more stable families and healthier relationships.

Rosalind C. Barnett is a clinical psychologist and expert on dual-earner issues, job-related stress, the American family, and work/family relations. She is a senior research scientist in the women's studies program at Brandeis University. Caryl Rivers is a professor of journalism at Boston University and the author of several books, including *Slick Spins and Fractured Facts: How Cultural Myths Distort the News* (1996). This piece is excerpted from the author's book, *He Works/She Works* (1996).

CRITICAL THINKING Are you familiar with the television programs *Leave it to Beaver*, *Father Knows Best*, *Ozzie and Harriet*, and *The Donna Reed Show*? If so, what kinds of families were portrayed in each? What was the established family structure, and how was this structure conveyed in these programs?

1   As he drops his daughter off at a very good day-care center staffed with well-trained, caring professionals, a father worries whether he's doing the right thing. Should he or his wife stay home with their daughter, even though they can't afford to? Will day care cause some problems for his child that he can't foresee? Is he doing something dreadfully wrong because his life is so different from that of his parents back in the 1960s?

2   Guilt is the universal malady of working parents today, and one to which parents in past generations were seemingly immune. Did the woman setting out in the covered wagon for a prairie homestead worry about whether her children would be well-adjusted out there on the plains? Did the women in colonial times, whose days were filled with manufacturing the clothing and food that would keep the family alive, brood about whether she and her children were "relating" well enough? Did Victorian men worry that their children were spending too much time with nannies?

3   It's safe to say that no modern working parent has completely escaped those sudden, painful stabs of guilt. It might help to understand its roots, and we will examine them in this essay. But first, it's important to realize how this guilt feeds into the mistaken conviction that today's parents can't quite measure up to those of the past.

4   It is imperative, we believe, to understand that those of us in the two-earner lifestyle have been as good or better parents—not worse ones—than the Ozzie and Harriet model. The two-earner lifestyle that has emerged in the past two decades of American life has been a positive development, fitting well with current economic realities. While it has not been easy, men and women have connected to the world of work and its demands while expending considerable energies on nurturing their children. If this meant that at times they felt they had to juggle too much, that there were times they wondered if they were going to be able to do it all, they lived with that problem—and, most often, survived it in good health and good humor.

5   We are already raising a generation of children in two-earner families; if we really want them to be stressed, let's tell them that what we are doing is all wrong, that what we should be doing was what their grandparents did in the 1950s, and that that's the ideal they, too, should aspire to.

6   In fact, we must prepare our children for the world they will really be facing—not some rosy image of a past that never was all that wonderful, and which is not going to return. With a global economy on the horizon and with the United States continually having to compete with the Pacific Rim and Europe, we will probably continue to see a pattern of downsizing of U.S. companies as high productivity becomes the watchword of industry. Men's real wages have been declining since 1960: The median income of employed white men in 1967 was about $19,800; by 1987 it was $19,008, adjusted for changes in earning power—roughly $750 less than it had been twenty years before.[1]

7   More and more, women's wages will become essential to a family's economic survival—as they are today in so many families. The days when women worked for "extras" are long gone and are not likely to return. More and more, in such an unstable work world, men will turn to their families as a way of finding self-esteem. And women, like men, will prepare early for careers or jobs in which they will be involved for most of their lives. Economists who predict the shape of the early twenty-

first century say that no longer will people remain in one job for a lifetime; the successful worker of the future will be one who is flexible, learns quickly, and can transfer skills from one work setting to another. Women may have to retool as the economy twists and turns, but few will have the chance to be full-time, lifelong homemakers.

8   Not until we accept the working woman as the norm can we adequately prepare our sons and daughters for the lives they will really be leading. Our study conclusively proves that holding up the rigid and outdated lifestyle of the 1950s as a sacred icon will only add stress to their busy and often difficult lives. Perhaps the most important finding of the study on which the book is based is the fact that for working couples, a gap in gender-role ideology is a major and consistent source of stress. It is not merely annoying when your image of the ideal family does not jibe with that of your spouse; it can be an important source of stress in your life.

9   On the whole, we do not help young women prepare for the flexible jobs that will protect their economic futures and that of their families if we plant in their heads the idea that what they really ought to be doing is staying home. We don't prepare young men for the deep involvement they are going to have with their families if we create in them the idea that the real man doesn't change a diaper or drive the kids to nursery school.

10   But the actual facts about what is good for real American couples and their families today may well be drowned out by the clamor of what we call the "new nostalgia," a combination of longing for the past and a fear of change. It not only feeds the guilt that can tie individuals in knots, but can be a major stumbling block to the creation of corporate and government policies that will help, not hinder, working families. The new nostalgia has already calcified in politics, in the media, in a spate of books that tell us we must retreat to the past to find solutions for the future. The messages of a reinvigorated right wing in politics pushes a brand of family values with which Ozzie and Harriet would have felt quite at home.

11   One steady, unblinking beacon of a message has been flashed to men and women over the past few years: Change is dangerous, change is abnormal, change is unhealthy. This message permeates our mass media, the books we read, the newscasts to which we listen, the advice from pop psychologists, the covers of news magazines. Men and women must stay in their traditional places, or there will be hell to pay.

12   The message comes in many guises. It comes from warnings that women are working themselves into sickness on the so-called second shift—the housework women do after they come home from work—doing so much that their health is in peril. It may be national magazines trumpeting the mommy track, concluding that women must seek achievement on a lower and slower track than men. It nests in headlines that claim women are simply unable to juggle the demands of work and home and are going to start having heart attacks just like men. It may be warnings that day care interferes with the mother-child bond—despite solid evidence to the contrary. It can be found in publications concluding that if people would just stay married or kids would stop having sex, all our social problems would disappear. It may be Robert Bly warning in *Iron John* that men have become weak, thanks to women, and they must find their warrior within.[2]

13   It is more than a backlash against the women's movement. Indeed, many of the warnings insist that men had better stay in the straitjacket of traditional masculinity. These warnings are implicit in the spate of action-adventure movies aimed at young men, in which manhood is defined as domination and mayhem, with no ongoing relationships with women or children. They are implicit also in the ease with which the word "wimp" is hurled at any political candidate who does not employ slash-and-burn macho tactics.

14   The flashing message is only intensified by widely held but outdated ideas from the behavioral sciences proclaiming that a man's emotional health is primarily based on his life at work, while a woman can only find her identity through being a wife and mother. So intense has this bias been that, until recently, social scientists rarely examined men's lives at home or women's at work.

15   The new nostalgia fuels the guilt that many working parents feel. The flames are fanned by forces that many working parents don't understand—and the media play a large role in keeping the bonfire going.

16   Never in the past were parents confronted with constant and ongoing images of how their grandparents raised children. Old folk remedies may have been passed down, mothers and grandmothers gave advice, but times changed and people changed with them. It was the natural order of things. But parents today see Ozzie and Harriet and Donna Reed and all their ilk as wonderful, ideal parents night after night on the tube. (Even the President and the First Lady, whose lives resemble most working families' more than those of the old sitcoms, admitted that one of their favorite TV shows was reruns of *The Donna Reed Show.*)

17   The power those TV parents still exercise has more to do with the durability of images than it does with today's reality. As Newsweek magazine points out, "The television programs of the fifties and sixties validated a family style during a period in which today's leaders—congressmen, corporate executives, university professors, magazine editors—were growing up or beginning to establish their own families. (The impact of the idealized family was magnified by the very size of the postwar generation.)"[3]

18   It can be somewhat frightening to think that the legislators who are voting on family leave plans, the aides who create policies for presidential candidates, the chairs of university departments who decide what courses should be staffed—all have inside their heads the very same model of the way our families ought to be.

19   Yale historian John Demos points out that "the traditional model reaches back as far as personal memory goes for most of us who currently teach and write and philosophize."[4] And in a time when parents seem to feel a great deal of change, "that image is comfortingly solid and secure, counterpoint to what we think is threatening to the future." In other words, an unreal past seems so much more soothing than a bumpy present.

20   In the manufacture of guilt, add another potent factor: the nature of the news media. The news media don't hold a mirror up to the world, despite what news executives like to say. The media not only select which facts and images will be churned out as news, but they determine the frame in which those images will be presented. This frame is most often one of conflict, tension, and bad news. It's no wonder everyone assumes that the American family is falling apart. That's all we read or hear about.

21   Of course, what the TV news anchor doesn't tell you is that in the past, "family" issues were rarely part of the news. Domestic violence and child abuse were shameful secrets, rarely written about. Dramatic images of violent crime were less a part of daily life. In Washington, D.C., where Caryl Rivers grew up in the 1950s, some 90 percent of crimes by young men were committed by juveniles who were graduates of one city reform school. But you never saw their victims on the evening news—because there were no minicams to capture the mayhem on video and the kids didn't spray the streets with automatic weapons fire. Americans now consume many hours of television each day—and research shows that people who watch a lot of TV see the world as a much more frightening place than it really is.

22   One of the bad-news frames of which the media is most fond today is the decline of the family. A Nexis search of the past five years reveals 15,164 references in the press to either the breakup or the decline of the American Family, a chorus that is relentless. Do you believe that the decline of the family is absolute fact? Many Americans do. However, most media coverage of the alleged decline of the family does not answer a key question: What position of lofty perfection is the family declining from? There must have been a golden age of family, since the words *decline* and *breakdown* imply that very notion. But when was it? And do we really want to go back there? . . . Many Americans believe that past family life was always—and should always be—like *Leave It to Beaver, Father Knows Best,* and *Ozzie and Harriet.*

23   In fact, the 1950s were a golden age—economically. Never before had Americans enjoyed a period of such affluence. Women reversed a long-standing trend of moving into the workforce, and went home. One would have thought that with women in such a traditional role, social critics would have approved. Mom was by the hearth with her kiddies nestled about her. But what happened? In perhaps no decade were women savaged as thoroughly as they were in the 1950s. Sweet Mom, baking cookies and smiling, was destroying her kids—the boys, anyway. While nostalgic articles in today's media hark back to the happy 1950s, the critics of the time had no such beatific vision.

24   Social critic Philip Wylie, in his best-seller *Generation of Vipers,* coined the term "Momism." Momism, Wylie decreed, had turned modern men into flaccid and weak creatures and was destroying the moral fiber of America.[5] When American soldiers sometimes failed to resist "brainwashing" when they were captured by the Communist Chinese in Korea, it was said that their overprotective mothers had made them weak and traitorous. Children often got too much Mom and not enough Dad. The memoirs of men who grew up in the 1950s reveal that their fathers were often distant and overly involved in work.

25   It's not surprising that depression was the malady that most affected women in those years. What Betty Friedan termed "the feminine mystique" came smack up against the lengthening life span. At a time when society was telling women that home and children must be their whole lives, technology and medicine were making those lives last longer than ever before in history. Women would outlive, by many years, the childhood of their last-born, and the notion that they could spend all their time in mothering was absurd. The cultural messages and the reality of the modern world were at odds. Kept out of the world of work in the suburban cocoons, physically healthier and longer-lived than their sisters in the past, women were far more

prone than men to depression, and in fact the mental health of married women had reached crisis proportions by the end of the 1960s. Statistics rolling in from all across the developed world were so grim that the noted sociologist Jessie Bernard called marriage a "health hazard" for women.[6] . . .

26   One reason we hear so much today about how wonderful the 1950s were is that the voices of male cultural critics are those most often heard. Men and women, it seems, remember that era differently. In many ways, the 1950s were good for men. It was the first era in history in which the average middle-class man could, on his salary alone, support a lifestyle that was available only to the upper classes in the past. The mental health of men was vastly superior to that of women. The daughters of 1950s homemakers rejected en masse a lifestyle that created so much depression and anxiety, and few women today would trade their lives for that of their mothers. But many men today would gladly opt for the financial security and economic opportunities their fathers had.

27   Because the 1950s live on endlessly in rerun land, it is hard for us to accept that the decade was such an atypical time. Stephanie Coontz warns that "the first thing to understand about the Fifties family is that it was a fluke, it was a seven-year aberration in contradiction to a hundred years of other trends."[7] And Arlene Skolnick notes that "far from being the last era of family normality from which current trends are a deviation, it is the family patterns of the 1950s that are deviant."

28   Deviant? Ozzie and Harriet? Indeed they were, from the point of view of history. Theirs was an atypical era, in which trends that had been firmly established since early in the century briefly reversed themselves in the aftermath of World War II. For years, women had been moving into the workforce in increasing numbers. The high point was epitomized by Rosie the Riveter, the symbol of the women who went to work in the factories to produce the tanks and the guns and the planes needed to win the war. After the war, during the brief period of unprecedented affluence when America's economic engine was unchallenged throughout the world, women went home, and the American birthrate suddenly jumped to approach that of India. A huge baby-boom generation grew up in middle-class affluence that no other generation had known. . . .

29   By the late 1970s, the 1950s were only a distant echo. The women's movement unleashed women's untapped brainpower and economic potential, and millions of women flooded into the marketplace. This movement of women into the workforce in the late twentieth century is one of the great mass migrations of history, comparable to the push westward and the move from the farms to the cities. And just as those mass movements changed not only the face of American society but the lives of individual citizens, so too did this new movement rearrange our social geography.

30   Despite the media drumbeat about the decline of the family, despite those thousands of references to its decay in the media, the American family is a thriving institution. We are both more centered on the family and more frantic about its problems than our European counterparts. Arlene Skolnick writes, "Paradoxically, Americans have a stronger sense of both familistic values and family crisis than do other advanced countries. We have higher marriages rates, a more home-centered way of life, and greater public devotion to family values."[8]

31   The notion that we can return to some mythic past for solutions to today's problems is tempting, but it is a will-o'-the-wisp that should not engage our attention.

The idea that we can find in Ozzie and Harriet and their lives workable solutions for today's rapidly changing economic and social patterns is a dream. Unfortunately, when we combine the new nostalgia with the old images, it's like taking a trip with only a 1955 road map to guide us. The old landmarks are gone, little backroads have become interstates, and the rules of the road have changed beyond recognition. Absurd as this image is, it is often precisely what we do when we think about the American family. Women who hurry out to work every morning can be trapped into thinking that this isn't what they are supposed to be doing; men with their hands in soapsuds after dinner can remember their fathers sitting and reading the newspaper while mom did the dishes. It's easy to feel resentful.

32   But the new nostalgia is more than harmless basking in the trivia of the past—it is, in fact, a major toxin affecting the health of today's men and women.

33   The "family values" crusade of the right wing, to the degree that it succeeds in invading people's thoughts, will only add to the stress of working couples by insisting on a model from the past that is increasingly impossible to achieve in the present. One newspaper poll showed that the proportion of adults who agreed with the statement "A preschool child is likely to suffer if his or her mother works" went up between 1989 and 1991.

34   As science, that statement is nonsense. There is plenty of evidence that no child is "likely to suffer" if his or her mother goes to work. But those adults agreeing with that statement—who are likely to be working parents—will get a huge dose of unnecessary stress. The family values crusade, to the extent that it glorifies homemakers and demonizes working mothers, will succeed only in making the lives of twenty-first-century Americans harder. The clock will not be turned back to the 1950s; that's as impossible as holding back the tide. If Americans feel guilty because they can't live up to some impossible, vanished ideal, their health will suffer.

35   The era of the two-earner couple may in fact create more closeness in families, not less. As the fast track becomes less available, men and women alike will turn to family for a strong sense of self-esteem and happiness. Divorces may decline as marriages become once again economic partnerships more like the ones they were before the industrial revolution. Today, of course, marriages will be overlaid with the demands for intimacy and closeness that have become a permanent part of modern marriage, but fewer people will be able to waltz easily out of marriage, as they might have in the days when a thriving economy made good jobs easy to come by. Middle-class couples are marrying later and many women are getting established in a career before having children. This pattern may promote more responsibility and happier marriages than those in the 1950s, when many young people felt they had to get married to have sex and discovered their emotional incompatibility only after they had children.

36   Negotiation and juggling, not the established gender roles of yesterday's marriages, are the features of modern coupledom. Who will stay home when a child is sick? Who will take over what jobs when one partner has to travel for an important meeting? Whose career will take first place? Who has to sacrifice what—and when? Such issues, ones that June and Ward and Ozzie and Harriet never had to confront, are the day-to-day problems that today's partners have to wrestle with.

37   Today's couples are facing the demands of very busy lives at home and at work. If you listen to the media tell their story, they are constantly stressed, the women are

disenchanted with trying to have it all, and the men are bitter about having to do work their fathers never had to do. Some of this is true—no lifestyle offers nirvana. On the other hand, today's couples have a better chance at achieving full, rich lives than did the men and women of the sitcom generation. While it may be no picnic to juggle the demands of work and family, research shows that working women are less depressed, less anxious, and more zestful about their lives than are homemakers. Today's man may have the stress of caring for children, but his relationship with his children may be warmer and more satisfying than was his own with his father. Most men who grew up in the 1950s don't tell stories about the warm, available dads we see in the sitcoms. More often, they speak of fathers who were distant, preoccupied, and unable to communicate with their sons on more than a superficial level. Many modern fathers, in fact, set out purposely to design lives that will be the exact opposite of their distant fathers'.

38   In their lifestyle, the men and women in our study are at the opposite end of the spectrum from Ozzie and Harriet. Both are breadwinners; and if they have children, both share the nitty-gritty everyday chores of parenting. They are true partners in supporting and nurturing their children and each other. They represent the new face of the American family, and the world they live in is not very much like the America of the 1950s.

39   Despite the ersatz glow of the new nostalgia, not much would be gained by a trip back in time—even if it were possible. How many women would want to return to the widespread depression and mental health problems of the 1950s? Catherine E. Ross, an Illinois University sociologist, says, "Any plea to return to the 'traditional' family of the 1950s is a plea to return wives and mothers to a psychologically disadvantaged position, in which husbands have much better health than wives."[9] And since research shows that the emotional health of the mother has a strong impact on her children, that's one bit of time travel we don't especially want to take. ◆

Notes

1. Janet Riblett Wilkie, "The Decline in Men's Labor Force Participation and Income and the Changing Structure of Family Economic Support," *Journal of Marriage and the Family* 53 (February 1991).
2. Robert Bly, *Iron John* (New York: Holiday House, 1994).
3. "What Happened to the Family?" *Newsweek* Special Issue (Winter 1990/Spring 1991).
4. "What Happened to the Family?" (Winter 1990/Spring 1991).
5. Philip Wylie, *Generation of Vipers* (New York: Holt, Rinehart & Winston, 1955).
6. Jessie Bernard, *The Future of Marriage* (New York: World-Times, 1972).
7. Stephanie Coontz, *The Way We Never Were: American Families and the Nostalgia Trap* (New York: Basic Books, 1992).
8. Cited in Arlene Skolnick, *Embattled Paradise: The American Family in an Age of Uncertainty* (New York: Basic Books, 1991).
9. Quoted in Betsy A. Lehman, "Parenting Pain—But Also Joy," *Boston Globe* (February 15, 1993).

FREEWRITING ASSIGNMENT

Why do parents in two-earner families feel guilty? What is the cause of their guilt and how is it perpetuated? How founded are their fears?

CRITICAL READING

1. What is "gender-role ideology" as described in paragraph 8? In paragraphs 8–14, how are traditional roles described as harmful to men? How do the authors feel about the current men's movement urging men to "find their warrior within"? How can you tell their opinions on this movement?
2. What are the authors' attitudes toward change—specifically toward changes in family roles and responsibilities? What phrases, images, and metaphors help you identify their attitudes in paragraphs 11–22?
3. The authors describe what the 1950s were really like for families in paragraphs 23–28. What were some of the problems these families had? What were some of the problems people faced fitting into these families? Why have we adopted this family model as the ideal?
4. Based on their response to the poll question in paragraphs 33 and 34, what do you think Barnett and Rivers would say to Barbara Dafoe Whitehead (later in this chapter) about the need to change divorce rates and policies? Do you think these authors would agree that marriages should be child-centered? Explain.
5. What improvements do the authors see in today's families? Why do they believe such families are becoming stronger, rather than falling apart? Do you agree with their conclusions? Explain.
6. What are the authors' attitudes toward the media? (See paragraphs 13, 20, and 21.) How important to their argument is the media's role in shaping American perceptions about the state of the family?

CRITICAL WRITING

7. *Exploratory Writing*: If you are a parent, or if you are thinking about marriage and children in your future, do you (or would you) feel the kind of guilt that Barnett and Rivers describe in this article? If so, what do you think would help you feel less guilty—support from family and friends? Different government policies? Media messages? More and better child-care facilities? Other factors? Explore your perspective in a well-considered essay.
8. *Personal Narrative*: Write a personal narrative in which you describe the structure of your family during your childhood. How does your family compare to the family situations described in this article? Did your family strive for the 1950s "ideal"? Explain.

GROUP PROJECTS

9. Working in small groups, discuss and compare the structures of families within your own experiences. Think about the families you grew up in, the families you know well, and the families you may have started. Evaluate the kinds of families you find. These may include two-earner families, traditional families, families with no children, blended families with stepparents and children, children raised by other relatives, and other groupings. Compare notes with your group. How well do your results match the description offered by Barnett and Rivers?

10. Working in small groups, research criticism and scholarly discussion of the four television shows the authors mention in this article, and try to watch a few episodes of each show. How do these shows reflect our expectations for family roles and values? Select four current programs that use a family unit as their central theme. How do the current programs compare to these 1950s prototypes?

Are the Conservatives Right?
Alex Kotlowitz

Recent decades have witnessed a shift in how society views single parenthood. High divorce rates and changing attitudes toward unwed motherhood are partially responsible for this shift. But is this greater acceptance of single parenthood good for children and their parents? Statistics reveal that children living in single-parent households are more likely to live in poverty and do less well academically. In fact, the government is initiating programs in some areas of the country to encourage marriages. Can government help poor communities by promoting marriage? In this essay, reporter Alex Kotlowitz discusses this issue prepared for a *Frontline* program, "Let's Get Married."

Alex Kotlowitz is the author of *There Are No Children Here: The Story of Two Boys Growing Up in the Other America* (1991) and *The Other Side of the River: A Story of Two Towns, a Death and America's Dilemma* (1998). His work has appeared in the *New Yorker,* the *New York Times Magazine,* the *Washington Post,* the *Chicago Tribune, Rolling Stone,* the *Atlantic Monthly* and the *New Republic.* He is currently a writer-in-residence at Northwestern University. This article first appeared on the *Frontline* web site for the program segment, "Let's Get Married," which aired in November of 2002.

CRITICAL THINKING   What is your opinion of single parenthood? Has society become too accepting of parents who decide to raise children out of wedlock?

1   There's not a single bridal shop on Chicago's West Side. Indeed, as an institution, marriage has virtually disappeared from inner-city communities. In the 10 years

since I wrote *There Are No Children Here*, which follows two young boys growing up in public housing on the West Side, I've been to half a dozen funerals in the neighborhood and only one wedding—and that marriage has since ended in divorce. In some impoverished urban communities, as few as one out of ten children are born to married parents.

2　For the families I got to know in Chicago while writing that book, marriage just didn't seem relevant. So many of the men were unemployed. The women were doing yeoman jobs while raising children. Their immediate concerns—like paying the rent or keeping their kids safe from the street violence or pushing the neighborhood school to do better by their children—seemed much weightier and more urgent than getting married. One friend who got out of the projects has moved to the suburbs with her partner and their seven children. She now works at a bank. Mother and father have been together for 19 years, and only now—finally feeling stable—has marriage entered the equation.

3　The Bush administration is pushing marriage as part of its welfare-reform strategy, the idea being that marriage can help lift people out of poverty. With the Republicans' victory in the mid-term elections, it now seems likely that Congress will indeed set aside funding for programs that promote marriage among the poor. A liberal friend of mine who runs an extraordinary program for inner-city children in Chicago declared this marriage push "nuts." Admittedly, that was my instinctive reaction as well. But while reporting this story, I've come to realize that there's been a shift in the winds. Could it be that the conservatives are on to something?

4　As we set out to make the documentary, we decided we should first go to the places where the marriage movement has taken hold. So we traveled to Oklahoma, the one state that has a significant pro-marriage program in place.

5　A few years ago, Oklahoma's governor, Frank Keating, had been concerned about the state's sagging economy, so he went to some local economists for advice. It turned out that Oklahoma—the buckle of the Bible Belt—had the second-highest divorce rate in the nation, second only to Nevada's. Stem the tide of divorce, the economists told Keating, and the state's high poverty rate would decrease.

6　So Keating set aside $10 million, a modest amount of money, to teach welfare recipients relationship skills. I sat in on some of those classes, and found the training benign enough, if unproven. The lessons were mostly on communication and sexuality. It was like Dr. Phil writ large. The thought that these quickie lessons were going to somehow change people's lives seemed awfully optimistic. In one class in Duncan, a small town in southern Oklahoma, virtually all of the women were running from relationships (many of them abusive), and yet they sat through four days of lessons on how better to communicate with their spouse. (To the instructor's credit, she realized the irony of the situation, and so steered much of the conversation to improving their relationships with their children.)

7　In Edin, a conservative small town in the northern part of the state, we met a teenaged couple. The girl, a junior in high school, was pregnant. She and her boyfriend had a contentious relationship, gushing over with teenaged melodrama, and whenever we visited we were never certain whether they'd be together or whether they'd be sparring. The girl attended one of the state's relationship training sessions at her high school. Brenda, a state worker who goes into the schools to teach family and consumer sciences, was running the session, and it turned out that Brenda's daughter was best friends with the girl, so Brenda knew her well. Brenda wanted her to get married, and even tried—unsuccessfully—to talk with the boyfriend.

8   I watched all of this unfold with some uneasiness. It seemed to be a case of government playing cupid. In the end, I'm not sure it's any of our business whether this couple stays together, let alone marries. And while yes, two parents might be best for this child, it was unclear that this couple, given their differences, would last—even with counseling.

9   From Oklahoma we traveled to Madison, Wisconsin, to hear Mike McManus, a pioneer of the marriage movement. McManus is essentially a marriage salesman. He goes from city to city, preaching to ministers and priests about the need to offer both pre-marital and marriage counseling. It's a fairly simple message: Let's take marriage more seriously. But listening to McManus made marriage feel like such a deliberate exercise. McManus has a questionnaire he uses to make sure that engaged couples are compatible. He's also given to moralizing, some of which can be alienating—as when he suggests that the collapse of marriage "creates monsters" because it leads to a greater likelihood that children will drop out of school or get involved in delinquency activity. Not exactly language that will win people over. Indeed, many in this young marriage movement look to stigmatize single parenthood. This seems both wrongheaded and misguided, especially since single parents are the very constituency the movement is trying to reach.

10   We then visited Chattanooga, Tenn., where a local organization, First Things First, was sponsoring a public contest in which the prize was an all-expenses paid wedding, honeymoon included. Couples sent in photos and wrote essays, and local television viewers voted for the most deserving of them. There were strings attached, however. The couples had to abstain from premarital sex and participate in premarital counseling. The organization had a strong Christian underpinning, and, again, as with McManus, moralizing played a big role.

11   To be honest, at this point I wasn't sure we had much of a program. None of this seemed terribly relevant to the poor, especially the urban poor. Marriage isn't part of the inner-city landscape. What's more, can you imagine someone like McManus extolling marriage to single mothers there, telling them that if they don't get married they're going to "create monsters"? The conservative Christian tone gave the movement a sense of piety. There were strong judgments made about single mothers. It wasn't uncommon to hear references to "illegitimate children," a term that for a while, at least, had disappeared from the lexicon.

12   What, I asked myself, does the marriage movement have to offer people in inner-city communities?

13   Back in Chicago, one of the first things I did was to sit down with a group of grandmothers from a hardscrabble neighborhood on the city's South Side. I was surprised, in part, by how much they sounded like the Bible Belt conservatives I'd met, at least inasmuch as they were dismayed at the fact that their children were having children without getting married. They couldn't understand what had happened, why marriage had become such a rarity in their community. They argued that the lo-

cal schools should give classes extolling the benefits of matrimony. They also talked about how the ministers in their churches often used their Sunday sermons to preach about marriage. But they had very different notions as to what answers were called for. They adamantly opposed the idea of government getting involved—and suggested that what would help couples find their way to the altar was not to push them but rather to ease the strains in their lives. More daycare. Better schools. Jobs. Adequate housing.

14   Research would seem to support this. The Fragile Families and Child Wellbeing Study, a long-term survey of 5,000 low-income couples sponsored by a consortium of universities, has found that eight out of ten couples surveyed planned to marry. "I was out in the field all of the time, interviewing low-income single mothers," Kathy Edin, the director of the study, told me. "And what really struck me in those interviews was how many people talked about the desire to get married. And I would go back, you know, and talk to my friends in academia, and they would say, 'Oh, they can't mean that.' But I would hear it again and again."

15   Still, although attitudes appear to be changing, there hasn't been a rush to the altar. In fact, Kathy Edin's survey has found that while most of the couples interviewed intend to wed, they never get there. They view marriage as the last step in life's progression, or as Edin says, "as icing on the cake." First, they want economic security. Remember my friend who grew up in public housing and with her partner of 19 years has raised seven children? She told me she's now considering marrying him. But there's one piece missing. "I really want everything in place," she tells me. "He has to have a job."

16   The news here, though, is that marriage is in the air. Ten years ago, when an African-American minister on the West Side, who speaks of marriage "as a traumatized tradition," tried to talk about the institution from the pulpit, his congregation scoffed at his preaching. But this year his church co-sponsored a marriage celebration, and weekly marriage enrichment classes have been so popular that he's had to put some parishioners on waiting lists. Another minister—a political progressive— will baptize children of unwed parents, but only if the parents agree to come into his office to hear his rap on marriage. In inner-city Baltimore, Joe Jones, who runs one of the nation's premiere fatherhood programs, plans to introduce marriage classes. And the Nation of Islam, which organized the Million Man March, now touts matrimony, calling it "a social institution in need of restoration."

17   If marriage has reentered the zeitgeist of the urban poor, we thought, why not try to find some couples who were considering getting married? I was surprised how easy that was. We went to pre-natal clinics and to two prominent Chicago organizations, the Ounce of Prevention Fund and Family Focus, and met numerous couples who had a child together or were about to give birth. Virtually all talked about getting married. One story in particular, that of Ashaki Hankerson, revealed how the marriage movement understands the need out there—and yet doesn't comprehend all the obstacles that lie in the way.

18   At Family Focus I was invited to sit in a class of single mothers. Afterwards, one of the young women, Ashaki, approached me. "Did you say you were a marriage counselor?" she asked. She was looking for some guidance. She was planning

to marry the father of her last child (she had seven in all) that coming weekend at City Hall, and was having second thoughts about whether she was really ready to exchange vows. She wanted certain things to be in place. She wanted her boyfriend, Steven Thomas, to have a job. That was important to her, and it was understandable. She lived in an apartment which for weeks had no gas service, and so had to cook on a hot plate. She couldn't afford furniture, so her rooms were virtually bare. Moreover, she worried about Steven. An affable, smart young man, he had had trouble finding employment, and when things got tight at home he would sell drugs. He eventually got caught and was sentenced to three months in boot camp.

19   I so hope it works out for them, especially because Steven has become a stand-in-father to all of the children. They're crazy about him. He'd take them to the park. He'd take them to school. He'd help them with their homework. And he got them to love oldies music. In fact, they so abided him, he had the five oldest doing a dance routine to the Temptations' "My Girl." Steven just got out of boot camp this past weekend, and Ashaki told me they still have plans to wed.

20   Talking about marriage can land you on treacherous turf. In 1965, Daniel Patrick Moynihan, then a young deputy in the Department of Labor, issued a report entitled "The Negro Family: The Case for National Action." It suggested that the breakdown of the black family—one-third of all black children at the time lived with only one parent—was keeping African-Americans from finding their way into the middle class. Moynihan was pilloried by progressives, accused of blaming the victim, and in the ensuing decades liberals essentially abdicated the discussion about family to the conservatives. They've had a tough time finding their way back ever since. "We've been dragged into this [conversation] kicking and screaming," one liberal sociologist told me.

21   The conservatives overstate their case when they suggest that marriage will lift people out of poverty. It won't. Certainly not without first easing the economic strains in people's lives. "Two broke people is just broke," the head of a men's group in Chicago told me.

22   Early on in the filming, a woman who directs an organization that works with African-American families laughed when I told her what I was working on. Marriage, she said, is not a subject around here. It's just not relevant to the lives of her clients, she told me. But when I sat down with her a couple of months later, she apologized. She'd given it some thought. Marriage, she said, was clearly critical to her community.

23   "The question is: What can we do to help people get there?" she said. "And not assume that they don't care about it. People do care [about getting married]. But there are so many obstacles in the way."

24   In the end, as Ashaki and Steven's situation made so clear, it all comes down to the kids. Social scientists from both the right and left are finding that, all things being equal, two parents are best for children. Indeed, I've become convinced that marriage, this very private institution, has very public consequences. That much, at least, the conservatives have right. What's missing from the marriage movement, though, is an understanding of the forces bearing down on couples in poor neighborhoods who are struggling just to get by. Liberals have much to contribute to this conversation. In fact, their voices are critical—both to counter the moralizing and to underscore the importance of strengthening families.

Postscript added in March 2004

I wrote this rather informal essay midway through the Bush administration. I was inclined to give President Bush the benefit-of-the-doubt, to believe that he had only good intentions in pushing marriage among the poor. I don't believe that anymore. President Buch has shown a disregard, if not outright hostility towards the nation's poor. He has proposed cutting public housing funds, turning Head Start over to the states, and paring back AmeriCorps. There is no conversation about how we might introduce jobs into communities where work has virtually disappeared. I can only conclude that the efforts to push marriage are a part of a larger, cynical effort to play to social conservatives. It's a shame. It's worthwhile having a real conversation about how we might fortify family, which could but doesn't necessarily include marriage—as well as talking about employment and housing, among other quite tangible matters. That conversation, I'm convinced, won't happen under President Bush's watch. ◆

FREEWRITING ASSIGNMENT

Should the government encourage unwed parents to marry? Why or why not? What is your viewpoint on this issue?

CRITICAL READING

1. What is the "marriage movement"? Who is promoting it and why?
2. In paragraphs 7 and 8, Kotlowitz writes about a pregnant teen couple from Oklahoma who are encouraged to marry by a social worker. Should the government be encouraging marriage to young pregnant couples? Is it a social and civil responsibility? Do you think it is a good idea for this couple to marry? Why or why not?
3. Kotlowitz describes the effort of Mike McManus, a "marriage salesman" who is the driving force behind "Marriage Savers." Visit McManus's web site at *http://www.marriagesavers.org/*. Based on what you read, evaluate his program from your own viewpoint.
4. Throughout his essay, Kotlowitz comments that one problem with marriage is that it isn't "relevant" to the urban poor. Why isn't it important? Is marriage relevant only to those individuals who are not financially struggling? Explain.
5. Kotlowitz notes that as he began his research for *Frontline*'s story, he felt that marriage wasn't important for the urban poor in the grand scheme of things. What makes him change his mind? Does the fact that the author admits this opinion shift influence your own opinion of this issue? Explain.
6. Evaluate the situation of Ashaki. In your opinion, should she marry the father of her seventh child? Why or why not? Is it more important that Steven have a job, or that he is a good father? Explain.
7. Why is the subject of marriage "treacherous territory" for conservatives to bring up? Why might urban communities resist the involvement of the conservative right?

CRITICAL WRITING

8. *Persuasive Writing*: Write a letter to Ashaki. Incorporating some of the points made in this essay and Farrell's preceding it, try to convince her to go through with her marriage to Steven. Or, alternatively, write a letter advising her against such a move.

9. *Research and Analysis*: You are a member of Kotlowitz's research team working on this assignment for *Frontline*. Using your school library resources and the Internet, trace the pattern of single motherhood over the last 20 years. Locate statistical data that breaks down single parenthood demographically and geographically. Add the data you uncover to Kotlowitz's essay and develop some of his ideas more fully.

10. *Research and Persuasive Writing*: Read the 2001 policy brief by the Brookings Institution, authored by Sara McLanahan, Irwin Garfinkel, and Ronald B. Mincy, outlining the social science evidence that both children and adults benefit from marriage (*http://www.brook.edu/es/research/projects/wrb/publications/pb/pb10.htm*). Drawing from their report, develop a hypothetical government program designed to help welfare families marry and stay married. Explain the reasoning behind your proposals.

GROUP PROJECTS

11. Using free association (writing down anything that comes to mind), brainstorm with your group to develop a list of terms associated with the phrase "single mother." The list could include anything from "latchkey kids" to "welfare" to "independent" and "community networking." Once you have developed a list, try and locate the source of the association, such as television, opinion editorials, government, political speeches, religion, and news media. What sources are grounded in modern fact, and what ones are not? What role does changing social opinion have on these associations? Explain.

12. Visit the *Frontline* web site associated with the program Kotlowitz was working on and take their quiz as a group (*http://www.pbs.org/wgbh/pages/frontline/shows/marriage/etc/quiz.html*). You can take the quiz even if you have not viewed the segment. Have one person write down your responses before submitting the quiz for scoring. Review your score. Did any of the statistics surprise you? As a class, discuss your results.

Nostalgia as Ideology
Stephanie Coontz

As Betty G. Farrell explained in the first essay in this chapter, most Americans feel that the family and marriage in general is in a state of decline. Underlying this feeling is that there is a loss of "traditional family values" that have contributed to the decay of marriage. How much of this belief is rooted in fact, and how much in hype? Stephanie Coontz maintains that the problem is that we are longing for a social construction that is based on a false memory, rather than fact. Culturally, we can't "go back," and Coontz wonders why would we even want to?

Stephanie Coontz is a professor of history and family studies at Evergreen State College in Olympia, Washington, and serves as the national co-chair of the Council on Contemporary Families. She is the author of *The Way We Never Were: American Families and the Nostalgia Trap* (1992) and *The Way We Really Are* (1998). Her work has been featured in many publications, including the *New York Times,* the *Wall Street Journal,* the *Washington Post, Newsweek, Harper's,* the *Chronicle of Higher Education,* and *National Forum.* She has also appeared on *The Oprah Winfrey Show, Crossfire,* CNN's *Talk Back Live,* and *CBS This Morning.* This article first appeared in the *American Prospect* in April 2002.

CRITICAL THINKING	Is marriage in danger of becoming an obsolete institution? Why do people marry today?

1 The more I listen to debates over whether we should promote marriage, the more I am reminded of one of my father's favorite sayings: "If wishes were horses, then beggars would ride." Yes, kids raised by married parents do better, on average, than kids raised in divorced- or single-parent homes. Yes, the long-term commitment of marriage confers economic, emotional, and even health benefits on adults as well. Certainly, we should remove marriage disincentives from government programs— 16 states, for instance, still discriminate against married couples in welfare policy. We should expand health coverage to include "couples counseling" for all who wish it. With better support systems, we may be able to save more potentially healthy marriages and further reduce rates of unwed childbearing among teenagers.

2 But there is no way to re-establish marriage as the main site of child rearing, dependent care, income pooling, or interpersonal commitments in the modern world. Any movement that sets this as a goal misunderstands how irreversibly family life and marriage have changed, and it will inevitably be dominated by powerful "allies" who are not interested in supporting the full range of families that exist today and are likely to in the future.

3 For more than 1,000 years, marriage was the main way that society transferred property, forged political alliances, raised capital, organized children's rights, redistributed resources to dependents, and coordinated the division of labor by age and gender. Precisely because marriage served so many political, social, and economic functions, not everyone had access to it. Those who did almost never had free choice regarding partners and rarely could afford to hold high expectations of their relationships.

4 During the last 200 years, the growth of bureaucracies, banks, schools, hospitals, unemployment insurance, Social Security, and pension plans slowly but surely eroded the political and economic roles that marriage traditionally had played. It increasingly became an individual decision that could be made independently of family and community pressures. By the early 1900s, love and companionship had become not just the wistful hope of a husband or wife but the legitimate goal of marriage in the eyes of society. But this meant that people began expecting more of married life than ever before in history—at the exact time that older methods of organizing and stabilizing marriages were ceasing to work. The very things that made

marriage more satisfying, and increasingly more fair to women, are the same things that have made marriage less stable.

5   The outlines of the problem were clear by the early twentieth century. The more that people saw marriage as their main source of intimacy and commitment, the less they were prepared to enter or stay in a marriage they found unsatisfying. Divorce rates shot up so quickly that by the 1920s many observers feared that marriage was headed for extinction. Books warned of "The Marriage Crisis." Magazines asked, "Is Marriage on the Skids?"

6   During the 1930s and 1940s, these fears took a backseat to more immediate survival issues, but abandonment rates rose during the Great Depression, out-of-wedlock sex shot up during the war, and by 1946 one in three marriages was ending in divorce. At the end of the 1940s, politicians and other concerned Americans began a campaign to reverse these trends. For a while it looked as if they would succeed. During the 1950s, the divorce rate dipped, the age at which people initially married plummeted, and fertility rates soared. But most historians agree that this decade was an aberration stimulated by the most massive government subsidization of young families in American history. And below the surface, the underpinnings of traditional marital stability continued to erode. Rates of unwed motherhood tripled between 1940 and 1948. The number of working mothers grew by 400 percent in the 1950s.

7   By the late 1960s, divorce rates were rising again, and the age of first marriage began to rise, too. The divorce rate peaked in the late 1970s and early 1980s, and has fallen by 26 percent since then. But the marriage rate has dropped at the same time, while the incidence of unmarried couples cohabiting, singles living alone, delayed marriage, and same-sex partnerships continued to increase throughout the 1990s.

8   Though welfare-state policies diverge, these trends are occurring in every industrial country in the world. Where divorce remains hard to get and out-of-wedlock birth is stigmatized, as in Italy and Japan, rates of marriage have plunged, suggesting that the historical trends undermining the universality of marriage will, if blocked in one area, simply spill over into another.

9   There is no way to reverse this trend short of a repressiveness that would not long be tolerated even in today's patriotic climate (and that would soon wipe out many of the benefits people now gain from marriage). Divorced families, stepfamilies, single parents, gay and lesbian families, lone householders, and unmarried cohabiting couples will never again become such a minor part of the family terrain that we can afford to count on marriage as our main institution for allocating income or caring for dependents.

10   I don't believe that marriage is on the verge of extinction—nor that it should become extinct. Most cohabiting couples eventually do get married, either to each other or to someone else. Gay men and lesbians are now demanding access to marriage—a demand that many marriage advocates perversely interpret as an attack on the institution. And marriage continues to be an effective foundation for interpersonal commitments and economic stability. Of course we must find ways to make marriage more possible for couples who want it and to strengthen the marriages they contract. But there's a big difference between supporting concrete measures to help marriages succeed and supporting an organized marriage movement.

11   Despite the benefits associated with marriage for most couples, unhappily married individuals are more distressed than people who are not married. Women in bad marriages lose their self-confidence, become depressed, develop lowered immune functions, and are more likely to abuse alcohol than women who get out of such marriages. A recent study of marriages where one spouse had mild hypertension found that in happy couples, time spent together lowered the blood pressure of the at-risk spouse. In unhappily married couples, however, even small amounts of extra togetherness led to increases in blood pressure for the at-risk spouse.

12   For children, living with two cooperating parents is better than living with a single parent. But high conflict in a marriage, or even silent withdrawal coupled with contempt, is often more damaging to children than divorce or growing up in a single-parent family. According to the National Center on Addiction and Substance Abuse at Columbia University, teens who live in two-parent households are less likely, on average, to abuse drugs and alcohol than teens in one-parent families; but teens in two-parent families who have a fair to poor relationship with their father are more likely to do so than teens who live with a single mother.

13   The most constructive way to support modern marriages is to improve work-life policies so that couples can spend more time with each other and their kids, to increase social-support systems for children, and to provide counseling for all couples who seek it. But many in the center-right marriage movement resist such reforms, complaining that single parents and unmarried couples—whether heterosexual or of the same sex—could "take advantage" of them. If we grant other relationships the same benefits as marriage, they argue, we weaken people's incentives to get married.

14   But that is a bullet we simply have to bite. I am in favor of making it easier for couples to marry and to sustain that commitment. But that cannot substitute for a more far-reaching, inclusive program to support the full range of relationships in which our children are raised and our dependents cared for. ◆

FREEWRITING ASSIGNMENT

Is marriage a goal for you in your life plan? Why or why not?

CRITICAL READING

1. Coontz's opening paragraph begins with a list of benefits marriage imparts. Why does she start her essay this way? How does this list contrast with the other points she makes in her essay? Explain.

2. What, according to Coontz, has contributed to the "erosion" of marriage?

3. Coontz states in her second paragraph that "there is no way to re-establish marriage as the main site of child rearing, dependent care, income pooling, or interpersonal commitments in the modern world." Respond to this statement in your own words. Do you agree with her? Is it a generalization, or a statement based largely on social fact? Explain.

4. Evaluate Coontz's use of statistics and facts. Do they support her points? Are they relevant to her thesis? Based on these facts, do you find yourself swayed by her argument? Why or why not?
5. Based on her essay, summarize Coontz's view of marriage. Cite specific areas of the text to support your summary.
6. How do you think Coontz would respond to the marriage programs described in Kotlowitz's essay? Explain.
7. What is Coontz's view of gay marriage? Connect her observations to those made in this chapter's *Viewpoints* section. Who do you think she would agree with, and why?

CRITICAL WRITING

8. *Personal Narrative*: Write a personal narrative in which you describe the structure of your family during your childhood, focusing specifically on the role of marriage in your family. Were your parents married? Divorced? If you could have changed anything about your parent's marital relationship, what would it have been?
9. If you are a member of an organized religious faith, research your religion's beliefs on marriage and family. If you are not a member of an organized religion, select one faith's doctrines to research. Be sure to include references. Describe your research in a short report.
10. Coontz notes that as people began to view marriage as more about love and intimacy, the divorce rate soared. Is marriage about love? Family? Children? If a couple has children, but find that they no longer feel the marriage is a loving one, should they stay together anyway? Write an essay in which you describe what you think marriage is, and what grounds individuals have to terminate it.

GROUP PROJECTS

11. As a group, make a list of the benefits of marriage Coontz cites in her essay. (Make sure you review the entire essay when compiling this list.) Discuss the list in terms of your own personal experience and perspective. Based on the list, decide whether marriage needs to be made more of a political priority.
12. In paragraph 2, Coontz asserts that "there is no way to re-establish marriage as the main site of child rearing, dependent care, income pooling, or interpersonal commitments in the modern world." Working in small groups, discuss and compare the structure of family and the role of marriage within your own experiences. Think about the family you grew up in, families you knew/know well, and the families you may have started. What marital structures did/do they have? Compare your observations with Coontz's statement.

The State of Our Unions

The National Marriage Project is a non-profit initiative at Rutgers, the State University of New Jersey, that provides research and analysis on the state of marriage in America, specifically addressing the social, economic, and cultural conditions affecting marriage. The project is co-directed by David Popenoe, Ph.D., a professor and former social and behavioral sciences dean at Rutgers, and Barbara Dafoe Whitehead, Ph.D., an author and social critic who has written extensively on marriage and divorce issues.

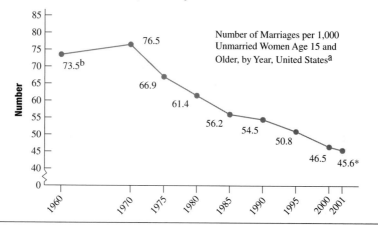

[a] We have used the number of marriages per 1,000 unmarried women age 15 and older, rather than the Crude Marriage Rate of marriages per 1,000 population to help avoid the problem of compositional changes in the population; that is, changes which stem merely from there being more or less people in the marriageable ages. Even this more refined measure is somewhat susceptible to compositional changes.

[b] Per 1,000 unmarried women age 14 and older

* Figure for 2001 was obtained using data from the Current Population Surveys, March 2001 Supplement, as well as *Statistical Abstract of the United States: 2002* page 88, Table 111. The CPS, March Supplement, is based on a sample of the U.S. population, rather than an actual count such as those available from the decennial census. See sampling and weighing notes at *http://www.bls. census.gov:80/ cps/ads/2002/ssamowgt.htm.*

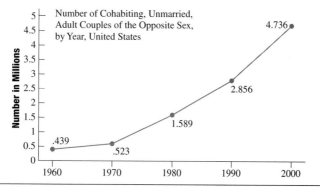

Sources: Data for both graphs from U.S. Department of Census, *Statistical Abstract of the United States: 2001*, Page 87, Tab. 117. *Statistical Abstract of the United States: 1988*, Page 79, Tab. 124; Current Population Reports, Series p 20–527; *America's Families and Living Arrangements: March 2000*, and earlier reports.

Did I Miss Something?

Lowell Putnam

Divorce has become an American way of life. Nearly half of all children will see their parents' marriage terminate by the time they turn 18. And although society may shake its collective head at such a statistic, lamenting the loss of the traditional family, not all children of divorce see it as a problem. In this piece, student Lowell Putnam wonders why divorce is still such a taboo topic. Having known no other way of life, children of divorced parents, explains Putnam, simply take such a lifestyle for granted.

Lowell Putnam is a junior majoring in English at Harvard University. When he is not living on campus in Cambridge, he splits his time between his mother's home in New York and his father's home in Massachusetts.

CRITICAL THINKING   In this essay, Lowell Putnam notes that people speak of divorce in hushed tones. If half of all marriages end in divorce, why does society still treat it as a taboo topic?

1   The subject of divorce turns heads in our society. It is responsible for bitten tongues, lowered voices, and an almost pious reverence saved only for life threatening illness or uncontrolled catastrophe. Growing up in a "broken home," I am always shocked to be treated as a victim of some social disease. When a class assignment required that I write an essay concerning my feelings about or my personal experiences with divorce, my first reaction was complete surprise. My second was a hope for large margins. An essay on aspects of my life affected by divorce seems completely superfluous, because I cannot differentiate between the "normal" part of my youth and the supposed angst and confusion that apparently comes with all divorces. The divorce of my parents over fifteen years ago (when I was three years old) has either saturated every last pore of my developmental epidermis to a point where I cannot sense it or has not affected me at all. Eugene Ehrlich's *Highly Selective Dictionary for the Extraordinarily Literate* defines divorce as a "breach"; however, I cannot sense any schism in my life resulting from the event to which other people seem to attribute so much importance. My parents' divorce is a true part of who I am, and the only "breach" that could arrive from my present familial arrangement would be to tear me away from what I consider my normal living conditions.

2   Though there is no doubt in my mind that many unfortunate people have had their lives torn apart by the divorce of their parents, I do not feel any real sense of regret for my situation. In my opinion, the paramount role of a parent is to love his or her child. Providing food, shelter, education, and video games are of course other necessary elements of successful child rearing, but these secondary concerns branch out from the most fundamental ideal of parenting, which is love. A loving parent will be a successful one even if he or she cannot afford to furnish his or her child

with the best clothes or the most sophisticated gourmet delicacies. With love as the driving force in a parent's mind, he or she will almost invariably make the correct decision. When my mother and father found that they were no longer in love with each other after nine years of a solid marriage, their love for me forced them to take the precipitous step to separate. The safest environment for me was to be with one happy parent at a time, instead of two miserable ones all the time. The sacrifice that they both made to relinquish control over me for half the year was at least as painful for them as it was for me (and I would bet even more so), but in the end I was not deprived of a parent's love, but merely of one parent's presence for a few short weeks at a time. My father and mother's love for me has not dwindled even slightly over the past fifteen years, and I can hardly imagine a more well-adjusted and contented family.

3   As I reread the first section of this essay, I realize that it is perhaps too optimistic and cheerful regarding my life as a child of divorced parents. In all truthfulness, there have been some decidedly negative ramifications stemming from our family separation. My first memory is actually of a fight between my mother and father. I vaguely remember standing in the end of the upstairs hallway of our Philadelphia house when I was about three years old, and seeing shadows moving back and forth in the light coming from under the door of my father's study, accompanied by raised voices. It would be naïve of me to say that I have not been at all affected by divorce since it has permeated my most primal and basic memories.

4   However, I am grateful that I can only recall one such incident, instead of having parental conflicts become so quotidian that they leave no mark whatsoever on my mind. Also, I find that having to divide my time equally between both parents leads to alienation from both sides of my family. Invariably, at every holiday occasion, there is one half of my family (either my mother's side or my father's) that has to explain that "Lowell is with his [mother/father] this year," while aunts, cousins, and grandparents collectively arch eyebrows or avert eyes. Again, though, I should not be hasty to lament my distance from loved ones, since there are many families with "normal" marriages where the children never even meet their cousins, let alone get to spend every other Thanksgiving with them. Though divorce has certainly thrown some proverbial monkey wrenches into some proverbial gears, in general my otherwise strong familial ties have overshadowed any minor snafus.

5   Perhaps one of the most important reasons for my absence of "trauma" (for lack of a better word) stemming from my parents' divorce is that I am by no means alone in my trials and tribulations. The foreboding statistic that sixty percent of marriages end in divorce is no myth to me, indeed many of my friends come from similar situations. The argument could be made that "birds of a feather flock together" and that my friends and I form a tight support network for each other, but I strongly doubt that any of us need or look for that kind of buttress. The fact of the matter is that divorce happens a lot in today's society, and as a result our culture has evolved to accommodate these new family arrangements, making the overall conditions more hospitable for me and my broken brothers and shattered sisters.

6   I am well aware that divorce can often lead to issues of abandonment and familial proximity among children of separated parents, but in my case I see very little

evidence to support the claim that my parents should have stayed married "for the sake of the child." In many ways, my life is enriched by the division of my time with my father and my time with my mother. I get to live in New York City for half of the year, and in a small suburb of Boston for the other half. I have friends who envy me, since I get "the best of both worlds." I never get double-teamed by parents during arguments, and I cherish my time with each one more since it only lasts half the year.

7   In my opinion, there is no such thing as a perfect life or a "normal" life, and any small blips on our karmic radar screen have to be dealt with appropriately but without any trepidation or self-pity. Do I miss my father when I live with my mother (and vice-versa)? Of course I do. However, I know young boys and girls who have lost parents to illness or accidental injury, so my pitiable position is relative. As I leave for college in a few short months, I can safely say that my childhood has not been at all marred by having two different houses to call home. ◆

FREEWRITING ASSIGNMENT

Is divorce detrimental to children or simply a way of life? Explain your point of view.

CRITICAL READING

1. Evaluate Putnam's description of the way people discuss divorce in "lowered voices, and an almost pious reverence saved only for life-threatening illness." What accounts for this attitude? Do you agree with his assessment? Explain.
2. At the end of his first paragraph, Putnam comments that "my parents' divorce is a true part of who I am." Why does Putnam associate his personal identity with his parents' marital status? Discuss how parent relationships influence how children view themselves and their world.
3. Analyze Putnam's definition of what makes a good parent. Do you agree or disagree with this viewpoint?
4. Critics of divorce say it is a selfish act of the parents, who put their wants before their children's needs. Putnam contends that his parents divorced out of love for him, and their divorce was a kind of sacrifice. Evaluate these two perspectives. Can divorce be a positive event for children?
5. Putnam comments that his parents' love for him has not dwindled as a result of their divorce, and that he "can hardly imagine a more well-adjusted and contented family." Why do you think he uses the singular "family"? Explain. How would his meaning change if he had used the plural form "families"?

CRITICAL WRITING

6. *Research and Analysis*: Using newspapers and newsmagazines, research a topic related to children and divorce. You might examine the issue of

"deadbeat dads," the psychological aspects of divorce on children, or so-cial perspectives of broken families. Write an essay analyzing the results of your research.

7. Draft a letter to a pair of married friends with children who are consider-ing divorce. Assume that both parents are working and they are consider-ing an amicable divorce in which they intend to continue a close relation-ship with their children.

8. *Personal Narrative*: Putnam's essay is a personal narrative describing his view of how his parents' divorce influenced his life. Write a personal narra-tive describing how your parents' marriage or divorce has influenced your own life. Can you relate to anything Putnam says in his essay? Explain.

GROUP PROJECTS

9. As a group, design and administer a poll for your classmates to answer anonymously, asking questions about family status (divorce, remarriage, single parenthood, absentee fathers or mothers, etc.). Then administer the same poll to a group of people a generation or two older than you (perhaps your professors or college staff members). How do the results compare? Are divorced families more "normal" than nondivorced families? Explain. What structures are more common among the different age groups? Dis-cuss your results with the class.

10. In your group, discuss the effects of divorce on children. Further develop Putnam's idea that it is just another way of life. Compare notes with class-mates to assemble a complete list. Based on this list, develop your own re-sponse about the effects of divorce on children.

Unmarried Bliss
Marshall Miller and Dorian Solot

Several of the essays in this chapter have lamented the decline of marriage as an inevitable, and regrettable, reality. The authors of the next piece argue that marriage isn't all it is chalked up to be. In fact, people can exist in meaningful and rewarding relationships without mar-riage, and children can grow up in nurtured and emotionally stable homes.

Marshall Miller and Dorian Solot are the founders of the Alternatives to Marriage Project, a national nonprofit organization that advocates for equality and fairness for unmarried peo-ple. They are the authors of the book, *Unmarried to Each Other: The Essential Guide to Living Together as an Unmarried Couple* (2002). They have appeared on *NBC News*, *CNN*, and *National Public Radio*, and have been mentioned in *USA Today*, *Time*, *Money*, and many other newspapers, radio, and television programs. Their work has been published in the *Boston Globe*, the *Washington Times*, and the *Arizona Daily Star*. This article first appeared in the *Providence Phoenix* in 1999.

CRITICAL THINKING   Many couples move in together without being married first, but eventually do so later. Others never marry. Do you think people should live together before getting married? Should they marry at all? Why or why not?

1   Duncan Smith remembers when, not so long ago, hotel check-in clerks requested evidence that he was married to his wife. Back then, he says, "If you wanted to be with someone, you had to be married."

2   Times have changed. Today, Smith, now divorced, lives with Lydia Breckon in the Edgewood neighborhood of Cranston with their three dogs and a cat. For 11 years, they've shared their lives, their cooking and cleaning, and their vacations. People sometimes assume they are married. But they have never taken a trip down the aisle together.

3   They describe themselves as pragmatists, not radicals. "I don't have a banner or a flag. I don't march around saying [being unmarried] is the right way to live. But on the other hand, I feel totally comfortable," Breckon says.

4   Living together without marriage, once unheard of, has become commonplace in America today. Parents often advise children to delay marriage and live with a partner to test the relationship, and growing numbers are forgoing marriage altogether. Unlike gay and lesbian couples, whose fight to legalize same-sex marriage has dominated recent headlines, those who choose not to marry receive little attention for their unique situation.

5   According to the US Census, 12,000 partners like Smith and Breckon live together in Rhode Island without being married. Nationally, there are 5.6 million, a fivefold increase since 1970. "Today, the 'Ozzie and Harriet' family only constitutes about 10 percent of all families. Family diversity is now the norm," says Los Angeles attorney Thomas Coleman, an expert on family diversity and marital status discrimination.

6   Coleman attributes the change to a list of factors, including women in the workforce, changing religious attitudes, no-fault divorce laws, and greater visibility of gay, lesbian, bisexual, and transgendered people. Yet many unmarried people say that government and private industry have been slow to keep up with the times by implementing laws and workplace policies that recognize the new structures of families.

7   Most cohabiting couples will marry eventually. For many, living together is a logical way to experience a relationship without making a lifelong commitment. Ken Heskestad of Providence says, "[Living together without marriage] makes me more conscious of what I have and makes me devote more of my energies to the relationship." Living together saves money as well, another common reason people decide to move in with a sweetheart.

8   Significant numbers of people, however, decide to stay together long-term without a formal exchange of "I do's." Their reasons vary. Some, like Jane Fronek, Heskestad's partner, say the choice not to marry allows her a freedom from assumed roles. "Once you are considered someone's wife, people treat you in a certain way, and that is something that really scares me," says Fronek.

9   Television talk shows label unmarried couples "commitment phobic," but many say that their level of commitment to a relationship has nothing to do with its legal status. In California, Amy Lesen's parents divorced when she was a child, and her father went on to have a successful 20-years-and-counting relationship without being married.

10   Today, Amy says she does not want to marry her partner. "I saw one marriage break up, and I saw two people who did not get married stay together for the rest of my life. I think that it drove a point home to me that [marriage] does not really matter," she says.

11   Some people find the institution of marriage too bound to religion. Some have experienced painful or expensive divorces and have sworn never to involve the legal system in their relationships again. Growing numbers of senior citizens find that they would lose a significant amount of the pension they receive from a deceased spouse if they were to wed again. So while college students may have been the first ones to thumb their noses at societal mores by moving in with a lover, today even some grandparents decide it's the way to go.

12   As a couple who long ago decided not to marry, this issue is a personal one for us. As children, neither of us dreamed of getting married when we grew up, possibly the legacy of our "you can do anything" feminist mothers. Our relationship was strong and felt stable and complete. We also didn't feel comfortable taking advantage of a privilege that wasn't available to many of our friends in same-sex relationships. Not getting married was an easy decision. Or so we thought.

13   After we'd been living together for a few years, an occasional family member would ask if we were considering marriage. One of our employers refused to give us the type of family health insurance policy for which married couples are eligible.

14   Then, in 1997 there was a news story about a Rhode Island man who wanted to legally adopt the biological son of his female domestic partner, a child he'd been parenting for years and considered his son. But a Family Court judge told the man that until he married the boy's mother, he would not consider the case.

15   Although the story was followed closely in the Rhode Island media, there was no public outrage—no letters to the editor or courthouse protests—as there had been in similar cases affecting transracial, gay, and single-parent adoptions. It was becoming clear to us that, in spite of our large and growing numbers, unmarried people didn't see themselves as a constituency, a group that could speak out and demand equal rights.

16   In case we weren't convinced yet, a few months later a potential landlord suggested he would not rent to us as an unmarried couple (breaking Massachusetts state law). A month later, a tenants' insurance company informed us we would have to buy separate policies, paying double what a married couple would. Finally, we got angry enough to do what we'd been talking about for years.

17   We decided to found a national organization to provide resources, advocacy and support for people who choose not to marry, are unable to marry, or are in the process of deciding whether marriage is right for them. The Alternatives to Marriage Project was born, and with it the beginning of a national community where none had existed before.

18   The conversations about what it's like to live without a ring, the challenges and the joys, are just beginning. Unmarried couples may not be harassed by hotel clerks now, but many say they still experience pressure to marry. Breckon remembers the day a newly-married friend of hers told her, "You've got to do this! Why are you holding out this back door in your relationship?"

19   But without marriage, Breckon says, there is a constant need to confirm her commitment to Smith. She told her friend, "There isn't a back door. The back door isn't open. Just because we're not married doesn't mean there's an escape path."

20   Things often get stickiest when unmarried couples decide to have children. Relatives turn up the heat, and for many, there is internal pressure to formalize the relationship. Marie Davis, who lives in Vermont and has participated in our Alternatives to Marriage Project, hasn't decided yet whether she wants to marry her partner of three years. But she says it's hard to know whether she could resist the pressure to marry if they decided to have children.

21   "A friend of mine recently got pregnant," Davis says. "She was married within three or four days of telling her parents. They flew out and did this clandestine little marriage ceremony, and now they're having a big wedding. And it kind of blew me away, like whoooah, those forces are strong!"

22   But even this last bastion of societal expectation is slowly shifting. Studies find that about one in 10 cohabitors give birth to a child while they live together, and an additional quarter bring children from a previous relationship to the current cohabiting relationship. The newest generation of children of unmarried parents, like Arthur Prokosch, a Brown University student, say it doesn't much matter.

23   "It never seemed to me to be that big of a deal that my parents weren't married," he says. "I was just a kid. My parents were there. And so I never really thought about it that much."

24   At a time when it is common for an elementary-school classroom to include children with single, divorced, foster or adoptive, and gay and lesbian parents, children raised with two unmarried parents usually don't see fitting in as a problem. Most say the issue would come up only occasionally, in insignificant ways.

25   Searching his mind for a way in which his parents' lack of a marriage license affected his life, Prokosch remembers, "Every so often, [a friend] would come over and say, 'Can I have another glass of milk, Mrs. Prokosch?' " And his mother would then have to decide whether to explain that she had a different last name than Arthur and his dad and that they weren't married.

26   Hillary Gross, a 19-year-old from New Jersey, says she and her college friends sometimes joke about families today. "We would tease somebody 'cause their parents are still married—'Oh, their parents are married! To each other? How weird!' "

27   When one thinks of gays and lesbians and marriage, images of the recent and ongoing high-profile cases to win the right to marry often come to mind. But while many same-sex couples eagerly await their chance to buy a plane ticket to whatever state first allows them to marry, others see themselves on the forefront of a movement pushing for a new definition of what constitutes a family.

28   "In my conception, what the gay and lesbian movement has been about has been tolerance of diversity," says Duncan A. Smith of Providence. Although he thinks same-sex couples should be allowed to marry, he says, "It just doesn't seem

like marriage really works effectively for the majority of those who decide to marry."

29 Paula Ettelbrick, a New York attorney, law professor, and activist in the field of "family recognition," points out that since gay and lesbian couples haven't historically had the option of marrying, they have been forced to re-think the very notion of what a family is. "Through our success in creating different kinds of families, we have shown that groups of people can constitute a family without being heterosexual, biologically related, married, or functioning under a male head-of-household," she says. Ettelbrick says LGBT people would be better off continuing to expand how family is defined "rather than confin[ing] ourselves to marriage."

30 For some in the LGBT community, marriage is even more complicated. Julie Waters of Providence, a pre-operative male-to-female transsexual, is in a relationship with a woman. And right now, she can't afford the expensive surgery involved in the medical transition process.

31 Since she is still considered a man legally, she points out, "If I could get married to someone whose health insurance happened to cover conditions related to transsexualism, I could get the insurance through them, go through the [sex change] process, and then, in most places, the marriage would be considered null and void after the process." Situations like this demonstrate how the notion of debating whether marriage should be limited to "one man and one woman" may be missing the point.

32 In many ways, American society is warming to the idea that families come in many shapes and sizes. A concrete example of this is the trend toward domestic-partner benefits, an option many employers have implemented to update human-resource definitions of "family" for employees of all sexual orientations.

33 The most common type of discrimination unmarried people face relates to equal pay for equal work. While most employers offer health insurance to the spouse and children of an employee, it's less common for policies to be available to unmarried partners. Still, the number of companies, colleges, nonprofit organizations, and municipalities offering domestic-partner benefits to their employees is on the rise.

34 According to a recent poll, 6 percent of large employers now offer domestic-partner benefits, and another 29 percent say they are considering offering them. Although details vary, the plans usually require that couples have lived together for a certain amount of time and that they are jointly responsible for living expenses and are in a caring, committed relationship.

35 In Rhode Island, two of the top 20 largest employers offer domestic-partner benefits: Brown University and BankBoston. Brown implemented the benefits first, in 1994, and in addition to getting a positive response from staff, the benefits have improved the university's ability to recruit and retain employees, says Brown spokesman Mark Nickel.

36 As of today, Brown's definition of domestic partners is limited to same-sex partners, because the policy was developed in response to staff requests, says Nickel. "Same-sex domestic partners have almost no avenue open to them, since same-sex marriage is not legal in Rhode Island or any other state," he explains. "At least opposite-sex domestic partners have some options open to them."

37 But as a result of this same-sex-only policy, Breckon and Smith, a Brown employee, had to weigh their options. At one point, Breckon was in danger of being

without health insurance, and Smith says they were frustrated by the fact that if Breckon had been a same-sex partner, she could have been added to his benefits plan.

38   Instead, Breckon says, "Briefly, on one Thursday, we considered getting married in a hurry." Breckon, however, was able to get a job quickly, so they ultimately avoided this newest kind of shotgun wedding.

39   Other employers are moving in the direction of offering domestic-partner benefits that are more inclusive, defining partners without regard for gender or sexual orientation. BankBoston's plan, which took effect just this summer, is an example. Employees now have the option of adding a spouse, dependent children, a domestic partner of any sex, or another adult dependent who meets certain criteria. "We wanted to expand eligibility with the goal to include as much of the diverse workforce as we could," says Martha Muldoon, a senior worklife consultant at BankBoston.

40   Los Angeles attorney Thomas Coleman is an advocate of broad-based benefits plans like BankBoston's. "I don't see why it is a legitimate business concern to an employer as to whether an opposite-sex couple chooses to be registered domestic partners rather than become legally married," he says. "If the opposite-sex couple is willing to sign the same affidavit and assume the same obligations as the employer has same-sex couples sign, then why should they not be able to do so and get the same employment benefits?"

41   Despite the "family values" rallying cry of politicos, the trend away from marriage and toward less traditional families is unlikely to change anytime soon. Coleman says, "Theoretically, the Constitution protects freedom of choice in certain highly personal decisions, such as those involving marriage, family, procreation, and child-rearing." And he hopes people's freedom to choose how they will structure their families will be increasingly respected by lawmakers, courts, and businesses.

42   Sometimes the freedom to choose results in some unusual benefits. Prokosch, son of unmarried parents, says that when telemarketers called and asked for "Mrs. Prokosch," he could tell them honestly, "There's no one here by that name."

43   "That was quite convenient," he laughs. ◆

FREEWRITING ASSIGNMENT ──────────────

If you could live together with a partner and enjoy the same benefits afforded to married couples, such as health and property insurance, inheritance rights, and retirement benefits, would you still get married? Why?

CRITICAL READING

1. In paragraph 5, Miller and Solot state that today, the "Ozzie and Harriet" family constitutes only about 10 percent of all families. What is the "Ozzie and Harriet" family structure? Why do Miller and Solot mention it?

2. Miller and Solot state that many people live together before getting married. In your opinion, does this arrangement make sense? Is it better to test

out a relationship before making a marriage commitment, or does it just make it easier for people to walk away from a relationship when the going gets rough? Would you live together with a sweetheart before making a commitment of marriage? Explain.

3. In paragraph 8, Jane Fronek cites that her reason for not marrying her partner is social fear. "Once you are considered someone's wife, people treat you in a certain way, and that is something that really scares me," she says. Are married women treated differently than unmarried ones? On what social concerns are Fronek's fears based?

4. Why do people object to marriage? Explain.

5. Why did the authors decide not to get married? What bias did they begin to notice? What did they decide to do about it? Explain.

6. Should unmarried couples living together have the same benefits, such as health insurance and life insurance coverage, as married ones? Explain.

7. Before you read this article, did you have any opinion on this issue? Did the essay change your ideas or give you something to think about that you had not considered before? Were they successful in persuading you to their point of view, if you did not already agree with them?

CRITICAL WRITING

8. *Research and Analysis*: Using newspapers and journals, research an issue related to unmarried couples living together. For example, you might research some of the issues mentioned in the article, such as health insurance, or adoption rights. Based upon your research, write a short essay in which you argue for or against "equal rights" for unmarried couples specifically addressing the issue you researched.

9. In 2000, the U.S. Census Bureau issued a report on married couples and unmarried partners living together. Review the report at *www.census.gov/prod/2003pubs/censr-5.pdf* and see where you fit in. Does your demographic group and geographic region influence your decision to marry? Parental viewpoint? Peer opinion? Write a short essay exploring the connection between your social and cultural ideology and your opinions of marriage. Refer to the Census Bureau report where appropriate.

GROUP PROJECTS

10. As a group, create a questionnaire on the issue of marriage and living together. Develop ten to twelve questions designed to gather information about people's opinions about marriage, living together before marriage, and nonmarried partnerships. Give the test to at least twenty people (try to survey a wide demographic). Compare your results to the information cited by the authors. As a class, discuss whether living together without marriage is better, or worse, than marriage itself. Do your results reveal a shift in social mores?

11. Miller and Solot note that only ten percent of families today mirror "Ozzie and Harriet" relationships. Working in a small group, make a list of at least ten prime time programs that depict families. (You may wish to visit the web pages of the major networks for guidance.) What is the family structure in these programs? How do they compare to the "Ozzie and Harriet" family structure. (If you are unfamiliar with this program, visit the American Heritage Center at the University of Wyoming for more information at *http://ahc.uwyo.edu/exhibits/ozzie*). With your group, conjecture what family structures might be depicted on programs ten or fifteen years from now.

What's Love Got to Do with It?

Anjula Razdan

In her essay Stephanie Coontz described how, for thousands of years, marriage was traditionally an arrangement based on economic and social considerations. It is only over the last century or so that marriage was the capstone of a loving relationship. But with over half of all marriages ending in divorce, are we going about this the wrong way? Many countries still view marriage as a political, social, and economic arrangement. The Western view of marriage is considered odd by many cultures that consider arranged marriages far more fruitful and intelligent than ones based on something as fickle as love. Are arranged marriages healthier than romantic attraction?

Anjula Razdan is associate editor of *Utne* magazine, in which this article was first published in the May/June 2003 issue.

CRITICAL THINKING	Is love the most important element in a marriage? What other factors are important for a successful marriage?

1   One of the greatest pleasures of my teen years was sitting down with a bag of cinnamon Red Hots and a new LaVyrle Spencer romance, immersing myself in another tale of star-crossed lovers drawn together by the heart's mysterious alchemy. My mother didn't get it. "Why are you reading that?" she would ask, her voice tinged with both amusement and horror. Everything in her background told her that romance was a waste of time.

2   Born and raised in Illinois by parents who emigrated from India 35 years ago, I am the product of an arranged marriage, and yet I grew up under the spell of Western romantic love—first comes love, then comes marriage—which both puzzled and dismayed my parents. Their relationship was set up over tea and samosas by their grandfathers, and they were already engaged when they went on their first date, a chaperoned trip to the movies. My mom and dad still barely knew each other on their wedding day—and they certainly hadn't fallen in love. Yet both were confi-

dent that their shared values, beliefs, and family background would form a strong bond that, over time, would develop into love.

3　"But, what could they possibly know of real love?" I would ask myself petulantly after each standoff with my parents over whether or not I could date in high school (I couldn't) and whether I would allow them to arrange my marriage (I wouldn't). The very idea of an arranged marriage offended my ideas of both love and liberty—to me, the act of choosing whom to love represented the very essence of freedom. To take away that choice seemed like an attack not just on my autonomy as a person, but on democracy itself.

4　And, yet, even in the supposedly liberated West, the notion of choosing your mate is a relatively recent one. Until the 19th century, writes historian E.J. Graff in *What Is Marriage For?: The Strange Social History of Our Most Intimate Institution*, arranged marriages were quite common in Europe as a way of forging alliances, ensuring inheritances, and stitching together the social, political, and religious needs of a community. Love had nothing to do with it.

5　Fast forward a couple hundred years to 21st-century America, and you see a modern, progressive society where people are free to choose their mates, for the most part, based on love instead of social or economic gain. But for many people, a quiet voice from within wonders: Are we really better off? Who hasn't at some point in their life—at the end of an ill-fated relationship or midway through dinner with the third "date-from-hell" this month—longed for a matchmaker to find the right partner? No hassles. No effort. No personal ads or blind dates.

6　The point of the Western romantic ideal is to live "happily ever after," yet nearly half of all marriages in this country end in divorce, and the number of never-married adults grows each year. Boundless choice notwithstanding, what does it mean when the marital success rate is the statistical equivalent of a coin toss?

7　"People don't really know how to choose a long-term partner," offers Dr. Alvin Cooper, the director of the San Jose Marital Services and Sexuality Centre and a staff psychologist at Stanford University. "The major reasons that people find and get involved with somebody else are proximity and physical attraction. And both of these factors are terrible predictors of long-term happiness in a relationship."

8　At the moment we pick a mate, Cooper says, we are often blinded by passion and therefore virtually incapable of making a sound decision.

9　*Psychology Today* editor Robert Epstein agrees. "[It's] like getting drunk and marrying someone in Las Vegas," he quips. A former director of the Cambridge Center for Behavioral Studies, Epstein holds a decidedly unromantic view of courtship and love. Indeed, he argues it is our myths of "love at first sight" and "a knight in a shining Porsche" that get so many of us into trouble. When the heat of passion wears off—and it always does, he says—you can be left with virtually nothing "except lawyer's bills."

10　Epstein points out that many arranged marriages result in an enduring love because they promote compatibility and rational deliberation ahead of passionate impulse. Epstein himself is undertaking a bold step to prove his theory that love can be learned. He wrote an editorial in *Psychology Today* last year seeking women to participate in the experiment with him. He proposed to choose one of the "applicants," and together they would attempt to fall in love—consciously and deliberately. After receiving more than 1,000 responses, none of which seemed right, Epstein yielded just a little to impulse, asking Gabriela, an intriguing Venezuelan woman he met on a plane, to join him in the project. After an understandable bout of cold feet, she eventually agreed.

11   In a "love contract" the two signed on Valentine's Day this year to seal the deal, Epstein stipulates that he and Gabriela must undergo intensive counseling to learn how to communicate effectively and participate in a variety of exercises designed to foster mutual love. To help oversee and guide the project, Epstein has even formed an advisory board made up of high-profile relationship experts, most notably Dr. John Gray, who wrote the best-selling *Men Are From Mars, Women Are From Venus*. If the experiment pans out, the two will have learned to love each other within a year's time.

12   It may strike some as anathema to be so premeditated about the process of falling in love, but to hear Epstein tell it, most unions fail exactly because they aren't intentional enough; they're based on a roll of the dice and a determination to stake everything on love. What this means, Epstein says, is that most people lack basic relationship skills, and, as a result, most relationships lack emotional and psychological intimacy.

13   A divorced father of four, Epstein himself married for passion—"just like I was told to do by the fairy tales and by the movies"—but eventually came to regret it. "I had the experience that so many people have now," he says, "which is basically looking at your partner and going, 'Who are you?' " Although Epstein acknowledges the non-Western tradition of arranged marriage is a complex, somewhat flawed institution, he thinks we can "distill key elements of [it] to help us learn how to create a new, more stable institution in the West."

14   Judging from the phenomenon of reality-TV shows like *Married By America* and *Meet My Folks* and the recent increase in the number of professional matchmakers, the idea of arranging marriages (even if in nontraditional ways) seems to be taking hold in this country—perhaps nowhere more powerfully than in cyberspace. Online dating services attracted some 20 million people last year (roughly one-fifth of all singles—and growing), who used sites like Match.com and Yahoo Personals to hook up with potentially compatible partners. Web sites' search engines play the role of patriarchal grandfathers, searching for good matches based on any number of criteria that you select.

15   Cooper, the Stanford psychologist and author of *Sex and the Internet: A Guidebook for Clinicians*, and an expert in the field of online sexuality, says that because online interaction tends to downplay proximity, physical attraction, and face-to-face interaction, people are more likely to take risks and disclose significant things about themselves. The result is that they attain a higher level of psychological and emotional intimacy than if they dated right away or hopped in the sack. Indeed, online dating represents a return to what University of Chicago Humanities Professor Amy Kass calls the "distanced nearness" of old-style courtship, an intimate and protected (cyber)space that encourages self-revelation while maintaining personal boundaries.

16   And whether looking for a fellow scientist, someone else who's HIV-positive, or a B-movie film buff, an online dater has a much higher likelihood of finding "the one" due to the computer's capacity to sort through thousands of potential mates. "That's what computers are all about—efficiency and sorting," says Cooper, who believes that online dating has the potential to lower the nation's 50 percent divorce

rate. There is no magic or "chemistry" involved in love, Cooper insists. "It's specific, operationalizable factors."

17 Love's mystery solved by "operationalizable factors"! Why does that sound a little less than inspiring? Sure, for many people the Internet can efficiently facilitate love and help to nudge fate along. But, for the diehard romantic who trusts in surprise, coincidence, and fate, the cyber-solution to love lacks heart. "To the romantic," observes English writer Blake Morrison in *The Guardian*, "every marriage is an arranged marriage—arranged by fate, that is, which gives us no choice."

18 More than a century ago, Emily Dickinson mocked those who would dissect birds to find the mechanics of song:

Split the Lark – and you'll find the Music –
Bulb after Bulb, in Silver rolled –
Scantily dealt to the Summer Morning
Saved for your Ear when Lutes be old.

Loose the Flood – you shall find it patent –
Gush after Gush, reserved for you –
Scarlet Experiment! Skeptic Thomas!
Now, do you doubt that your Bird was true?

19 In other words, writes Deborah Blum in her book, *Sex on the Brain*, "kill the bird and [you] silence the melody." For some, nurturing the ideal of romantic love may be more important than the goal of love itself. Making a more conscious choice in mating may help partners handle the complex personal ties and obligations of marriage; but romantic love, infused as it is with myth and projection and doomed passion, is a way to live outside of life's obligations, outside of time itself—if only for a brief, bright moment. Choosing love by rational means might not be worth it for those souls who'd rather roll the dice and risk the possibility of ending up with nothing but tragic nobility and the bittersweet tang of regret.

20 In the end, who really wants to examine love too closely? I'd rather curl up with a LaVyrle Spencer novel or dream up the French movie version of my life than live in a world where the mechanics of love—and its giddy, mysterious buzz—are laid bare. After all, to actually unravel love's mystery is, perhaps, to miss the point of it all. ◆

FREEWRITING ASSIGNMENT

In this essay, Razdan notes that she wouldn't let her parents arrange a marriage for her because to take away that choice "seemed like an attack not just on my autonomy . . . but on democracy itself." Expand on this idea. Is the right to choose one's mate a democratic ideal? Explain.

CRITICAL READING

1. Why is Razdan's mother both amused and horrified at her daughter's delight in romance novels? How does her concern mirror the difference between their generations and social experience?

2. Despite the fact that Razdan's parents no longer live in India, they clearly still want their daughter to follow in their marital footsteps. Furthermore, their arranged marriage seems to be working out well. The idea of arranged marriages seems to be outrageous to most Americans. In your opinion, could arranged marriages ever have a place in the American social system? Why or why not?

3. Robert Epstein, editor of *Psychology Today*, argues that marrying for love alone is "like getting drunk and marrying someone in Las Vegas." Does he have a point? Consider the reasons you have ended romantic relationships. Would they have been more successful if they had been based on things other than love first?

4. Razdan makes several references to reality programs designed to help people make successful matches. Do these programs serve as modern "matchmakers"? Why or why not?

5. How is the Internet becoming a major conduit for matchmaking? Explain.

6. How does the author feel about romantic love? Identify passages from the essay that reveal her viewpoint.

7. What is the meaning of the Dickinson poem? How does it connect to the point Razdan is trying to make?

CRITICAL WRITING

8. Arranged marriages differ from culture to culture. Some involve a matchmaker, who asks the participants to describe themselves and what they are looking for in a mate (much like a Western dating service). Prepare an information package about yourself, to give to a matchmaker. What does your description tell you about yourself? About what you hope for in a partner? Based on your description, answer the question Razdan raises in her title, "What's Love Got to Do with It?"

9. *Research and Analysis*: Razdan states that her parents' marriage was arranged by their grandfathers. Research arranged marriages online. Why are they promoted and encouraged? Are they longer lasting? Happier? Prepare a report based on your research.

10. Razdan was raised in the United States by Indian parents. Interview a student from another country and inquire about their culture's marriage practices and traditions. How do they differ from the U.S.? What is their opinion of American marriage?

GROUP PROJECT

11. Razdan notes that in the west, marriage is driven by love, often with unsuccessful long-term results. As a group, discuss whether you feel arranged marriages could work in the United States. Outline your reasons why you feel they could or could not work. Be sure to consider the pros and cons of the issue.

VIEWPOINTS

► Unveiled

Andrew Sullivan

► The Danger in Same-Sex Marriage

Jeff Jacoby

► Assault on Family Values (cartoon)

Dan Wasserman

This chapter's Viewpoints section addresses the issue of gay marriage. The issue has been hotly argued for the past few years, as some states ban and others begin to permit same-sex marriage. Supporters of gay marriage argue that it reduces sexual promiscuity, promotes stronger family units, is healthier for same-sex partners, and legitimizes the relationship both socially and legally. In "Unveiled," Andrew Sullivan reasons that marriage should be a bond between two loving adults who wish to make a life-long commitment to each other, regardless of gender.

But not everyone believes that gay marriage should be a human right. Religious fundamentalists and social conservatives argue that same-sex unions are not natural or moral. Other people just do not see the need to attach a conventional social institution such as marriage to an unconventional lifestyle. They argue that marriage and same-sex unions are simply not the same thing. In "The Danger of Same-Sex Marriage," Jeff Jacoby argues that same-sex marriage undermines the institution of marriage itself. Writing a year after a Vermont law authorizing same-sex civil unions, Jacoby fears that marriage will cease to have any meaning at all. (Three years after this ruling, nearly 5,700 gay and lesbian couples have registered their relationship.)

Andrew Sullivan is a senior editor for the *New Republic*, a magazine of cultural and political opinion. He is gay, conservative, and a Roman Catholic. His 1996 book, *Virtually Normal: An Argument About Homosexuality*, argues that the best way to tackle antigay prejudice is to shape public laws and policies so that they extend the same rights and protections to all U.S. citizens, regardless of sexual orientation. His latest book is *Love Undetectable: Notes on Friendship, Sex, and Survival* (1998). The essay reprinted here first appeared in the August 13, 2001, issue of the *New Republic*.

Jeff Jacoby is an editorial columnist for the *Boston Globe*, and is considered that newspaper's "conservative voice." His editorial appeared in the *Boston Globe*.

Dan Wasserman is also employed by the *Boston Globe* as an editorial cartoonist. He has illustrated many books and is the author of *Paper Cuts: The American Political Scene from Bush to Newt* (1995). One of his political cartoons on the issue of gay marriage and the political area appears after the articles.

CRITICAL THINKING   In your opinion, should gay men and women be permitted to legally marry? Explain your perspective with a reasonable argument.

Unveiled

Andrew Sullivan

1 In the decade or so in which same-sex marriage has been a matter of public debate, several arguments against it have been abandoned. Some opponents initially claimed marriage was about children and so gays couldn't marry. But courts made the obvious point that childless heterosexuals can marry and so the comparison was moot. Others said a change in the definition of marriage would inexorably lead to legal polygamy. But homosexuals weren't asking for the right to marry anyone. They were asking for the right to marry someone. Still others worried that if one state granted such a right, the entire country would have to accept same-sex marriage. But legal scholars pointed out that marriage has not historically been one of those legal judgments that the "full faith and credit" clause of the U.S. Constitution says must be recognized in every state if they are valid in one state. And if there were any doubt, the Defense of Marriage Act, designed expressly to prohibit such a scenario, was passed by a Republican Congress and President Clinton in 1996.

2 None of this stopped the Vermont Supreme Court, legislature, and governor from establishing "civil unions," the euphemism for gay marriage in the Ben & Jerry's state. It's been almost exactly a year since civil unions debuted, and social collapse doesn't seem imminent. Perhaps panicked by this nonevent, the social right last month launched a Federal Marriage Amendment, which would bar any state from enacting same-sex marriage, forbid any arrangement designed to give gays equal marriage benefits, and destroy any conceivable claim that conservatives truly believe in states' rights. Even some movement conservatives—most notably the *Washington Times*—demurred. The *Wall Street Journal* ran its only op-ed on the matter in opposition.

3 Perhaps concerned that their movement is sputtering, the opponents of same-sex marriage have turned to new arguments. Stanley Kurtz, the sharpest and fairest of these critics, summed up the case last week in *National Review Online*. For Kurtz and other cultural conservatives, the deepest issue is sex and sexual difference. "Marriage," Kurtz argues, "springs directly from the ethos of heterosexual sex. Once marriage loses its connection to the differences between men and women, it can only start to resemble a glorified and slightly less temporary version of hooking up."

4 Let's unpack this. Kurtz's premise is that men and women differ in their sexual-emotional makeup. Men want sex more than stability; women want stability more than sex. Heterosexual marriage is therefore some kind of truce in the sex wars. One side gives sex in return for stability; the other provides stability in return for sex. Both sides benefit, children most of all. Since marriage is defined as the way women tame men, once one gender is missing, this taming institution will cease to work. So, in Kurtz's words, a "world of same-sex marriages is a world of no-strings heterosexual hookups and 50 percent divorce rates."

5 But isn't this backward? Surely the world of no-strings heterosexual hookups and 50 percent divorce rates preceded gay marriage. It was heterosexuals in the 1970s who changed marriage into something more like a partnership between equals, with both partners often working and gender roles less rigid than in the past.

All homosexuals are saying, three decades later, is that, under the current definition, there's no reason to exclude us. If you want to return straight marriage to the 1950s, go ahead. But until you do, the exclusion of gays is simply an anomaly—and a denial of basic civil equality.

6   The deeper worry is that gay men simply can't hack monogamy and that any weakening of fidelity in the Clinton-Condit era is too big a risk to take with a vital social institution. One big problem with this argument is that it completely ignores lesbians. So far in Vermont there have been almost twice as many lesbian civil unions as gay male ones—even though most surveys show that gay men outnumber lesbians about two to one. That means lesbians are up to four times more likely to get married than gay men—unsurprising if you buy Kurtz's understanding of male and female sexuality. So if you accept the premise that women are far more monogamous than men, and that therefore lesbian marriages are more likely to be monogamous than even heterosexual ones, the net result of lesbian marriage rights is clearly a gain in monogamy, not a loss. For social conservatives, what's not to like?

7   But the conservatives are wrong when it comes to gay men as well. Gay men— not because they're gay but because they are men in an all-male subculture—are almost certainly more sexually active with more partners than most straight men. (Straight men would be far more promiscuous, I think, if they could get away with it the way gay guys can.) Many gay men value this sexual freedom more than the stresses and strains of monogamous marriage (and I don't blame them). But this is not true of all gay men. Many actually yearn for social stability, for anchors for their relationships, for the family support and financial security that come with marriage. To deny this is surely to engage in the "soft bigotry of low expectations." They may be a minority at the moment. But with legal marriage, their numbers would surely grow. And they would function as emblems in gay culture of a sexual life linked to stability and love.

8   So what's the catch? I guess the catch would be if those gay male couples interpret marriage as something in which monogamy is optional. But given the enormous step in gay culture that marriage represents, and given that marriage is entirely voluntary, I see no reason why gay male marriages shouldn't be at least as monogamous as straight ones. Perhaps those of us in the marriage movement need to stress the link between gay marriage and monogamy more clearly. We need to show how renunciation of sexual freedom in an all-male world can be an even greater statement of commitment than among straights. I don't think this is as big a stretch as it sounds. In Denmark, where de facto gay marriage has existed for some time, the rate of marriage among gays is far lower than among straights, but, perhaps as a result, the gay divorce rate is just over one-fifth that of heterosexuals. And, during the first six years in which gay marriage was legal, scholar Darren Spedale has found, the rate of straight marriages rose 10 percent, and the rate of straight divorces decreased by 12 percent. In the only country where we have real data on the impact of gay marriage, the net result has clearly been a conservative one.

9   When you think about it, this makes sense. Within gay subculture, marriage would not be taken for granted. It's likely to attract older, more mainstream gay couples, its stabilizing ripples spreading through both the subculture and the wider society. Because such marriages would integrate a long-isolated group of people into the world of love and family, they would also help heal the psychic wounds that

scar so many gay people and their families. Far from weakening heterosexual marriage, gay marriage would, I bet, help strengthen it, as the culture of marriage finally embraces all citizens. How sad that some conservatives still cannot see that. How encouraging that, in such a short time, so many others have begun to understand. ◆

The Danger in Same-Sex Marriage
Jeff Jacoby

1   It was a year ago last month that the Vermont law authorizing same-sex civil unions—marriage by another name—took effect, and *The New York Times* marked the anniversary with a story on July 25. "Quiet Anniversary for Civil Unions," the double headline announced. "Ceremonies for Gay Couples Have Blended Into Vermont Life." It was an upbeat report, and its message was clear: Civil unions are working just fine.

2   The story noted in passing that most Vermonters oppose the new law, and that many support a constitutional amendment confirming that marriage is the union of a man and a woman. Presumably they have reasons for not wanting legal recognition conferred on homosexual couples, but the *Times* had no room to mention them. It did have room, though, to dismiss those reasons—whatever they might be—as meritless:

3   "The sky has not fallen, Governor Howard Dean said, 'and the institution of marriage has not collapsed. None of the dire predictions have come true. . . . There was a big rhubarb, a lot of fear-mongering, and now people realize there was nothing to be afraid of.' "

4   In *The Wall Street Journal* two days later, much the same point was made by Jonathan Rauch, the esteemed Washington journalist and vice president of the Independent Gay Forum.

5   Opponents of same-sex marriage, he wrote, worry "that unyoking marriage from its traditional male-female definition will destroy or severely weaken it. But this is an empirical proposition, and there is reason to doubt it. Opponents of same-sex marriage have done a poor job of explaining why the health of heterosexual marriage depends on the exclusion of a small number of homosexuals."

6   The assertion that same-sex marriage will not damage traditional family life is rarely challenged, a fact seized on by US Representative Barney Frank during the 1996 congressional debate over the Defense of Marriage Act.

7   "I have asked and I have asked and I have asked and I guess I will die . . . unanswered," Frank taunted. "How does the fact that I love another man and live in a committed relationship with him threaten your marriage? Are your relations with your spouses of such fragility that the fact that I have a committed, loving relationship with another man jeopardizes them? . . . Whose marriage does it threaten?" When another congressman replied that legitimizing gay unions "threatens the institution of marriage," Frank was scornful:

8   "That argument ought to be made by someone in an institution because it has no logical basis whatsoever."

9   But Frank's sarcasm, Rauch's doubts, and Dean's reassurances notwithstanding, the threat posed by same-sex unions to traditional marriage and family life is all

too real. Marriage is harmed by anything that diminishes its privileged status. It is weakened by anything that erodes the social sanctions that Judeo-Christian culture developed over the centuries for channeling men's naturally unruly sexuality into a monogamous, lasting, and domestic relationship with one woman. For proof, just look around.

10 Over the last 40 years, marriage has suffered one blow after another. The sexual revolution and the Pill made it much easier for men to enjoy women sexually without having to marry them. The legalization of abortion reduced the pressure on men to marry women they impregnated, and reduced the pressure on women to be sexually responsible, or to wait for lasting love. The widespread acceptance of unmarried cohabitation—an arrangement that used to be disdained as "shacking up"—diminished marriage even further. Why get married if intimate companionship can be had without public vows and ceremony?

11 The rise of the welfare state with its subsidies for single mothers subverted marriage by sending the unmistakable message that husbands were no longer essential for family life. And the rapid spread of no-fault divorce detached marriage from any presumption of permanence. Where couples were once expected to stay married "for as long as you both shall live"—and therefore to put effort into making their marriage work—the expectation today is that they will remain together only "for as long as you both shall love."

12 If we now redefine marriage so it includes the union of two men or two women, we will be taking this bad situation and making it even worse.

13 No doubt the acceptance of same-sex marriage would remove whatever stigma homosexuality still bears, a goal many people would welcome. But it would do so at a severe cost to the most basic institution of our society. For all the assaults marriage has taken, its fundamental purpose endures: to uphold and encourage the union of a man and a woman, the framework that is the healthiest and safest for the rearing of children. If marriage stops meaning even that, it will stop meaning anything at all. ◆

FREEWRITING ASSIGNMENT

What are the "virtues" of marriage? Why do people marry? What do they hope to gain by marriage? What does society expect from married couples compared with non-married couples?

CRITICAL READING

1. Identify the primary points of argument Sullivan uses to support his case. Make a list of his reasons, and respond to each one. How do you think Jacoby would respond to Sullivan's points in an editorial?

2. According to Sullivan, why do homosexual couples want to marry—what motivates them? Do heterosexual couples marry for the same reasons as gay couples?

3. If marriage is more about keeping men in monogamous, committed relationships, as Jacoby implies, does it apply to same-sex unions? Why or why not? Explain.

4. Consider Wasserman's cartoon. How are the subjects presented? How does Wasserman portray each character through clothing, manner, words, and typeface? What "side" of the argument do you think he is on? Explain.

5. Sullivan notes that, one year after Vermont instituted same-sex civil unions, "social collapse" has not occurred. Jacoby quotes Vermont governor Howard Dean as proclaiming, "The institution of marriage has not collapsed." Can such assessments be made only one year after the passing of a law? How might a conservative argue against these statements?

6. Sullivan says that Stanley Kurtz is the "sharpest and fairest" of the anti-gay marriage movement. On what grounds does Kurtz argue against same-sex marriage? Do you agree or disagree with his argument? Explain.

7. In his conclusion, Jacoby states that the fundamental purpose of marriage is to "uphold and encourage the union of a man and a woman . . ." In your own words, state what the "fundamental purpose" of marriage is. How do you think Jacoby and Sullivan would react to your definition?

CRITICAL WRITING

8. *Persuasive Writing*: Write a letter to a minister, rabbi, or other religious leader. Explain why you think he or she should agree to perform a marriage ceremony celebrating the commitment of two of your best friends—a gay couple. Assume that this leader has not given much thought to gay marriage. Use Sullivan's comments about the reasons why gays want to marry as support for your case. Alternatively, you may write a letter arguing against such a marriage. Assume that you care about your friends, and know that your opinions can cause them pain, but that you still must advise against such a union.

9. *Exploratory Writing*: Gay couples have been more prominent in the media over the past few years. What images of gay life has television presented to its viewers? How do the images correspond to Sullivan's claims that many gay men and women just want what marriage affords—"social stability, anchors in relationships, and family and financial security"? Write an essay in which you explore the portrayal of gay relationships in the media, and how this portrayal may or may not influence public opinion on the issue of gay marriage.

10. *Persuasive Writing*: Will legalizing gay marriage increase or decrease the problems involved in gaining the social acceptance gay men and women now encounter in America? What benefits might all gay people receive, whether or not they choose to marry? Do you think that a legal change in marriage will help to change the beliefs of people who now disapprove of homosexuality? Why or why not? Explain.

GROUP PROJECTS

11. Working as a team using Internet resources, see what information you can find about gay and lesbian marriages. Check out the "Right to Marry Resource" at *http://grasshopperdesign.com/gay_marriage/index.htm* and the

American Family Association at *www.afa.org* to help get you started. Can you locate additional information for or against gay marriage? Assemble a list of resources and compare it with other groups. Then select a more narrow topic for each group to research online. Prepare a brief description of what Internet users might find at each site. What cultural and social conclusions about gay marriage can you make based on your research? Explain.

12. Should marriage be a public and political institution? Alternatively, should it be a religious, private, and moral institution? Or should it have features of both? List the qualities that a marriage draws from each of these realms. After you have compiled your list, discuss with your group what marriage should be and for whom.

13. Design a survey that you will administer anonymously to other members of your class or students in the student union asking for their opinions on gay marriage. Design your survey to allow people to formulate opinions and express their views while incorporating some of the ideas presented in this *Viewpoints* section. Collect the surveys and discuss the results. How do the responses connect to the arguments presented in this section? Explain.

Assault on Family Values

Dan Wasserman

Cohabiting Is *Not* the Same as Commitment

Karen S. Peterson

Are couples who live together less likely to marry? Some experts believe that rather than serving as a test run for marriage, cohabitation deters many men from tying the knot. This article, by reporter Karen S. Peterson, appeared in the July 8, 2002, edition of *USA Today*.

1 Women living unmarried with guys and expecting a lasting, committed marriage down the line had better review their options [says] researcher Scott Stanley. His research finds that men who cohabit with the women they eventually marry are less committed to the union than men who never lived with their spouses ahead of time. Stanley presented his findings at a 2002 conference sponsored by the Coalition for Marriage, Family and Couples Education in Washington, D.C.

2 But rather than settle anything for the more than 5 million unmarried American couples who live together, the research will likely spark the ongoing dispute over living together vs. marriage, and true commitment vs. a spirit of "maybe I do," in Stanley's words. And it will also raise fresh questions about who's more of a slacker in the commitment department: men or women.

3 Stanley, co-director of the Center for Marital and Family Studies at the University of Denver, says the evidence from his research is so strong that cohabiting women "should be very careful about how aligned they are with a particular man if he does not show any strong sense of marriage and a future together."

4 Men who either drift into marriage "through inertia" following a cohabiting arrangement or who are "dragged down the aisle" by women who finally put their feet down are not good marriage risks, he says.

5 Many researchers agree with Stanley: It is young men, not women, who move toward marriage with the speed of a wounded sloth. Their findings will reinforce stereotypes and infuriate many of both sexes who want to look before they leap. But still it is men, these researchers say, who drag their feet—big time.

Testing the Relationship

6 Stanley says his results do not mean there are not "a lot of super men out there," who have cohabited and are dedicated to their women both before and after heading down the aisle. But his findings do hold up on average, he says, and are reinforced by another of his current research projects.

7 The cohabiting women in Stanley's small but pioneering study did not show differences in commitment to their unions before or after marriage. He speculates that men who want "to test marriage out first" are less committed to the institution in general and their partners specifically than men who move directly to marriage without cohabiting. And he speculates that women are still socialized to put relationships first and tend to be as committed to both the union and the partner, after marriage as they were before it.

8   His findings will interest those who monitor marriage trends. Setting up shop together—before marriage or without any plans to marry—has become common-place. Between 50% and 60% of new marriages now involve couples who have lived together first.

9   Many who live together feel it is a vaccination against divorce. "I've been dat-ing the same girl for three years, and it just seemed the natural progression for our relationship, the next step to take," says Scott Tolchinsky, 23, of Bethesda, Md., who has just set up housekeeping with his girlfriend. "You see so many get divorced that you want to try things out."

10   Divorce is "just a huge issue for my generation," says Rosanne Garfield, 28, of Arlington, Va. "My family has not had good success with marriage. I was living with my boyfriend for the last year. I told him to make a decision (about marriage), and that ended it. But it would never cross my mind not to live together with some-one before marrying him." Ironically, the divorce rate among those who once lived together is higher than among those who have not. Experts say that is often because those who choose to cohabit are not great believers in marriage in the first place.

11   Stanley sees other factors at play. In his study on live-ins who married, less reli-gious men were particularly apt to be less committed. It may be that higher divorce rates among onetime cohabitors are a result of "the presence of males who are less dedicated, less religious and more negative" than males who didn't cohabit, he says.

12   The co-author of *Fighting for Your Marriage*, Stanley helped develop a com-munication skills course for couples based on 20 years of the center's research. Much of its work is funded by the National Institute of Mental Health. His current study is based on a sub-sample of 207 men and women married 10 years or less and culled from ongoing marital research on 950 adults nationwide. Standard assess-ments of commitment were employed during telephone interviews.

13   Stanley says his results dovetail with those from a controversial Rutgers Uni-versity study released June 25. That research by sociologist David Popenoe has be-come a hot topic. Popenoe will elaborate further on his findings at the "Smart Mar-riages" conference.

14   The Rutgers study found that young men are reluctant to marry because just liv-ing with a woman is easier. They fear the cost of a divorce. They are not excited about sharing the everyday chores of parenting with their future wives. And they'd like to be financially stable first.

15   Both he and Popenoe agree, Stanley says, that "it is a bigger switch for men than women to go from being non-married to married. And men are more reluctant to throw that switch."

16   Women, Stanley says, are more willing to sacrifice for others, more willing to undergo the burdens that babies bring. And women's fertile years are limited. They hear their biological clocks ticking while men hear only the sounds of silence.

Seekers of Commitment

17   Many experts agree men are the foot-draggers. Atlanta psychiatrist Frank Pittman, author of *Grow Up!*, says men still have not been raised to be good candidates for today's egalitarian marriages. "Marriage is by its nature, total, permanent and equal.

In that way it is different from any other relationship or activity." Men are still reluctant to move toward such a binding relationship, he says.

18   But the Rutgers study is causing a fuss elsewhere. The Alternatives to Marriage Project (AtMP) debunks the concept that men would rather have a live-in lover than a wife. Marshall Miller and Dorian Solot, live-ins themselves and co-founders of the non-profit group supporting non-marrieds, say that "men actually tend to be more interested in marriage than women." Among the polls and surveys they cite:

- A 1996 Gallup poll found 39% of unmarried men would prefer to be married; 29% of unmarried women would.
- A government-funded survey of high-schoolers, from 1996–2000, found 38% of senior boys believe marriage leads to a fuller and happier life; 29% of senior girls said so.
- A 1994 government-funded survey found 59% of unmarried men ages 18–35 want to get married; 48% of women agreed.

19   Men are committed to women, Miller says. "Their only hesitation is whether to commit to the institution of marriage."

20   Steve Penner of Brighton, Mass., called *USA Today* to object to the Rutgers survey. Over the last 20 years, he says, he has talked to more than 21,000 singles as head of LunchDates, an upscale dating service in the Boston area. Both the men and women of today seek commitment, he says. "I really think we are picking on men. Men and women are equally looking for relationships."

21   Whether or not anyone wants to commit depends on age, financial situation and life experiences, not gender, many others say. "People are always saying all men are dogs," Tolchinsky says. "But there are lots of nice men out there who are looking to settle down. Maybe women are looking in the wrong places."

Days of Delayed Unions

22 Both sexes are delaying marriage today for financial reasons, Penner says. "They both want to buy a house first. They both want to pursue a career. These are the children of the baby boom generation, and the men and women are very similar." Indeed, both sexes are tending to marry later. The median age for first marriage for men is now about 27; for women, it is 25.

23   Her generation is waiting, says Garfield. "We have had experiences with functional and dysfunctional families all around us." A lasting commitment really depends on "trial and error," she says. And living together first is a good option.

24   Maybe, says researcher Scott Stanley. But still, there are his findings on men who cohabit first vs. those who don't, the men who live with a woman but 10 years after marriage don't feel a solid commitment to them. He says to women: "If you want someone to marry, choose someone who won't live with you."

CRITICAL THINKING

1. Stanley's study reveals that men and women who live together before marriage are in fact less likely to have successful marriages in the future.

What reasons does he attribute to this statistic? Can you think of any other reasons that might bear on the outcome of marriages between people who have lived together first? Explain.

2. What reasons do people give for living together before marriage? What cultural factors influence this decision? Explain.

RESEARCH PROJECTS

3. Visit the Coalition for Marriage, Family, and Couples Education web site at *http://www.smartmarriages.com/articles.html* and review some of the statistical and research information posted there. Pick a topic related to marriage and divorce on the coalition's web site that interests you and re-search it using the information on the web site and additional web re-sources. Write a short research report on your topic, connecting it to the subject of trends in marriage in the twenty-first century.

4. Stanley's study indicates that men are less likely to marry the women they cohabitate with, and when they do marry, more likely to later divorce. Prepare a survey and interview at least 20 men and 20 women between the ages of 18 to 24 for their opinions about cohabitation versus marriage. Would they live together with someone before marrying them? Would they live together regardless of future marriage plans? Do they view co-habitation as the natural precursor to marriage? Should the possibility of a future marriage even be a factor when deciding to live together? Compare your data to Stanley's and write an essay based on your research. Like Stanley, try to draw some conclusions from your data, and what it might mean for the future of marriage for your generation.

Additional essay topics, writing assignments, research guidelines, and readings for this chapter can be found online at **www.ablongman.com/goshgarian**.

Humans Inc.

Cloning and Our Genetic Future

5

That discussion every parent dreads—the talk about the birds and the bees—may get even harder for parents. Reproductive technology has moved beyond test tube babies into what seems to many people the realm of science fiction. It is now possible for us to clone animals and, presumably, ourselves. With the mapping of the human genome, there is the selective possibility of creating "perfect" children. In light of these dramatic scientific breakthroughs, parents might need more than a biology textbook to answer Junior's question, "Where did I come from?"

In June 2000, scientists announced that they had completed a working draft of the human genome. Now that they had isolated and identified every gene within the 23 pairs of human chromosomes, they could begin research on the connection between these genes and human disease.

The first piece, "Baby, It's You and You and You," by Nancy Gibbs, presents an overview of human cloning and genetic engineering. The mapping of the human genome means we are opening the door to understanding how these genes work, and will soon be able to manipulate DNA to achieve certain predictable outcomes. Such genetic manipulation may also mean cloning the first human could be only months away, if it hasn't already happened since this book entered production. Gibbs warns that the ethical issues around abortion and euthanasia will seem "tame" compared to the issues genetic manipulation raises.

Now that researchers had identified every gene within the 23 pairs of human chromosomes, they could begin to probe the mysteries contained within these genes. In "Designer Babies," Sharon Begley discusses how future parents might use genomic technology to not only prevent genetic diseases, but also to create the "perfect baby."

Her piece is followed by "The Last Human," in which Gregory Stock asserts that genetic technology *will* be used on humans—we just haven't decided how yet. And while we may be changing the very definition of what it means to be human, it would be inhuman *not* to use it. Humans have always dared to test the boundaries; when such acts are successful, they are known as pioneers. And why not make humans even better?

Bill McKibben, in "Enough," doesn't agree that genetic manipulation will make humans better. Sure, they may be smarter, stronger, and live longer than their creators, but what happens to the people who aren't genetically modified? Genetic manipulation could create a power shift in which the regular guys simply can't compete. This idea is further explored by Ruth Hubbard and Stuart Newman in "Yuppie Eugenics," in which they wonder, "are we creating a world of genetic haves and have-nots?"

This section's Viewpoints presents an argument over the ethics of human cloning. When people say that they are against cloning, they usually mean human cloning in a lab. Human clones have always existed—identical twins and triplets are technically clones, each containing exact matching sets of DNA. But identical twins still start out the same way everyone else does—DNA from a sperm cell joins with DNA from an egg cell. However, in 1997, scientists at Roslin Institute in Scotland announced that they had successfully cloned an adult sheep, named Dolly. Soon after, they cloned Cedric, Cecil, Cyril, and Tuppence from cultured embryo cells—

four Dorset rams that are genetically identical to one another. And everything we thought we knew about reproduction was turned upside down.

After Roslin Institute made their announcement, researchers, religious leaders, politicians, legal experts, and journalists responded to the news with strong opinions—especially as this new technology could someday relate to humans. What dangers does human cloning pose for cloned children, and for society? What measures must we take to prevent the abuse of this technology? Could cloned children become shunned by society as scientific freaks? In "Should Human Cloning Be Permitted?" Patricia A. Baird presents reasons why it should not—spanning from unknown genetic alterations generations from now, to concern for the social status of the clones themselves.

But not everyone is concerned. It is unlikely that a cloned human would be a perfect replica of its DNA parent—the conditions in the uterus, the health of the mother, and environmental factors can all influence fetal development. After birth, external factors help create who we are. Supporters of human cloning, such as Chris MacDonald in "Yes, Human Cloning Should Be Permitted," argue that scientific horror stories, such as cloning for body parts, are just that—horror stories that will never happen in the real world.

The final piece proposes a "Genetic Bill of Rights" drafted by the Council for Responsible Genetics. The Council believes that we must take steps now to ensure that our genetic future is not compromised. Do we have a right to our own genetic integrity? Could our genetic rights be at risk? This Research Issue explores the concept of genetic rights in greater depth.

Baby, It's You and You and You
Nancy Gibbs

When researchers at Roslin Institute in Scotland announced that they had cloned a sheep in 1997, no one could have prepared them for the calls and letters from people eager to clone their loved ones. Said Ian Wilmut, one of the scientists who created Dolly the first cloned sheep, "Such pleas are based on a misconception that cloning of the kind that produced Dolly confers instant, exact replication—a virtual resurrection." As anyone who has taken college biology knows, we are more than our DNA—we are products of our environment, beginning with the first divisions of fetal cells. Nevertheless, many people are indeed interested in human cloning; and one sect, the Raelians, has even claimed to have done just that. In this article, Nancy Gibbs discusses the various reasons why people wish to pursue human cloning and some of the arguments against it.

Nancy Gibbs is a senior editor at *Time* magazine, where she divides her time between writing major stories on national affairs and domestic policy issues and editing various sections of it. She has taught a seminar "Poltics and the Press" at Princeton University. In addition to publication in *Time* and other magazines and journals, Gibbs's work is included in the *Princeton Anthology of Writing*. This article was first printed in the February 19, 2001, issue of *Time*.

CRITICAL THINKING	What do you know about human cloning? Do you think it should be banned? After reading the articles in this section, reevaluate your position and see if your position remains the same.

1　Before we assume that the market for human clones consists mainly of narcissists who think the world deserves more of them or neo-Nazis who dream of cloning Hitler or crackpots and mavericks and mischief makers of all kinds, it is worth taking a tour of the marketplace. We might just meet ourselves there.

2　Imagine for a moment that your daughter needs a bone-marrow transplant and no one can provide a match; that your wife's early menopause has made her infertile; or that your five-year-old has drowned in a lake and your grief has made it impossible to get your mind around the fact that he is gone forever. Would the news then really be so easy to dismiss that around the world, there are scientists in labs pressing ahead with plans to duplicate a human being, deploying the same technology that allowed Scottish scientists to clone Dolly the sheep four years ago?

3　All it took was that first headline about the astonishing ewe, and fertility experts began to hear the questions every day. Our two-year-old daughter died in a car crash; we saved a lock of her hair in a baby book. Can you clone her? Why does the law allow people more freedom to destroy fetuses than to create them? My husband had cancer and is sterile. Can you help us?

4　The inquiries are pouring in because some scientists are ever more willing to say yes; perhaps we can. Last month a well-known infertility specialist, Panayiotis Zavos of the University of Kentucky, announced that he and Italian researcher Severino Antinori, the man who almost seven years ago helped a 62-year-old woman give birth using donor eggs, were forming a consortium to produce the first human clone. Researchers in South Korea claim they have already created a cloned human embryo, though they destroyed it rather than implanting it in a surrogate mother to develop. Recent cover stories in *Wired* and the *New York Time*s Magazine tracked the efforts of the Raelians, a religious group committed to, among other things, welcoming the first extraterrestrials when they appear. They intend to clone the cells of a dead 10-month-old boy whose devastated parents hope, in effect, to bring him back to life as a newborn. The Raelians say they have the lab and the scientists, and—most important, considering the amount of trial and error involved—they say they have 50 women lined up to act as surrogates to carry a cloned baby to term.

5　Given what researchers have learned since Dolly, no one thinks the mechanics of cloning are very hard: take a donor egg, suck out the nucleus, and hence the DNA, and fuse it with, say, a skin cell from the human being copied. Then, with the help of an electrical current, the reconstituted cell should begin growing into a genetic duplicate. "It's inevitable that someone will try and someone will succeed," predicts Delores Lamb, an infertility expert at Baylor University. The consensus among biotechnology specialists is that within a few years—some scientists believe a few months—the news will break of the birth of the first human clone.

6　At that moment, at least two things will happen—one private, one public. The meaning of what it is to be human—which until now has involved, at the very least, the mysterious melding of two different people's DNA—will shift forever, along with our understanding of the relationship between parents and children, means and ends, ends and beginnings. And as a result, the conversation that has occupied scientists and ethicists for years, about how much man should mess with nature when it comes to reproduction, will drop onto every kitchen table, every pulpit, every politician's desk. Our fierce national debate over issues like abortion and euthanasia will seem tame and transparent compared with the questions that human cloning raises.

7   That has many scientists scared to death. Because even if all these headlines are hype and we are actually far away from seeing the first human clone, the very fact that at this moment, the research is proceeding underground, unaccountable, poses a real threat. The risk lies not just with potential babies born deformed, as many animal clones are; not just with desperate couples and cancer patients and other potential "clients" whose hopes may be raised and hearts broken and life savings wiped out. The immediate risk is that a backlash against renegade science might strike at responsible science as well.

8   The more scared people are of some of this research, scientists worry, the less likely they are to tolerate any of it. Yet variations on cloning technology are already used in biotechnology labs all across the country. It is these techniques that will allow, among other things, the creation of cloned herds of sheep and cows that produce medicines in their milk. Researchers also hope that one day, the ability to clone adult human cells will make it possible to "grow" new hearts and livers and nerve cells.

9   But some of the same techniques could also be used to grow a baby. Trying to block one line of research could impede another and so reduce the chances of finding cures for ailments such as Alzheimer's and Parkinson's, cancer and heart disease. Were some shocking breakthrough in human cloning to cause "an overcompensatory response by legislators," says Rockefeller University cloning expert Tony Perry, "that could be disastrous. At some point, it will potentially cost lives." So we are left with choices and trade-offs and a need to think through whether it is this technology that alarms us or just certain ways of using it.

10   By day, Randolfe Wicker, 63, runs a lighting shop in New York City. But in his spare time, as spokesman for the Human Cloning Foundation, he is the face of cloning fervor in the U.S. "I took one step in this adventure, and it took over me like quicksand," says Wicker. He is planning to have some of his skin cells stored for future cloning. "If I'm not cloned before I die, my estate will be set up so that I can be cloned after," he says, admitting, however, that he hasn't found a lawyer willing to help. "It's hard to write a will with all these uncertainties," he concedes. "A lot of lawyers will look at me crazy."

11   As a gay man, Wicker has long been frustrated that he cannot readily have children of his own; as he gets older, his desire to reproduce grows stronger. He knows that a clone would not be a photocopy of him but talks about the traits the boy might possess: "He will like the color blue, Middle Eastern food and romantic Spanish music that's out of fashion." And then he hints at the heart of his motive. "I can thumb my nose at Mr. Death and say, 'You might get me, but you're not going to get all of me,'" he says. "The special formula that is me will live on into another lifetime. It's a partial triumph over death. I would leave my imprint not in sand but in cement."

12   This kind of talk makes ethicists conclude that even people who think they know about cloning—let alone the rest of us—don't fully understand its implica-

tions. Cloning, notes ethicist Arthur Caplan of the University of Pennsylvania, "can't make you immortal because clearly the clone is a different person. If I take twins and shoot one of them, it will be faint consolation to the dead one that the other one is still running around, even though they are genetically identical. So the road to immortality is not through cloning."

13   Still, cloning is the kind of issue so confounding that you envy the purists at either end of the argument. For the Roman Catholic Church, the entire question is one of world view: whether life is a gift of love or just one more industrial product, a little more valuable than most. Those who believe that the soul enters the body at the moment of conception think it is fine for God to make clones; he does it about 4,000 times a day, when a fertilized egg splits into identical twins. But when it comes to massaging a human life, for the scientist to do mechanically what God does naturally, is to interfere with his work; and no possible benefit can justify that presumption.

14   On the other end of the argument are the libertarians who don't like politicians or clerics or ethics boards interfering with what they believe should be purely individual decisions. Reproduction is a most fateful lottery; in their view, cloning allows you to hedge your bet. While grieving parents may be confused about the technology—cloning, even if it works, is not resurrection—their motives are their own business. As for infertile couples, "we are interested in giving people the gift of life," Zavos, the aspiring cloner, told *Time* this week. "Ethics is a wonderful word, but we need to look beyond the ethical issues here. It's not an ethical issue. It's a medical issue. We have a duty here. Some people need this to complete the life cycle, to reproduce."

15   In the messy middle are the vast majority of people who view the prospect with a vague alarm, an uneasy sense that science is dragging us into dark woods with no paths and no easy way to turn back. Ian Wilmut, the scientist who cloned Dolly but has come out publicly against human cloning, was not trying to help sheep have genetically related children. "He was trying to help farmers produce genetically improved sheep," notes Hastings Center ethicist Erik Parens. "And surely that's how the technology will go with us too." Cloning, Parens says, "is not simply this isolated technique out there that a few deluded folks are going to avail themselves of, whether they think it is a key to immortality or a way to bring someone back from the dead. It's part of a much bigger project. Essentially the big-picture question is: To what extent do we want to go down the path of using reproductive technologies to genetically shape our children?"

16   At the moment, the American public is plainly not ready to move quickly on cloning. In a *Time*/CNN poll, 90% of respondents thought it was a bad idea to clone human beings. "Cloning right now looks like it's coming to us on a magic carpet, piloted by a cult leader, sold to whoever can afford it," says ethicist Caplan. "That makes people nervous."

17   And it helps explain why so much of the research is being done secretly. We may learn of the first human clone only months, even years, after he or she is born—if the event hasn't happened already, as some scientists speculate. The team that cloned Dolly waited until she was seven months old to announce her existence. Creating her took 277 tries, and right up until her birth, scientists around the world were saying that cloning a mammal from an adult cell was impossible. "There's a signifi-

cant gap between what scientists are willing to talk about in public and their private aspirations," says British futurist Patrick Dixon. "The law of genetics is that the work is always significantly further ahead than the news. In the digital world, everything is hyped because there are no moral issues—there is just media excitement. Gene technology creates so many ethical issues that scientists are scared stiff of a public reaction if the end results of their research are known."

18   Of course, attitudes often change over time. In-vitro fertilization was effectively illegal in many states 20 years ago, and the idea of transplanting a heart was once considered horrifying. Public opinion on cloning will evolve just as it did on these issues, advocates predict. But in the meantime, the crusaders are mostly driven underground. Princeton biologist Lee Silver says fertility specialists have told him that they have no problem with cloning and would be happy to provide it as a service to their clients who could afford it. But these same specialists would never tell inquiring reporters that, Silver says—it's too hot a topic right now. "I think what's happened is that all the mainstream doctors have taken a hands-off approach because of this huge public outcry. But I think what they are hoping is that some fringe group will pioneer it and that it will slowly come into the mainstream and then they will be able to provide it to their patients."

19   All it will take, some predict, is that first snapshot. "Once you have a picture of a normal baby with 10 fingers and 10 toes, that changes everything," says San Mateo, Calif., attorney and cloning advocate Mark Eibert, who gets inquiries from infertile couples every day. "Once they put a child in front of the cameras, they've won." On the other hand, notes Gregory Pence, a professor of philosophy at the University of Alabama at Birmingham and author of Who's Afraid of Human Cloning?, "if the first baby is defective, cloning will be banned for the next 100 years."

20   "I wouldn't mind being the first person cloned if it were free. I don't mind being a guinea pig," says Doug Dorner, 35. He and his wife Nancy both work in health care. "We're not afraid of technology," he says. Dorner has known since he was 16 that he would never be able to have children the old-fashioned way. A battle with lymphoma left him sterile, so when he and Nancy started thinking of having children, he began following the scientific developments in cloning more closely. The more he read, the more excited he got. "Technology saved my life when I was 16," he says, but at the cost of his fertility. "I think technology should help me have a kid. That's a fair trade."

21   Talk to the Dorners, and you get a glimpse of choices that most parents can scarcely imagine having to make. Which parent, for instance, would they want to clone? Nancy feels she would be bonded to the child just from carrying him, so why not let the child have Doug's genetic material? Does it bother her to know she would, in effect, be raising her husband as a little boy? "It wouldn't be that different. He already acts like a five-year-old sometimes," she says with a laugh.

22   How do they imagine raising a cloned child, given the knowledge they would have going in? "I'd know exactly what his basic drives were," says Doug. The boy's dreams and aspirations, however, would be his own, Doug insists. "I used to dream of being a fighter pilot," he recalls, a dream lost when he got cancer. While they are at it, why not clone Doug twice? "Hmm. Two of the same kid," Doug ponders. "We'll cross that bridge when we come to it. But I know we'd never clone our clone

to have a second child. Once you start copying something, who knows what the next copies will be like?"

23   In fact the risks involved with cloning mammals are so great that Wilmut, the premier cloner, calls it "criminally irresponsible" for scientists to be experimenting on humans today. Even after four years of practice with animal cloning, the failure rate is still overwhelming: 98% of embryos never implant or die off during gestation or soon after birth. Animals that survive can be nearly twice as big at birth as is normal, or have extra-large organs or heart trouble or poor immune systems. Dolly's "mother" was six years old when she was cloned. That may explain why Dolly's cells show signs of being older than they actually are—scientists joked that she was really a sheep in lamb's clothing. This deviation raises the possibility that beings created by cloning adults will age abnormally fast.

24   "We had a cloned sheep born just before Christmas that was clearly not normal," says Wilmut. "We hoped for a few days it would improve and then, out of kindness, we euthanized it, because it obviously would never be healthy." Wilmut believes "it is almost a certainty" that cloned human children would be born with similar maladies. Of course, we don't euthanize babies. But these kids would probably die very prematurely anyway. Wilmut pauses to consider the genie he has released with Dolly and the hopes he has raised. "It seems such a profound irony," he says, "that in trying to make a copy of a child who has died tragically, one of the most likely outcomes is another dead child."

25   That does not seem to deter the scientists who work on the Clonaid project run by the Raelian sect. They say they are willing to try to clone a dead child. Though their outfit is easy to mock, they may be even further along than the competition, in part because they have an advantage over other teams. A formidable obstacle to human cloning is that donor eggs are a rare commodity, as are potential surrogate mothers, and the Raelians claim to have a supply of both.

26   Earlier this month, according to Brigitte Boisselier, Clonaid's scientific director, somewhere in North America, a young woman walked into a Clonaid laboratory whose location is kept secret. Then, in a procedure that has been done thousands of times, a doctor inserted a probe, removed 15 eggs from the woman's ovaries and placed them in a chemical soup. Last week two other Clonaid scientists, according to the group, practiced the delicate art of removing the genetic material from each of the woman's eggs. Within the next few weeks, the Raelian scientific team plans to place another cell next to the enucleated egg.

27   This second cell, they say, comes from a 10-month-old boy who died during surgery. The two cells will be hit with an electrical charge, according to the scenario, and will fuse, forming a new hybrid cell that no longer has the genes of the young woman but now has the genes of the dead child. Once the single cell has developed into six to eight cells, the next step is to follow the existing, standard technology of assisted reproduction: gingerly insert the embryo into a woman's womb and hope it implants. Clonaid scientists expect to have implanted the first cloned human embryo in a surrogate mother by next month.

28   Even if the technology is basic, and even if it appeals to some infertile couples, should grieving parents really be pursuing this route? "It's a sign of our growing

despotism over the next generation," argues University of Chicago bioethicist Leon Kass. Cloning introduces the possibility of parents' making choices for their children far more fundamental than whether to give them piano lessons or straighten their teeth. "It's not just that parents will have particular hopes for these children," says Kass. "They will have expectations based on a life that has already been lived. What a thing to do—to carry on the life of a person who has died."

29   The libertarians are ready with their answers. "I think we're hypercritical about people's reasons for having children," says Pence. "If they want to re-create their dead children, so what?" People have always had self-serving reasons for having children, he argues, whether to ensure there's someone to care for them in their old age or to relive their youth vicariously. Cloning is just another reproductive tool; the fact that it is not a perfect tool, in Pence's view, should not mean it should be outlawed altogether. "We know there are millions of girls who smoke and drink during pregnancy, and we know what the risks to the fetus are, but we don't do anything about it," he notes. "If we're going to regulate cloning, maybe we should regulate that too."

30   Olga Tomusyak was two weeks shy of her seventh birthday when she fell out of the window of her family's apartment. Her parents could barely speak for a week after she died. "Life is empty without her," says her mother Tanya, a computer programmer in Sydney, Australia. "Other parents we have talked to who have lost children say it will never go away." Olga's parents cremated the child before thinking of the cloning option. All that remains are their memories, some strands of hair and three baby teeth, so they have begun investigating whether the teeth could yield the nuclei to clone her one day. While it is theoretically possible to extract DNA from the teeth, scientists say it is extremely unlikely.

31   "You can't expect the new baby will be exactly like her. We know that is not possible," says Tanya. "We think of the clone as her twin or at least a baby who will look like her." The parents would consider the new little girl as much Olga's baby as their own. "Anything that grows from her will remind us of her," says Tanya. Though she and her husband are young enough to have other children, for now, this is the child they want.

32   Once parents begin to entertain the option of holding on to some part of a child, why would the reverse not be true? "Bill" is a guidance counselor in Southern California, a fortysomething expectant father who has been learning everything he can about the process of cloning. But it is not a lost child he is looking to replicate. He is interested in cloning his mother, who is dying of pancreatic cancer. He has talked to her husband, his siblings, everyone except her doctor—and her, for fear that it will make her think they have given up hope on her. He confides, "We might end up making a decision without telling her."

33   His goal is to extract a tissue specimen from his mother while it's still possible and store it, to await the day when—if—cloning becomes technically safe and socially acceptable. Late last week, as his mother's health weakened, the family began considering bringing up the subject with her because they need her cooperation to take the sample. Meanwhile, Bill has already contacted two labs about tissue storage, one as a backup. "I'm in touch with a couple of different people who might be

doing that," he says, adding that both are in the U.S. "It seems like a little bit of an underground movement, you know—people are a little reluctant that if they announce it, they might be targeted, like the abortion clinics."

34   If Bill's hopes were to materialize and the clone were born, who would that person be? "It wouldn't be my mother but a person who would be very similar to my mother, with certain traits. She has a lot of great traits: compassion and intelligence and looks," he says. And yet, perhaps inevitably, he talks as though this is a way to rewind and replay the life of someone he loves. "She really didn't have the opportunities we had in the baby-boom generation, because her parents experienced the Depression and the war," he says. "So the feeling is that maybe we could give her some opportunities that she didn't have. It would be sort of like we're taking care of her now. You know how when your parents age and everything shifts, you start taking care of them? Well, this would be an extension of that."

35   A world in which cloning is commonplace confounds every human relationship, often in ways most potential clients haven't considered. For instance, if a woman gives birth to her own clone, is the child her daughter or her sister? Or, says bioethicist Kass, "let's say the child grows up to be the spitting image of its mother. What impact will that have on the relationship between the father and his child if that child looks exactly like the woman he fell in love with?" Or, he continues, "let's say the parents have a cloned son and then get divorced. How will the mother feel about seeing a copy of the person she hates most in the world every day? Everyone thinks about cloning from the point of view of the parents. No one looks at it from the point of view of the clone."

36   If infertile couples avoid the complications of choosing which of them to clone and instead look elsewhere for their DNA, what sorts of values govern that choice? Do they pick an uncle because he's musical, a willing neighbor because she's brilliant? Through that door lies the whole unsettling debate about designer babies, fueled already by the commercial sperm banks that promise genius DNA to prospective parents. Sperm banks give you a shot at passing along certain traits; cloning all but assures it.

37   Whatever the moral quandaries, the one-stop-shopping aspect of cloning is a plus to many gay couples. Lesbians would have the chance to give birth with no male involved at all; one woman could contribute the ovum, the other the DNA. Christine DeShazo and her partner Michele Thomas of Miramar, Fla., have been in touch with Zavos about producing a baby this way. Because they have already been ostracized as homosexuals, they aren't worried about the added social sting that would come with cloning. "Now [people] would say, 'Not only are you a lesbian, you are a cloning lesbian,'" says Thomas. As for potential health problems, "I would love our baby if its hand was attached to its head," she says. DeShazo adds, "If it came out green, I would love it. Our little alien . . ."

38   Just as women have long been able to have children without a male sexual partner, through artificial insemination, men could potentially become dads alone: replace the DNA from a donor egg with one's own and then recruit a surrogate mother to carry the child. Some gay-rights advocates even argue that should sexual preference prove to have a biological basis, and should genetic screening lead to termina-

tions of gay embryos, homosexuals would have an obligation to produce gay children through cloning.

39   All sorts of people might be attracted to the idea of the ultimate experiment in single parenthood. Jack Barker, a marketing specialist for a corporate-relocation company in Minneapolis, is 36 and happily unmarried. "I've come to the conclusion that I don't need a partner but can still have a child," he says. "And a clone would be the perfect child to have because I know exactly what I'm getting." He understands that the child would not be a copy of him. "We'd be genetically identical," says Barker. "But he wouldn't be raised by my parents—he'd be raised by me." Cloning, he hopes, might even let him improve on the original: "I have bad allergies and asthma. It would be nice to have a kid like you but with those improvements."

40   Cloning advocates view the possibilities as a kind of liberation from travails assumed to be part of life: the danger that your baby will be born with a disease that will kill him or her, the risk that you may one day need a replacement organ and die waiting for it, the helplessness you feel when confronted with unbearable loss. The challenge facing cloning pioneers is to make the case convincingly that the technology itself is not immoral, however immorally it could be used.

41   One obvious way is to point to the broader benefits. Thus cloning proponents like to attach themselves to the whole arena of stem-cell research, the brave new world of inquiry into how the wonderfully pliable cells of seven-day-old embryos behave. Embryonic stem cells eventually turn into every kind of tissue, including brain, muscle, nerve and blood. If scientists could harness their powers, these cells could serve as the body's self-repair kit, providing cures for Parkinson's, diabetes, Alzheimer's and paralysis. Actors Christopher Reeve, paralyzed by a fall from a horse, and Michael J. Fox, who suffers from Parkinson's, are among those who have pushed Congress to overturn the government's restrictions on federal funding of embryonic-stem-cell research.

42   But if the cloners want to climb on this train in hopes of riding it to a public relations victory, the mainstream scientists want to push them off. Because researchers see the potential benefits of understanding embryonic stem cells as immense, they are intent on avoiding controversy over their use. Being linked with the human-cloning activists is their nightmare. Says Michael West, president of Massachusetts-based Advanced Cell Technology, a biotech company that uses cloning technology to develop human medicines: "We're really concerned that if someone goes off and clones a Raelian, there could be an overreaction to this craziness—especially by regulators and Congress. We're desperately concerned—and it's a bad metaphor—about throwing the baby out with the bath water."

43   Scientists at ACT are leery of revealing too much about their animal-cloning research, much less their work on human embryos. "What we're doing is the first step toward cloning a human being, but we're not cloning a human being," says West. "The miracle of cloning isn't what people think it is. Cloning allows you to make a genetically identical copy of an animal, yes; but in the eyes of a biologist, the real miracle is seeing a skin cell being put back into the egg cell, taking it back in time to when it was an undifferentiated cell, which then can turn into any cell in the body." Which means that new, pristine tissue could be grown in labs to replace damaged or

diseased parts of the body. And since these replacement parts would be produced using skin or other cells from the suffering patient, there would be no risk of rejection. "That means you've solved the age-old problem of transplantation," says West. "It's huge."

44   So far, the main source of embryonic stem cells is "leftover" embryos from IVF clinics; cloning embryos could provide an almost unlimited source. Progress could come even faster if Congress were to lift the restrictions on federal funding—which might have the added safety benefit of the federal oversight that comes with federal dollars. "We're concerned about George W.'s position and whether he'll let existing guidelines stay in place," says West. "People are begging to work on those cells."

45   That impulse is enough to put the Roman Catholic Church in full revolt; the Vatican has long condemned any research that involves creating and experimenting with human embryos, the vast majority of which inevitably perish. The church believes that the soul is created at the moment of conception, and that the embryo is worthy of protection. It reportedly took 104 attempts before the first IVF baby, Louise Brown, was born; cloning Dolly took more than twice that. Imagine, say opponents, how many embryos would be lost in the effort to clone a human. This loss is mass murder, says David Byers, director of the National Conference of Catholic Bishops' commission on science and human values. "Each of the embryos is a human being simply by dint of its genetic makeup."

46   Last week 160 bishops and five Cardinals met for three days behind closed doors in Irving, Texas, to wrestle with the issues biotechnology presents. But the cloning debate does not break cleanly even along religious lines. "Rebecca," a thirtysomething San Francisco Bay Area resident, spent seven years trying to conceive a child with her husband. Having "been to hell and back" with IVF treatment, Rebecca is now as thoroughly committed to cloning as she is to Christianity. "It's in the Bible—be fruitful and multiply," she says. "People say, 'You're playing God.' But we're not. We're using the raw materials the good Lord gave us. What does the doctor do when the heart has stopped? They have to do direct massage of the heart. You could say the doctor is playing God. But we save a life. With human cloning, we're not so much saving a life as creating a new being by manipulation of the raw materials, DNA, the blueprint for life. You're simply using it in a more creative manner."

47   A field where emotions run so strong and hope runs so deep is fertile ground for profiteers and charlatans. In her effort to clone her daughter Olga, Tanya Tomusyak contacted an Australian firm, Southern Cross Genetics, which was founded three years ago by entrepreneur Graeme Sloan to preserve DNA for future cloning. In an e-mail, Sloan told the parents that Olga's teeth would provide more than enough DNA—even though that possibility is remote. "All DNA samples are placed into computer-controlled liquid-nitrogen tanks for long-term storage," he wrote. "The cost of doing a DNA fingerprint and genetic profile and placing the sample into storage would be $2,500. Please note that all of our fees are in U.S. dollars."

48   When contacted by *Time,* Sloan admitted, "I don't have a scientific background. I'm pure business. I'd be lying if I said I wasn't here to make a dollar out of it. But I would like to see organ cloning become a reality." He was inspired to launch the business, he says, after a young cousin died of leukemia. "There's

megadollars involved, and everyone is racing to be the first," he says. As for his own slice of the pie, Sloan says he just sold his firm to a French company, which he refuses to name, and he was heading for Hawaii last week. The Southern Cross factory address turns out to be his mother's house, and his "office" phone is answered by a man claiming to be his brother David—although his mother says she has no son by that name.

49   The more such peddlers proliferate, the more politicians will be tempted to invoke prohibitions. Four states—California, Louisiana, Michigan and Rhode Island—have already banned human cloning, and this spring Texas may become the fifth. Republican state senator Jane Nelson has introduced a bill in Austin that would impose a fine of as much as $1 million for researchers who use cloning technology to initiate pregnancy in humans. The proposed Texas law would permit embryonic-stem-cell research, but bills proposed in other states were so broadly written that they could have stopped those activities too.

50   "The short answer to the cloning question," says ethicist Caplan, "is that anybody who clones somebody today should be arrested. It would be barbaric human experimentation. It would be killing fetuses and embryos for no purpose, none, except for curiosity. But if you can't agree that that's wrong to do, and if the media can't agree to condemn rather than gawk, that's a condemnation of us all." ◆

FREEWRITING ASSIGNMENT

Would you clone yourself or a loved one for any reason—such as to save a living child, or even yourself?

CRITICAL READING

1. What reasons does Gibbs list for why people are interested in human cloning? Are these the same reasons cited by researchers? How are the expectations of the general population different from the expectations of the scientific world?
2. What "backlash" do "responsible" scientists fear will happen as a result of human cloning research? Are their fears well-founded? Explain.
3. What are some of the misconceptions people seem to have about cloning themselves? Explain.
4. Gibbs notes that the issue of human cloning is "so confounding that you envy the purists at either end of the argument." What are the opinions of the "purists"? Do you find one side of the argument more compelling than another? Explain.
5. Ian Wilmut observes that there is a tragic twist to parents' desire to clone their dead children—that the success rate is so miniscule that they are more likely to end up with another dead child. Should parents be able to pursue this option? Is any chance—no matter how remote—worthy of the risk? Why or why not?

6. In paragraph 20, Doug Dorner states that he "wouldn't mind being a guinea pig." Would the donor of the cells used to create a human clone be the "guinea pig"? Or is the clone the "guinea pig"?

7. In paragraph 29, Pence comments that cloning is "merely another reproductive tool" now available to us. Respond to his statement expressing your own viewpoint.

8. Gibbs observes that many people who support human cloning seem to do so without considering the point of view of the clone. How do the examples of people who support cloning in her article support this viewpoint?

CRITICAL WRITING

9. *Research and Analysis*: In 1997, the National Bioethics Advisory Council recommended against human cloning because of the dangers it presented to the child born of such reproductive technology. In 2000, researchers reported that Dolly's cells appeared to age faster than normal. Through online and library research, track Dolly's development. If Dolly were human, what biological problems would she face? Based on your research, can you make a recommendation for or against human cloning at this time?

10. Research the cloning claims of the Raelians and their efforts to clone a human being. After the announcement of the cloning of Dolly, Rael, the founder of the Raelian movement, founded Clonaid, a company offering human cloning services (*http://www.clonaid.com*). Visit the Clonaid web site. Are their efforts dangerous? Noble? Write a short newspaper report on the most recent activities of Clonaid.

GROUP PROJECTS

11. Obtain a copy of the President's Council on Bioethics' report on human cloning at its web site at *http://www.bioethics.gov/reports/cloningreport/ index.html*. Your group has been appointed to revisit the issues addressed by the commission developed in 2002. Individually, research current cloning technology, addressing the section on children and research in particular, and then discuss your viewpoints on this issue with your group. Based on group discussion, revise the 2002 report and make a recommendation to the president.

12. One of the arguments against human cloning is that the technology could be abused to create clones of exceptional people, such as athletes, geniuses, and supermodels. With your group, discuss the likelihood of such an application of cloning technology. Who are possible candidates for cloning and why? In your discussion, also address the idea of "the right to genetic identity." Should such a right exist? How could it be violated?

Designer Babies
Sharon Begley

When scientists announced the mapping of the human genome in 2000, it was only the beginning, rather than the end, of a huge scientific endeavor. By identifying every gene within
the 23 pairs of chromosomes that make a human being, scientists may now hold the keys to
unlocking miracle cures for genetic diseases. Many researchers believe gene therapy could
allow physicians to cure genetic diseases while a fetus is still growing—before it is even
born. But other possibilities, perhaps more sinister, come with this technology. If scientists
can manipulate genes to treat diseases, could they also use this knowledge to create kids
with made-to-order traits? Will the twenty-first century usher in the age of the designer baby?
Newsweek writer Sharon Begley explores the connection between the promise of genetic engineering and its implications for generations of future children.

**CRITICAL
THINKING** Many people blame their genes for characteristics they consider undesirable
about themselves. If your parents could have genetically designed you, what
physical traits would you have wanted them to select? Or are you happy with
your genetic profile just the way you are?

1 It is only a matter of time. One day—a day probably no more distant than the first
wedding anniversary of a couple who are now teenage sweethearts—a man and a
woman will walk into an in vitro fertilization clinic and make scientific history.
Their problem won't be infertility, the reason couples now choose IVF. Rather, they
will be desperate for a very special child, a child who will elude a family curse. To
create their dream child, doctors will fertilize a few of the woman's eggs with her
husband's sperm, as IVF clinics do today. But then they will inject an artificial human chromosome, carrying made-to-order genes like pearls on a string, into the fertilized egg. One of the genes will carry instructions ordering cells to commit suicide.
Then the doctors will place the embryo into the woman's uterus. If her baby is a
boy, when he becomes an old man he, like his father and grandfather before him,
will develop prostate cancer. But the cell-suicide gene will make his prostate cells
self-destruct. The man, unlike his ancestors, will not die of the cancer. And since the
gene that the doctors gave him copied itself into every cell of his body, including his
sperm, his sons will beat prostate cancer, too.

2   Genetic engineers are preparing to cross what has long been an ethical Rubicon.
Since 1990, gene therapy has meant slipping a healthy gene into the cells of one organ of a patient suffering from a genetic disease. Soon, it may mean something much
more momentous: altering a fertilized egg so that genes in all of a person's cells, including eggs or sperm, also carry a gene that scientists, not parents, bequeathed them.
When the pioneers of gene therapy first requested government approval for their experiments in 1987, they vowed they would never alter patients' eggs or sperm. That

was then. This is now. One of those pioneers, Dr. W. French Anderson of the University of Southern California, recently put the National Institutes of Health on notice. Within two or three years, he said, he would ask approval to use gene therapy on a fetus that has been diagnosed with a deadly inherited disease. The therapy would cure the fetus before it is born. But the introduced genes, though targeted at only blood or immune-system cells, might inadvertently slip into the child's egg (or sperm) cells, too. If that happens, the genetic change would affect that child's children unto the nth generation. "Life would enter a new phase," says biophysicist Gregory Stock of UCLA, "one in which we seize control of our own evolution."

3   Judging by the 70 pages of public comments NIH has received since Anderson submitted his proposal, the overwhelming majority of scientists and ethicists weighing in oppose gene therapy that changes the "germline" (eggs and sperm). But the opposition could be a boulevard wide and paper thin. "There is a great divide in the bioethics community over whether we should be opening up this Pandora's box," says science-policy scholar Sheldon Krimsky of Tufts University. Many bioethicists are sympathetic to using germline therapy to shield a child from a family disposition to cancer, or atherosclerosis or other illnesses with a strong genetic component. As James Watson, president of the Cold Spring Harbor Laboratory and codiscoverer of the double-helical structure of DNA, said at a recent UCLA conference, "We might as well do what we finally can to take the threat of Alzheimer's or breast cancer away from a family." But something else is suddenly making it OK to discuss the once forbidden possibility of germline engineering: molecular biologists now think they have clever ways to circumvent ethical concerns that engulf this sci-fi idea.

4   There may be ways, for instance, to design a baby's genes without violating the principle of informed consent. This is the belief that no one's genes—not even an embryo's—should be altered without his or her permission. Presumably few people would object to being spared a fatal disease. But what about genes for personality traits, like risk-taking or being neurotic? If you like today's blame game—it's Mom's fault that you inherited her temper—you'll love tomorrow's: she intentionally stuck you with that personality quirk. But the child of tomorrow might have the final word about his genes, says UCLA geneticist John Campbell. The designer gene for, say, patience could be paired with an on-off switch, he says. The child would have to take a drug to activate the patience gene. Free to accept or reject the drug, he retains informed consent over his genetic endowment.

5   There may also be ways to make an end run around the worry that it is wrong to monkey with human evolution. Researchers are experimenting with tricks to make the introduced gene self-destruct in cells that become eggs or sperm. That would confine the tinkering to one generation. Then, if it became clear that eliminating genes for, say, mental illness also erased genes for creativity, that loss would not become a permanent part of man's genetic blueprint. (Of course, preventing the new gene's transmission to future generations would also defeat the hope of permanently lopping off a diseased branch from a family tree.) In experiments with animals, geneticist Mario Capecchi of the University of Utah has designed a string of genes flanked by the molecular version of scissors. The scissors are activated by an enzyme that would be made only in the cells that become eggs or sperm. Once acti-

vated, the genetic scissors snip out the introduced gene and, presto, it is not passed along to future generations. "What I worry about," says Capecchi, "is that if we start messing around with [eggs and sperm], at some point—since this is a human enterprise—we're going to make a mistake. You want a way to undo that mistake. And since what may seem terrific now may seem naive in 20 years, you want a way to make the genetic change reversible."

6   There is no easy technological fix for another ethical worry, however: with germline engineering only society's "haves" will control their genetic traits. It isn't hard to foresee a day like that painted in the film "Gattaca," where only the wealthy can afford to genetically engineer their children with such "killer applications" as intelligence, beauty, long life or health. "If you are going to disadvantage even further those who are already disadvantaged," says bioethicist Ruth Macklin of Albert Einstein College of Medicine, "then that does raise serious concerns." But perhaps not enough to keep designer babies solely in Hollywood's imagination. For one thing, genetic therapy as done today (treating one organ of one child or adult) has been a bitter disappointment. "With the exception of a few anecdotal cases," says USC's Anderson, "there is no evidence of a gene-therapy protocol that helps." But germline therapy might actually be easier. Doctors would not have to insinuate the new gene into millions of lung cells in, say, a cystic fibrosis patient. They could manipulate only a single cell—the fertilized egg—and still have the gene reach every cell of the person who develops from that egg.

7   How soon might we design our children? The necessary pieces are quickly falling into place. The first artificial human chromosome was created in 1997. In 2000, the Human Genome Project decoded all 3 billion chemical letters that spell out our 70,000 or so genes. Animal experiments designed to show that the process will not create horrible mutants are underway. No law prohibits germline engineering. Although NIH now refuses to even consider funding proposals for it, the rules are being updated. And where there is a way, there will almost surely be a will: none of us, says USC's Anderson, "wants to pass on to our children lethal genes if we can prevent it—that's what's going to drive this." At the UCLA symposium on germline engineering, two thirds of the audience supported it. Few would argue against using the technique to eradicate a disease that has plagued a family for generations. As Tuft's Krimsky says, "We know where to start." The harder question is this: do we know where to stop? ◆

FREEWRITING ASSIGNMENT

The "nature vs. nurture" argument has a long history. What role, if any, do you think genetics has on a person's professional and personal success?

CRITICAL READING

1. Science policy scholar Sheldon Krimsky comments that using genetic technology to cure diseases before birth is a "Pandora's box." What does

he mean? What was "Pandora's box"? What did it do to the world? Is this analogy appropriate? Explain.

2. How could our understanding of genetics change reproduction? Would it be considered parental irresponsibility *not* to alter offspring genetically? For example, if a woman has the gene for breast cancer, and bears children without genetic engineering to prevent the transmission or activation of this gene, could she potentially face a charge of manslaughter if her daughter developed the disease?

3. Although "designer babies" are not yet possible, the probability of our ability to determine the genetic makeup of our children is very real. What type of genetic control does "genetic foreknowledge" offer future parents? Are there ethical and unethical applications of this technology? Explain.

4. Begley comments that one ethical worry connected to genetic engineering of humans is that "only society's 'haves' will control their genetic traits." How could genetic testing create even greater disparity between the rich and the poor? How does genetics influence our current economic hierarchy? Explain.

5. Evaluate Begley's quote from Sheldon Krimsky as the concluding sentence to her essay. Is this quote an effective ending? Why or why not? How does it connect to her article overall? Explain.

CRITICAL WRITING

6. *Exploratory Writing*: Would you want to know the genetic blueprint of your future child? If you would want to know, explain how you would use such knowledge. If you would not want to know, explain why not.

7. *Critical Analysis*: Consider W. French Anderson's comment that genetic engineering will bring "life into a new phase, one in which we seize control of our own evolution." Explore the ethical implications of his statement.

8. *Exploratory Writing*: Write about what impact the ability to determine a child's genetic makeup could have on future generations. Besides medical benefits and problems, discuss the social ramifications of such power. For example, some societies prefer male children to female, and others consider certain traits more desirable. What could the long-term ramifications of genetic control have on the world?

GROUP PROJECTS

9. Discuss the social ramifications of moving reproduction to the laboratory. With your group, develop a picture of what society would be like in such a world. You may want to view the movie *Gattica,* Begley refers to as a starting point for discussion. Share your views with the class.

10. With your group, develop a set of rules that controls the use of genetic engineering in humans. In your rules, consider the possibility of altering the "germline," disease prevention, and the potential for human error. Share your draft with the class, and explain the reasons behind your decisions.

Future Scientific Convention
Michael Ramirez

While the completion of the Human Genome Project was a much anticipated and highly publicized event for journalists, it also provided fodder material for editorial cartoonists. This cartoon by Michael Ramirez, an editorial cartoonist, was published in the *Los Angeles Times*.

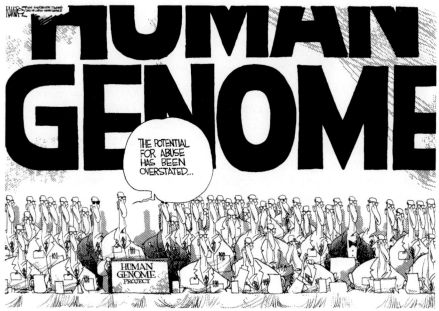

Michael Ramirez and Copley News Service

1. What is the visual cliché in this cartoon? How long does it take you to discern what the cliché is and how it works in the image?
2. Is this cartoon funny? Why or why not?
3. What does the viewer need to know about the subject in order to understand the cartoon? How important is timing to this cartoon? Explain.

The Last Human
Gregory Stock

With advances in DNA technology, we may be confronting the most difficult decisions ever to face humanity. While many ethicists worry that this technology may irrevocably alter the human genome and humanity as we now define it, others argue that if we have the ability, why not use it? In the next piece, Gregory Stock agrees that there are many ethical issues we must address with genetic technology, but like it or not, the question is no longer whether we will use DNA technology to improve human lives, but how we will use it.

Gregory Stock is director of the Program on Medicine, Technology, and Society at the University of California School of Medicine at Los Angeles. He is the author of several books, including *Metaman: The Merging of Humans and Machines into a Global Superorganism* (1993), and *The Book of Questions* (1987). The following essay is an excerpt from the introduction of Stock's latest book, *Redesigning Humans: Our Inevitable Genetic Future* (2002).

CRITICAL THINKING	Is biotechnology eroding our definitions of what it means to be human? Could the way we view ourselves, and our sense of identity, change because of this new technology? Why or why not?

God and Nature first made us what we are, and then out of our own created genius we make ourselves what we want to be. . . . Let the sky and God be our limit and Eternity our measurement.

—Marcus Garvey (1887–1940)

1   We know that *Homo sapiens* is not the final word in primate evolution, but few have yet grasped that we are on the cusp of profound biological change, poised to transcend our current form and character on a journey to destinations of new imagination.

2   At first glance, the very notion that we might become more than "human" seems preposterous. After all, we are still biologically identical in virtually every respect to our cave-dwelling ancestors. But this lack of change is deceptive. Never before have we had the power to manipulate human genetics to alter our biology in meaningful, predictable ways.

3   Bioethicists and scientists alike worry about the consequences of coming genetic technologies, but few have thought through the larger implications of the wave of new developments arriving in reproductive biology. Today *in vitro* fertilization is responsible for fewer than 1 percent of births in the United States; embryo selection numbers only in the hundreds of cases; cloning and human genetic modification still lie ahead. But give these emerging technologies a decade and they will be the cutting edge of human biological change.

4   These developments will write a new page in the history of life, allowing us to seize control of our evolutionary future. Our coming ability to choose our children's genes will have immense social impact and raise difficult ethical dilemmas. Biological enhancement will lead us into unexplored realms, eventually challenging our basic ideas about what it means to be human.

5   Some imagine we will see the perils, come to our senses, and turn away from such possibilities. But when we imagine Prometheus stealing fire from the gods, we are not incredulous or shocked by his act. It is too characteristically human. To forgo the powerful technologies that genomics and molecular biology are bringing would be as out of character for humanity as it would be to use them without concern for the dangers they pose. We will do neither. The question is no longer whether we will manipulate embryos, but when, where, and how.

6   We have already felt the impact of previous advances in reproductive technology. Without the broad access to birth control that we take so for granted, the popu-

lations of Italy, Japan, and Germany would not be shrinking; birth rates in the developing world would not be falling. These are major shifts, yet unlike the public response to today's high-tech developments, no impassioned voices protest birth control as an immense and dangerous experiment with our genetic future. Those opposing family planning seem more worried about the immorality of recreational sex than about human evolution.

7   The arrival of safe, reliable germline technology will signal the beginning of human self-design. We do not know where this development will ultimately take us, but it will transform the evolutionary process by drawing reproduction into a highly selective social process that is far more rapid and effective at spreading successful genes than traditional sexual competition and mate selection.

8   Dismissal of technology's role in humanity's genetic future is common even among biologists who use advanced technologies in their work. Perhaps the notion that we will control our evolutionary future seems too audacious. Perhaps the idea that humans might one day differ from us in fundamental ways is too disorienting. Most mass-media science fiction doesn't challenge our thinking about this either. One of the last major sci-fi movies of the second millennium was *The Phantom Menace*, George Lucas's 1999 prequel to *Star Wars*. Its vision of human biological enhancement was simple: there won't be any. Lucas reveled in special effects and fantastical life forms, but altered us not a jot. Despite reptilian sidekicks with pedestal eyes and hard-bargaining insectiods that might have escaped a Raid commercial, the film's humans were no different from us. With the right accent and a coat and tie, the leader of the Galactic Republic might have been the president of France.

9   Such a vision of human continuity is reassuring. It lets us imagine a future in which we feel at home. Space pods, holographic telephones, laser pistols, and other amazing gadgets are enticing to many of us, but pondering a time when humans no longer exist is another story, one far too alien and unappealing to arouse our dramatic sympathies. We've seen too many apocalyptic images of nuclear, biological, and environmental disaster to think that the path to human extinction could be anything but horrific.

10   Yet the road to our eventual disappearance might be paved not by humanity's failure but by its success. Progressive self-transformation could change our descendants into something sufficiently different from our present selves to not be human in the sense we use the term now. Such an occurrence would more aptly be termed a pseudoextinction, since it would not end our lineage. Unlike the saber-toothed tiger and other large mammals that left no descendants when our ancestors drove them to extinction, *Homo sapiens* would spawn its own successors by fast-forwarding its evolution.

11   Some disaster, of course, might derail our technological advance, or our biology might prove too complex to rework. But our recent deciphering of the human genome (the entirety of our genetic constitution) and our massive push to unravel life's workings suggest that modification of our biology is far nearer to reality than the distant space travel we see in science fiction movies. Moreover, we are unlikely to achieve the technology to flit around the galaxy without being able to breach our own biology as well. The Human Genome Project is only a beginning. Considering the barrage of press reports about the project, we naturally wonder how much is

hype. Extravagant metaphor has not been lacking. We are deciphering the "code of codes," reading the "book of life," looking at the "holy grail of human biology." It is reminiscent of the enthusiasm that attended Neil Armstrong's 1969 walk on the moon. Humanity seemed poised to march toward the stars, but 2001 has come and gone, and there has been no sentient computer like HAL, no odyssey to the moons of Jupiter. Thirty years from now, however, I do not think we will look back at the Human Genome project with a similar wistful disappointment. Unlike outer space, genetics is at our core, and as we learn to manipulate it, we are learning to manipulate ourselves.

12   Many bioethicists do not share my perspective on where we are heading. They imagine that our technology might become potent enough to alter us, but that we will turn away from it and reject human enhancement. But the reshaping of human genetics and biology does not hinge on some cadre of demonic researchers hidden away in a lab in Argentina trying to pick up where Hitler left off. The coming possibilities will be the inadvertent spinoff of mainstream research that virtually everyone supports. Infertility, for example, is a source of deep pain for millions of couples. Researchers and clinicians working on *in vitro* fertilization (NF) don't think much about future human evolution, but nonetheless are building a foundation of expertise in conceiving, handling, testing, and implanting human embryos, and this will one day be the basis for the manipulation of the human species. Already, we are seeing attempts to apply this knowledge in highly controversial ways: as premature as today's efforts to clone humans may be, they would be the flimsiest of fantasies if they could not draw on decades of work on human IVF.

13   Similarly, in early 2001 more than five hundred gene-therapy trials were under way or in review throughout the world. The researchers are trying to cure real people suffering from real diseases and are no more interested in the future of human evolution than IVF researchers. But their progress toward inserting genes into adult cells will be one more piece of the foundation for manipulating human embryos.

14   Not everything that can be done should or will be done, of course, but once a relatively inexpensive technology becomes feasible in thousands of laboratories around the world, and a sizable fraction of the population sees it as beneficial, it *will* be used.

15   We cannot hold ourselves apart from the biological heritage that has shaped us. What we learn from fruit flies, mice, or even a cute Dorset ewe named Dolly is relevant to us. No matter how much the scientists who perform basic research in animal genetics and reproduction may sometimes deny it, their work is a critical part of the control we will soon have over our biology. Our desire to apply the results of animal research to human medicine, after all, is what drives much of the funding of this work.

16   Over the past hundred years, the trajectory of the life sciences traces a clear shift from description to understanding to manipulation. At the close of the nineteenth century, describing new biological attributes or species was still a good Ph.D. project for a student. This changed during the twentieth century, and such observations became largely a means for understanding the workings of biology. That too is now changing, and in the first half of the twenty-first century, biological understanding will likely become less an end in itself than a means to manipulate biology. In one century, we have moved from observing to understanding to engineering.

17   The best gauge of how far we will go in manipulating our genetics and that of our children is not what we say to pollsters, but what we are doing in those areas in which we already can modify our biology. On August 2, 1998, Marco Pantani cycled along the Champs Elysees to win the eighty-fifth Tour de France, but the race's real story was the scandal over performance enhancement—which, of course, means drugs.

18   The banned hormone erythropoietin was at the heart of this particular chapter in the ongoing saga of athletic performance enhancement. By raising the oxygen-carrying capacity of red blood cells, the drug can boost endurance by 10 to 15 percent. Early in the race, a stash of it was found in the car of the masseur of the Italian team Festina—one of the world's best—and after an investigation the entire team was booted from the race. A few days later, more erythropoietin was found, this time in the possession of one of the handlers of the Dutch team, and several of its cyclists were kicked out. As police raids intensified, five Spanish teams and an Italian one quit in protest, leaving only fourteen of the original twenty-one teams.

19   The public had little sympathy for the cheaters, but a crowd of angry Festina supporters protested that their riders had been unfairly singled out, and the French minister of health insisted that doping had been going on since racing began. Two years later in a courtroom in Lille, the French sports icon Richard Virenque, five-time winner of the King of the Mountains jersey in the Tour de France, seemed to confirm as much when the president of the court asked him if he took doping products. "We don't say doping, replied Virenque. "We say we're 'preparing for the race.'"

20   The most obvious problem with today's performance-enhancing drugs—besides their being a way of cheating—is that they're dangerous. And when one athlete uses them, others must follow suit to stay competitive. But more than safety is at issue. The concern is what sports will be like when competitors need medical pit crews. As difficult as the problem of doping is, it will soon worsen, because such drugs will become safer, more effective, and harder to detect. Professional sports offers a preview of the spread of enhancement technology into other arenas. Sports may carry stronger incentives to cheat, and thus push athletes toward greater health risks, but the nonsporting world is not so different. A person working two jobs feels under pressure to produce, and so does a student taking a test or someone suffering the effects of growing old. When safe, reliable metabolic and physiological enhancers exist, the public will want them, even if they are illegal. To block their use will be far more daunting than today's war on drugs. An antidrug commercial proclaiming "dope is for dopes" or one showing a frying egg with the caption "your brain on drugs" would not persuade anyone to stop using a safe memory enhancer.

21   Aesthetic surgery is another budding field for enhancement. When we try to improve our appearance, the personal stakes are high because our looks are always with us. Knowing that the photographs of beautiful models in magazines are airbrushed does not make us any less self-conscious if we believe we have a smile too gummy, skin too droopy, breasts too small, a nose too big, a head too bald, or any other such "defects." Surgery to correct these nonmedical problems has been growing rapidly and spreading to an ever-younger clientele. Public approval of aesthetic surgery has climbed some 50 percent in the past decade in the United States. We may not be modifying our genes yet, but we are ever more willing to resort to

surgery to hold back the most obvious (and superficial) manifestations of aging, or even simply to remodel our bodies. Nor is this only for the wealthy. In 1994, when the median income in the United States was around $38,000, two thirds of the 400,000 aesthetic surgeries were performed on those with a family income under $50,000, and health insurance rarely covered the procedure. Older women who have subjected themselves to numerous face-lifts but can no longer stave off the signs of aging are not a rarity. But the tragedy is not so much that these women fight so hard to deny the years of visible decline, but that their struggle against life's natural ebb ultimately must fail. If such a decline were not inevitable, many people would eagerly embrace pharmaceutical or genetic interventions to retard aging.

22   The desire to triumph over our own mortality is an ancient dream, but it hardly stands alone. Whether we look at today's manipulations of our bodies by face-lifts, tattoos, pierced ears, or erythropoietin, the same message rings loud and clear: if medicine one day enables us to manipulate our biology in appealing ways, many of us will do so—even if the benefits are dubious and the risks not insignificant. To most people, the earliest adopters of these technologies will seem reckless or crazy, but are they so different from the daredevil test pilots of jet aircraft in the 1950s? Virtually by definition, early users believe that the possible gains from their bravado justify the risks. Otherwise, they would wait for flawed procedures to be discarded, for technical glitches to be worked through, for interventions to become safer and more predictable. In truth, as long as people compete with one another for money, status, and mates, as long as they look for ways to display their worth and uniqueness, they will look for an edge for themselves and their children.

23   People will make mistakes with these biological manipulations. People will abuse them. People will worry about them. But as much could be said about any potent new development. No governmental body will wave some legislative wand and make advanced genetic and reproductive technologies go away, and we would be foolish to want this. Our collective challenge is not to figure out how to block these developments, but how best to realize their benefits while minimizing our risks and safeguarding our rights and freedoms. This will not be easy.

24   Our history is not a tale of self-restraint. Ten thousand years ago, when humans first crossed the Bering Strait to enter the Americas, they found huge herds of mammoths and other large mammals. In short order, these Clovis peoples, named for the archaeological site in New Mexico where their tools were first identified, used their skill and weaponry to drive them to extinction. This was no aberration: the arrival of humans in Australia, New Zealand, Madagascar, Hawaii, and Easter Island brought the same slaughter of wildlife. We may like to believe that primitive peoples lived in balance with nature, but when they entered new lands, they reshaped them in profound, often destructive ways. Jared Diamond, a professor of physiology at the UCLA School of Medicine and an expert on how geography and environment have affected human evolution, has tried to reconcile this typical pattern with the rare instances in which destruction did not occur. He writes that while "small, long-established egalitarian societies can evolve conservationist practices, because they've had plenty of time to get to know their local environment and to perceive their own self-interest," these practices do not occur when a people suddenly colonizes an unfamiliar environment or acquires a potent new technology.

25   Our technology is evolving so rapidly that by the time we begin to adjust to one development, another is already surpassing it. The answer would seem to be to slow down and devise the best course in advance, but that notion is a mirage. Change is accelerating, not slowing, and even if we could agree on what to aim for, the goal would probably be unrealistic. Complex changes are occurring across too broad a front to chart a path. The future is too opaque to foresee the eventual impacts of important new technologies, much less whole bodies of knowledge like genomics (the study of genomes). No one understood the powerful effects of the automobile or television at its inception. Few appreciated that our use of antibiotics would lead to widespread drug resistance or that improved nutrition and public health in the developing world would help bring on a population explosion. Our blindness about the consequences of new reproductive technologies is nothing new, and we will not be able to erase the uncertainty by convening an august panel to think through the issues.

26   No shortcut is possible. As always, we will have to earn our knowledge by using the technology and learning from the problems that arise. Given that some people will dabble in the new procedures as soon as they become even remotely accessible, our safest path is to not drive early explorations underground. What we learn about such technology, while it is imperfect and likely to be used by only a small number of people, may help us figure out how to manage it more wisely as it matures. ◆

FREEWRITING ASSIGNMENT

If humans were to use genetic engineering to alter their DNA, would they still be human, or something else?

CRITICAL READING

1. Stock states, "Biological enhancement will lead us into unexplored realms, eventually challenging our basic ideas about what it means to be human" (paragraph 4). What does he mean? What are the implications of this statement? Does it seem frightening? Exciting? Explain.

2. Stock observes that in *The Phantom Menace*, despite fantastic intergalactic creatures, humans were altered "not a jot." In what ways has the media considered the future of genetic engineering? In addition to the *Star Wars* movies, can you think of other sci-fi movies that feature humans in the future? How are they depicted? Do your examples back up Stock's observations, or refute them?

3. How does Stock feel about genetic engineering? Summarize his argument in a paragraph.

4. When comparing the promise of the mapping of the human genome to the 1969 moonwalk, Stock states, "Thirty years from now, however, I do not think we will look back at the Human Genome project with a similar wistful disappointment." What assumptions does he make of his audience with this statement? Explain.

5. Stock makes a reference to Hitler's eugenics plan to create a master race. Could DNA technology be abused this way? Theoretically, could a dictator use genetic engineering to create smarter, stronger citizens?

6. Stock notes that dismissal of the role of technology in our genetic future is common even among biologists, perhaps because the "notion that we will control our evolutionary future seems too audacious." Are so many people opposed to genetic technology because it poses legitimate risks, or because it is intellectually upsetting? What is at the root of their objections? Explore this issue.

7. Stock uses the case of cyclists doping with erythropoietin during the 1998 Tour de France as a parallel to what is likely to happen with genetic engineering. How effective is this example? Does it serve as a good indicator of what humans will do to achieve and succeed? Explain.

CRITICAL WRITING

8. Is there such a thing as "genetic identity?" Should we have such a right? How could our genetic identity be violated? Could we someday have a situation where "identity theft" is more than a case of stolen credit cards but the theft of our DNA? Write an essay exploring the concept of genetic identity, and what it might mean for the future.

9. *Exploratory Writing*: Stock predicts that in thirty years, unlike the space program, we will be actively using genetic technology to "manipulate ourselves." Write an exploratory essay in which you predict what genetic technology might be used for in actual practice thirty years from now.

10. Stock makes a reference to Hitler's eugenics plan to create a master race. Could DNA technology be abused this way? Theoretically, could a dictator use genetic engineering to create smarter, stronger citizens? Research Hitler's eugenics efforts during World War II, and apply your research to the possibility of such efforts being repeated in the future.

11. Many of the writers in this chapter have argued against the things for which Stock advocates in this essay. Write a response to Stock from the viewpoint of another author in this chapter. Refer to points made in each writer's essays in your response.

GROUP PROJECTS

12. The year is 2040, and the U.S. government, concerned that tinkering with human DNA could have dire consequences generations from now, has banned the practice of human genetic engineering. However, routine genetic screening, a common health practice, reveals that a young boy has been genetically altered to make him smarter than he normally would have been. His parents are arrested, having admitted to paying for the genetic engineering at a center in Europe. They argue that they obtained this service because they felt it was in the best interest of their child. Your group, a jury, must decide what to do. Do you incarcerate the couple? Fine

them? Discuss the case and present your decision to the class as part of a larger discussion.

13. Stock makes the argument that if a safe genetically engineered product were available to make us smarter, more youthful, or have better memories, we would use them. With your group, discuss whether such usage is ethical. If so, are they any different from athletes using erythropoietin? Why or why not?

Enough
Bill McKibben

In the preceding essay, Gregory Stock extolled the promise of genetic engineering. In the next piece, Bill McKibben takes a more grim perspective on the issue. He warns that we are approaching the transformation of our species as if we were "sleepwalking." Unless we open our eyes and take a good hard look at what genetic technology means for the future of the human race, we will soon reach a point of no return. We must consider the implications before it is too late.

Bill McKibben is a scholar in residence at Middlebury College. He is a regular contributor to many publications, including the *New York Review of Books*, the *New York Times*, and *The Atlantic*. He is the author of many books, most recently *Maybe One*, *Long Distance: A Year of Living Strenuously*, and *Enough*, from which this essay was excerpted.

CRITICAL THINKING   Twenty years ago, we were raising serious questions about the ethics of *in vitro* fertilization and "test tube" babies—a practice that most people find acceptable. Do you think its likely that we will feel the same way about human genetic engineering? Will it become acceptable as time passes? Why or why not?

---

1   For the first few miles of the marathon, I was still fresh enough to look around, to pay attention. I remember mostly the muffled thump of several thousand pairs of expensive sneakers padding the Ottawa pavement—an elemental sound, like surf, or wind. But as the race wore on, the herd stretched into a dozen flocks and then into a long string of solitary runners. Pretty soon each of us was off in a singular race, pitting one body against one will. By the halfway point, when all the adrenaline had worn off, the only sound left was my breath rattling in my chest. I was deep in my own private universe, completely absorbed in my own drama.

2   Now, this run was entirely inconsequential. For months I'd trained with the arbitrary goal of 3 hours and 20 minutes in my mind. Which is not a fast time: it's an hour and a quarter off the world record. But it would let a forty-one-year-old into the Boston Marathon. And given how fast I'd gone in training, I knew it lay at the outer edge of possible. So it was a worthwhile target, a number to live with through one

early-morning run after another, a number to multiply and divide against the read-outs on the treadmill display when downpours kept me in the gym. It's rare enough in my life to have a goal so concrete and unambiguous.

3   By about, say, mile 23, two things were becoming clear. One, my training had worked. I'd reeled off one 7:30 mile after another. Two, my training wouldn't get me to the finish by itself. My legs were starting to slow and wobble, my knees and calves were hard pressed to lift and push at the same pace as an hour earlier. I could feel my goal slipping away, my pace dropping. With every hundred yards the race became less a physical test and more a mental one, game spirit trying to rally sagging flesh before sagging flesh could sap game spirit and convince it the time had come to walk. Someone stronger passed me, and I slipped onto her heels for a few hundred crucial yards, picking up the pace. The finish line swam into my squinted view, and I stagger-sprinted across. With 14 seconds to spare.

4   A photographer clicked a picture, as he would of everyone who finished. I was a cipher to him—a grimacing cipher, the 324th person to cross, an unimportant finisher in an unimportant time in an unimportant race. In the picture you can see the crowd at the finish, looking right past me toward the middle distance, waiting for their mom or dad, son or daughter to move into sight. It mattered not at all what I had done.

5   But it mattered to me. When it was done, I had a clearer sense of myself, of my power and my frailty. For a period of hours, and especially those last gritty miles, I had been absolutely, utterly *present*, the moments desperately, magnificently clarified. As meaningless as it was to the world, that's how meanig*ful* it was to me. I met parts of myself I'd never been introduced to before, glimpsed more clearly strengths and flaws I'd half suspected. A marathon peels you down toward your core for a little while, gets past the defenses we erect even against ourselves. That's the high that draws you back for the next race, a centering elation shared by people who finished an hour ahead and two hours behind me. And it must echo in some small way what runners have always felt—the Tarahumara Indians on their impossible week-long runs through the canyons of Mexico, the Masai on their game trails. Few things are more basic than running.

6   And yet it is entirely possible that we will be among the last generations to feel that power and that frailty. Genetic science may soon offer human beings, among many other things, the power to bless their offspring with a vastly improved engine. For instance, scientists may find ways to dramatically increase the amount of oxygen that blood can carry. When that happens, we will, though not quite as Isaiah envisioned, be able to run and not grow weary.

7   This is one small item on the long list of "improvements" that the proponents of human genetic engineering envision, and one of the least significant comers of human life they propose to alter. But it serves as a decent template for starting to think about all the changes they have in mind, and indeed the changes that may result from a suite of other new engineering marvels like advanced robotics and nanotechnology.

8   Consider sports. Attempts to alter the human body are nothing new in sports, of course. It's been more than a century since Charles-Edouard Brown-Sequard, the French physiologist called "the father of steroids," injected himself with an extract derived from the testicle of a guinea pig and a dog.[1] Athletes have been irradiated

and surgically implanted with monkey glands; they have weight-trained with special regimens designed to increase mitochondria in muscle cells and have lived in special trailers pressurized to simulate high altitudes.[2] For endurance athletes, the drug of choice has for the last decade been erythropoietin, or EPO, a man-made version of a hormone released by the kidneys that stimulates the production of red blood cells, so that the blood can carry extra oxygen. With EPO, the red blood cells can get so thick that the blood curdles, turns into a syrupy ooze—in the early days of the drug, elite cyclists started dropping dead across their handlebars, their hearts unable to pump the sludge running through their veins.

9   In 1995, researchers asked two hundred Olympic hopefuls if they'd take a drug that would guarantee them a five-year winning streak and then kill them. Almost half said yes.[3] The Tour de France has been interrupted by police raids time and again; in 2001, Italian officials found what they described as a "mobile hospital" trailing the Giro d'Italia bike race, well-stocked with testosterone, human growth hormone, urofillitophin, salbutamol, and a synthetic blood product called HemAssist.[4] The British sports commentator Simon Eassom said recently that the only people likely to be caught for steroid abuse were from Third World countries: everyone else could afford new-generation drugs that didn't yet show up on tests.[5] Some sports, like power lifting, have had to give in and set up "drug-free" or "natural" divisions.[6]

10   In other words, you could almost say that it makes no difference whether athletes of the future are genetically engineered—that the damage is already done with conventional drugs, the line already crossed. You could almost say that, but not quite. Because in fact, in the last couple of years, the testing has gotten better. The new World Anti-Doping Agency has caught enough offenders to throw a scare into dirty athletes, and some heart into clean ones. Some distance athletes who had decided to retire because they felt they couldn't compete have gone back into training; a new group of poststeroids shotputters and discus hurlers have proved their point by winning meets with shorter throws than the records of a decade ago.[7] And both athlete and fan remain able to draw the line in their minds: no one thought Ben Johnson's 1988 dash record meant anything once the Olympic lab found steroids in his system. It was erased from the record books, and he was banned from competition. Against the odds, sports just manages to stay "real."

11   But what if, instead of crudely cheating with hypodermics, we began to literally program children before they were born to become great athletes? "Picture this," writes one British journalist. "It is 2016. A young couple are sitting in a doctor's waiting room. They know that what they are about to do is illegal, but they are determined. They have come to make their child a world-beating athlete," by injecting their embryo with the patented genes of a champion.[8] Muscle size, oxygen uptake, respiration—much of an athlete's inherent capacity derives from her genes. What she makes of it depends on her heart and mind, of course, as well as on the accidents of where she's born, and what kind of diet she gets, and whether the local rulers believe that girls should be out running.

12   And her genes aren't entirely random: perhaps her parents were attracted to each other in the first place because both were athletes, or because they were not. But all those variables fit within our idea of fate. Flipping through the clinic catalogue for athletic genes does not; it's a door into another world.

13   If it happens—and when that girl grows up to compete—it won't be as if she is "cheating." "What if you're born with something having been done to you?" asks the Olympic dash champion Maurice Greene. "You didn't have anything to do with it."[9] But if that happens, what will be the point of running? "Just what human excellences are we supposed to be celebrating?" asks the medical ethicist Eric Juengst. "Who's got the better biotech sponsor?"[10]

14   Soon, says Simon Eassom, most sport may become Evel Knievelish pageantry: "'Roll up, roll up, let's see somebody who'll break six seconds for the hundred meters.'" Spectacle will survive, and for many fans that may be enough. But the emptiness will be real.

15   To get a small sense of what it will feel like, consider the 2002 Winter Olympics in Salt Lake City. While the North American media obsessed over figure skating disputes, the highest drama may have come on the Nordic skiing trails. Erling Jevne of Norway, a grand old man of the sport, was readying himself for one last race, the 50-kilometer, the marathon of winter. He was the sentimental favorite, in part because he had one of those sad stories that, were he an American, would have earned him hours of maudlin airtime. Raking hay on his fifth-generation family farm one day, he'd watched helplessly as his four-year-old son climbed a fence, stumbled onto a road, and was killed by a car. "I don't have a single workout where I don't think about Erich Iver," he said before the Games. "Yes, I would go far enough to say that he is an inner inspiration for my training now"—which makes Jevne not so different from all the thousands of people who run marathons in honor of their mothers, their fathers, their sons, their daughters, their friends who have died before their time or live amidst tragedy.[11] Half the people running next to me in Ottawa seemed to be wearing T-shirts with the image of some dead or dying relative.

16   Once before Jevne had won Olympic silver, losing to a Finn who, years later, was caught doping. This was his final stand—and he was crushed. Not long after the start, the Spaniard Johann Muehlegg caught up with him and cruised past. "His pace was simply too fast for me. He skied faster than I've ever done in my life," said Jevne.[12] As one commentator put it, Muehlegg "looked like he was skiing on another planet."[13] As indeed he was—the Planet NESP, a new EPO derivative discovered in his urine right after the race. He was stripped of his medal, although he's still appealing.

17   Before he heard the news—when he thought he'd simply been passed by a stronger man, or one who'd trained harder—Jevne said, "I'll recover from the disappointment. It's after all just a skiing race."[14] Which is, I suppose, the right way to think about it; for those of us who will never win a race, it should be easy to nod. But as we move into this new world of genetic engineering, we won't simply lose races, we'll lose racing: we'll lose the possibility of the test, the challenge, the celebration that athletics represents. Forget elite athletes—they drip one drop of sweat for every thousand that roll off the brows of weekend warriors. It's the average human, once "improved," who will have no more reason for running marathons. Say you've reached Mile 23, and you're feeling strong. Is it because of your hard training and your character, or because the gene pack inside you is pumping out more red blood cells than your body knows what to do with? Will anyone be impressed with your dedication? More to the point, will you be impressed with your dedication?

Will you know what part of it is you, and what part is your upgrade? Right now we think of our bodies (and our minds) as givens; we think of them as us, and we work to make of them what we can. But if they become equipment—if your heart and lungs (and eventually your character) are a product of engineering—then running becomes like driving. Driving can be fun, and goodness knows there are people who care passionately about their cars, who will come to blows on the question Ford vs. Chevy. But the skill, the engagement, the meaning reside mostly in those who design the machines. No one goes out and drives in honor of a dying sister.

18   Sport is the canary in a miner's cage. It's possible the canary will die; there are those who think, with good reason, that genetic engineering of the human organism may be crude and dangerous, especially at first. But the even greater danger is that the canary will be souped up into an ever perkier, ever tougher, ever "better" specimen. Not a canary anymore, but a parrot, or a golden eagle, or some grand thing we can only guess at. A canary so big and strong that it . . . won't be a canary anymore. It will be something else entirely, unable to carry the sweet tune it grew up singing.

19   No one needs to run in the twenty-first century. Running is an outlet for spirit, for finding out who you are, no more mandatory than art or music. It is a voluntary beauty, a grace. And it turns out to be a fragile beauty. Its significance depends on the limitations and wonders of our bodies as we have known them. Why would you sign up for a marathon if it was a test of the alterations some embryologist had made in you, and in a million others? If 3 hours and 20 minutes was your design spec? We'll still be able to run hard; doubtless we'll even hurt. It's not the personal challenge that will disappear. It's the personal. ◆

Notes

1. John M. Hoberman, Mortal Engines: *The Science of Performance and the Dehumanization of Sport* (New York: 1992), p. 72.
2. Ibid., pp. 136, 102; Sharon Begley, "Good Medal Workouts," *Newsweek*, Dec. 17, 2001.
3. Mark Compton, "Enhancement Genetics: Let the Games Begin," *DNA Dispatch*, July 2001.
4. "More Giro Shocks Still to Come," *Pro Cycling*, March 5, 2002.
5. Amanda Swift, "The Sports Factor," ABC radio [Australia], July 12, 2001.
6. Ira Berkow, "This Lifter Is Fueled by Natural Power," *New York Times*, Feb. 6, 1994.
7. Rod Osher, "Hot Performances," *Time.com*, Sept. 6,1999.
8. Michael Butcher, "Next: The Genetically Modified Athlete," *The Guardian*, Dec. 15, 1999.
9. Jere Longman, "Getting the Athletic Edge May Mean Altering Genes," *New York Times*, May 11, 2001.
10. Compton, "Enhancement Genetics."
11. "Erling Jevne: Down to Earth," *Skisport* magazine, translated and archived at *www. xcskiworld.com.*
12. "Jevne's Last Campaign," *www.langrenn.com*, Feb. 25, 2002.
13. J. D. Downing, "GoldenJustice," *www.xcskiworld.com*, Feb. 25, 2002.
14. "Jevne's Last Campaign."

FREEWRITING ASSIGNMENT ————————————

Would knowing you were genetically enhanced to perform better at sports or mathematics reduce your pride when you excelled in these areas? Why or why not?

CRITICAL READING

1. Why does McKibben choose to open his argument with a story of his first marathon? How does this story frame the points that follow? Is it an effective way to draw in his readers? How does it relate to his thesis? Explain.
2. McKibben comments, "you could almost say that it makes no difference whether athletes of the future are genetically engineered—the damage is already done with conventional drugs, the line already crossed." On what grounds does he disprove this statement?
3. Several authors in this section have brought up the issue of biological enhancement as it relates to athletics. If genetic engineering were used to create better athletes, how would it change sports in general? Would people still be impressed by excellence? Would athletes have to undergo genetic screenings before they could compete? Would it create a different "race"—a race of athletes bred for muscle? Discuss.
4. McKibben wonders if we were genetically engineered to be stronger runners, the inherent challenge in running a race would disappear. "It's not the personal challenge that will disappear. It's the personal." What does he mean?
5. How do you think Stock would respond to McKibben's concerns regarding genetic engineering? Explain.

CRITICAL WRITING

6. McKibben warns that genetic engineering will change what it means to be human—for the worse. But are people likely to heed his concerns and of others like him? Imagine that we could go back in time 150 years ago and warn government leaders that weapons of war soon to be invented—such as automatic weapons, missiles, gases, mines and grenades—would result in millions of deaths in a 30-year time period between 1915 and 1945. Would they have banned such technology? Would this have been good for humanity? (Remember that many forms of technology used in modern weaponry are also used in modern medicine.) Explore this idea from your own viewpoint.
7. A deeper issue connected to genetic alteration that McKibben raises is that it could irrevocably alter how we feel about ourselves as individuals and how we relate to others. Imagine a world in which there are genetically enhanced individuals who have been made smarter, stronger, or more beautiful than conventionally conceived children. What issues are likely to arise? How would the nonenhanced people function in a world in which there was no hope to ever compete on the same level as the enhanced?

8. *Personal Narrative*: McKibben describes how a marathon made him realize things about himself he never knew. "For a period of hours, and especially those last gritty miles, I had been absolutely, utterly *present*, the moments desperately, magnificently clarified. As meaningless as it was to the world, that's how meaning*ful* it was to me." Write a personal narrative describing a time when you pushed yourself beyond your expectations. What did you learn about yourself, and why?

GROUP PROJECT

9. McKibben wonders what a world of genetically modified super athletes would be like. With your group, outline the reasons we compete in sports, or watch them. If you knew that other players had been enhanced, would that change your opinion of athletic competition? Discuss this issue with your group, writing down important points. Share your points as part of a larger class discussion.

Yuppie Eugenics
Ruth Hubbard and Stuart Newman

The concept of eugenics is nothing new. In *The Republic*, the ancient philosopher Plato proposed that, in an effort to create a more perfect state, the government should control the procreation of children. Tall people would reproduce with short ones, fat with thin, comely with ugly, and, in so doing, create a more uniformly perfect population. Of course, we know that such techniques wouldn't work, but we are approaching a time when we could manipulate the genetic code in order to create taller, stronger, or more healthy children. In the next piece, Ruth Hubbard and Stuart Newman claim that a form of eugenics is being practiced right now among those who can afford it. Genetic testing allows parents to terminate "disappointing" pregnancies, and select embryos known to be free of certain genetic diseases such as cystic fibrosis. But such technology isn't available to everyone, and Hubbard and Newman fear that we may create a world of genetic haves and have-nots.

Ruth Hubbard is professor emerita of biology at Harvard University and author of *The Politics of Women's Biology* and co-author of *Exploding the Gene Myth*. Stuart Newman is professor of cell biology and anatomy at New York Medical College. They are founding members of the Council for Responsible Genetics in Cambridge, Massachusetts. This article first appeared in *Z Magazine*, in March 2002.

CRITICAL THINKING   What is eugenics? What connotations does the word have?

---

[1]   We have entered the era of Yuppie Eugenics. A contemporary, ostensibly voluntary form of older ideas and practices, Yuppie Eugenics is based in modern molecular

genetics and concepts of "choice," and has begun to raise the high-tech prospect of employing prenatal genetic engineering. What it shares with the earlier doctrines is the goal of improving and perfecting human bloodlines and the human species as a whole.

2   The eugenics movement arose in the late 19th century in the wake of new scientific thinking about animal and plant breeding that culminated in evolutionary biology and genetics. While thus part of the scientifically-influenced "progressive" thinking of the time, it was based on the fallacious argument that since nature had yielded "fit" species by "natural selection" and humans had "improved" domesticated animal breeds by "artificial selection," there was now a scientific warrant to use social and political means to discourage propagation of biologically "inferior" sorts of people. It soon gave rise to a set of State-directed programs in the United States and Europe.

3   The legal assault against people of "bad heredity" began in the United States with compulsory sterilization bills. The first of these was introduced into the Michigan legislature in 1897, but was defeated. A second bill, aimed at "idiots and imbecile children," passed the Pennsylvania legislature in 1905, but was vetoed by the governor. Indiana was the first state to actually enact a compulsory sterilization law in 1907 and it was followed by some 30 others. California did not repeal its law until 1979 and, in 1985, around 20 states still had laws on their books that permitted the involuntary sterilization of "mentally retarded" persons. The United States was by no means alone. In that liberal paragon Sweden, compulsory sterilizations of "unfit" persons were performed into the 1970s. All these laws were meant to improve the genetic make-up of the population, and especially of poor people, by preventing those judged to be "defective" from passing on their "defects" to future generations.

4   State Eugenics reached an abhorrent extreme in the Nazi extermination programs of the 1930s and 1940s. Initially directed at people with similar health or social problems as were targeted by the U.S. and Swedish sterilization laws, these were eventually expanded to cover entire populations—Jews, Gypsies, Poles—judged by the Nazi regime to represent "worthless lives" ("lebensunwerte Leben"). While certain overt State policies such as the use of gas chambers are now avoided, "ethnic cleansing," practiced on three continents in recent times, shows that eugenic cruelties have far from disappeared.

5   Technologies developed in the past three decades, however, have permitted a change in focus in the implementation of eugenics, at least in more affluent countries, from the State to the individual. Increasing numbers of diagnostic tests have been developed that enable physicians to assess some aspects of a fetus's future health status early enough to permit termination of a pregnancy during the second or even the first trimester. Though all such predictions have pitfalls and problems, they have made it possible for prospective parents not to bear a child they expect to be too ill or disabled to knowingly make part of their family. Though the intent of these methods is to widen choice in matters of procreation, they are eugenic in that they are meant to prevent the birth of people who are expected to perpetuate certain types of inborn conditions, such as cystic fibrosis, Huntington's disease, sickle cell disease, or phenylketonuria (PKU). Some scientists and physicians, indeed, have explicitly argued that it is wrong to permit ill or disabled people to procreate unless so-

ciety is prepared to provide them with the "choice" to abort any fetus likely to manifest a condition like their own.

6   The new profession of genetic counseling has arisen to meet the need for information about the availability and significance of appropriate preconceptive and prenatal tests and about the decisions with which such tests confront prospective parents. Now a central factor in the shift of "scientific" selection from coercive state programs to socially-sanctioned personal initiatives, advice about Choice Eugenics has become a routine part of prenatal care. In fact, practitioners have been sued by parents of children born disabled for not offering such information. Meanwhile, other prospective parents complain that their obstetrician or genetic counselor was excessively insistent that they accept a prenatal test and terminate a pregnancy that was predicted to produce a disabled child. So, though Choice Eugenics is not comparable to the earlier, compulsory state practices, some people experience it as coercive. Indeed, anxiety about social disapproval can sometimes be a more compelling dictator of choice than the law.

7   Extending the range of such "choices" since the 1970s and increasingly in the 1990s, hospital-based, non-profit fertility clinics, as well as a growing for-profit fertility industry, have been devising new technologies and social practices and expanding the use of the traditional ones, such as artificial insemination. The basis for most of the newer reproductive practices is in vitro fertilization (IVF). Initially, IVF was intended to help women whose ovaries and uterus were intact, so that they could produce eggs and gestate an embryo, but whose fallopian tubes were missing or blocked. It involves hyper-stimulation of the ovaries to induce several ova to mature simultaneously and then extracting a few of these and incubating them with fertile sperm outside the body ("in vitro"). Once an egg and sperm have fused and the first few cell divisions have occurred, several embryos are inserted into the woman's uterus in the hope that at least one of them will become implanted and develop into a baby.

8   Since the first successful attempt, in 1977, resulted in the birth of Louise Brown, IVF has become a widely offered and virtually routine part of reproductive medicine. It is covered by some state and private insurance programs in the United States and by the national health insurance programs of other countries. In addition to its procreative potential, it also enables prospective parents to have predictive tests performed on the embryos before they are implanted. It has therefore become an option for Choice Eugenics, especially for couples who strongly object to aborting an initiated pregnancy.

9   The access to human embryos offered by IVF has also made the technology a point of departure for a range of previously unavailable manipulations that raise complex questions not just for the individuals they affect directly, but for society at large. The technically least challenging of these involves the participation of two women, instead of just one, in producing a child—one who produces the egg, the other who gestates the embryo. This arrangement raises the novel question of which of them is the child's biological mother. In cases of disagreement, judges have often come down on the side of genes—hence of the egg donor—but that simply acts out our current genomania, because it ignores the biological major role of the woman who gestates and gives birth.

10   The explosive proliferation of preconceptive and prenatal tests has provided more and more reasons to terminate pregnancies in the hope of a better roll of the dice. Given certain features of modern prosperous societies, there is an increasing tendency to exercise such options on the basis of notions of biological perfectibility. This tendency is transforming Choice Eugenics into Yuppie Eugenics. What was once a preventative choice has become a pro-active entitlement, exacerbated by the sense prevailing among current elites that one has the right to control all aspects of one's life and shape them by buying and periodically upgrading the best that technology has to offer, be it a computer, a car, or a child. Because this trend enjoys broadly based, mainstream sanction in the United States, what may begin as elite yuppie-ism is poised to become more widely disseminated as the technologies become cheaper and their use becomes more routine.

11   Fair-minded people differ on the point at which Choice Eugenics grades into Yuppie Eugenics. For some people with congenital disabilities, much Choice Eugenics, directed to preventing the birth of people like themselves, is going too far. People with congenital disabilities typically feel whole, and consider themselves victimized not by their genes, but by disaccomodating social arrangements. At the same time, a lack of extended family and health support systems can, for many, shift the balance against "preventable diversity." All eugenics defines some people as biologically unacceptable. Each turn of the screw en route to Yuppie Eugenics potentially excludes more and more people.

12   The false hope that scientists can alter an embryo genetically so as to "enhance" its potential and to make it conform to the future parents' image of a desirable child is also part of Yuppie Eugenics. Such unrealistic expectations, built on intrinsically unreliable genetic foreknowledge as well as on unscientific notions of the correspondence of specific genes to complex traits, can tempt prospective parents to agree to novel biological manipulations that are at least as likely to introduce problems as to remedy them. Also called germ-line genetic engineering or germ-line "gene therapy," this possibility has aroused widespread opposition. There are religious, but also secular, philosophical reasons for resisting a technology that plays into the idea of the developing human as a perfectible item. The goal of perfection encourages a view of existing life as imperfect. It transforms life into an ahistorical object, without context and eventually artifactual.

13   Objections also center on the fact that a genetic alteration introduced into an embryo is likely to become a permanent part of the genetic endowment of the person into whom that embryo develops and thus also of all of her or his progeny. Considering that the procedures themselves are experimental and the results are unpredictable (laboratory mice on which such procedures are performed often produce progeny with malformations, behavioral abnormalities, or increased cancer rates), germ-line genetic engineering poses unacceptable risks for "persons" who have just barely been conceived. There is no justification for undertaking such manipulations. If the prospective parents of the child into whom the embryo would develop are concerned that it may not meet their expectations, they need not gestate it.

14   Unfortunately this insidious prospect of germline engineering has found advocates among scientists such as James D. Watson, the Nobel Prize winning co-discoverer of the structure of DNA and the first director of the Human Genome Pro-

ject, and Princeton University biologist Lee Silver. In his book *Remaking Eden* and in numerous appearances on television and the college speaking circuit, Silver has been trying to persuade the public to get used to the prospect of a world with genetic haves and have-nots that would eventually lead to separate, and intentionally unequal, human species.

15   Fortunately, other more responsible scientists, writers, and activists have warned about the ominous safety and social implications of following this path, and have called for a ban on producing genetically-engineered humans. Indeed many European countries already prohibit such procedures.

16   This makes it particularly discreditable that the American Association for the Advancement of Science (AAAS), the largest professional organization of scientists in the United States, has gone on record with a statement that dances around the hazards of germline modification without even raising the possibility of a ban. Although the panel that prepared the AAAS report considers that the time is not yet ripe for implementing inheritable genetic modifications (IGM), it leaves the door open for future uses: "Although there are major technical obstacles to developing human IGM in the responsible ways that we have recommended," they write, "it is possible that at some time in the future scientific advances will make it feasible to undertake IGM." The AAAS panel failed to explain that only an unethical line of research, in contravention of the internationally endorsed Nuremburg Code on human experimentation, would have to be undertaken before any assurances can be made as to the risks of these procedures.

17   Cloning, another experimental genetic technology touted as a new "reproductive option," is being advocated by maverick physicians and scientists despite wide evidence of pathology in animals produced in this fashion. Some of these proponents, including a representative of the Raelians, a Canadian religious cult that claims to have received an extraterrestrial directive to clone its adherents, were given a respectful hearing at a forum at the prestigious National Academy of Sciences in August 2001.

18   Yuppie Eugenics also has its boosters among journalists and professional bioethicists. Michael Kinsley, writing in *Slate* (April 2000), suggested that genetic tests should eventually be used as qualifications for employment. He was seconded by Andrew Sullivan in the *New York Times Magazine* (July 2000), where he argued that genetic testing for future capacities is less objectionable than using SAT scores or letters of recommendation, since genetic tests are "more reliable." Arthur Caplan, Glenn McGee, and David Magnus of the University of Pennsylvania Institue of Bioethics follow the Kinsley-Sullivan thesis to its logical conclusion when they state, in a 1999 *British Medical Journal* article, "it is not clear that it is any less ethical to allow parents to pick the eye color of their child or to try to create a fetus with a propensity for mathematics than it is to permit them to teach their children the values of a particular religion or require them to play the piano." Here the intersubjective nature of the parent-child relationship is conflated with the one-way imposition of a chancy, irreversible genetic alteration during the earliest stages of embryonic development.

19   What is generally ignored in such prescriptions is that each gene contributes to numerous traits, and that any trait of significance depends on the functions of many

different genes. Genes and other features involved in growth and development constitute integral wholes that genetic alterations are more likely to disturb than enhance.

20   Yuppie Eugenics builds on the mirage that applications of genetics and biotechnology will be able to make us more perfect as well as to counter all forms of pain, illness, and death. The best way to restore us to sanity is to remember that genetics will never tell us what it takes to make a worthy human being and that the major causes of human illness and death continue to be not enough healthful food and too much unhealthful work. Eugenic and other gene dreams will not cure what ails us. ◆

FREEWRITING ASSIGNMENT

Is genetic testing of embryos for certain diseases technically ethical? Why or why not?

CRITICAL READING

1. Why do the authors call genetic selection, including genetic testing, "Yuppie Eugenics"? What does this term tell you about their position on this issue?
2. Are the extermination programs conducted by the Nazis during the 1930s and 1940s parallel to the types of genetic practices used now? How are they similar, and how are they different?
3. In paragraph 6, the authors state that the "anxiety about social disapproval" couples may face when deciding what to do about a pregnancy predicted to produce a disabled child might compel them to terminate a pregnancy against their deeper wishes. Is such pressure a form of forced eugenics? Could HMOs one day make couples terminate a pregnancy if genetic tests reveal the fetus to have abnormalities?
4. Why do the authors put quotation marks around the words, "reproductive option" in paragraph 17?
5. The authors observe that genetic testing is being used to weed out unhealthy pregnancies. Do they approve or disapprove of this practice? Explain.
6. In paragraph 13, the authors state that there "is no justification for undertaking [genetic] manipulation." What do they suggest be done to embryos that do not "meet [parental] expectations" instead of genetic manipulation? How does their solution correspond to other positions they have taken on genetic technology in the essay? Explain.

CRITICAL WRITING

7. In paragraph 18, the authors quote several well-known journalists and bioethicists. Look up the articles to which they refer and evaluate the arguments presented by these prominent names: Michael Kingsley, *Baby Needs a New Set of Genes*, *http://slate.msn.com/id/80604/*; Andrew Sullivan, *Promotion of the Fittest* (see Lexis/Nexis); and Caplan, McGee, and Magnus, *What is Immoral about Eugenics?* *http://cmgm.stanford.edu/*

biochem118/Papers/Genome%20Papers/Eugenics.pdf. Are these writers really encouraging eugenics, or engaging in intellectual argument? Did the authors correctly convey the position of these individuals? Explain.

8. Many politicians are calling for a ban on human cloning. Research the issue online at web sites such as *http://bioethics.gov*, *www.ornl.gov*, *www.nsplus.com/nsplus/insight/clone/clone.html*, and others you locate through search engines using key words such as "human cloning," "ethics," and "cloning debate." How has the cloning debate changed since the creation of Dolly was announced? Is a moratorium on human cloning likely to be lifted within the next few years? Write an essay in which you advocate either for, or against, a ban on human cloning.

GROUP PROJECTS

9. If genetic manipulation could be performed with accuracy and was made available to the general population, what rules should govern its use to prevent a gap between the haves, and the have-nots? Develop a set of recommendations with your group, considering points raised by the authors.

10. One of the arguments against human cloning is that the technology could be abused to create clones of exceptional people, such as athletes, geniuses, and supermodels. With your group, discuss the likelihood of such an application of cloning technology. Who are possible candidates for cloning and why? In your discussion, also address the idea of "the right to genetic identity." Should such a right exist? How could it be violated?

VIEWPOINTS

▶ **Should Human Cloning Be Permitted?**
Patricia A. Baird, M.D.

▶ **Yes, Human Cloning Should Be Permitted**
Chris MacDonald, Ph.D.

Many of the authors in this section focus on how human cloning can benefit, or harm, individuals. In the next piece, Dr. Patricia A. Baird explains why such a perspective is "dangerously" incomplete. The implications of human cloning must be viewed in its entire *social* context. How will human cloning affect our society, not just in the present, but for generations down the line? How would a cloned child be viewed by society, and how might he or she feel about being a cloned person? If we pursue human cloning, will future generations look back on our actions as reckless and irresponsible? And why endanger the future if there is no true need to create human clones in the first place?

Responding directly to her argument, ethicist Chris MacDonald explains why he disagrees with Baird's argument. He feels that Baird is too severe in her condemnation of human cloning, and fails to provide sufficient evidence that human cloning should be banned. Moreover, he disagrees with her point that if a majority of society wishes to ban something, we should heed the voice of the people. In principle, he explains, a majority shouldn't impose its viewpoint on a minority, and this applies to human cloning as well.

Patricia A. Baird is a geneticist and head of the Department of Medical Genetics at the University of British Columbia. She frequently writes on the social, ethical, and health consequences connected to human reproductive biology and genetics, and the resulting implications for public policy. Baird presented this paper to an ethics committee created by the California state legislature, addressing the issue of human cloning. The committee invited individuals to present their recommendations on what position should be taken on human cloning, and the reasons for their position. This abridged version of her presentation was published in the June 2000 *Annals of the RCPSC*.

Chris MacDonald teaches ethics, philosophy, and moral theory at Dalhousie University in Halifax, Nova Scotia. His research spans health care ethics, professional ethics, business ethics, and moral theory. This response to Patricia Baird's paper was published in the October 2000 issue of the *Annals of the RCPSC*.

CRITICAL THINKING

Baird raises some questions about the well-being of the cloned person, and how cloned people would feel about themselves, their identity, and how they fit into a society where most people were not cloned. She also wonders how society would treat cloned people. How do you think a cloned person would fit into our society today? Would he or she be the object of curiosity? A celebrity? A freak? Would he or she ever be able to lead a normal life? Explain.

 ## Should Human Cloning Be Permitted?
Patricia A. Baird, M.D.

A Qualitatively Different Type of Reproduction

Producing humans by somatic-cell nuclear-transfer cloning differs from sexual reproduction—it separates reproduction from recombination. Normally, in an outbred species such as humans, we cannot predict what the overall characteristics of an embryo will be. In sexual reproduction, it is unpredictable which combination of the parents' thousands of genes will occur. To date, in creating the next generation, we have had to give ourselves over to chance. But if nuclear transfer is used, the nucleus can be taken from an adult whose characteristics are known—and the process reproduces the biology of the former individual. It becomes possible to select by known characteristics which humans will be copied. The new technology allows the asexual replication of a human being, the ability to predetermine the full complement of a child's nuclear genes, and the easier alteration of the genes of prospective individuals. Cloning is a change in the integrity of our species, and we must think about the long-term consequences.

Public Reaction to Human Cloning

Cloning used to produce a human is rejected by the overwhelming majority of people. Polls on new scientific developments have limitations, but the *Economist* reported that over 90 percent of Americans were opposed to human cloning.[1] Other polls have shown similar results.[2,3] Polls, however, are affected by how the questions are asked, so an in-depth approach is needed. Many experts believe that lay people cannot understand complicated scientific topics, but there are data showing that they can assimilate and make judgments about complex issues. The Wellcome Trust did a qualitative focus-group study, and reported that opposition to human cloning was "nearly universal" among participants.[4] Most were against the idea of using cloning for reproductive purposes, stemming from concerns for the children and society, as much as from fears about interfering with nature. When over 90 percent of citizens in a democracy oppose human cloning, it is difficult for a government to justify a policy that permits it. There are a few people, however, who would pursue cloning because they see potential advantages for themselves.

Foreseeable Requests for Cloning

There are foreseeable situations where individuals may want to pursue cloning—for example, for couples where both are infertile and have neither eggs nor sperm, or where the male produces no sperm. Given that there are new treatment techniques using cells from testicular biopsy, such problems are rare. A second example is where a lesbian couple might wish to use one partner's body cell and the enucleated egg of the other to produce a child together. In these scenarios, there are other options available to form a family—such as sperm donation, egg and embryo donation, or adoption. Other situations where cloning may be pursued is when a couple's child is dying or is killed, and they want to replace him or her by using one of his or her cells in nuclear-transfer cloning; or when a clone could provide a genetically compatible organ for transplantation. There will be instances where people wish to pursue cloning for particular reasons.[5-7]

The arguments about physical and psychological harm to clones have also been well-delineated.[8,9] For example, with regard to possible physical harms, congenital malformations, handicap, early death, increased risk of cancer, premature aging, and death have all been raised. Possible psychological harms to cloned individuals (replicands) have also been outlined, including diminished individuality, a sense of foreclosed future, or a disturbed sense of identity. An important part of human identity is the sense of arising from a maternal and a paternal line while at the same time being a unique individual. Many children who are adopted, or conceived from donor insemination, show a deep need to learn about their biological origins. Making children by cloning means that they do not have this dual genetic origin; they are not connected to others in the same biological way as the rest of humanity. The first person born this way would have to cope with being the first not to come from the union of egg and sperm. Social, family, and kinship relationships that support human flourishing have evolved over millennia—but there is no way to place replicands. Is the DNA source the twin? The mother? The father?

Widening the Frame

Most debate on human cloning focuses on a weighing of harms and benefits to indi-
5   viduals. This is a dangerously incomplete framing. Looking at the issue as a matter of reproductive technology choice, although it focuses on individual autonomy, reproductive freedom, and protection of children, means that other issues are omitted.[10] We need to shift from the framing as individual choice, to a framing that reveals how permitting cloning affects future generations and society. I am reminded of one of the consultations of the Royal Commission on New Reproductive Technologies with an aboriginal group in Canada. They told the commission about their seventh-generation rule. They said that when they had to make a big decision in their community, they always considered what the consequences were likely to be in the seventh generation. This is a useful perspective to have, because viewing cloning as a personal matter inappropriately minimizes potentially serious social consequences. Individual choices in reproduction are not isolated acts—they affect the child, other people, and future generations. The wider consequences must be considered because we all have a stake in the type of community that we live in. We do not want it to be one where the use of cloning commodifies children, commercializes family formation, or increases social injustice. Cloning raises issues about the future of our species. We have not yet found the wisdom to deal with hunger, poverty, and environmental degradation—we are unlikely to have the wisdom to direct our own evolution.

Nuclear-transfer cloning allows third parties to choose the genotypes of people
6   who will be cloned. Before, when two people mated, no one could control which genes the child received out of a myriad of possibilities. This lottery of reproduction has been a protection against people being predetermined, chosen, or designed by others—including parents.

Cloning directs the production of human beings in an unprecedented way.
7   When a child of a particular genetic constitution is "made," it is easier to look on him or her as a product, rather than a gift of providence. If we can, and some people do, make children "to order," it is likely to change the way we view children.

An impetus to developing nuclear-transfer cloning for producing animals has
8   been that it could then be combined with genetic enhancement—genes could be added to give the animals desired traits. Genes are inserted into cells in culture, then the cells screened to pick the ones that have incorporated the desired genes. These altered cells are used as the donors of nuclei for cloned animals. It is then possible to create transgenic cloned animals with commercially desirable genetic traits (for example, heavier meat yield or production of insulin in the milk).[11]

9   Reproduction by nuclear-transfer cloning makes it possible to think about genetically enhancing humans. A person's cells could be cultured, genes inserted, and those cells taking up the desired genes used to produce a cloned "improved" individual. We could insert genes for viral-disease resistance, or to protect against baldness or degenerative diseases, or insert genes related to height or intelligence. If nuclear-transfer cloning is permitted, what will stop genetic enhancement being used eventually? There would be strong individual motivation to have a taller or disease-resistant child. We would then be taking human evolution into our own hands. Are we wise enough to manage it or the social consequences? Most people will want their child to be brighter, taller, disease-resistant—so this technology could make people more standard, based on individual choices and market forces. If it works, it is likely to become used more often than just occasionally.

10   Who would have access to cloning or genetic improvements? Everyone? It is likely that those with financial resources would have access, but not other people, because cloning or enhancement would have to be provided as a socially underwritten "good" if it were to be available to everyone. And it is unlikely that most countries would provide publicly supported cloning, given that there are few social benefits and many potential harms.

11   If cloning or enhancement technology were provided as a public good to ensure equality of access, the government would have to decide in what circumstances people may clone themselves, and what traits were desirable. Docility? Height? Ability to provide a tissue transplant? Unless the market is to decide, criteria as to who may clone themselves, and a regulatory body will be needed.

12   If cloning is used, will we undermine the unconditional parental acceptance of offspring that is central to nurturing human beings? Parental acceptance is likely to become conditional when we are able to program for certain characteristics. If cloning technology or genetic enhancement is permitted, people with disabilities, or members of racial or ethnic minorities, will be affected differently, and in a way unlikely to lead to greater equality and respect.

13   There are forces favoring the use of cloning—particular individuals will pursue it, and it will benefit financially those who provide it, so it is likely to be marketed to the public.

14   Many issues arising from cloning cannot be resolved in the framework of individual autonomy and reproductive choice. The focus on autonomy leads us to overlook the collective and transgenerational consequences of leaving the use of reproductive technologies to individual choices.[12] The use of scientific technology focused on individual wishes may result in social harms because individual interests differ from the public good at times. It is analogous to the tragedy of the commons,[13] which is exemplified by ranchers sharing grazing land, or fishers sharing a fishing ground. There is an incentive for individuals to overgraze or overfish because the benefits of doing so accrue to the individual, whereas the costs and harms occur to the community. The aggregate effect of individually beneficial choices may harm the long-term common good, and the cumulative impact of individual choices can result in an unethical system. Public policy-making differs from individual-based decision-making—because the moral unit of a physician is the patient, while the moral unit of public policy is all citizens.[14] If there is a conflict between the total social good and the good of an individual, public policy must uphold the public interest.

15   All members of the public have a stake in whether cloning is permitted, because if cloned people exist, the changes affect everyone. Even though a majority do not want to allow it, if it is permitted, we would all live in a world where people are cloned. Even though initially, individuals on whom cloning technology had a direct impact would be a minority, their collective experiences would influence social values. In public policy-making, it is inappropriate to subordinate every consideration to the question of whether it helps a couple to have a family. Society has a legitimate role in deciding whether cloning will be used. The far-reaching nature of this choice means more voices must be involved in making decisions. The decisions should not be taken preemptively by a clinical facility or a group of scientists who ignore the wishes of the rest of the community. We need the perspectives not just of those who are knowledgeable in biology or science; we also need the perspectives of sociologists, humanists, and citizens from a variety of life experiences. On something that affects our species' future, it would be valuable to have the perspectives of people from many countries.

Conclusions Regarding Policy

16   There is no compelling case to make people by asexual means; human reproductive cloning is without potential benefits to almost all citizens, and other options are available in most situations. Many institutions have come to this conclusion; the prospects of making human beings by cloning have elicited concern in many countries, and there have been calls for a worldwide ban on cloning used to produce humans by many political and religious leaders, and by organizations such as the World Health Organization, the World Medical Organization, the American Medical Association, and UNESCO. Nineteen countries in the Council of Europe have signed an agreement that bans human cloning. Medicine, science, and technology are worldwide endeavors, so this is an issue facing humans as a species. For this reason, WHO is making an international effort to cooperate on guidelines for cloning in humans.

17   History shows that where there is a demand for a new service and the ability of a few to pay for it, unless there is legislation, there will be professionals willing to provide it. There is licensing of fertility clinics in several European countries, but in some other countries, reproductive technologies are highly commercialized and little regulated. If human cloning were permitted in the United States, it would likely proceed in the billion-dollar private reproductive-medicine sector. In this market-driven context, its use is unlikely to be controlled. It is now possible to peruse catalogues if you wish to buy eggs or surrogate pregnancies; so it seems likely that if human cloning is permitted in the United States, it is only a matter of time before pressure from individuals with specific interests would open up the field. Legislation is needed to ban the implantation into a woman of an egg cell that has had its nucleus transferred from a body cell. When such legislation is written, its wording should not inadvertently ban nonreproductive cloning research, or animal cloning research that may be of benefit, and that many people see as acceptable.

18   How we use cloning is not an individual or medical matter. It is a matter of social policy that cannot be viewed in a narrow framework of reproductive technology and individual choice. How we choose to use this technological capacity will shape

society for our children, their children, and after. How it is used is likely to entrench existing inequalities, and create new ones.

19   In conclusion, using nuclear-transfer cloning to allow people to have a child introduces a different way of reproduction for our species. Once we breach this barrier, it leaves us with no place to stop. Given all the problems outlined, the reasons for permitting cloning to produce a person are insufficiently compelling. Even in the few circumstances where the case for human cloning seems justified, there are alternative solutions. We are at an appropriate stopping place on a slippery slope. Not all reasons why a person might wish to copy his or her cells are unethical, but given there are other options open to people wishing to form a family, concerns about individual and social harms from cloning are strong enough that it is not justified to permit it. These issues affecting the creation of the next generation are important for the future of our species; we must deal with them wisely. I hope we can. ◆

References

1. "Whatever next?" *The Economist*, 1997, March 1;79–81.
2. *Time*/CNN poll. 1997 March.
3. International Food Information Council. Wirthlin group quorum survey, 1997 March 21–24.
4. Public perspectives on human cloning, Medicine in society program. The Wellcome Trust, 1999 June (http://www.wellcome.ac.uk/en/1/awtpubrepcln.html).
5. McGee G. *The Human Cloning Debate*. Berkeley: Berkeley Hills Books, 1998.
6. Hummer J, Almeder R. *Human Cloning. Biomedical Ethics Reviews*. Totowa: 1998.
7. Andrews L. *The Clone Age: 20 Years at the Forefront of Reproductive Technology*. New York: Henry Holt, 1999.
8. Wilson JQ, Kass L. *The Ethics of Human Cloning*. Washington: American Enterprise Press, 1999:10(2).
9. "Cloning Human Beings." Report of the national bioethics advisory commission. Hastings Centre Report 1997:27(5).
10. Baylis F. *Human Cloning: Three Mistakes and a Solution*. Unpublished manuscript.
11. Pennis E. "After Dolly, a Pharming Frenzy." *Science* 1998:279;646–8.
12. Baird PA. "Individual Interests, Societal Interests, and Reproductive Technologies." *Perspectives Biology Medicine* 1997;40(3):440-51.
13. Hardin G. "The Tragedy of the Commons." *Science* 1968;162:1243–8.
14. Lamm RD. "Redrawing the Ethics Map." Hastings Centre Report 1999;29(2):28–9

Yes, Human Cloning Should Be Permitted
Chris MacDonald, Ph.D.

1 Patricia Baird's discussion of human cloning challenges the prospect of nuclear-transfer cloning for the purposes of human reproduction. Baird reviews a long list of familiar worries about human cloning, but the most striking feature of her discussion is its frankness in placing the onus of justification on the shoulders of those who would permit human cloning. The reasons for permitting cloning, she argues, are "insufficiently compelling," so cloning should be prohibited. The implication is

that any new technology should be forbidden unless and until enough justification can be found for allowing its use.

2   Baird is to be commended for her frankness. But the onus is misplaced, or at least too severe. One need not be a single-minded defender of liberty to think that, contrary to Baird's implication, we need good reasons to limit the actions of others, particularly when those actions do no clear and specific harm. The fact that a portion of society—even a majority—finds an activity distasteful is insufficient grounds for passing a law forbidding it. For example, it is presumably true that at one point, roughly 90 percent of the public (the same proportion that Baird says is against human cloning) was opposed to homosexuality. Does (or did) this justify action on the part of government to ban homosexual lifestyles? Surely not.

3   There may be a flaw in my analogy. Human cloning, according to critics, has harmful effects (or at least risks). Indeed, Baird suggests that the arguments regarding potential physical and psychological harm to clones have been "well-delineated." In fact, a convincing case has yet to be made for the claim that the physical and psychological risks to clones are more severe than, or different in kind from, those faced by children produced in more traditional ways. Identical twins live with the psychological "burden" of not being genetically unique. Children born to women over 35 are at an increased risk of genetic illness. Children resulting from in vitro fertilization or other reproductive technologies live with the knowledge that their origins were unusual. They may even live with the knowledge that their genetic profile has been manipulated (for example, through pre-implantation selection of embryos). Human cloning for reproductive purposes is another novel—and as yet untested—medical technology. As such, it should be approached with caution. Thorough animal trials should be completed before attempts on humans are contemplated. But this is true of any new medical technology.

4   Baird worries about the shift that human cloning might provoke in the way that we view children. This in turn would change the type of community that we are. The central worry is that human cloning "commodifies" children (i.e., that cloning may make us think of children as a commodity or product to be bought and sold). Why would cloning have this effect? Is it simply because it is likely to be expensive, so that it costs money to have children? Surely this is insufficient to worry us. Raising children already costs money—the statistics show us how many hundreds of thousands of dollars it costs to raise a child through to adulthood. Yet no one has suggested that we see our children as products, or love them any less. (In the mid 1940s—before publicly funded health care—my grandparents sold their car to pay the hospital bill related to my father's birth, so "purchasing" the birth of a child is nothing new!)

5   Baird argues that an "important part of human identity is the sense of arising from a maternal and a paternal line while at the same time being a unique individual." Yet without supporting evidence, this sounds like pop psychology. And we can reply in kind: most people I know do not identify with both their maternal and paternal lineages. One of my friends, who was raised by a single mother, identifies with her maternal Eastern European heritage, and not with the French paternal heritage implied by her surname. Another friend identifies with his fa-

ther's black heritage, rather than with his maternal Chinese lineage, despite his Asian physical features. Such patterns are not unusual. Dual heritage may be normal, but it hardly seems central to our conception of ourselves as humans. And identical twins seem none the worse for the knowledge that they are not genetically unique individuals. Claims about challenges to what makes us "human" may be powerful rhetorical devices, but they must be substantiated if they are to be convincing.

6   Baird is correct to exhort us to look beyond harms to identifiable individuals, to the social implications that human cloning might have. As a comparison, think of fetal sex selection. Most of us think that sex selection is a bad thing—not because of any purported harm to the child, but because we worry about the social implications of valuing children of one sex over those of another. So Baird rightly reminds us that focusing on potential harms to individuals constitutes a "dangerously incomplete framing" of the problem. Furthermore, cloning (and genetic technology in general) is sufficiently new—and its implications sufficiently poorly understood—to warrant a healthy respect, and even the allowance of a margin of safety. But this does not suggest the need for the ban that Baird (with others) proposes. What these worries suggest is a need for caution, for discussion, and for regulation. For instance, laws limiting the number of clones that might be created from one individual, restricting the combination of cloning with genetic modification, and defining lines of parental obligation, would alleviate many of the concerns associated with human cloning. (Françoise Baylis argues that cloning is so likely to be used in combination with gene transfer that we should think of cloning as an enhancement technology rather than as a reproductive technology, in her article "Human cloning: three mistakes and a solution," which has been accepted for publication in the *Journal of Medicine and Philosophy*.)

7   What I have said here should not be taken as an absolute defense of human cloning in all circumstances. (Indeed, there may be only a few circumstances in which cloning is appropriate.) Nor have I suggested that public monies should be spent on cloning research. All I have suggested is that a ban on research leading toward human cloning is unwarranted by the arguments raised thus far. Caution and discretion are warranted; a ban is not.

8   Finally, I worry that Baird's point of view exemplifies the way in which human reproductive cloning is being singled out, among cloning-related techniques, as a bogeyman. Almost in chorus, scientists are pleading with regulators not to place restrictions on cloning experimentation per se. At the same time, most scientists seem to be more than willing to swear off reproductive cloning, and indeed to wring their hands over the moral implications of its use. Yet this has the air of a too-hasty concession. The scientific community seems to be too willing to condemn one unpopular application of cloning technology, on the basis of too little convincing argumentation, to appease those who oppose cloning technology in general. But human cloning for reproductive purposes has legitimate, morally acceptable applications— for example, for infertile couples, and for gay couples. And none of the criticisms have been convincingly made. We should not let reproductive human cloning be abandoned as the moral sacrificial lamb of the cloning debate. ◆

FREEWRITING ASSIGNMENT

Because no one has actually cloned a human being (that has been proven), much of the debate on this issue is theoretical. Are hypothetical arguments sufficient grounds to create laws against something like human cloning? Why or why not?

CRITICAL READING

1. What does Baird mean when she says that human cloning will create a change in the "integrity" of reproduction? What does this word mean? What does it imply when used this way? Explain.

2. MacDonald presents an analogy between the acceptance, or nonacceptance, of homosexuality and the controversy over human cloning. Are these two subjects similar? Does it support his point? Why or why not?

3. In paragraph 3, MacDonald argues that no convincing case has been made that human clones would suffer more physical and psychological risks than children "produced in more traditional ways." How do you think Baird would respond to this claim? Other authors in this section? Explain.

4. What is the "seventh generation rule"? How does Baird apply it to the issue of human cloning? Do you think her use of this rule is an effective way to support her argument? Explain.

5. Baird comments that "we have not yet found the wisdom to deal with hunger, poverty, and environmental degradation—we are unlikely to have the wisdom to direct our own evolution." Are these examples parallel? Why or why not? Does she make a good point? Explain.

6. How does MacDonald argue against Baird's essay? Identify the points he selects to argue against, how he addresses these points. Does he address all of the points in Baird's piece? Explain.

7. In paragraphs 9–11, Baird raises questions connected to creating "improved" babies that possess the genetic traits we prefer, such as creating children to be taller, brighter, or more disease resistant. Why does she feel such an application of this nuclear-transfer cloning would be harmful? Explain.

8. Analyze Baird's conclusion. How does she end her argument? What ideas and points does she leave with her audience?

9. Consider the perspective from which MacDonald writes. Baird is a medical professional, MacDonald is an ethicist. Does he convince his audience that he has the credentials to debate this issue? Is it important to Baird's argument that she is herself a geneticist? Does the fact that MacDonald is not a physician undercut his argument? Why or why not?

10. MacDonald argues that just because most people (90%) want to ban human cloning, we should not bend to majority rule because such concessions can be dangerous. Do you agree? Why or why not?

CRITICAL WRITING

11. Is human cloning likely to "change the way we view children"? Why or why not? Frame your answer in terms of how society may view cloned children.

12. Baird raises the question, if there is no real need to clone, why try it at all? Respond to her statements by expressing your own opinion on this aspect of the cloning debate.

13. *Personal Narrative:* Write a personal narrative from the point of view of a teenager who has just found out that they were a clone of a dead sibling. Until this point, you had grown up thinking you were just like any other person. Now, you discover you are actually a clone. How do you feel? Would you be angry? Accepting? Explain.

14. Scientists warn that once DNA is altered in a human being, there is no going back. An alteration may continue with each new generation. Moreover, such DNA alteration may become undesirable, with some people discriminating against genetically altered people out of a desire to produce "pure" genetic lines. (Consider the controversy concerning genetically enhanced foods). Write an essay in which you explore some of the future issues genetic engineering in humans may cause. Support your predictions with information provided in the chapter.

GROUP PROJECTS

15. Baird states, "Cloning raises issues about the future of our species. . . . Before, when two people mated, no one could control which genes the child received out of a myriad of possibilities. This lottery of reproduction has been a protection against people being predetermined, chosen, or designed by others—including parents." With your group, discuss this idea. Would human cloning remove the "lottery" aspect of human reproduction? Would this be a bad thing? Debate the issue, and, later, summarize the discussion in a short essay.

16. With your group, develop a policy statement in which you ban, allow, or partially allow certain aspects of human cloning. Under what conditions is it acceptable, if ever, and why? Share your policy statement with the class as part of a larger group discussion.

17. Baird conjectures that human cloning technology could lead to the creation of "genetically enhanced" humans—a possibility to which she objects. However, if such technology was successfully applied, could it be considered parental irresponsibility not to genetically alter offspring? For example, if a woman has the gene for breast cancer, and bears children without genetic engineering to prevent the transmission or activation of this gene, could she potentially face a charge of manslaughter if her daughter developed the disease? With your group, develop a short list of possible ethical scenarios of this nature for a broader class discussion.

Dolly the sheep made scientific history when her birth was announced in 1997 by researchers at Roslin Institute in Great Britain. The first successfully cloned mammal, Dolly's creation and birth became a sensation—the apex of heated debate over cloning ethics and the future of the human race.

In February 2003, scientists at Roslin decided to put down Dolly via lethal anesthetic injection. She was six- and one-half-years old, arthritic, and suffering from lung cancer caused by a virus. Sheep can live up to 10 to 12 years, so Dolly's relatively early death raised even more questions, fueling the debate about the ethics of cloning research and the long-term health of clones.

RESEARCH ISSUE ## The Genetic Bill of Rights

The Board of Directors of the Council for Responsible Genetics

The Council for Responsible Genetics (CRG) drafted the Genetic Bill of Rights in order to introduce "a global dialogue on the fundamental values that have been put at risk by new applications of genetics." The council explains that the Genetic Bill of Rights is a basic set of common principles that are "essential for creating a framework for understanding the ethical, legal, social, and environmental implications of biotechnology." Although this document has not been adopted by any official government agency, the CRG hopes it will assist in the process of regulation and governance of new genetic technologies. Founded in 1983, the Council for Responsible Genetics is a nonprofit, nongovernmental organization based in Cambridge, Massachusetts. CRG aims to "foster public debate about the social, ethical, and environmental implications of genetic technologies." This "bill of rights" was posted in Spring 2000 by CRG.

Preamble

1   Our life and health depend on an intricate web of relationships within the biological and social worlds. Protection of these relationships must inform all public policy.

2   Commercial, governmental, scientific and medical institutions promote manipulation of genes despite profound ignorance of how such changes may affect the web of life. Once they enter the environment, organisms with modified genes cannot be recalled and pose novel risks to humanity and the entire biosphere.

3   Manipulation of human genes creates new threats to the health of individuals and their offspring, and endangers human rights, privacy, and dignity.

4   Genes, other constituents of life, and genetically modified organisms themselves are rapidly being patented and turned into objects of commerce. This commercialization of life is veiled behind promises to cure disease and feed the hungry.

5   People everywhere have the right to participate in evaluating the social and biological implications of the genetic revolution and in democratically guiding its applications.

6   To protect our human rights and integrity and the biological integrity of the earth, we, therefore, propose this Genetic Bill of Rights.

The Genetic Bill of Rights

7   All people have the right to preservation of the earth's biological and genetic diversity.

8   All people have the right to a world in which living organisms cannot be patented, including human beings, animals, plants, microorganisms, and all their parts.

9   All people have the right to a food supply that has not been genetically engineered.

10   All indigenous peoples have the right to manage their own biological resources, to preserve their traditional knowledge, and to protect these from expropriation and biopiracy by scientific, corporate, or government interests.

11   All people have the right to protection from toxins, other contaminants, or actions that can harm their genetic makeup and that of their offspring.

12   All people have the right to protection against eugenic measures such as forced sterilization or mandatory screening aimed at aborting or manipulating selected embryos or fetuses.

13   All people have the right to genetic privacy including the right to prevent the taking or storing of bodily samples for genetic information without their voluntary informed consent.

14   All people have the right to be free from genetic discrimination.

15   All people have the right to DNA tests to defend themselves in criminal proceedings.

16   All people have the right to have been conceived, gestated, and born without genetic manipulation. ◆

CRITICAL THINKING

1. What is a "bill of rights"? Why was it written and what does it seek to protect? What motivated the creation of this document? In what ways does the document reflect current issues connected to human cloning and genetic enhancement and testing?
2. Is there such a thing as "genetic identity"? Should we have such a right? How could our genetic identity be violated? Write an essay exploring the concept of genetic identity and what it might mean for the future.
3. Draft your own genetic bill of rights. Referring to the CRG document as a prototype, list your articles, and any preamble you wish to preface it, expressing your own position on the issue of genetic enhancement and human cloning.

RESEARCH PROJECTS

4. Download the report on human cloning by the President's Council on Bioethics at its web site at *http://www.bioethics.gov/reports/cloningreport/index.html.* You have been appointed as a member of a commission who must reassess the position drafted by the commission in 2002. Research current cloning technology, addressing the section on children and research in particular. Based on your research, revise the 2002 report and make a recommendation to the president.
5. Go to the GeneWatch web site at *http://www.gene-watch.org/programs/privacy.html* and review the resources and articles addressing the issue of genetic privacy. Write a letter to the editors of *GeneWatch* magazine expressing your own viewpoint on the issue of genetic privacy, referring to the Genetic Bill of Rights and its articles.

Additional essay topics, writing assignments,
research guidelines, and readings for this chapter can
be found online at **www.ablongman.com/goshgarian**.

Making
the Grade
Education Today

6

By the time you have reached college, you have spent over 20,000 hours in school between the ages of 5 to 18—not including the time used to complete homework or participate in extracurricular activities. Most people would agree that a good education is the key to success later in life, whether students pursue a professional career, enter a technical field, raise a family, pursue public service, or join the military. Basic tasks, from balancing a checkbook, filling out a job application, or reading a set of instructions, all depend on what we learned as children in school. So it isn't surprising that education has been the subject of much political, intellectual, and social debate.

Mounting criticism on how schools are run and what students learn has formed the foundation of many political campaigns and reform movements. In his inaugural address, Bill Clinton called for test preparation manuals to be available to every child. George W. Bush's "No Child Left Behind" Act demands that schools provide "report cards" based on standardized tests designed to assess student knowledge and academic proficiency. Parents worry if their children's schools are safe. And teachers wonder how standardized testing will change the quality of education in general.

This chapter examines a few of the issues facing education today. It begins with two essays that address the role of test scores as a measure of student and school achievement. In "Turning Schools into Profit Centers," Peter Sacks questions the movement toward adopting corporate models to reshape public school systems. Under such systems, he argues, kids become "products" sorted by test scores which determine the "market" (real estate value) of the school district. On a more personal level, science teacher Stephen Kramer writes a "Letter to a Washington State Test Scorer," in which he explains that many of his students are much more complex than a test could ever reveal.

Thirty-year public school veteran Evan Keliher discusses the resurgence of school reform movements, arguing that such plans have failed to improve education, despite years of innovative teaching techniques and alternative classroom models. In "Forget the Fads—The Old Way Works Best," Keliher explains that the best way to improve education is to look to the past, when a room of eager students faced a teacher with a chalkboard. It was with little more than a chalkboard that journalist-turned-teacher Christina Asquith taught a year in an inner city school in Philadelphia. In "A Real Education," Asquith puts human faces on the educational issues many politicians discuss in broad terms. What she learned from her experience changed the way she viewed the education debate.

While teachers like Asquith face many daunting challenges in the classroom, few expect that they could be sued for failing a student. Janelle Brown, in "'L' Is for Lawsuit," discusses a growing trend in litigation—parents suing teachers when their children fail in school. Such lawsuits may even have their roots in racism. While most people associate racial profiling as something that happens on the streets, it may also be happening in the classroom. Jodie Morse describes the practice as "Learning While Black" and describes how some students may be suffering this unexpected form of racism.

The next piece moves to the college campus, where James Shapiro wonders what is happening to the great works of literature. In "When Brevity Rules the Syllabus, 'Ulysses' Is Lost," Shapiro explains that long novels are being cut in favor of shorter ones of less quality in an effort to accommodate students' busy lifestyles. Will such books disappear from the literary canon? And are college students getting the short end of the stick in addition to the shorter books?

S. I. Hayakawa and Lourdes Rovira present different perspectives on the highly controversial issue of bilingual education in this chapter's Viewpoints. The bilingual education question is particularly significant in many Spanish-speaking areas of the country, such as California, the Southwest, and Florida. English-only advocates insist that linguistic divisions prevent national unity, isolate ethnic groups, and impede educational goals. They also argue that programs providing bilingual education provide little inducement for non-English speakers to participate in mainstream American culture, preventing them from pursuing higher education and professional employment. On the other side of the controversy is the concern that the English-only movement denies children their heritage, is elitist, and even racist. But the question remains, what is best for the students? The chapter closes with a Research Issue interview with education professor Linda Darling Hammond who discusses some of the issues facing schools and teachers today.

Turning Schools into Profit Centers
Peter Sacks

School reform has been a hot topic in recent years. Parents are demanding higher standards, and politicians are calling for accountability. In response, the testing trend has swept the nation, and administrators are considering ways to apply business models to educational structures. In the next essay, Peter Sacks questions some of these trends in school reform. Schools, he argues, are not minicorporations, and students are not "products." Bonuses and cash awards based on a school's performance in standardized tests should not be a measure of success. Such measures, he contends, could do more harm than good.

Peter Sacks is an author and essayist who writes frequently about education. His most recent book is *Standardized Minds: The High Price of America's Testing Culture and What We Can Do to Change It* (2001). This article was first published in the January issue of *Education Week*.

CRITICAL THINKING   Can schools improve administrative and educational techniques by applying practices traditionally used in businesses and corporations? Are there similarities between running a business and running a school? Or are the two entities vastly different?

1   Beware former corporate executives who take control of public schools. Before you can say "accountability," they're yakking about how the dowdy world of education ought to be handed over to the slick M.B.As and run like a corporation, allowing self-interested individuals and unfettered competition to transform the neighbor-

hood school into a pseudo-profit center. Like Adam Smith's proverbial invisible hand, the CEOs say the tools of capital will magically improve the nation's education system.

2   Under the corporate model of education, schools are businesses and kids are "products," as former Chrysler Chairman Lee Iococca once called schoolchildren when speaking to a group of educators. "Your product needs a lot of work, and in the end it's your job," he said.

3   Children in this corporate vision of public education are to be measured, sorted, and processed on the basis of standardized-test results. When test scores, and test scores alone, become the coin of the realm, the "market value" of individual schools themselves is simply and unquestionably indicated by those test scores, as any real estate agent will gladly tell you.

4   Now comes the J.A. and Kathryn Albertson Foundation, the philanthropic arm of the giant supermarket conglomerate Albertson Inc., which says it will hand out "cash awards" to cash-strapped schools in Idaho based on standardized-test results.

5   The Albertson Foundation finds itself in good corporate company. For instance, Joel I. Klein, the former Bertelsmann Inc. chief executive officer who is now the chancellor of the New York City school system, the nation's largest, wants to give bonuses to superintendents of up to $40,000 a year, largely on the basis of standardized-test performance. The way Mr. Klein talks about the proposal, it seems as if he had little choice, owing to the widely accepted rules of capitalism. "It's the way most systems of accountability and reward work in America," he told a reporter.

6   To the economist or the CEO, nothing could be more elegant than to reward and punish superintendents and teachers on the basis of simple productivity measures, like test scores. Following the money, school managers will do whatever it takes to improve the performance of their profit centers by, for example, firing supposedly incompetent teachers who aren't getting the job done.

7   But there's at least one glaring problem with this scenario, which Joel Klein, the Albertson Foundation, and others have neglected to realize or simply ignored because it inconveniently muddles the apparent elegance of their corporate-inspired incentives. The problem lies in the very self-interested behavior they are hoping to tap in to in order to improve schools: With the promise of such hefty bonuses, superintendents will, in fact, do whatever it takes to boost test scores, regardless of the educational wisdom of the methods employed to accomplish that end.

8   Indeed, the lessons of the recent research literature on the effects of high-stakes testing in schools is quite clear, and should give pause to policymakers when contemplating these test-laden incentive systems. Schools operating in high-stakes environments can rapidly engineer impressive gains in test scores by installing intensive test-preparation programs narrowly focused on drilling for a specific exam.

9   At bottom, children end up being the real losers of such gaming strategies. Among the unintended consequences of these narrowly focused test-prep programs is that test-score gains don't transfer into real and lasting learning, because the test-specific gains typically cannot be detected in other assessments of achievement.

10   As just one example, in a recent study of overall learning gains in 18 states with high-school "exit" exams, David C. Berliner and Audrey L. Amrein of Arizona State University could find little evidence that improvements on the state tests trans-

ferred to meaningful gains on other tests, such as the SAT or the National Assessment of Educational Progress. The researchers concluded, "Analyses of these data reveal that if the intended goal of high-stakes testing policy is to increase student learning, then that policy is not working."

11   Hence, the bonuses that Mr. Klein and the Albertson Foundation would give to superintendents and schools will likely be based upon illusory, unsustainable gains, for the simple reason that the outcome measures, as well as the means to effect those outcomes, are overly narrow.

12   Incentives for performance might work for schools, but the prevailing paradigm of school accountability must change to include far broader definitions of school quality than is presently the norm. For example, what if superintendents and teachers were rewarded not just on short-term snapshots of test results, but based on how many of a district's graduates go on to enroll in four-year colleges? Or, were rewarded on the basis of periodic, external reviews of actual portfolios of student work and other broader measures of academic achievement?

13   Yes, educators do respond to incentives—and the results aren't always pretty when school quality is defined by test scores. In some cases, school managers have invented ways to exclude the test results of certain classes of students, such as those with limited English proficiency, thus making the schools appear more "profitable" than in reality. And, in the most egregious cases, schools and teachers, operating under these test-score imperatives, have resorted to cheating to get their numbers up.

14   In short, schools operating in such "corporatized" environments have, in due course, adopted some of the tricks of the Enrons and WorldComs, fudging the numbers and hiding the losses to inflate their performance.

15   Reasons abound to be skeptical of former corporate CEOs when they talk about the imperative of running schools more like businesses. A bit of retrospection is in order, especially considering the recent systemic failings of the American corporation itself when individuals act upon incentives that enrich themselves at the expense of the public good. ◆

FREEWRITING ASSIGNMENT

In the second paragraph, Sacks quotes Lee Iococca's comment to a group of teachers, "Your product needs a lot of work, and in the end it's your job." Respond to this statement in your own words. Is he right?

CRITICAL READING

1. Why are business leaders getting involved in educational issues? How are business models being applied to schools?
2. Why is Sacks concerned with school reforms that apply business models to traditional educational practices? What specific concerns does he express, and what is his position on these concerns? Explain.
3. Why does Sacks object to financial incentives to schools and bonuses to administrators based on test performance? What can go wrong? How do you feel about such incentives? Explain.

4. What is Sacks's tone in this essay? Identify phrases and words he uses that reveal his position on this issue.

5. In paragraph 12, Sacks proposes alternative ways to measure success other than standardized testing. Do you think his suggestions are better than testing? Why or why not? Identify the pros and cons of his solution.

CRITICAL WRITING

6. Write a letter to the J. A. and Kathryn Albertson Foundation, explaining why you support or oppose their proposal to hand out cash awards to Idaho schools based on standardized test results.

7. *Exploratory Writing*: Sacks notes that bonuses to superintendents and cash incentives to schools with higher scores is fundamentally flawed. Write an exploratory essay identifying the flaws in this practice. Alternatively, write about why this model could serve to improve school performance and education overall.

GROUP PROJECTS

8. As a group, print and take the fifth grade European history test featured at *http://cresst96.cse.ucla.edu/CRESST/Sample/5EURO.PDF*. After taking the test, discuss the questions. Is the content appropriate for fifth graders? Is it relevant to children across the country? Does it contain questions that might be considered ambiguous? Discuss the content of the test as a class.

9. Visit the web site of the National Center for Education Statistics and view the "nation's report card," detailing last year's test results in the area of reading at *http://nces.ed.gov/nationsreportcard/*. What do the results reveal? As a group, discuss the results and their possible relationship to standardized testing. For example, what do the results imply on a national level (National Results), and what might you infer from the "Subgroup" results? Explain.

Letter to a Washington State Test Scorer
Stephen Kramer

The movement towards standardized testing in the nation's schools was driven by the desire to have measurable standards to evaluate academic success, and to ensure that schools were teaching comparable material. While many of the principles behind testing make sense, some teachers argue that a test is not an accurate measure of student performance because it doesn't allow for variables and special situations. In the next piece, educator Stephen Kramer writes a hypothetical letter to the test scorer destined to evaluate his class. Kramer notes some of the special circumstances he wishes the scorer could consider, but can't, as the tests are graded.

Stephen Kramer teaches fifth grade in Brush Prairie, Washington. He is the author of several science books for children, including *Lightning, How to Think Like a Scientist, Eye of the Storm*, and *Hidden Worlds*. This "letter" was published in the September 2003 online issue of *EdWeek*.

CRITICAL THINKING   In the next piece, teacher Stephen Kramer "writes" a letter to the test scorer who will grade his class tests. Rather than grading with a number, he wishes that the scorer knew more about the individual students who took the tests. Should tests have areas for teachers to explain special cases or exceptions or give background on students?

> *Not everything that can be counted counts,*
> *And not everything that counts can be counted.*
> —Albert Einstein

Dear Washington State Science Test Scorer:

1   I've been thinking about you this summer. I know that one of these days you'll be opening a box of test booklets my students worked on last spring. For three hours, approximately one hour per day, my 5th graders read and answered multiple-choice, short-answer, and longer-response questions designed to measure their knowledge of Washington State's Essential Academic Learning Requirements for science.

2   Now it's your turn. You've been hired and trained to score my students' papers with a checklist/rubric. When you are finished, there will be 26 numbers—one for each pupil—that indicate how proficient my students are in science. This year the test is being piloted. Once it's finalized, however, annual science scores for my school will be published every autumn in our local newspaper, along with scores in reading, math, writing, and listening. People in both Washington state and in Washington, D.C., will make judgments about our school based on those scores and any increases or decreases they show in the next few years.

3   The funny thing is, I could have told you who was going to do well and who was going to struggle before my class had even sharpened their No. 2 pencils. The test, like many assessments we're being asked to give elementary students these days, contained many open-ended items requiring students to think, analyze, and write at cognitive levels at the upper limit of their developmental abilities. I love posing such questions to students. They're at the heart of any good science lesson, and we use them in classroom discussions to learn about science and to learn from each other. But there's a different dynamic at work when such items are given to 10- and 11-year-olds in test booklets. Under those conditions—when students work in isolation and aren't allowed to ask questions or clarify their thoughts through discussion—student performance is highly correlated with factors such as IQ, general background knowledge, attention span, and writing ability.

4   There are stories behind the names on the test booklets I'm sending you—things I think you should know. If I could sit at your side while you evaluate my students' work, here are some things I'd say:

5   I realize you'll have to give Vitaly a failing score. Except for the name on the cover, his test book is completely blank. But I hope you don't think he doesn't care or didn't try. Vitaly's family recently immigrated to the United States. He didn't attend school much before he came to this country. Vitaly is excited about learning to read, and he's making good progress. However, he's just now entering what English-as-a-second-language teachers call the "speech immersion stage" of language development—meaning that he's beginning to try out short phrases in English conversation. A couple of weeks ago, when I was checking with Vitaly about his lunch, I asked whether he knew what a peanut butter and jelly sandwich was. He smiled and shook his head "no." According to the rules of the federal No Child Left Behind Act of 2001, I had to give Vitaly the science test along with the rest of my class. After he wrote his name on the cover, I kneeled by his desk and we looked at the first page together. I asked him if he understood any of the questions. He wrinkled his brow, stared at the page for a long moment, and then shook his head "no." At that point, I patted his shoulder and smiled to let him know it was OK. Then I closed the test booklet and put it away. Vitaly now knows what a peanut butter and jelly sandwich is; we haven't been able to communicate much yet about the scientific method. But I wish you could see the smile on Vitaly's face when he runs across the field behind our school with an insect net in his hands. And last spring, when we were doing a lab using baking soda to compare the acid content of various liquids, you should have seen how carefully he measured fruit juices with his syringe. Maybe Vitaly will grow up to become a veterinarian or a medical researcher.

6   Lindsey left quite a few of the essay-type questions unanswered. Reading has never been easy for her, and she sometimes goes off on a tangent when she has to follow written instructions on her own. But you should see Lindsey during our class discussions—when I'm explaining how metamorphic rocks are formed or how diabetes affects people. She's like a sponge, soaking up information—and she remembers what she hears. That's the way she learns. Lindsey doesn't say much, but when she raises her hand, I frequently hear a question or a comment that's full of insight. Last fall, our class built rubber-band-powered go-carts. When other students became exasperated by the technical problems of finding ways to increase wheel diameter or rubber-band-engine power, Lindsey was the one with the ideas and persistence who got things going again. She's also an excellent facilitator, a person who can help three other squabbling students get back on task. I believe Lindsey has a future as a mechanical engineer.

7   Logan's test booklet has some excellent answers—and some questions you may think that he skipped. Actually, it's not Logan's style to skip anything. You see, whether I give Logan an art project or a writing assignment, he needs lots of time to process and think things through before he can even make the first mark on his paper. Before I understood this, I sometimes tried to keep him moving along at the pace of his classmates. I quickly found that made both of us unhappy. I eventually discovered that if I let Logan work at his own pace, he would often complete a piece of artwork or writing that was so creative, detailed, and thoughtful that it would give

me goose bumps. Even though the instructions in the science booklet said that Logan could have taken as much time as he needed, he was overwhelmed by the number of items on the test. Remember, he's only been an 11-year-old for a month! Although he left many items blank, I'll bet some of his answers are as thoughtful as any you'll see. I'm guessing that Logan will grow up to become a biological illustrator, or perhaps a children's science-book author/artist.

8   I know that the science test I gave was just the pilot. I also know that a committee has yet to evaluate the results and establish a cutoff point that will identify which students pass and which don't. But this emphasis on testing has a downside. I keep thinking about recent in-service trainings I've attended on teaching reading, writing, and math. The people in charge were all good presenters. They were enthusiastic and had the interests of students at heart. But as I left the trainings, I was saddened by the fact that in each one I'd heard about how the activities I was learning would improve my students' scores on state-mandated tests. I didn't hear, in any of them, how the activities would help my students develop a greater love of reading, writing, or math.

9   I could tell you stories about Michael, Jennifer, Richard, and every other child in my class—but I hope you understand my point. Evaluating students is a complex task. The science tests I just gave—and others like them—can turn out to be more like sieves than measuring cups. Some of the most important things we do in the classroom end up leaking through the holes. A well-constructed test can give teachers important information about what students know and where to focus instructional time. It's just that I'd hate for anyone to think that a single number represents what the 5th graders in our school know about science. It's a lot more complicated than that. ◆

FREEWRITING ASSIGNMENT

How do you perform on standardized tests? Do you think they were useful in rating your achievements? Explain.

CRITICAL READING

1. What is Kramer asking for in his letter? Does he think that his letter will matter? What does he want to accomplish, and why?
2. How does Kramer appeal to the emotions with this letter? Cite some examples.
3. Why do you think Kramer chose the quote preceding his letter? How does it connect to the points he makes? Explain.
4. To what aspects of standardized testing does Kramer object? Why does he feel that they are flawed? Do you agree?
5. What hopes does Kramer express, and what guesses does he make regarding the future of some of his students?
6. What kind of teacher do you think Kramer is? Would you want him to teach your child? Why or why not?

CRITICAL WRITING

7. You are the test scorer who received Kramer's letter along with a packet containing his class tests. Write a letter to him responding to his comments. Draw from information from your own experience, and from the other articles in this section, as you formulate your response.

8. *Exploratory Writing*: At the end of his letter, Kramer notes that in each training seminar he had attended on teaching recently, the focus has not been on promoting love of learning but on how to improve student test scores. In your opinion, are standardized tests changing the way students learn? Should teachers be trying to get students to love learning, or teaching them information needed to pass tests? Or is there a happy medium? Explain.

GROUP PROJECTS

9. With your group, develop a questionnaire of 10–12 questions designed to gather public opinion on standardized tests, such as the respondent's opinion of standardized tests, the penalties for failing such tests, school rewards, incentives, etc. Try to interview a variety of people, including students, teachers, and parents of school-age children. Tabulate the responses and present a general overview statement to the rest of the class as part of a broad discussion on testing in schools.

10. Testing is connected to reward in many schools. By the time they reach college, most students have taken many standardized tests, from academic achievement tests, to placement tests, to PSATs and SATs, and other college entrance examinations. As a group, discuss the impact testing has on students—the pressure, the success, the preparation involved. Are tests accurate measures of success and indicators of future performance? Should we have more, or less, testing in schools? Write a short summary of your discussion, addressing any key observations that were brought up by the group.

Forget the Fads—The Old Way Works Best
Evan Keliher

School reform movements since the 1960s have sought the educational holy grail—a system that engages students, promotes learning, advances graduation rates, and prepares students to be responsible adults. If all the political hullabaloo is any indicator, so far, we haven't found the magic formula. But are we trying too hard? In this piece, Evan Keliher says he knows what will fix public education. It is as simple as a teacher, a chalkboard, and a roomful of willing students. With 30 years of teaching under his belt, he ought to know.

Evan Keliher is a retired public school teacher and the author of several books, including *Guerrilla Warfare for Teachers: A Survival Guide* (1996), *Motor City Miracles* (2001), and

Triple Play (2001). This editorial appeared in the September 30, 2002 "My Turn" column in *Newsweek*.

CRITICAL THINKING

Think about the classroom format and educational system(s) you experienced in your elementary and high schools. Did you have team teaching, open classrooms, traditional classrooms, peer-tutoring, or group mentoring styles? Did any format work better, or worse, than others?

1   I've never claimed to have psychic powers, but I did predict that the $500 million that philanthropist Walter Annenberg poured into various school systems around the country, beginning in 1993, would fail to make any difference in the quality of public education. Regrettably, I was right.

2   By April 1998, it was clear that the much-ballyhooed effort had collapsed on itself. A *Los Angeles Times* editorial said, "All hopes have diminished. The promised improvements have not been realized." The program had become so bogged down by politics and bureaucracy that it had failed to create any significant change. How did I know this would be the result of Annenberg's well-intentioned efforts? Easy. There has never been an innovation or reform that has helped children learn any better, faster or easier than they did prior to the 20th century. I believe a case could be made that real learning was better served then than now.

3   Let me quote Theodore Sizer, the former dean of the Harvard Graduate School of Education and the director of the Annenberg Institute for School Reform, which received some of the grant money. A few years ago a reporter asked him if he could name a single reform in the last 15 years that had been successful. Sizer replied, "I don't think there is one."

4   I taught in the Detroit public-school system for 30 years. While I was there, I participated in team teaching, supervised peer-tutoring programs and tussled with block scheduling plans. None of it ever made a discernible difference in my students' performance. The biggest failure of all was the decentralization scheme introduced by a new superintendent in the early 1970s. His idea was to break our school system into eight smaller districts—each with its own board of education—so that parents would get more involved and educators would be more responsive to our students' needs. Though both of those things happened, by the time I retired in 1986 the number of students who graduated each year still hadn't risen to more than half the class. Two-thirds of those who did graduate failed the exit exam and received a lesser diploma. We had changed everything but the level of student performance.

5   What baffles me is not that educators implement new policies intended to help kids perform better, it's that they don't learn from others' mistakes. A few years ago I read about administrators at a middle school in San Diego, where I now live, who wanted a fresh teaching plan for their new charter school and chose the team teaching model. Meanwhile, a few miles away, another middle school was in the process of abandoning that same model because it hadn't had any effect on students' grades.

6   The plain truth is we need to return to the method that's most effective: a teacher in front of a chalkboard and a roomful of willing students. The old way is the best way. We have it from no less a figure than Euclid himself. When Ptolemy I,

the king of Egypt, said he wanted to learn geometry, Euclid explained that he would have to study long hours and memorize the contents of a fat math book. The pharaoh complained that that would be unseemly and demanded a shortcut. Euclid replied, "There is no royal road to geometry."

7   There wasn't a shortcut to the learning process then and there still isn't. Reform movements like new math and whole language have left millions of damaged kids in their wake. We've wasted billions of taxpayer dollars and forced our teachers to spend countless hours in workshops learning to implement the latest fads. Every minute teachers have spent on misguided educational strategies (like building kids' self-esteem by acting as "facilitators" who oversee group projects) is time they could have been teaching academics.

8   The only way to truly foster confidence in our students is to give them real skills—in reading, writing and arithmetic—that they can be proud of. One model that incorporates this idea is direct instruction, a program that promotes rigorous, highly scripted interaction between teacher and students.

9   The physicist Stephen Hawking says we can be sure time travel is impossible because we never see any visitors from the future. We can apply that same logic to the subject of school reforms: we know they have not succeeded because we haven't seen positive results. But knowing that isn't enough. We should stop using students as lab rats and return to a more traditional method of teaching. If it was good enough for Euclid, it is good enough for us. ◆

FREEWRITING ASSIGNMENT

In your opinion, what is the best way for students to learn? If you could give the department of education advice based on your own educational experience, what would it be?

CRITICAL READING

1. Keliher states in his introduction that he knew that the Annenberg project in public educational reform would fail to make any difference in the quality of public education. Review the Annenberg Foundation's report on this effort at *www.lessonsandreflections.org/lessons/report.pdf.* Would the foundation agree with Keliher that the project was unsuccessful? What is your opinion?
2. Keliher notes that he has taught in many different classroom models and educational formats, including team teaching. Team teaching was very popular in the late 1960s and 1970s, but many schools are abandoning this style because it has been judged ineffective. Research this classroom model online. What made it popular? Why did it fail?
3. What words reveal Keliher's opinion of "fad" teaching styles? Identify adjectives and phrases in his essay that reveal his position. How do these words influence his audience? Explain.
4. In paragraph 6, Keliher states that we must return to traditional teaching methods—"the old way is the best way." What is the "old way"? Can we truly go back to the old way? Or has technology made this an unlikely possibility?

CRITICAL WRITING

5. *Personal Narrative*: Write a personal narrative describing your memories of a favorite teacher. What made that teacher special? What teaching methods did he or she use? What could other teachers learn from this person? Explain.

6. *Research and Analysis*: What causes poor academic performance? Poor schools? Ineffective teachers? Inattentive or uninterested parents? Student apathy? Is it a combination of factors? Write an essay in which you discuss the factors that contribute to school performance, drawing from your own experience, and information you gather online.

GROUP PROJECT

7. In paragraph 8, Keliher states that the way to foster confidence in students is to give them "real skills—in reading, writing, and arithmetic." As a group, discuss the skills that a student should have upon graduation from high school. Are these skills as simple as reading, writing, and arithmetic? Are others required to successfully live in today's world? Or do these basics provide the foundation everyone needs?

A Real Education
Christina Asquith

In 1999, a young journalist with no teaching experience decided to answer the call to teach. As a reporter, Christina Asquith had taken a special interest in stories on education, and trying her hand at teaching seemed like a logical step to give her the "inside scoop." Responsible for a sixth grade class in one of Philadelphia's toughest middle schools, Asquith soon found that things are not quite what they seem. The challenges facing urban schools exceeded her worst fears. In the narrative that follows, Asquith describes her experience and what it taught her.

Christina Asquith is a reporter who spent one year in a Philadelphia middle school as an emergency certified teacher. She has written a book describing her experience, and is currently working on a book with her sister, a teacher, called *The 10 Golden Rules to Surviving Your First Year Teaching*. This piece was published in the March 14, 2002 issue of the *Columbia Journalism Review*.

CRITICAL THINKING   The issue of problems facing urban schools is often reported in the newspapers. What are some of these issues? Are urban school systems different from suburban ones? Do they face different challenges?

1 One sunny July morning in 1999, on a whim, I called the Philadelphia School district and made an appointment with a recruiter. I thought of myself as a reporter, but I was looking for a job. Like many cities suffering from a teacher shortage, Philadelphia still needed 1,200 teachers and was taking almost anyone with a college degree. I had written hundreds of stories about education and always harbored an interest in teaching. Still, I'd never considered actually doing it, until then. "We need you more than you need us," the recruiter said. He gave me a folder of paperwork including a background check for the state police, and there wasn't much more involved. I had mixed feelings. My colleagues at *The Philadelphia Inquirer*—we were finishing a two-year reporting program there—were heading to staff positions at papers like the *Orlando Sentinel* and the Raleigh *News & Observer*. I didn't want to throw away the journalism career I'd worked hard for since my college newspaper days. I'd interned unpaid through college and reported for a year from Chile, primarily for AP/Dow Jones. When I returned, the *Inquirer* hired me as one of its "two-year correspondents" to cover southern Chester County, Pennsylvania, a beat that included three school districts, twenty-seven townships, and a mushroom industry that employed 10,000 Mexican immigrants. I gravitated to school stories out of interest and a sense that they were important. From my suburban outpost, I made page one occasionally by regionalizing a story on subjects like revolving-door principals or questionable strategies to raise test scores. But I always felt uncertain about my stories about schools, as though I were guessing at what was really happening inside them.

2 When the two years ended, I interviewed for a staff position on the *Inquirer's* city education desk, but the beat went to an education reporter with a decade of experience. Meanwhile, my affection for newspapers was waning; there had been a lot of deflating news about corporate ownership and declining circulation. At age twenty-five, I was already questioning if newspaper journalism could be the vehicle for change I wanted it to be. I was eager to make a difference.

3 So, when I saw the article about the teacher shortage I got excited. If I taught for a year I would be able to see the real issues firsthand. I could have an effect on education in a way I wasn't having with journalism. And I wasn't throwing away my career, I reasoned, because if I wanted to come back to newspapers, I would be an even stronger education reporter. I decided to do it. Six weeks later, I stepped into my story.

4 My school was Julia de Burgos Bilingual Middle Magnet School, a 100-year-old stone building in The Badlands, the nickname for a heroin-ravaged Puerto Rican neighborhood in North Philadelphia. City test scores ranked it as the worst middle school in the city. At my first teachers' meeting in September, the new principal, Jayne Gibbs, warned us, "We can't fail any special-education students this year because the government is breathing down our neck." As the teachers nodded and murmured, I sheepishly glanced around. I needed to remind myself that I wasn't a reporter sneaking into a meeting. Other teachers were talking openly to me, without that guarded, clipped manner that I was accustomed to. To them, I was Ms. Asquith, a sixth grade bilingual teacher, with a classroom of forty desks, two blackboards, bars over the windows, and a scenic view of the boiler room roof.

5 My sixth graders ranged in age from ten to fourteen, and were mostly first- or second-generation Puerto Ricans. Half the class spoke little or no English. The first week, the school was still missing another sixth grade teacher so I got two classes.

They shuffled in carrying composition notebooks and wearing puffy jackets, tapered jeans, and Timberland boots. They called me "miss," and were shy, obedient, and eager to please. They wanted stickers for their notebooks and to read the Harry Potter books. A couple of boys wore gangster-style skullcaps and looked tough, but beyond appearances, they were not the drug-dealing street-toughs fitting my stereotype.

6   My journalistic interests were immediately eclipsed by the reality and enormity of teaching. I had Jose, a thirteen-year old boy from the Dominican Republic, who spoke mostly Spanish and had been left back twice already; Darnell, a mentally troubled boy who jumped out of his seat constantly; and Evelyn, a diligent, articulate eleven-year old who aspired to be a doctor. I didn't know how to teach a lesson, let alone how to teach a class with such a range in abilities.

7   The school didn't help. When I asked the vice principal for a curriculum, I was promised one that never appeared. By the fourth week, I was finally given a set of grammar textbooks and a set of social studies textbooks, but they were too difficult for my English-as-a-second-language students. I had to invent everything myself. When the *Philadelphia Daily News* ran a story in October reporting that 100 new teachers across the city had quit, complaining of lack of support and supplies, I understood. For the first few months, each day felt like a churning, eight-hour tempest. I invented lame writing assignments—"What would you do with a million dollars?"—and read *Chicken Soup for the Kid's Soul.* Several of the administrators were also new, and just as overburdened by the remaining seven teacher vacancies. Whether and what I taught were secondary concerns to them. So I used my journalism skills, asked a lot of questions of other teachers, and wrote everything down. A significant handful of teachers were so incompetent that it was dangerous. They screamed at the students all day and created a climate of fear, abuse, and violence. But by November, I was finally picking up enough tricks and materials from the good ones to put together a semblance of a daily lesson. I got by with the help of my nicer colleagues, who amazed me with their ingenuity. In my class, instead of the typical reading and writing assignments we read newspaper and magazine articles, and wrote letters to the editor. The *Daily News* printed a short letter from one of my most easily discouraged students. Seeing his face light up pushed me forward.

8   At night, after grading and planning, I wrote in a journal all that I was learning in my new world. Details I had never focused on as a journalist fascinated me, such as who kept student attendance and how easy it was to fudge upwards. Schools get higher ratings and award money from the state for high attendance, and as a teacher I saw how attendance could fluctuate depending on what time it's taken, whether suspended students are considered absent, and whether a school counts excused absences in its total.

9   And from the inside, I could see how some education stories really miss the mark. For example, in late winter the school board announced plans to spend millions of dollars on a new "discipline school," a place for kids with behavior problems. From an outsider's point of view, that might seem like a good idea. Indeed, our school had about thirty or forty students who needed to be removed. They roamed the hallways, picking fights, threatening teachers with scissors, and destroying the learning environment. These students were often victims of abuse themselves and needed help. But they remained in our school year after year. The problem was not a lack of discipline schools. The fact was that the city's existing

discipline schools were half empty. The reason: the stacks and stacks of paperwork required by the city and state to transfer a dangerous student into one of the city's discipline schools. It could take up to eight months to put a transfer through, so few teachers bothered. When the *Inquirer* wrote a long feature story about the proposed new million-dollar discipline school, the article made only brief mention of the fact that the existing discipline schools were not being used, and no mention at all of the many roadblocks involved in moving a student to a discipline school.

10   The issues I had worried myself with, as a reporter, suddenly seemed quite esoteric and bureaucratic in comparison to what the students and teachers had to deal with. Most of my sources as a reporter had been administrators, union members, and school board members—instead of students, parents, and teachers. And yet, much of what the school board dealt with was unrelated to what really happened on the ground. For example, the school board fussed for months over prohibiting social promotion, finally deciding that a failing student could not be passed on, regardless of age. Yet our principal is allowed to change grades, and about failing students she told us, "If you retain them we will have to deal with them again." When I turned in two failing report cards they came back to me with the grades raised.

11   Journalists' assumptions, I was finding out, can be off the mark. An example of this arose when I was given a $ 1,200 iMac computer for my classroom. As a reporter, I had written a number of stories involving the effort to put technology in the classroom, and just assumed it was a positive goal. I am now less certain. My class's computer collected dust in the back because one, two, even five computers are not that helpful with thirty-three kids. I always believed that increased funding would help schools, but now I saw how existing money was sometimes misspent. The sad truth was that many teachers used the computers to busy the tough-to-control special-education students so that they wouldn't destroy the school. A reporter is not likely to get that story from just talking to a school board member. What the school really needed was not fancy technology but someone to design a curriculum, coordinate the grades, and order appropriate books.

12   One morning I saw a thirteen-year-old girl crying in the hallway. The security guard was screaming at her, so I offered to walk her back to her classroom. Her name was Angela, she was mentally disabled, one of some seventy students placed in "special education classes" out of about 700 students in the school. When we reached her classroom I understood why she preferred the hallways. Students were fighting and overturning desks and the substitute teacher was shouting, "they're animals." The ceiling was peeling, and exposed nails stuck up from a piece of wood on the floor. Angela was attacked. When I turned to get help, I saw that the security guard was already there and had just been overpowered. This was not an emergency; this was a typical day for special-education students. Yet here was a kind of story that reporters tend not to find—the routine and systematic abuse of special-ed students.

13   Later I learned that Angela's group was one of five special-education classes that would not have a teacher all year. They were bounced from room to room each period. One substitute pushed his desk in front of the door and turned on the TV. Occasionally, a substitute wouldn't show up, and the students were left alone in the room. In the spring, at a school in the same neighborhood, a girl in special education was raped during the school day. The overwhelming reaction at my school was

"thank god it didn't happen here." But it easily could have. With no teacher or program, Angela and the other special-education students just ran loose in the hallways, starting fires that nearly torched the school, pushing and hospitalizing a teacher, molesting younger students, getting arrested, and shredding the learning environment for the rest of the students. We were dependent on the school district to find real special-education teachers, but it never sent us any. Much of the time of our special-education teacher was spent on completing paperwork that glossed over such problems. Indeed, when our special-ed program was reviewed by federal auditors in May, the school passed.

14   Seeing this abuse daily made me feel personally frustrated with the media, which—while investigating the police and other public departments—tended to treat the schools as a feature beat. In October, the *Daily News* wrote its "special report" about new teachers quitting. In the spring, there were stories about a rape and a shooting that occurred at two different schools, and in between there were many stories about contract negotiations and administrative matters. Not much about actual education, its successes *or* failures. And when something was written about the schools, it often carried the intonation that the students were at fault. After a vice principal was shot during a scuffle in a West Philadelphia school, the *Daily News* followed up with a cover story: WHY THE SCHOOLS ARE STUCK WITH SO MANY BAD KIDS. It was illustrated with a shadowy image of a student lurking in the background. The underlying assumption—that the students were to blame—reflected a sentiment popular with many in the school board, teachers union, and the administration—none of whom want to take responsibility for their failings. But what I experienced as a teacher showed me the opposite. The story should have read: WHY THE KIDS ARE STUCK WITH SO MANY BAD SCHOOLS. The ongoing failure of our nation's urban school system is a scandal—it's hurting millions of children, stealing from taxpayers, and creating violence and desperation that has a ripple effect on all corners of society. And it doesn't have to be that way. It's time for the education desk to shed its reputation as a soft beat, for reporters and editors to take a sharper pencil to the schools.

15   Having once dealt with deadlines, editors, and the pressure for copy, I feel I have some understanding of the complacency that affects the coverage of education. But I can no longer justify it. Too many reporters think that nothing can be done. They allow the protectors of the status quo to use sensitive issues of race and culture and poverty as a shield against their critics. They feed the sense of hopelessness that is encouraged by bad teachers, self-aggrandizing union leaders, and hapless administrators. All those things affected me, too, when I was a reporter. It took a classroom of them to convince me that the kids really do deserve a chance, and that they won't have one until the news organizations act as if they believe it. ◆

FREEWRITING ASSIGNMENT ————————————————

Asquith mentions many disturbing situations she experienced while working in an urban middle school in Philadelphia. Pick one such situation and write about it. Did something seem particularly alarming? Were you outraged, concerned, saddened? Explain.

CRITICAL READING

1. Asquith admits that until she became a teacher herself, she didn't speak to the right people or ask the right questions when reporting on educational issues. What did she discover as an insider? What does she recommend reporters do differently when reporting on educational issues?

2. Asquith presents her experience as a first-person narrative. Evaluate the effectiveness of her narrative. What information does she think the reader should know about her, and why?

3. As a reporter with no teaching experience, Asquith is challenged to learn how to run a classroom with no direction, no mentoring, and for a while, no textbooks. How does she address these challenges?

4. This article was published in the *Columbia Journalism Review*, an academic, professional publication. Why do you think she chose this venue to print her story?

5. What does Asquith hope to accomplish by publishing her narrative? Are her goals different now than when she first started this self-imposed assignment? Explain.

6. Several of the readings in this section discuss the role of standardized testing to measure success and even award performance bonuses. Based on what you have read, does testing seem possible in schools such as the Julia de Bergos Bilingual Magnet School? Explain.

CRITICAL WRITING

7. In this essay, Christina Asquith becomes a teacher in order to see "first hand" the issues facing teachers and students in urban schools. Using a similar approach, prepare a newspaper article about an industry, business concern, or discipline from the perspective of an insider. For example, if you worked in the fast food industry, or a retail outfit, you could report on what that experience was like that outsiders are unlikely to know or realize. Or if you have participated in sports, you could prepare a story on that experience. Address some of the assumptions outsiders may have, and why they are right or wrong about them. Did you learn anything from the experience that surprised you?

8. *Research and Analysis*: Many essays in this chapter address the issue of education reform. Asquith notes that applying innovative teaching methods and new approaches was almost impossible in light of the daily challenges faced by many teachers in urban schools. Go to the Education Reform map web site maintained by the White House at *www.whitehouse.gov/infocus/education/edmap.html*. Visit the pages of several states to see what assistance and proposals the White House is making to improve education. After researching the information and articles posted on this site, write an essay on how the White House plans are likely to improve, or not improve, the situation facing many inner-city schools.

9. *Personal Narrative*: Asquith presents her experience in the form of a personal narrative. Write a personal narrative describing an experience in which you faced a daunting challenge, and explain how you dealt with it.

GROUP PROJECTS

10. Asquith comments that she received a $1,200 computer for her classroom, but that it "collected dust in the back because one, two, even five computers are not that helpful with thirty-three kids." As a group, discuss ways that Asquith could have used the computer in her sixth grade class, bearing in mind that the computer itself was probably the only technology she had access to. After developing a few ideas, share them with the class. The class should examine each idea and determine the applicability and/or potential pitfalls facing each project.

11. In paragraph 9, Asquith describes the frustrating situation of "discipline schools" to which students with behavior problems are sent, only after a load of paperwork is processed to have them removed from the regular school system. Research "discipline schools" (You may try *http://www.cms.k12.nc.us/ discover/goals/equityScorecard/studentDiscipline.pdf* as a starting point). Are more discipline schools needed, as the city of Philadelphia seems to believe, or are there alternatives? Do they hold the key to creating schools for the majority of students who should have a safe and orderly learning environment? Discuss this issue as a group.

"L" Is for Lawsuit
Janelle Brown

Most students know that if they fail to study and apply themselves, their grades will suffer. But not all students have to face the ramifications of their failure to make the grade. Angry that their darling Johnny flunked, an increasing number of parents are threatening to sue teachers. And this practice has teachers, and many parents, furious. Are lawsuits against teachers the next wave of troubles to face educators in the twenty-first century?

Janelle Brown is a contributing writer for *Salon* magazine, in which this article first appeared online on July 12, 2002. Her articles have appeared in many magazines and newspapers, including *Spin*, *Rolling Stone*, *Ms.*, *Wired*, the *Utne Reader*, the *New York Times,* and *Variety.*

CRITICAL THINKING

Have you ever received a grade that you felt you didn't deserve? Do you believe you were singled out unfairly by a teacher? How did you react? How did you deal with the situation? Explain.

1 One of the students in Elizabeth Joice's senior English class at Sunrise Mountain High School in Peoria, Ariz., was flirting with failure. In fact, it was much more than a dalliance—she was flunking. The student, whose name Joice wishes to keep private, had plagiarized a test, skipped classes, failed assignments and even missed a make-up session that might have allowed her to raise her grade. Joice had been sending notices to the girl's parents since April, warning them about the failing grade; and both the girl and her parents had met with assorted district administrators, counselors and Joice herself. But it was all to no avail: It was almost graduation, the girl had blown too many tests, and she wasn't going to walk.

2 Imagine Joice's surprise then, when on May 22, just one day before senior graduation, she received a letter from a lawyer representing the girl's family. The family felt that the teacher had graded unfairly, the letter said; they believed that their daughter hadn't been given enough of a chance, and unless Joice took "whatever action is necessary to correct this situation" they were going to file a lawsuit.

3 The girl graduated with her class the next day, igniting a local battle that has yet to be settled. Parents and students are furious that the girl (whose name has been withheld from the media) was given what they believe to be an unfair boost. Teachers are livid at the school district, which forced Joice to retest the student at the last minute. The Arizona state bar is investigating the ethics of the girl's lawyer. And the Peoria school district is defending its decision by claiming that the teacher hadn't applied appropriate grading procedures.

4 Welcome to high school in America, where grades are an irritating annoyance that can be swept aside by a well-placed threat, and where teachers and administrators only have authority as long as they don't displease parents. Bad grades, discipline problems, shocking attendance records: Offenses that in the past warranted school action as strong as suspension, dismissal from school or refusal to grant a diploma are easily blocked or reversed—as long as Dad's got a good lawyer.

5 The struggle for classroom control comes in an increasingly intimidating school environment where teachers are commanded—by parents, administrators and the government—to usher students through a gantlet of tests to graduation without displeasing litigious families or failing to meet performance standards that bring schools added funding or, at the very least, ensure their survival for another year.

6 Says John Mitchell, deputy director of the American Federation of Teachers, "Teachers are under incredible pressure right now from two places: from policymakers to raise standards and teach to those higher standards. Then on the other side you have parents giving pressure to teachers not to hold kids up to the high standards. Teachers are between a rock and a hard place. . . . It's an area ripe for lawsuits."

7 Indeed, the number of threats and lawsuits against teachers and schools—many of which fail to grab the attention of national media—has risen dramatically over the last decade, forcing schools to spend limited funds on lawyers and insurance, and teachers to spend more time protecting themselves from potential litigation; and, in the process, instituting defense strategies that are changing education in the country's public schools—and not for the better. As classroom creativity is curbed by the fear of lawsuits, kids lose the benefits of their teachers' inspiration and replace it with a different kind of lesson: that anything is possible if you have money or a capacity to complain.

8   Up until the moment when Elizabeth Joice received the letter from lawyer Stan Massad, her struggle with the failing senior was fairly typical. The warnings, the second chances—it was standard fare until May 22, the day before graduation and the day after a final meeting with the student's parents.

9   The letter that Massad sent Joice represented the nadir in her long history of parent-teacher relations. The girl had been "scarred for life" by the flunking grade, the letter claimed. "Since hearing this devastating news, the student has been very sick, unable to sleep or eat and she has been forced to seek medical attention." The letter went on to threaten Joice with a lawsuit and its attendant personal discomforts: "Of course, all information regarding your background, your employment records, all of your class records, past and present, dealings with this and other students become relevant, should litigation be necessary," it said.

10   After she received the letter, Joice immediately sent it to the Sunshine Mountain High School principal and the school district. She also composed her own defiant response: "The student would be a very capable student if she would apply herself, study and get her assignments in on time," she wrote. "Instead of being scarred for life, perhaps she will learn these lessons now, rather than when she is in college or in the work force. I think your clients would be better off investing their money in summer school tuition for the student rather than wasting their money on attorney fees, litigating a case with little likelihood of success."

11   On the morning of May 23, however, Joice was informed by the school district that she needed to give the student a second chance. "I was told 'You better decide what you are going to do, because that girl is going to walk tonight,'" Joice recalls. Just hours before graduation, Joice was instructed to give the student a second shot at a multiple-choice test she had already flunked once. The girl squeaked by, and was allowed to graduate.

12   Jack Erb, superintendent of the Peoria School District, swears that the district's decision had nothing to do with the threat of a lawsuit, and claims that he didn't see the lawyer's letter until after they had decided to retest the student. "It isn't an issue; people threaten us all the time and most of the time they don't follow through with it," he says. He posits that the decision to retest the student was based on a quirk in Joice's curriculum and grading system.

13   But after outraged parents and teachers from across the state sent furious letters to the local papers, complaining that the student shouldn't have been granted special privileges, the district finally offered a general apology for its "lack of clear and appropriately enforced internal guidelines regarding grading and curriculum standards." It said nothing about the legal threats, however. (The lawyer, in turn, is now being investigated by the state board of Arizona as to whether his veiled threats to Joice were ethical.)

14   Regardless of whether the district ultimately caved because it feared a lawsuit, the entire affair draws into relief the conflict currently taking place in classrooms across the country. Higher standards linked to higher stakes for schools have caused educators to be more rigorous. Concerned parents, facing tougher college entrance requirements for their kids, panic when their children falter, often blaming the teachers and schools for their children's failures. The result, of late, is lawsuits, or, most often, threats of lawsuits.

15   An astounding 25 percent of all secondary schools were involved with lawsuits of all sorts—from accidental injuries to discipline squabbles—between 1997 and 1999, according to a 1999 survey by the American Tort Reform Association—a huge increase over the decade before. While some of these lawsuits were no doubt justifiable, there is no shortage of egregious litigation: Legal expert Walter Olson's site Overlawyered.com, which chronicles legal ugliness in schools in order to point out the frivolous nature of American litigiousness, lists dozens of overzealous-parent lawsuits similar to the threats in Peoria.

16   There was the lawsuit, for example, filed by 15-year-old Elizabeth Smith in Bath Township, Ohio, who sued her school district and 11 teachers in 2000 for $6 million, claiming that her grades were unfair. The school had lowered her grades because of frequent absences and tardiness, which the Smith family blamed on "chronic tonsillitis" and the fact that she stayed home to put her siblings on the school bus. Meanwhile, in Riverside, Calif., a football player sued his former high school teachers at Murrieta Valley High School for giving him grades that were too high: He claimed that his education suffered because they cut him too much slack so that he could play football.

17   School discipline is another area where teachers and parents struggle for the upper hand. Lacey Renfro, a high school student in Tennessee, sued the cheerleading coach after she was suspended from a game for disciplinary reasons; Justin Swindler in Pennsylvania sued because he was expelled for soliciting a hit man via his Web site to kill his English teacher; and a father in Tennessee sued two teachers after they confiscated his son's yo-yo on a school trip where toys had been expressly forbidden.

18   Olson, a senior fellow at the Manhattan Institute, explains that, in the past, most schoolyard litigation grew out of incidents in which kids were barred from sports teams, or fell on the playground, or felt that they were discriminated against under the Individuals with Disabilities Education Act. It is rare that a simple grading squabble, such as the one in Peoria, will make it all the way to a court case—in part because of a 1978 Supreme Court ruling that held that courts shouldn't second-guess a school on academic decisions (those grading squabbles that do make it all the way to lawsuits are usually under the purview of the Disabilities Act—i.e.: "My kid was disabled and deserved special treatment.").

19   This doesn't mean that parents still don't threaten lawsuits over grades, however. Olson increasingly hears from school administrators who have received legal threats because of grading complaints and discipline issues. Few of these cases, he says, emerge in the media. "My guess is that the sort of strong-arming seen in the [Peoria] case is not in fact all that rare, but that the great majority of disputes never result in formal court filings and never result in publicity because neither side seeks it," he explains.

20   Pressure exerted behind the scenes tends to be more insidious than the interaction involved in public lawsuits, which, because they are argued in the open, lack some of the more vicious personal threats and allegations. In Washington D.C., for example, a teacher at the competitive Wilson Senior High School recently discovered that in at least 11 cases, student grades had been raised without the teacher's knowledge, apparently by an administrator who had felt pressured to help the stu-

dents graduate (although no one has confessed to the act). Teachers who had flunked their students were appalled to see those same students walking across the stage at graduation.

21   One of those students had been in the Spanish class of teacher Anexora Skvirsky, who had given her a generous D—and was promptly threatened by the student's father. Although she held her ground against the parent at the time, a year later someone in the administration apparently did not. Although Skvirsky has been teaching for 19 years, she says it's only been in the last few years that she's witnessed such "an incredible advocacy" on the part of parents. Although she's never received a legal threat, parents regularly try to get her fired by complaining to the principal.

22   "It is hellish," she says. "So many times I've had stomachaches, headaches, insomnia, because a parent would call and try to intimidate me or complain about me to the principal with a letter."

23   Skvirsky places the guilt for the 11 anonymous grade changes squarely on the shoulders of the school's administrators, who she says regularly cave to powerful parents who "move mountains by just complaining." This, say teacher advocacy groups, is becoming a common occurrence, particularly in schools with rigorous academics and demanding parents.

24   "I'm afraid Peoria is not an anomaly; it's not commonplace but it's not unusual for teachers to be told to change grades," says Mitchell of the American Federation of Teachers. "In most cases the teacher refuses to do it and the administrator does it over their protestations."

25   But this is not a totally new phenomenon, either. According to Kathleen Lyons, spokesperson for the National Education Foundation, the occasional case in which unhappy parents threatened teachers with lawsuits and retribution if grades weren't raised has always existed. The difference now is that behavior of the last resort has become almost routine.

26   "There have always been some parents who want a special deal for their child," Lyons says. "There's nothing new there, except that a higher-stakes educational environment and the high stakes of standardized testing has led to high stress. Parents now know it does make a difference how your kids do in school."

27   "I think there's a lot more riding on it," she adds, "and that does tend to bring out the worst in people: When the stakes are high, you find transgressions."

28   One solution is to completely standardize education—testing, grading and discipline—so that there is no wiggle room in the system for outraged parents and their lawyers. But that resolution already has prompted other kinds of parent lawsuits—in California and Texas—that claim that the system is too rigid, and discriminates against their children's special needs.

29   Worse, total standardization can extinguish all creativity from the classroom. In Peoria, where the school district has reacted to the controversy by writing a new series of standardized rules for the classroom, Joice worries that teachers are ultimately going to become automatons. "We may not be able to be as creative with the units we use, which will be a travesty because every teacher has a specialty and if we can't share that with our students, if it's all black and white, then that's sad," she

says. "If that's the case, why they don't just put computers out in the classroom as teachers?"

30   Even in districts that haven't bowed to pressure with standardized grading, the fear of lawsuits and parental retribution has undermined school programs and teachers' daily routines. Twenty percent of the respondents to the American Tort Reform Association survey, for example, reported spending five to 10 hours a week in meetings or documenting every little action they took with a student, in case of future litigation.

31   "It takes a lot of time to document everything: You have to document conversations, what you did, what the kids said in class," says Joice. "It will take more effort on the part of teachers if they want to stand up and say what happened."

32   Besides the simple question of time, lawsuits also come at a high cost for school districts and teachers: even a frivolous lawsuit over a grading dispute, which might be thrown out after just one hearing, can cost $10,000 in lawyers fees. School districts do have liability insurance, of course, as do teachers (some professional teachers organizations, such as the Texas State Teacher's Association, lure members with the promise of $6 million in liability insurance for those moments when "people are reacting with emotion rather than reason"). But that costs money, too.

33   "Lawsuits have become a great cost for school districts," says Julie Underwood, general counsel for the National School Boards Association. "The entire sub-specialty of education law didn't exist 25 years ago, and now it's a big, recognized sub-specialty. You can't keep track of the number of times that someone comes in to a principal's office and says, 'If you don't do this, I'll sue you.' It's just so commonplace." In fact, she says, all principals now have to undergo education-law classes before they can receive certification.

34   Finally, the students risk both the quality of their education and their faith in the system. Kids with lackluster achievement records who nevertheless head off to college with satisfactory grades thanks to Mom's strong-arm tactics are probably not going to make it far in higher education. Their classmates, who actually worked hard for their grades, will probably be demoralized, too.

35   "It undermines the hard work of other kids in the classroom, when they see standards change for one student. It erodes the standards, when we really want students to know that standards are meaningful. And for students involved, it really cheats them of a meaningful experience," says Mitchell. "Sometimes failure is the best teacher a student could have." ◆

FREEWRITING ASSIGNMENT

John Mitchell is quoted at the end of the article as saying, "Sometimes failure is the best teacher a student could have." Write about a time in which you learned from failure. It could be an experience in school, at work, or with an outside project. What did you learn, and why?

CRITICAL READING

1. What steps did high school teacher Elizabeth Joice take to warn her student and her parents of the student's failing situation? Could she have done anything else to avert the threat of the lawsuit? Explain.
2. John Mitchell comments that some of the best lessons a student can learn can stem from failure. What "lesson" did Joice's student likely learn from the experience? In what ways might this lesson harm Joice's student in the future? Explain.
3. In what ways does standardized education bar some lawsuits while permitting grounds for others? Explain.
4. How do frivolous lawsuits harm other students who do apply themselves and earn good grades?
5. What is Brown's opinion of parents suing teachers over grades? Is her essay balanced? Biased? Does she discuss both sides of the issue? Explain.

CRITICAL WRITING

6. *Exploratory Writing*: You are a parent of "Susan," who has received a failing grade. Because of this grade, your child will be unable to graduate with her class. You know "Susan" has let a few things slide in her final months of school, but overall, she is a good kid who you believe deserves to graduate. A friend suggests you speak with a lawyer to strong-arm your child's teacher into giving her a second chance at passing. Write an essay explaining why you would, or would not, employ such a tactic and why.
7. Kathleen Lyons observes of academic performance, "I think there's a lot more riding on it. . . . Parents now know it does make a difference how your kids do in school." Write a short essay describing your academic performance in high school. Were you a high achiever? Did you tend to coast? Were you more focused on extracurricular activities than on academics? Did your parents pressure you to get good grades? Explain.

GROUP PROJECT

8. Each member of your group should visit the website of the National School Board Association at *www.nsba.org* and select one recent legal case listed under its "School Law Issues" section. Each group member should prepare a one-paragraph summary of the case. After reviewing the summaries as a group, choose one to research in greater depth. As a group, serve as the judiciary body deciding the case (you may do this even if a verdict was already rendered). Explain the reasoning behind your verdict. As part of a larger class discussion, each group should report on the case it chose and discuss its verdict.

Learning While Black
Jodie Morse

We hear of racial profiling on the roads and in the skies, but are minority kids also being unfairly singled out for discipline in schools? Although some school administrators claim discipline is merely a reflection of behaviors, the N.A.A.C.P. and other research groups argue that African American students receive harsher punishments for less significant transgressions. The result, reporter Jodie Morse explains in this May 27, 2002, story published in *Time,* may be that African American students are getting an incomplete education.

CRITICAL THINKING
Were you ever disciplined in school for inappropriate behavior? Did you feel your punishment was fair or excessive? If you were never disciplined in school, what did you think of the behavior of those students who were? Were some students disciplined more than others?

1   No one is saying Kenneth Russell is an angel. The 16-year-old high school junior from Salida, California, is a C student with a filthy mouth who has been known to saunter into class on his own schedule. And, yes, as Russell readily admits, after a bout of name-calling with a white classmate last fall, he threw the first punch in a fistfight that left him battered and his adversary with five stitches over his left eye.

2   But is Russell actually a victim? The N.A.A.C.P. and some of his teachers think so. His father John has filed a civil rights complaint with the U.S. Department of Education, charging that Kenneth was unjustly punished for the fight. Although officials from the local Modesto school district ruled the scuffle "mutual," the white classmate received a three-day suspension while Russell was sent home for a little more than a month and later expelled from his school and assigned to one farther from where he lives. "It's been hard catching up with my work," says Kenneth. "I lost out on a month of my high school life."

3   For years black parents have quietly seethed about stories like Russell's. Now civil rights groups have given those silent suspicions a recognizable name: racial profiling. They contend that not unlike police who stop people on the basis of race, teachers and school officials discipline black students more often—and more harshly—than whites. The result: black students are more likely to slip behind in their studies and abandon school altogether—if they're not kicked out first. In Modesto, black students are 2 1/2 times as likely as their white peers to be expelled. This kind of treatment persists not only in the farm country of Modesto but also in urban districts like Minneapolis, Minnesota. During the 1998-99 school year, only one state (South Carolina) suspended 9% or more of its white students, but 35 states suspended that percentage of blacks, according to The Civil Rights Project at Harvard University. The syndrome has even acquired a catchphrase: "learning while black."

4   In the past two years, advocacy groups in a dozen cities have taken up the cause, and the N.A.A.C.P. called on every state to submit a plan to redress discipline and other educational inequities. Legislators in Maryland and Rhode Island have set up task forces to study school discipline. In April 2002, under a new state law, Ohio released suspension data broken down by race for each of its school districts.

5   Despite the current concern, the school-discipline gap is actually an old problem, first noted by social scientists a quarter-century ago. But with schools suspending nearly twice as many pupils as they did in the early '70s, the racial disparities have widened sharply. And today the penalties are stiffer. In the post-Columbine era, which has seen administrators reach for one-strike-and-you're-out, or zero-tolerance, policies, many schools no longer grant students a warning and a second chance, turning over even the most routine disciplinary matters to local police. "Schools now call in the police if a student is talking too much or doesn't do his homework," says Pedro Noguera, a professor at the Harvard Graduate School of Education.

6   There is some evidence that black students are more likely to wind up in the dragnet. A study released by the Advancement Project, a Washington-based advocacy group, reports that black students, although they made up just 30% of the population of Miami-Dade County public schools in 2000-01, accounted for half the school arrests in that district. Says Judith Browne, senior attorney with the project: "This is no different from what happens on the street, only now it's school administrators abusing authority."

7   Predictably, talk of racial profiling turns very nasty very quickly. No matter the venue, the debate revolves around the same set of slippery questions: Do differences in data equal racism? Or could it be that blacks actually drive more recklessly or, in the case of schools, behave worse? Perhaps race is just incidental, and gender or class is the overriding factor. "This is not a simple matter, where the numbers speak for themselves," says Samuel Walker, a professor of criminal justice at the University of Nebraska, Omaha. "In the past two years there have been five or six conferences on traffic-stop data, and there's still no consensus."

8   The school-discipline picture is even cloudier. "In isolated cases, there appears to be a difference in treatment," says Susan Bowers, an enforcement director with the U.S. Department of Education's Office for Civil Rights who investigates claims like the one filed in Modesto. "But often school districts have a justification, and race goes away." Researchers have theorized that anything from lead exposure to passive smoke may drive some students to act out more than others. The National Association of Secondary School Principals has deemed the discipline gap "an issue of socioeconomic status." The interim findings of the Rhode Island task force bolster this view. The group, after considering a student's race and whether he or she qualified for free lunch, concluded that "poverty is the single most pressing factor" associated with the disproportionate suspension of minority students in as many as a third of Rhode Island schools.

9   But a major study to be released in the *Urban Review* journal squarely shows the opposite. Russell Skiba, an associate professor of educational psychology at Indiana University, charted the discipline patterns of 11,000 middle-school students in a major urban district in Indiana, in which black students were more than twice as

likely as their white peers to be sent to the principal's office or suspended—and four times as likely to be expelled. When Skiba factored in the financial status of the students and their families, the discipline gap did not budge. But a second finding smacks more overtly of discrimination: while white students were typically reprimanded for behaviors like smoking and vandalism, black students were more often disciplined for nebulous infractions like excessive noise and disrespect. "It's pretty clear that black students are referred for more subjective behaviors," he says. "You can choose not to use the word racism, but districts need to look seriously at why this is going on."

10   The more closely districts look, the less transparent the diagnoses. Beginning last year, Texas' Austin Independent School District began requiring principals to track discipline data by race to discern if any specific teachers were using a heavier hand with black students. The answer was yes, but the reasons were far from straightforward. Cornel Jones, principal of Austin's Oak Springs Elementary School, does not blame racism but chalks the problem up to "cultural misunderstandings" between his white teachers and the 97%-minority student body. One insidious source of confusion: When a teacher scolds a black or Latino student for a simple matter like talking out of turn, Jones says, that student typically looks away out of respect. Feeling her authority challenged, the teacher may send the student to the office. "It cycles up into a big monster, and then nothing the child can do is right," says Jones.

11   But when does misunderstanding slip over the line into prejudice? "There are racial misunderstandings, but there is also racial paranoia," says Beverly Cross, an associate professor at the University of Wisconsin-Milwaukee School of Education. "We see this a lot with black boys who are cute until about the fourth grade, and then teachers start to fear them." Linelle Clark, Austin's dropout-prevention coordinator, sees some evidence of this in her district. She recalls that "one principal noticed a teacher with a pattern of sending the same black kid to the office, and when he called her on it, she said, 'I'm scared of that child.'"

12   Because racial-profiling claims are difficult to prove in court, civil rights activists urge parents to bypass the legal system and confront school officials directly. In some cities, the N.A.A.C.P. accompanies families to expulsion hearings. Another tactic popular among advocates is to gather a district's discipline statistics—which are collected by the government and can be obtained by filing a Freedom of Information Act request—and prepare self-published reports for local news broadcasts. After enough badgering, some districts have begun to bend their discipline codes. Last fall Chicago public-schools chief Arne Duncan directed principals to stop handing out suspensions for picayune infractions like "gum chewing" and reserve the punishment for violent offenses. The district is working with local activists and civil rights attorneys to launch a program allowing students to be tried by a peer jury for violations such as arguing with a teacher or using profanity.

13   The conversation in Modesto has thus far been much less conciliatory. Despite repeated calls for reform from a small but vocal black parents' group, the district is not weighing any changes to its discipline code. Administrators will not comment on particular cases, but Jim Pfaff, Modesto's associate superintendent, points out

that district policy stipulates a stiffer penalty for a student, like Russell, who inflicts injuries causing "stitches, loss of consciousness or a fracture." Pfaff attributes the high rate of black expulsions to an influx of black families from San Francisco "who do not understand" Modesto's discipline code, which provides few second chances—just consequences. He has little patience for charges of profiling. "Because we expel more males than females, does it mean that we discriminate against men too?" he asks. Even the black community has splintered over the issue, with some parents who want change accusing others of kowtowing to the district. "[She's] dealing with the people we're fighting, running to the white man with everything," sniffs Mack Wilson, education chairman of the local N.A.A.C.P., speaking of a black mother who joined with school officials to form Project Success, a group that tries to defuse small disciplinary matters before they escalate.

14 Russell is indifferent to the charges flying around him. He has more urgent matters to attend to, like the D and the F on his latest report card and whether they will affect his prospects for studying architecture in college. While parents and administrators continue to bicker, he has found his own remedy for the discipline gap. "You learn which teachers treat different ethnicities differently," he says. "And you learn when you're around them to stay quiet and keep to yourself." ◆

FREEWRITING ASSIGNMENT

Think back to when you were in high school. What was your classroom environment like? How important was the classroom environment, and the relationship between students in the classroom, to your ability to learn? Explain.

CRITICAL READING

1. Was Russell a victim? If you were a judge hearing the civil lawsuit Russell brought against the school, would you rule for or against his suit? Explain.
2. In paragraph 3, Morse describes the expulsion rate of black students as a "syndrome." Why does she use this word to describe the circumstances? What is a "syndrome"? What does her word choice reveal about how she feels about this issue? Explain.
3. In what ways are students facing racial profiling issues in the classroom? How is this issue being addressed by parents, lawyers, and school administrators?
4. In paragraph 5, Pedro Noguera, a professor at the Harvard Graduate School of Education, observes, "Schools now call in the police if a student is talking too much or doesn't do his homework." Is this statement substantiated? Does it seem true? Based on your own high school experience in the "post-Columbine era," are schools resorting to these disciplinary extremes?

5. How do school administrators respond to the allegations that African American students tend to be singled out for more disciplinary action than their peers?

CRITICAL WRITING

6. *Research and Analysis*: Visit the Harvard Civil Rights Project at *http://www.civilrightsproject.harvard.edu* and read about some of the civil rights issues facing education today. Select a topic and research it in greater depth. Write a short essay discussing your issue and its implications for education in the twenty-first century.

7. The year 2004 marks the fiftieth anniversary since the passage of the *Brown v. Topeka Board of Education* decision. Learn more about this landmark case at the National Teachers Association website at http://www.nea.org/brownvboard/#overview. Drawing from the information on the website as well as in this article, write an essay drawing connections between the promise of *Brown* and the racial profiling situation in many of America's schools.

GROUP PROJECT

8. The ERASE Initiative challenges racism in public schools and promotes racial justice and academic excellence for all students. The program is coordinated by the Applied Research Center, a public policy, education, and research institute that emphasizes issues of race and social change. Download the report "Racial Profiling and Punishment in U.S. Schools," prepared as part of the ERASE Initiative's national program at http://www.arc.org/erase/downloads/profiling.pdf. Have each member of your group read a section of the report (it is about 40 pages of reading) and prepare a summary of that section or essay. Discuss the issue of racism in schools today and some solutions to end it. Prepare a short (bullet points) recommendation report of strategies that administrators and teachers can use to prevent racism in the classroom. Review your recommendations with the rest of the class as part of a larger class discussion on this issue.

When Brevity Rules the Syllabus, 'Ulysses' Is Lost

James Shapiro

You may not realize it, but the great works of literature you read in college may be quite different from the ones the generations before you read. But this isn't because better books have been written—just shorter ones. James Shapiro explains that in an effort to preserve favorite authors, many English teachers are forced to abandon longer works in favor of shorter ones. He fears that students are being shortchanged. Even worse, great writers will be forgotten as literary selections become more uniform, and brevity dictates the curriculum.

James Shapiro is a professor of English and comparative literature at Columbia University and a regular contributor to the *Chronicle of Higher Education* in which this article was first published.

CRITICAL THINKING	Think about the great works of literature you have read in high school and in your college courses. What other works and authors that you haven't read come to mind?

1   If there's one thing that teachers of literature across the ideological spectrum would agree upon, it's that size matters. Given the way that books are taught in today's college classrooms, in courses that meet for an hour or so a few times a week for 15 weeks, it has become increasingly difficult to assign long and complex works of literature. No doubt, that is due in part to the extraordinary demands placed upon today's college students (a far higher percentage of whom now commute, hold down a job or two, and even raise children than did students a generation ago). But the explanations don't much change the inexorable logic of canon formation: In America today, if a book is not taught, it's unlikely to remain part of the literary canon for long.

2   And novels that are more than 350 pages long—even if they are by celebrated writers like Charles Dickens, James Joyce, George Eliot, and Henry James—are regularly rejected by professors who have learned from experience that it's wiser to play it safe and substitute a shorter work, one that students will be more likely to finish. I learned my lesson after asking hard-pressed undergraduates to read Eliot's 900-page Daniel Deronda over a 10-day stretch; I won't try that again soon.

3   Those who teach the history of the novel tell me that classics like Henry Fielding's *Tom Jones* and Laurence Sterne's *Tristram Shandy* appear less and less frequently in courses. And you can forget about Samuel Richardson's influential *Clarissa*—it's hard to imagine a teacher with the nerve to assign its more than one million words. (I can imagine the revenge students would exact in their course evaluations, if anyone dared.) Who out there is still regularly assigning heavyweight books? And who will be teaching the next generation of readers the current crop of important long books, including Don DeLillo's *Underworld*, Thomas Pynchon's *Mason & Dixon*, Philip Roth's *American Pastoral*, and A.S. Byatt's *Possession*?

4   Long poems are already headed toward extinction. John Milton's *Paradise Lost* and *Paradise Regained* are taught far less frequently in their entirety than they once were, as are Edmund Spenser's *The Faerie Queene* and Alexander Pope's *Dunciad*. These epics have either been reduced to anthologized fragments or consigned to the limbo where the once-loved though no-longer-much-read long poems of Dryden, Byron, Tennyson, Longfellow, and Pound wander aimlessly in search of readers.

5   In this age of literary triage, teachers know that they have to abandon longer works if they are to rescue their favorite authors from oblivion. I informally polled a

number of friends around the country who teach English, and they all offered versions of the same story. One scuttled his favorite Faulkner novel, *Absalom, Absalom!*, and assigned instead the shorter and less vexing *As I Lay Dying*. A Joyce scholar taught *Portrait of the Artist as a Young Man* rather than the all too formidable *Ulysses*. Triage means that Gertrude Stein's *The Autobiography of Alice B. Toklas* has displaced her brilliant but now nearly unread *Making of Americans*, despite Stein's efforts to trim the first edition of that book from 925 pages or so down to a more manageable 416. Friends who teach Henry James and love *The Golden Bowl* and *The Wings of the Dove* nonetheless ask their students to read *Daisy Miller* or *The Turn of the Screw*. Dickens seems to have suffered more than most; gone are *Bleak House*, *Dombey and Son*, and *Our Mutual Friend*, replaced more often than not by *Hard Times*. *Billy Budd* apparently gets far more readers these days in college classes than *Moby-Dick*. Conrad's *Heart of Darkness* has firmly displaced *Nostromo* and *Lord Jim*. Admirers of Pynchon's *Gravity's Rainbow* still end up teaching *The Crying of Lot 49*. One friend wondered how many people now know that Charlotte Bronte wrote *Villette*. The Bronte novel of choice, overwhelmingly, is the comparatively brief *Jane Eyre*. Writers lacking the foresight to have left behind a teachable short novel—their numbers include Proust, Cervantes, Rabelais, and Sir Walter Scott—have no one to blame but themselves.

6   Colleagues in comparative literature tell me that the same holds true for novels in French, Russian, and German, even in translation. For every student assigned Dostoevsky's *Idiot*, many more are asked to read the more manageable *Notes From the Underground*. Forget about *War and Peace*—*The Death of Ivan Ilyich* is fast becoming Tolstoy's representative work. Franz Kafka's brief *The Metamorphosis* outpaces *The Castle*, arguably his greatest work. Several colleagues who teach German literature told me that not too long ago, students could be counted on to read Thomas Mann's *Doctor Faustus* and *The Magic Mountain*; today, what is read of Mann by American students has shrunk to *Death in Venice*. Again and again, it comes down to relative length; all other things being equal, the shortest novel almost always wins out.

7   Curious to see whether the views of my friends were representative, and armed with the recent Modern Library list of the top 100 English-language novels of the 20th century—an arbitrary list, but as useful for my purposes as any other—I headed off to Labyrinth Bookstore (perhaps the best scholarly bookstore in New York City, and the preferred bookstore for those who teach literature at Columbia and Barnard).

8   It turned out that 21 of the 100 novels on the list were ordered last semester at Labyrinth, for a wide range of undergraduate and graduate courses. Of those, only three were over the unspoken cutoff of 350 pages: Richard Wright's *Native Son* (398 pages), Ralph Ellison's *Invisible Man* (568 pages), and Theodore Dreiser's *An American Tragedy* (874 pages). Of the other 18 novels, seven were under 200 pages.

9   Clearly, only the longer novels have suffered neglect, and suffered badly. If the statistics are representative, such books will remain untaught and sooner or later will disappear from the canon.

10   Setting the Modern Library list aside, the most popular works of American, British, or Continental fiction ordered at Labyrinth were, again, quite short. Mary

Shelley's *Frankenstein* (196 pages) was the most popular, ordered for seven classes. Three novels, each ordered for six classes, tied for second place: Joseph Conrad's *Heart of Darkness* (126 pages), Aphra Behn's *Oroonoko* (86 pages), and Daniel Defoe's *Robinson Crusoe* (252 pages). Right behind were two books assigned in five courses: Kafka's *The Metamorphosis* (127 pages) and Virginia Woolf's *Mrs. Dalloway* (296 pages). Once again, brevity seems to have been the common denominator.

11   The problem with today's choices is not their reputed ideological leanings, but the fact that they are increasingly cut off from the literary conversations that their authors took for granted: To read *Frankenstein* without having the familiarity with *Paradise Lost* that Mary Shelley would have assumed, or to come to *Heart of Darkness* without recognizing the ways in which Conrad invoked Dante, is to diminish the resonance of literary masterpieces. The current classroom practice (facilitated by the growing popularity of critical editions) of substituting snippets of cultural context—situating the work historically, biographically, and theoretically—only exacerbates the problem. I'm as guilty of assigning those supplementary readings as anyone, torn between a desire for my students to have some kind of historical and intellectual context for what they are reading and the desire just to have them read more (and longer) important literary works.

12   Until recently, anthologies included briefer works of fiction supplementing the longer novels that teachers ordered separately for their courses. Today's anthologies have rendered additional readings superfluous: They simply reproduce, in their entirety, the most popular short novels. Flip through the pages of the major anthologies that are the basis for most students' exposure to English literature and you'll discover the exact same choices. The forthcoming edition of *The Norton Anthology of English Literature* and its newly released competitor, *The Longman Anthology of British Literature,* include the complete texts of—you guessed it—*Oroonoko, Frankenstein*, and *Heart of Darkness*.

13   Such anthologies take their own approach to triage. Rather than abandoning texts, they prefer to save nearly all of them, even if doing so requires performing radical surgery on long ones—amputating parts and leaving what's left frailer and lesser, if still alive. So, for example, the 6,000-page *Longman Anthology* makes room for 23 pages of Joyce's 783-page *Ulysses* and 11 pages of his 628-page *Finnegans Wake*. The editors' implicit argument is that, in exposing students to fragments, they will inspire them to read the full version in subsequent courses. But that works only if those courses actually assign the longer books. To offer just one ominous example, over the past quarter-century, classroom orders of Ulysses have fallen steadily. It's also hard to imagine students inspired to read long works after exposure to truncated versions. What the anthologies seem to be offering is a kind of validation: Students with 20 pages of *Ulysses* under their belts get the desired credential of having read Joyce.

14   The culture warriors are right about one thing: A canon embodies values. But they are mistaken in assuming that such values are necessarily defined along political lines. Not too long ago, many of the books that were passed down from one generation of teachers and students to the next took a while to read. We no longer have the time or patience for that. Today's literature classes increasingly reflect and perpetuate the values that our society holds most dear: expediency, brevity, uniformity. ◆

FREEWRITING ASSIGNMENT

Consider Shapiro's final sentence, "Today's literature classes increasingly reflect and perpetuate the values that our society holds most dear: expediency, brevity, uniformity." What is Shapiro saying here? Respond to this statement with your own opinion.

CRITICAL READING

1. Why are some books being cut from college literature courses? What are the reasons behind their removal? What could happen to the works that are cut over the long run? Explain.
2. What is the literary "canon"? What books are traditionally ascribed to the canon?
3. Have you read any of the works or authors Shapiro cites in his essay? Did you read the shorter pieces, or the longer ones? If you read a longer work, did you find it too lengthy for the course? If you haven't read any of the longer pieces, do you feel that you are missing out?
4. Should the factors Shapiro cites in his first paragraph that have contributed to the shift in reading assignments in college English classes be the concern of educators and college curricula? Why or why not?
5. What are the inherent problems with assigning short pieces, such as Mary Shelly's *Frankenstein,* at the expense of longer ones? How are educators addressing these problems?
6. How does Shapiro feel about the move many literature anthologies have made to include excerpts of longer works in their selections. Is an excerpt better than omission? Is it likely to encourage students to read the longer work? Why or why not?

CRITICAL WRITING

7. Respond to Shapiro's essay writing from your own experience. Do you agree that your exposure to literature is suffering because shorter works are selected in favor of longer ones? Explain.
8. *Exploratory Writing*: Shapiro laments that many great works of literature are being replaced by shorter works of lesser quality. He fears that the great works of the canon will be lost. However, a list of best books is open to debate. What do you think should be the criteria for judging the best works? What makes a book one of the best? Should it be required reading regardless of its length? Why or why not?

GROUP PROJECTS

9. In paragraph 7, Shapiro mentions the Modern Library's list of the top 100 novels in the English language. Access the most recent Modern Library list at *http://www.randomhouse.com/modernlibrary/100bestnovels.html.* Do you agree with this list? What books would you recommend be on the

Modern Library list that are not there, and why? Compare your list with those developed by other groups.

10. List all of the works that Shapiro cites in his essay. As a group, identify all of the ones members of your group have read. How many have you heard of, but have not read? How many are completely unknown to you? Based on your discussion, does Shapiro's argument that great works are likely to disappear and be forgotten hold weight? Explain.

VIEWPOINTS

▶ **Bilingualism in America: English Should Be the *Only* Language**
S. I. Hayakawa

▶ **Let's Not Say Adios to Bilingual Education**
Lourdes Rovira

The late S. I. Hayakawa was a leading advocate of the English-only movement. A former U.S. senator from California and a professor of linguistics who published several books on language, Hayakawa was born in Vancouver, British Columbia, to Japanese parents. Hayakawa served as honorary chairman of U.S. English, a public-interest organization based in Washington, D.C., that is working to establish English as the nation's only official language.

In June of 1998, California voters passed Proposition 227, terminating bilingual education in that state. Although supporters of bilingual education blamed politicians, educators, and the white power structure for this decision, opinion polls indicated that a significant number of Hispanics themselves had doubts about bilingual education. Since then, several other states followed suit. In 2002, Massachusetts governor Mitt Romney made the debate over bilingual education a major issue of his election campaign. He promised to make "English only" a priority educational initiative.

In the essay that follows, Hayakawa explains why he feels that English must be the only recognized official language of the United States. This article originally appeared in *USA Today* magazine in July of 1989, by which time English had been made the official language in 17 states.

Following his article, Lourdes Rovira, the executive director for bilingual education for the Miami-Dade County school system, criticizes the California vote that passed Proposition 227. According to Rovira, denying students the option of bilingual education isn't simply a poor educational decision, it is an outright injustice.

CRITICAL THINKING   Have you ever been in a place where you did not speak the language? How did you feel? What if you were a child entering a school in which you did not speak the local language? Does your experience influence your perspective on bilingual education?

Bilingualism in America: English Should Be the *Only* Language

S. I. Hayakawa

1 During the dark days of World War II, Chinese immigrants in California wore badges proclaiming their original nationality so they would not be mistaken for Japanese. In fact, these two immigrant groups long had been at odds with each other. However, as new English-speaking generations came along, the Chinese and Japanese began to communicate with one another. They found they had much in common and began to socialize. Today, they get together and form Asian-American societies.

2 Such are the amicable results of sharing the English language. English unites us as Americans—immigrants and native-born alike. Communicating with each other in a single, common tongue encourages trust, while reducing racial hostility and bigotry.

3 My appreciation of English has led me to devote my retirement years to championing it. Several years ago, I helped to establish U.S. English, a Washington, D.C.-based public interest group that seeks an amendment to the U.S. Constitution declaring English our official language, regardless of what other languages we may use unofficially.

4 As an immigrant to this nation, I am keenly aware of the things that bind us as Americans and unite us as a single people. Foremost among these unifying forces is the common language we share. While it is certainly true that our love of freedom and devotion to democratic principles help to unite and give us a mutual purpose, it is English, our common language, that enables us to discuss our views and allows us to maintain a well-informed electorate, the cornerstone of democratic government.

5 Because we are a nation of immigrants, we do not share the characteristics of race, religion, ethnicity, or native language which form the common bonds of society in other countries. However, by agreeing to learn and use a single, universally spoken language, we have been able to forge a unified people from an incredibly diverse population.

6 Although our 200-year history should be enough to convince any skeptic of the powerful unifying effects of a common language, some still advocate the official recognition of other languages. They argue that a knowledge of English is not part of the formula for responsible citizenship in this country.

7 Some contemporary political leaders, like the former mayor of Miami, Maurice Ferre, maintain that "Language is not necessary to the system. Nowhere does our Constitution say that English is our language." He also told the *Tampa Tribune* that, "Within ten years there will not be a single word of English spoken [in Miami]— English is not Miami's official language—[and] one day residents will have to learn Spanish or leave."

8 The U.S. Department of Education also reported that countless speakers at a conference on bilingual education "expounded at length on the need for and eventually of, a multilingual, multicultural United States of America with a national language policy citing English and Spanish as the two 'legal languages.'"

9   As a former resident of California, I am completely familiar with a system that uses two official languages, and I would not advise any nation to move in such a direction unless forced to do so. While it is true that India functions with ten official languages, I haven't heard anyone suggest that it functions particularly well because of its multilingualism. In fact, most Indians will concede that the situation is a chaotic mess which has led to countless problems in the government's efforts to manage the nation's business. Out of necessity, English still is used extensively in India as a common language.

10   Belgium is another clear example of the diverse effects of two officially recognized languages in the same nation. Linguistic differences between Dutch- and French-speaking citizens have resulted in chronic political instability. Consequently, in the aftermath of the most recent government collapse, legislators are working on a plan to turn over most of its powers and responsibilities to the various regions, a clear recognition of the diverse effects of linguistic separateness.

11   There are other problems. Bilingualism is a costly and confusing bureaucratic nightmare. The Canadian government has estimated its bilingual costs to be nearly $400,000,000 per year. It is almost certain that these expenses will increase as a result of a massive expansion of bilingual services approved by the Canadian Parliament in 1988. In the United States, which has ten times the population of Canada, the cost of similar bilingual services easily would be in the billions.

12   We first should consider how politically infeasible it is that our nation ever could recognize Spanish as a second official language without opening the floodgates for official recognition of the more than 100 languages spoken in this country. How long would it take, under such an arrangement, before the United States started to make India look like a model of efficiency?

13   Even if we can agree that multilingualism would be a mistake, some would suggest that official recognition of English is not needed. After all, our nation has existed for over 200 years without this, and English as our common language has continued to flourish.

14   I could agree with this sentiment had government continued to adhere to its time-honored practice of operating in English and encouraging newcomers to learn the language. However, this is not the case. Over the last few decades, government has been edging slowly towards policies that place other languages on a par with English.

15   In reaction to the cultural consciousness movement of the 1960s and 1970s, government has been increasingly reluctant to press immigrants to learn the English language, lest it be accused of "cultural imperialism." Rather than insisting that it is the immigrant's duty to learn the language of this country, the government has acted instead as if it has a duty to accommodate an immigrant in his native language.

16   A prime example of this can be found in the continuing debate over Federal and state policies relating to bilingual education. At times, these have come dangerously close to making the main goal of this program the maintenance of the immigrant child's native language, rather than the early acquisition of English.

17   As a former U.S. senator from California, where we spend more on bilingual education programs than any other state, I am very familiar with both the rhetoric and reality that lie behind the current debate on bilingual education. My experience

has convinced me that many of these programs are shortchanging immigrant children in their quest to learn English.

18   To set the record straight from the start, I do not oppose bilingual education *if it is truly bilingual.* Employing a child's native language to teach him (or her) English is entirely appropriate. What is not appropriate is continuing to use the children of Hispanic and other immigrant groups as guinea pigs in an unproven program that fails to teach English efficiently and perpetuates their dependency on their native language.

19   Under the dominant method of bilingual education used throughout this country, non-English-speaking students are taught all academic subjects such as math, science, and history exclusively in their native language. English is taught as a separate subject. The problem with this method is that there is no objective way to measure whether a child has learned enough English to be placed in classes where academic instruction is entirely in English. As a result, some children have been kept in native language classes for six years.

20   Some bilingual education advocates, who are more concerned with maintaining the child's use of their native language, may not see any problem with such a situation. However, those who feel that the most important goal of this program is to get children functioning quickly in English appropriately are alarmed.

21   In the Newhall School District in California, some Hispanic parents are raising their voices in criticism of its bilingual education program, which relies on native language instruction. Their children complain of systematically being segregated from their English-speaking peers. Now in high school, these students cite the failure of the program to teach them English first as the reason for being years behind their classmates.

22   Even more alarming is the Berkeley (Calif.) Unified School District, where educators have recognized that all-native-language instruction would be an inadequate response to the needs of their non-English-speaking pupils. Challenges by a student body that spoke more than four different languages and by budgetary constraints, teachers and administrators responded with innovative language programs that utilized many methods of teaching English. That school district is now in court answering charges that the education they provided was inadequate because it did not provide transitional bilingual education for every non-English speaker. What was introduced 20 years ago as an experimental project has become—despite inconclusive research evidence—the only acceptable method of teaching for bilingual education advocates.

23   When one considers the nearly 50 percent dropout rate among Hispanic students (the largest group receiving this type of instruction), one wonders about their ability to function in the English-speaking mainstream of this country. The school system may have succeeded wonderfully in maintaining their native language, but if it failed to help them to master the English language fully, what is the benefit?

Alternatives

24   If this method of bilingual education is not the answer, are we forced to return to the old, discredited, sink-or-swim approach? No, we are not, since, as shown in Berkeley and other school districts, there are a number of alternative methods that have been proven effective, while avoiding the problems of all-native-language instruction.

25   Sheltered English and English as a Second Language (ESL) are just two programs that have helped to get children quickly proficient in English. Yet, political recognition of the viability of alternate methods has been slow in coming. In 1988, we witnessed the first crack in the monolithic hold that native language instruction has had on bilingual education funds at the Federal level. In its reauthorization of Federal bilingual education, Congress voted to increase the percentage of funds available for alternate methods from four to 25 percent of the total. This is a great breakthrough, but we should not be satisfied until 100 percent of the funds are available for any program that effectively and quickly can get children functioning in English, regardless of the amount of native language instruction it uses.

26   My goal as a student of language and a former educator is to see all students succeed academically, no matter what language is spoken in their homes. I want to see immigrant students finish their high school education and be able to compete for college scholarships. To help achieve this goal, instruction in English should start as early as possible. Students should be moved into English mainstream classes in one or, at the very most, two years. They should not continue to be segregated year after year from their English-speaking peers.

27   Another highly visible shift in Federal policy that I feel demonstrates quite clearly the eroding support of government for our common language is the requirement for bilingual voting ballots. Little evidence ever has been presented to show the need for ballots in other languages. Even prominent Hispanic organizations acknowledge that more than 90 percent of native-born Hispanics currently are fluent in English and more than half of that population is English monolingual.

28   Furthermore, if the proponents of bilingual ballots are correct when they claim that the absence of native language ballots prevents non-English-speaking citizens from exercising their right to vote, then current requirements are clearly unfair because they provide assistance to certain groups of voters while ignoring others. Under current Federal law, native language ballots are required only for certain groups: those speaking Spanish, Asian, or Native American languages. European or African immigrants are not provided ballots in their native language, even in jurisdictions covered by the Voting Rights Act.

29   As sensitive as Americans have been to racism, especially since the days of the Civil Rights Movement, no one seems to have noticed the profound racism expressed in the amendment that created the "bilingual ballot." Brown people, like Mexicans and Puerto Ricans; red people, like American Indians; and yellow people, like the Japanese and Chinese, are assumed not to be smart enough to learn English. No provision is made, however, for non-English-speaking French-Canadians in Maine or Vermont, or Yiddish-speaking Hassidic Jews in Brooklyn, who are white and thus presumed to be able to learn English without difficulty.

30   Voters in San Francisco encountered ballots in Spanish and Chinese for the first time in the elections of 1980, much to their surprise, since authorizing legislation had been passed by Congress with almost no debate, roll-call vote, or public discussion. Naturalized Americans, who had taken the trouble to learn English to become citizens, were especially angry and remain so. While native language ballots may be a convenience to some voters, the use of English ballots does not deprive citizens of their right to vote. Under current voting law, non-English-speaking voters are permitted to bring a friend or family member to the polls to assist them in casting their

31   ballots. Absentee ballots could provide another method that would allow a voter to receive this help at home.

Congress should be looking for other methods to create greater access to the ballot box for the currently small number of citizens who cannot understand an English ballot, without resorting to the expense of requiring ballots in foreign languages. We cannot continue to overlook the message we are sending to immigrants about the connection between English language ability and citizenship when we print ballots in other languages. The ballot is the primary symbol of civic duty. When we tell immigrants that they should learn English—yet offer them full voting participation in their native language—I fear our actions will speak louder than our words.

32   If we are to prevent the expansion of policies such as these, moving us further along the multilingual path, we need to make a strong statement that our political leaders will understand. We must let them know that we do not choose to reside in a "Tower of Babel." Making English our nation's official language *by law* will send the proper signal to newcomers about the importance of learning English and provide the necessary guidance to legislators to preserve our traditional policy of a common language. ◆

Let's Not Say Adios to Bilingual Education

Lourdes Rovira

1   A great travesty occurred in California on June 2, 1998. By passing Proposition 227, California's voters elected to terminate bilingual education in their state. It was a sad day for our country because we allowed ill-informed politicians and xenophobic voters to dictate educational policy.

2   The United States is a country of immigrants—immigrants who have come seeking freedom and the pursuit of the American dream. Throughout history, English has been the common language that has united these immigrants from all over the world. English is the language of this great country. None of us who support bilingual education question the validity or the importance of the English language, as some would like the public to believe. Quality bilingual programs emphasize the acquisition of English. English is taught to all immigrant students; it is required, and we aim to perfect it in the school setting.

3   Yet to learn English, students need not forget the language they bring to school with them—be it Spanish, Vietnamese, or Urdu. Bilingual education is not like an antibiotic that we give to children who are sick, their illness being lack of English. As soon as the children are well, that is, as soon as they know English, the antibiotic—bilingual education—is removed. Good bilingual programs are not remedial but enrichment programs.

4   One common misunderstanding is that bilingual education is the exclusive domain of immigrant students. No: studying a second language is a right that belongs

to all students—recently arrived refugees, African Americans, and, yes, white Americans. Languages expand a child's cognitive development. Knowing more than one language is not an impediment to intellectual capacity. If it were, the rest of the world's children outside of the United States would be intellectually inferior to ours. After all, the majority of them are bilingual.

5 Years ago, being bilingual was a privilege reserved for those who could afford to send their children to private tutors or to a finishing school in Europe. It was a privilege reserved for those who traveled and went to the opera. In today's global economy, being bilingual can no longer remain a privilege reserved for the elite. To-day, being bilingual is a right that must transcend all socioeconomic strata. Denying all students that right is not only a mistake, it is an injustice.

6 Students are enabled—not disabled—by being bilingual; they are empowered by knowing more than one language. The American experience is strengthened, not weakened, by citizens who can cross languages and cultures. The United States can no longer afford to remain a monolingual country in a multilingual world. Being bilingual and biliterate not only gives people a political and economic advantage, it also allows them to be bridges between people of different cultures.

7 For immigrant students, being bilingual means having the best of two worlds—their home culture and language and our nation's culture and English language. For native speakers of English, knowing a second language means opening up their horizons to the richness of cultural diversity and becoming active participants in—and not merely spectators of—today's global society. In no way does it require sup-planting one language and culture with another.

8 This may come as a surprise to many, but bilingual education is not a recent phenomenon in this country. Its history in the U.S. falls into two distinct periods: the first from 1840 to 1920 and the second beginning in the early 1960s.

9 In 1840 a form of bilingual education originated in Cincinnati with a state law designed to draw German children into the American schools. Several other similar initiatives, which provided instruction in Dutch, Italian, and Polish, among others, took place during the latter part of the 19th century and the beginning of the 20th. During World War I, strong anti-German sentiments increased, and by the end of the war bilingual programs were terminated and 'Americanism' and English-only instruction were promoted. Some states went so far as to impose restrictions on the instruction of foreign languages.

10 Instruction in and through two languages disappeared from the U.S. from 1920 until 1963, when thousands of Cuban refugees poured into the Miami area, opening up a second phase of bilingual schooling in this country. In an effort to meet the needs of the Cuban refugee children, the Miami-Dade County Public Schools orga-nized a dual-language instructional program at Coral Way Elementary with a stu-dent population evenly divided between Spanish speakers and English speakers. Both groups spent half of their day being instructed in English and the other half in Spanish, thus immersing themselves in two languages and cultures.

11 Since then, federal and state laws and court decisions have not only allowed but directed local school districts to create special programs to meet the academic needs of non-English-speaking students. But almost 30 years after the passing of the Bilin-gual Education Act, the debate over the benefits of bilingual education continues to

be politically and emotionally charged. Also lingering after 30 years seems to be a dreadful ignorance over the definition of bilingual education and its goals and practices. Those who make for themselves a political agenda over the issue attack bilingual education as a failure based on a very limited knowledge of one specific bilingual-education model while ignoring others that have been extremely successful, not only in this country but throughout the world.

12   Critics of bilingual education who regard it as a dismal failure claim that children enrolled in bilingual programs do not learn English and that the research regarding the benefits of bilingual programs is contradictory and inconsistent. They assert that immersion programs are superior to bilingual programs and believe that after one year of English immersion, non-English-speaking students will be ready to be mainstreamed into regular, English-speaking classes.

13   Much of educational policy, whether it is bilingual education or reading, stems from pendulum swings from one extreme to another. Unfortunately, immersion programs have failed to prove a successful track record. To wipe out bilingual programs in favor of a sink-or-swim curriculum is a simplistic political solution to a complex educational issue. Moreover, it hardly seems fair to blame bilingual education for all the ills of California's 1.4 million limited-English-proficient students when less than 30 percent of them are enrolled in bilingual programs.

14   Those of us who have dedicated our professional lives to the promotion of bilingual education can assert that properly organized and executed bilingual programs not only work, they work extremely well. This does not mean that some bilingual models cannot be improved. However, there is ample research that demonstrates without a doubt that good bilingual programs are successful—and none that could claim such success for one-year immersion programs.

15   The school district I work for, Miami-Dade County Public Schools, the fourth largest in the country, has been in the forefront of bilingual education since the establishment of Coral Way Elementary in 1963. Our programs are recognized nationally and internationally as programs that promote excellence in English and another language for all students who want to avail themselves of that opportunity.

16   Bilingual programs in our district provide instruction in English for Speakers of Other Languages (ESOL) to students with limited English proficiency as soon as they enroll in school. Students are provided instruction in their home language for approximately 20 percent of the instructional time, but the primary goal is the rapid acquisition of English. At the same time, Miami-Dade County Public Schools embraces diversity and offers all our students the opportunity to enroll in quality programs that promote literacy in a language other than English. We promote high standards for all of our students whether the instruction is in English, Spanish, Haitian-Creole, or French.

17   As the waves beat against the shore and drag everything in sight, it sometimes seems that whenever California voters make an earthshaking decision at the polls, the rest of the country wants to follow suit. How will California's decision affect bilingual education in the rest of the country? Thankfully, the Miami-Dade County Public Schools and districts in many other states (e.g., New York, New Jersey, and Connecticut) have no interest in eliminating bilingual education. Bilingual education is viewed as quintessential to living in this part of the country. In South Florida,

and much of the rest of the world for that matter, being bilingual and biliterate is not a liability but an asset.

18   Bilingualism not only prepares students for today's increasingly global economy and promotes cognitive development and creative thinking, it also instills pride. And, as a Catholic, I would also argue that bilingualism is rooted in gospel values and based on justice. What position should Catholics, and Christians in general, take in the continuing public debate of this issue? It seems to me that we are called to be more informed and compassionate toward immigrants than the average California voter.

19   In 1963 Pope John XXIII addressed the treatment of minorities in his encyclical letter Pacem in terris (On Peace on Earth): "It is especially in keeping with the principles of justice that effective measures be taken by civil authorities to improve the lot of the citizens of an ethnic minority, particularly when that betterment concerns their language [and] . . . their ancestral customs." Language, notes a document of the Southeast Regional Office for Hispanic Ministry in Miami, "expresses the soul of the people."

20   The 1985 Vatican-sponsored World Congress on the Pastoral of Emigration observed in its final document: "Experience has shown that the inability of expression in the mother tongue and the elimination of religious traditions . . . greatly damage the conscience, impoverish the cultural surroundings, provoke separation and even schism, and reduce the numbers of the faithful."

21   Those who question the need for bilingual education are often the same people who question why Masses have to be said in Spanish. Perhaps the words of Pope Paul VI in his 1975 apostolic exhortation Evangelii nuntiandi can do a better job of persuading them than those of us in bilingual education have been able to do: "Evangelization loses much of its force and effectiveness if it does not take into consideration the actual people to whom it is addressed, if it does not use their language, their signs and symbols, if it does not answer the questions they ask; and if it does not have an impact on their particular lives. . . . The split between the Gospel and culture is without a doubt the drama of our time, just as it was of other times."

22   It is unfortunate that California's Proposition 227 passed. It is revolting that bilingual education has been killed at the hands of people who do not understand its virtues. It is offensive that bilingual education continues to be solely associated with immigration. And it is shameful that we have forgotten that when this nation was founded, English was not the exclusive language of the country.

23   Unlike the western waves, South Florida's waves are of a different nature. They embrace the shores with the linguistic plurality needed to fortify the shores, not destroy them. ◆

● FREEWRITING ASSIGNMENT

Consider how information is articulated in your community. Do you live in a multilingual area? Do signs feature other languages in addition to English? If so, how does this multilingual environment affect your social and linguistic experience?

CRITICAL READING

1. Why does Hayakawa feel it is particularly important for a nation of immigrants to communicate in a single, common tongue? Does the fact that he is an immigrant himself lend credence to his argument? Do you agree with this viewpoint? Why or why not?

2. What is Hayakawa's assessment of countries that recognize two or more official languages? From what you know of multilingual countries, do you tend to agree or disagree with his assessment?

3. Do you think that the option of bilingual education should be a right? In light of the fact that Spanish is the second-most-spoken language in the United States, should it be a legally protected option for all children of Hispanic descent?

4. In the third paragraph, Rovira states that students shouldn't forget their native language, whether it is "Spanish, Vietnamese, or Urdu." Do you think she is advocating that bilingual programs be established for languages other than Spanish?

5. How does Hayakawa define bilingual education? What does he feel is its biggest flaw? Drawing from your own experience, do you agree with him? Explain your answer.

6. What alternative to current bilingual education does Hayakawa suggest? Do his alternatives seem like reasonable and feasible solutions?

7. Rovira asserts that the vote to determine bilingual education in California was driven by xenophobic motives. What does she mean by this? Explain.

8. Evaluate Rovira's comparison of the right to learn other languages in school to the principles of bilingual education. How do you think other authors in this section would respond to her statement?

CRITICAL WRITING

9. Write an essay supporting or opposing an amendment to the U.S. Constitution making English the official language.

10. A national language is the language of public discourse, control, and power. Do you think that English instruction for non-English-speaking children should be left to chance or be approached by early, intensive instruction in school? Write a paper in which you explore your thoughts on this question. Consider in your discussion the effects of home language and culture on personal pride.

11. One argument against bilingual education is that language-minority children cannot be separated from language-majority speakers if they are to enjoy the maximum benefits of public-school education. The argument further maintains that if children are taught separately, they will never properly integrate into blended classrooms and, later, the professional community. Write a paper in which you take a stand for or against this argument.

12. An argument in favor of bilingual education is that mother-tongue instruction increases cultural and ethnic pride of the heritage of the mother coun-

try. Immigrant children are allowed to take pride in their home culture, while learning in their native tongue. Write a paper in which you explore your feelings on this pro-bilingual perspective.

GROUP PROJECTS

13. Contact some local schools and ask what bilingual programs they have. If possible, interview some teachers familiar with the programs, and write a group report evaluating the effectiveness of such programs.
14. *Education Week on the Web* is an online magazine addressing the issues facing education today and the pedagogical concerns of teachers. They have compiled a balance fact sheet on bilingual education, including links to online articles that explore the issue (*www.edweek.org/context/topics/biling.htm*). You are a member of a government subcommittee which must develop an official recommendation to the governor on the issue of bilingual education in your state. Based on your research, write a position statement in which your committee makes a recommendation for, or against, bilingual education. Support your perspective with facts and information from the web site.

What could be a new language is evolving in Spanish-speaking countries and areas of the United States: *Spanglish*. While some linguists categorize Spanglish as a dialect of Spanish, others believe that this blending of two languages—English and Spanish—is a new language. Spanglish may interject an English word with a predominantly Spanish phrase or combine English root words or prefixes with Spanish verb conjunctions or suffixes. Some critics fear that Spanglish threatens the integrity of the Spanish language by discouraging Spanglish speakers from using the correct language to communicate. Others argue that it is simply a natural evolution of language as the world becomes a smaller place. This photo depicts a company that is using Spanglish to reach its English/Latino clientele. Wateria is a company that sells purified water, ice, and other water-related products. The California company's name mixes the English word "water" with the Spanish suffix "ria" to mean "a place which sells water."

1. Can you think of any Spanglish words that are used in common speech today? Go online and look up "Spanglish" for more information, or see if your library carries any books on Spanglish.
2. What cultural implications does the evolution of Spanglish have for Americans? What does it reveal about the power of language and communication?
3. Do you think Spanglish is likely to become more prevalent? Do you think it could influence English speakers the way it is influencing Spanish ones? Explain.

RESEARCH ISSUE **Interview with Linda Darling Hammond**

Linda Darling Hammond is a professor of education at Stanford University and director of the National Commission on Teaching and America's Future. This interview was conducted by the Public Broadcasting Service (PBS) for *Only a Teacher*, a documentary series exploring the diverse faces and many roles of the American teacher. Today's teachers must deal with challenges their predecessors never dreamed of. Many view their multiple roles as educator, mentor, public servant, and counselor, as almost a calling. But it isn't an easy job. As PBS explains, "America's attitude toward its teachers is frequently ambivalent. We admire them and at the same time lament that they don't do more. We limit their resources, and then ask them to do the most important job in the world." In this interview, Darling Hammond explains what it means to be a teacher in modern America.

Q: What problems do we need to address in the structure of schools today?

Well, I actually think there are two big problems in the way that we run schools today. One is that the schools we have now are constructed as though teaching doesn't matter, and secondly they're constructed as though relationships don't matter. We have this idea that if we just give them the textbooks to follow and the test to give and the procedures to, you know, pursue, that the kids will just magically get taught adequately, without realizing that teaching, when it's good teaching, is reciprocal. What the kids do determines what the teacher needs to do; the teacher needs to know a lot in order to be able to do that. She needs to know a lot about children, about learning, about subject matter, about curriculum and how to build it so that it's in some kind of a logical order, and so on. And if we don't give teachers the supports to do that well, the knowledge, the time to plan, the opportunity to work with one another to get better at it, we don't get very high quality teaching. The other problem is that we have schools structured as though relationships don't matter. If you want to teach well to very high standards, you have to know the students well, you have to have that relationship that allows you to both challenge them, and adapt what you're doing for them so that it works. So schools have to be redesigned to focus on teaching and to enable relationships.

Q: There's a lot of talk about reform that's gone nowhere. What should be the heart of any reform today?

We've had waves of reform for this entire century, in the 1900s, in the 1930s, in the 1960s. Every single time we try to do reform by changing the curriculum, changing the management structure, changing the budgeting process, whatever, without paying attention to helping teachers learn how to teach kids well, the reform fails. And then we say, "Oh, we tried that and it didn't work." Because teachers were not enabled to use the curriculum materials, to use whatever the new innovation was that was coming down the pike. The sine qua non of learning is to enable really high quality teaching.

Q: What can we do to help teachers do their best work?

Unfortunately kids don't learn at the same rate. They don't learn in the same way. So whenever teachers are given a single way to teach, they're actually made less effective in meeting the needs of the students. And I think a lot of the folks outside of the profession don't realize that some efforts to improve teaching can actually harm it. Obviously, lack of time to work individually with students or collaboratively with colleagues is a huge hindrance in American schools. In many other countries like France, Germany, China, Japan, and so on, teachers will have 10, 15 even as much as 20 hours a week to work with one another on planning lessons, on doing demonstration lessons, on observing one another in the classroom, meeting individually with parents and students, all the stuff that enables what goes on in the classroom to be effective. In this country teachers have 3-5 hours a week for planning their lessons, period, and they do it by themselves. So all of that support for developing high quality teaching and enabling kids not to fall behind is not available to them. Things like class sizes and so on obviously can make a difference, but in fact, even more so than that, we found that not having access to the knowledge you need to do the job is probably the single biggest hindrance that American teachers have. We have very thin, uneven teacher education experiences; there are some great programs in this country; there are some that are truly awful; many of them are just cash cows on the University campus that are there to fund the education of lawyers, accountants, architects, doctors and everyone but the teachers who are paying the tuition. Very little opportunity for ongoing learning. So when a teacher comes into the classroom and is confronted with kids who have a variety of needs, learning disabilities, many who may not speak English as their first language, who learn at different rates and different ways, the likelihood that she will have encountered the knowledge that would help her address these learning needs, understand how children develop, know what to do about learning difficulties, have an adequate grounding in the content area, is relatively small in this country. And so teachers have to learn by trial and error. And it's not fair to them. And of course it's not fair to the kids.

Q: How does teaching compare to other professions?

In this country, teaching is not yet a profession. A profession really has at least three features. First of all, everyone who is admitted to entry into the profession commits themselves to practice with the welfare of clients first and foremost as their major goal. It's like the Hippocratic oath in medicine. Second, everyone who's admitted to practice in a profession has demonstrated that they've mastered a common knowledge base and that they know then how to use that knowledge on behalf of the clients that they're there to serve. And third, a profession takes responsibility for defining, transmitting, and enforcing some standards of practice to protect the people who they're there to serve. Teaching has not acquired those three traits yet.

Q: Why doesn't teacher certification ensure good teaching?

Often the standards that states have enacted are not up to date, do not incorporate current knowledge about teaching, and they're remarkably willing to waive the standards. So forty states still will allow people to practice teaching without any training for the job, and without having pledged themselves to the welfare of the students. Basically it's the feather test: after September first, when there's a vacant slot, where if you breathe on it and it moves, you've passed the test. You can get hired. And there's not a single state that will do this, for example, for the hiring of cosmetologists, plumbers, not to mention lawyers, doctors, architects. We are much more willing to take chances with the lives of our children than we are with the condition of our hair, for example, in this country. Fortunately there's a lot of change underfoot in the way that we, you know, certify teachers to come into the profession.

Q: What about the new national certification for teachers?

The National Board for Professional Teaching Standards now issues a certificate like board certification for doctors, in pediatrics or oncology, and so on, for advanced teachers who are highly accomplished. And they can, over the course of a year, document their practice and have it assessed so they can receive, if they meet the standards, which are very high, a certificate of accomplished practice. Some states are now acknowledging that expert teaching with salary stipends, with the opportunity for teachers to become lead teachers or mentor teachers to help their colleagues. They're, in fact, beginning to incorporate these standards into teachers' evaluation processes, so they are using it to help bring the profession along in terms of increasing the quality of teaching widely available to kids.

Q: How does teacher compensation correlate with their responsibilities?

Teachers are paid about twenty-five percent less than other professionals with similar levels of education. Although the public may look at that short work day, they actually work ten to twelve hours a day with much of the work for planning and grading papers and calling students and meeting with parents outside, you know, what we think of as traditional school hours. And they're responsible for being sure that the children in their care often are fed as well as educated, are supported through family crisis and problems, and are raised to be moral, you know, human beings who can live in a democracy. All of that is on the teacher's plate—increasingly with inadequate support from the society at large, I think.

Q: Are there examples of reforms that are working?

There are a few places where a new image of what a teaching career might be is being invented: Cincinnati, Ohio, comes to mind, Rochester, New York, comes to mind. There are others where there is a real effort to bring people into teaching in a supportive way, to enable people to become competent and not burn out and leave right away and to enable them to grow throughout their careers as they might in another profession.

Q: What are the prospects for teaching today?

Now, in the mid-1990s, the late-1990s, very high ability young people are going into teaching because salaries have begun to increase, because teachers are being given more decision-making responsibility, because in many communities teachers are involved in redefining schools, in developing new kinds of reforms. We're attracting some of the best and brightest back into teaching. But to keep them there we've got to really be able to ensure that they get the respect that they deserve, the access to knowledge that they need to feel competent and successful in the job, and the supports within the schools to do high quality teaching well. And that's the challenge we have. ◆

CRITICAL THINKING

1. What specific problems facing education today does Darling Hammond cite? Based on your experience as a student, respond to her comments with your own opinion.
2. How do you think teachers would respond to Darling Hammond's comments? For example, what might they say about teacher certification? About teaching as a profession?
3. Darling Hammond notes that teachers are paid, on average, 25 percent less than their similarly educated peers. She points out that the general public may feel this disparity is acceptable because of a teacher's shorter workday, but observes that most teachers work 10 to 12 hours a day. What is the public's perception of teachers? Why do they think teachers don't work as hard as other professionals? If you consider the multiple responsibilities of teachers, would you want to be one? Why or why not?

RESEARCH PROJECTS

4. This interview was one of 14 conducted with people connected to education and teaching—current and former teachers and professors of education. Read the other interviews at *www.pbs.org/onlyateacher/today.html* and learn more about the multifaceted opinions and viewpoints regarding education today. Select some questions provided on the website, and conduct your own interview of several teachers for their firsthand opinion about education. Write a research essay addressing a particular challenge facing teachers today.
5. The National Commission on Teaching and America's Future, a nonprofit organization addressing educational issues in American schools, claims high teacher turnover and attrition is becoming a national crisis. Its report aims to improve teacher retention by at least 50 percent by 2006. Review their "No Dream Denied" report posted on their website at *www.nctaf.org* (under Research, Reports and Presentations). What reasons does the commission identify for poor teacher retention and high turnover, and what do they suggest doing about it?

Additional essay topics, writing assignments,
research guidelines, and readings for this chapter can
be found online at **www.ablongman.com/goshgarian**.

Gender
Perceptions
Has Anything Changed?

7

We have witnessed enormous changes in the social and professional lives of men and women over the past century. Traditional ways of defining others and ourselves along gender lines have been irrevocably altered. Only 100 years ago, the full financial responsibility of a family was squarely on the shoulders of men. Women could not vote and had limited legal resources at their disposal. Sex was something that happened within the confines of marriage. Women were expected to remain at home, relegated to housework and childrearing. Men were expected to be the disciplinarians of family life, with limited involvement in the daily lives of their children. Now, women may pursue many different career options and lifestyles. Men are not expected to be the sole breadwinner, and men and women together often share financial responsibilities. Sexual mores have relaxed, and both men and women enjoy greater freedoms socially, professionally, and intellectually than they ever have before.

Most college-age men and women were born after the "sexual revolution" and the feminist movement of the 1970s. But it was largely the movements of the 1960s and 1970s that have shaped the way men and women interact, view each other, evaluate opportunity, and envision the future. However, while much has changed and we have moved toward greater gender equality, vestiges of gender bias and sexism remain. The essays in this section examine how society has changed its expectations of gender, and how these changes have affected men and women as they continue to define themselves and their relationships with each other and society as a whole.

In "My Most Attractive Adversary," Madeleine Begun Kane, a former lawyer, describes how expressions of subtle sexism, such as physical compliments paid by men to women in professional settings, belittle women, and reinforce dated notions about women in the workforce. Michael Abernethy questions the way men are portrayed by the popular media in "Male Bashing on TV." Why is it acceptable, he wonders, to make men look stupid on television? Scott Russell Sanders continues the exploration of male stereotypes in "The Men We Carry in Our Minds," challenging the widely held assumption that men enjoy power and privilege.

The next two pieces take a look at how women may be sabotaging themselves. In "Girls, We Really Are Our Own Worst Enemies," student Lyz Baranowski observes that it is women who are the most critical of women. Instead of supporting each other intellectually, women are more likely to gossip, criticize, and judge other women's hair, makeup, and clothing. Such petty behavior, says Baranowski, just shows that women are losing the battle for gender equality. Then Andre Mayer examines how the pop music industry seems to be slinking back to the caves. Demeaning images and lyrics, designed to glorify male debauchery and female subservience, are now the norm in the music industry. Female artists, such as the "Britneys and the Christinas and the Jessicas" are helping to promote sexualized images of women as nothing more than eye candy for male audiences. While the rest of the world moves forward, the music industry seems bent on going "Back to the Stone Age."

Christine Rosen presents a historical picture of patriarchy and why she feels that it has gotten a bum rap by many feminists. In "Three Cheers for Patriarchy!"

Rosen explains why this institution, blamed by many as the reason women were kept chained to stoves and relegated to the home, actually paved the way for many of the freedoms women now enjoy.

The Viewpoints section explores how feminism has—or hasn't—changed the way women perceive themselves. Why has feminism, a movement meant to improve the lives of women, and men, by gaining greater gender equality, suffered from so much negative press? Why are some young women, who are essentially feminist in their thinking, hesitant to identify themselves as such? Susan Faludi and Karen Lehrman go head to head about what it means to be a feminist and discuss the phenomenon known as "Revisionist Feminism."

The Viewpoints section is followed by an opinion piece addressing an issue facing women living in the most patriarchal societies, Muslim countries. Semeen Issa and Laila Al-Marayati explain in the Research Issue entitled "An Identity Reduced to a Burka" that this clothing does not represent all Muslim women, nor do all Muslim women feel oppressed by it. Such assumptions are stereotypical and demeaning, ignoring the rich diversity of Muslim women across the world.

My Most Attractive Adversary

Madeleine Begun Kane

In the next essay, Madeleine Begun Kane holds that subtle sexism maintains gender differences. Women may seem to have made tremendous progress professionally and academically, but they are held back by indirect sexist comments and attitudes. They are caught in a catch-22. If they react against these seemingly small slights, they appear to be overreacting or too sensitive. But to let them pass may signal that such comments are somehow acceptable.

Madeleine Begun Kane is a New York writer and humor columnist. This article was first published in *Women's Village*.

CRITICAL THINKING Do we have certain ingrained gender expectations when it comes to job positions? For example, do we expect men to be mechanics or lawyers or firefighters, and women to be teachers or nurses or secretaries? Are these expectations changing, or are they still common assumptions?

1 "Our Portia has come up with an excellent solution." A trial judge said this about me several years ago in open court, when I was still a full-time litigator. I've never forgotten it. Not because it was a compliment to be compared to so formidable a lawyer as Shakespeare's Portia, although I think he meant it as a compliment. But what I really remember is my discomfort at being singled out as a woman in what, even today, remains a predominantly male world.

2   Despite our progress in the battle against workplace discrimination, the fact of being a female is almost always an issue. It may not be blatant, but it usually lurks just below the surface. We are not lawyers, executives and managers. We are *female* lawyers, *female* executives and *female* managers. Just when we are lulled into believing otherwise, something happens to remind us and those around us of our gender, in subtle yet unsettling ways.

3   Men often use physical compliments to call attention to the fact that we are different. References to "my lovely opponent" or "my most attractive adversary" remain remarkably common. It's a clever technique because any response, other than a gracious "thank you," seems like a petty over-reaction.

4   Consequently, unless the remark is obviously offensive, as in references to certain unmentionable body parts, a simple nod or "thank you" is usually the prudent response. Of course if you're feeling less cautious, you may want to return the compliment. Done with a slight note of irony, this can be an effective way to get your point across. But saying, "You look very handsome yourself, Your Honor," is probably not a good idea.

5   Concern for the tender female sensibility rivals compliments in the subtle sexism department. I've experienced this most often during business meetings—high-powered meetings where a lone female is surrounded by her peers and superiors. At some point during the meeting the inevitable will happen. One of the men will use an expletive—a minor one in all likelihood. The expedient course is to ignore it. She is a woman of the world. She has heard and possibly used such language—and even worse.

6   But is she allowed to ignore it? Of course not! That would be too easy. The curser inevitably turns to the lone female (who until this moment has somehow managed not to blush) and apologizes. This singles her out as a delicate female who doesn't quite belong and needs to be protected. This also reminds everyone that the rest of the group would be ever so much more comfortable, at ease and free to be themselves, if only a woman hadn't invaded their turf.

7   This has happened to me more times than I care to recall. And I still don't know the proper response. Should I ignore both the profanity and the apology? Is it best to graciously accept the apology, as if one were appropriate? Or should I say what I'm always tempted to say: "That's all right, I swear like a sailor too."

8   Most women, myself included, overlook these subtle forms of sexism. I'm troubled by this, and I worry that by being silent, I'm giving up an opportunity to educate. For while some men use these tactics deliberately, others don't even know they're being offensive. Nevertheless, I usually smile discreetly and give a gracious nod. And wonder if I'm doing the right thing, or if I'm mistaking cowardice for discretion. ◆

FREEWRITING ASSIGNMENT ─────────────────────────

What profession do you hope to pursue? Is your profession a male or female dominated one? Or is it balanced with both sexes? Do you think that gender will ever be an issue in your chosen profession?

CRITICAL READING

1. Kane opens her essay with a story about how she was called Portia by a judge. Who is Portia? Why is Kane uncomfortable with what she believes to be a compliment by the judge? Explain.
2. Kane objected to physical compliments made by male professionals, such as "my lovely opponent," and "my most attractive adversary." How do such compliments undermine her role as a lawyer and a professional? Do you think the men intended to slight her? Why or why not?
3. In paragraphs 5 and 6, Kane describes a situation in a business meeting in which men apologize to a woman for their offensive language. Why does she object to such apologies? What assumptions do the men make in making such an apology?
4. Kane observes that it is difficult for women to openly object to physical compliments because to do so could backfire on them. How could their objections work against them? Explain.
5. Why does Kane worry about remaining silent against subtle sexism? What could happen if she doesn't remain silent? What would you do?

CRITICAL WRITING

6. In her second paragraph, Kane states that women are not "lawyers, executives and managers." Instead, they are "*female* lawyers, *female* executives, and *female* managers." Interview a woman who holds a professional position in law, medicine, or business and ask her about this observation. Does she feel that the word "female" floats in front of her professional title, unspoken but still "lurking beneath the surface"? Summarize your interview and analyze the discussion.
7. *Personal Narrative*: Write about a time when you felt awkward because of your gender. Describe the situation, the experience, and why you felt uncomfortable. With a critical eye, analyze the situation and think about how social expectations of gender may have contributed to your feelings of discomfort.

GROUP PROJECTS

8. Kane argues that gender bias "lurks beneath the surface," reminding women that they are women in what were traditionally male professions. When does referencing gender cross a line into sexism? Is it sexist to refer to a woman as a "lady doctor" or a man as a "male nurse"? Are such references as common as Kane maintains? As a group, make a list of professions and their titles. Include old titles and their newer ones (for example, "mailman" to "postal carrier"). Has renaming the titles of these professions decreased sexism in the workplace?

9. In paragraph 7, Kane laments that she has experienced the apology for swearing scenario at many business meetings. As a group, consider her situation and develop a few comebacks she could use if she faced the situation again. Share your comebacks with the class.

Male Bashing on TV
Michael Abernethy

Because television reaches a broad and diverse audience, it can influence cultural and social opinion. For example, homosexuality was a taboo topic before programs such as *Ellen* and *Will and Grace* made the topic more acceptable television fare. Now, every major television network includes a program with at least one gay character. Before programs such as *The Mary Tyler Moore Show*, women were primarily depicted on television as subservient housewives. Television helped promote, and thereby make acceptable, the concept of women in the workforce with independent personalities. Such is the influence of television. But as a conduit for social persuasion, could television harm one group of people as much as it may help another? In the next essay, Michael Abernethy questions the depiction of men as lazy, incompetent, insensitive, or simply stupid on television programs and in commercials. While such depictions may seem funny, stereotypical "male bashing," argues Abernethy, hurts men, and society as a whole.

Michael Abernethy is an adjunct writing instructor at Indiana University Southeast. He is a film and television critic for the online magazine *PopMatters*, in which this essay was first published in January 2003.

CRITICAL THINKING	Think about the ways men and women are portrayed on television and television commercials. Are there certain gender-based stereotypes that seem common? What makes a male character interesting and engaging? What makes a female character noteworthy and interesting? Is the criterion different?

1 Warning for our male readers: The following article contains big words and complex sentences. It might be a good idea to have a woman nearby to explain it to you.

2 It's been a hard day. Your assistant at work is out with the flu and there is another deadline fast approaching. Your wife is at a business conference, so you have to pick up your son at daycare, make dinner, clean the kitchen, do a load of laundry, and get Junior to bed before you can settle down on the sofa with those reports you still need to go over.

3 Perhaps a little comedy will make the work more bearable, you think, so you turn on CBS's Monday night comedies: *King of Queens, Yes, Dear, Everybody Loves Raymond,* and *Still Standing.* Over the next two hours, you see four male lead characters who are nothing like you. These men are selfish and lazy, inconsiderate husbands and poor parents.

4   And the commercials in between aren't any better. Among them: A feminine hygiene ad: Two women are traveling down a lovely country road, laughing and having a great time. But wait. One of them needs to check the freshness of her mini-pad, and, apparently, the next rest area is six states away. A women's voice-over interjects, "It's obvious that the interstate system was designed by men."

5   A digital camera ad: A young husband walks through a grocery store, trying to match photos in his hand with items on the shelves. Cut to his wife in the kitchen, snapping digital pictures of all the items in the pantry so that hubby won't screw up the shopping.

6   A family game ad: A dorky guy and beautiful women are playing Trivial Pursuit. He asks her, "How much does the average man's brain weigh?" Her answer: "Not much."

7   A wine ad: A group of women are sitting around the patio of a beach house, drinking a blush wine. Their boyfriends approach, but are denied refreshment until they have "earned" it by building a sand statue of David.

8   Welcome to the new comic image of men on TV: incompetence at its worst. Where television used to feature wise and wonderful fathers and husbands, today's comedies and ads often feature bumbling husbands and inept, uninvolved fathers. On *Still Standing*, Bill (Mark Addy) embarrasses his wife Judy (Jamie Gertz) so badly in front of her reading group, that she is dropped from the group. On *Everybody Loves Raymond*, Raymond (Ray Romano) must choose between bathing the twin boys or helping his daughter with her homework. He begrudgingly agrees to assist his daughter, for whom he is no help whatsoever.

9   CBS is not the only guilty party. ABC's *My Wife and Kids* and *According to Jim*, Fox's *The Bernie Mac Show, The Simpsons, Malcolm in the Middle,* and (the recently cancelled) *Titus*, and the WB's *Reba* also feature women who are better organized and possess better relational skills than their male counterparts. While most television dramas tend to avoid gender stereotypes, as these undermine "realism," comic portrayals of men have become increasingly negative. The trend is so noticeable that it has been criticized by men's rights groups and some television critics.

10   It has also been studied by academicians Dr. Katherine Young and Paul Nathanson in their book, *Spreading Misandry: The Teaching of Contempt for Men in Popular Culture.* Young and Nathanson argue that in addition to being portrayed as generally unintelligent, men are ridiculed, rejected, and physically abused in the media. Such behavior, they suggest, "would never be acceptable if directed at women." Evidence of this pattern is found in a 2001 survey of 1,000 adults conducted by the Advertising Standards Association in Great Britain, which found that 2/3 of respondents thought that women featured in advertisements were "intelligent, assertive, and caring," while the men were "pathetic and silly." The number of respondents who thought men were depicted as "intelligent" was a paltry 14%. (While these figures apply to the United Kingdom, comparable advertisements air in the U.S.)

11   Some feminists might argue that, for decades, women on TV looked mindless, and that turnabout is fair play. True, many women characters through the years have had little more to do than look after their families. From the prim housewife whose only means of control over her children was, "Wait till your father gets home!" to

the dutiful housewife whose husband declares, "My wife: I think I'll keep her," women in the '50s and '60s were often subservient. (This generalization leaves out the unusual someone like Donna Reed, who produced her own show, on which she was not subservient.)

12   Then, during the "sexual revolution," TV began to feature independent women who could take care of themselves (Mary and Rhoda on *The Mary Tyler Moore Show*, Julia; Alice and Flo on *Alice*; Louise and Florence on *The Jeffersons*). So now, 30 years later, you'd think that maybe we'd have come to some parity. Not even.

13   Granted, men still dominate television, from the newsroom to primetime. And men do plenty on their own to perpetuate the image of the immature male, from Comedy Central's *The Man Show* to the hordes of drunken college boys who show up every year on MTV's *Spring Break*. What's the problem with a few jokes about how dumb men can be? C'mon, can't we take a few jokes?

14   If only it was just a few. The jokes have become standard fare. Looking at a handful of sitcoms makes the situation seem relatively insignificant, but when those sitcoms are combined with dozens of negative ads which repeat frequently, then a poor image of men is created in the minds of viewers.

15   According to *Gender Issues in Advertising Language*, television portrayals that help create or reinforce negative stereotypes can lead to problems with self-image, self-concept, and personal aspirations. Young men learn that they are expected to screw up, that women will have the brains to their brawn, and that childcare is over their heads. And it isn't just men who suffer from this constant parade of dumb men on TV. *Children Now* reports a new study that found that 2/3 of children they surveyed describe men on TV as angry and only 1/3 report ever seeing a man on television performing domestic chores, such as cooking or cleaning. There are far too few positive role models for young boys on television.

16   Moreover, stereotypical male-bashing portrayals undermine the core belief of the feminist movement: equality. Just think. What if the butt of all the jokes took on another identity? Consider the following fictional exchanges:

"It is so hard to get decent employees."
"That's because you keep hiring blacks."

"I just don't understand this project at all."
"Well, a woman explained it to you, so what did you expect?"

"I can't believe he is going out again tonight."
"Oh please, all Hispanics care about is sex."

17   All of these statements are offensive, and would rightfully be objected to by advocates of fair representation in the media. However, put the word "man" or "men" in place of "blacks," "woman," and "Hispanics" in the above sentences and they're deemed humorous. Are men who ask to be treated civilly overly sensitive or are we as justified in our objections as members of NOW, the NAACP, GLAAD, and other groups which protest demeaning television portrayals, whether those portrayals are on sitcoms, dramas, advertisements, or moronic TV like *The Man Show*.

18   Most of the shows I'm talking about are popular. Maybe that means I am being too sensitive. Yet, many U.S. viewers didn't have a problem with *Amos and Andy* or *I Dream of Jeannie*, both famous for their offensive stereotypes. These shows enjoyed good ratings, but neither concept is likely to be revived anytime soon, as "society" has realized their inappropriateness.

19   All this is not to say buffoonery—male or female—isn't a comic staple. Barney on *The Andy Griffith Show*, Ted on *The Mary Tyler Moore Show*, and Kramer on *Seinfeld* were all vital characters, but the shows also featured intelligent males. And these clowns were amusing because they were eccentric personalities, not because they were men. The same could be said of many female characters on TV, like *Alice's* Flo, *Friends'* Phoebe, or Karen on *Will & Grace*. Good comedy stems from creative writing and imaginative characterizations, not from degrading stereotypes.

20   Fortunately, some people are working to change the way television portrays men. J. C. Penney recently ran an ad for a One Day sale, with a father at the breakfast table, with his infant crying and throwing things. The father asks the child when his mother will be home. Lana Whited of *The Roanoke Times*, Syndicated columnist Dirk Lammers, and the National Men's Resource Center were just a few who objected to this image of an apparently incompetent and uncaring father, one who would let his child cry without making any attempt to calm him. Penney's got the message; their recent holiday ad features a father, mother, and son all happily shopping together.

21   Few men I know want a return to the "good ole days." Those generalizations were as unrealistic as the idea that all men are big slobbering goofballs. Hope lies beyond such simplistic oppositions, in shows like *The Cosby Show or Mad About You*, which placed their protagonists on level playing fields. Paul Reiser and Cosby did, on occasion, do moronic things, but so did Helen Hunt and Phylicia Rashad. People—because they are people, not just gendered people—are prone to fall on their faces occasionally.

22   Undoubtedly, there are men out there who are clones of Ward Cleaver, just as there are men who resemble Al Bundy. But the majority is somewhere in between. We're trying to deal the best we can with the kids, the spouse, the job, the bills, the household chores, and the countless crises that pop up unexpectedly. After all that, when we do get the chance to sit down and relax, it would be nice to turn on the TV and not see ourselves reflected as idiots. ◆

FREEWRITING ASSIGNMENT

Consider the contrast between male sitcom characters and men in real life. Do male characters on television mirror men in the real world? Explain.

CRITICAL READING

1. Evaluate how the author supports the thesis of his essay. First, identify Abernethy's thesis. Then, analyze each supporting element he uses to prove his point. Does the author allow for alternative points of view? Does he try to see multiple sides of the issue? Explain.

2. Dr. Katherine Young and Paul Nathanson observe (paragraph 10) that the portrayal of men as "generally unintelligent" would "never be acceptable if directed at women." Respond to this statement in your own words. Support your response with examples from the essay and your television viewing experience.

3. In paragraph 15, Abernethy notes that "television portrayals that help create or reinforce negative stereotypes can lead to problems with self-image, self-concept, and personal aspirations." In your opinion, what is the cultural influence of the programs Abernethy cites? Does he make a valid point? Explain.

4. Watch a television program Abernethy cites in his essay and write a short description of the male and female characters. Then reverse the gender of these characters.

5. Abernethy's essay identifies *Everybody Loves Raymond* in several places as a program that particularly portrays men as insensivitive and inept. Watch the program and evaluate it for yourself. How are other characters depicted in the program, such as Robert, Debra, and Ray's parents? Is Debra a role model? His parents? Robert? Explain.

6. Abernethy notes that "some feminists may argue" that the portrayal of men as mindless on television could be "fair play," and mere justice for the many years women were stereotyped. Is this a valid argument? Why or why not? Explain.

7. What does Abernethy want to happen as a result of his essay? For what is he advocating? What solutions does he offer?

8. Paragraph 17 outlines some fictitious exchanges in which the word "man" or "men" is replaced by another group. How do these examples demonstrate his point? Do they support his argument? Are they compelling? Respond to his examples with your own opinion of each.

CRITICAL WRITING

9. *Research and Analysis*: Abernethy observes in paragraph 8 that television programs used to present men as "wise and wonderful husbands and fathers." How were women portrayed on these programs? Make a list of programs before 1970 featuring husbands or fathers. How were the men portrayed? What about the women? Could the argument be made that women used to serve as the comic "foil," and now men have assumed this role? Is that fair? Acceptable? Write a short essay describing your results and conclusion.

10. Write a response to Abernethy in which you either agree or disagree, in whole or in part, with his argument. Cite specific areas in his essay with which you agree or disagree, and provide supporting evidence of your own to back up your point of view.

11. *Exploratory Writing*: Write about a male or female television character that you particularly enjoy watching. Explain why you chose this character and what made him or her so appealing to you. Do you see this character as a role model, or simply entertaining? Explain.

12. *Exploratory Writing*: Consider the ways Hollywood influences our cultural perspectives of gender and identity. Write an essay exploring the influence, however slight, film and television have had on your own perceptions of gender. If you wish, interview other students for their opinion on this issue, and address some of their points in your essay.

GROUP PROJECTS

13. Visit the network web sites of CBS, NBC, FOX, ABC, and the WB. Working as a group, identify the male lead characters in prime time programs (exclude dramas as Abernethy does), and try to categorize each character. Provide a brief explanation next to each, supporting your categorization of the character. Do any characters not fall into any category? If so, which ones and why? Share your list with the class. Did other groups categorize characters differently? Discuss.

14. Consider Abernethy's ideas in the context of our broader culture. Do you agree that producers present men as inept or stupid because that is what our society thinks is funny? Working as a group, prove or disprove this idea, using movies, television, and printed media, such as advertisements and popular music.

The Men We Carry in Our Minds
Scott Russell Sanders

Statistically, men tend to hold more positions of power and wealth than women do. Many women feel that simply being born male automatically confers status and power, or at the very least, makes life easier. This cultural assumption, however, may only apply to a very small segment of the male population. Is it fair to stereotype men this way?

Scott Russell Sanders grew up in rural Tennessee and Ohio, where men aged early from lives of punishing physical labor or died young in military service. When he got to college, Sanders was baffled when the daughters of lawyers, bankers and physicians accused him and his sex of "having cornered the world's pleasures." Sanders is the author of several award-winning books, including *Hunting for Hope* (1999) and *The Force of Spirit* (2000). He recently collaborated with several other writers on a collection of essays, *Coming to Land in a Troubled World* (2004).

CRITICAL THINKING   Consider the stereotypical view that being male automatically grants one power, status, and privilege. Then think about three men you know well, such as a father, brother, or friend. Do their everyday life experiences bear out this generalization?

1   "This must be a hard time for women," I say to my friend Anneke. "They have so many paths to choose from, and so many voices calling them."

2   "I think it's a lot harder for men," she replies.

3   "How do you figure that?"

4   "The women I know feel excited, innocent, like crusaders in a just cause. The men I know are eaten up with guilt."

5   "Women feel such pressure to be everything, do everything," I say. "Career, kids, art, politics. Have their babies and get back to the office a week later. It's as if they're trying to overcome a million years' worth of evolution in one lifetime."

6   "But we help one another. And we have this deep-down sense that we're in the right—we've been held back, passed over, used—while men feel they're in the wrong. Men are the ones who've been discredited, who have to search their souls."

7   I search my soul. I discover guilty feelings aplenty—toward the poor, Native Americans, the whales, an endless list of debts. But toward women I feel something more confused, a snarl of shame, envy, wary, tenderness, and amazement. This muddle troubles me. To hide my unease I say, "You're right, it's tough being a man these days."

8   "Don't laugh," Anneke frowns at me. "I wouldn't be a man for anything. It's much easier being the victim. All the victim has to do is break free. The persecutor has to live with his past."

9   How deep is that past? I find myself wondering. How much of an inheritance do I have to throw off?

10   When I was a boy growing up on the back roads of Tennessee and Ohio, the men I knew labored with their bodies. They were marginal farmers, just scraping by, or welders, steelworkers, carpenters; they swept floors, dug ditches, mined coal, or drove trucks, their forearms ropy with muscle; they trained horses, stoked furnaces, made tires, stood on assembly lines wrestling parts onto cars and refrigerators. They got up before light, worked all day long whatever the weather, and when they came home at night they looked as though somebody had been whipping them. In the evenings and on weekends they worked on their own places, tilling gardens that were lumpy with clay, fixing broken-down cars, hammering on houses that were always too drafty, too leaky, too small.

11   The bodies of the men I knew were twisted and maimed in ways visible and invisible. The nails of their hands were black and split, the hands tattooed with scars. Some had lost fingers. Heavy lifting had given many of them finicky backs and guts weak from hernias. Racing against conveyor belts had given them ulcers. Their ankles and knees ached from years of standing on concrete. Anyone who had worked for long around machines was hard of hearing. They squinted, and the skin of their faces was creased like the leather of old work gloves. There were times, studying them, when I dreaded growing up. Most of them coughed, from dust or cigarettes, and most of them drank cheap wine or whiskey, so their eyes looked bloodshot and bruised. The fathers of my friends always seemed older than the mothers. Men wore out sooner. Only women lived into old age.

12   As a boy I also knew another sort of men, who did not sweat and break down like mules. They were soldiers, and so far as I could tell they scarcely worked at all. But when the shooting started, many of them would die. This was what sol-

diers were for, just like a hammer was for driving nails. Warriors and toilers: those seemed, in my boyhood vision, to be the chief destinies for men. They weren't the only destinies, as I learned from having a few male teachers, from reading books, and from watching television. But the men on television—the politicians, the astronauts, the generals, the savvy lawyers, the philosophical doctors, the bosses who gave orders to both soldiers and laborers—seemed as remote and unreal to me as the figures in Renaissance tapestries. I could no more imagine growing up to become one of these cool, potent creatures than I could imagine becoming a prince.

13   A nearer and more hopeful example was that of my father, who had escaped from a red dirt farm to a tire factory, and from the assembly line to the front office. Eventually, he dressed in a white shirt and tie. He carried himself as if he had been born to work with his mind. But his body, remembering the earlier years of slogging work, began to give out on him in his fifties, and it quit on him entirely before he turned 65.

14   A scholarship enabled me not only to attend college, a rare enough feat in my circle, but even to study in a university meant for the children of the rich. Here I met for the first time young men who had assumed from birth that they would lead lives of comfort and power. And for the first time I met women who told me that men were guilty of having kept all the joys and privileges of the earth for themselves. I was baffled. What privileges? What joys? I thought about the maimed, dismal lives of most of the men back home. What had they stolen from their wives and daughters? The right to go five days a week, 12 months a year, for 30 or 40 years to a steel mill or a coal mine? The right to drop bombs and die in war? The right to feel every leak in the roof, every gap in the fence, every cough in the engine as a wound they must mend? The right to feel, when the layoff comes or the plant shuts down, not only afraid but ashamed?

15   I was slow to understand the deep grievances of women. This was because, as a boy, I had envied them. Before college, the only people I had ever known who were interested in art or music or literature, the only ones who read books, the only ones who ever seemed to enjoy a sense of ease and grace were the mothers and daughters. Like the menfolk, they fretted about money, they scrimped and made do. But, when the pay stopped coming in, they were not the ones who had failed. Nor did they have to go to war, and that seemed to me a blessed fact. By comparison with the narrow, ironclad days of fathers, there was an expansiveness, I thought, in the days of mothers. They went to see neighbors, to shop in town, to run errands at school, at the library, at church. No doubt, had I looked harder at their lives, I would have envied them less. It was not my fate to become a woman, so it was easier for me to see the graces. I didn't see, then, what a prison a house could be, since houses seemed to be brighter, handsomer places than any factory. I did not realize—because such things were never spoken of—how often women suffered from men's bullying. Even then I could see how exhausting it was for a mother to cater all day to the needs of young children. But if I had been asked, as a boy, to choose between tending a baby and tending a machine, I think I would have chosen the baby. (Having now tended both, I know I would choose the baby.)

16   So I was baffled when the women at college accused me and my sex of having cornered the world's pleasures. I think something like my bafflement has been felt by other boys (and by girls as well) who grew up in dirt-poor farm country, in mining country, in black ghettoes, in Hispanic barrios, in the shadows of factories, in Third World nations—any place where the fate of men is just as grim and bleak as the fate of women.

17   When the women I met at college thought about the joys and privileges of men, they did not carry in their minds the sort of men I had known in my childhood. They thought of their fathers, who were bankers, physicians, architects, stockholders, the big wheels of the big cities. They were never laid off, never short of cash at month's end, never lined up for welfare. These fathers made decisions that mattered. They ran the world.

18   The daughters of such men wanted to share in this power, this glory. So did I. They yearned for a say over their future, for jobs worthy of their abilities, for the right to live at peace, unmolested, whole. Yes, I thought, yes yes. The difference between me and these daughters was that they saw me, because of my sex, as destined from birth to become like their fathers, and therefore as an enemy to their desires. But I knew better. I wasn't an enemy, in fact or in feeling. I was an ally. If I had known, then, how to tell them so, would they have believed me? Would they now? ◆

FREEWRITING ASSIGNMENT

As you read, list the occupations and obligations of the men mentioned in the article. What socioeconomic segment of society is Sanders describing? What does this suggest about the relationship between gender and class?

CRITICAL READING

1. In paragraph 7, Sanders states he has feelings of guilt toward a number of minority groups or social causes, but his feelings toward women are more complicated. What do you think might be the reasons for his feelings? Can you identify with this perspective?

2. Do you think Sanders feels women, not men, are the privileged class? Explain.

3. How do you think women from the different socioeconomic groups Sanders mentions in his essay would respond to his ideas? For example, how would the educated daughters of the lawyers and bankers respond? How about the women from Sanders's hometown?

4. Sanders relates his argument entirely in the first person, using personal anecdotes to illustrate his point. How does this approach influence the reader? Would this essay be different if he told it from a third-person point of view? Explain.

5. In paragraph 8, Sanders's friend Anneke says she "wouldn't be a man for anything. It is much easier being the victim." What does Anneke mean by this statement? Do you agree with her view? Why or why not?

6. What effect do Anneke's comments have on Sanders's audience? Why do you think he quotes her? How do her comments support his argument?

CRITICAL WRITING

7. *Exploratory Writing*: Write an essay in which you consider your own sense of cultural conditioning. Do you think your behavior has been conditioned by sex-role expectations? In what ways? Is there a difference between the "real" you and the person you present to the world? If there is a difference, is it the result of cultural conditioning?
8. What does it mean to be a man today? Write an essay explaining what you think it means to be male in today's society. How do men factor into current social, intellectual, political, economic, and religious arenas? What opportunities are available—or not available—to men? Do you think it is easier or better to be male in American culture?

GROUP PROJECT

9. With your group, try to define the terms "masculine" and "feminine." You might include library research on the origins of the words or research their changing implications over the years. Develop your own definition for each word, and then discuss with the rest of the class how you arrived at your definitions.

Girls, We Really Are Our Own Worst Enemies
Lyz Baranowski

Feminism has paved the way for many young women to pursue life choices that were largely inaccessible or unacceptable to women only a generation ago. As the feminist movement picked up speed in the 1970s, many activists blamed male-dominated social structures for confining women to prescribed social roles. But should women be pointing the finger back at themselves? In the next editorial, student Lyz Baranowski argues that women are their own "worst enemies" when it comes to gender equality. It is women's criticism of other women, their tendency to judge a woman on her looks or clothing rather than her intellect, which prevents women from truly being liberated.

Lyz Baranowski is a student majoring in English at Gustavus Adolphus College in Saint Peter, Minnesota. This editorial was published in the *Gustavian Weekly*, the college's student newspaper on May 2, 2003.

CRITICAL THINKING How has feminism changed American society over the last thirty years? How has it affected your life and the lives of your parents?

1 "A woman needs a man like a fish needs a bicycle," is Gloria Steinem's famous declaration of feminism. It asserts the ideology many associate with feminism: no woman needs a man.

2   Nearly three years ago Gloria Steinem married a man twice her age and many feminist activists declared her a hypocrite. In a time when an overwhelming number of young women refuse to call themselves feminist and headlines declare the death of feminism, we have to ask, was it all just wasted bras?

3   It is clear through the marriage of Steinem and the similar yoking of many strong and admirable women that feminism is no longer a rejection of men. Women need men like a fish needs water and men need women like a toilet needs to flush. The sexes balance one another, we compliment and augment, knowing that without black there can be no white.

4   This does not always translate into marriage, nor does it have to, but the companionship of a brother, a father or a friend adds perspective (who else is going to make sure you see *The Matrix: Reloaded*, over and over and over again?).

5   The truth is that a new generation of women are becoming strong by realizing the balance and the nature of the world is that Adam needed Eve in the garden, so we fish need our water.

6   Yet, with this new feminist attitude comes a realization that men are no longer the biggest threat; it is ourselves. Feminism isn't just a reaction against men anymore. A study by the University of Chicago found that in a race, women run slower when other women run with them. (The author concluded that women are less responsive to competition.) Merely walking out of your dorm room with two different colored socks on would prove otherwise. Just think about it, who is going to look at you with that "Girl, don't you know what you are doing?" look? It is not the men, it's the women.

7   As a member of the speech and debate team I am constantly attending tournaments, wearing nice suits and speaking pretty. The speech and debate crowd is one of people interested in learning, debating and discussing, so I was not prepared when a judge commented that I needed to use more lipstick. She later thanked me when I did use more lipstick at the next tournament. A friend received a similar comment and a girl from California gave a speech on how a female judge told her she ought to stop wearing suit pants because they were not professional. She won nationals with that speech.

8   While she may have won, our experiences and the everyday experiences of girls commenting and gossiping on everything from clothes to the amount of time a girl raises her hand in class, show that women are still losing. The problem is not others, the problem is us.

9   We are the ones editing *Vogue* and giving girls weight issues and eating disorders, we are the ones backstabbing and gossiping about that outspoken girl who wears weird clothes. Women act relationally aggressive toward each other, as Rachel Simmons points out in her book, *Odd Girl Out*. She explains that women view one another as competition and attack each other in non-physically aggressive ways. While this form of aggression is neither worse nor better than the usually labeled male physical aggression, it is more difficult to discover.

10   As Phyllis Chesler, author of *Woman's Inhumanity to Woman,* is clear to point out, even that supposed solid and united front of women in the 60s and 70s was fraught with backstabbing and tension. Many argue that this is a symptom of social convention and gender bias, yet Chesler suggests otherwise. She takes the stance

that female aggression may in part be biological while also perpetuated by cultural ideas of gender.

11   This concept is almost as liberating as the legal use of contraceptives or suffrage, because it allows us to stop blaming other people (i.e., those stupid white males) for our problems, to take matters into our own hands and to be more responsible for our actions rather than pawning them off to history and repression. Blaming and criticizing the world for problems we are just as responsible for perpetuating is not feminism, it is just a cycle of self-oppression.

12   I will tell you what feminism is: pride. Pride in the fact that we are women who can play sports, make millions and still look good in spaghetti straps. Pride in the fact that we are not men and we never will be; we are women and we are a valid, powerful force. Feminism is the realization that no matter what a woman does, even if she is a homemaker, or didn't even graduate from high school, whether she loves babies and can't wait to embrace motherhood, she is just as important and in need of support as the independent woman with an education, a great job and a loft apartment in New York. Feminism is me saying I love being a woman and I wouldn't have it any other way. ◆

FREEWRITING ASSIGNMENT

In this piece, Baranowksi notes that many young women refuse to call themselves feminist, although without feminism, they would not be enjoying the freedoms and lifestyle they currently do. What accounts for this backlash? What has tarnished feminism for these young women?

CRITICAL READING

1. Baranowski opens her essay with a quote from Gloria Steinem. Who is Gloria Steinem? What is her role in the feminist movement? What did her often quoted statement mean? In what context and climate did she say it? Does the fact that Steinem later married change the impact of her words, or does it simply reflect that culture has changed? Explain.
2. Why, according to Baranowski, are some women "their own worst enemies" in terms of promoting gender equality?
3. Baranowski notes that women are more critical of women than men are critical of women. In your opinion, is this true? Explain.
4. What problems facing women does Baranowski blame on women? Could these things also be blamed on men? Social expectations?
5. Evaluate Baranowski's final paragraph in which she "defines" feminism. Do you agree with her definition? If not, provide one of your own.

CRITICAL WRITING

6. *Field Research and Analysis*: In paragraph 6, Baranowski conjectures that if you left your dorm room with two different colored socks on, it would be the women who would give you questioning looks, not men. If you are

female, test this claim and see how men and women react to your faux pas. If you are male, perform the same test, and see if anyone notices. If they do, do they forgive you because you are a guy? Are they critical of your mistake?

7. Baranowski wrote this piece for a column in her student newspaper, the *Gustavian Weekly*. Write a column about feminism from your own perspective, but begin your column by repeating Baranowski's first line, "A woman needs a man like a fish needs a bicycle."

GROUP PROJECT

8. As a group, develop a list of questions designed to elicit student opinion on perceptions of feminism in the first decade of the 21st century. What does feminism mean to the people you interview? How do men and women feel about it? Would they define themselves as supporting feminism? How do the definitions they provide compare to a dictionary definition of feminism? To Baranowski's definitions at the end of her essay? Discuss your results with the class as part of a broader discussion on perceptions of feminism.

The New Sexual Stone Age
Andre Mayer

Although the Western world is moving toward greater gender equality, you wouldn't know it from watching and listening to many popular music groups, says Andre Mayer in this essay. After a wave of strong women vocalists, many female artists are allowing the music industry to present them as highly sexualized "tramps," catering to popular men's magazines such as *Maxim* and *FHM*. Male groups present women in videos as "bitches and hos" and use lyrics that demean women. Mayer examines what he feels is a disturbing trend in the music industry—a culture where "pimps and hos" are sentimentalized, and women are objectified. Is the music industry indeed "slouching back to the caves"?

Andre Mayer is a reporter living in Toronto, Canada, and a regular columnist for *Shift Magazine*, in which this article first appeared in its Autumn 2001 issue.

CRITICAL THINKING Who are your favorite pop artists? How are men and women portrayed in videos and music jackets by these artists? How do the artists portray themselves?

---

1 Boys will be louts and girls will be hos: at a time when outmoded notions about gender roles are relaxing, pop music is slouching back to the caves. Everywhere you

look, people are taking a more open-minded stance on gender roles. In October 2000, Dutch parliament implemented legislation that would make it the first country in the world to recognize gay marriages. Ohio University announced it would designate thirty campus bathrooms "unisex" to accommodate transgendered students. The number of male nurses is rising, as is the overall viewership of women's sports. Outmoded notions about the roles of men and women are relaxing; except, that is, in pop music, where quite the opposite is true. Glance at magazine covers, at videos, at lyric sheets: We've returned to an age of rampant chauvinism, where men swagger about in a testosterone rage and women are reduced to sexual ornaments.

2   The most visible advocates are artists like Kid Rock, Limp Bizkit and Crazy Town, who not only resemble eighties hair metal in their thudding guitar assault, but in their celebration of male debauchery and female subservience. In song, females are oppugned; in videos, they're totted up like bimbos and objectified. Limp Bizkit's "Nookie" does both: The track is a misogynistic kiss-off to a girlfriend, and when singer Fred Durst shouts "I did it all for the nookie," he's blatantly admitting that he exploited her for sex. Critics have long reproved hip hop for its too-enthusiastic use of words like "bitches" and "hos," but rappers could always deflect accountability by claiming that their lyrics were a stark reflection of ghetto reality. With the advent of rap-metal, however, artists like Kid Rock and Limp Bizkit have taken the gritty argot of their hip hop heroes and are passing it off as their own. With widespread use, such hateful language becomes more accepted.

3   The same can be said for the current prevalence of pimp iconography. Echoing rappers like the Notorious B.I.G. and Too $hort, Kid Rock fancies himself an "American pimp," but he's part of a greater trend that includes apparel (Phat Pimp Clothing, Pimpdaddy.com), movies (the Hughes brothers' documentary *American Pimp* and the upcoming comedy *Lil' Pimp*, about a nine-year-old procurer), and staged events, like Boston's annual "Pimps and Hos Ball." It stems from the general nostalgia for blaxploitation flicks like *Cleopatra Jones* and *The Mack,* in which pimps are the pinnacle of camp, dressing in garish attire and spouting comical jive. Real pimps are far less cuddly—as we know, they insult, abuse and unscrupulously lord over their female charges. Most people would agree that pimping is abhorrent, but the image has become so widespread—and in many cases, sentimentalized— that a new generation of pop culture consumers blithely embraces it.

4   Unfortunately, the current contingent of female stars is doing little to correct these primitive attitudes. Many of them—the Britneys, the Christinas, the Jessicas— dress like prostitutes, or at the very least, extras in a Van Halen video. When these chirpy, vacuous singers swept into vogue, they knocked more intelligent and progressive gals like Tori Amos and Alanis Morissette off the charts. Every new video or awards show is an opportunity for immodest types like Mariah Carey and Toni Braxton to set new standards for libidinous spectacle, and while they pay lip service to positive messages, the only thing they offer their distaff fans is an unattainable image of female sexuality.

5   So what's the cause of this retrograde sexism? Many critics have pointed to the feelings described by Susan Faludi in her book *Stiffed*: *The Betrayal of the American Man,* in which she claims that feelings of emasculation (due to a number of factors, including joblessness and feminism) have spurred many men to reassert their

manhood. The most glaring consequence of this may be the popularity of so-called "lad mags," of which *Maxim* was arguably the catalyst. Started in the mid-nineties, *Maxim* captured an immense demographic of horny males by offering *Playboy*-type titillation (stopping just short of pornography) and insolent commentary. The effect inevitably snowballed into other media—while pop has always used sex to help sell albums, record executives undoubtedly felt that increasing the T&A in the marketing of female artists would also satisfy the booming *Maxim* niche.

6   The music press seems eerily complicit with the problem. While some writers have commented on the inherent virgin-whore complex in Britney Spears' image, for example, many seem only too happy to defend it, or at the very least excuse it. The Spears profile in the September 13th issue of *Rolling Stone* typifies the music press's soft treatment of gender. The cover features Spears with trademark bared midriff and salacious leer and carries the kicker "Britney talks back: Don't treat me like a little girl." Like most Spears interviews, it's a shameless red herring. The story is punctuated with Spears' cheerily oblivious musings on the nature of her appeal, and in lieu of any remotely revealing quotes, writer Jenny Eliscu comes to the shrugging conclusion that "Britney and her image are one and the same—she is as much of a delightful contradiction as she seems." The title of Spears' single, "I'm a Slave 4 U," suggests that her provocative image shows no signs of flagging.

7   Meanwhile, those females who assert their strength often seem misguided. The catchphrase "independent women" is as hollow as the shrieks of "girl power!" back in 1997. Destiny's Child equates self-sufficiency with having the wherewithal to buy their own clothes, shoes and cars. Then again, any assertion of dignity seems practical at a time when Eminem proteges D12 spout, "Independent women in the house / Show us your tits and shut your motherfucking mouth" ("Ain't Nuttin' But Music").

8   This prevailing machismo not only denigrates women, but inherently scorns anyone whom it deems less than "manly" (i.e., impervious to sensitivity and militantly hetero). Barring gender benders like Marilyn Manson and Placebo's Brian Molko, few artists seem interested in exploring the androgyny of David Bowie and Freddie Mercury. And why would they? Right now, pop seems not only unreceptive but hostile to such liberalism.

9   The easiest qualification of music's current homophobia is taking a tally of the number of openly gay stars. There are few beyond Elton John, k.d. lang, Melissa Etheridge and Rufus Wainwright. Has anyone heard from George Michael lately? He's probably wary of returning to this increasingly homophobic milieu. Given the current inclination for close-mindedness, sitting out until pop emerges from the Stone Age seems like a sound idea. ◆

FREEWRITING ASSIGNMENT ————————————————

Mayer notes that in many pop music videos, the image of "pimps and hos" are sentimentalized, glorifying people and a profession that is really pretty awful for women. Are they just for fun, as the "Pimp and Ho Ball" in Boston suggests, or could glorifying such images be harmful?

CRITICAL READING

1. What groups or singers does Mayer specifically identify as examples that we have returned to an "age of rampant chauvinism"? From what you know of these artists, in what ways are they sexist? Explain.
2. What does Mayer mean when he says that in many pop songs, females are "oppugned"? What message might these lyrics promote?
3. Mayer indicates that hip hop's use of sexist language may be more acceptable than its use by other artists such as Limp Bizkit and Kid Rock. On what does he argue his claim? Do you agree?
4. What is "pimp iconography"? How does it apply to pop music? Explain.
5. In what ways are female pop stars encouraging the chauvinistic lyrics and images in the music industry?
6. Mayer comments that the music industry "seems eerily complicit with the problem" of sexism and chauvinism in pop music, and that, in fact, they seem to be encouraging it. Can you think of some examples of this complicity that Mayer doesn't mention?
7. How does Mayer's title connect to his essay's thesis? Explain.

CRITICAL WRITING

8. In this essay, Andre Mayer expresses his concern that the way some pop artists "celebrate male debauchery and female subservience" could be harmful to our culture. Write an essay expressing your own viewpoint on this issue. Can lyrics and images be harmful? Are they just in fun? Or maybe to shock but not to be taken seriously? Explain.
9. Compare the images of females on pop and hip hop music covers and videos to real women. What images of women are they promoting? Assume you are a foreign visitor to the U.S. who has never seen a music video or listened to pop and hip hop music. What might you assume about the cultural attitude toward American women based on what you see and hear? Explain.

GROUP PROJECTS

10. Mayer notes that many female pop music icons are allowing themselves to be promoted as sex objects rather than as strong independent women. Even those who claim to be empowered are still referring to sex in their lyrics and in the way they dress and present their public image. Visit the *Billboard*'s top 50 singles and tracks (*www.billboard.com*) and list the female groups and vocalists. After compiling your list, discuss the image of these women in pop culture. How does your list compare to the observations Mayer makes in his essay?
11. Susan Faludi, in her book, *Stiffed: The Betrayal of the American Man*, claims that men, spurred on by feminism and joblessness, are reasserting

their manhood. Mayer wonders if one example of this reassertion is through the emergence of many "lad mags" such as *Maxim* and *FHM* (For Him Magazine) that feature sexy photographs of female pop culture icons and "insolent commentary." Go to the *Maxim* web site at *http://www. maximonline.com/index.html,* and the *FHM* web site at *http://www.fhm. com/.* (Or look at similar magazines such as *Stuff for Men, Razor, Blender.*) As a group, discuss the images and content of the magazines. If you are female, do you feel the content promotes the objectification of women, or is it just a typical male magazine? Could such images be harmful to women and the way men view women in general? If you are male, answer the same question. Discuss as a group.

Three Cheers for Patriarchy!

Christine Rosen

If you look up the word "patriarchy" in the dictionary, the definition will probably read something along the lines of, "a social institution with the father as the head of the family with legal oversight of wives and children, with the descent of inheritance and authority contained in the male line; a society organized according to these principles." For many feminists, it is not a nice word. Patriarchal society was the primary social institution for most western cultures for over 2000 years. Feminists identify patriarchy as the primary reason women have suffered from social, political, sexual, religious, and academic inequality for centuries. Until the middle of the nineteenth century, women were considered either the property of their fathers or husbands, unable to hold property, make legal decisions, or pursue lifestyles other than that of wife and mother. But was this social organization so very bad for women? In this essay, Christine Rosen argues that while patriarchy might not have been perfect, it actually improved women's lot. Instead of tearing it apart and blaming it for social ills, Rosen says we should be thankful for the good things patriarchy has done for women.

Christine Rosen holds her doctoral degree in history and is currently a fellow at the American Enterprise Institute and a former senior fellow of the Independent Women's Forum. She is the author of *Preaching Eugenics: Religious Leaders and the American Eugenics Movement* (2004). This essay was first published in the *Women's Quarterly* in Spring 2002.

CRITICAL THINKING   Think about how the word "patriarchy," defined above and in the following essay, has become feminism's "dirty word." Before you read, consider the role of patriarchy in history. What institutions did it support? How did it contribute to social stability? How did it encourage the subjugation of women?

---

1 Praise for patriarchy? Surely only a victim of false consciousness would utter such blasphemy. Any sane person with a liberal arts degree knows that patriarchy is a

pernicious beast—still only partly subdued by the efforts of the women's movement—that has ravaged the talents of women for thousands of years.

2   But can patriarchy be as bad as some would have us believe? Defined narrowly, patriarchy is "a social organization marked by the supremacy of the father in the clan or family, the legal dependence of wives and children, and the reckoning of descent and inheritance in the male line." This is not always the preferred arrangement in modern families. But the brief against patriarchy encompasses more than relationships inside the family.

3   Since everything to emerge from western civilization bears the stamp of patriarchy, the argument goes, western civilization is inherently suspect. If you think this sounds nutty, then clearly you, dear reader, have fallen prey to patriarchy's wiles. For as theorists such as Andrea Nye—author of *Words of Power: A Feminist Reading of the History of Logic*—tell us, because of its roots in ancient patriarchal Greece, logic itself is suspect.

4   So is rigorous debate. Law professor Lani Guinier, for example, who had her fifteen minutes of fame when she was nominated as attorney general by former President Bill Clinton, took Socrates to task for developing a method of instruction that, two millennia later, supposedly still wounds the self-esteem of female law students. In *Becoming Gentlemen: Women, Law School, and Institutional Change*, Guinier argues that the often-combative Paper Chase-style Socratic method of teaching places far too much emphasis on combativeness, which is masculine. Guinier prefers inclusive, mentoring relationships to the orgies of Socratic rigor.

5   Patriarchy has for some time been the star of the women's studies classroom. There, it appears as a hyphenate epithet, as in "hetero-patriarchy," or in combinations such as feminist theorist bell hooks' "heterosexist white supremacist patriarchal culture." University presses churn out big-ticket titles such as *Patriarchy* and *Incest* from Shakespeare to Joyce, and *Refiguring the Father: New Feminist Readings of Patriarchy* that document this menace.

6   One women's studies professor told Daphne Patai and Noretta Koertge in their book, *Professing Feminism*, "If there were no patriarchy, there would be no oppression. If there were no oppression, there would be no need for affirmative action. If there were no affirmative action, we wouldn't be here acting like pigs trying to shoulder each other away from the trough!"

7   Patriarchy even serves as a convenient villain for a generation of young women who are some of the wealthiest and best situated on the planet. At the University of Oregon at Eugene, for example, students recently organized a conference called "Against Patriarchy." Conference participants engaged questions such as "How do we identify male privilege?" and "How does male domination connect to other oppressions, like racism, heterosexism, ableism, classism and capitalism, government and speciesism?"

8   Patriarchy—read: western civilization—doesn't deserve this treatment. In fact, it could be argued that it's the best thing that ever happened to women. To understand how womankind has benefited from the last two thousand years of patriarchy, one must examine the status of women at the dawn of the present era.

9   Athens, whose name is synonymous with high cultural and philosophical achievement, did not allow women to be citizens or own property. Roman husbands

were free to engage in any kind of sexual adventure, but a wife who committed adultery could be put to death—the doctrine of patria potestas guaranteed it. A Roman father acted as priest, judge, legislator, and, indeed, high executioner in his own household, with nary a concern for the rights of his wife and children. If this were all patriarchy had to offer, feminists would be right to regard it as the epitome of evil.

10   Truth be told, however, the patriarchal institution that feminist scholars most love to hate—the Catholic Church—began to make the earliest inroads into this system. First, there was the revolutionary idea that all people—including women—were precious and important beings. That was so attractive to downtrodden—truly downtrodden—women that they flocked to that now maligned institution—so much so that a pagan emperor once forbade missionaries to set foot in any pagan house where women resided—there was too much danger of conversion.

11   Second, women in the ancient world rarely had a say in choosing their spouses. But the medieval Church insisted that the woman's consent was of equal importance with the groom's. No, this didn't mean that there were no politically arranged marriages between royal infants or that fathers immediately ceased forcing their daughters into miserable marriages. But it did mean that there was now a new ideal, a new right of women that, over time, became a reality instead of an abstraction. Another change: Fidelity, long demanded of women, was now required from men.

12   Chivalry and honor codes are outgrowths of patriarchal societies that bound men to protect king and country—and women and children in the process. Knights didn't merely fight. They committed themselves to elaborate codes of behavior that included respect for women and a certain mannerly decorum. Such ideals still appeal, as evidenced by a trend in popular culture toward chivalrous and manly heroes in movies, such as *Kate & Leopold,* and in the public's praise of tough 'n' tender males, such as former New York Mayor Rudy Giuliani and Secretary of Defense Donald Rumsfeld.

13   Some of patriarchy's supposedly oppressive strictures—particularly those surrounding questions of sex and marriage—seem more appealing than onerous compared to our modern alternatives. Who wouldn't prefer courtly love, which sprang up in an obviously patriarchal medieval Europe, to the crass hooking-up culture of contemporary times? Then, troubadours and trouvères praised the virtues of women and, as historian Jacques Barzun has argued, helped establish "in theory the rights and privileges that women deserve and that many have enjoyed in reality, beginning with respect of their person and admiration of their qualities." Today, women's qualities are "admired" in venues such as Temptation Island and *Maxim*; perusing *Playboy*, not penning poetry, is the more acceptable male medium for marveling at women's charms.

14   The evolution of legal rights for women was slow. The ancients weren't keen on granting women property rights. Why should they have been? Women were regarded as property. By the still-patriarchal nineteenth century, this had changed. Single women enjoyed the legal status of femme sole, giving them the right to own property in their own names and to make contracts. Married women fared differently. "Coverture," the norm by the nineteenth century, wherein women lost all independent legal status upon marriage, wasn't something any modern wife would permit. However, it was, at the very least, a small step for womankind because, unlike the ancient Roman, the husband now had a legal obligation to protect his wife.

As Sir William Blackstone described it in his *Commentaries on the Laws of England*, the wife was under her husband's "wing, protection, and cover." By the 1830s, legal reforms in the United States extended the right to own property to married women as well, effectively abolishing coverture. While progress was slow, it was steady.

15   Despite their strictures (of which, admittedly, there were many), patriarchal societies didn't entirely stifle women's ambitions; many maidenly and even matronly malcontents made their mark. Eleanor of Acquitaine (1122–1204) is but the best known of a cohort of medieval women who scorned convention. In 1147, she and her phalanx of female attendants went on the Second Crusade to Palestine with her husband, Louis VII. Rumored to have warmed her bed with men other than the dour Louis on her adventures, she returned home and promptly divorced him, resuming rule of her hereditary lands, the valuable region of Acquitaine. After frenzied wooing from the most eligible bachelors on earth, Eleanor chose Henry Plantagenet, heir to the English throne, as her next conquest.

16   Her marriage to Henry was stormy, and eventually Eleanor, fed up with his royal philandering, established her own glittering court in Poitiers, where she promoted courtly love and patronized important poets of the day. The marriage produced two kings of England, Richard the Lionhearted and the less reputable John. Eleanor helped both to intrigue against Henry. When Richard was held captive in Palestine, Eleanor was a key player in English politics. She lived into her eighties, always an important figure on the world's stage.

17   Women also transgressed the literary boundaries of patriarchal societies. Left widowed and with three children to support, Christine de Pisan (1363–1430) had the gumption to put her knowledge of Italian and Latin to work in the French court, producing poems, such as "Epistle to the God of Love" (1399), where she criticized male behavior by channeling Cupid, and prose works such as *The Book of the City of Ladies*, where she rallied Reason, Rectitude, and Justice to defend her sex against a host of charges.

18   Feminist theorists' attacks on patriarchy might be more palatable if their recommended replacement made any sense at all. But it does not. The most active theorists wrestling with this demon offer something far less robust: spurious theories of ancient matriarchies, for one. These matriarchal utopias, though popular in women's history courses, have no basis in historical fact, as Cynthia Eller has shown in *The Myth of Matriarchal Prehistory*. Other theorists become mired in semantics. A few years ago on a women's studies academic listserv, for example, a heated debate erupted over the usefulness of the term "patriarchy," with alternatives such as "gender binaries," "phallocentrism," and "phallic drift" offered as replacements.

19   Granted, patriarchy has taken some puzzling turns, particularly today. Participants in the contemporary American subculture of "Christian Patriarchy," for example, argue that "biblical patriarchy has provided for the greatest measure of liberation for women." Fans of Christian patriarchy extol "Jesus Christ the Bridegroom" as a "model of monogamy" for the modern man. The editor of *Patriarch* magazine (motto: "Equipping men to be godly leaders in family, church, and society") sees his mission as calling men "back to their manly duties" in the home, especially their duties as fathers. Still, questions of ecumenical etiquette aside, who could object to a movement that encourages men to become more attentive fathers?

20   At the other end of the spiritual spectrum are the "pioneers of feminist spiritual-ity," as Barbara Walker describes them in her book, *Restoring the Goddess*. Walker and her ilk are less than pleased with patriarchy's past triumphs, particularly the Judeo-Christian tradition's reference to God as male. Citing the work of nameless "feminist scholars," Walker argues that they "have shown that our traditional reli-gious organizations have been dedicated to denial or demonization of the Goddess, all the way from biblical times to the present."

21   In many ways patriarchal societies have made good on the promises of those medieval swains who honored their ladies. It is patriarchal societies, after all, that have produced triumphs of logic, science, art, and literature; and, for the most part, it was a patriarchal clique that developed the liberal political philosophies that led to notions of democracy, individual rights—and women's liberation. Therein lies the rub: Patriarchy was the dominant social arrangement for most of the history of western civilization, a civilization that has produced the expres-sions of human freedom and individual rights that radical feminists now want to reject. ◆

FREEWRITING ASSIGNMENT

One hundred and fifty years ago, where would you fall in the order of a patriarchal society? Would you be under the control of a father or hus-band? Would you be the son in line to inherit a family business? Could you be pursuing the lifestyle you are now? Would it matter? Explain.

CRITICAL READING

1. What tone does Rosen use in this essay? Does her tone promote a neutral interpretation of her points? Does it engage a wide audience, or could it alienate some readers? Identify specific passages or words she uses to support your response.
2. What sorts of things are blamed on patriarchy? Why?
3. In paragraph 8, Rosen argues that patriarch is "the best thing that ever happened to women." What proof does she offer to support her claim?
4. Rosen gives Rudy Giuliani and Donald Rumsfeld as examples of males who project the "tough n' tender" male image that the public adores, the legacy of chivalric patriarchy. Why do you think she chose these two men to support her point? What public image do they project? How do you feel about these individuals?
5. In paragraph 13, Rosen wonders, "Who wouldn't prefer courtly love, which sprang up in patriarchal medieval Europe, to the crass hooking-up culture of contemporary times"? Respond to her statement expressing your own point of view.
6. Rosen provides many examples of how patriarchy has been good for women. Review her essay and make a list of her examples. Critically eval-uate each one. Do some examples provide stronger support than others? Could some undermine her argument? Explain.

CRITICAL WRITING

7. *Exploratory Writing*: Rosen provides many examples of patriarchy's influence on our contemporary world, as well as making connections to the improvement of women. Write a short essay on how patriarchy has influenced your life. Was it a positive or negative influence? Explain.

8. *Persuasive Writing*: Write an essay in which you respond to Rosen's argument with your own perspective. Do you agree with her claim that patriarchy was good for women? Why or why not? Try to specifically address the examples Rosen provides in her essay, by either building upon them or identifying flaws in her argument.

9. *Research and Analysis*: As a social historian, Rosen connects how the social institutions of the past have influenced the present. Select one of Rosen's examples of how patriarchy helped women (chivalry, marriage, religion, etc.), and research its historical role on society. Write an essay describing how the patriarchal social institution you chose affected women in the past, and present.

GROUP PROJECT

10. Interview at least 15 to 20 students outside of your class and ask them what they think patriarchy means. If they do not know, provide a dictionary definition of the word. Then, ask them if they can think of positive and negative influences patriarchy has had on contemporary culture, for both men and women. Summarize your interviews and discuss as a class. Do the responses reflect Rosen's comment at the beginning of her essay that patriarchy is a "pernicious beast"? Is the concept of patriarchy fading? Is it a hot topic of debate? What do students on your campus think?

VIEWPOINTS

► **Revisionist Feminism: A Dialogue**
Susan Faludi and Karen Lehrman

The next article is the beginning of a multiletter dialogue between feminist writers Susan Faludi and Karen Lehrman featured in *Slate MSN,* in which the two women discuss the meaning of "real feminism." Faludi objects to the "revisionist feminists," who seem to feel that feminism denies them their femininity. Lehrman responds by explaining that the leftist political agenda of conventional feminism has clouded the goals of the movement, and has alienated both men and women.

Susan Faludi is the author of the critically acclaimed books *Backlash: The Undeclared War Against American Women* (1991) and *Stiffed: The Betrayal of the American Man* (1998). Her articles have appeared in many journals and magazines, including *Newsweek* and *Esquire.* Karen Lehrman is the managing editor of *Consumer's Research* magazine and the author of *The Lipstick Proviso: Woman, Sex & Power in the Real World* (1997).

<table>
<tr>
<td>

CRITICAL THINKING

</td>
<td>

Look up the word "feminism" in the dictionary. Does the definition surprise you? Does American society seem to have a different understanding of what feminism means? Explain.

</td>
</tr>
</table>

Dear Karen,

1   I enter into this conversation with you about feminism with some misgivings. Not because I don't want to talk to you. It's just that I suspect it will be like a phone conversation where the connection's so bad neither party can hear the other through the static. I say this because in my experience, there's no getting through to the group of "feminists" (and I use that word with heavy quotation marks and highly arched brows) who are your sister travelers. I mean the group that maintains that an "orthodoxy" of "reigning feminists" (your terms) torments the American female population with its highhanded fiats, its litmus tests of "proper" feminist behavior, its regulatory whip seeking to slap the femininity out of the American girl. Christina Hoff Sommers, Katie Roiphe, Laura Ingraham, Danielle Crittenden, and the rest of the inside-the-Beltway "revisionist feminists" (as the media would have it) condemn feminism for its "excesses" over and over on the *New York Times* and *Washington Post* op-ed pages and the major TV talk shows (while complaining they are viciously "silenced" by the "reigning" feminists, who hardly ever get an airing in the aforementioned forums).

2   And you, too, Karen. Your own book-length addition to this chorus repeats the argument that feminism has turned women off by denying them the right to display and revel in their feminine beauty and sexuality. You then adorn that old can of "revisionist" contents with a fancy new label, The Lipstick Proviso, which you define as "women don't have to sacrifice their individuality, or even their femininity— whatever that means to each of them—in order to be equal."

3   For the longer version of my response to the "revisionists" and their charges against feminism. For the shorter version, to your book specifically, here 'tis:

4   Earth to Karen! Do you read me? . . . 'Cuz back on planet Earth, feminists don't "reign" and they certainly don't stop women at checkpoints to strip them of their "individuality" by impounding their lipstick (though what a pathetic "individuality" that must be if it depends on the application of Revlon to achieve it). Bulletin from the front: I wear lipstick, and I've spotted it on other feminists, too. I've watched, in fact, legions of "militant" feminists apply makeup brazenly in public ladies' rooms, and no femi-Nazi police swooped down and seized their compacts. And you know why? Because lipstick is not what feminism is about.

5   What's clear in your book is you feel gypped by feminism. You feel the feminists of the '60s and '70s made a promise to your generation of women that they didn't keep. Let us assume you are sincere, and I have no reason—in your case—to think otherwise. But why do you feel so betrayed? Maybe the answer lies in your definition of feminism. You write in your book that "as a young woman eager to escape the confines of a traditional household," you embraced feminism, which, you believed, "was going to turn all women into liberated women, into women who

would unfailingly exhibit serene confidence, steely resolve, and steadfast courage. Unburdened by the behavioral and sartorial restrictions of traditional femininity, we would all want to trek alone through the wilds of Indonesia, head IBM, run for president." You then go on to lament, "Yet it doesn't seem as though the first generation of women to come of age with feminism . . . has metamorphosed en masse into briefcase-toting, world-wandering Mistresses of the Universe."

6   Now here's the problem: Your definition of feminism is gleaned not from '70s feminism but from '70s advertising. In that decade, Madison Avenue and Hollywood and the fashion industry and mass media all saw a marketing opportunity in "women's lib" and they ran with it. Feminism as reinterpreted through television commercials for pantyhose and marketing manuals for Dress for Success bow ties would do just what advertising is supposed to do: Inflame your hungers and your anxieties, then offer to mollify them with a product that makes ludicrously inflated promises. So just as Hanes tried to convince shoppers that slipping on a pair of pantyhose would turn them into raving beauties with a million suitors, so the faux-feminism of Consumer America tried to convince a younger generation of women that "liberation" led to Banana Republicesque treks in the Himalayas and starring roles in the executive penthouse suite. All young women had to do to get that liberation was smoke Virginia Slims. As Christopher Lasch (that raving liberal!) wrote prophetically in 1979 in *The Culture of Narcissism,* "The advertising industry thus encourages the pseudo-emancipation of women, flattering them with its insinuating reminder, 'You've come a long way, baby,' and disguising the freedom to consume as genuine autonomy."

7   Now you are trying to reclaim that promise, proclaiming in your book that women have the "right" to liberate themselves via the marketplace. You champion women's right to express themselves through makeup, lingerie, cosmetic surgery, aerobics classes, and corsets. You even say that "entering a wet T-shirt contest" can be a "liberating" act for some women.

8   But, but, but . . . you are mad at the wrong folks. Feminists never promised you a rose garden in Lotusland; the consumer culture did. Feminism, unlike advertising, is not about gulling you into believing you could win the sweepstakes. Feminism is and always has been about women acting in the world as full-fledged citizens, as real participants in the world of ideas and policy and history. That doesn't have anything to do with wearing lipstick or not wearing lipstick or even about making obscene amounts of money. It's about insisting on the right of women to dignity, a living wage, meaningful work, and active engagement in the public arena. As for lipstick: For most women who work in the cruddy lower reaches of American employment, the problem isn't being denied the "right" to wear makeup and lingerie; it's about the right not to be forced to dress and act the way their male bosses demand. You may recall that flight attendants in the '60s fought one of the earliest battles of feminism's second wave so that male corporate bosses could no longer fire them over their weight, age, dress, or marital status. (Stewardesses were also, by the way, required to wear girdles—and didn't consider it liberating when their supervisors conducted company-mandated "touch checks.") Feminism, real feminism, is about freeing women to be genuine individuals—and recognizing that such individuality doesn't come in one size only or out of a bottle.

9   You propose that we cleanse feminism of political content and even "abolish" the term "women's movement." "This next wave" of feminism, you say, "needs to be primarily devoted to developing our emotional independence." Well, we certainly are in an "emotional" era. That's because we are steeped in a consumer culture where emotional manipulation is the name of the game and political analysis interferes with the Big Sell and so is discouraged. Now you are asking that feminism junk the politics and join in on the consumerizing of the American female public. Well, you can ask. You can cheerlead for that all you like, of course. And I'm sure a lot of powerful institutions will be only too glad to enable your cheerleading for their own selfish ends. But you can't call what you're asking for feminism, or progress. You can't say we've come a long way when you are still championing our "right" to stand on the stage in a wet T-shirt and be called baby.

10   . . . Am I getting through, or does this all sound like static on the line?

Sincerely,
Susan

Dear Susan,

11   Well, I think there would be much less static between us if you had read my book more carefully, did not take my words out of context, and did not lump me in with women with whom I clearly have little in common. I also think we'd have a much better connection if you'd drop the sneery, condescending tone you always seem to adopt when writing about women with whom you disagree. I respect you; I'd probably even like you if we met under slightly less fraught circumstances. Yes, I disagree with some of your philosophical and political views. But those views don't make you any less of a feminist. As long as you believe that women should have the same rights, opportunities, and responsibilities as men, you can have whatever political agenda, lifestyle, or wardrobe you wish.

12   Unfortunately, you don't seem to feel the same way about me or millions of other women. You say that "feminism, real feminism, is about freeing women to be genuine individuals—and recognizing that such individuality doesn't come in one size only or out of a bottle." But much of what you've written on the subject—in your book, magazine articles, and already in this dialogue—would indicate that you don't really mean it. And the same, I'm afraid, is true about most of the other self-appointed spokeswomen for feminism.

13   You each appear to believe that, to be allowed to use the term feminist, a woman has to adhere to a well-defined leftist political agenda, consisting of, at the very least, affirmative action, nationally subsidized day care, and "pay equity" (formerly known as comparable worth). In your *Ms.* article, you call a handful of women who happen to disagree with you politically (myself included) "pod" or "pseudo" feminists. You say that we're right-wing misogynists or pawns of right-wing misogynists. Perhaps most curiously, you imply that we're also racist. In 1992, the National Organization for Women tried to start a "women's party," offering a distinctly leftist "women's agenda." During the last election, NOW president Patricia Ireland said women should vote only for "authentic" female candidates, Gloria Steinem called Texas Republican Sen. Kay Bailey Hutchinson a "female imperson-

ator," and Naomi Wolf described the foreign-policy analysis of Jeane Kirkpatrick as being "uninflected by the experiences of the female body." The desire to enforce political conformity is even worse in academia. Many women's-studies professors regularly judge texts and opinions in terms of their agreement with the orthodox political agenda. (For an honest "insider" account, check out *Professing Feminism*, by Daphne Patai and Noretta Koertge.)

14   Fortunately, all women don't think alike, and as far as feminism is concerned they certainly don't have to. The only items on the real feminist agenda are equal rights and opportunities, a society capable of accepting the widest array of women's choices, and women strong and independent enough to make rational ones. This in no way means that feminists should "junk the politics." It means that feminism is a moral ideal; how women achieve it is a matter of political debate.

15   It's true that some of the women you mention above and in your *Ms.* article do oppose abortion rights, do deny that discrimination exists, and do believe that it is a woman's God-given duty to have children and stay home with them—all anti-feminist notions. Some have minimized the very real problems of sexual harassment and date rape, and seem far more interested in self-promotion than in the future of feminism. Yet the surveys suggest that the vast majority of women—and men—who have criticized the women's movement in recent years do believe in women's essential equality and are simply unhappy with the fact that feminism has turned into an orthodoxy, that it now means precisely the opposite of what it was intended to mean—namely, freedom.

16   Feminist theorists have gotten much better at not explicitly stating that women need to follow a certain lifestyle or dress code to be a feminist. But an implicit criticism of more traditional choices is still quite apparent. In *Backlash*, for instance, you blame the fact that women are still primarily clustered in the "pink ghetto" or low- to mid-level management positions entirely on discrimination. Some of it surely is discrimination, and some of it is due to the fact that women are still working their way up. But much of the explanation can be found in the choices of women themselves. The vast majority of women—even young women with college degrees who have grown up with nearly every option open to them—still prefer to give their families higher priority than their careers. According to the Women's Education and Research Institute (hardly a bastion of conservative thought), employed mothers are significantly more likely than fathers to want to stay at their current levels of responsibility and to trade job advancement to work part time, work at home, or have control over their work schedules. Four-fifths of mothers who work part-time do so by choice.

17   The larger problem is that most feminist theorists still refuse to acknowledge that there appear to be significant biological differences between the sexes. They still seem to believe that equality with men has to mean sameness to men, that until all aspects of traditional femininity are abolished, women will not be free. Thankfully, this is far from necessary. Women, on average, may always have a stronger need than men to nurture, a need that will at times eclipse their desire for power. Restructuring the corporate world to better accommodate two-career families may certainly help women to deal with these conflicting goals, but I don't think they will ever disappear. We may not like the choices many women continue to make, but not only are they really none of our business, there's precious little we could do about them if they were.

18   Biology also still seems to be turning up in courtship (the desire of the vast majority of women to want men to pursue them), sex (the ambivalence most women have toward casual sex), and beauty (the energy most women give toward making themselves attractive). As you well know, I do not say anywhere in the book that women have to wear lipstick to be feminist or even feminine. I use lipstick as a metaphor for all of the traditionally feminine behaviors that feminist theorists have at some point condemned as being degrading and exploitative—from being a mother to staying home full-time with one's children to wearing miniskirts and makeup. In *Backlash*, you implicitly argue that the desire of many women to buy feminine or sexy clothing and indulge in cosmetic products and services is wholly the result of manipulation by the beauty and fashion industries. You call women's desire for sexy lingerie "fashion regression," and argue that happy and confident women don't care about clothes. Actually, I think the desire of most women to not hide their sexuality is a sign of progress, evidence that many women now feel they no longer have to renounce a fundamental aspect of themselves in order to make a symbolic point.

19   I do not feel "gypped" by feminism. On the contrary, feminism has offered me the opportunity to live my life in a way that was considered reprehensible just 40 years ago. What I do feel is that the feminist revolution is not complete, and it's incomplete in ways that differ from the orthodox feminist line. There's still more political work to be done, to be sure, especially involving the issues of rape and domestic violence. But there's also much personal work to be done. This is a major theme of my book, yet for some reason you have chosen to purposefully misread what I wrote about it. Where do I say anything about "the consumerizing of the American female public"?

20   Of course the advertising industry exploited feminism; that's their job. But that has nothing to do with what I'm talking about. I use the term emotional independence to refer to self-development, which was a prominent part of feminist theorizing and activism in the early days of the Second Wave. Actually, it's not that surprising that you chose to ignore what I was saying and turn the focus back on how society has victimized women. Feminists have unfortunately been doing that for the past 20 years, which may partly explain why women lag so far behind in their emotional development. While enormous attention has been paid to how the "patriarchy" mistreats women, little has been written about how women mistreat themselves. Even focusing on how women should take responsibility for their problems is often dismissed as naive, sexist, or "blaming the victim."

21   (By the way, you also took my point about "entering a wet T-shirt contest" completely out of context. As you well know, I was actually saying that just because women now have the freedom to do something doesn't mean it's the most rational thing to do. "Only each woman can decide if her actions are self-destructive and thus unfeminist," I wrote. "What is self-destructive for one woman—entering a wet T-shirt contest, for instance, or being a full-time housewife—may be liberating for another.")

22   It's true that the orthodoxy is breaking up, and other feminist voices are finally being heard. But that's no thanks to you, Susan. I think you have focused more energy on stifling dissent than perhaps any other feminist writer. In your book, you castigate Susan Brownmiller, Betty Friedan, and Erica Jong for having the gall to

suggest that the women's movement's refusal to acknowledge biological differences between the sexes is hurtful to women. You can't blame the media for the fact that two-thirds of women still don't call themselves feminist. The media may very well highlight the extremes, but it has also given Gloria Steinem, Naomi Wolf, Patricia Ireland, and yourself plenty of space and air time to alienate the majority of women through your restrictive view of feminism.

23 Feminism—real feminism—deserves to be respected and honored. Every woman today should proudly call herself a feminist. But that is not going to happen until prominent feminist writers such as yourself admit to a couple of things. One, that a Republican housewife who annually has her face lifted and daily greets her husband at the door wearing only heels can be a feminist if she knows her mind, follows her desires, and believes that every woman has the right to do the same. Two, that the notion of sisterhood is false, outdated, and sexist. Women don't "owe" each other anything: They don't have to like each other, agree with each other, vote for each other, or hire each other for feminism to succeed.

24 Three, the notion of a "women's movement" has outlived its usefulness. Men must be just as aware and involved as women—on both a personal and political level—for feminism to work. Four, women can act differently from men. Even if that means that Congress, corporate boards, and CEOs will never be 50 percent female, as long as women are making their choices freely, feminism will not be undermined. And finally, each woman is fundamentally unique. No assumptions can be made about her politics, values, goals, and beliefs.

25 Instead of fighting about whether or not feminism has turned into an orthodoxy, I think it would be far more useful if this dialogue—as well as the larger feminist debate—were focused on the complexities that women must deal with today. For instance, how does the corporate world learn to judge women strictly on their merits yet recognize the obvious differences—e.g., that women are the only ones who get pregnant? How do we help women deal with their ambivalence toward responsibility and power? How do we help women develop the strength and independence to demand boyfriends who don't abuse them, and raises that they deserve? These are tough questions, and I'd really like to know what you think about them.

Sincerely,
Karen

FREEWRITING ASSIGNMENT

What does the word "feminism" mean to you? Explain.

CRITICAL READING

1. Why does Faludi express "misgivings" about entering into a conversation on feminism with Lehrman? What tone does she set for the dialogue? How does Lehrman respond to this tone?
2. Summarize Faludi's argument. What is her definition of "real feminism"? Why does she object to "revisionist feminism"? Explain.

3. Summarize Lehrman's argument. What is her definition of "real feminism"? Why does she object to Faludi, and other "self-appointed spokeswoman for feminism?" Explain.

4. In what ways has consumer culture clouded the goals of feminism? How has advertising exploited feminism? Explain.

5. On what points do Faludi and Lehrman agree? If you were the moderator of this dialogue, how would you use these points of agreement to help them reach a consensus?

6. Do Faludi and Lehrman enter this dialogue on feminism in order to reach an understanding or middle ground? What evidence is there, if any, on either side of their discussion to try to reach a consensus or at least understand the other's point of view?

CRITICAL WRITING

7. You have been asked to write an article about feminism at the beginning of the twenty-first century for inclusion in a time capsule to be opened at the beginning of the next century. Describe your own perception of feminism, and include examples from popular culture and your experience. How are women portrayed by the media? How are they perceived in American culture? How do you think things will have changed in 100 years? Explain.

8. *Research and Analysis*: Is it harder to grow up male or female in America today? Using information from the articles in this section, as well as outside resources, write an essay explaining which gender faces the greatest and most daunting challenges, and why. Will this situation get worse? Offer suggestions to help ease the gender-related challenges children face growing up in today's culture.

9. *Exploratory Writing*: Write an essay in which you consider your own sense of cultural conditioning. Do you feel your behavior has been conditioned by sex-role expectations? In what ways? Is there a difference between the "real" you and the person you present to the world? If there is a difference, is it the result of cultural pressure? Explain.

GROUP PROJECT

10. Thirty years ago, men were expected to earn more than women. Do we still hold such beliefs? Poll students outside of class as well as other people on campus to find out their opinions regarding income status. Create some questions that will allow both men and women to discuss how they feel about this issue. Do males feel that they should earn more? Would they feel less masculine if their girlfriends or wives earned more then they did? Do females look for higher incomes when they consider a partner? Analyze your results and draw some conclusions from your survey.

RESEARCH ISSUE **An Identity Reduced to a Burka**
Semeen Issa and Laila Al-Marayati

With much media attention focused on the Middle East, generalizations can become misconceptions. As these two Muslim women explain in the opinion section of the *Los Angeles Times* (January 20, 2002), the issues Middle Eastern women face are much more complex than the burkas they wear. Semeen Issa is president of the Muslim Women's League and a teacher in Arcadia. Laila Al-Marayati is a Los Angeles physician.

1   A few years ago, someone from the Feminist Majority Foundation called the Muslim Women's League to ask if she could "borrow a burka" for a photo shoot the organization was doing to draw attention to the plight of women in Afghanistan under the Taliban. When we told her that we didn't have one, and that none of our Afghan friends did either, she expressed surprise, as if she'd assumed that all Muslim women keep burkas in their closets in case a militant Islamist comes to dinner. She didn't seem to understand that her assumption was the equivalent of assuming that every Latino has a Mexican sombrero in their closet.

2   We don't mean to make light of the suffering of our sisters in Afghanistan, but the burka was—and is—not their major focus of concern. Their priorities are more basic, like feeding their children, becoming literate and living free from violence. Nevertheless, recent articles in the Western media suggest the burka means everything to Muslim women, because they routinely express bewilderment at the fact that all Afghan women didn't cast off their burkas when the Taliban was defeated. The Western press' obsession with the dress of Muslim women is not surprising, however, since the press tends to view Muslims, in general, simplistically. Headlines in the mainstream media have reduced Muslim female identity to an article of clothing—"the veil." One is hard-pressed to find an article, book or film about women in Islam that doesn't have "veil" in the title: "Behind the Veil," "Beyond the Veil," "At the Drop of a Veil" and more. The use of the term borders on the absurd: Perhaps next will come "What Color is Your Veil?" or "Rebel Without a Veil" or "Whose Veil is it, Anyway?"

3   The word "veil" does not even have a universal meaning. In some cultures, it refers to a face-covering known as niqab; in others, to a simple head scarf, known as hijab. Other manifestations of "the veil" include all-encompassing outer garments like the ankle-length abaya from the Persian Gulf states, the chador in Iran or the burka in Afghanistan.

4   Like the differences in our clothing from one region to another, Muslim women are diverse. Stereotypical assumptions about Muslim women are as inaccurate as the assumption that all American women are personified by the bikini-clad cast of "Baywatch." Anyone who has spent time interacting with Muslims knows that, despite numerous obstacles, Muslim women are active, assertive and engaged in society. In Qatar, women make up the majority of graduate-school students. The Iranian parliament has more women members than the U.S. Senate. Throughout the world,

many Muslim women are educated and professionally trained; they participate in public debates, are often catalysts for reform and champions for their own rights. At the same time, there is no denying that in many Muslim countries, dress has been used as a tool to wield power over women.

5   What doesn't penetrate Western consciousness, however, is that forced uncovering is also a tool of oppression. During the reign of Shah Mohammad Reza Pahlavi in Iran, wearing the veil was prohibited. As an expression of their opposition to his repressive regime, women who supported the 1979 Islamic Revolution marched in the street clothed in chadors. Many of them did not expect to have this "dress code" institutionalized by those who led the revolution and then took power in the new government.

6   In Turkey, the secular regime considers the head scarf a symbol of extremist elements that want to overthrow the government. Accordingly, women who wear any type of head-covering are banned from public office, government jobs and academia, including graduate school. Turkish women who believe the head-covering is a religious obligation are unfairly forced to give up public life or opportunities for higher education and career advancement.

7   Dress should not bar Muslim women from exercising their Islam-guaranteed rights, like the right to be educated, to earn a living and to move about safely in society. Unfortunately, some governments impose a strict dress code along with other restrictions, like limiting education for women, to appear "authentically Islamic." Such laws, in fact, are inconsistent with Islam. Nevertheless, these associations lead to the general perception that "behind the veil" lurk other, more insidious examples of the repression of women, and that wearing the veil somehow causes the social ills that plague Muslim women around the world.

8   Many Muslim men and women alike are subjugated by despotic, dictatorial regimes. Their lot in life is worsened by extreme poverty and illiteracy, two conditions that are not caused by Islam but are sometimes exploited in the name of religion. Helping Muslim women overcome their misery is a major task. The reconstruction of Muslim Afghanistan will be a test case for the Afghan people and for the international community dedicated to making Afghan society work for everyone. To some, Islam is the root cause of the problems faced by women in Afghanistan. But what is truly at fault is a misguided, narrow interpretation of Islam designed to serve a rigid patriarchal system.

9   Traditional Muslim populations will be more receptive to change that is based on Islamic principles of justice, as expressed in the Koran, than they will be to change that abandons religion altogether or confines it to private life. Muslim scholars and leaders who emphasize Islamic principles that support women's rights to education, health care, marriage and divorce, equal pay for equal work and participation in public life could fill the vacuum now occupied by those who impose a vision of Islam that infringes on the rights of women.

10   Given the opportunity, Muslim women, like women everywhere, will become educated, pursue careers, strive to do what is best for their families and contribute positively according to their abilities. How they dress is irrelevant. It should be obvious that the critical element Muslim women need is freedom, especially the freedom to make choices that enable them to be independent agents of positive change. Choosing to dress modestly, including wearing a head-scarf, should be as respected

as choosing not to cover. Accusations that modestly dressed Muslim women are caving in to male-dominated understandings of Islam neglect the reality that most Muslim women who cover by choice do so out of subservience to God, not to any human being.

11   The worth of a woman—any woman—should not be determined by the length of her skirt, but by the dedication, knowledge and skills she brings to the task at hand. ◆

CRITICAL THINKING

1. What is a burka? Why are they worn? What do they represent to most Westerners?
2. According to the authors, why are Westerners misguided by the concept of burkas, chadors, and hijabs? In what ways can banning these items be just as extremist as mandating their use?
3. Consider the authors' title for their essay. What does the title mean? How can identity be reduced to a burka? Could their title also be ironic? Explain.

RESEARCH PROJECTS

4. The authors of this essay point out that Muslim women are diverse. Depending on where they live, they can be highly educated and involved in political and economic arenas or oppressed to the point where they cannot leave their homes without a chaperone. Visit the web site of the Muslim Women's league and read more about Muslim women in America. Write a short essay describing one of the issues American Muslim women are dealing with today (racial profiling, civil rights, cultural misconceptions, etc.). Share your own opinion about the issue as well.
5. In paragraph 2, the authors note that most discussions about Muslim women concentrate on their wearing "the veil." Research the Muslim tradition of the veil and write a short history about it. A good resource to begin your research is About.com's guide at *http://womensissues.about.com/cs/abouttheveil.* Include in your report modern opinions about the veil, and if possible, interview a Muslim female student for her opinion about this article of clothing.

Additional essay topics, writing assignments,
research guidelines, and readings for this chapter can
be found online at **www.ablongman.com/goshgarian**.

Sports
Culture
Not Just a Game

8

Sports form an integral part of our culture, touching many facets of our lives. They serve as entertainment and a means to bond with individuals, community, and even a nation. Internationally, sports unify us with the Olympic games and world championships. On a more personal level, children learn teamwork, self-reliance, and motor skills participating in school soccer and baseball games. As a community, we root for our favorite local teams. For hopeful teens, sports may present a way to go to college, if not to a professional career. When asked to name heroes, many children will name several famous sports figures as the people they most admire. And the advertising industry knows that the largest market for their commercials will be during the Super Bowl.

We are a nation fully immersed in sports culture—a nation in which most major newspapers feature a sports section as large as the sections devoted to international, national, and regional news. This chapter takes a look at the role of sports in our society: the business of sports, its influence on our lives and the lives of children, gender equality in athletics, and legal issues.

The first article explores the issue of the commercialization of college sports by the National Collegiate Athletic Association (NCAA), and college athletes as "Unpaid Professionals." Andrew Zimbalist presents the background of the NCAA, and its cartel-like hold over college sports. He raises many troubling ethical questions concerning the big business of college sports, and the academic institutions they help support. As Zimbalist explains, the rampant commercialization of college sports lines the pockets of coaches and administrators while damaging the spirit of athletic competition and the college athletic experience. Sports-journalists Skip Rozin and Susan Zegel continue the discussion on college sports teams in "A Whole New Ball Game?"

The next article examines our national obsession with sports. In "Sports Centered," Jay Weiner discusses how our preoccupation with sports has, in fact, ruined the game for many players and fans. Indeed, for many people, sports are a serious business. Weiner examines how the financial aspects of sports are affecting the game. In addition to evaluating the current state of sports in our culture today, Weiner presents some ways we can help "save" sports and preserve the thrill of the game for future generations.

In "Where Are the Heroes?" media critic Ed Siegel laments that our one-time ideals of heroism have passed from public life—that myths of strength, courage, and achievement have disappeared from the realm of politics, religion, and art. But our culture still has its heroes—found now on the playing fields and courts across the country.

It has been over thirty years since Title IX secured educational opportunities for women, both in the classroom and on the playing field. In 2003, the law came under review by the Bush administration. Mary Ann Cooper presents opposing sides of the argument in "Point/Counterpoint—Title IX: The Battle of the Sexes Continues."

This chapter's Viewpoints section examines the issue of drug testing athletes. In "Just Say No to Random Drug Testing," American Civil Liberties Union lawyer David Rocah explains how the drug testing of athletes is an invasion of their personal rights. Claude Lewis, however, maintains that drug testing should routinely be performed not only on athletes, but on all students. Drug testing, says Lewis, will protect students and send a clear message that drugs will not be tolerated on or off the playing fields.

This chapter's Research Issue addresses parental violence in sports. Sports psychologist Michael L. Sachs discusses the growing problem of the behavior and interaction of parents, coaches, and referees during or after youth sporting events. In "Lighten Up, Parents!" Sachs gives some suggestions on how to get parents in check and allow kids to enjoy the game.

Unpaid Professionals
Andrew Zimbalist

The National Collegiate Athletic Association (NCAA) is the governing body of college athletics. The NCAA exerts tremendous control over college athletics and their financial ventures. For example, in November of 1999, the NCAA signed a six billion dollar contract extension with CBS for the rights to broadcast the "March Madness" annual basketball tournament and several other NCAA athletic championships. Such deals can mean millions in additional revenue for the schools involved. However, critics question the integrity of the NCAA. If the NCAA is a commercial enterprise, how can it effectively regulate the actions of college teams, especially when millions of dollars are at stake? In this article, Andrew Zimbalist discusses some of the ethical quandaries facing athletic departments and university administrations today.

Andrew Zimbalist is an economics professor at Smith College in Northampton, Massachusetts. He is the author of many books on development and comparative economics and is a recognized authority in sports economics. In 1998, Zimbalist was named *Village Voice* Sports Journalist of the Year. This article is excerpted from his latest book, *Unpaid Professionals: Commercialism and Conflict in Big-Time College Sports* (1999).

CRITICAL THINKING

What is your opinion about the media coverage and attention given to "big-time" college sports? If colleges and universities are supposed to be primarily academic institutions, is it fair that they lavish so much attention on their teams and athletes?

A college racing stable makes as much sense as college football. The jockey could carry the college colors; the students could cheer; the alumni could bet; and the horse wouldn't have to pass a history test.

—Robert Hutchins, former president of the University of Chicago

1 On page one of the 1997–98 NCAA Manual, the basic purpose of the National Collegiate Athletic Association is written: "to maintain inter-collegiate athletics as an integral part of the educational program and the athlete as an integral part of the

student body and, by doing so, retain a clear line of demarcation between intercollegiate athletics and professional sports." Some may wonder whom do they think they are kidding?

In December 1996, Notre Dame was playing its final regular season football game against the University of Southern California. The Notre Dame placekicker missed an extra point at the end of the fourth quarter and the game went into overtime where Notre Dame lost, 27–21. The loss quashed Notre Dame's bid to go to an Alliance Bowl game, which would have been worth $8 million to the school. The Fighting Irish turned down an invitation to the $800,000 Independence Bowl. The placekicker blew an $8 million extra point![1]

Notre Dame has a 7-year, $45 million contract with NBC to televise its regular season football games. The major conferences have a $700 million, 7-year contract with ABC to televise the bowl championship series beginning in 1998–99.[2] The NCAA has a $1.725 billion 8-year contract with CBS to broadcast its annual men's basketball tournament.

Like the professional leagues, the NCAA promotes its own line of licensed clothing, as do its leading colleges. Like the National Basketball Association (NBA) and the National Football League (NFL), the NCAA has its own traveling tent show—NCAA Hoop City. It has its own marketing division. Its corporate sponsorships have increased roughly sevenfold in the nineties, with guaranteed income of $75 million between 1997 and 2002. It has its own real estate subsidiary and even its own Learjet. In 1997, the NCAA cut a deal with the city of Indianapolis to build it a new headquarters and provide an estimated $50 million in subsidies, leaving three-hundred employees and forty-five years of tradition behind in Kansas City.[3]

The NCAA's total budget, which surpassed $270 million in 1997–98, has grown at an annual rate of 15 percent since 1982. Its Executive Director, Cedric Dempsey, has done even better than this. His salary and benefits package grew 30.2 percent in fiscal 1997 to $647,000, as part of a new five-year deal. Dempsey replaced Dick Schultz in 1993 when the latter ran into ethical problems. As punishment, the Association gave Schultz a golden parachute worth at least $700,000.[4]

Dempsey also gets treated well when he attends the Final Four of the annual basketball tournament. The *Kansas City Star* reports that "the manual for cities holding Final Fours requires a series of gifts to be delivered every night to the hotel rooms of NCAA officials. These momentos cost Indianapolis an estimated $25,000 [in March 1997]. . . . At a minimum, gifts for each official included a Samsonite suit bag, a Final Four ticket embedded in Lucite, a Limoges porcelain basketball and Steuben glass."[5] And to maximize revenue at the Final Four, the NCAA has spurned normal basketball-sized venues and instead has chosen cavernous arenas such as the New Orleans Superdome, the San Antonio Alamodome, the St. Louis Trans World Dome, the Indianapolis RCA Dome, and the Georgia Dome, all with seating capacities in excess of forty thousand.

With big bucks dangling before their eyes, many NCAA schools find the temptations of success too alluring to worry about the rules. Schools cheat. They cheat by arranging to help their prospective athletes pass standardized tests. They cheat by providing illegal payments to their recruits. They cheat by setting up special rinky-dink curricula so their athletes can stay qualified. And when one school cheats, oth-

ers feel compelled to do the same. Then the NCAA passes new rules to curtail the cheating. Sometimes these rules are enforced, sometimes not, but rarely is the penalty harsh enough to be a serious deterrent. The solution, it turns out, is more rules. The NCAA Manual has grown in size from 161 pages in 1970–71 to 579 pages in 1996–97 (and the pages increased in size from $6 \times 8\frac{1}{2}$ inches prior to 1989 to $8\frac{1}{2} \times 11$ inches after). In 1998–99, the Manual became so long that the NCAA
8 broke it into three volumes, with 1,268 pages (some are repeats).

So what is "the clear line of demarcation between intercollegiate athletics and professional sports"? It certainly is not the presence or absence of commercialism and corporate interests. Rather, two differences stand out. First, unlike their handsomely remunerated coaches and athletic directors (ADs), college athletes don't get paid. Second, the NCAA and its member schools, construed to be amateur organizations promoting an educational mission, do not pay taxes on their millions from TV
9 deals, sponsorships, licensing, or Final Four tickets.

In the end, college sports leads a schizophrenic existence, encompassing both amateur and professional elements. The courts, the IRS, and sometimes the universities themselves cannot seem to decide whether to treat intercollegiate athletics as part of the educational process or as a business. The NCAA claims that it manages college sports in a way that promotes both the goals of higher education and the financial condition of the university. Critics say it does neither.
10

The NCAA wants it both ways. When confronted by the challenges of Title IX and gender equity, the NCAA and its member schools want to be treated as a business. ADs argue that it is justifiable to put more resources into men's than women's sports, because men's sports generate more revenue. But when the IRS knocks on its door, the NCAA and its member schools want their special tax exemptions as part of the nonprofit educational establishment and they claim special amateur status in order to avoid paying their athletes.
11

Big-time intercollegiate athletics is a unique industry. No other industry in the United States manages not to pay its principal producers a wage or salary. An athlete's financial aid package tops out at around $30,000 in the late-1990s. Given that the leading college basketball teams generate over five million dollars and the leading football teams over twenty million dollars annually in revenues,[6] it seems obvious that the star players on these teams are worth many times more than their financial aid packages. One study, based on data from 1988–89, estimated that the top college football players generated over $500,000 in revenues annually for their schools.[7] The figure today would be at least 50 percent higher.[8] Another study estimates that individual top college basketball players in the early 1990s produced revenues of $870,000 to $1 million each year.[9]
12

Herein lies a powerful incentive for colleges to cheat. Since schools are not allowed to offer overt cash payments to athletes, schools are obliged to seek more creative or surreptitious forms of remuneration to their student-athletes.[10] Still, payment to the players is constrained, so the schools divert large sums, on the one hand, to compensate more handsomely their top coaches and athletic directors and, on the other, to recruit their student-athletes and to build facilities that appeal to the athletes. While some of the more egregious forms of covert compensation have been curtailed in recent years, the NCAA has never devoted sufficient resources or energy to ameliorate the problem significantly. Rather, it seems that the NCAA has concentrated its meager efforts on levying exemplary punishments on select schools which, some allege, are out of political favor with the Association. Tom McMillen, University of Maryland and NBA star, former U.S. Congressman, and presently co-chair of the President's Council on Physical Fitness, commented during a congressional hearing in July 1991: "The NCAA's response to the crisis has been inadequate: its members have promulgated an ironic system of rules that severely penalize the most minor infraction while ignoring the larger, corrupt practices which 13 are evident in the system."[11]

Even after under-the-table payments from boosters and player agents, the special dormitories and meals, the high-paying summer sinecures, solicitous tutors, tailored gut courses, free clothing, and a myriad of other perquisites, the majority of the top student-athletes are creating considerably more value for their colleges than they are receiving. And this disparity becomes even more glaring when one takes into account that only 54 percent of Division IA football and 41 percent of men's basketball players receive college degrees; among black athletes these proportions 14 fall to 44 percent and 35 percent, respectively.[12]

Complementing the dubious treatment of the student-athletes, the cultural dominance of intercollegiate sports over campus life raises still more serious questions. University administrators' quest for publicity and media coverage leads them to genuflect at the door of the athletic director's (AD's) office. Resources are lavished on the recruitment of top athletes, not top scholars.[13] Full financial scholarships go to the best athletes, not the best students. During the academic year 1993–94, Duke University awarded $4 million to its 550 student-athletes, and only $400,000 in academic merit grants for its 5,900 other undergraduates. The University of North Carolina at Chapel Hill offered almost $3.2 million to its 690 athletes and only 15 $636,000 in academic merit scholarships to the rest of its 15,000 student body.[14]

Special living conditions, meals, and curricula reinforce a class system within the student body. Underqualified students, some without elementary reading and mathematical skills, are admitted, sometimes by arranging for surrogates to take their SAT exams. The institutional logic evolves to support athletic prominence rather than intellectual inquiry. The president of the University of Oklahoma reflected this poignantly when he went before the state legislature in search of a larger university budget and asserted: "I hope to build a university of which our football 16 team can be proud."[15]

A 1989 Harris poll found that 80 percent of Americans surveyed felt that college sports were out of control.[16] The 1991 Knight Commission report on college athletics concurred, and Creed Black, the president of the Knight Foundation, told the U.S. Congress that university athletic programs were being corrupted by big money, and "the rules violations undermined the traditional role of universities as places where the young people learn ethics and integrity."[17] When college basketball players seek to protest the working conditions and wages at a Nike factory in Asia by taping over the Nike label on their sneakers, but their school's endorsement contract with the company obligates the players to remove the tape, then has not the 17 sacred principle of free speech been violated?

Acknowledging that intercollegiate sports have lost all sense of proportion, however, is not to deny them their rightful place in the university. Participation in

sports can promote physical and emotional well-being. Physical activity, whatever its form, is a healthy antidote to the sedentary lifestyle of a student. Participation in competitive sports can enhance one's self-image and teach discipline. Team sports can build character, friendships, and community. Spectator sports can provide re-
18 lease and enrich school spirit. Athletes need not be counterposed to students.

This is clear in the case of women participants in school sports. An emerging body of research has found that female participants in school sports are more likely to graduate high school,[18] 92 percent less likely to use drugs, less likely to be depressed or experience low self-esteem, and 55 percent less likely to have an unwanted pregnancy.[19] At the university level, women student-athletes graduate at a 69 percent rate, compared to 59 percent for all women. Eighty percent of women who were identified as key leaders in Fortune 500 companies had a background in sports.[20] Regular exercise has also been shown to reduce significantly the risk of breast cancer, and to lower the incidence of obesity (currently experienced by 25 percent of children and 30 percent of adults in the United States) and of osteoporosis
19 (loss of bone mass).[21]

It is precisely these positive attributes of sports participation along with an abiding ethos of fairness that drive the struggle for gender equity in athletic programs. In 1972, notwithstanding an aggressive NCAA lobbying effort against it, Congress passed Title IX of the Educational Amendments to the 1964 Civil Rights Act. Title IX declared it to be illegal for institutions receiving federal aid to discriminate in any of its activities on the basis of sex. While the initial implementation of Title IX in intercollegiate athletics was delayed and its progress proceeded in fits and starts, by the mid-1990s enormous gains for female student-athletes had been achieved. For instance, the number of women athletes involved in intercollegiate sports increased from 31,852 in 1971–72 to 129,285 in 1996–97. Still, in 1996–97 women represented only 39 percent of all student-athletes and received a smaller (37.3) percentage of all scholarship aid to athletes. Thus, much ground remains to be traveled
20 before gender equality is attained.

It is no longer fashionable for the NCAA, its member schools, or athletic directors to argue against the principles of gender equity. Virtually all proclaim their commitment to the goals of Title IX; the only impediment, they say, is economic.
21 There is simply not enough money to go around. Women must be patient.

Since the vast majority of college athletic programs operate in the red, finding funds to promote equal athletic opportunity for women is no easy matter. Title IX not only presents a budgetary problem for U.S. colleges, it raises the basic question
22 of the role of athletics in the university.

College presidents see two difficult choices: attempt to develop new revenue sources by further commercializing intercollegiate athletics or move decisively away from big-time athletics. While level-headed thinking might seem to dictate the latter option, cultural momentum and key alumni, boosters, and corporate interests
23 favor the former.

The business of college sports took a dramatic turn in 1984 when the Supreme Court struck down the NCAA's centralized control over the national televising of college football. This decision ended the NCAA's monopoly and resulted in more games being televised. So far, so good (suspending critical judgement about its cultural impact). The other outcome of the high court's ruling was that strong football schools and conferences began to earn television revenue for themselves instead of sharing it with all NCAA colleges. The rich programs eventually got richer, and the middle and poor programs got poorer. This growing inequality has been enhanced in the 1990s by increased corporate penetration of the top programs, the formation of the Bowl Championship Series (né Bowl Super Alliance), and the NCAA's "restructuring," which allows for Division I colleges to run their own show as well as for control to be vested in the Division's most powerful conferences.

24   Thus, many of the sixty-odd top schools in the Big Ten, the Pac-10, the Big East, the Atlantic Coast Conference, the Big 12, and the Southeastern Conference are being bathed in cash, while the 40 Division IA schools in other conferences, the 198 schools in Divisions IAA and IAAA, the 267 schools in Division II, and the 387 schools in Division III are drowning in red ink. Save the handful of colleges with excellent academic reputations, college public relations, admissions, and development departments behave as if successful athletic teams are the *sine qua non* of financial health and more qualified student bodies. The logic is that athletic triumphs bring notoriety which, on the one hand, entice more student applications, thereby allowing for greater selectivity in admissions.

25   The struggle for gender equity has put the traditional conflict of college sports between professionalism and amateurism into sharp relief. At once, the NCAA must deal, *inter alia,* with growing legal challenges to its rules and regulations, the rigidifying class structure among its member schools, the push for sexual parity, the unpaid professional athletes who are jumping early to the pro leagues, and the glut of sports programming on television. Intercollegiate athletics is at a crossroads.

26   Externalities is the word economists use for a phenomenon that arises when a producer or consumer takes an action but does not bear all the costs (negative externality) or receive all the benefits (positive externality) of the action. College sports generates both positive and negative externalities. Among the positive externalities are that they provide a source of entertainment for tens of millions of Americans and of school spirit for college students.[22] Among the negative externalities are that college sports compromise the intellectual standards and educational process at U.S. universities. The challenge is to reform the system in a way that preserves the positives and minimizes the negatives. If the experience with the contradictions and imperfections of college sports over the last hundred years has taught us anything, it is that there are no quick fixes or ideal outcomes. ◆

Notes

1. *Chronicle of Higher Education,* December 20, 1996, p. A35.
2. Jim Naughton, "Debate Over Championship Game in Football Reflects Larger Tensions in College Sports," *Chronicle of Higher Education,* September 19, 1997.
3. Welch Suggs, "A Different Final Four to Win," *Kansas City Star,* March 11, 1997, p. D1.
4. Mike McGraw et al., *Money Games: Inside the NCAA,* reprint from the *Kansas City Star,* 1997, p. 6.
5. Ibid., p. 2. In the summer of 1998 the NCAA issued new rules that limit the amount Final Four host cities can spend to $500,000. In March 1998 San Antonio had a budget of $1.2 million for hosting the Final Four. The apparent reason behind this limit is to help protect the investment of the NCAA's national corporate sponsor. The more local money

spent, the more local sponsorship is needed and the more the national sponsor's presence is diluted.

6. Daniel Fulks, *Revenues and Expenses of Intercollegiate Athletics Programs,* Overland Park, Kansas: NCAA, August 1994, pp. 13–18.

7. Robert Brown, "An Estimate of the Rent Generated by a Premium College Football Player," *Economic Inquiry,* vol. 31, October 1993, pp. 671–84.

8. The average Division IA men's football had reported revenues of $4.34 million in 1989 and $6.44 million in 1995 (an increase of 48.4%), while the average men's basketball team had reported revenues of $1.64 million in 1989 and $2.5 million in 1995 (an increase of 52.4%). Unreported revenues, such as off-budget contributions to the coaches' incomes from sneaker companies and booster groups, have skyrocketed since the 1980s. Daniel Fulks, *Revenues and Expenses of Intercollegiate Athletics Programs: Financial Trends and Relationships,* 1995, Overland Park, Kansas: NCAA, 1996.

9. Robert Brown, "Measuring Cartel Rents in the College Basketball Player Recruitment Market," *Applied Economics,* January 1994, pp. 27–34.

10. There is a large literature on the transgressions and excesses in college sports. Some of the more interesting treatments are: Murray Sperber, *College Sports, Inc.,* New York: Henry Holt, 1991; James Michener, *Sports in America,* New York: Random House, 1976, esp. chap. 7; John Thelin, *Games Colleges Play,* Baltimore: Johns Hopkins University Press, 1994; Tom McMillen with Paul Coggins, *Out of Bounds,* New York: Simon & Schuster, 1992; Don Yaeger, *Undue Process: The NCAA's Unjustice for All,* Champaign, Illinois: Sagamore, 1991; Francis Dealy, *Win at Any Cost: The Sell Out of College Athletics,* New York: Birch Lane, 1990; Gary Shaw, *Meat on the Hoof: The Hidden World of Texas Football,* New York: St. Martin's Press, 1972; David Whitford, *A Payroll to Meet: A Story of Greed, Corruption, and Football at SMU,* New York: Macmillan, 1989; Rick Telander, *The Hundred Yard Lie: The Corruption of College Football and What We Can Do to Stop It,* New York: Simon & Schuster, 1989; and Peter Golenbock, *Personal Fouls,* New York: Penguin Books, 1989.

11. *Intercollegiate Sports.* Hearings Before the Subcommittee on Commerce, Consumer Protection, and Competitiveness of the Committee on Energy and Commerce. House of Representatives. 102d Congress, 1st Session. Washington, D.C.: USGPO, 1992, p. 83.

12. NCAA, *1997 NCAA Division I Graduation-Rates Report,* Overland Park, Kansas: NCAA, June 1997, p. 626. These percentages refer to the four-class average for the entering classes between 1987–88 and 1990–91.

13. Some schools are beginning to offer full scholarship rides to high school valedictorians and other top students, but this practice is still not nearly as prevalent or extensive as athletic grants-in-aid. See Michael McPherson and Morton Schapiro, *The Student Aid Game,* Princeton: Princeton University Press, 1998.

14. Cited in Sperber, 1991, p. 506.

15. Thelin, p. 115. Statement was made in February 1951.

16. A 1997 CBS News poll of 1,037 adults found that 47 percent believed sports in college were overemphasized and among college graduates 62 percent thought so. Porto, "Completing the Revolution," p. 394.

17. *Intercollegiate Sports.* Hearings, House of Representatives, p. 9.

18. Women's Sports Foundation, *Women's Sports Facts,* East Meadow, N.Y., 1995, p. 1.

19. This result is from a 1998 study of a nationally representative sample of 11,000 students in grades 9 through 12. It found that female athletes of this age cohort were less likely to have sex and more likely to use contraceptives. Women's Sports Foundation, "Sport and Teen Pregnancy," East Meadow, N.Y.

20. Norma Cantu, Assistant Secretary of Civil Rights, U.S. Department of Education, Statement before the Subcommittee on Consumer Affairs, Foreign Commerce and Tourism, Committee on Commerce, Science and Transportation, U.S. Senate, October 18, 1995, p. 4.
21. Ibid., p. 2.
22. Presumably, college sports also produce consumer surplus. Even though college sporting events employ price discrimination through ticket pricing and premiums (e.g., booster contributions), there are likely tens of thousands, if not millions, of fans who derive more utility from attending these events.

FREEWRITING ASSIGNMENT

Read the quotation. Analyze the quotation preceding this article and explain what Hutchins is saying about the nature of college football.

CRITICAL READING

1. Evaluate the author's tone and style in this article. How does he feel about this subject? What do you think he is trying to accomplish by writing this piece? Explain.
2. Based on the information Zimbalist presents in this article, discuss the role of the NCAA in college sports. Is the NCAA forwarding the cause of college sports? If so, in what ways? According to the author, what influence does the NCAA exert over college sports, and how does this influence harm colleges, students, and athletes? Explain.
3. How do you think Mary Ann Cooper ("The Battle of the Sexes Continues") would respond to the points Zimbalist raises in paragraphs 18–25 about the role of women in college sports? Explain.
4. What is the role of the college athlete? If athletes are on the team to promote the economic interests of the school, should they be paid for their work? If so, how?
5. What is the "schizophrenic existence" of college sports? Do you agree with Zimbalist's assessment? Why or why not?
6. Evaluate the information Zimbalist provides in paragraphs 14 and 15 about the allocation of supportive resources for the overall student body as compared to the athletic program. Does the disparity of resource allocation surprise you? Explain.
7. According to Zimbalist, what are the positive qualities of college sports? Where can these positive influences still be found? How do college sports help the overall student body and the economic and spiritual health of the school? Explain.

CRITICAL WRITING

8. *Exploratory Writing*: How do college sports encourage many NCAA schools to cheat? How do they cheat, and why? What does this cheating do to the rest of the student body, and to the athletes themselves? Write an

essay addressing the multiple issues connected to rule bending and cheating by college athletic departments. Support your essay with information from Zimbalist's article.

9. *Research and Evaluation*: Zimbalist presents some interesting facts about female athletes in college sports. With a graduation rate of 69 percent, more female athletes finish college than their nonathletic female counterparts. This number is significantly higher than that of male athletes—only 54 percent of Division IA football and 41 percent of men's basketball players receive college degrees. What accounts for this disparity? Are their goals different? Have financial considerations corrupted men's college sports? Write an essay exploring this issue. Use outside research from critics, coaches and, if possible, some college athletes themselves, to support your essay.

10. *Personal Narrative*: Supporters of the money-making ability of college sports teams explain that athletic triumph brings the school publicity, which in turn attracts higher quality students to the school. Write about the role of college sports teams in your current and pre-college experience. Was the sports reputation of your college a factor in your decision to attend? Explain. If it was not, write about your personal opinion about your college's sporting teams, and how, and if, they influence your college experience today.

GROUP PROJECTS

11. As a group, discuss the controversy surrounding the fact that college athletes are not paid. Treated as professional athletes, and held accountable for the revenue they do and do not generate, big-time college athletes raise up to $500,000 annually for their schools, but receive financial aid packages averaging about $30,000 a year. Is this a fair trade? Have one member of the group write down the points your group makes about this issue to share with the class after the discussion period.

12. Each member of your group should obtain at least two "mission statements" from a division IA or IAA school. How do college athletics factor into the mission statement? Are sports directly addressed? How do college sports contribute to the overall goals of the school for its student body? After you discuss this issue as a group, share your impressions with the rest of the class, reading the mission statements of several schools.

A Whole New Ball Game?

Skip Rozin, with Susan Zegel

Over the last ten years, several universities have shocked college students, alumni, and the media by cutting college teams and even programs. Concerned that colleges are spending too much money on sports, and worried about scandals, some colleges are deciding that organized athletics are just not worth the sacrifice. In 1997, Boston University terminated its football program, followed by Swarthmore in 2000. In 2003, Vanderbilt disbanded the entire athletic department. Such sweeping reforms promise to change college sports forever as Skip Rozin and Susan Zegel report in this article.

Susan Zegel is a reporter and staff writer for *Business Week.* Skip Rozin is a freelance sportswriter whose articles have appeared in many sports magazines and newspapers, including *The New York Times, The Washington Post, Time,* and *Harper's.* He has written and collaborated on several books, *One Step from Glory* (1979*), Daley Thompson: The Subject is Winning* (1983), *Garvey* (1986, with Steve Garvey), and *The Name of the Game* (1994, with Jerry Gorman and Kirk Calhoun). This article appeared in the October 20, 2003, issue of *Business Week.*

CRITICAL THINKING

Did the reputation of your college's athletic program influence your decision to attend it? Are you involved in organized collegiate athletics? Would you decide not to attend a college that doesn't have a football team, or an athletic department?

---

1 A glorious autumn day. School colors flying. Bands blaring fight songs. Cheerleaders in skimpy skirts kicking up their heels. Stands vibrating from the stomping feet of fans. Fearsome young men raging with the fire of competition. Isn't this what college is all about?

2 Er . . . not according to a killjoy named Gordon Gee. In September, Vanderbilt Chancellor Gee grabbed headlines when he announced that he was disbanding the university's athletic department. Granted, no teams were cut, no athletic scholarships lost. But Gee did strike a chord. In trying to pull the athlete back into the academic community, he became the public face of a movement that is making a serious stab at reforming college sports. "Other universities have called and said: 'Good, you jump off that cliff, and if it works, get back to me,'" says Gee. "I suspect they're sweating bullets, with all this national attention."

3 Why? Because Gee's success or failure just might help foretell the future of an extracurricular activity that has grown into a $ 3 billion-a-year annual industry, according to Smith College economist Andrew S. Zimbalist, author of *Unpaid Professionals.* Behind the crowds and TV hype, pressure is building either to turn class-skipping athletes into students or recognize that—at least at big-time sports schools—it's too late to turn back the clock. And that's pitting reformers against an army of alumni boosters, politicians who control state schools, TV networks, and commercial interests—all of whom would feel the impact of downsizing college sports.

4 The endless debate over the proper role of sports in university life would probably not be raging so fiercely if it weren't for a particularly troubling spate of scandals. Months after Maurice Clarett led Ohio State to the national title in football, the running back was charged with receiving special treatment on an exam and accused of lying to police about what was stolen from a car loaned to him by a school

booster. The men's basketball team at Fresno State was put on probation after some-one else did players' course work. The University of Washington was hit with a two-year probation for recruiting violations.

5   And it isn't just the players. Georgia basketball coach Jim Harrick resigned amid charges of academic fraud. Alabama fired head football coach Mike Price for "indecorous" behavior involving a drinking spree and a stripper. Iowa State basket-ball coach Larry Eustachy resigned after photos surfaced showing him drinking and kissing coeds at a party after a game. Most bizarre, Baylor basketball coach Dave Bliss threw in the towel after trying to cover up illegal payments to a player—before he was murdered—by allegedly spreading rumors that he dealt drugs.

6   Some reforms have already been put in place: stricter academic requirements for entering freshmen and for athletes to remain eligible. Others are long-range and more ambitious. They include shortening the football and basketball seasons, and, most fundamental, pulling back from the commercial forces that have turned college sports into an entertainment spectacle.

7   Leading the charge are faculty senates, including many from the six athletic conferences that form the Bowl Championship Series (BCS); the powerful Associa-tion of Governing Boards of Universities & Colleges; and the National Collegiate Athletic Assn. (NCAA)—generally considered the marketing arm of college sports. "What's unusual here is having a faculty group and a trustee group aligned," says Robert Eno, co-chair of the faculty group, the Coalition on Intercollegiate Athletics (COIA), alluding to trustees' usual fervent support of athletics. "It's odd. It's un-precedented. We're all surprised, but it seems to be working well."

8   Crisis is nothing new to college sports. Violent deaths in football led President Teddy Roosevelt in 1905 to threaten the game's abolition, which spurred the form-ing of the NCAA that same year. What's different now is the amount of money sloshing around. Schools that make it to the top bowl games can pull in up to $13 million apiece. And in March, 1999, CBS signed an 11-year, $6 billion TV contract, mostly for basketball. (Football contracts are awarded by individual conferences.) As a result, schedules and seasons have expanded, expenses have skyrocketed, and scandals have multiplied.

9   "Follow the money now," says Myles Brand, head of the NCAA since January, "change is in the air." Predictably, the current reform movement started over money. The coalition of faculty members was born in the fall of 2002 after a profes-sor of classic languages at the University of Oregon, James Earl, became alarmed by a single act of university spending. "I picked up my newspaper one morning and read about the university spending $90 million to expand the football stadium," says Earl. "The faculty had never been told about it. We went nuts. We're poor as church mice here. How could you spend $90 million on a stadium when we can't even pay the faculty's salaries?"

10   Earl was then president of the Oregon faculty senate, and he wrote to the presi-dents of the other universities in the Pacific 10 Conference. By the beginning of 2003, faculty senates at 45 to 50 universities had contacted the COIA to voice their support. In January, the Association of Governing Boards of Universities & Col-leges, the advisory group representing the trustees of over 1,200 institutions elected to join the COIA in its reform push. The final member of the triumvirate to weigh in

was the NCAA. Says Brand, the first university president to head the NCAA and the man who fired basketball legend Bobby Knight at Indiana: "Reform was one of the conditions under which I took this job."

11   The three groups met in Chicago in April and endorsed a series of educational and budgetary reforms. Some had already been enacted by the NCAA over the previous two years, all of them aimed at improving academic performance. One rule stipulates that athletes complete a set percentage of the requirements to graduate each year. Another raises grade-point-averages athletes must achieve in college, and a third boosts the academic qualifications athletes must have to enter.

12   The reformers also back a carrot-and-stick plan, rewarding teams that do well academically with more scholarship slots and money from television and punishing teams doing poorly by taking away scholarships and ultimately barring them from post-season play. These measures will be voted on by Division 1 presidents in April and are expected to pass. "We are also looking at the kinds of courses that student-athletes should be taking," says Brand. "We want general education courses, not any old course."

13   Critics, however, point out that stronger regulations aren't enough. They require accurate and honest reporting. "You can toughen up academic standards, but that leads to more academic fraud," says Howard Chudacoff, a history professor at Brown and the university's NCAA faculty representative. Brand insists that maintaining academic integrity is a primary objective and says the NCAA will modestly boost its investigative staff, which now numbers 15.

14   The April meeting also set longer-term goals involving "transparency" in athletic budgets. The sources of money for college sports are often murky: Cash from boosters often goes unreported and can cover under-the-table payments to coaches and even players. Facilities can be a mystery all their own. "It's always difficult to account for capital spending, athletic or otherwise," says Brand. On Aug. 6, the NCAA received a $50,000 grant from the Mellon Foundation to back a study of capital spending on athletics.

15   What's not murky is that as more money goes to new stadiums, celebrity coaches, and better training facilities, critics of the so-called "athletics arms race" have become more vocal. Some schools have independent athletic departments that support themselves, but the majority are funded by the university. "About 30 schools have separate athletic budgets," says reformer Earl, but around 100 in Division 1 are "sucking money from the schools."

16   And it isn't just the money that bothers the reformers but the deals made to get that money—like the Nike swoosh on uniforms at many schools and ads on arena walls. "That's an unpleasant message to a lot of people who care about the idea of the university as a place of inquiry free of commercial taint," says Derek Bok, former president of Harvard and author of *Universities in the Marketplace*.

17   The reformers are also training their guns on what may be the most powerful force in today's college sports landscape: television. They believe that TV's scheduling needs—games during the week, long travel to tournaments—increasingly clash with academic requirements. One of the movement's long-term goals is regaining control of schedules. They would like to see shorter seasons and smaller squads. The Drake Group, a four-year-old reform organization of about 100 dues-

paying professors across the country, wants "to return control of the classroom to the faculty," says its president, Linda Bensel-Meyers of the University of Denver. The group believes many athletic departments currently have the power to get grades changed, and encourage plagiarized papers.

18   Major ammunition for the reform movement has come from a persuasive set of statistics—"myth-breaking," Brand calls them—that challenge the benefits long thought to flow from strong sports programs. One of the biggest myths was shattered when Brand announced in August that "fewer than a dozen universities" make a profit from sports. All of those were Division 1-A schools with major basketball and football programs.

19   Universities that can't rely on football and men's basketball to pay the bills are often forced into painful downsizing of their sports programs. Since 2000, 31 Division I schools have eliminated at least one intercollegiate sports team, according to the *Chronicle of High Education.* This year, West Virginia University swung the ax at five, including men's cross-country and men's tennis.

20   Four studies in the past eight years—the latest by the NCAA this year—conclude that winning sports teams do not necessarily inspire alumni to donate, and in those cases when they do, the boost is short-lived. "We only saw an impact in alumni giving if a school wins a bowl game, on average 7.3%," says economist Thomas A. Rhoads, who co-authored a 2000 study. "But when a basketball team was put on probation, there was a decrease of 13.6% in alumni contributions."

21   The most shocking findings came from a 2001 study by the Mellon Foundation that demonstrated the importance afforded athletics at Ivy League and other prestigious schools that downplay sports and profess to give no athletic scholarships. "We say we don't give scholarships, but we really do—the whole Ivy League does," says Brown's Chudacoff. "We give money to needy students, and we have a lot of needy athletes." The Mellon report revealed that nearly all top schools also lowered admission standards for athletes, opening the door more readily for jocks than for minorities or the children of alumni. Once enrolled, athletes do more poorly than nonathletes—as much as 20% worse.

22   "It makes it harder for faculty to teach the way they want to teach because they don't get the commitment or the preparation from the recruited athletes that they get from the other students," says William G. Bowen, head of the Mellon Foundation and co-author of two books based on the study. Bowen adds that nonathletes resent what they see as domination of the campus by athletes, who can make up as much as 35% to 40% of the student body of smaller schools, compared with about 3% at big state universities. The result, he says, is "an athletic divide."

23   Some schools have already taken action to rein in sports. Boston University dropped football in 1997 after 113 years, and Swarthmore ended a 122-year football tradition in 2000—both citing an overconcentration on sports. In 2002, 5 of the 11 members of the New England Small College Athletic Conference (NESCAC) decided to reduce the number of athletes it accepted, and the Council of Ivy League Presidents in June voted for the first time to limit the athletes its eight universities can recruit.

24   "We were willing to trade off SATs and GPAs to get a kid who's a great violinist or a student of color, but we were more willing to make that trade-off for ath-

letes," says President Morton O. Schapiro of Williams, which voted for the NESCAC cuts.

25 How many schools will follow suit remains to be seen—and some of the reformers' proposals clearly amount to pigskin in the sky. Many university leaders argue that the benefits of a major sports program still far outweigh the drawbacks. "The idea of sports is to shine a light on the university in a positive manner and to help enrollment," says Robert J. Dwyer, chairman of the board of trustees of Niagara University and a 1965 graduate who helped fund the school's first hockey rink. "Our [men's hockey team] went to the Final Eight in 2000, and our women to the Final Four in 2002. Enrollment has risen steadily."

26 Rabid fans aside, college sports are deeply woven into America's tapestry. "Sports offers high visibility that in some mysterious way creates a bond between the university and a broader public," says James Duderstadt, former president of the University of Michigan. The pull that collegiate sports has on the populace is especially true at state schools, where traditions are storied and fans rabid. It was no accident that Gee waited until he had left his previous positions at Ohio State, Colorado, and West Virginia before making his stand at private Vanderbilt. "If I were to try to do this at Ohio State," says Gee, "I would end up pumping gas."

27 And it is not just emotions that are at play at state schools but money and politics. The governor and legislatures control school budgets, and they stand for election answerable to a sports-crazed electorate. "Because the state has deeper pockets than any single institution, state universities are more likely to spring for new facilities," says sports economist Zimbalist. "Once that investment is made, perhaps hundreds of millions of dollars, it ups the pressure to win."

28 That's why many think the reform movement will get nowhere—at least at bigtime sports schools. "I can't believe that a Michigan or a Penn State, schools with good academics and successful sports programs, are going to want to cut back," says Bill Cella, chairman of Magna Global USA, the TV negotiating arm of the communications conglomerate Interpublic Group. "I think the reverse is happening. There are efforts now on behalf of the networks to convince the [BCS] conference to go into a real playoff structure. That would generate some real money, and money rules the day." Zimbalist adds that shortening seasons might not loosen money's grip: "With less supply, the price for sponsorship and advertising could go up," he points out.

29 The question is: Where is it all going to end? Reformer Eno sees a nightmarish future: "If the situation continues to evolve the way it has," he says, "there's going to be increased pressure for the payment of athletes in the revenue sports, even for the outsourcing of big-time football and basketball, to try to distance the universities from the negative associations of commercialism."

30 That may not be far off. State legislatures in California, Utah, and Nebraska last summer introduced bills to pay athletes and allow them to share in money earned from bowl games, TV, and endorsements. The NCAA firmly opposes "pay-for-play" but is studying a plan to increase scholarship support.

31 "We're at a crossroads," says Brand. "If this reform fails and schools adopt a pay-for-play professional model, it is the end of college sports as we know it and a

serious loss to the educational system." That's why the reformers plan to keep grinding it out on the ground until they make some serious yardage. ◆

Who's Tops in Alumni Giving?* It's not all big-time sports schools	
	Millions
USC	$585.2
Harvard	$477.6
Stanford	$454.8
Cornell	$363
University of Pennsylvania	$319.7
Johns Hopkins	$318.7
University of Wisconsin	$307.2
University of California	$282.3

* Totals include all private giving for 2002
Data: RAND's Council for Aid in Education

FREEWRITING ASSIGNMENT

How important are sports to your overall college experience? How would your life be different, if at all, without a college athletics program?

CRITICAL READING

1. Why are so many colleges making drastic changes to their sports programs? List several reasons cited in the article. Do you think such changes are necessary to preserve the academic integrity of the college experience?
2. What is the "athletic divide"? How does it separate students? Have you experienced it at your college? Explain.
3. In their opening paragraphs, Rozin and Zegel state that Gordon Gee, the chancellor of Vanderbilt, is a "killjoy." Why do they use this word? Is it used sarcastically, or do they feel that Vanderbilt made a poor decision?
4. What benefits do sports teams afford colleges? In your opinion, do the benefits outweigh the negatives? Explain, referencing the article for additional support.
5. What is the "carrot-and-stick" incentive to athletes? Should it be necessary to create such incentives? Explain.
6. How have television and the media contributed to the college athletics reform movement?
7. If college athletes are being paid (pay-for-play), should they really be in college? Are they students, or professional athletes? Can they be both? What do you think of pay-for-play? Will it change college sports?

8. *Exploratory Writing and Opinion*: What is the role of sports in universities and colleges? Are they an essential and integral part of the college experience, or are they a separate entity apart from the overall mission of the university? Explain.

9. Rozin and Zegel wonder if it is too late to "turn back the clock" on college sports. NCAA president Myles Brand fears that if athletic reform fails, and college athletes are paid according to the professional model, college sports will cease to exist. Research this issue online. Write an essay in which you argue either for or against "pay-for-play." How could it change college sports?

10. *Research and Analysis*: Rozin and Zegel cite several recent scandals in college sports that have contributed to the reform measures adopted by colleges and universities. Research one of these scandals and analyze its relationship to the athletic reform movement. Describe the scandal and the circumstances that contributed to it.

GROUP PROJECTS

11. *Group/Class Project*: Originally, college athletes received financial aid packages based on both their abilities and their scholastic aptitude. Now, however, most "big-time" division IA colleges recruit their athletes on athletic ability alone. What role, if any, should academic ability play in college sports? What ethical issues are raised if athletes are chosen solely on ability and are not held to the same scholastic standards of other students? With your group, discuss this issue either from the perspective of nonathletic students or from the perspective of NCAA administrators. Then debate the issue with the rest of the class.

12. As a group, research your college's athletic program. What teams does your college have? Are they in a division? How important is your athletic department to school pride and unity? What do you think the reaction of students and alumni would be if your school cut its sports teams? (If you attend a school that has already taken such a step, discuss the long-term ramifications of this measure.) Will it matter 10, 20 years from now? Summarize your discussion.

Sports Centered

Jay Weiner

Sports play an important role in American culture. Historically, sports have served as a social and political arena for change. Over the past century, sports have served as a means to protest racism, bring down social barriers, and demonstrate equality. In this piece, Jay

Weiner discusses how the spirit of sports has changed from a social and political force that mattered to an empty forum of entertainment that lacks meaning and focuses on greed.

Jay Weiner is a sportswriter for the Minneapolis *Star Tribune* and author of the book *Stadium Games: Fifty Years of Big League Greed and Bush League Boondoggles* (2000). This article first appeared in the January–February 2000 issue of the *UTNE Reader.*

CRITICAL THINKING   Consider the role sports occupy in our society. Why do we value sports and why do they command so much of our attention?

---

1 How far back must we go to remember that sports matter? How deeply into our personal and national pasts must we travel to recall that we once cared?

2   Do we have to return to 1936? Adolf Hitler tried to make the Olympics into a propaganda machine for anti-Semitism and racism. In that case, American track star Jesse Owens, demonstrating that the master race could be mastered at racing, stole Hitler's ideological show. Were not sports a vehicle of significant political substance then?

3   Or should we return to 1947 and Jackie Robinson? A baseball player integrated our "national pastime" a year before the U.S. Army considered African Americans equal. Robinson's barrier-break may have been largely based on ticket-selling economics for the Brooklyn Dodgers' owners, but didn't sports do something good?

4   Their fists raised, their dignity palpable, track stars Tommie Smith and John Carlos spread the American black power and student protest movements to the world when they stood on the victory stand at the 1968 Olympics in Mexico City. Politics and sports mixed beautifully then.

5   Remember when tennis feminist Billie Jean King took on an old fart named Bobby Riggs in 1973, boldly bringing the women's movement to the playing fields? That moment of sports theater stirred up sexual politics as much as any Betty Friedan essay or Miss America bra burning could ever do.

6   Sports had meaning. And sports were accessible.

7   Remember when your grandfather or your uncle—maybe your mother—took you to a game when you were a little kid? The hot dog was the best. The crowd was mesmerizing. The colors were bright. The crack of the bat under the summer sun, or the autumn chill wrapped around that touchdown run, was unforgettable. Back then, some nobody became your favorite player, somebody named Johnny Callison or Hal Greer or Clarence Peaks or Vic Hadfield, someone who sold cars in the off-season and once signed autographs for your father's men's club for a $50 appearance fee. Those "heroes" were working-class stiffs, just like us.

8   Now you read the sports pages—or, more exactly, the business and crime pages—and you realize you've disconnected from the institution and it from you. Sports is distant. It reeks of greed. Its politics glorify not the majestic drama of pure competition, but a drunken, gambling masculinity epitomized by sports-talk radio, a venue for obnoxious boys on car phones.

9   How can we reconcile our detachment from corporatized pro sports, professionalized college sports—even out-of-control kids' sports—with our appreciation for

athleticism, with our memories? And how, after we sort it all out, can we take sports back?

10   Part of the problem is that we want sports to be mythological when, in our hearts, we know they aren't. So reclaiming sports requires that we come to grips with our own role in the myth-making. Owens, Robinson, Smith, Carlos, and King played to our highest ideals and so have been enshrined in our sports pantheon. But we've also made heroes of some whose legacies are much less clear-cut. Take Joe Namath, the 1960s quarterback who represented sexual freedom, or Bill Walton, the 1970s basketball hippie who symbolized the alienated white suburban Grateful Dead sports antihero. Neither deserves the reverence accorded Owens or Robinson or even King, but both captured the essence of their era. Or how about relief pitcher Steve Howe, who symbolized the evils of drug addiction in the '80s, or Mike Tyson, who currently plays the archetypal angry black male? No less than Tommie Smith and John Carlos, these anti-icons were emblematic of their age.

11   It may be discomfiting, but it's true: The power of sports and sports heroes to mirror our own aspirations have also contributed to the sorry state of the institution today. The women's sports movement Billie Jean King helped create proved a great leap forward for female athletes, but it also created a generation of fitness *consumers,* whose appetite for Nikes and Reeboks created a new generation of Asian sweat-shops.

12   Fans applauded the courage of renegade Curt Flood, the St. Louis Cardinals outfielder who in 1969 refused to be traded, arguing that baseball players should be free to play where they want to play. We cheered—all the way to the Supreme Court—his challenge to the cigar-smoking owners' hold on their pinstripe-knick-ered chattel. Now players can sell their services to the highest bidder, but their astro-nomical salaries—deserved or not—alienate us from the games as much as the own-ers' greed.

13   The greed isn't new, of course. The corporate betrayal of the fan is as tradi-tional as the seventh-inning stretch. The Boston Braves moved to Milwaukee in 1953, and the Dodgers and New York Giants fled to California in 1958, for money, subsidized facilities, and better TV contracts. But what has always been a regret-table by-product of sports has suddenly become its dominant ethos. Our worship of sports and our worship of the buck have now become one and the same. So it shouldn't surprise us that we get the heroes we expect—and maybe deserve.

14   So how do we as a society reclaim sports from the corporate entertainment be-hemoth that now controls it? Some modest proposals:

15   • *Deprofessionalize college and high school sports.* Let's ban college athletic scholarships in favor of financial aid based on need, as for any other student. And let's keep high school athletics in perspective. Why should local news cov-erage of high school sports exceed coverage given to the band, debating society, or science fair? Sports stars are introduced to the culture of athletic privilege at a very young age.

16   • *Allow some form of public ownership of professional sports teams.* Leagues and owners ask us to pay for the depreciating asset of a stadium but give us no share of the appreciating asset of a franchise. Lease agreements between teams and

publicly financed stadiums should also include enforceable community-involvement clauses.

17 • *Make sports affordable again.* Sports owners call their games "family entertainment." For whose family? Bill Gates'? Owners whose teams get corporate subsidies should set aside 20 percent of their tickets at prices no higher than a movie admission. And, like any other business feeding at the public trough, they should be required to pay livable wages even to the average schmoes who sell hot dogs.

18 • *Be conscious of the messages sports are sending.* Alcohol-related advertising should be banned from sports broadcasting. Any male athlete convicted of assaulting a woman should be banned from college and pro sports. Fighting in a sports event should be at least a misdemeanor and maybe a felony, rather than a five-minute stay in the penalty box.

19 Let's take the sports establishment by its lapels and shake it back toward us. Because even with all the maddening messages of male dominance, black servility, homophobia, corporate power, commercialism, and brawn over brains, sports still play an important role in many lives. When we watch a game, we are surrounded by friends and family. There are snacks and beverages. We sit in awe of the players' remarkable skills. We can't do what they do. They extend our youth. The tension of the competition is legitimate. The drama is high.

20 And therein lies the essence of modern American sport. It's a good show, albeit bread and circuses. And we just can't give it up. So why not take it back for ourselves as best we can, looking for ways to humanize an institution that mirrors our culture, understanding that those who own sport won't give it up without a fight, knowing that we like it too much to ever just walk away. ◆

FREEWRITING ASSIGNMENT

What, according to Weiner, gives sports "meaning?" How have we "lost" the meaning in sports today? Explain.

CRITICAL READING

1. How, according to Weiner, have sports served our society? How have they forwarded social and political agendas? Explain.
2. Evaluate Weiner's modest proposal at the end of his essay. What steps are necessary to actualize his proposals? How plausible are they? If they could be successfully implemented, would they indeed "save" sports? Why or why not?
3. Is this essay fair and balanced, or does it present some bias in the argument? Analyze how Weiner's examples support his argument, and conversely, how his selective use of particular athletes may serve to weaken his argument.
4. Evaluate Weiner's examples of historic sports heroes with his list of current athletes. Can you identify any modern heroes that embody the social

and political revolutionizing spirit of past heroes, such as Robinson and
Owens? Explain.

5. What problems does free agency present the modern sports arena? Do you
agree or disagree with Weiner's assessment of this issue?

CRITICAL WRITING

6. *Research and Evaluation*: Weiner opens his essay by citing the history-
making actions of some great athletes of the past. Select one of these athletes and research how their sports-related heroism changed the social and
political landscape. In your essay, describe the long-term ramifications of
their actions. What imprint did they leave on their sport, and on our culture as a whole?

7. *Exploratory Writing*: How do sports act as an "institution that mirrors our
culture"? How do the actions of athletes, owners, franchises, and fans reflect greater society? Write an essay in which you explore the connection
between sports and society.

GROUP PROJECTS

8. Weiner presents a short list of remedies that he believes can help "save"
sports. As a group, compile your own list of solutions that you feel will
make sports better. If you wish, you can focus on college or professional
sporting issues. Explain why each "solution" you list is important and
why it is necessary. Share your list with the class for discussion.

9. Do sports heroes deserve the salaries and acclaim they currently receive?
Why or why not? Discuss this issue with the rest of the group, presenting
your personal perspective. Should athletes be held to higher standards
than other entertainers? Or do we hold our sports heroes to unfair standards? What are these standards? Explain.

Where Are the Heroes?
Ed Siegel

Would a composer of classical music be your first choice for a hero? Or would you wish to
emulate a painter or a playwright? If you are like most people, the answer to both questions is
"no." More likely, a sports hero would be your heroic first choice, especially if you are male
and under 25, or so argues *Boston Globe* arts critic Ed Siegel. Siegel laments that the world of

contemporary art has become so antiheroic that few people can relate to it. But there is one last place we can find true heroic behavior—on the athletic field.

Ed Siegel is a critic-at-large covering local arts and entertainment for the *Boston Globe*, in which this article first appeared on the morning of January 26, 1997—the day of Super Bowl XXXI. The New England Patriots met the Green Bay Packers at the Louisiana Super-dome. The Packers won the laurels by 14 points. Five years later, the New England Patriots would win Super Bowl XXXVI; and two years after that, Super Bowl XXXVIII.

CRITICAL THINKING   As a society, many of us raise athletes to the status of "hero." What is a hero? Why do so many people, especially youth, find their heroes on the basketball courts and football fields? Do they deserve this status? Why or why not?

1   Toward the end of his first "Young People's Concert" telecast in 1958, Leonard Bernstein played an excerpt from the finale of Tchaikovsky's Fifth Symphony, turned to a national audience and described the music this way: "The whole orchestra sounds joyful and triumphant, like someone who has just made a touchdown and is the hero of the football game."

2   As virtually the entire region, if not the nation, settles in front of their television sets at about 6 o'clock tonight for Super Bowl XXXI between the New England Patriots and the Green Bay Packers, hoping that Drew Bledsoe or Curtis Martin or Terry Glenn becomes the hero of this larger-than-life event, the last thing on anyone's mind will be Tchaikovsky's Fifth, or classical music—or any work of art.

3   That's a shame. That the world of professional sports and the world of contemporary art exist in separate orbits may seem like the natural state of affairs, but as Bernstein suggested, it wasn't always so. Arts organizations and their audiences may sneer at the amount of money and attention devoted to what is only, after all, a game. And they are right to lament how art of all kinds has been taken out of the schools, as well as bemoaning the media's continuing drift toward popular culture, the Republican sacking of national endowments and all the other reasons for their troubles.

4   It may be, though, that the art world sealed its own diminished fate when, not long after Tchaikovsky's Fifth was first performed in 1888, modernists began to reject the heroic ideal as a primary topic for artistic consideration. If, as mythologist and folklorist Joseph Campbell suggested, we are all drawn to the hero's adventure as a universal myth, is it any wonder that we turn to sports and turn away from contemporary art to see those myths played out? Particularly when the idea of heroism has also been erased from public life, be it politics, religion or the media?

5   Sports is one of the last places where those myths can be experienced. One of the reasons the Patriots are in the Super Bowl, for example, is because they won their final regular-season game, which led to a first-round bye and home-field advantage in the playoffs. Few fans at halftime of that game thought the Patriots had a chance. They were losing, 22–0, to the New York Giants, and the mood was akin to

the beginning of that Tchaikovsky symphony—"sad and gloomy and depressed" in Bernstein's words.

6   In order to win, the Patriots had to summon up every ounce of heroism as individuals and as a collective. The punt-return team had to block impeccably to free Dave Meggett for a stunning touchdown return. Bledsoe had to be fearless against Giants trying to crush him, and he had to throw perfect passes, including the winning one to Ben Coates, who may have surprised even himself by getting into the end zone with three tacklers hanging onto him. And the defense had to play as if divinely possessed.

7   There was, in that second half, almost everything that we get from myth—selflessness, determination, ingenuity, courage, nobility. Even if those myths are played out in terms of brute strength and athletic achievement, they are still metaphors for the human struggle, just as are those in "Ulysses," either the Homer or James Joyce version.

8   Can those myths be found today in the music of Pierre Boulez? The plays of David Mamet? The paintings of Willem De Kooning? This isn't to say that these artists don't have other things to offer or that it was undesirable to undermine the bombast of Wagnerian opera and romantic literature.

9   The question is whether too much of contemporary art has gone too far in divorcing itself from mythic and heroic concerns. In a 1995 lecture at Massachusetts Institute of Technology, in acceptance of the Killian Faculty Achievement Award, Pulitzer Prize-winning composer John Harbison welcomed "the end of a historical period, an interesting one but not always the best one for the production of works of music, a sort of heroic age, which I call the 'Masterpiece Age.' "

10   Granted, not every piece of music has to be a soundtrack for a Patriots' victory, and not every novel and play has to touch on universal myth. But Harbison, who has written distinguished music, speaks to the problems that the arts face today. If the arts are alienated from striving toward some ideal, then doesn't it stand to reason that potential patrons will be alienated from the arts?

11   When Eugene O'Neill, in "Long Day's Journey Into Night," changed Shakespeare's quote from "We are such stuff as dreams are made on" to "We are such stuff as manure is made on," he was shouldering a banner for a tough and bold standard of how art would measure human life. O'Neill's is quite likely the best play written in this country, but its call to anti-heroic arms speaks volumes about why people shrink from contemporary art.

12   The concept of heroism hasn't exactly disappeared and has even gone through some fascinating permutations in Joyce and elsewhere. There is May Sarton's great quote, "One must think like a hero to behave like a merely decent human being." John le Carré used that in his epigraph to "The Russia House" and Tom Stoppard incorporated it in his screenplay of the novel.

13   Another Pulitzer Prize-winning composer, the late Stephen Albert, believed that we have lost the narrative thread to our lives and that abstraction in 20th-century art was part of the problem. Albert and Yo-Yo Ma both won Grammys for one of his final compositions, the Cello Concerto, which reconnected the thread. As Ma says in the liner notes, "It is like one of the old romantic concertos—an autobiography of

the wounded hero. This music is in the strongest sense personal and soulful, and it takes us through the same emotional journey Stephen was going through when he composed it."

14   You can find similar hero's journeys in John Corigliano's Symphony No. 1, the plays of Athol Fugard, the jazz of Wynton Marsalis or Abdullah Ibrahim. But by and large, the idea of art as heroic seems to be acceptable only in pursuit of a political issue.

15   One of the few other places besides sports we can regularly turn to for heroes is pop culture—rock music and film in particular. The divide between so-called high art and pop art was symbolized a few weeks ago in a *New York Times* classical-music column. Bernard Holland announced he had little desire to see the movie "Shine" because of the triviality of the music it showcased—Rachmaninoff's Third Piano Concerto.

16   He has a point, in that the piece does symbolize the dull excesses of romanticism, but the reason the movie is such a huge arthouse hit is because both David Helfgott's life and the music are mythic in nature. Helfgott, of course, had to fight back from mental illness. And imagine if he had been rehearsing something like Anton Webern's "Variations for Piano." Audiences would have said that's why he flipped out, as they were leaving the theater halfway through the movie.

17   There are variations of heroism everywhere you look in movies, ranging from the light entertainment of "Jerry Maguire" to "Hamlet" to "Secrets and Lies." Movies go too far in the other direction, making something heroic out of everything, even such questionable figures as Eva Peron and such unquestionably unheroic figures as Larry Flynt.

18   Rock music has its share of unsavory "heroes" as well, particularly gangsta rappers. But Bruce Springsteen, Beck and the ex-Prince all give their fans a heroic pose along with relatively sophisticated content. And it's not an all-boys' myth-making club anymore, either, as Madonna, Queen Latifah, Alanis Morissette and Joan Osborne can attest to. Whatever you think of their music, all four of these women speak to taking charge of their lives, and it's easy to see why they are heroes to their fans.

19   But sports still seems to be the pop-culture form that possesses many of the noblest attributes we used to look to high art to illuminate, despite the increasing thuggery professional sports tolerates and the free agency that makes a joke out of the idea of loyalty.

20   Still, only on rare occasions like the tearing down of the Berlin Wall, has a performance of Beethoven's Ninth so captured the ideals of that music, as well as the aftermath of the Celtics beating the Philadelphia 76ers in the seventh game of their semifinal series in 1981 by one point. Perfect strangers were hugging each other on Causeway Street in celebration.

21   The world doesn't offer us many heroes anymore, so Mayor Thomas M. Menino had better beware, even if the Patriots don't win today. If the team leaves the city, it won't matter how many good things he does in office. If the Cleveland Patriots are in some future Super Bowl, Menino will always be remembered as the villain who forced the heroes out of the city.

22   Win or lose, the Patriots have already spoken to us about what most of us strive for—working well with other people, interracial harmony, determination, fortitude, and, most of all, a sense that we can all share in something larger than ourselves. The art world should take note:

23   Look down your nose if you want. If the Patriots win today, I'll be celebrating with a fifth of Tchaikovsky. ◆

FREEWRITING ASSIGNMENT

Make a list of the qualities that you think fit the definition of a hero, and write about why one, or several, of these qualities are particularly heroic to you.

CRITICAL READING

1. What makes the Patriots' victory in the playoff game against the Giants particularly heroic? For Siegel, how does this game represent many of the qualities found in heroic myth?
2. Discuss the difference between Shakespeare's line, "We are such stuff as dreams are made on," and O'Neill's representation, "We are such stuff as manure is made on" (paragraph 11). What do each of these lines suggest about the nature of humanity? How do they support Siegel's point?
3. Summarize Siegel's thesis. How well does he support this thesis? Explain.
4. Do you agree with Siegel that movies have gone too far in making heroes of such "questionable figures as Eva Peron and . . . Larry Flynt" (paragraph 17)? Who else would you add to the list of people who have been unjustifiably glamorized by the movies?

CRITICAL WRITING

5. *Exploratory Writing*: Siegel argues that sports allow us to "share in something larger than ourselves." Write an essay developing this idea. Use examples from your own experience, the articles in this chapter, and personal research and evaluation to support your perspective.
6. *Persuasive Writing*: Siegel feels that sports offer the public an arena to see heroes and heroic behavior. However, many stories about sports figures focus on their misdeeds—drug abuse, gambling, sexual escapades, violent behavior, and egotistical temper tantrums. Write an essay discussing whether you think the media's reporting of athletes' foibles has gone too far, or if this scrutiny is necessary to avoid blind hero worship.
7. *Personal Narrative*: Write a narrative about a sporting event—either one you watched or one in which you participated—where you feel the athletes demonstrated heroic behavior. What qualities did the team's players display that made for an uplifting experience? How did the crowd react?

GROUP PROJECTS

8. Throughout his essay, Siegel argues that the modern arts—particularly drama, art, and music—have failed to offer audiences works that celebrate human achievement and possibility, thus alienating audiences. Because of this alienation, audiences turn to sports and popular culture figures for role models. Research Siegel's theory. As a group, visit a local museum featuring a modern art exhibit, or attend a dramatic or musical production. Discuss your reactions to the experience. Did different group members react to the experience in different ways? After discussing your impressions, each group member should write a brief essay about how he or she felt about their cultural experience. (Refer back to the essay in your discussion.)

9. Many athletes advertise products ranging from sneakers to soft drinks to mutual fund companies. Discuss the use of athletes in advertising. Watch several different channels, including sports networks, and list as many advertisements featuring athletes as you can. Combine your personal list with the rest of the group. What is the appeal of athletes pitching products in our culture? Share your collective viewpoint with the rest of the class for discussion on this issue.

Point/Counterpoint—Title IX: The Battle of the Sexes Continues

Mary Ann Cooper

Since Title IX became law, it has been instrumental in increasing women's educational opportunities. In 1971, 18 percent of female high school graduates completed at least four years of college, as compared to 26 percent of male high school graduates. Today, there is no longer an education gap. In fact, women now make up the majority of students in America's colleges and universities, a statistic many credit to Title IX. While Title IX centers on equal educational opportunity, it is most known for the debate it generates regarding athletics. In this article, Mary Ann Cooper explores the arguments made for and against reforming this landmark legislation—arguments spurred largely by issues connected to college sports. This article appeared in *Hispanic Outlook in Higher Education*, July 13, 2003.

CRITICAL THINKING Should men's and women's programs receive equal financial support and provide students with equal opportunities to participate? Is a law necessary to ensure that women are provided opportunities to participate in athletic programs and receive athletic scholarships? Why or why not?

1 Thirty years after its creation, the future of Title IX is the subject of heated debate. While the statute is best known for increasing the number of female athletes and sports teams, it actually is a federal law that prohibits sex discrimination in education. Here is the actual language of the statute:

2 "No person in the United States shall, on the basis of sex, be excluded from participation in, be denied the benefits of, or be subjected to discrimination under any education program or activity receiving Federal financial assistance."

3 Since its passage, the prohibition against being "excluded from participation" in "any education program or activity" has opened the door to many educational opportunities for females, but an increase in sports programs for women has attracted the most controversy. When the Commission on Opportunity in Athletics raised the possibility of reforming the act—a move embraced by the Bush administration—the war of words began. Here are some of the key arguments for and against revising Title IX as it currently exists.

Title IX Is Only About Sports Programs

4 Both sides agree that Title IX is broad-based and deals with outlawing discrimination in educational opportunity. Title IX opponents believe that it has been co-opted by feminists with a political agenda to secure more scholarship money for women at the expense of men. Proponents assert that Title IX merely attempts to level the playing field throughout the education experience without harming male opportunities. According to the Department of Education, in 1999 to 2000, women were awarded 43 percent of the degrees in medicine and 46 percent of the law degrees. As a comparison, in 1972 to 1973 those percentages were 9 and 8 percent.

Title IX Penalizes Male Athletes and Universities

5 Opponents point to the fact that since passage of Title IX, 171 college wrestling teams have been cut (according to the National Wrestling Coaches Association), representing 40 percent of the national total. Proponents contend that the Government Accounting Office report issued in March 2001 at the behest of House Speaker Dennis Hastert showed that, indeed, some men's sports programs had been slashed, but were replaced with new programs. In all, men's sports programs actually increased between 1982 and 1999, a net gain of 36 new men's teams. Despite some high-profile exceptions, most men's football and basketball programs run at a deficit. College and university athletic programs don't generate enough income to pay for themselves. They certainly don't generate enough revenue to fund other sports. The GAO also reports that for every two sports initiatives launched for women, men were afforded 1.5 additional sports opportunities. Proponents also argue that nothing in the Title IX guidelines dictates that schools shut down male sports programs in favor of women's programs. However, opponents insist that the allocation of funds between women's programs and men's programs makes the elimination of programs a fact of life.

Title IX Is Nothing But a Sexual Quota Program

6 Use of the word "proportionality" infuriates opponents of Title IX as it currently exists. This term is used to describe one of the tests of compliance, which dictates that the number of female athletes should be in direct proportion to the number of females in an institution. If the female student population numbers 60 percent, then 60 percent of the student-athletes at that school should be female. Proponents say that "proportionality" is only one of three tests for compliance. Another test is of the institution's history of expanding athletic programs for women and a plan to continue that practice. The third test is evidence that the school is taking a special interest in addressing the needs and abilities of its female athletes. Opponents concede this is true, but insist that the Department of Education has singled out proportionality and used it as its sole criterion for compliance. Proponents refute that claim by pointing to the records of the Office of Civil Rights, which show that of the 74 cases it handled between 1994 and 1998 involving disputes over Title IX's implementation, only 21 schools were using proportionality as their method of compliance.

Title IX Proves Men Play Sports More Than Women Do

7 Proponents contend that women athletes are every bit as much a part of the sports scenes as men athletes are; opponents says there is no reasonable way to measure that claim. They instead point to their own anecdotal reasoning to support their position. Conservative columnist Phyllis Schlafly opined in one of her recent columns, "It's a fact of human nature that female college students do not seek to play on athletic teams in anywhere near the percentage that male students do. Furthermore, a significant percentage of the female college population is made up of 're-entry' women. They are older women who return to college after their children are grown or after divorce, and they surely aren't going to college to play basketball or soccer." Proponents of Title IX point to Department of Education statistics which point to fewer than 32,000 women being involved in collegiate sports prior to the passage of Title IX. Today that number is more than 150,000, proving, they say, that "If you build it, they will come" (to paraphrase "Field of Dreams").

Title IX Is Not Needed Any Longer

8 Opponents insist that while Title IX has afforded women many educational opportunities, we are living in a different world than that of 1972 when the law was first passed. Proponents point to the fact that women still receive $133 million less in athletic scholarships than men do, proving that there is still a long way to go. Opponents applaud the January 2003 report to Education Secretary Rod Paige recommending changes in the interpretation of Title IX compliance tests and procedures to allow schools more "flexibility" in implementing Title IX at their institutions. Proponents see changing Title IX's regulations as a way to take the teeth out of this 30-year-old program to make it ineffective. The ball is in Secretary Paige's court as the Bush administration weighs its options. ◆

CRITICAL READING

1. Cooper presents her essay as a point/counterpoint; that is, she lists an objection to Title IX, and then provides responses to it. Evaluate this technique. Can you tell the author's opinion on the issue of restructuring Title IX? Explain.
2. What is "proportionality"? Do you think that athletic programs should be based on proportionality? Why or why not?
3. Conservative columnist Phyllis Schlafly stated that "it's a fact of human nature that female college students do not seek to play on athletic teams in anywhere near the percentage that male students do." Is this indeed a fact or an opinion? If it were indeed fact, should that have a bearing on Title IX?
4. What could happen if title IX were reformed? In your opinion, should it stay as is, or should it be changed? If so, in what ways?
5. In your opinion, was the implementation of Title IX necessary thirty years ago? Is it necessary today? Refer to information Cooper provides in her article to support your response.
6. Cooper subtitles her piece "The Battle of the Sexes Continues." Does this title reflect your campus' attitude toward Title IX and sports programs? Is it indeed a "battle"? Or do students seem to agree that sports programs are important to both sexes? Explain.

CRITICAL WRITING

7. *Research and Analysis*: Research the history of Title IX. Why was it passed and what does it protect/guarantee? Arrange an interview with a coach in your athletic department to discuss Title IX. How has this piece of legislation changed the athletic program in your school over the last 30 years? Would your life be any different if Title IX had not been implemented in 1972?
8. Cooper lists five objections that opponents to Title IX have made in their effort to reform the federal law. Interview at least ten students on the issue of Title IX. Ask them what they know about it, and if they think it is a necessary law. Separate their responses into either for or against the law, and create your own point/counterpoint essay following Cooper's format of point/counterpoint.

GROUP PROJECTS

9. Cooper's title refers to the famous tennis match between Billie Jean King and Bobby Riggs in 1973. Research this tennis match and the media attention leading up to it. In addition to Internet research, discuss the event with people who were adults in the early 1970s for their memory of the match. Why was the match so hyped? Would a similar match, say between John McEnroe and Venus Williams, have the same implications to-

day? After discussing these questions with your group, write a short paper on your research, highlighting your group's opinion of the event, and its impact on sports culture today.

10. Visit several sports-related web sites, such as ESPN.com and sportsillus-trated.com, and locate some articles about women in sports. Are the stories about female athletes parallel to the reporting on male athletes? Are women judged by similar or different criteria? If photographs accompany the articles, do they parallel photographs of men (action shots, etc.)? Discuss your findings.

▶ **Just Say No to Random Drug Testing**
David Rocah

▶ **Naïve Court Didn't Go Far Enough with Drug Testing**
Claude Lewis

Most people will agree that athletics and drugs are a bad mix. Drug use impairs academic and athletic performance, encourages antisocial behavior, and may even lead to crime. Some schools are turning to mandatory drug testing of athletes to curtail the problem. In 1997, the American Civil Liberties Union (ACLU) filed suit against the Ridgefield Park Board of Education on behalf of Bryan Wilson, a Ridgefield Park High School student. Wilson had played on the football team during his first two years of high school but was barred from continuing because he refused to agree to random drug testing. A preliminary injunction prohibited the school district from conducting the tests until a trial could be held.

In the first essay in this section, David Rocah, representing the ACLU, explains why they felt compelled to defend this case. The case never was tried. In 1998, the Ridgefield Park Board of Education agreed to rescind the policy on the advice of Judge Sybil R. Moses, who found that the school district had no evidence of a more severe drug problem among student athletes, and, thus, had not demonstrated a sufficient need for the random drug testing program. The policy could be reimplemented, however, if a serious drug problem among students could later be demonstrated.

In the next article, columnist Claude Lewis presents a different view, arguing that drug testing shouldn't be limited to just athletes; all students should be randomly tested for drugs, for their own safety as well as the general population.

David Rocah is a staff attorney with the American Civil Liberties Union of New Jersey. The following article was published online on the ACLU's webzine, *Voices of Liberty*.

Claude Lewis has worked as a writer and editor for many publications including *Newsweek*, the *New York Herald Tribune*, and the *Philadelphia Inquirer*. He is also the founder of the National Association of Black Journalists. Lewis is the author of six books, including a biography of Muhammad Ali. Now retired, he still writes a column twice a month for the *Philadelphia Inquirer*.

CRITICAL
THINKING
Would you sign a random drug testing agreement with your school's athletic department in order to play sports?

Just Say No to Random Drug Testing
David Rocah

In our system, state-operated schools may not be enclaves of totalitarianism. School officials do not possess absolute authority over their students. Students in school as well as out of school are "persons" under our Constitution.

—Justice Abe Fortas, *Tinker* v. *Des Moines* (1969)

1 Ridgefield Park, like at least nine other school districts in New Jersey, recently decided that it would not permit its junior and senior high school students to participate in interscholastic sports unless they agreed to have their urine tested for traces of certain illicit drugs at random intervals during the athletic season. Because we believe that this intrusive and demeaning search of students' bodily fluids violates fundamental constitutional principles, the American Civil Liberties Union of New Jersey is representing a student and his parents in a legal challenge to the Ridgefield Park program.

2 One of the fundamental features of our legal system is that we are presumed innocent of any wrongdoing unless and until the government proves otherwise. Random drug testing of student athletes turns this presumption on its head, telling students that we assume they are using drugs until they prove to the contrary with a urine sample. The overwhelming majority of student athletes in Ridgefield Park, and throughout New Jersey, are law abiding citizens, and there is no basis in law or logic to presume otherwise or to treat them worse than accused criminals.

3 An equally cherished constitutional command is the rule that government officials may not search us without an adequate reason. Thus, for example, even though we know there is a drug problem in our society, we do not allow the police to randomly stop us on the street to see if we are carrying drugs.

4 The constitutional prohibition against "unreasonable" searches also embodies the principle that merely belonging to a certain group is not a sufficient reason for a search, even if many members of that group are suspected of illegal activity. Thus, for example, even if it were true that most men with long hair were drug users, the police would not be free to stop all long-haired men and search them for drugs.

5 Unfortunately, many school officials concerned about drug use by students seem willing to ignore these principles. There is no doubt that the concern is well-placed, and it is one that we share. Drug use is a scourge on our society, exacting a terrible toll in lost lives. And no one is arguing that we should tolerate students' use of illegal drugs. But zero tolerance for drugs should not lead us to have zero tolerance for constitutional limits. Sadly, that is exactly what is happening.

6   Parents and school officials currently have a wide variety of tools at their disposal to address drug use by students. Educating students about the dangers of drug use can be highly effective. A recent study by the Parent's Resource Institute for Drug Education shows that students who are warned about drugs by their parents use them 30 percent less often than those who are not, and students who said their parents set "clear rules" regarding drugs used them 57 percent less than those whose parents did not.

7   In addition, school officials currently have the power to require any student whom they reasonably suspect of using drugs to submit to a drug test. Indeed, if the affidavits submitted in court by the Ridgefield Park School Board are to be believed, school officials there have been grossly irresponsible in failing to act when they had reason to suspect particular students were using drugs. Not only did they not conduct drug tests, there is no indication that they even informed the parents of their suspicions.

8   Acting on the basis of individual suspicion ensures both that hundreds of innocent children are not subjected to a degrading search, and demonstrates that school officials care about all students who use drugs, not just student athletes. The Board also could have implemented a truly voluntary drug testing program, rather than coercing parents to consent by denying their children the opportunity to participate in interscholastic athletics. Had the Board done so, it is likely that no one would have objected, and the ACLU could not and would not have challenged it.

9   Given these tools, which, when employed vigorously can be an effective and constitutional means of dealing with drug use by the entire student body, why are school districts resorting to random drug testing of athletes? Because they improperly read a 1995 U.S. Supreme Court decision as giving them carte blanche. In a case involving a school district in Vernonia, Oregon, the Court decided that the district could constitutionally require student athletes to submit to random drug testing where officials testified that they were no longer able to maintain discipline in the school system because of a culture of pervasive drug use and disrespect for authority, and where student athletes were the leaders of the drug culture.

10   Are the parents and administrators in Ridgefield Park prepared to admit that they cannot maintain order and discipline in their schools? There is no evidence of this, and we would be surprised if it were so. Ridgefield Park has a fine school system, which sent 73 percent of its graduates to college last year.

11   Are student athletes leaders of the drug culture? Although the Ridgefield Park School Board's court papers scandalously attempted to portray its student athletes as a pack of drug addled alcoholics, these same athletes won state championships in football for the past two years. Nationally, student athletes have been found to have higher academic achievement and fewer disciplinary problems than nonathletes, due in large part to the tremendous discipline required to balance a full academic program and the time demanded by practice and competition schedules. Singling out athletes in New Jersey because of a problem in Vernonia, Oregon, is both ridiculous and unfair.

12   School officials argue that random drug testing will deter drug use. But students should not use drugs because they are harmful and illegal, not because they might get caught. Moreover, random drug testing simply encourages students to defer drug

use until after the athletic season is completed, rather than completely refraining from drug use.

13   School officials also argue that participating in interscholastic athletics is a privilege, not a right, and that they may therefore impose any conditions on the exercise of that privilege that they see fit. This ignores the well-established constitutional doctrine that the government may not condition the receipt of a governmental benefit on the waiver of constitutional rights. Just as a school could not condition participation in interscholastic athletics on students giving up their right to free speech, they also may not condition participation on students giving up their right to be free from unreasonable searches.

14   Some also argue that students who aren't doing anything wrong have nothing to fear. This ignores the fact that what they fear is not getting caught, but the loss of dignity and trust that the drug test represents. And we should all be afraid of government officials who believe that a righteous cause warrants setting aside bedrock constitutional protections. The lesson that our schools should be teaching is respect for the Constitution and for students' dignity and privacy, not a willingness to treat cherished constitutional principles as mere platitudes. ◆

Naïve Court Didn't Go Far Enough with Drug Testing
Claude Lewis

1   This nation has so badly botched the war on drugs that I find myself in painful agreement with a Supreme Court ruling that public schools can require students to take drug tests as a condition of playing sports.

2   Indeed, my concern for an end to the devastation of drug abuse and addiction is so great that I find myself wondering why such tests should be restricted to athletes. Why not apply the pain all at once and permit random testing of all students? If such draconian solutions are necessary, why single out those who play sports? What about the millions of other students who don't? Should they not be required to undergo random drug tests?

3   Random drug testing is the antithesis of a free society. Yet, I am persuaded that since the drug problem is so pervasive, destructive and corrupt, and since the government has failed so miserably for so long in ending its corrosive effects, we have few alternatives other than poking our noses in places where they don't belong.

4   When it comes to drugs, we have reached a point where the only cure may have to be worse than the disease. We "must" take the strongest possible action to protect the young and the unsuspecting.

5   Most Americans have never seen firsthand the powerful and depraved activity in the world of illicit drugs. I have talked with addicts for years and have witnessed the demise and deaths of countless young men and women who were unable to end their enslavement.

6   I have seen young people with old faces, the result of persistent experimenting with drugs. Because government has failed at containing addiction and our nation has no sure method of treating the army of addicts living among us, extreme measures must be adopted.

7   No longer is it possible, if it ever was, to accept the pathetic lie that drug addicts exist mainly in the inner city. The problem has grown so great that in almost any community, children and errant adults can locate drugs within a half-hour of their homes.

8   If the court's decision is, as some say, a victory, it is one of the saddest victories I can imagine. It is distressing that we must resort to limiting Fourth Amendment privacy rights to student athletes in order to protect them from the danger of drugs. Students spend more time in school than in any other institution outside their homes. And it is the school where initial exposure to illegal drugs often takes place.

9   The irony in all this is that it is not the students who have failed, but the adults who are responsible for them. In Washington, the court's ruling was met with wide acceptance among young athletes.

10   Others argue if there's no reason to suspect illegal drug use, students should not be subjected to random testing. Such notions were valid in another era. No more.

11   How else do we begin to get at the problem? Drug education is good but won't provide a total solution. Education must be a part of the solution along with other firm approaches. Few of us come new to this problem. America is one of the world's most drug-dependent nations and the problem threatens to grow worse.

12   An enormous number of crimes committed every year—from petty thefts to bank robberies to murders—are connected to addiction.

13   Supreme Court Justice Sandra Day O'Connor holds a naïve notion on the matter, calling the collection of urine samples "particularly destructive of privacy and offensive to personal dignity."

14   What could be more offensive to personal dignity than addiction itself? The court's ruling may contain some frightening implications, but not nearly as frightening as the growing new armies of addicts who will poison the future of many young people for generations. ◆

FREEWRITING ASSIGNMENT

Does drug testing assume guilt until innocence is proven? How does drug testing apply to the rights guaranteed U.S. citizens by the Constitution? Does the Bill of Rights apply to the drug testing of athletes?

CRITICAL READING

1. Rocah comments that the "overwhelming majority of student athletes are law-abiding citizens, and there is no basis to presume otherwise." If this is true, why do you think Ridgefield Park decided to implement a drug testing policy? If this statement were not true, would it then be permissible to test students for drug abuse?

2. Evaluate Rocah's argument in paragraph 8. Can Rocah project what people will and will not object to? Does he make other statements in his article in which he anticipates group opinions? What effect does this have on his overall argument?

3. Rocah points out that 73 percent of Ridgefield Park's graduates went on to college in 1996. He also claims that student athletes have higher academic achievement rates than nonathletes do. How might these statements be red herrings? Do they strengthen or weaken his argument? Explain.

4. In paragraph 4, Lewis says that drug testing is necessary to "protect the young and unsuspecting." Do today's students and athletes fit this description? How would you respond to Lewis's statement?

5. If most Americans have "never seen" the world of illicit drugs (paragraph 5), is drug testing really needed? Or is it necessary only for some areas and some groups, such as athletes? How might Lewis's statement be used to argue *against* his point?

6. Evaluate the tone of each article. Is it angry, militant, resigned, sad? How does tone contribute to the message of the arguments?

7. Why does Lewis think the court's decision is "one of the saddest victories I can imagine"? Do you agree? Explain your viewpoint.

CRITICAL WRITING

8. *Exploratory Writing*: Are student athletes the leaders of the drug culture in academic institutions? Write an essay addressing this issue. Support your essay with information from the articles in this section, your personal experience, and outside research on this topic.

9. *Personal Narrative*: Have you ever been forced to take a drug test to participate in an athletic event? If so, write about this experience. If not, consider your feelings and reactions if you were asked to perform such a test. Explain in a personal narrative why you would, or would not, agree to take a drug test in order to participate on a sports team or in an athletic event.

10. From the standpoint of a school administrator, write a letter to parents in which you explain why the school will be implementing a mandatory drug-testing program for student athletes. Frame your argument by drawing from information gathered from the essays in this section as well as from personal experience. How do you address the controversial aspects of this issue? What approach would you take to avoid the most conflict?

11. Research the drug-testing policies of the NFL and/or the NBA. Find examples of policy violations. How were the violations dealt with and what was the penalty for breaking the rules? Did the punishment fit the crime? Explain.

GROUP PROJECTS

12. What is the objective behind the drug testing of athletes (and all students in general)? Are athletes the logical population to routinely test for drug

abuse? Why or why not? Survey college students and college administrators for their response to this question. After conducting your survey, discuss the data you collect as a group. Are there differences between the athletes' responses and the administrators'? Did any of the responses surprise you? If so, why?

13. Ridgefield Park dropped its drug-testing policy when faced with a lawsuit. Ridgefield Park football coach Tony Gonzalez expressed that he was "one thousand percent in favor" of mandatory drug screening because it gave student-athletes a way to counter peer pressure to drink alcohol or do drugs at parties. "It gives them an out . . . they can say, if I get tested I lose football." Write a group essay in which you address the pros and cons of mandatory drug testing from a student's perspective. Consider Gonzalez's comment when framing your evaluation.

RESEARCH ISSUE **Lighten Up, Parents!**
Michael L. Sachs

Youth sports can instill social and team-building skills, self-reliance, and confidence. But they can also drive parents to the edge. Television newscasts report incidents of parental violence at youth sporting events with distressing frequency. Are parents getting out of control? Michael L. Sachs is a sports psychologist and a professor in the department of kinesiology at Temple University. He is co-author of *The Total Sports Experience for Kids: A Parents' Guide to Success in Youth Sports.* This story appeared in the November 2000 issue of *USA Today Magazine.*

1   On July 5, 2000, in Reading, Massachusetts, Thomas Junta beat Michael Costin to the point that he died two days later from his injuries. Junta has been charged with manslaughter and, if found guilty, could serve up to 20 years in prison.

2   Why did he attack Costin? Junta apparently thought that the hockey game in which his son and Costin's sons were playing (Costin was supervising the practice) had gotten too rough. The two men had an argument about this, and Junta was asked to leave the rink. He came back, however, and attacked Costin. If only he had stayed away, Costin, the single father of four young children, might be alive today.

3   Sports psychologists have long been concerned about what has been labeled "Little League parent syndrome" (LLPS), named for those adults who get so wrapped up in their children's play that they yell and scream verbal abuse and, occasionally, get physically abusive. More recently, with the Reading example as exhibit A, things seemingly have gotten more violent. There have always been cases of parents and coaches, referees, or other parents getting into verbal and, sometimes, physical confrontations. Indeed, parents have even had physical contact with players on their offspring's and opposing teams. However, this is the first instance within memory where death has been the result of such an altercation.

4   How is this possible? What are parents doing intruding on their youngsters' games? These are, after all, children's games, whether baseball, soccer, hockey, football, swimming, whatever. Adults should be there in a supportive role, helping the kids enjoy the best experience they could possibly have, not creating, as too often happens, a pressure-filled, unhappy situation for all concerned.

5   It is important to note that LLPS is symptomatic of only a minority of parents (although the percentage seems to be growing each year). This minority is adept, though, at making youth sports an unpleasant experience for all. These parents expect perfection from their children, coaches, and referees. While winning may be at the top of their priority list, playing time for their offspring is critical.

6   A task-oriented approach is required—can't let fun get in the way of winning! Youth sports is a stressful time with victory the only acceptable result, and even there, playing time and quality play on the part of the youngster is expected.

7   These parents have forgotten why their kids are participating in the first place. What do children say when you ask them why they play? The number-one reason is to have fun! This is so critical that it cannot be overemphasized. Youth sports is a voluntary activity, and it should be a place where youngsters can be supported in a chance to play. When kids play, they're supposed to have fun.

8   Children also say they want to improve their skills and get some exercise and/or stay in shape. Kids like to play with their friends and make new friends. Winning is way down on the list, ranking tenth. The source for these reasons is a survey of 10,000 students and their feelings about sports, published by the American Footwear Association.

9   Sports psychologists and sociologists lament the tremendous decrease in informal play. Many of you remember the days when you would come home after school and then hurry back outside to be with your friends on your block or at a local park. You had special games, many similar to those of kids in other areas, but with slightly different names and rules, depending on the neighborhood. You had a chance to be active, have a challenging game, have everyone play (from the highly skilled kid to the less-skilled), and decide on the roles and make decisions as the game progressed. You had to learn to negotiate so that everyone got in the game and all felt a part of the process. If not, the game would disintegrate, and no one could play.

10   Nowadays, what is called formal play has taken over. Rarely does one see informal play going on anymore. (When was the last time you saw kids playing on your street or at your local park or playground, or at least saw many of them doing so?) Because of safety concerns, families where both parents are wage earners, and a drive to get children into organized leagues so they can learn the game faster and be on the road toward fame and fortune, the move, in many cases, has been to organized youth sport leagues. These can still be fun for youngsters, but in many instances are not.

11   Children often feel pressured to succeed. Asking your offspring "Did you win today" indicates that winning is important. It really is not important in youth sports! Trying to win is certainly part of the experience. But it doesn't or shouldn't matter whether they win or lose. There's always another game tomorrow and another chance to try to win. More important is the chance to be active and have fun with friends.

12   What should a parent ask? How about "Did you have fun today?" "Did you have a good time?" or "What did you learn today?" All these are good alternatives and send the right message.

13   When kids wrote what they liked and didn't like about youth sports and their parents' roles, the youngsters indicated that parents do good things (like being supportive), but they often put too much pressure on their offspring, are critical, and behave in ways that embarrass them. You probably have seen parents act in a matter that is quite embarrassing. How do you think their children feel when they see their parents acting so foolishly?

14   Why would parents behave this way? They may feel pressured (although they shouldn't), given that they may be investing considerable time and money in Johnny or Susie's activity. They may have hopes or expectations that their child will one day be an Olympic gold medalist, professional athlete, or, at the very least, earn a scholarship to college. Most parents really don't realize what a minuscule percentage attains such stardom. Even if they are aware of this, they also know that a select few do make it, so why can't that one person be their son or daughter?

15   Parents may feel their offspring's performance is a reflection on them—if Johnny or Susie plays poorly, I must be seen as a bad parent. Some adults may be living vicariously through their kids' athletic accomplishments. The parents could never achieve the level of excellence they see in their children, and their youngsters' success (read winning) means they can vicariously bask in the glory that has been achieved.

16   There are many reasons, therefore, why parents may act the way they do. These may help us to understand them, but it is still difficult to grasp why parents would become verbally and, especially, physically abusive. In some cases, role models like former Indiana University basketball coach Bob Knight make it seem all right to be abusive—but it is not all right! Parents would not want to be treated that way, and they have no right to do so to children, coaches, and referees.

17   Success in youth sports does not necessarily mean winning. Rather, it means having put out 100% effort and done the best you could on a given day. Winning a Little League baseball game or youth soccer game does not really matter; giving all that you can and doing the best you can are what is important. Learning that playing sports means trying your hardest, playing fairly (sportsmanship), and having fun are the messages we should be sending. Parents are guests at youth sports and should be supporters of their children, not adding pressure to kids' already hectic lives of school, sports, music lessons, etc.

18   What can be done to stem the growth in the number of LLPS adults? In Jupiter, Fla., parents are required to take a sportsmanship course developed by the National Alliance for Youth Sports and sign a code of conduct. This will surely be seen elsewhere as other youth sports associations adopt this strategy. Violate the code of conduct (e.g., be verbally abusive, threaten others, interfere with the game) and you are ejected from the game and prohibited from attending the next one. Should you commit further infractions, your child doesn't play. Refuse to sign, and your child doesn't play.

19   This general approach is eminently reasonable. Many youth sport groups may simply be able to review with parents what expectations are for appropriate behavior from them, as well as players, coaches, and referees. That will be enough for many

groups. Others, especially those with past problems in this area (a surplus of LLPS parents!), may need to move toward signing such a code of conduct or even requiring such a class before signing the code. These steps may be necessary to make it perfectly clear to parents that these are their children's games, and adults are there to support the kids, not create conflict.

20 It is not hard to find examples in one's neighborhood of the LLPS adult. As has been seen in the papers all too often recently, the level of violence may be escalating. (Some of it is a result of increased media attention. Physical confrontations—especially between parents and referees or coaches—have been going on for decades.)

21 It is to be hoped that the death of a parent such as Michael Costin is a unique occurrence, never to happen again. To assure this, parents and youth sport supporters must control their behavior as well as that of people with whom they work and play. ◆

CRITICAL THINKING

1. According to Sachs, why are parents "intruding" on their children's games? Why are they acting violently toward other parents, coaches, and referees?

2. In what ways have organized sports changed children's play? Are children's sports different from the way they were 10, 20, or 30 years ago? Explain.

3. What recommendations does Sachs make to help control parents? Do you think his recommendations are feasible? Why or why not?

RESEARCH PROJECTS

4. In paragraph 3, Sachs describes "Little League parent syndrome" (LLPS). What is LLPS? (In Australia, it is called "ugly parent syndrome.") Research this phenomenon in greater detail. Cite some recent cases in which parents have injured each other or game officials because of uncontrolled anger during or after a game. Summarize the cases and public reaction following each incident.

5. The National Alliance for Youth Sports has developed a sportsmanship course with a code of conduct designed to help parents participate more positively in their children's sporting events. Visit their web site at *http://www.nays.org/* and read about their program. Develop a code of conduct for parents based on the information you gather online, your personal experience with youth sports, and discussions with youth coaches. After you draft your code, explain whether you would require parents to sign it before allowing their children to participate in community or school-based sports.

Additional essay topics, writing assignments, research guidelines, and readings for this chapter can be found online at **www.ablongman.com/goshgarian**.

Stereotyping
and
Profiling
Looking Beyond Race

9

As a nation of immigrants, the United States is made up of many races, ethnic traditions, religions and languages. Under a common political and legal system, we agree that we have the right to life, liberty, and the pursuit of happiness. Many of us take pride in our differences—what makes us distinct from one another. That is what makes America so special. But it is these differences that can pose challenges as well. Stereotyping—generalized assumptions about groups of people based on characteristics such as race, ethnic origin, social class, religion, gender, or physical appearance—may marginalize some groups and even persecute them because of their ethnic background. When these stereotypes are used in law enforcement, it is called racial profiling. Many of the pieces in this chapter address the controversy surrounding racial profiling—both of African Americans, and, after September 11, individuals who look like they could be from the Middle East.

The first article is an excerpt from a report commissioned by the U.S. State Department in November 2000 to provide guidelines on collecting data on racial profiling by law enforcement. Three professors of law and criminal justice at Northeastern University prepared "The Nature of the Problem of Racial Profiling." The section reproduced here explores the scope of the problem and provides some definitions that will help frame the essays that follow.

After September 11, many people who looked as if they could be of Middle Eastern descent found themselves eyed with suspicion. Some were even victims of physical violence. "Racial Profiling Goes Beyond Black and White," relates the experience of one young man of Brazilian and Indian heritage, who experiences hostility on a train from an African American man. He is shocked to be treated with such animosity by someone he feels should certainly understand the injustice of racial profiling. But as Sasha Polakow-Suransky explains, racial profiling can come from unexpected sources, especially when it is fueled by fear.

Bryonn Bain describes his experience in a New York City jail after he is arrested for crimes he did not commit. Unbelievably, Bain, a graduate of Harvard Law School, had been arrested before on suspicion for another crime merely because of his skin color. Bain relates his latest experience in "Three Days in a New York City Jail," in which he wonders when black people will be treated fairly and with dignity by the legal system. His piece is followed by an experience of Shelby Steele, who reflects on how the simple act of hailing a cab now serves as a tableau in America's ongoing cultural war in "Hailing While Black." Will a cab stop for a black man in New York City, or will Steele be another victim of racism?

Sometimes stereotypes can stimulate suspicion, which leads to racial profiling. Laura Fokkena wonders how much Hollywood's depiction of Middle Eastern people as terrorists has influenced current racial profiling practices in airports today. In "Are You a Terrorist, or Do You Play One on TV?" Fokkena concedes that September 11 put many Americans on edge, but must every Middle Eastern man be viewed as a potential threat? And why does Hollywood think it is okay to keep promoting negative images of Muslims?

The Viewpoints section in this chapter focuses on two opinions concerning the issue of racial profiling, as applies to African Americans. Harvard Law Professor

Randall Kennedy argues that while racial profiling may seem to be based on logical premises, it is morally wrong. John Derbyshire presents another view in his editorial, "In Defense of Racial Profiling," in which he explains that while racial profiling is based on a negative stereotype, it is still a useful tool.

Alton Fitzgerald White gives another personal perspective on the issue of racism as he describes his nightmarish experience of being arrested for a crime he did not commit in the Research Issue, "Ragtime, My Time." In the wrong place at the wrong time, White explains the painful ramifications of racial profiling.

The Nature of the Problem of Racial Profiling
A Resource Guide on Racial Profiling Data Collection Systems: Promising Practices and Lessons Learned
Deborah Ramirez, Jack McDevitt, and Amy Farrell

Despite media hype implying the contrary, on a national level we have actually witnessed a decline in crime over the last decade. During this same time, however, tensions and mistrust between the police and urban communities has risen, especially in issues connected to race. One of the ways that law enforcement agencies are addressing concerns and allegations regarding discriminatory policing is through data collection. To help assist in the collection of racial profiling data in areas across the country, the U.S. Department of Justice funded *A Resource Guide on Racial Profiling Data Collection Systems*. What follows is the introduction to the final document, describing the scope and nature of racial profiling.

This document was prepared in November of 2000 by Deborah Ramirez, Jack McDevitt, and Amy Farrell, professors of law and criminal justice at Northeastern University, with funding support from the U.S. Department of Justice. The opinions, findings, and conclusions or recommendations expressed in this document are those of the authors and do not necessarily represent the official position or policies of the U.S. Department of Justice.

CRITICAL THINKING   We have all heard of racial profiling, but what does it mean to you? Is it something you have experienced yourself? Is it something you hear about on television but doesn't directly affect you? Do you think something needs to be done about racial profiling?

The problem of racial profiling is complex and multifaceted. Dedicated police officers and professional police practices have contributed to making our communities safer. The majority of police officers are hard-working public servants who perform a dangerous job with dedication and honor; however, the perception that some police officers are engaging in racial profiling has created resentment and distrust of the police, particularly in communities of color. These communities applaud the benefits of community policing in reducing crime, but they also believe that truly effective policing will only be achieved when police both protect their neighborhoods from crime and respect the civil liberties of all residents. When law enforcement practices are perceived to be biased, unfair, or disrespectful, communities of color are less willing to trust and confide in police officers, report crimes, participate in problem-solving activities, be witnesses at trials, or serve on juries.

Defining Racial Profiling

2 When seeking to determine whether allegations of racial profiling are accurate, any analysis concerning the nature and scope of the problem depends on the definition of racial profiling used. Racial profiling is defined as any police-initiated action that relies on the race, ethnicity, or national origin rather than the behavior of an individual or information that leads the police to a particular individual who has been identified as being, or having been, engaged in criminal activity.

3   There is almost uniform consensus on two corollary principles that follow from adopting this definition of racial profiling: police may not use racial or ethnic stereotypes as factors in selecting whom to stop-and-search, and police may use race or ethnicity to determine whether a person matches a specific description of a particular suspect.[1]

4   Developing consensus on whether race can be used when police are addressing a crime committed by a group of individuals who share racial or ethnic characteristics is more difficult. Of course, when police know that a particular individual is a member of a criminal organization, police may legitimately use that information as a factor in the totality of the circumstances that may indicate ongoing criminal activity. For example, many criminal organizations are composed of persons with similar ethnic, racial, or national origin characteristics. Under the definition provided above, however, if police use a person's race, ethnicity, or national origin in determining whether a specific individual is a member of a criminal organization, they have engaged in racial profiling.

Nature and Extent of Perceptions of Racial Profiling

5 In the late 1990s, the American news media exploded with coverage of the problem of racial profiling. Indeed, the allegations have become so common that the community of color has labeled the phenomenon with the derisive term "driving while black" or "driving while brown." Front-page news stories and editorials in both the national and local press began to illustrate the individual and social costs of racial profiling.

6   National surveys have confirmed that most Americans, regardless of race, believe that racial profiling is a significant social problem. According to a Gallup Poll released on December 9, 1999, more than half of Americans polled believed that police actively engage in the practice of racial profiling and, more significantly, 81

percent of them said they disapprove of the practice.[2] In a national sample of adults, 59 percent said that racial profiling is widespread.[3] When the responses to the survey question were broken down by race, 56 percent of whites and 77 percent of blacks responded that racial profiling was pervasive. Additionally, the Gallup survey asked respondents how often they perceived having been stopped by the police based on their race alone. Six percent of whites and 42 percent of blacks responded that they had been stopped by the police because of their race, and 72 percent of black men between ages 18 and 34 believed they had been stopped because of their race.

7   Recent survey data also confirm a strong connection between perceptions of race-based stops by police and animosity toward local and state law enforcement. In addition to gathering data on individual perceptions of stops by the police, the 1999 Gallup Poll asked respondents how favorably they viewed the police. Eighty-five percent of white respondents had a favorable response toward local police and 87 percent of white respondents had a favorable response to state police. Black respondents, overall, had a less favorable opinion of both state and local police, with just 58 percent having a favorable opinion of the local police and 64 percent having a favorable response to the state police. Fifty-three percent of black men between ages 18 and 34 said they had been treated unfairly by local police.

8   Similarly, a 12-city survey conducted by the Department of Justice in 1998 demonstrated that, although most people in the African-American community felt satisfied with police services in their neighborhoods, their level of dissatisfaction was approximately twice that of the white community.[4] This wide schism in all 12 cities surveyed indicates the need for law enforcement to work harder to restore the confidence of communities of color in the critical work being done by law enforcement. Police departments that fail to address the perception of racially discriminatory policing within minority neighborhoods may find their law enforcement efforts undermined.

Evidence of Racial Profiling

9 Anecdotal and empirical evidence confirm national perceptions about the pervasiveness of racial profiling. To better understand the issues associated with identifying racial profiling in police stops, concerns about police discretion have been broken into two stages: an officer's decision to stop a vehicle or person and the actions of the officer during the stop. The second issue may include a number of questions: Are passengers and drivers ordered to step out of the car? Is the suspect treated with respect? Are police questioning the occupants about subjects unrelated to the traffic-stop violation? Were drug-sniffing dogs summoned to the scene? Did the officer request permission to search the car and its contents? How long did the encounter last? The answers to these and other questions are critical for understanding the complexities and nuances of racial profiling. Evidence from anecdotal accounts and statistical studies has begun to address these important issues.

Anecdotal Evidence

10 Personal anecdotes and stories help illustrate the experiences of those who believe they have been stopped because of racial profiling and, in turn, give rise to a set of common concerns about police stop-and-search practices. A 1999 report by David Harris, *Driving While Black: Racial Profiling on Our Nation's Highways*, cites numerous accounts of disparate treatment toward minorities by police from a variety of state and local jurisdictions.[5] A sample of these accounts illustrates the emotional impact of such incidents.

11   The concern that police stop drivers because they or their passengers do not appear to "match" the type of vehicle they occupy is common in racial profiling accounts. This "driving in the wrong car" concern is illustrated by the experiences of Dr. Elmo Randolph, a 42-year-old African-American dentist, who commutes from Bergen County to his office near Newark, New Jersey. Since 1991, he has been stopped by New Jersey troopers more than 50 times. Randolph does not drive at excessive speeds and claims he has never been issued a ticket.[6] Instead, troopers approach his gold BMW, request his license and registration, and ask him if he has any drugs or weapons in his car. The experience of Randolph and many other minority drivers on New Jersey's highways led to the recent consent decree and settlement between the state of New Jersey and DOJ. As a result of the settlement, New Jersey State Police (NJSP) are collecting data on the race and ethnicity of persons stopped by state troopers and improving their supervision and training.

12   Another common complaint is that police stop people of color traveling through predominately white areas because the police believe that people of color do not "belong" in certain neighborhoods and may be engaged in criminal activity. This type of profiling was reported by Alvin Penn, the African-American deputy president of the Connecticut State Senate. In 1996, a Trumbull, Connecticut, police officer stopped Penn as he drove his van through this predominately white suburban town. After reviewing Penn's license and registration, the officer asked Penn if he knew which town he was in (Bridgeport, the state's largest city, where blacks and Latinos comprise 75 percent of the population, borders Trumbull, which is 98 percent white). Penn, recalling that he had been turning around on a dead-end street when the officer stopped him, responded by asking why he needed to know which town he was in. The officer told him that he was not required to give Penn a reason for the stop and that, if he made an issue of it, the officer would cite him for speeding.[7] Three years after this incident, Penn sponsored legislation that made Connecticut the second state to begin collecting data on the demographics of individuals stopped by state police.

13   By far the most common complaint by members of communities of color is that they are being stopped for petty traffic violations such as under-inflated tires, failure to signal properly before switching lanes, vehicle equipment failures, speeding less than 10 miles above the speed limit, or having an illegible license plate. One example of this is the account of Robert Wilkins, a Harvard Law School graduate and a public defender in Washington, D.C., who went to a family funeral in Ohio in May 1992. On the return trip, he and his aunt, uncle, and 29-year-old cousin rented a Cadillac for the trip home. His cousin was stopped for speeding in western Mary-

land while driving 60 miles per hour in a 55-mile-per-hour zone of the interstate. The group was forced to stand on the side of the interstate in the rain for an extended period while officers and drug-sniffing dogs searched their car. Nothing was found. Wilkins, represented by the ACLU, filed suit and received a settlement from the state of Maryland.[8]

14   Although this small sample of anecdotal evidence does not prove that police officers actively engage in racial profiling, it is representative of the thousands of personal stories cataloged in newspaper articles, interviews, ACLU commentary, and court battles.

Empirical Research on Racial Profiling

15   In addition to a growing body of individual accounts of racial profiling, scholars have begun examining the relationship between police stop-and-search practices and racial characteristics of individual drivers. The majority of empirical research collected to date has been used in expert testimony accompanying lawsuits. Wilkins v. Maryland State Police (1993) was one of the first cases to introduce empirical evidence of racial profiling into the court record.

16   In 1995 and 1996, as a result of Wilkins' settlement with the Maryland State Police (MSP), Dr. John Lamberth, a professor of psychology at Temple University, conducted an analysis of police searches along I-95 in Maryland. Using data released by MSP pursuant to the settlement, Lamberth compared the population of people searched and arrested with those violating traffic laws on Maryland highways. He constructed a violator sample using both stationary and rolling surveys of drivers violating the legal speed limit on a selected portion of the interstate. His violator survey indicated that 74.7 percent of speeders were white, while 17.5 percent were black.[9] In contrast, according to MSP data, blacks constituted 79.2 percent of the drivers searched. Lamberth concluded that the data revealed "dramatic and highly statistically significant disparities between the percentage of black I-95 motorists legitimately subject to stop by the Maryland State Police and the percentage of black motorists detained and searched by troopers on this roadway."[10]

17   Empirical data on stop-and-search practices in New Jersey also originated through actions of the court. In the late 1980s and early 1990s, black drivers were reporting that they were being stopped disproportionately by New Jersey troopers. In response to these complaints, in 1994, the Gloucester County public defender's office, while representing Pedro Soto and others, filed a motion to suppress evidence obtained in a series of searches, alleging that the searches were unlawful because they were part of a pattern and practice of racial profiling by New Jersey troopers.[11] As part of that litigation, the defendants received traffic-stop and arrest data compiled by NJSP in selected locations from 1988 through 1991.[12] Lamberth served as the statistical expert for the defendants and conducted a comparative violator survey to weigh the percentage of blacks stopped and arrested by New Jersey troopers against a comparative percentage of blacks who violated traffic laws on New Jersey highways. His analyses found that blacks comprised 13.5 percent of the New Jersey Turnpike population and 15 percent of the drivers speeding. In contrast, blacks represented 35 percent of those stopped and 73.2 percent of those arrested. In

other words, in New Jersey, black drivers were disproportionately more likely to be stopped and arrested than white drivers. The Superior Court of New Jersey relied on Lamberth's study in its decision to suppress the evidence seized by New Jersey troopers in 19 consolidated criminal prosecutions and concurred with his opinion that the troopers relied on race in stopping and searching turnpike motorists.

18   Recent data collection efforts in New Jersey and New York have confirmed the independent empirical findings used in court cases. In April 1999, the Attorney General of New Jersey issued a report indicating that New Jersey troopers had engaged in racial profiling along the New Jersey Turnpike.[13] This report tracked the racial breakdowns of traffic-stops between 1997 and 1998. The information indicated that people of color constituted 40.6 percent of the stops made on the turnpike. Although few stops resulted in a search, 77.2 percent of those individuals searched were people of color. An analysis of the productivity of these searches indicated that 10.5 percent of the searches that involved white motorists resulted in an arrest or seizure, and that 13.5 percent of the searches involving black motorists resulted in arrest or seizure. Finally, the New Jersey report demonstrated that minority motorists were more likely to be involved in consent searches than nonminority motorists. Eighty percent of consent searches involved minority motorists.[14]

19   In December 1999, New York Attorney General Eliot Spitzer released the results of an investigation by his office of the "stop and frisk" practices in New York City. It showed that blacks and Latinos were much more likely to be stopped and searched, even when the statistics were adjusted to reflect differing criminal participation rates in some neighborhoods.[15] After reviewing 175,000 incidents in which citizens were stopped by the police during the 15-month period that ended in March 1999, the attorney general found that blacks were stopped six times more often than whites, while Latinos were stopped four times more often. Blacks made up 25 percent of the city population but 50 percent of the people stopped and 67 percent of the people stopped by the New York City Street Crimes Unit.[16] International data suggest that racial profiling is not an isolated American experience. A 1998 study by the British Government's Home Office examined the racial and ethnic demographics of the stop-and-search patterns of 43 police forces in England and Wales. The study indicated that blacks were 7.5 times more likely to be stopped and searched and 4 times more likely to be arrested than whites.[17] This is true even though, according to census population figures, Great Britain is 93 percent white and 7 percent ethnic minority.[18] Although the high proportion of searches of people of color has been a constant feature of police searches in London, England, and elsewhere, the proportion of searches that result in an arrest does not differ by race or ethnicity. That is, the arrest rate differs little regardless of whether the search was of a white or black person. In London, the arrest rate was 11.1 percent for light-skinned Europeans, 11.4 percent for dark-skinned Europeans, and 11.7 percent for black people. In the case of Asians, the arrest rate was lowest at 9.4 percent.[19]

20   Anecdotal and empirical evidence has helped state and local activists, community members, and government officials understand the problem of racial profiling and has raised new questions about police stop-and-search practices. However, more expansive and systematic data collection is needed to address the concerns surrounding police practices of racial profiling.

Origin of Racial Profiling and the Complexities of Police Discretion

21 Although empirical research, anecdotal evidence, and survey data confirm the existence of racial profiling as a social problem, many still question how such profiling could arise. Throughout all areas of their daily routine, police exercise a great deal of individual discretion. Within the area of traffic-stops, for example, police must use reasoned judgment in deciding which cars to stop from among the universe of cars being operated in violation of the law. Since many traffic enforcement and vehicle code laws apply to all cars on the road, and since more vehicles are being operated in violation of the local traffic laws than police have the resources to stop them, officers have a wide discretion in selecting which cars to stop.

22   Many traffic officers say that by following any vehicle for 1 or 2 minutes, they can observe a basis on which to stop it.[20] Many police departments have not developed formal, written, standards directing officers on how to use this discretion. Instead, officers often develop ad hoc methods of winnowing suspicious from innocent motorists. This intuition, often learned by young officers observing the actions of more experienced officers, can vary widely across individual officers even within a particular department. Police departments often use traffic-stops as a means of ferreting out illicit drugs and weapons. Consequently, some officers routinely use traffic stops as a means of tracking down drug or gun couriers. These discretionary decisions are seldom documented and rarely reviewed. As a result, individual officers are infrequently made accountable for these decisions.

Levels of Police Discretion

23 Several factors may influence an officer's decision to stop-and-search an individual, but the various types of potential scenarios can easily be broken down into high- and low-discretion realms. Traffic and pedestrian stops can be viewed on a continuum from low-discretion stops, in which an officer's decision not to make a stop is limited, to high-discretion stops, in which the decision to stop someone is often based on an officer's experiences in the field.

24   *Low discretion.* Although the nature and scope of low-discretion stops vary by place and context, they are common in policing. Low-discretion stops can include those based on externally generated reports of a crime or suspicious activity, such as when a victim describes a particular suspect. In the traffic-stop context, for jurisdictions in which traffic enforcement is a priority, speeding more than 10 miles above the speed limit or running a red light may also be placed in the category of low-discretion stops. Some jurisdictions have actually calculated the percentage of stops that fall in this low-discretion category. The New York attorney general's Stop and Frisk study, for example, shows that only 30 percent of the stops were based on victims' descriptions.[21] Similarly, in London, England, only 25 percent of searches in selected study sites were considered low discretion.[22]

25   *High discretion.* The complexities of police discretion emerge more often in the high-discretion stop category. In the traffic-stop context, these stops include checks for under-inflated tires, safety belt warnings, failures to signal lane changes, and other minor vehicle code and nonmoving violations. In the pedestrian-stop

context, high-discretion stops involve those who may look suspicious but are not engaged in any specific criminal violation or activities. These high-discretion stops invite both intentional and unintentional abuses. Police are just as subject to the racial and ethnic stereotypes they learn from our culture as any other citizen. Unless documented, such stops create an environment that allows the use of stereotypes to go undetected.

The Perception That Minorities Are More Likely to Carry Contraband

26 The perception that African Americans, Hispanics, Asians, and other minorities are more likely to carry drugs than their white counterparts intensifies the complexities of police discretion in stops and searches.[23] The escalating pressure from the war on drugs has led some police officers to target people of color whom police believe to be proportionately involved in drug use and trafficking. Although some members of the police community suggest that race-based searches are justified because more minority drivers are found with contraband, the empirical evidence amassed to date tends to discredit such arguments.[24] In Lamberth's study on I-95 in Maryland, he found that 28.4 percent of black drivers and passengers who were searched were found with contraband, and 28.8 percent of white drivers and passengers who were searched were found with contraband.[25]

27   Thus, the probability of finding contraband was the same for blacks and whites. Race did not matter. According to the New Jersey attorney general's Interim Report (April 1999), the "hit rates" at which contraband was found among those searched did not differ significantly by race. Only 10.5 percent of the searches of whites resulted in an arrest or seizure compared to a rate of 13.5 percent for black motorists.[26] Similarly, in the New York study of "stop and frisk" practices, between 1998 and 1999, the attorney general found that 12.6 percent of whites stopped were arrested, compared to only 10.5 percent of blacks and 11.3 percent of Latinos.[27] In a recent U.S. Customs Service study, nationwide data revealed that, while 43 percent of those searched were either black or Latino, the hit rates for blacks and Latinos were actually lower than the hit rates for whites. The study found that 6.7 percent of whites, 6.3 percent of blacks, and 2.8 percent of Hispanics had contraband. This finding is particularly surprising because the study does not involve car stops, but involves stops and searches in airports. Presumably, if the perception that drug couriers are more likely to be black or Latino were true, a widespread survey of airport searches should reveal differing hit rates.[28] Similarly, in London, England, the probability of finding contraband as a result of a search did not significantly differ among races.[29] Although sound empirical research on the relationship between race and hit rates for contraband is limited, to date the evidence indicates that blacks and Latinos are no more likely than whites to be in possession of narcotics or other contraband.[30]

28   In many cases, disproportionate minority arrests for drug possession and distribution have fueled perceptions by police and others that race is an appropriate factor in the decision to stop or search an individual.[31] However, existing data on the productivity of searches across racial groups suggest that stop-and-search practices have become a game of "search and you will find." Police officers who aggressively

and disproportionately search people of color will arrest more people of color than whites, not because of differences in behavior, but because they are stopping and searching many more people of color than whites. Regardless of whether the perception that blacks and Latinos are more likely to be found in possession of contraband could be empirically verified, United States laws do not, and should not, permit race to be used as a basis for stopping and searching individuals.[32] ◆

Notes

1. The U.S. Supreme Court has addressed the issue of ethnicity and immigration stops in *United States* v. *Brignoni-Ponce* 422 U.S. 873 (1975) and *United States* v. *Martinez-Fuerte* 428 U.S. 543 (1976). More recently, the Ninth Circuit addressed the use of race in border stops in *United States* v. *Montero-Camargo*, 208 F. 3d 1122 (9th Cir. 2000).
2. Gallup Poll Organization Poll Release, *Racial Profiling Is Seen as Widespread, Particularly Among Young Black Men,* Princeton, NJ: Gallup Poll Organization, December 9, 1999, at 1.
3. Gallup Poll Organization Poll Release, see note 2, at 1.
4. Bureau of Justice Statistics, *Criminal Victimization and Perceptions of Community Safety in 12 Cities, 1998,* Washington, DC: U.S. Department of Justice, May 1999 (NCJ 173940).
5. David Harris, *Driving While Black: Racial Profiling on Our Nation's Highways*, Washington, DC: American Civil Liberties Union, 1999.
6. Mark Hosenball, "It Is Not the Act of a Few Bad Apples: Lawsuit Shines the Spotlight on Allegations of Racial Profiling by New Jersey State Troopers," *Newsweek,* May 17, 1999, at 34–35.
7. Richard Weizel, "Lawmaker Pushes for Racial Profiling Bill," *Boston Globe,* May 2, 1999, at D21.
8. *Wilkins* v. *Maryland State Police,* Civil Action No. CCB-93-483, Maryland Federal District Court (1993). For a discussion of the settlement, see John Lamberth, "Driving While Black: A Statistician Proves That Prejudice Still Rules the Road," *Washington Post,* August 16, 1999, at C1.
9. Lamberth, see note 8. For a discussion of the Lamberth study, see David Harris, "The Stories, the Statistics, and the Law: Why Driving While Black Matters," *Minnesota Law Review* 84(2), 1999, at 280–281.
10. Lamberth, see note 8, at 4.
11. *State of New Jersey* v. *Pedro Soto et al.,* Superior Court of New Jersey, 734 A.2d 350, 1996.
12. The stop-and-arrest information was compiled using patrol charts, radio logs, and traffic tickets for selected dates from April 1988 to May 1991.
13. Peter Verniero and Paul Zoubek, *New Jersey Attorney General's Interim Report of the State Police Review Team Regarding Allegations of Racial Profiling (N.J. Interim Rep.),* April 20, 1999.
14. Verniero and Zoubek, see note 13, at 27–28.
15. Kevin Flynn, "State Cites Racial Inequality in New York Police Searches," *New York Times,* December 1, 1999, at 22.
16. New York Attorney General, New York City Police *"Stop and Frisk" Practices: A Report to the People of New York From the Office of the Attorney General,* New York, NY: December 1, 1999, at 95.
17. *Statistics on Race and the Criminal Justice System: A Home Office Publication Under Section 95 of the Criminal Justice Act of 1991,* London, England: Home Office, 1998, chapters 3 and 4.

18. *The UK in Figures,* London, England: Office of National Statistics, Government Statistical Service, 1999.

19. Marian FitzGerald, *Searches in London, Interim Evaluation of Year One of the Programme of Action*, London, England: Home Office, August 1999, at 21.

20. For a discussion of this practice, see Gary Webb, "Driving While Black," *Esquire Magazine*, April 1999, at 119–127.

21. New York Attorney General, see note 16, at 141–145.

22. Marion FitzGerald, *Final Report Into Stop-and-Search*, London, England: Metropolitan Police, 1999.

23. This idea has been perpetuated by some police training materials. For example, in the mid-1980s, the Florida Department of Highway Safety and Motor Vehicles issued guidelines for the police on common characteristics of drug couriers that warned officers to be suspicious of drivers who do not "fit the vehicle" and "ethnic groups associated with the drug trade." For a discussion of this practice, see O.W. Wisotsky, *Beyond the War on Drugs: Overcoming a Failed Public Policy,* Buffalo, NY: Prometheus Books, 1990.

24. Note that only a limited number of empirical studies have examined the relationship between an individual's race and the probability that they are carrying contraband. More research is needed to address such questions.

25. Lamberth, see note 8.

26. Verniero and Zaubek, see note 13. Note that the New Jersey report is based on a sample size of only 78 searches. Although the hit rate of 38 percent for Latinos was higher than for whites or blacks, the smaller number of searches involving Latinos makes any conclusion about the proportionality of those searches more difficult to determine statistically.

27. New York Attorney General, see note 16, at 111.

28. U.S. Customs Service, *Personal Searches of Air Passengers Results: Positive and Negative*, Washington, DC, 1998, at 1. For a discussion of the Customs study, see Harris, note 9, at 277–288.

29. FitzGerald, see note 29.

30. National research conducted by the Substance Abuse and Mental Health Services Administration (SAMHSA) *National Household Survey of Drug Abuse* indicates that the rate at which blacks use illegal drugs is 8.2 percent, only slightly higher than the white or Hispanic rates, both at 6.1 percent. This research indicates that the vast majority of people across all racial groups do not use drugs and should not be seen as targets of suspicion. Similarly, the National Institute of Drug Abuse found that 12 percent to 14 percent of those who abuse drugs are black. This percentage mirrors the proportion of blacks in the general population. For more information, see National Clearinghouse for Alcohol and Drug Information, Research and Statistics, *National Household Survey on Drug Abuse*, Washington, DC: U.S. Department of Health and Human Services, 1998, at 16.

31. The racial demographics of arrest statistics for narcotics show more blacks, Hispanics, and minorities tend to be arrested on drug charges than whites. However, most drug possession and distribution go undetected. Those activities are private and conducted outside the ambit of police view. Only a small percentage of these crimes are given the attention of law enforcement. Thus, the number of drug arrests may only reflect law enforcement patterns.

32. Just as we do not allow insurance companies to charge differential life insurance rates to women because they live longer than men, we ought not allow empirical racial profiling to impose costs on the entire community of color. It would be unfair to stigmatize an entire community based on the conduct of a few. By allowing police to use race as a factor in determining whom to stop-and-search, many innocent black and Hispanic individuals are subjected to searches. For more discussion on this issue, see Randall Kennedy, *Race, Crime and the Law,* New York, NY: Pantheon Books, 1997, at 147.

FREEWRITING ASSIGNMENT

Has racial profiling influenced your perception of law enforcement and the justice system? Why or why not?

CRITICAL READING

1. According to the Department of Justice document, what is racial profiling? Do you agree with this definition? Explain.
2. Under what circumstances may law enforcement consider race a factor? Is it ever acceptable? Should it be?
3. What are the ambiguous areas of racial profiling?
4. What is empirical evidence? Why is it important to the study of racial profiling? Explain.
5. Dr. John Lamberth served as the statistical expert for the defense in a case involving a traffic stop that resulted in the seizure of illegal contraband (see paragraph 17). The defense argued that because the traffic stop was the result of racial profiling, the evidence obtained from such an inherently illegal stop should be suppressed. The judge agreed and suppressed the evidence in 19 consolidated criminal prosecutions. What is your own opinion on this case? Did the judge make the right decision, even if it did dismiss criminal activity? Explain.
6. What is "police discretion?" What is "high" and "low" discretion? How does police discretion connect to the issue of racial profiling? Explain.
7. In paragraphs 26 and 27, the Northeastern professors observe that minority drivers are no more likely to carry contraband than their white counterparts. On what evidence do they base this determination? If it is accurate, what accounts for the police perception that minorities are more likely to be carrying contraband?
8. If empirical evidence proved that certain racial groups were indeed more likely to engage in criminal activities, would racial profiling be justified? Why or why not?

CRITICAL WRITING

9. *Exploratory Writing*: Nancy E. Gist, director of the Bureau of Justice Assistance at the U.S. Department of Justice, said in her forward to the resource guide, "The guarantee to all persons of equal protection under the law is one of the most fundamental principles of our democratic society. Law enforcement officers should not endorse or act upon stereotypes, attitudes, or beliefs that a person's race, ethnicity, or national origin increases that person's general propensity to act unlawfully. There is no tradeoff between effective law enforcement and protection of the civil rights of all Americans; we can and must have both." Write an essay in which you build upon her statement. Do you agree with her statement that there can be no "tradeoff" between civil protection and civil rights? Why or why not?

10. *Research and Analysis*: The report on racial profiling was completed one year before September 11. While racial profiling for African Americans and Latinos is still of great concern, much attention is now on the profiling of people of Middle Eastern descent. Visit the ACLU's web site on racial equality at *http://www.aclu.org/RacialEquality/RacialEqualityMain. cfm* and review their information on racial profiling. What are the most pressing issues concerning racial profiling today? Select an issue or case described on the ACLU web site and research it in greater depth. Write a short essay summarizing the situation, the issue, and your position on it.

GROUP PROJECTS

11. Visit the U.S. Department of Justice web site and read the "Racial Profiling Fact Sheet" posted online at *http://www.usdoj.gov/opa/pr/2003/ June/racial_profiling_fact_sheet.pdf.* Review the entire fact sheet and discuss it as a group. What is the government's official position on racial profiling? What exceptions do they make concerning racial profiling, and why? Identify any areas of the document that you find questionable or particularly compelling, and share them with the rest of the class as part of a larger class discussion of this document.

12. Paragraphs 2–4 attempt to define racial profiling. As a group, develop your own definition, drawing from information provided in the article and from online research. After preparing your definition, write a position statement on racial profiling for your own school's public safety department.

Racial Profiling Goes Beyond Black and White
Sasha Polakow-Suransky

Many people immediately equate racial profiling with discrimination against African Americans. But racial profiling takes many forms and affects many different groups. This reality was made very apparent after the terrorist attacks on September 11, 2001. Suddenly, racial profiling shifted to Arab Americans and people who looked like they could be from the Middle East. Even groups who had experienced racial profiling first-hand endorsed its use in law enforcement, as this essay reveals.

Sasha Polakow-Suransky is a journalist and a fellow at the *American Prospect* magazine. He has been published in the *Chronicle of Higher Education*, the *Brown Alumni Magazine*, and has presented as a speaker at the American Educational Research Association. This article was published in *Africana*, November 2001, two months following the terrorist attacks of September 11.

In your opinion, do you consider racial profiling ever justifiable? If so, under what circumstances? If not, why?

1   Eric Hotchandani, a 20-year-old University of California-Santa Barbara student, boarded a packed rush-hour train on the evening of September 21. When the train emptied out, he took the first open seat, next to a middle-aged black man in a suit, and began reading his newspaper. The black man stared at him coldly.

2   "How're you doing?" Hotchandani greeted him.

3   "Not so good anymore," the man replied.

4   "Why is that?" Hotchandani asked.

5   "Look who's sitting next to me," the man snapped back.

6   Hotchandani was taken aback. "Just go ahead and spell this one out for me," he said.

7   The man turned to him and asked, "Where were you born?"

8   Although shocked by the question, Hotchandani answered. "I was born in Brazil, but I have this Indian side to me, which darkens my skin and probably makes you think I'm a terrorist," he said.

9   The black man seemed surprised. "Sorry, I thought you were from the Middle East," he said. But Hotchandani was not satisfied.

10   "Let's go ahead and assume that I was," he said to the man, raising his voice. "What happened in New York on September 11 was done by an extreme group of Muslims who don't represent Islam or people of my skin color. I'm not here to inflict harm on anyone. I'm just minding my own business."

11   "I'm not going to let you do any harm to me," the black man retorted. "I just don't feel comfortable with you sitting next to me."

12   To the shock and dismay of many African American leaders, polls released in the weeks following September 11 indicate that the views expressed by this black man on a Bay Area train are not uncommon. A Zogby International poll conducted between September 25 and October 8 showed that African American approval of racially profiling Arab Americans reached a peak of 60% on September 30, compared to 45% among the overall population. The statistics later leveled out with African Americans showing a 45% approval rating by October 8, virtually in line with the 41% figure for other racial groups. Similarly, an October 25 Africana.com poll found that 34% of respondents thought it was "okay" for U.S. law enforcement to racially profile Arabs.

13   These results have provoked a range of reactions. Urban League President Hugh Price is disturbed. "We should see in these polls' findings more evidence of the perniciousness of racial profiling itself, no matter how it's seemingly bolstered by glib or urgently declared rationalizations," he said. "These polls show that whenever people speak in favor of racial profiling, they always favor its use against some other group, not theirs."

14   Others, such as Henry L. Taylor, a University of Buffalo professor of Architecture and Urban Planning, claim that the results are not representative of general black attitudes because they are based solely on immediate fears of terrorism. "A lot of people, African Americans included, have not looked at the civil implications of

these questions," said Taylor. "Right now we're in a time period where anything that looks like it will preserve the security of a nation is going to be embraced."

15   While the statistics indicating widespread black approval of Arab racial profiling can certainly be attributed in part to a knee-jerk reaction after September 11, there are deeper causes as well. Syndicated columnist Earl Ofari Hutchinson points to religious intolerance and ingrained distrust of Muslims within the African American community. Complex issues such as the presence of Arab-owned convenience stores in predominantly black neighborhoods and the tension between the two communities play into this equation as well. As Hutchinson contends, "Many [blacks] still view all Muslims with the same mix of caution, distrust and hostility, as many white Americans do."

16   While such views may be widespread, they are largely based on a false premise. In fact, the majority of Arabs in the United States are not Muslims, they are Syrian and Lebanese Christians. According to the Arab-American Institute, 77 percent of Arabs in America are Christians and only 23 percent practice Islam. Another little known fact further complicates matters: the majority of American Muslims are not Arabs. Statistics from the Council on American-Islamic Relations reveal that most Muslims in the U.S. are of African or South Asian descent—only 25 percent are Arab.

17   Hutchinson concludes his column, "When the Profiled Become Profilers," by observing that black support for the racial profiling of others could very well backfire: "Bush has implored Americans to return life back to normalcy. Unfortunately, those blacks who approve racial profiling against Muslims run the grave risk of making sure that racial profiling could be part of that normalcy, and with them once more the prime targets."

18   Columnist Clarence Page has similar worries. Page argued in an October 3 *Chicago Tribune* column that African Americans who say they support the racial profiling of Arabs haven't thought it through. "The first casualty of war is often rational thinking," he writes. "It is not going to be easy for us to argue against the unfair profiling of blacks if most of us favor the unfair profiling of Arabs."

19   NAACP leaders have expressed similar dismay. "It is unfortunate that it would be African Americans that have suffered this kind of terror and profiling at the hands of the police . . . to then support this type of profiling," says Buffalo NAACP President Frank Mesiah.

20   But *New York Daily News* columnist Stanley Crouch disagrees. Crouch insists that racial profiling of blacks is qualitatively different than the current profiling of Arabs. While pulling over black motorists involves police officers' frequently incorrect assumptions about who might commit a crime, Crouch claims that profiling Arabs is not comparable.

21   "The Arabs-in-America question removes us from the area of speculation and abstract theories about individual freedom," he argues. "We have had war declared on us by a spider at the center of a web of terrorist cells. Followers of that spider are hiding in the Arab-American community."

22   And finally there are some in the African American community who are simply relieved that someone else is the target for once, as a group of black and Latino teenagers in Brooklyn told the *New York Times*. "The police would probably

racially profile everyone that's here. . . . But now they don't really bother us. They, like, stop everyone that has Middle Eastern features. They stop them. They ask them questions like that," said Louis Johnson, an 18-year-old whose parents are from Trinidad.

23   "We've become a little more at ease with the policemen," agreed Johnson's Latino friend, Miqueo Rawell-Peterson, 17. "We realize what they've done. Now we look at them more as heroes, instead of—I guess, what you'd say, enemies."

24   But while black and Latino teenagers enjoy their reprieve from racial profiling, a series of complaints has emerged from profiling's newfound targets. In the post-September 11 climate, "driving while black" has become "flying while brown" and the most egregious cases to emerge involve men who look "Middle Eastern" being kicked off airplanes after passing through security. All in all, over a dozen men have been denied the right to board or been removed from planes.

25   In Orlando, two Pakistani businessmen invited to attend a conference by the U.S. Department of Commerce were kicked off a US Airways flight on September 17, despite the fact that they showed a letter of invitation from the U.S. consul. The same day, in San Antonio, Ashraf Kahn was ejected from a Delta flight and, as a result, missed his brother's wedding in Pakistan. In Minneapolis, Kareem Alasady and two companions were not allowed to board a Northwest flight on September 20.

26   In Tampa, Mohamed el-Sayed, a U.S. citizen born in Egypt, was barred from boarding a United flight to Washington. United has also kicked several other men off its flights in recent weeks; in Phoenix, Iraqi-American businessman Younadam Youkhana and his companions were forced off a United flight to Chicago, and in Boston, businessman Muhammad Ali was removed, questioned extensively and cleared by law enforcement, and still not allowed to re-board his United flight to Washington.

27   Worse yet, Ali Khadraoui, an American citizen originally from Algeria, was strip-searched and detained by French police after being kept off of his United flight home to Washington from Paris. Finally, in Seattle, Vahid Zohrehvandi, an Iranian-American engineer and part-time employee of American Airlines, was kicked off a flight operated by his own employer. He was not allowed to fly home to Dallas until the airline found a pilot who agreed to fly with a "Middle Eastern" man on board.

28   Zohrehvandi's lawyers, Kelli Evans and Christy Lopez, belong to the Washington-based civil rights firm Relman and Associates, whose attorneys are best known for winning large class action settlements in the recent Denny's restaurant and Avis Rent-a-Car discrimination suits. The firm is representing several other men kicked off planes as well. Evans and Lopez, both veterans of the U.S. Department of Justice Civil Rights Division, compare Zohrehvandi's having to wait for a pilot willing to fly him to forcing a customer in a restaurant to wait until a non-discriminatory waitress is willing to serve him. Refusal to provide service to a passenger because of his or her race is illegal, they argue, and federal law appears to be on their side.

29   The U.S. Code states clearly, "An air carrier or foreign air carrier may not subject a person in air transportation to discrimination on the basis of race, color, national origin, religion, sex, or ancestry." Secretary of Transportation Norman Mineta, himself a victim of Japanese internment during World War II, has vowed to enforce the law. "Protecting the civil rights of our passengers is essential to

maintaining the security of our nation, because those civil rights are essential to our most fundamental values," he declared. "There have been times in our history as a nation when that has been forgotten. I am committed, and the administration is committed, to ensuring that it is never forgotten again."

30   But that is not all. Evans and Lopez claim that the airlines' refusal to transport their clients and other Middle Eastern men is also a violation of contract law—Title 42, Section 1981 of the U.S. Code, to be exact. This provision, an important stride towards racial equality in the Reconstruction era, was originally created in 1870 to ensure that freed slaves could enter the marketplace. It guarantees: "All persons within the jurisdiction of the United States shall have the same right in every State and Territory to make and enforce contracts . . . and to the full and equal benefit of all laws and proceedings for the security of persons and property as is enjoyed by white citizens." Today, the same law—designed to dismantle institutionalized anti-black racism in the post-civil war South—could be invoked to defend the civil rights of brown-skinned Middle Eastern and South Asian men kicked off planes.

31   That the victims of the new racial profiling are being represented by the same firm that brought black Americans some of the most notable antidiscrimination class action victories in recent history is no coincidence. The potential for a broad alliance against arbitrary and unfounded racial profiling has never been greater. But whether the current climate of racial division between blacks and Arabs will give way to such a coalition remains to be seen.

32   Poll results aside, some Middle Eastern Americans, and others singled out because they look like Arabs, have found that more African Americans seem supportive than suspicious. According to Evans and Lopez, when one of their clients finally managed to board a flight, he received a sympathetic reception from a black flight attendant in first class, who expressed his empathy by offering the beleaguered coach passenger some champagne.

33   And when confronted with the hostile black man on the Bay Area train, Eric Hotchandani seized the opportunity to speak out, and found a sympathetic audience.

34   "Do you want me to go to the back of the train? Do we have to redo Rosa Parks all over again?" Hotchandani asked the man who had expressed discomfort at his presence, as the whole train grew silent, looking on. "To me you are beyond ignorant. I'm sure you've experienced some sort of racism considering that you're black. If you knew anything about your own history you wouldn't be doing this. I can't believe you're reciprocating this kind of hate—you're kicking me down when you've been kicked before."

35   A black man in his mid-20s seated near the two men broke the silence.

36   "At first I thought this guy was joking with you," he said, addressing Hotchandani. "Please don't think all black people think like this."

37   The middle-aged black man did not respond. At the next stop, he gathered his belongings and left the train. The passengers clapped as he stepped off. ◆

FREEWRITING ASSIGNMENT

In the days following September 11, did you consider the race or ethnicity of the people around you? If you are of Middle Eastern descent, did you notice any differences in the way people treated you?

CRITICAL READING

1. How does the case of Eric Hotchandani serve to support Polakow-Suran-sky's argument? Is Hotchandani even from the Middle East? What is the irony of his situation on the train? How does he handle it?
2. Evaluate how the author presents and supports the thesis of his essay. First, identify his thesis, then analyze the supporting elements he uses to prove his point. Does the author allow for alternative points of view? Does he try to see multiple sides of the issue? Explain.
3. In paragraph 13, Urban League President Hugh Price says, "polls show that whenever people speak in favor of racial profiling, they always favor its use against some other group, not theirs." What are the sociological implications of this statement? What does it reveal about the motivation behind racial profiling in general?
4. Henry L. Taylor notes that racial profiling of African American men who looked Middle Eastern followed in the immediate aftermath of a terrorist attack perpetrated by Middle Eastern men. Therefore, the "civil implications" of the situation were not evaluated—people were reacting from the gut. Is this understandable? Justifiable? Explain.
5. In what ways did September 11 ease racial profiling practices against other minority groups? Explain.
6. Eric Hotchandani asks the man on the train if they have to "do Rosa Parks all over again?" Who is Rosa Parks? What did she do? Why does Hotchandani refer to her? What effect did mentioning her probably have on the other people on the train? Explain.

CRITICAL WRITING

7. Henry L. Tayor notes that while racial profiling of any group is not admirable or right, it sometimes can be a knee-jerk reaction to specific events, such as those connected to September 11. Explore the psychology of such reactions from your own perspective.
8. How would you have reacted if you were in Eric Hotchandani's situation? What would you have said? Would you have left? Moved? Reacted with anger? Write a fictitious dialogue between yourself and the man on the train, being honest to your temperament and personality.

GROUP PROJECT

9. In the aftermath of the attacks of September 11, many individuals who were or looked to be of Arab descent were questioned on airplanes, harassed by security officials, and even shunned by neighbors in their own communities, as the situation in the preceding essay describes. The consensus, however, was that, under the circumstances, such suspicions were justified, putting a new spin on the debate over racial profiling. As a group, discuss this issue and formulate your own position on racial profiling in times of crisis.

Three Days in a New York City Jail
Black = Terrorist = Thug: The New Racial Profile?
Bryonn Bain

On October 18, 1999, Harvard Law School student Bryonn Bain was arrested for a crime he didn't commit; for the crime, says Bain, of simply being black. He described his experience in an essay prepared for his Cultural Perspectives on the Law class, and later submitted it to the *Village Voice*, which printed it as the cover story in April 2000. Over 40,000 people have responded to the article, pushing Bain to the forefront of a debate on racial profiling and justice. Then, on November 23, 2002, Bain was, unbelievably, put through the anguish of yet another arrest, incarcerated for three days for crimes committed through the identity theft of his name (due to the media attention he generated from his original arrest). In this essay, also printed in the *Village Voice*, Bain describes his experience.

A musician and poet, Byronn Bain is a graduate of Columbia University and Harvard Law School. He is the founder of the Blackout Arts Collective and teaches poetry at New York University. He is considering pursuing legal action against the New York Police Department. Says Bain, "I have a cause, not a complaint." He published the account of his first experience in the hope that it would lead to meaningful dialogue and public action to end racial profiling.

CRITICAL THINKING   What assumptions do you have regarding our legal system? Do you believe that you will be treated fairly? That we are innocent until proven guilty? As you read Bain's essay describing his three days in jail, consider how your assumptions match his experience.

1   Saturday night, November 23, 2002, I was pulled over on the Bruckner Expressway because of a broken taillight. The police officer who ran my license claimed I had multiple warrants out for my arrest, and I was thrown in jail to begin a weekend I will not soon forget.

2   During the next three days, I was interrogated about "terrorist activity"—whether I was involved with a terrorist group or knew anyone else who was—without an attorney present. My Legal Aid lawyer claimed she was also a medical professional and diagnosed me as mentally ill when I told her I teach poetry at New York University. After my bail was posted, I was held behind bars another night because central booking ran out of the receipts required for my release. On my third day in jail, accused of two misdemeanors and a felony I knew nothing about, I was finally found innocent, and allowed to go home.

3   These events are not in themselves that extraordinary. Black men and women in this country have for centuries experienced far worse episodes with law enforcement. This incident is striking because it occurred at a time when I have been working to expose the injustice and inhumanity of the prison crisis in America, and because it was not the first time I was unjustly jailed.

4   Six months after I was racially profiled in 1999, the *Village Voice* published a story I wrote entitled "Walking While Black," recounting the wrongful arrest I experienced with my brother and cousin outside the now defunct Latin Quarter nightclub in Manhattan. The story was read by several hundred thousand people and received a response unprecedented in the paper's history. The 400 pages of mail sent to me in the following weeks indicated how widespread the epidemic of police misconduct is across the nation.

5   By May 2000, months after my initial arrest, the organization my family founded to empower communities of color using the arts, education, and activism began developing a national campaign to raise awareness about the prison-industrial complex. Months later, Blackout Arts Collective launched the Lyrics on Lockdown Tour—an annual road trip that brings hip-hop and spoken-word poetry to correctional facilities and community venues around the country. In November 2002, Blackout received the Union Square Award for our grassroots organizing efforts. The next day, I was arrested, strip-searched, and thrown into jail. (As a result of events detailed here, a notice of claim has been filed reserving the right to sue the culpable parties involved with the second case.)

Day 1: Saturday, November 23

6   It began with a familiar request: "License and registration, please." My truck had a flickering light bulb from a recent accident. I expected a traffic ticket, but one of the policemen said they were required to run a routine check. With the requested documents in hand, Officer Caraballo and his partner returned to their vehicle. Ten minutes later, I heard, "Get out of the car and come here!" As I walked nervously toward them, the partner approached me with his hand on his gun. I was told to place my hands on the hood of their car. I was searched, then handcuffed.

7   "Why are you arresting me"? I asked. "I haven't done anything wrong." The partner removed the wallet from my pocket and rummaged through its contents. He confiscated my driver's license, saying it was suspended. There were warrants out for my arrest, I was told. We raced to the 41st Precinct, where I was fingerprinted and had my mug shot taken. No one ever told me what charges were on the warrants that bore my name. I was not allowed to call a lawyer. I was in jail for the night, period.

8   Hours later, I sat in a Bronx cell with 12 other inmates and a backed-up toilet. An elderly man in the adjacent cell insisted he needed desperately to use the bathroom. He was ushered into our space. As they let him in, he ignored all of us and went straight to the stool. "Spray, spray! Guard, get the spray!" yelled an inmate who knew we were entitled to disinfectant. The guard said they had run out of spray. The older man was taken back to his cell, but we were left with an inescapable reminder of his visit.

Day 2: Sunday, November 24

9   As the next day crept by, I watched a pair of inmates trying to break into a pay phone. Another boasted of how adept his attorney was at getting him acquitted of major felonies he had actually committed. We were given bologna sandwiches for

lunch. When asked for my dietary restrictions the previous day, I had informed them I am a vegetarian.

10   I was later moved to a second cell with another set of inmates. Shortly thereafter, I was taken to an interrogation room. A court-appointed attorney walked in. Rachel Dole, a brunette of medium height and build, handed me a card identifying her as an employee of the Bronx Legal Aid Society. She sat across from me and talked as she looked through a file. Her questions were general and our dialogue direct. Recalling our conversation to the best of my ability, I wrote it down the next day.

11   "Have you ever been arrested?"

12   "Yes," I said, "but I was racially profiled. The case was dismissed."

13   "Did you know about these warrants?" she asked.

14   "No, I didn't."

15   Dole never looked up from the file or made eye contact with me. "Just promise me that you'll show up in court," she said.

16   "Of course, I'll show up," I said. "Can you just tell me what these warrants are for?"

17   She got up from her chair and walked away. She stopped at the door and turned to me before exiting. "You know what these warrants are for," she said.

18   I was led back to the second cell to wait some more. After a half-hour, I was led to a third cell. Then a guard came for me, and I was taken to a hallway where six other inmates waited. Every 10 minutes or so, a door at the end of the hall opened and a guard would come to take one of us into a courtroom. The inmates tried to guess what kind of mood to expect from the judge. I was still wondering why I was there.

19   Inside the courtroom, Dole stood before a podium, where I was to stand at her side. I was still a few feet away when she spoke to me, loud enough for the judge to hear.

20   "You actually have three warrants out for your arrest," Dole said.

21   "I don't know anything about those. They have nothing to do with me," I answered.

22   Dole said she could have my fingerprints taken again so they could be compared against those that generated the arrest warrants. I told her to go ahead; I had done nothing wrong. She asked that I be taken back to my cell until I could be reprinted.

23   Dole told the *Voice* she could not comment, as she had no recollection of the case, but added that it was likely that she would have recommended redoing the fingerprints.

24   Twenty minutes later, I was once again in the interrogation room. This time, Alison Webster, a slender blonde attorney also employed by Bronx Legal Aid, came in and sat across from me. She said she was just in the courtroom and had witnessed what occurred. Webster took the card given to me by Dole, scratched out the name, and wrote hers above it, along with her phone number. She told me not to take Dole's behavior personally; sometimes things like that happen. They were busy. Overwhelmed. But she was there to help.

25   Webster's words were comforting, but her appearance was alarming. Her face was hidden behind a surgical mask. Wearing plastic gloves, she extended a hand to

shake one of my shackled hands. Then she flipped through my file. "This doesn't add up," Webster said, according to my notes from the next day. "You say you started college in 1991, but what did you say was your date of birth?" Realizing the cause for her confusion, I told her I had skipped two grades before college. "That may be why your numbers seem off," I explained. Webster questioned me further.

26 "When did you go to high school?"

27 "I finished in 1991."

28 "And how did you pay for college?"

29 "Scholarships and loans."

22 "You say you went to law school?"

31 "In Cambridge, Massachusetts."

32 The questioning continued as I told her I was a graduate of Columbia University, where I had been president of my class all four years, before earning a master's from NYU, and then studying law at Harvard. But my résumé was no match for what she believed to be my rap sheet. She asked why I hadn't responded to the notices mailed to me about the warrants. I told her I knew nothing about them, and then shared with her that I had been out of the country for the past month.

33 "Where were you?" she asked.

34 "In India," I said. "Writing and doing research. I teach downtown at NYU."

35 After that, Webster changed her approach.

36 "In addition to being an attorney," she said, "I am also a registered nurse specializing in mental illness. And it is my professional obligation to inform you that you may have a bipolar disorder."

37 I was so shocked I had no idea how to respond. "You probably don't teach at NYU," she continued. "You probably never went to India last month. Frankly, I'm not sure anything you've told me is the truth." I still couldn't speak. "It's nothing bad," Webster assured me. "Sometimes people create alternate realities for themselves as a coping mechanism for dealing with stress."

38 I told her that if she checked my fingerprints, she would see my real background.

39 "This isn't anything racist," Webster replied, apropos of nothing. "Sometimes these things just happen."

40 After she was faxed a privacy waiver required for her to answer questions, Webster failed to respond to at least six *Voice* calls.

41 Webster never asked me about my medical history. She never asked if there was any history of mental illness in my family. I was returned to my cell. As I waited, I recalled some lyrics from a poem by Assata Shakur: "They say you're crazy/'cause you not crazy enough/ to kneel when told to kneel . . . /'cause you expose their madness."

42 I looked around at the cell. Someone had tagged "Problem Child" on the wall. I stared at those words so long they began taking shape in my own impromptu poem. More time passed. I wondered how long I would be in jail. The poetry was flowing, but there was nothing poetic or just about where I was. No one took my prints again.

43 At a poetry reading during my last semester of law school, a Liberian filmmaker who had been a finalist at the Sundance Film Festival the year before asked me to audition for his latest project. I had no prior interest in acting, but read for the role anyway. Several months later, I received a call from the director, Kona Khasu, asking me to play the lead. His movie, *Hunting in America*, told the story of a young

attorney who is racially profiled while driving a black truck, almost exactly as I had been. Khasu knew nothing about my incident with the NYPD. And here I was, in jail again. This was life imitating art imitating life.

44   I wondered if anyone would believe me when they heard I had been wrongfully arrested again. I could hardly believe it myself. Since I was interviewed on *60 Minutes* in 2001 about the first incident, I have had more than a dozen cases of identity theft. Funds have been removed from my bank account; credit cards obtained with my Social Security number have been maxed out.

45   A security guard at Columbia University arrested a young man carrying an ID card with my name and his picture. My law school dean was called by a judge in New Jersey who claimed I had interviewed with him, clerked at his courthouse for a week, and then stolen his bankruptcy files. During a telephone conversation a few days later, I discovered several inconsistencies on the résumé he had with my name. It was only after the judge received a copy of my law school photo ID that the judge believed I was not the thief in question.

46   Later that same day, while prepping me to return to court, Alison Webster advised me not to mention having a law degree or teaching at a university. The judge gave me a $50 ticket for having a busted taillight. (Months later, I received a notice from the Department of Motor Vehicles. The reason my license had been suspended and confiscated was that the DMV had failed to process records proving insurance coverage for my truck.) But there were still three warrants for my arrest, one of which included a felony charge of grand larceny. The judge said I would have to return to Manhattan Criminal Court for another hearing. He set bail for me. My family arrived that evening with the money. The clerk counted out $3,000, then apologized.

47   "I'm sorry," she said. "We don't have any more bail receipts. Mr. Bain will not be able to go home with you today." The prison was out of paper. So I spent another night in jail.

Day 3: Monday, November 25

48 Before the sun came up, I was among a dozen or so inmates chained together to board a bus for Rikers Island. An iron-barred door was locked to separate the driver and a correctional officer from the rows of inmates seated in the back of the bus. Just before we pulled off, I overheard a senior officer change our destination to a place he called "The VCBC." We went to a dock at Hunts Point in the Bronx, and drove onto a boat. It was a floating jail. The sign in front of the gates read: "Vernon C. Bain Correctional Center."

49   The irony was overwhelming. This boat shared the name of the family that once owned my ancestors. And here I was, centuries later, being loaded back onto a ship in chains.

50   We were ordered to strip naked and prepare for cavity searches. A young inmate who voiced his reluctance to do so was dragged into a back room by three guards. Every man in line heard his cries as he was beaten.

51   At dawn, I was taken with several inmates to the criminal courthouse in Manhattan. The officer who processed my paperwork laughed when I said I wasn't guilty. His response echoed a cliché from countless films: "Sure you're innocent. So is everybody here."

52   A well-dressed young attorney, Eric Williams, introduced himself to me. I began to discuss strategy with the namesake of the man who fought to liberate my parents' native Trinidad from colonial rule. This Williams was a former student of one of the leading defense attorneys in the U.S.: Jill Soffiyah Elijah, whom I had called collect from jail the day before. We had met at Harvard's Criminal Justice Institute, where she teaches and represents clients from Dorchester and Roxbury.

53   Williams asked the court for my prints and photos, but his request was denied. He told Judge Robert M. Stolz that this was the seventh case of identity theft I had experienced since I was unjustly arrested two years prior. The assistant district attorney, Justin Herdman, interrupted him. "Your honor," began the dark-haired young man in a blue suit, "to avoid any potential conflict of interest, I should inform you that I know the defendant. He was in my law school class at Harvard."

54   The press secretary of the Manhattan district attorney's office and Herdman both said the ADA could not comment on the case.

55   Stolz ordered the delivery of the arrest photos and fingerprints just before the afternoon recess. He ordered me released on my own recognizance, but I was told to return after lunch. I was then taken back to my cell to sign release forms. Three documents were handed to me.

56   One had my name printed on it, and the others had the name "Anwar Bostick" typed above my Social Security number. The papers seemed to suggest that Bostick had obtained my name and personal information. When arrested for the crimes with which I had been charged that weekend, he somehow passed off my identity as his own, was released after making bail, and then failed to show up for his court date. His three arrest warrants were thus reissued—in my name. Because our arrest photos and fingerprints were never compared when I was arrested, it was nearly Monday evening by the time anyone in the system found out we were not the same person.

57   I refused to sign the release forms. "You'll sign them if you want to get out of here," a guard said. Another officer agreed.

58   "Anwar Bostick is your alias," the second officer informed me while flipping through the forms. "Are you refusing to sign this? Because if you are, you'll just have to sit in jail and wait until whenever they get around to calling you back to court." I refused to incriminate myself. They ignored the judge's ruling that I be released, and returned me to a basement holding cell.

59   After lunch, a captain and lieutenant for the Department of Corrections showed up to settle the dispute. Following a lengthy debate, it was discovered that my signature was not even necessary. According to the captain, someone without the authority to do so had introduced the mandatory signature policy as "a rule" and it had become the standard.

60   "You do the wrong thing long enough," he explained, "and it becomes right." ◆

FREEWRITING ASSIGNMENT ────────────────────────────────

Have you ever been pulled over by a police officer for a traffic violation? What was the experience like? If not, what would you expect to happen, and how do you think you would react?

CRITICAL READING

1. Is Bain's experience a case of racial profiling, as his subtitle suggests, or a case of identity theft? Did some members of the legal system act appropriately in this case, and others inappropriately? Discuss the actions of each person connected to the legal system that Bain encounters.
2. How do you feel after reading this essay? Are there particular points in his narrative that seem more powerful than others? Do you find yourself becoming emotionally involved with his narrative? Explain.
3. Identify Bain's references to racism in his article. Evaluate Bain's recounting of his experience as it relates to racism.
4. How does Bain describe the lawyers from Legal Aid?
5. Do the questions asked of Bain by his lawyers seem strange? What do you think they should have asked him? What do you think he should have said to his lawyers?
6. Bain mentions that he was a student at Harvard Law School. In light of this fact, does his reaction and behavior during this experience seem surprising? How would you have acted in this situation if you held a law degree?

CRITICAL WRITING

7. *Analytical Writing*: Bain mentions that he was a victim of racial profiling, which led to his first arrest. Read about his experience described in the *Village Voice* at *www.villagevoice.com/issues/0017/bain.php*. Evaluate the effectiveness of his technique of using "articles" based on the Bill of Rights to demonstrate the injustice he feels and how these articles reflect his actual experience.
8. Read the letters to the editor at the *Village Voice* written in response to Bain's second article. Write your own letter to the editor describing your own impressions and opinions regarding Bain's experience.

GROUP PROJECTS

9. Visit *Horizon Magazine*'s online site at *www.horizonmag.com/6/racial-profiling.asp* and take the racial profiling test. Discuss the test as a group, and summarize your results in preparation for a class discussion.
10. Visit Bryonn Bain's web site at *http://www.bryonnbain.com/*. In light of what you know about Bain based on his articles in the *Village Voice*, discuss how Bain is trying to increase awareness of racism in America. Evaluate his efforts and how they do, or do not, contribute to a broader dialogue on racism.

Hailing While Black
Shelby Steele

Many articles in this section describe how racial profiling has created a sense of social and political distrust. But has the high-profile exposure of this issue created an atmosphere where we have come to expect racism? To test it everyday in the ordinary actions of our lives? In this piece, Shelby Steele explains how even the simple act of hailing a cab in New York City can become fraught with social and political implications.

Shelby Steele is a research fellow at the Hoover Institution of Stanford University, specializing in the study of race relations, affirmative action, and multiculturalism. He is the author of *The Content of Our Character: A New Vision of Race in America* (1990), for which he was honored with the National Book Critic's Circle Award, and *A Dream Deferred: The Second Betrayal of Black Freedom in America* (1998). This essay appeared in the July 30, 2001, issue of *Time* magazine.

CRITICAL THINKING What expectations and assumptions do we harbor in how we expect to be treated by others? When hailing a cab, for example, do we expect an empty cab to stop and pick us up? Do we expect courteous service at a restaurant? What happens to our feelings when we do not receive the service we expect?

1 In Manhattan recently I attempted something that is thought to be all but impossible for a black man: I tried to hail a cab going uptown toward Harlem after dark. And I'll admit to feeling a new nervousness. This simple action—black man hailing cab—is now a tableau in America's ongoing culture war. If no cab swerves in to pick me up, America is still a racist country, and the entire superstructure of contemporary liberalism is bolstered. If I catch a ride, conservatives can breath easier. So, as I raise my hand and step from the curb, much is at stake.

2 It's all the talk these days of racial profiling that has set off my nerves in this way. Having grown up in the era of segregation, I know I can survive the racial profiling of a cabby. What makes me most nervous is the anxiety that I have wrongly estimated the degree of racism in American life. I am a conservative. But conservatism is a misunderstood identity in blacks that would be much easier to carry in a world where New York City cab drivers stopped for black fares, even after dark.

3 It is easy to believe that racial profiling is a serious problem in America. It fits the American profile, and now politicians have stepped forward to give it credence as a problem. But is it a real problem? Is dark skin a shorthand for criminality in the mind of America's law-enforcement officers? Studies show that we blacks are stopped in numbers higher than our percentage in the population but lower than our documented involvement in crime. If you're trying to measure racism, isn't it better to compare police stops to actual black involvement in crime than to the mere representation of blacks in the population? The elephant in the living room—and the tragedy in black America—is that we commit crimes vastly out of proportion to our numbers in society.

4   But I can already hear "so what"? from those who believe profiling is a serious problem. And I know that the more energetic among them will move numbers and points of reference around like shells in a shill game to show racism. In other words, racial profiling is now an "identity" issue like affirmative action, black reparations or even O.J.'s innocence. It is less a real issue than a coded argument over how much racism exists in society today. We argue these issues fiercely—make a culture war around them—because the moral authority of both the left and right political identities hangs in the balance.

5   Racial profiling is a boon to the left because this political identity justifies its demand for power by estimating racism to be high. The more racism, the more power the left demands for social interventions that go beyond simple fairness under the law. Profiling hurts the right because it makes its fairness-under-the-law position on race seem inadequate, less than moral considering the prevalence of racism. The real debate over racial profiling is not about stops and searches on the New Jersey Turnpike. It is about the degree of racism in America and the distribution of power it justifies.

6   Even as individuals, we Americans cannot define our political and moral identities without making them accountable to an estimate of racism's potency in American life. Our liberalism or conservatism, our faith in government intervention or restraint and our concept of social responsibility on issues from diversity to school reform—all these will be, in part, a response to how bad we think racism is. The politically liberal identity I was born into began to fade as my estimate of American racism declined. I could identify with a wider range of American ideas and possibilities when I thought they were no longer tainted by racism. Many whites I know today, who are trying to separate themselves from the shame of America's racist past, will overestimate racism to justify a liberal identity that they hope proves that separateness. First the estimation, then the identity.

7   Recently, after a talk on a college campus, a black girl stood up and told me that she was "frequently" stopped by police while driving in this bucolic and liberal college town. A professor on the same campus told me that blacks there faced an "unwelcome atmosphere"—unwelcomeness being a newly fashionable estimation of racism's potency on college campuses today. Neither of these people offered supporting facts. But I don't think they were lying so much as "spinning" an estimation of racism that shored up their political identities.

8   We are terrible at discussing our racial problems in America today because we just end up defending our identities and the political power we hope those identities will align us with. On that day in Manhattan, I caught the first cab that came along. And I should have been happy just for the convenience of good service. That I also saw this minor event as evidence of something, that I was practicing a kind of political sociology as well as catching a cab—that is the problem. ◆

FREEWRITING ASSIGNMENT

In this essay, Steele presents a black conservative's point of view on racial profiling and social fairness. Does the fact that Steele is black make his argument more compelling? A conservative? Why or why not?

CRITICAL READING

1. Steele labels himself a "conservative." How does such an identifier influence his discussion? What does it tell you about how he views himself and his expectations of his audience? Explain.
2. What is the "elephant in the living room" Steele alludes to in paragraph 3? How does it relate to the argument in favor of racial profiling?
3. Steele comments that racial profiling has become "an identity issue, like affirmative action." In what ways are these issues similar? What is the coded argument that they both veil? Explain.
4. Steele admits that the first available cab stops to pick him up, much to his relief. Do you think he would have written the same essay if he had been passed by instead?

CRITICAL WRITING

5. *Personal Narrative*: Have you ever anticipated or expected that you might be mistreated due to your race, age, or gender? If so, describe the situation and its outcome.
6. Steele is concerned that a cab may not pick him up because of his appearance—a black male trying to hail a cab at night, in New York City. In other words, he is concerned about how the way he looks to others. Write an essay in which you consider the connection between how others "see" you and how you perceive yourself. Critically analyze how your physical appearance may be "interpreted" by others.

GROUP PROJECT

7. While much of the discussion on racial profiling addresses legal injustice, an often overlooked but vitally important element is the impact such experiences have on a person. Steele describes the internal conflict he faces by simply raising his hand to hail a cab. Discuss the psychology at work here, and its impact on a person. As a group, discuss incidents where you have felt wronged because of a stereotype—it could be related to gender, age, social group, financial status, race, or religion.

Are You a Terrorist, or Do You Play One on TV?

Laura Fokkena

Sometimes stereotypes can be more than simply insulting; they can interfere with the daily lives of the people victimized by them. As Laura Fokkena observes in this essay, Hollywood has long cast people from the Middle East as terrorists. This stereotype wasn't helped by the tragic events of September 11. The perpetuation of the Arab-as-terrorist stereotype has caused Fokkena, who is American, and her husband, who is Egyptian, to face the scrutiny of airport security, to be kept off of flights, and to be eyed with suspicion merely because he resembles the same ethnicity as the Muslim extremists who committed acts of terrorism. As Fokkena explains, for some people racial profiling, on the street or on the screen, is nothing new.

Laura Fokkena's writing has been published in a variety of newspapers and magazines in the United States and Middle East, including *HipMama* and *Home Education Magazine*. This essay first appeared in the November 2002 edition of *PopPolitics*.

CRITICAL THINKING   In this piece, Laura Fokkena comments on the negative way Hollywood depicts people from the Middle East on film. Before you read her essay, consider the way Hollywood traditionally presents terrorists in the movies. How can Hollywood's stereotyping hurt people of Middle Eastern descent living in America? Or is it "just Hollywood"?

1   Several years ago I came home from work one night to find my Egyptian husband and his Jordanian friend up past midnight watching *Aladdin*. Our daughter—then a toddler and the rightful owner of the video—had gone to bed hours earlier and left the two of them to enjoy their own private cultural studies seminar in our living room.

2   "Oh, God, now the sultan's marrying her off!" cried Jordanian Friend. "It's barbaric, but hey, it's home," quipped my husband, repeating lyrics from the film while rolling his r's in a baritone imitation of an accent he's never had.

3   I admit it: I purchased Disney crap. In my own defense, I try to avoid all strains of happily-ever-after princess stories. But, other than a few grainy videos that you can order from, say, Syria, *Aladdin* is one of the rare movies with an Arab heroine available for the 2-to-6-year-old set. And so I had taken my chances with it.

4   My husband preferred to tell my daughter bedtime stories taken straight out of *1,001 Nights*, before they'd been contorted at the hands of Hollywood. (Tales of Ali Baba's clever servant Morghana are far more feminist than the big screen version of *Aladdin* ever was.) For my daughter's sake, I think this is wonderful. But it's also disappointing to see yet another example of unadulterated Middle Eastern literature trapped in Middle Eastern communities, told in whispers to children at bedtime, while the world at large is bombarded with a mammoth distorted Hollywood version replete with hook-nosed villains, limping camels, a manic genie and Jasmine's sultan dad who is (of course) a sexist.

5   While Native Americans, Asian Americans and numerous other ethnic groups have had significant success in battling racist and inaccurate media images of their communities, Muslims and Middle Easterners are just beginning to decry stereotypical portrayals of Arabs and Islam. In April, following another crisis in the West Bank, Edward Said wrote a short piece, published in both the American and Arab press, stressing the importance of media savvy. "We have simply never learned the importance of systematically organizing our political work in this country on a mass level, so that for instance the average American will not immediately think of 'terrorism' when the word 'Palestinian' is pronounced."

6   After Sept. 11, an astonishing number of films and television programs were cancelled, delayed or taken out of production due to unfortunate coincidences between their violent plotlines and, well, reality. It went without saying that all this mad scrambling was for the benefit of a nation momentarily unwilling to see the fun in shoot-em-up action adventures, and that it was not—at least in the case of movies with Middle Eastern characters—indicative of a sudden dose of sensitivity towards anti-Arab stereotyping.

7   But apparently Hollywood has either declared the grieving period over, or has decided that what we need most right now are more escapist fantasies of Americans kicking the asses of aliens and foreigners. A number of films initially pushed back have since been released (some, like *Black Hawk Down* and *Behind Enemy Lines* were actually moved up), and television series that were hastily rewritten to eradicate any terrorist references have now been rewritten again, this time to highlight them.

8   This first became obvious back in March, when CBS was bold enough to broadcast *Executive Decision* (albeit opposite the Oscars). *Executive Decision*, originally released in 1996, is a mediocre thriller that depicts Muslim terrorists hijacking a 747 en route to Washington, D. C. Like most films in its genre, wild-eyed Arabs are foiled by the technological, intellectual and ultimately moral superiority of Americans.

9   *Executive Decision* has since appeared repeatedly on various cable networks, along with *True Lies* (1994), *The Siege* (1998) and *Not Without My Daughter* (1991). NBC's *The West Wing* has written a fictional Arab country into its plotline (and assassinated its defense minister); *Law and Order* opened this year's season with the story of an American convert to Islam who murders a women's rights activist. Islam is treated with varying degrees of nuance in each of these works, but it is always approached as a dilemma to be overcome—one always needs to do something about these troublesome Muslims—rather than folded unproblematically into the background, the way Josh and Toby's Judaism is presented on *The West Wing*, or the way Betty Mahmoody's Christianity is portrayed in *Not Without My Daughter*.

10   According to a recently released report from *Human Rights Watch*, the federal government received reports of 481 anti-Muslim hate crimes in 2001, 17 times the number it received the year before. It also noted that more than 2,000 cases of harassment were reported to Arab and Muslim organizations. The Bush administration and the Department of Justice have responded on the one hand by condemning hate crimes against the Muslim and Middle Eastern community, and on the other by rounding up Muslims and Middle Easterners for questioning. Most notoriously, the FBI and Justice Department announced last fall their intent to schedule "interviews" with 5,000 men of Arab descent between the ages of 18 and 33. More than 1,000 men were detained indefinitely and incommunicado in the aftermath of Sept. 11, most of them on minor visa charges.

11   Yet racial profiling and ethnic stereotyping are nothing new to Americans of Middle Eastern descent. Hollywood has long used images of bumbling, accented Arabs and Iranians as shorthand for "vile enemy," depicting them as stupid (witness the terrorist lackey in *True Lies* who forgets to put batteries in his camera when making a video to release to the press), yet nevertheless deeply threatening to all that is good and right with America. So ingrained is the image of Arab-as-terrorist that Ray Hanania, an Arab-American satirist, titled his autobiography *I'm Glad I*

Look Like a Terrorist ("almost every TV or Hollywood Arab terrorist looks like some uncle or aunt or cousin of mine. The scene where Fred Dryer [of TV's *Hunter*] pounces on a gaggle of terrorists in the movie *Death Before Dishonor* (1987) looks like an assault on a Hanania family reunion").

12   Within hours of the Oklahoma City bombing in 1995, there were rumors of Arab or Muslim involvement, and real fear within the Middle Eastern community about being falsely associated with the atrocity. Despite the regular drum of tension in Northern Ireland and the civil wars that burn throughout Africa and the Americas, only those who look Middle Eastern—even Sikhs, young women and members of the Secret Service—have been the targets of this particular brand of racial profiling.

13   Nowhere is this game of Pin The Bomb Threat On The Muslim more obvious than at the airport. A few years ago I flew out of Cairo with my husband and discovered that F.W.A. (Flying While Arab) is no joke. We landed in Paris with a crying baby and were ushered to the back of the line while the airline attendants processed every other passenger. My husband was unconcerned; he was used to the routine. But I was acutely aware of two things: (1) that the baby was on her last diaper; and (2) that diaper was feeling heavy.

14   Our turn finally came a good three hours later, whereupon we spent another 45 minutes having our carry-on luggage examined and re-examined, answering the same questions again and again, and waiting while security checked and re-checked their computer database. All this over a graduate student from Egypt, married to an American citizen, during a time when world politics were calm enough that Bill Clinton's main preoccupation was rubbing lipstick smudges off his fly.

15   As it happened, most of the French airline workers were on strike that week (imagine that!) so we were sent to an airport hotel for the night and told we could take our connecting flight to D. C. the next day. While the other Americans and Europeans on our flight took the opportunity to spend a free night in Paris, my husband was instructed not to leave the hotel. I suppose the baby and I could have taken our crisp blue passports and gone into the city without him, but the thought of taking advantage of my American citizenship—something I'd just been born into by chance, mind you—while he stayed behind watching bad French television in the hotel lounge was too much to take.

16   Of course, it would be a mistake to assume that the most egregious offenses of racial profiling take place at the airport. The Council on American-Islamic Relations reports that half of the discrimination complaints it received in 2001 were work-related, and there has been a leap in the number of outright hate crimes, including at least three murders, since Sept. 11.

17   April's *Atlantic Monthly* featured an essay by Randall Kennedy, Harvard law professor and author of *Nigger: The Strange Career of a Troublesome Word*, comparing racial profiling to its "alter ego," affirmative action. "Supporters of profiling, who are willing to impose what amounts to a racial tax on profiled groups, denounce as betrayals of 'color blindness' programs that require racial diversity," he wrote. "A similar turnabout can be seen on the part of many of those who support affirmative action. Impatient with talk of communal needs in assessing racial profiling, they very often have no difficulty with subordinating the interests of individual white candidates to the purported good of the whole."

18   Kennedy's piece reaches no conclusions—other than to affirm the need for the debate in the first place—but I see no contradiction here. When workers are paid unequally for doing equivalent work, union organizers naturally argue that all workers should be paid what the highest-earning worker is paid, a process called "leveling up." Both the opposition to racial profiling and the support of affirmative action are about leveling up.

19   In both cases, marginalized groups who have suffered from stereotyping and injustice are asking to be considered full-fledged participants in our culture, to be given the same benefit of the doubt that white people have been given for centuries. Membership has its privileges, including job promotions, tenure, the ability to speed in a school zone and get off with a warning, and impromptu nights in Paris cafes. Whether one considers these things rights or luxuries, they are the aspects of citizenship that make one feel both accepted in and loyal to one's community and culture.

20   Some, like Ann Coulter—a columnist so out of touch even *The National Review* fired her—call those who complain about such matters "crazy," "paranoid," "immature nuts" and (my favorite) "ticking time bombs." Though most people would find her language over-the-top, there are many people who agree with the sentiment: that an increase in security, even if it means engaging in racial profiling, is a necessary evil in these dark times.

21   Lori Hope, in a My Turn column published in *Newsweek* last spring, worried that in alerting a flight attendant of a suspicious-looking traveler ("He was olive-skinned, black-haired and clean-shaven, with a blanket covering his legs and feet"), she might have "ruined an innocent man's day" when the man was removed from the flight. Nevertheless, she said, "I'm not sure I regret it . . . it's not the same world it was half a lifetime ago."

22   And for her, it probably isn't. But for the thousands of people who have been falsely associated with a handful of extremists for no reason other than their ancestry or their religion, for those who have been targeted not for their crimes but for color of their skin, not a whole lot has changed.

23   The assumption in all these discussions is that getting kicked off a plane is merely a hassle. Granted, no one should be hassled because of their race or ethnicity, but c'mon, be reasonable. This is just a little annoyance we're talking about, the way watching the mad professor getting chased around by psychotic Libyans in *Back to the Future* is "fun," "just a joke," you know, like someone in blackface. National security is the real issue. Anyone who can't see that must have something to hide.

24   But those who argue that it's an inevitable necessity should look to countries like Egypt, where racial and religious profiling as a manner of combating Islamic extremism is obviously unworkable. Ethnic stereotyping, whether by Hollywood or by the FBI, solidifies the wedge between what we call "mainstream" culture and those who are perceived to be on the outside of it. "Ruining an innocent man's day" isn't the point, just as the hassle of moving to a different seat on the bus wasn't the point for Rosa Parks. Didn't we hammer all this out 40 years ago? ◆

FREEWRITING ASSIGNMENT

Fokkena notes that immediately following the attacks, many movie studios delayed the release of violent films, especially ones featuring Arabs as the bad guys. In light of the events of September 11, what new obstacles do Arab Americans face in dispelling the film stereotype Fokkena describes?

CRITICAL READING

1. How has Hollywood promoted the stereotype of Arabs as terrorists? What do you think of this stereotype? Is it art imitating life? Is it unfair? Explain.
2. How has racial profiling affected Fokkena's life and her family? Explain.
3. Evaluate Fokkena's connection between racial profiling and affirmative action. In what ways are they similar, and how are they different?
4. In paragraph 21, Fokkena refers to an essay written by Lori Hope that appeared in *Newsweek*. Read about the Lawyers Committee for Civil Rights suit (*http://www.lccr.com/khan.doc*) against the airline that ejected a passenger from a flight on the recommendation of another passenger. Was Hope correct in voicing her concerns? What about the airline? Explain.
5. What does Fokkena allude to in her final sentence? Why does she end her essay with this reference?

CRITICAL WRITING

6. Fokkena opens her essay with a reference to Disney's *Aladdin*, a movie she purchases because of its Arab heroine. Consider the ways Hollywood influences our cultural perspectives of race and ethnicity. Write an essay exploring the influence, however slight, film and television have had on your own perception of race. You may interview other students for their opinions on this issue and address their observations in your essay.
7. Write an essay discussing your own family's sense of ethic or racial identity. What are the origins of some of your families' values, traditions, and customs? Have these customs ever been questioned by people who did not understand them? What assumptions do you think other people may have about your family?
8. Fokkena comments that Ann Coulter was a columnist "so out of touch even the *National Review* fired her." Read her controversial column at *http://www.nationalreview.com/coulter/coulter091301.shtml.* Respond to her column in your own words.

GROUP PROJECTS

9. The Patriot Act was designed to "deter and punish terrorist acts in the United States and around the world, to enhance law enforcement investigatory tools, and for other purposes." Research the Patriot Act online (try *www.epic.org/privacy/terrorism/hr3162.html and http://www.lifeandliberty. gov/,* as well as an article on Slate at *http://slate.msn.com/id/ 2087984/*

"Guide to the Patriot Act"). What does the Patriot Act allow the government to do? How does it connect to racial profiling and issues of freedom? Discuss as a group.

10. As a group, identify as many movies as you can involving highjackings, espionage, and terrorist activity over the last 15 years (you may try the Internet Movie Database at *http://www.imdb.com/* to assist your research). Who are the villains? Prepare a demographic pie chart depicting the data you collect. Is the stereotyping as bad as Fokkena indicates? Explain.

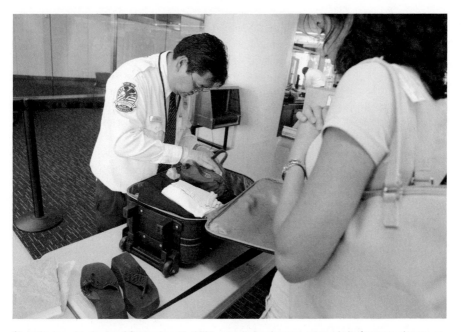

Since the terrorist attacks of September 11, 2001, security has become a top priority for many airports, especially international ones. In the months following the attacks, many individuals who looked Middle Eastern were detained and subjected to luggage and personal searches. While this posed a complication for air travel, many people felt such measures were worth the effort. Racial profiling is only one of several factors that security personnel use, but can it be the only one? Is it reasonable to ethnically profile individuals based on experience, or is that simple racism? Or is airport security a situation in which we must sacrifice principles for safety?

1. What is happening in this photo? If you saw the photograph in 1994, what would you assume is happening and why? Do you think our interpretation of this photo is different now? Explain.

2. Are security measures at airports unbiased and fair? Do you think they single out certain people? Explain.

3. Do you think that ethnic profiling is justifiable in considering whom to stop and search at airport security checkpoints? Should everyone be stopped? Would this make air travel tedious, or is it a safety measure worth the time and effort? Explain your point of view.

VIEWPOINTS

► **You Can't Judge a Crook by His Color**
Randall Kennedy

► **In Defense of Racial Profiling**
John Derbyshire

Racial profiling is the practice by law enforcement of considering race as an indicator of the likelihood of criminal behavior. Based on statistical assumptions, racial profiling presumes that certain groups of people are more likely to commit, or not commit, certain crimes. The Supreme Court officially upheld the constitutionality of this practice, as long as race is only one of several factors leading to the detainment or arrest of an individual.

In the first essay in this Viewpoints section, law professor Randall Kennedy argues that while racial profiling may seem justifiable, it is still morally wrong. His essay is followed by a piece by John Derbyshire, who argues that while we can rhetorically debate in principle why racial profiling may be morally reprehensible, it will continue to be a tool of law enforcement not because of racism, but because it is "common sense."

Randall Kennedy is a professor at Harvard Law School where he teaches courses on freedom of expression and the regulation of race relations. Educated at Princeton, Oxford, and Yale Law School, he is a member of the bar of the District of Columbia and the Supreme Court of the United States. He is the author of several books, including *Race, Crime, and the Law* (1998), for which he won the 1998 Robert F. Kennedy Book Award. In addition to contributing to many general and scholarly publications, he sits on the editorial boards of the *Nation, Dissent,* and the *American Prospect.*

Political conservative John Derbyshire is a contributing editor to the *National Review* and a columnist for the *National Review Online* (NRO). He is the author of the books *Seeing Calvin Coolidge in a Dream* (1996) and *Fire from the Sun* (2000). Kennedy's article first appeared in the *New Republic* in 1999, and Derbyshire's was printed in the February 19, 2001 issue of the *National Review.*

CRITICAL THINKING

Derbyshire argues that much of the public outcry against racial profiling stems from its exposure as a political issue by aspiring public figures. Why is racial profiling such a popular political issue? Is there truth to Derbyshire's assertion that "anyone who wants a public career in the United States must place himself on record as being against it"?

You Can't Judge a Crook by His Color
Randall Kennedy

1   In Kansas City, a Drug Enforcement Administration officer stops and questions a young man who has just stepped off a flight from Los Angeles. The officer has focused on this man because intelligence reports indicate that black gangs in L.A. are flooding the Kansas City area with illegal drugs. Young, toughly dressed, and appearing nervous, he paid for his ticket in cash, checked no luggage, brought two carry-on bags, and made a beeline for a taxi when he arrived. Oh, and one other thing: The young man is black. When asked why he decided to question this man, the officer declares that he considered race, along with other factors, because doing so helps him allocate limited time and resources efficiently.

2   Should we applaud the officer's conduct? Permit it? Prohibit it? This is not a hypothetical example. Encounters like this take place every day, all over the country, as police battle street crime, drug trafficking, and illegal immigration. And this particular case study happens to be the real-life scenario presented in a federal lawsuit of the early '90s, *United States* v. *Weaver,* in which the 8th U.S. Circuit Court of Appeals upheld the constitutionality of the officer's action.

3   "Large groups of our citizens," the court declared, "should not be regarded by law enforcement officers as presumptively criminal based upon their race." The court went on to say, however, that "facts are not to be ignored simply because they may be unpleasant." According to the court, the circumstances were such that the young man's race, considered in conjunction with other signals, was a legitimate factor in the decision to approach and ultimately detain him. "We wish it were otherwise," the court maintained, "but we take the facts as they are presented to us, not as we would like them to be." Other courts have agreed that the Constitution does not prohibit police from considering race, as long as they do so for bona fide purposes of law enforcement (not racial harassment) and as long as it is only one of several factors.

4   These decisions have been welcome news to the many law enforcement officials who consider what has come to be known as racial profiling an essential weapon in the war on crime. They maintain that, in areas where young African American males commit a disproportionate number of the street crimes, the cops are justified in scrutinizing that sector of the population more closely than others—just as they are generally justified in scrutinizing men more closely than they do women.

5   As Bernard Parks, chief of the Los Angeles Police Department, explained to Jeffrey Goldberg of the *New York Times Magazine:* "We have an issue of violent crime against jewelry salespeople. . . . The predominant suspects are Colombians. We don't find Mexican Americans, or blacks, or other immigrants. It's a collection of several hundred Colombians who commit this crime. If you see six in a car in front of the Jewelry Mart, and they're waiting and watching people with briefcases, should we play the percentages and follow them? It's common sense."

6   Cops like Parks say that racial profiling is a sensible, statistically based tool. Profiling lowers the cost of obtaining and processing crime information, which in

turn lowers the overall cost of doing the business of policing. And the fact that a number of cops who support racial profiling are black, including Parks, buttresses claims that the practice isn't motivated by bigotry. Indeed, these police officers note that racial profiling is race-*neutral* in that it can be applied to persons of all races, depending on the circumstances. In predominantly black neighborhoods in which white people stick out (as potential drug customers or racist hooligans, for example), whiteness can become part of a profile. In the southwestern United States, where Latinos often traffic in illegal immigrants, apparent Latin American ancestry can become part of a profile.

7   But the defenders of racial profiling are wrong. Ever since the Black and Latino Caucus of the New Jersey Legislature held a series of hearings, complete with testimony from victims of what they claimed was the New Jersey state police force's overly aggressive racial profiling, the air has been thick with public denunciations of the practice.

8   Unfortunately, though, many who condemn racial profiling do so without really thinking the issue through. One common complaint is that using race (say, blackness) as one factor in selecting surveillance targets is fundamentally racist. But selectivity of this sort can be defended on nonracist grounds. "There is nothing more painful to me at this age in my life," Jesse Jackson said in 1993, "than to walk down the street and hear footsteps and start to think about robbery and then look around and see somebody white and feel relieved." Jackson was relieved not because he dislikes black people, but because he estimated that he stood a somewhat greater risk of being robbed by a black person than by a white person. Statistics confirm that African Americans—particularly young black men—commit a dramatically disproportionate share of street crime in the United States. This is a sociological fact, not a figment of a racist media (or police) imagination. In recent years, victims report blacks as perpetrators of around 25 percent of violent crimes, although blacks constitute only about 12 percent of the nation's population.

9   So, if racial profiling isn't bigoted, and if the empirical claim upon which the practice rests is sound, why is it wrong?

10   Racial distinctions are and should be different from other lines of social stratification. That is why, since the civil rights revolution of the 1960s, courts have typically ruled—based on the 14th Amendment's equal protection clause—that mere reasonableness is an insufficient justification for officials to discriminate on racial grounds. In such cases, courts have generally insisted on applying "strict scrutiny"—the most intense level of judicial review—to government actions. Under this tough standard, the use of race in governmental decision making may be upheld only if it serves a compelling government objective and only if it is "narrowly tailored" to advance that objective.

11   A disturbing feature of this debate is that many people, including judges, are suggesting that decisions based on racial distinctions do not constitute unlawful racial discrimination—as long as race is not the only reason a person was treated objectionably. The court that upheld the DEA agent's action at the Kansas City airport, for instance, declined to describe it as racially discriminatory and thus evaded strict scrutiny.

12   But racially discriminatory decisions typically stem from mixed motives. For example, an employer who prefers white candidates to black candidates—except for those black candidates with superior experience and test scores—is engaging in racial discrimination, even though race is not the only factor he considers (since he selects black superstars). In some cases, race is a marginal factor; in others it is the only factor. The distinction may have a bearing on the moral or logical justification, but taking race into account at all means engaging in discrimination.

13   Because both law and morality discourage racial discrimination, proponents should persuade the public that racial profiling is justifiable. Instead, they frequently neglect its costs and minimize the extent to which it adds to the resentment blacks feel toward the law enforcement establishment. When O. J. Simpson was acquitted, many recognized the danger of a large sector of Americans feeling cynical and angry toward the system. Such alienation creates witnesses who fail to cooperate with police, citizens who view prosecutors as the enemy, lawyers who disdain the rules they have sworn to uphold, and jurors who yearn to get even with a system that has, in their eyes, consistently mistreated them. Racial profiling helps keep this pool of accumulated rage filled to the brim.

14   The courts have not been sufficiently mindful of this risk. In rejecting a 1976 constitutional challenge that accused U.S. Border Patrol officers in California of selecting cars for inspection partly on the basis of drivers' apparent Mexican ancestry, the Supreme Court noted in part that, of the motorists passing the checkpoint, fewer than 1 percent were stopped. It also noted that, of the 820 vehicles inspected during the period in question, roughly 20 percent contained illegal aliens.

15   Justice William J. Brennan dissented, however, saying the Court did not indicate the ancestral makeup of *all* the persons the Border Patrol stopped. It is likely that many of the innocent people who were questioned were of apparent Mexican ancestry who then had to prove their obedience to the law just because others of the same ethnic background have broken laws in the past.

16   The practice of racial profiling undercuts a good idea that needs more support from both society and the law: Individuals should be judged by public authorities on the basis of their own conduct and not on the basis of racial generalization. Race-dependent policing retards the development of bias-free thinking; indeed, it encourages the opposite.

17   What about the fact that in some communities people associated with a given racial group commit a disproportionately large number of crimes? Our commitment to a just social order should prompt us to end racial profiling even if the generalizations on which the technique is based are supported by empirical evidence. This is not as risky as it may sound. There are actually many contexts in which the law properly enjoins us to forswear playing racial odds even when doing so would advance legitimate goals.

18   For example, public opinion surveys have established that blacks distrust law enforcement more than whites. Thus, it would be rational—and not necessarily racist—for a prosecutor to use ethnic origin as a factor in excluding black potential jurors. Fortunately, the Supreme Court has outlawed racial discrimination of this sort. And because demographics show that in the United States, whites tend to live

longer than blacks, it would be perfectly rational for insurers to charge blacks higher life-insurance premiums. Fortunately, the law forbids that, too.

19   The point here is that racial equality, like all good things in life, costs something. Politicians suggest that all Americans need to do in order to attain racial justice is forswear bigotry. But they must also demand equal treatment before the law even when unequal treatment is defensible in the name of nonracist goals—and even when their effort will be costly.

20   Since abandoning racial profiling would make policing more expensive and perhaps less effective, those of us who oppose it must advocate a responsible alternative. Mine is simply to spend more money on other means of enforcement—and then spread the cost on some nonracial basis. One way to do that would be to hire more police officers. Another way would be to subject everyone to closer surveillance. A benefit of the second option would be to acquaint more whites with the burden of police intrusion, which might prompt more of them to insist on limiting police power. As it stands now, the burden is unfairly placed on minorities—imposing on Mexican Americans, blacks, and others a special kind of tax for the war against illegal immigration, drugs, and other crimes. The racial element of that tax should be repealed.

21   I'm not saying that police should never be able to use race as a guideline. If a young white man with blue hair robs me, the police should certainly be able to use a description of the perpetrator's race. In this situation, though, whiteness is a trait linked to a particular person with respect to a particular incident. It is not a free-floating accusation that hovers over young white men practically all the time—which is the predicament young black men currently face. Nor am I saying that race could never be legitimately relied upon as a signal of increased danger. In an extraordinary circumstance in which plausible alternatives appear to be absent, officials might need to resort to racial profiling. This is a far cry from routine profiling that is subjected to little scrutiny.

22   Now that racial profiling is a hot issue, the prospects for policy change have improved. President Clinton directed federal law enforcement agencies to determine the extent to which their officers focus on individuals on the basis of race. The Customs Service is rethinking its practice of using ethnicity or nationality as a basis for selecting subjects for investigation. The Federal Aviation Administration has been re-evaluating its recommended security procedures; it wants the airlines to combat terrorism with computer profiling, which is purportedly less race-based than random checks by airport personnel. Unfortunately, though, a minefield of complexity lies beneath these options. Unless we understand the complexities, this opportunity will be wasted.

23   To protect ourselves against race-based policing requires no real confrontation with the status quo, because hardly anyone defends police surveillance triggered *solely* by race. Much of the talk about police "targeting" suspects on the basis of race is, in this sense, misguided and harmful. It diverts attention to a side issue. Another danger is the threat of demagoguery through oversimplification. When politicians talk about "racial profiling," we must insist that they define precisely what they mean. Evasion—putting off hard decisions under the guise of needing more information—is also a danger.

24   Even if routine racial profiling is prohibited, the practice will not cease quickly. An officer who makes a given decision partly on a racial basis is unlikely to acknowledge having done so, and supervisors and judges are loath to reject officers' statements. Nevertheless, it would be helpful for President Clinton to initiate a strict anti-discrimination directive to send a signal to conscientious, law-abiding officers that there are certain criteria they ought not use.

25   To be sure, creating a norm that can't be fully enforced isn't ideal, but it might encourage us all to work toward closing the gap between our laws and the conduct of public authorities. A new rule prohibiting racial profiling might be made to be broken, but it could set a new standard for legitimate government. ◆

◉ In Defense of Racial Profiling
John Derbyshire

1 Racial profiling "has become one of the shibboleths of our time." Anyone who wants a public career in the United States must place himself on record as being against it. Thus, ex-senator John Ashcroft, on the eve of his confirmation hearings: "It's wrong, inappropriate, shouldn't be done." During the vice-presidential debate last October, moderator Bernard Shaw invited the candidates to imagine themselves black victims of racial profiling. Both made the required ritual protestations of outrage. Lieberman: "I have a few African American friends who have gone through this horror, and you know, it makes me want to kind of hit the wall, because it is such an assault on their humanity and their citizenship." Cheney: "It's the sense of anger and frustration and rage that would go with knowing that the only reason you were stopped . . . was because of the color of your skin. . . ." In the strange, rather depressing, pattern these things always follow nowadays, the American public has speedily swung into line behind the Pied Pipers: Gallup reports that 81 percent of the public disapproves of racial profiling.

2   All of which represents an extraordinary level of awareness of, and hostility to, and even passion against ("hit the wall . . .") a practice that, up to about five years ago, practically nobody had heard of. It is, in fact, instructive to begin by looking at the history of this shibboleth.

3   To people who follow politics, the term "racial profiling" probably first registered when Al Gore debated Bill Bradley at New York's Apollo Theatre in February 2000. Here is Bradley, speaking of the 1999 shooting of African immigrant Amadou Diallo by New York City police: "I . . . think it reflects . . . racial profiling that seeps into the mind of someone so that he sees a wallet in the hand of a white man as a wallet, but a wallet in the hand of a black man as a gun. And we—we have to change that. I would issue an executive order that would eliminate racial profiling at the federal level."

4   Nobody was unkind enough to ask Senator Bradley how an executive order would change what a policeman sees in a dark lobby in a dangerous neighborhood at

night. Nor was anyone so tactless as to ask him about the case of LaTanya Haggerty, shot dead in June 1999 by a Chicago policewoman who mistook her cell phone for a handgun. The policewoman was, like Ms. Haggerty, black.

5   Al Gore, in that debate at the Apollo, did successfully, and famously, ambush Bradley by remarking that: "You know, racial profiling practically began in New Jersey, Senator Bradley." In true Clinton-Gore fashion, this is not true, but it is sort of true. "Racial profiling" the thing has been around for as long as police work, and is practiced everywhere. "Racial profiling" the term did indeed have its origins on the New Jersey Turnpike in the early 1990s. The reason for the prominence of this rather unappealing stretch of expressway in the history of the phenomenon is simple: The turnpike is the main conduit for the shipment of illegal drugs and other contraband to the great criminal marts of the Northeast.

6   The career of the term "racial profiling" seems to have begun in 1994, but did not really take off until April 1998, when two white New Jersey state troopers pulled over a van for speeding. As they approached the van from behind, it suddenly reversed towards them. The troopers fired eleven shots from their handguns, wounding three of the van's four occupants, who were all black or Hispanic. The troopers, James Kenna and John Hogan, subsequently became poster boys for the "racial profiling" lobbies, facing the same indignities, though so far with less serious consequences, as were endured by the Los Angeles policemen in the Rodney King case: endless investigations, double jeopardy, and so on.

7   And a shibboleth was born. News-media databases list only a scattering of instances of the term "racial profiling" from 1994 to 1998. In that latter year, the number hit double digits, and thereafter rose quickly into the hundreds and thousands. Now we all know about it, and we are, of course, all against it.

8   Well, not quite all. American courts—including (see below) the U.S. Supreme Court—are not against it. Jurisprudence on the matter is pretty clear: So long as race is only one factor in a generalized approach to the questioning of suspects, it may be considered. And of course *pace* Candidate Cheney, it always is only one factor. I have been unable to locate any statistics on the point, but I feel sure that elderly black women are stopped by the police much less often than are young white men.

9   Even in the political sphere, where truth-telling and independent thinking on matters of race have long been liabilities, there are those who refuse to mouth the required pieties. Alan Keyes, when asked by Larry King if he would be angry with a police officer who pulled him over for being black, replied: "I was raised that everything I did represented my family, my race, and my country. I would be angry with the people giving me a bad reputation."

10   Practically all law-enforcement professionals believe in the need for racial profiling. In an article on the topic for the *New York Times Magazine* in June 1999, Jeffrey Goldberg interviewed Bernard Parks, chief of the Los Angeles Police Department. Parks, who is black, asked rhetorically of racial profiling: "Should we play the percentages? . . . It's common sense." Note that date, though. This was pretty much the latest time at which it was possible for a public official to speak truthfully about racial profiling. Law-enforcement professionals were learning the importance of keeping their thoughts to themselves. Four months before the Goldberg piece saw print, New Jersey state-police superintendent Carl Williams, in an interview, said that certain

crimes were associated with certain ethnic groups, and that it was naïve to think that race was not an issue in policing—both statements, of course, perfectly true. Superintendent Williams was fired the same day by Governor Christie Todd Whitman.

11   Like other race issues in the U.S., racial profiling is a "tadpole," with an enormous black head and a long but comparatively inconsequential brown, yellow, and red tail. While Hispanic, "Asian American," and other lesser groups have taken up the "racial profiling" chant with gusto, the crux of the matter is the resentment that black Americans feel toward the attentions of white policemen. By far the largest number of Americans angry about racial profiling are law-abiding black people who feel that they are stopped and questioned because the police regard all black people with undue suspicion. They feel that they are the victims of a negative stereotype.

12   They are. Unfortunately, a negative stereotype can be correct, and even useful. I was surprised to find, when researching this article, that within the academic field of social psychology there is a large literature on stereotypes, and that much of it—an entire school of thought—holds that stereotypes are essential life tools. On the scientific evidence, the primary function of stereotypes is what researchers call "the reality function." That is, stereotypes are useful tools for dealing with the world. Confronted with a snake or a fawn, our immediate behavior is determined by generalized beliefs—stereotypes—about snakes and fawns. Stereotypes are, in fact, merely one aspect of the mind's ability to make generalizations, without which science and mathematics, not to mention, as the snake/fawn example shows, much of everyday life, would be impossible.

13   At some level, everybody knows this stuff, even the guardians of the "racial profiling" flame. Jesse Jackson famously, in 1993, confessed that: "There is nothing more painful to me at this stage in my life than to walk down the street and hear footsteps and start thinking about robbery, then look around and see somebody white and feel relieved." Here is Sandra Seegars of the Washington, D.C., Taxicab Commission:

14   Late at night, if I saw young black men dressed in a slovenly way, I wouldn't pick them up. . . . And during the day, I'd think twice about it.

15   Pressed to define "slovenly," Ms. Seegars elaborated thus: "A young black guy with his hat on backwards, shirttail hanging down longer than his coat, baggy pants down below his underwear, and unlaced tennis shoes." Now there's a stereotype for you! Ms. Seegars is, of course, black.

16   Law-enforcement officials are simply employing the same stereotypes as you, me, Jesse, and Sandra, but taking the opposite course of action. What we seek to avoid, they pursue. They do this for reasons of simple efficiency. A policeman who concentrates a disproportionate amount of his limited time and resources on young black men is going to uncover far more crimes—and therefore be far more successful in his career—than one who biases his attention toward, say, middle-aged Asian women. It is, as Chief Parks said, common sense.

17   Similarly with the tail of the tadpole—are racial-profiling issues that do not involve black people. China is known to have obtained a top-secret warhead design. Among those with clearance to work on that design are people from various kinds of national and racial background. Which ones should investigators concentrate on? The Swedes? The answer surely is: They should first check out anyone who has

family or friends in China, who has made trips to China, or who has met with Chinese officials. This would include me, for example—my father-in-law is an official of the Chinese Communist Party. Would I then have been "racially profiled"?

18   It is not very surprising to learn that the main fruit of the "racial profiling" hysteria has been a decline in the efficiency of police work. In Philadelphia, a federal court order now requires police to fill out both sides of an 8½-by-11 sheet on every citizen contact. Law-enforcement agencies nationwide are engaged in similar statistics-gathering exercises, under pressure from federal lawmakers like U.S. Rep. John Conyers, who has announced that he will introduce a bill to force police agencies to keep detailed information about traffic stops. ("The struggle goes on," declared Rep. Conyers. The struggle that is going on, it sometimes seems, is a struggle to prevent our police forces from accomplishing any useful work at all.)

19   The mountain of statistics that is being brought forth by all this panic does not, on the evidence so far, seem likely to shed much light on what is happening. The numbers have a way of leading off into infinite regresses of uncertainty. The city of San Jose, Calif., for example, discovered that, yes, the percentage of blacks being stopped was higher than their representation in the city's population. Ah, but patrol cars were computer-assigned to high-crime districts, which are mainly inhabited by minorities. So that overrepresentation might actually be an underrepresentation! But then, minorities have fewer cars. . . .

20   Notwithstanding the extreme difficulty of finding out what is actually happening, we can at least seek some moral and philosophical grounds on which to take a stand either for or against racial profiling. I am going to take it as a given that most readers of this article will be of a conservative inclination, and shall offer only those arguments likely to appeal to persons so inclined. If you seek arguments of other kinds, they are not hard to find—just pick up your newspaper or turn on your TV.

21   Of arguments against racial profiling, probably the ones most persuasive to a conservative are the ones from libertarianism. Many of the stop-and-search cases that brought this matter into the headlines were part of the so-called war on drugs. The police procedures behind them were ratified by court decisions of the 1980s, themselves mostly responding to the rising tide of illegal narcotics. In U.S. vs. Montoya De Hernandez (1985) for example, Chief Justice Rehnquist validated the detention of a suspected "balloon swallowing" drug courier until the material had passed through her system, by noting previous invasions upheld by the Court:

22   First class mail may be opened without a warrant on less than probable cause. . . . Automotive travellers may be stopped . . . near the border without individualized suspicion *even if the stop is based largely on ethnicity.* . . . (My italics.) The Chief Justice further noted that these incursions are in response to "the veritable national crisis in law enforcement caused by smuggling of illegal narcotics."

23   Many on the political Right feel that the war on drugs is at best misguided, at worst a moral and constitutional disaster. Yet it is naïve to imagine that the "racial profiling" hubbub would go away, or even much diminish, if all state and federal drug laws were repealed tomorrow. Black and Hispanic Americans would still be committing crimes at rates higher than citizens of other races. The differential criminality of various ethnic groups is not only, or even mainly, located in drug crimes. In 1997, for example, blacks, who are 13 percent of the U.S. population, comprised

35 percent of those arrested for embezzlement. (It is not generally appreciated that black Americans commit higher levels not only of "street crime," but also of white-collar crime.)

24   Even without the drug war, diligent police officers would still, therefore, be correct to regard black and Hispanic citizens—other factors duly considered—as more likely to be breaking the law. The Chinese government would still be trying to recruit spies exclusively from among Chinese-born Americans. (The Chinese Communist Party is, in this respect, the keenest "racial profiler" of all.) The Amadou Diallo case—the police were looking for a rapist—would still have happened.

25   The best nonlibertarian argument against racial profiling is the one from equality before the law. This has been most cogently presented by Professor Randall Kennedy of Harvard. Kennedy concedes most of the points I have made. Yes, he says:

26   Statistics abundantly confirm that African Americans—and particularly young black men—commit a dramatically disproportionate share of street crime in the United States. This is a sociological fact, not a figment of the media's (or the police's) racist imagination. In recent years, for example, victims of crime report blacks as the perpetrators in around 25 percent of the violent crimes suffered, although blacks constitute only about twelve percent of the nation's population.

27   And yes, says Professor Kennedy, outlawing racial profiling will reduce the efficiency of police work. Nonetheless, for constitutional and moral reasons we should outlaw the practice. If this places extra burdens on law enforcement, well, "racial equality, like all good things in life, costs something; it does not come for free."

28   There are two problems with this. The first is that Kennedy has minimized the black-white difference in criminality, and therefore that "cost." I don't know where his 25 percent comes from, or what "recent years" means, but I do know that in Department of Justice figures for 1997, victims report 60 percent of robberies as having been committed by black persons. In that same year, a black American was eight times more likely than a non-black to commit homicide—and "non-black" here includes Hispanics, not broken out separately in these figures. A racial-profiling ban, under which police officers were required to stop and question suspects in precise proportion to their demographic representation (in what? the precinct population? the state population? the national population?), would lead to massive inefficiencies in police work. Which is to say, massive declines in the apprehension of criminals.

29   The other problem is with the special status that Professor Kennedy accords to race. Kennedy: "Racial distinctions are and should be different from other lines of social stratification." Thus, if it can be shown, as it surely can, that state troopers stop young people more than old people, relative to young people's numerical representation on the road being patrolled, that is of no consequence. If they stop black people more than white people, on the same criterion, that is of large consequence. This, in spite of the fact that the categories "age" and "race" are both rather fuzzy (define "young") and are both useful predictors of criminality. In spite of the fact, too, that the principle of equality before the law does not, and up to now has never been thought to, guarantee equal outcomes for any law-enforcement process, only that a citizen who has come under reasonable suspicion will be treated fairly.

30   It is on this special status accorded to race that, I believe, we have gone most seriously astray. I am willing, in fact, to say much more than this: In the matter of race,

I think the Anglo-Saxon world has taken leave of its senses. The campaign to ban racial profiling is, as I see it, a part of that large, broad-fronted assault on common sense that our over-educated, over-lawyered society has been enduring for some forty years now, and whose roots are in a fanatical egalitarianism, a grim determination not to face up to the realities of group differences, a theological attachment to the doctrine that the sole and sufficient explanation for all such differences is "racism"—which is to say, the malice and cruelty of white people—and a nursed and petted guilt towards the behavior of our ancestors.

31   At present, Americans are drifting away from the concept of belonging to a single nation. I do not think this drift will be arrested until we can shed the idea that deference to the sensitivities of racial minorities—however overwrought those sensitivities may be, however overstimulated by unscrupulous mountebanks, however disconnected from reality—trumps every other consideration, including even the maintenance of social order. To shed that idea, we must confront our national hysteria about race, which causes large numbers of otherwise sane people to believe that the hearts of their fellow citizens are filled with malice towards them. So long as we continue to pander to that poisonous, preposterous belief, we shall only wander off deeper into a wilderness of division, mistrust, and institutionalized rancor—that wilderness, the most freshly painted signpost to which bears the legend RACIAL PROFILING. ◆

FREEWRITING ASSIGNMENT

What assumptions do Kennedy and Derbyshire make regarding their audiences?

CRITICAL READING

1. Kennedy argues that racial profiling is racist. In what ways it is racist? Alternatively, how can it be defended on nonracist grounds? Is it always racist? Explain.
2. A critical reader may argue that Kennedy contradicts himself in some places, such as in paragraph 21 when he follows his argument against racial profiling with the statement that in "extraordinary circumstances" it may be permissible. Is this, indeed, a contradiction? Explain.
3. Derbyshire presents a "history" of the emergence of racial profiling into the political arena. How does this history help frame and support the rest of his discussion? Explain.
4. According to Derbyshire, what influence have politicians had on the "racial profiling" debate? How have they influenced public opinion? If Americans feel so strongly against racial profiling, why does it seem to have emerged as a political issue as recently as ten years ago? Or does it have a much longer history? Explain.
5. In paragraph 17, Kennedy presents two examples of how the law "properly enjoins us to forswear playing racial odds even when doing so would advance legitimate goals." Do these examples support his argument that all racial profiling should be illegal? Explain.

6. According to Derbyshire, what is the "fruit" of the racial profiling hysteria? In his opinion, how does the "national hysteria about race" serve to drive Americans apart as a nation? Explain.

7. How plausible are the solutions Kennedy offers? For example, he proposes that to end racial profiling cities should hire more police officers so that the "time saving" element of racial profiling would no longer be a factor. What issues does he not address that an opponent could use to counterargue this solution? What information would you recommend he include to deflect objections? Explain.

8. Evaluate Kennedy's observation that the practice of racial profiling keeps "the pool of accumulated [minority] rage filled to the brim." How does this reaction affect other areas of law enforcement? How can racial profiling backfire in the courtroom and on the streets? Explain.

9. Evaluate Kennedy's practice of posting questions to his readers and then providing them with his answers. In what ways could this article serve as a class lecture?

10. What does Derbyshire imply when he says that Bernard Park's interview with the *New York Times Magazine* was "pretty much the latest time at which it was possible for a public official to speak truthfully about racial profiling." How does he support this statement?

CRITICAL WRITING

11. Both Kennedy and Derbyshire quote LA police chief Bernard Parks. Does the fact that Parks is a black law enforcement official influence your opinions of racial profiling?

12. Look up some of the cases described by Kennedy and Derbyshire in their essays and evaluate the role racial profiling played in legal incidents. Write an analysis of the issue based on your research. Support your analysis with additional information provided by the two authors in their essays.

13. How would Kennedy and Derbyshire debate Byronn Bain's experiences described earlier in this chapter? Based on the essays of the three men, and drawing from their specific statements, create a fictitious debate among the three, using Bain's arrest as the subject for the debate.

GROUP PROJECTS

14. Teenagers often complain that they are watched more closely in stores because they could be potential shoplifters. John Derbyshire reasons that young white males are probably more likely to be stopped by the police than elderly black females. Consider as a group the validity of other kinds of profiling such as age, income, and gender. What criminal assumptions accompany these groups? If racial profiling is wrong, is it also wrong to profile on other criteria? Why or why not?

15. Select one of the cases described by Kennedy or Derbyshire, or a more recent case involving racial profiling. After you have made a selection, divide the group into two sections—one section will argue that racial profil-

ing is justified, the other that it is not, referring specifically to the details of the case. After developing your arguments, present them to the class. The class should vote on which side makes the more compelling case, and why.

RESEARCH ISSUE **Ragtime, My Time**

Alton Fitzgerald White

As Americans, we are raised to believe in the values of justice and freedom. We believe that we are entitled to certain rights, opportunities, and protections as citizens. But what happens when we feel our rights have been violated by the very system supposed to uphold them? As this personal account by Broadway actor Alton Fitzgerald White attests, the damage can be deep, undermining not only our feelings of justice, but our entire perspective of how we fit into society. White is best known for his performances in the Broadway shows *Smokey Joe's Café* and *Ragtime,* in which he played the starring role of Coalhouse Walker, Jr. He has released two CDs, *How Do I Feel* and *Ecstasis,* and has written a book of poetry, *Uncovering the Heart Light.* This article was first published in the *Nation.*

1   As the youngest of five girls and two boys growing up in Cincinnati, Ohio, I was raised to believe that if I worked hard, was a good person and always told the truth, the world would be my oyster. I was taught to be courteous and polite. I was raised a gentleman and learned that these fine qualities would bring me one very important, hard-earned human quality: Respect!

2   While respect is indeed something one has to earn, consideration is something owed to every human being, even total strangers. On Friday, June 16, 1999, when I was wrongfully arrested while trying to leave my building in Harlem, my perception of everything I had learned as a young man was forever changed—not only because of the fact that I wasn't given even a second to use any of the wonderful manners and skills my parents had taught me as a child, but mostly because the police, who I'd always naïvely thought were supposed to serve and protect me, were actually hunting me.

3   I had planned the day to be a pleasant one. The night before was not only pay-day but also I received a rousing standing ovation after portraying the starring role of Coalhouse Walker, Jr. in *Ragtime* on Broadway. It is a role I've worked very hard for professionally, and emotionally as well. A role that requires not only talent but also an honest emotional investment, including the morals and lessons I learned as a child.

4   Coalhouse Walker, Jr. is a victim (an often misused word but in this case the true definition) of overt racism. His story is every black man's nightmare. He is hard-working, successful, talented, charismatic, friendly and polite. Perfect prey for someone with authority and not even a fraction of those qualities. The fictional character I portrayed on Thursday night became a part of my reality on Friday afternoon.

Nothing in the world could have prepared me for it. Nothing I had seen on television. Not even stories told to me by other black men who had suffered similar injustices.

5   Most Fridays for me mean a trip to the bank, errands, the gym, dinner and then to the theater. On this particular day, I decided to break my usual pattern of getting up and running right out of the house. Instead, I took my time, slowed down my pace and splurged by making myself some homemade strawberry pancakes. It was a way of spoiling myself in preparation for my demanding, upcoming four-show weekend. Before I knew it, it was 2:45, and my bank closes at 3:30, leaving me less than forty-five minutes to get to midtown on the train. I was pressed for time but in a relaxed, blessed state of mind. When I walked through the lobby of my building, I noticed two light-skinned Hispanic men I'd never seen before. Not thinking much of it, I continued on to the vestibule, which is separated from the lobby by a locked door.

6   As I approached the exit, I saw people in uniforms rushing toward the door. I sped up to open it for them, especially after noticing that the first of them was a woman. My first thought was that they were paramedics, seeing as many of the building's occupants are retired and/or elderly. It wasn't until I had opened the door and greeted the woman that I recognized that they were the police. Within seconds I was told to "hold it" because they had received a call about young Hispanics with guns. I was told to get against the wall. I was searched, stripped of my backpack (which was searched repeatedly), put on my knees, handcuffed and told to be quiet when I tried to ask any questions.

7   With me were three other innocent black men. They had been on their way to their U-Haul, parked on the side of the building. They were moving into the apartment beneath me and were still glowing from the tour I'd given them of the beautiful historic landmark building. I had just bragged to them about how safe it was and how proud I was to have been living there for over five years. And now here the four of us were being told to get on our knees, handcuffed and not allowed to say a word in our defense. As a matter of fact, it was one of these gentlemen who got off his knees, still handcuffed, and unlocked the door for the policemen to get into the lobby where the two strangers were. Instead of being thanked or even acknowledged, we were led out the door past our neighbors, who were all but begging the police in our defense.

8   We were put into cars with the two strangers and taken to the 33rd Precinct at 165th and Amsterdam. The police automatically linked us to them with no questions and no regard for our character or our lives. No consideration was given to where we were going or what we were in need of doing before they came into our building. Suppose I had an ailing relative upstairs in my apartment waiting for me to return with her emergency remedy? Or young children who were told Daddy is running to the corner store for milk and will be right back? These three gentlemen weren't even allowed to lock their apartment or check on the U-Haul full of their personal belongings.

9   After we were lined up in the station, the younger of the two Hispanic men was immediately identified as an experienced criminal, and drug residue was found in a pocket of the other. I now realize how naïve I was to think the police would then uncuff me, apologize for their terrible mistake and let me go. Instead, they continued to search my backpack repeatedly, questioned me and put me in jail with the criminals.

10   The rest of the nearly five-hour ordeal was like a horrible dream, putting me in a surreal state of shock. Everything from being handcuffed, strip-searched, taken in

and out for questioning, to being told that they knew exactly who I was and my responsibility to the show and that in fact they knew they already had whom they wanted, left me in absolute disbelief.

11   When I asked how they could keep me there, or have brought me there in the first place with nothing found and a clean record, I was told it was standard procedure. As if the average law-abiding citizen knows what that is and can dispute it. From what I now know, "standard procedure" is something that every citizen, black and white, needs to learn, and fast. Even though they knew I was innocent, they made me feel completely powerless. All for one reason. Why do you think? Here I was, young, pleasant and successful, in good physical shape, dressed in clean athletic attire. I was carrying a backpack, containing a substantial paycheck and deposit slip, on my way to the bank and to enjoy a well-deserved great day. Yet after hours and hours I was sitting at a desk with two officers who not only couldn't tell me why I was there but seemed determined to find something on me, to the point of making me miss my performance.

12   *It was because I am a black man!*

13   I sat in that cell crying silent tears of disappointment and injustice with the realization of how many innocent black men are convicted for no reason. When I was handcuffed, my first instinct had been to pull away out of pure insult and violation as a human being. Thank God I was calm enough to do what they said. When I was thrown in jail with the criminals and strip-searched, I somehow knew to put my pride aside, be quiet and do exactly what I was told, hating it but coming to terms with the fact that in this situation I was powerless. I was a victim. They had guns!

14   Before I was finally let go, exhausted, humiliated, embarrassed and still in shock, I was led to a room and given a pseudo-apology. I was told that I was at the wrong place at the wrong time. My reply? "I was where I live."

15   As a result, what I learned growing up in Cincinnati has been shattered. Life will never be the same.

CRITICAL THINKING

1. Why were White and the other men in the lobby arrested by the police? What was the charge? On what grounds did the police arrest them? After the real criminals were identified, why were they retained?

2. White states in several places in his essay that he felt his arrest was connected solely to his race. In your opinion, was this indeed a case of racial profiling or one of mistaken identity? Or could it be a bit of both? Explain.

3. White clearly believes that he was unfairly judged by the officers involved in his arrest based on the color of his skin. What does he feel was most violated by his experience? How does his reaction resonate with the reader? Explain.

RESEARCH PROJECTS

4. Read about White's lawsuit against the New York City police department for wrongful arrest at *http://www.nyclu.org/white_complaint.html.* After

reading the document posted on the New York Civil Liberties Union web site, write a response to it as if you were a member of a jury. If you wish, you may research this issue further on the Internet for more information.

5. Review the information on racial profiling on the ACLU's web site on racial equality at *www.aclu.org/RacialEquality/RacialEqualityMain.cfm*. What are the most pressing issues concerning racial profiling today? Select an issue or case described on the ACLU web site and research it in greater depth. Write a short essay summarizing the situation or issue and your position on it.

Additional essay topics, writing assignments, research guidelines, and readings for this chapter can be found online at **www.ablongman.com/goshgarian**.

The
American
Experience
One Nation, Many Faces

The United States of America is a union predicated on similar moral values, political and economic self-interest, a common legal system, and a democratic form of government. While we have much in common, we are also a nation of immigrants—people of different ethnic backgrounds, religions, traditions, languages and cultures. We are a nation whose motto *e pluribus unum* ("one out of many") bespeaks a pride in its multicultural heritage. In this chapter, we explore issues connected to our concept of nationhood, diversity, and patriotism.

Although America has been a multiethnic and multiracial society since its founding, in the last few decades different groups of Americans have reasserted their ethnic and racial identities. While this attention to native roots has created greater tolerance and celebration of differences, it has also challenged our definition of ourselves as Americans. Furthermore it compels us to think about how to balance ethnic heritage and identity, and how we fit into broader American culture. Are we no longer the "great melting pot" that Arthur Schlesinger, Jr., extols in his essay, "The Return of the Melting Pot"? Or, should we rethink our definitions of cultural "melting"—an idea that Gregory Rodriguez advances in "Forging a New Vision of America's Melting Pot." Rodriguez explains that the concept of the melting pot shouldn't be all or nothing. Rather, we need to rethink the notion of what melting means in a multicultural nation.

A century ago, immigrant populations tended to marry within their group, while still assimilating into broader American culture. Two world wars, mass media, and modern transportation systems helped make the nation a smaller place—and encouraged intermixing of cultures and backgrounds. By the last quarter of the twentieth century, it was common for an individual to proclaim Italian, English, Irish, Armenian, or Polish heritage. With the greater social acceptance of interracial relationships, that same person could now have children with someone who claimed Moroccan, Japanese, German, Native American ancestry. Donna Jackson Nakazawa, the mother of two interracial children, explores the challenges they may face in "A New Generation Is Leading the Way." Such children will literally change the face of America and how we perceive race in this country. But while America is becoming increasingly multiethnic, divisions are still common, often by choice. In "People Like Us," David Brooks hazards to state the obvious—that no matter how much lip service we might pay publicly to diversity, we still tend to gather with people who are "basically like ourselves."

Suzanne Fields discusses the national holiday of Thanksgiving—America's first "multicultural holiday" in "When Fair is Foul." Thanksgiving, she explains, is a day that unites us as a nation—transcending the secular and spiritual. And Jordan Lite wonders why it is so important in our multicultural nation to know each other's ethnic origins as she requests "Please Ask Me 'Who,' Not 'What' I Am."Aurora Levins Morales's "Ending Poem" presents her view of being a "child of the Americas."

This chapter's Viewpoints presents some opinions on what it means to be a patriot in the United States today. After September 11, 2001, many Americans found new reasons to express their love for their country. Such patriotism came with a steep price—American lives both in the U.S. and abroad, and the sacrifice of some personal freedom. Sam Smith begins the section with "How to Be a Patriot," in which he wonders why it took violence to inspire Americans to express their love of country. He also fears patriotism's "dark side"—the side that blindly follows propaganda and threatens the freedoms guaranteed by the Constitution. Charley Reese presents his view on this issue in "What Is Patriotism"? As you read the opinions of these writers, consider your own position on American patriotism and political conscience.

The last Research Issue of this book addresses the topic of immigration. More people than ever are coming to America to make new lives for themselves. But many are content to live in the U.S. with green cards. Should the government push to make these newcomers naturalized citizens? Tamar Jacoby explores this issue in depth in "How to Turn More Immigrants into Americans."

The Return of the Melting Pot
Arthur Schlesinger, Jr.

What exactly is the "American melting pot"? At the turn of the century, most people felt it meant educating one's children in American schools, learning the English language, and blending into mainstream American society. But a century later, the concept of the melting pot has changed. To some groups, it symbolizes the loss of individual cultures and beliefs at the expense of a blended idea helped by the status quo. In this piece, Arthur Schlesinger, Jr., questions this new desire to challenge the ideals of *e pluribus unum*.

Arthur Schlesinger, Jr. is a well-known historian and a former columnist for the *New York Times*. The recipient of two Pulitzer Prizes for history, he is the author of *The Disuniting of America: Reflections on a Multicultural Society* (1992), in which he questions the rising popularity of radical multiculturalism. His most recent books are *A Life in the 20th Century: Innocent Beginnings, 1917–1950* (2000) and *Taught to Lead: The Education of the Presidents* (2004). This essay was first published in the *Wall Street Journal*.

CRITICAL THINKING	What is "multicultural education"? Where do you stand on the issue of multicultural education? Is it important? Why or why not?

1   "What then is the American, this new man?" a French immigrant asked two centuries ago. Hector St. John de Crevecoeur gave the classic answer to his own question. "He is an American, who, leaving behind him all his ancient prejudices and manners, receives new ones from the new mode of life he has embraced, the new government he obeys, and the new rank he holds. . . . Here individuals of all nations are melted into a new race of man."

2   The conception of America as a transforming nation, banishing old identities and creating a new one, prevailed through most of American history. It was famously reformulated by Israel Zangwill, an English writer of Russian Jewish origin, when he called America "God's crucible, the great melting pot where all the faces of Europe are melting and re-forming." Most people who came to America expected to

become Americans. They wanted to escape a horrid past and to embrace a hopeful future. Their goals were deliverance and assimilation.

3 Thus, Crevecoeur wrote his "Letters from an American Farmer" in his acquired English, not in his native French. Thus, immigrants reared in other tongues urged their children to learn English as speedily as possible. German immigrants tried for a moment to gain status for their language, but the effort got nowhere. The dominant culture was Anglo-Saxon and, with modification and enrichment, remained Anglo-Saxon.

Repudiation of the Melting Pot

4 The melting pot was one of those metaphors that turned out only to be partly true, and recent years have seen an astonishing repudiation of the whole conception. Many Americans today righteously reject the historic goal of "a new race of man." The contemporary ideal is not assimilation but ethnicity. The escape from origins has given way to the search for "roots." "Ancient prejudices and manners"—the old-time religion, the old-time diet—have made a surprising comeback.

5 These developments portend a new turn in American life. Instead of a transformative nation with a new and distinctive identity, America increasingly sees itself as preservative of old identities. We used to say *e pluribus unum*. Now we glorify *pluribus* and belittle *unum*. The melting pot yields to the Tower of Babel.

6 The new turn has had marked impact on the universities. Very little agitates academia more these days than the demands of passionate minorities for revision of the curriculum: in history, the denunciation of Western civilization courses as cultural imperialism; in literature, the denunciation of the "canon," the list of essential books, as an instrumentality of the existing power structure.

7 A recent report by the New York State Commissioner of Education's task force on "Minorities: Equity and Excellence" luridly describes "African Americans, Asian Americans, Puerto Ricans/Latinos and Native Americans" as "victims of an intellectual and educational oppression." The "systematic bias toward European culture and its derivatives," the report claims, has "a terribly damaging effect on the psyche of young people of African, Asian, Latino and Native American descent"—a doubtful assertion for which no proof is vouchsafed.

8 Of course teachers of history and literature should give due recognition to women, black Americans, Indians, Hispanics and other groups who were subordinated and ignored in the high noon of male Anglo-Saxon dominance. In recent years they have begun belatedly to do so. But the *cult of ethnicity,* pressed too far, exacts costs—as, for example, the current pressure to teach history and literature not as intellectual challenges but as psychological therapy.

9 There is nothing new, of course, about the yearnings of excluded groups for affirmations of their own historical and cultural dignity. When Irish Americans were thought beyond the pale, their spokesmen responded much as spokesmen for blacks, Hispanics and others respond today. Professor John V. Kelleher, for many years Harvard's distinguished Irish scholar, once recalled his first exposure to Irish American history—"turgid little essays on the fact that the Continental Army was 76 percent Irish, or that many of George Washington's closest friends were nuns and priests, or that Lincoln got the major ideas for the Second Inaugural Address from the Hon. Francis P. Mageghegan of Alpaca, New York, a pioneer manufacturer of

cast-iron rosary beads." John Kelleher called this "the there's-always-an-Irishman-at-the-bottom-of-it-doing-the-real-work approach to American history."

10   Fortunately, most Irish Americans disregarded their spokesmen and absorbed the American tradition. About 1930, Kelleher said, those "turgid little essays began to vanish from Irish-American papers." He added, "I wonder whose is the major component in the Continental Army these days?" The answer, one fears, is getting to be blacks, Jews and Hispanics.

11   There is often artificiality about the attempts to use history to minister to psychological needs. When I encounter black insistence on inserting Africa into mainstream curricula, I recall the 1956 presidential campaign. Adlai Stevenson, for whom I was working, had a weak record on civil rights in America but was a champion of African nationalism. I suggested to a group of sympathetic black leaders that maybe if Stevenson talked to black audiences about Africa, he could make up for his deficiencies on civil rights. My friends laughed and said that American blacks couldn't care less about Africa: That is no longer the case; but one can't escape the feeling that present emotions are more manufactured than organic.

12   Let us by all means teach women's history, black history, Hispanic history. But let us teach them as *history,* not as a means of *promoting group self-esteem.* I don't often agree with Gore Vidal, but I liked his remark the other day: "What I hate is good citizenship history. That has wrecked every history book. Now we're getting 'The Hispanics are warm and joyous and have brought such wonder into our lives,' you know, and before them the Jews, and before them the blacks. And the women. I mean, cut it out!"

13   Novelists, moralists, politicians, fabulators can go beyond the historical evidence to tell inspiring stories. But historians are custodians of professional standards. Their objective is critical analysis, accuracy and objectivity, not making people feel better about themselves.

14   Heaven knows how dismally historians fall short of their ideals; how sadly our interpretations are dominated and distorted by unconscious preconceptions; how obsessions of race and nation blind us to our own bias. All historians may in one way or another mythologize history. But the answer to bad history is not "good citizenship history"—more bad history written from a different viewpoint. The answer to bad history is better history.

15   The ideological assault in English departments on the "canon" as an instrument of political oppression implies the existence of a monolithic body of work designed to enforce the "hegemony" of a class or race or sex. In fact, most great literature and much good history are deeply subversive in their impact on orthodoxies. Consider the American canon: Emerson, Whitman, Melville, Hawthorne, Thoreau, Mark Twain, Henry Adams, William and Henry James, Holmes, Dreiser, Faulkner. Lackeys of the ruling class? Agents of American imperialism?

16   Let us by all means learn about other continents and other cultures. But, lamentable as some may think it, we inherit an American experience, as America inherits a European experience. To deny the essentially European origins of American culture is to falsify history.

17   We should take pride in our distinctive inheritance as other nations take pride in their distinctive inheritances. Certainly there is no need for Western civilization, the source of the ideas of individual freedom and political democracy to which most of

the world now aspires, to apologize to cultures based on despotism, superstition, tribalism, and fanaticism. Let us abjure what Bertrand Russell called the fallacy of "the superior virtue of the oppressed."

18   Of course we must teach the Western democratic tradition in its true proportions—not as a fixed, final and complacent orthodoxy, intolerant of deviation and dissent, but as an ever-evolving creed fulfilling its ideals through debate, self-criticism, protest, disrespect and irreverence, a tradition in which all groups have rights of heterodoxy and opportunities for self-assertion. It is a tradition that has empowered people of all nations and races. Little can have a more "terribly damaging effect on the psyche" than for educators to tell young blacks and Hispanics and Asians that it is not for them.

One Step at a Time

19 Belief in one's own culture does not mean disdain for other cultures. But one step at a time: No culture can hope to ingest other cultures all at once, certainly not before it ingests its own. After we have mastered our own culture, we can explore the world.

20   If we repudiate the quite marvelous inheritance that history has bestowed on us, we invite the fragmentation of our own culture into a quarrelsome spatter of enclaves, ghettos and tribes. The bonds of cohesion in our society are sufficiently fragile, or so it seems to me, that it makes no sense to strain them by encouraging and exalting cultural and linguistic apartheid. The rejection of the melting pot points the republic in the direction of incoherence and chaos.

21   In the 21st century, if present trends hold, non-whites in the U.S. will begin to outnumber whites. This will bring inevitable changes in the national ethos but not, one must hope, at the expense of national cohesion. Let the new Americans foreswear the cult of ghettoization and agree with Crevecoeur, as with most immigrants in the two centuries since, that in America "individuals of all nations are melted into a new race of man." ◆

FREEWRITING ASSIGNMENT

Schlesinger argues that "no culture can hope to ingest other cultures all at once." Respond to his statement, stating your own opinion.

CRITICAL READING

1. In paragraph 5, Schlesinger states that instead of working toward common goals and a common identity, we now "glorify *pluribus* and belittle *unum*." Explain what you think he means by this statement.
2. How does Schlesinger use American history to support his argument? Is it an effective way to bolster his argument? Could history be also used to discredit his points? Explain.
3. In paragraph 10, Schlesinger says that it was fortunate that Irish Americans disregarded their "spokesman and absorbed the American tradition." What is the "American tradition"? What does he mean by the term?

4. Why does Schlesinger think it was important that Irish Americans assimilate into mainstream American culture? Do you agree? How might the Irish immigration experience be different if it happened now?
5. What support does Schlesinger provide to buttress his statement "[We] inherit an American experience, as America inherits a European experience" (paragraph 16)? Is this true? Explain.
6. Schlesinger implies that multiculturalism isn't teaching history or literature as subjects in themselves, but as a means to promote one's "self-esteem." Analyze and formulate a response to this statement in which you either support or refute his claim.

CRITICAL WRITING

7. *Research and Analysis*: How was the subject of multiculturalism approached in your high school? Speak to local high school teachers of history and literature (English) who have taught for at least 15 years. Has the instruction of these subjects changed? How? Outline Schlesinger's primary points and ask the teachers you interview to respond with their own viewpoints. Prepare an essay evaluating your information and the likely role of multiculturalism in the nation's school systems in the future.
8. Many universities and schools over the last twenty years have embraced multicultural approaches to education. With the upsurge in standardized testing practices, however, the subject matter and content of literature and history is influencing what is taught in the classroom. Research the possible implications of standardized testing on multicultural education.

GROUP PROJECT

9. As a group, discuss what "traditional American" and "American mainstream society" mean. If you were to define these terms for a foreign visitor, what would you say? Discuss this question as a group, and develop a definition. Share your group's definition with the rest of the class.

Forging a New Vision of America's Melting Pot
Gregory Rodriguez

Mexican Americans comprise the second largest immigrant population in American history, and they are poised to become America's largest minority group. Influences of Latino culture are pervading mainstream society, from style and architecture, to art and music. One

Californian historian comments, "the Latinization of America is so profound that no one really sees it." In the next piece, Gregory Rodriguez explains how this group could change how the nation views itself in the next century.

Gregory Rodriguez is a senior fellow at the New America Foundation, a nonpartisan public policy institute "dedicated to bringing exceptionally promising new voices and ideas to the fore of the nation's public discourse." He is a contributing editor to the opinion section of the *Los Angeles Times* and a political analyst for MSNBC. This article was published in the February 11, 2001, edition of the *New York Times*.

CRITICAL THINKING	Think about your own family's experience in the United States. Did it take them long to be accepted? Did they assimilate quickly, or did it require generations to complete? Or is the processes of assimilation still a daily reality for your family? Explain.

1   While visiting Ellis Island at the turn of the 20th century, Henry James wondered how the sweeping tide of immigrants would ultimately affect "the idea of" America. Comparing the incorporation of foreigners to sword- and fire-swallowing feats at a circus, James reflected on what it meant for America to share its patrimony with those "inconceivable aliens."

2   Yet throughout American history, immigrants and minority groups, seeking to make room for themselves, have broadened the definition of America. Minority experiences have acted as a powerful force in the creation of America's self-image.

3   For the first half of the 20th century, Jews were the paradigmatic American minority by which all other minority experiences were understood. In the second half, African Americans, the descendants of a forced migration, set the standard for a racial debate that altered the nation's vision of itself. Now, with Hispanics poised to become the largest minority group, Mexican Americans—who make up two-thirds of all Latinos in the United States—could change how the nation sees itself in the 21st century.

4   Their unique perspectives on racial and cultural synthesis may fundamentally alter the nation's attitudes, for they are the second largest immigrant group in American history—the largest when including illegal immigrants. Mexicans, themselves the product of the clash between the Old and New Worlds, could shift this country's often divisive "us versus them" racial dialogue.

5   A Census Bureau study released in January 2001 found that about 10 percent of United States residents are foreign-born, midway between the high of 15 percent at the turn of the 20th century and the low of 5 percent in 1970. And Mexicans are by far today's biggest immigrant group. As such, they are the most likely to leave a permanent imprint on the culture.

6   For instead of simply adding one more color to the multicultural rainbow, Mexican Americans may help forge a unifying vision. With a history that reveals an ability to accept racial and cultural ambiguity, Mexican Americans could broaden the definition of America unlike any earlier immigrants.

7 The early 20th-century debate about the "melting pot" evolved as Jewish writers envisioned an America that might better accommodate Jews. Their historic experience as a minority prompted them to take the lead in re-imagining America for an entire wave of immigrants. The playwright Israel Zangwill, in a 1908 drama about a Jewish immigrant rejecting his faith's prohibition against intermarriage, developed the optimistic American civic faith that a fusion of ethnicities will create a stronger nation. For Zangwill, the United States was both a safe harbor and a crucible that melted Old World ethnics into a distinctly new American culture.

8 But by the 1960s, America's exclusion of African Americans from the mainstream forged a new vision based on multiculturalism. Though it encompassed other minority groups, including women and gays, blacks gave the multicultural movement its key moral impetus. The civil rights movement had begun by advocating racial integration, but by the late 1960s its message had fused with a reemergent black separatism that fueled the nascent multicultural movement.

9 Multiculturalism—the ideology that promotes the coexistence of separate but equal cultures—essentially rejects assimilation and considers the melting-pot concept an unwelcome imposition of the dominant culture. Race became the prism through which all social issues were perceived.

10 But because their past and present is characterized by a continual synthesis, a blending of the Spanish and indigenous cultures, Mexican Americans could project their own melting pot vision onto America, one that includes mixing race as well as ethnicity. Rather than upholding the segregated notion of a country divided by mutually exclusive groups, Mexican Americans might use their experience to imagine an America in which racial, ethnic and cultural groups collide to create new ways of being American.

11 It was never clear where Mexican Americans belonged on the American racial scale. In 1896, two white politicians in Texas grew worried that more Mexican immigrants would naturalize and vote. They filed suit against a Mexican-born citizenship applicant, Ricardo Rodriguez, because he was not white, and so, like Asians and American Indians, not eligible to become a citizen. Citing the Treaty of Guadalupe Hidalgo, in which citizenship was granted to Mexicans in the conquered region of the Southwest after 1848, the court rejected the suit on the grounds that Mr. Rodriguez's national origins qualified him for citizenship regardless of his racial background.

12 In the 1920 census, Mexicans were counted as whites. Ten years later, they were reassigned to a separate Mexican "racial" category, though in 1950 they were white again. Mexican Americans and Hispanics as a whole are commonly viewed as a mutually exclusive racial, linguistic and cultural category in a country of competing minorities. But Mexican Americans do not share the overarching ethnic narrative of Jews or the shared history of suffering that has united African Americans. For all the discrimination and segregation Mexican Americans suffered in the region, the Southwest was never the Deep South. In any case, as the memoirist John Phillip Santos wrote recently, "Mexicans are to forgetting what the Jews are to remembering."

13 By the late 1990s, both the largely ethnic-Mexican Hispanic Congressional Caucus and the powerful California Latino Legislative Caucus had adopted "Latino issues are American issues" as their mantra. Mexican Americans are using their

growing political power to enter the American mainstream, not to distance themselves from it. The new chairman of the Hispanic Congressional Caucus, Representative Silvestre Reyes, Democrat of Texas, was once a high-ranking Border Patrol official and the architect of Operation Hold the Line, the labor-intensive strategy to stem illegal immigration along the West Texas border.

14   Perhaps assuming that Mexicans would (or should) follow the organizational model of Jews or African Americans, East Coast-based foundations contributed to the founding of national ethnic-Mexican institutions. The New York-based Ford Foundation was instrumental in creating three of the most visible national Mexican-American organizations—all modeled after similar black organizations.

15   But with the exception of some scattered homegrown social service organizations and political groups, Mexican Americans have developed little parallel ethnic infrastructure. One national survey has shown that Mexican Americans are far more likely to join a non-ethnic civic group than a Hispanic organization. There is no private Mexican American college similar to Yeshiva University or Morehouse College. In Los Angeles, which has the largest Mexican population in the country, there is no ethnic-Mexican hospital, cemetery or broad-based charity organization. Nor does Los Angeles have an English-language newspaper for Mexican Americans similar to the black Amsterdam News and the Jewish Forward in New York.

16   Though the Spanish-language media is often referred to as the "Hispanic media," it generally serves first generation immigrants and not their English-dominant children and grandchildren.

17   In the late 1920s, Representative John C. Box of Texas warned his colleagues on the House Immigration and Naturalization Committee that the continued influx of Mexican immigrants could lead to the "distressing process of mongrelization" in America. He argued that because Mexicans were the products of mixing among whites, Indians and sometimes blacks, they had a casual attitude toward interracial unions and were likely to mix freely with other races in the United States.

18   His vitriol notwithstanding, Mr. Box was right about Mexicans not keeping to themselves. Apart from the cultural isolation of immigrants, subsequent generations are oriented toward the American mainstream. But because Mexican identity has always been more fluid and comfortable with hybridity, assimilation has not been an either/or proposition. For example, Mexican Americans never had to overcome a cultural proscription against intermarriage. Just as widespread Mexican-Anglo intermarriage helped meld cultures in the 19th-century Southwest, so it does today. In fact, two-thirds of intermarriages in California involve a Latino partner.

19   According to James P. Smith, an economist and immigration scholar at the RAND Corporation, by 2050 more than 40 percent of United States Hispanics will be able to claim multiple ancestries. "Through this process of blending by marriage in the U.S.," he says, "Latino identity becomes something even more nuanced."

20   The fact that people of mixed ancestry came to form a greater proportion of the population of Latin America than in Anglo America is the clearest sign of the difference between the two outlooks on race. Mexican Americans bring the New World notion encompassed by the word *mestizaje*, or racial and cultural synthesis, to their American experience. In 1925, the romantic Mexican philosopher Jose Vasconcelos wrote that the Latin American mestizo heralds a new post-racialist era in human de-

velopment. More recently, the preeminent Mexican-American essayist Richard Rodriguez stated, "The essential beauty and mystery of the color brown is that it is a mixture of different colors."

21   "Something big happens here at the border that sort of mushes everything together," says Maria Eugenia Guerra, publisher of *LareDos,* an alternative monthly magazine in Laredo, Texas, a city that has been a Latino majority since its founding in 1755. As political and economic power continues to shift westward, Mexican Americans will increasingly inject this mestizo vision onto American culture. "The Latinization of America is so profound that no one really sees it," asserts Kevin Starr, the leading historian of California, who is writing a multivolume history of the state. The process of they becoming us will ultimately force us to reconsider the very definition of who we are. ◆

FREEWRITING ASSIGNMENT

How do the points made in the preceding essay by Arthur Schlesinger, Jr. contrast with the issues Rodriguez addresses? Does one author seem more credible than the other? More culturally aware? Explain.

CRITICAL READING

1. What is the "idea" of America? How have immigrants and minority groups broadened the "definition" of America? Does the term "melting pot" seem appropriate? Why or why not?
2. What influence does Rodriguez foresee Mexican Americans having on national identity in the twenty-first century? Explain.
3. Respond to Rodriguez's statement that as the second largest immigrant population, Mexican Americans could "shift the country's often divisive 'us verses them' racial dialogue" (paragraph 4). What does he mean? Who is "us"; who is "them"?
4. According to the author, how could Mexican American's legacy of "mixed ancestry" in turn influence America's melting pot?
5. In what ways are Mexican Americans different from other immigrant populations? How could this difference ultimately provide them with more political and social power? Explain.

CRITICAL WRITING

6. *Exploratory Writing*: Write a paper assessing the influence of multiculturalism on your life and education. For example, how has multiculturalism changed the way you look at literature and history? Has it allowed your family a stronger sense of its own culture and history? Or, if not, has multiculturalism influenced the way you view people of other cultures and backgrounds? Explain.
7. Many of the essays in this section refer to the concept of "mainstream" society. Write an essay in which you identify and describe "mainstream

society." Who is part of it, and how do they belong to it? Who decides what is "mainstream" and what is not? Or, if you wish, you may argue that such an entity does not exist in modern America.

8. *Personal Narrative*: Write an essay about what is important to your own sense of identity. In addition to race, you should consider other factors, such as gender, age, religious background, education, etc. In your opinion, on what criteria do the people you meet judge you? How does it compare to your personal standards of identity?

GROUP PROJECTS

9. As a group, discuss how ethnic and racial differences divide and unite us as a nation. According to the report *Changing America* by the President's Initiative on Race, the gaps among races and ethnic groups in the areas of education, jobs, economic status, health, housing, and criminal justice are substantial. Access this report at *http://w3.access.gpo.gov/eop/ca/index.html*. Choose one subject area from its table of contents, and read through that chapter and charts. Then, summarize what you have learned about the differences among racial and ethnic groups, and discuss how you think these disparities affect our chances of creating a society in which all Americans can participate equally.

10. What does American life look like? Visit American 24/7 on MSN at *http://www.msnbc.com/news/910248.asp* and view the archive of photos submitted by people across the country on what it means to be American—in terms of family, work, play, faith, community, and country. Discuss as a group how you feel about the presentation, and what it says about what it means to be an American. If you could add photos to the presentation, which ones would you submit, and why?

A Population of Changing Dimensions

In 25 years, non-Hispanic whites will not be a majority in four states, including the two most populous ones, and in 60 years, they will make up barely half the U.S. population.

1960   **1995**   **2025**

Non-Hispanic whites as percentage of state population

☐ More than 75 percent   ▨ 50–75 percent   ■ Less than 50 percent

Sources: www.Washingtonpost.com

One in 10 U.S. Residents Was Born Abroad

In 1960, foreign-born Americans were mostly from Europe. Now most come from Asia and Latin America.

Foreign born, by country of origin

1960		1996	
Germany	990,000	Mexico	6,679,000
Canada	963,000	Philippines	1,164,000
Poland	748,000	China	801,000
Soviet Union	691,000	Cuba	772,000
Mexico	576,000	India	757,000
England	528,000	Vietnam	740,000
Ireland	339,000	El Salvador	701,000
Austria	305,000	Canada	650,000
Hungary	245,000	Korea	550,000
Czechoslovakia	228,000	Germany	523,000

Sources: www.Washingtonpost.com. Data from U.S. Census Bureau; World Bank. Foreign-born data for other nations from 1994.

A New Generation Is Leading the Way
Donna Jackson Nakazawa

We have long recognized that America has been a melting pot of many different peoples, but for much of our nation's history, races, as we define them, remained discretely separate in terms of marriage. Over the last two generations, however, social barriers associated with race have broken down significantly. Racial intermarriage has become common, bringing with it a whole new way to think about race. The children of interracial relationships are literally changing the face of America. But fitting in isn't always easy. These children are, in many respects, pioneers. In this article, Donna Jackson Nakazawa, the mother of two children from an interracial marriage, discusses some of the challenges interracial children face.

Donna Jackson Nakazawa is the author of *Does Anybody Else Look Like Me? A Parent's Guide to Raising Multiracial Children* (2003). She is from a western European background, while her husband is Japanese-American. Although they hoped to raise their son and daughter to be "color blind," they couldn't ignore the many comments made by both adults and children concerning their children. When her son was still small, he was asked if he spoke Chinese, and Nakazawa was assured that her daughter didn't "even look Asian." This article was printed in the July 6, 2003, issue of *Parade Magazine*.

CRITICAL THINKING   What is "race"? Why do we classify race at all? Will the children of interracial relationships change how we define race in the future?

1   As a white woman who had grown up in white America, nothing quite prepared me for the reactions that I and my Japanese-American husband encountered when we began our multiracial family a decade ago. The curious stares in the grocery store and the intrusive questions from strangers ("What are they?", "Wow, do you ever get used to the fact that they don't look anything like you?") took me by surprise.

2   Later, my son brought home his own playground stories. ("That's your mom? No way!", "What are you, anyway?") I began to wonder how my multiracial children would find their identities in our color-conscious world. And I decided to speak with as many young people of mixed race as I could, to discover what they had learned growing up in America.

"You Can't Be Both"

3   My children and I are part of a trend that is changing the face of our nation. According to the latest U.S. Census estimates, 4.5 million children now under 18 in this country are multiracial. The rate of interracial marriages is skyrocketing. In some areas, one in six babies born today is of two or more racial heritages—making multiracial youth one of the fastest-growing segments of our population.

4   Yet numbers don't necessarily signal acceptance. Most of the kids I spoke with said they struggled, often painfully, with their racial identity as they grew up. They

found that many people became uncomfortable when they couldn't easily categorize them into one of the five standard racial pigeonholes (Caucasian, African American, Native American, Asian or Latino).

5   "Kids would ask, 'Is that your mom?' or, 'Are you adopted?' " recalls Nicole Brown, 22, of Los Angeles, who is African American and Caucasian. "Even my closest friend—my 'pretend sister' in grade school—told me one day that I had to say whether I was black or white. She said that I couldn't be both. I had to choose."

6   Nicole, like most multiracial students, found junior high and high school even more challenging. That's when friends start dividing up along racial lines, most visibly at lunch in the cafeteria. "As a teenager, you really want to belong," says Nicole. "You need to have a group where you know you fit in. But I felt torn. I spent half my time, at school, playing one role—as part of that white world—and half my time, at home, hanging out with the black kids. I fit into each world I was in, but I never got to be all of myself at the same time."

7   Matt Kelley, 23, of Korean and Caucasian heritage, said he felt uncomfortable when forced to fill out school forms that provided no space for having a mixed-race background. Matt, who grew up in Seattle, either had to check "Other" or choose between Asian or White.

8   "Identity is based on how you see yourself and how others see you," he notes. "And when every form you fill out tells you that how you identify yourself is not an identity you can have, how can that not affect how you see yourself? You end up feeling, 'I'm a freak.' "

Choosing a Broader Identity

9 Many multiracial young people say they came into their own during the college years, as they began to broaden their own sense of identity in settings with a wide variety of people. Jamie Mihoko Doyle, 23, of Philadelphia, whose parents are Japanese and Irish, remembers the time she went to an Asian sorority party at the University of Texas and was greeted by whispers and stares. "Students at my university separated by rigid racial lines," she says. Instead, Jamie sought out a diverse group of friends. "They encompass just about every shade in the racial spectrum."

10   Students also noted that college offers an opportunity to explore a racial heritage that may not have been emphasized at home: They can join different ethnic organizations, take ethnic-studies classes or learn a foreign language that is in their family background. As a result, some students even change their primary racial identity.

11   "I was raised practically as a white person," says Tracy Scholl, 29, now a political fundraiser in Washington, D.C., who is of African American and German roots and grew up in the Philadelphia suburbs. "But in college I became an African American person. I became immersed in African American history courses. I learned the black kids' language—their slang—even though at first I couldn't understand a word of it." Scholl says her racial identity has continued to evolve. "Now I'm both," she says. "I want to have a multicultural life."

Feeling Whole

12 Indeed, mixed-race students on university campuses are increasingly forming their own student groups. Today, more than 25 colleges have multiracial student organizations—including Brown, the University of Pennsylvania, the University of Virginia, the University of Michigan, Smith, Wellesley and the University of Texas.

13   As a freshman at Wesleyan University, Matt Kelley founded *Mavin*, a magazine for multiracial young people. He says he chose the name because it means "one who understands" in Hebrew. "I wanted the magazine to be a forum where we could come together and talk about our experiences and be understood," he says.

14   Jamie Mihoko Doyle helped form Neapolitan, a multiracial group, at the University of Texas. "When I was growing up, I'd often have to explain myself to other people in parts," she says. "Neapolitan has allowed me to be all that I am—a whole person."

Becoming a Bridge

15 As I spoke with young people of mixed race in every part of the country, it became clear what an extraordinary group they are: self-aware, open-minded, optimistic— and eager to use their own experiences and insights to promote understanding and to work to close the racial gap in our country. I found their words and perspective both inspiring and comforting as I thought about the road that lay ahead for my own children. Multihued and multiethnic, these young men and women are leading the way toward a society in which race may simply become an interesting background note to a person's identity.

16   Bethany Bastinelli, 24, of Nazareth, Pa.—whose parents are Native American and Italian—works in the Fraternity and Sorority Affairs Office at Lehigh University. "I want to help incoming freshmen to understand that in college they're surrounded with people from all different backgrounds, and they can choose to erase the stereotypical tapes we all have in our minds," she says. "When they do have a racist thought, they can say to themselves, 'Hey, this is stupid. This isn't how I want to think.'"

17   Nicole Brown, a graduate of Columbia University who is now an executive at a film-production company in L.A., says: "Because of my multiracial background, I can connect with and make relationships with so many different types of people. It's something extra that I have that others don't have."

18   That perspective is echoed by Naomi Reed, 22, a math graduate student at Rice University in Texas, whose roots are African American and Jewish Caucasian: "Being multiracial has allowed me to see things from both sides of the color line," she says. "It opens my mind to differences of all types, so that I don't prejudge anything or anyone. That's something I wish we could all do. If I could have any wish, it would be to be able to go inside people's heads and flip the little switch that controls racial categorization and racism. I think people would be surprised at how many more genuine friends they would have if we all met each other in the dark." ◆

FREEWRITING ASSIGNMENT

Many college applications ask students to check off their race as part of the form. What box did you check off? Did you think about your choice? Why or why not?

CRITICAL READING

1. Nakazawa notes in her opening paragraph that she had grown up in "white America." What is "white America"? What does such a term imply? Explain.
2. Nakazawa cites several questions and comments that people would make concerning her interracial children. What is her reaction to such questions? Are people just curious? Is she missing an opportunity to educate people, or are they completely out of line in speaking about her children at all? Explain your view.
3. What unique challenges do children of interracial relationships face? Consider Nicole Brown's dilemma. Should she have to make such choices? Why or why not?
4. In paragraph 11, Tracy Scholl explains that she changed her "primary" racial identity after going to college. Why do we wish to classify others and ourselves into "primary" racial identities? What is the psychology behind such classifications? Explain.
5. Why do you think Jamie Mihoko Doyle named her student group "Neapolitan"? Why is it an appropriate name? Explain.
6. Nakazawa ends her article with a quote from Naomi Reed: "I think people would be surprised at how many more genuine friends they would have if we all met each other in the dark." Respond to this statement in your own words.

CRITICAL WRITING

7. *Exploratory Writing*: Do you think we will be more ethnically/racially melded as a nation in the next century? Write an essay postulating what race might mean one hundred years from now. What about two hundred years?
8. *Personal Narrative*: Examine your own racial and/or ethnic background. Write about how your racial/ethnic background has contributed (or has not contributed) to your perception of yourself and how you relate to others.
9. *Personal Narrative*: Many of the children of interracial relationships quoted in this article describe challenges they faced or decisions they had to make because of their unique circumstances. Write about a time when your own racial or ethnic background influenced a decision you made in your life. Explain in detail the internal and external forces influencing your decision.

GROUP PROJECTS

10. With your group, construct a demographic picture of the future. Try to conjecture what the face of the nation will look like after a century has passed. Are there still check boxes asking for one's race on job applications? Does affirmative action still exist? What about school clubs and organizations? Consider history as you formulate your vision for the future. Share your vision, and the reasoning behind it, with the rest of the class.

11. Print out a copy of the college common application form available at *http://app2.commonapp.org/Additional_Forms/common2004_app.pdf.* On page two or three of this application form, there is a box listing ethnic preference. With your group, make a list of the contributions that a particular ethnic group has made to mainstream American culture. Select one ethnic group only for this project. When did such contributions become mainstream? Cite specific examples in many areas, such as music, art, drama, dance, sports, television, food, literature, etc.

People Like Us
David Brooks

Acording to writer David Brooks, we all pay lip service to the melting pot, but we really prefer the congealing pot.

David Brooks is a columnist for the *New York Times*, a senior editor at the *Weekly Standard*, a contributing editor at *Newsweek* and the *Atlantic Monthly*, and a commentator on *The NewsHour with Jim Lehrer*. He is the author of *Bobos in Paradise: The New Upper Class and How They Got There* (2000). This essay was published in the September 2003 issue of the *Atlantic Monthly*.

CRITICAL THINKING When you were growing up, with whom did your parents socialize? Where did they live and what social functions were they likely to attend? Now that you are an adult, with whom do you chose to socialize? What is the demographic anatomy of your social group?

---

1 Maybe it's time to admit the obvious. We don't really care about diversity all that much in America, even though we talk about it a great deal. Maybe somewhere in this country there is a truly diverse neighborhood in which a black Pentecostal minister lives next to a white anti-globalization activist, who lives next to an Asian short-order cook, who lives next to a professional golfer, who lives next to a postmodern-literature professor and a cardiovascular surgeon. But I have never been to or heard of that

neighborhood. Instead, what I have seen all around the country is people making strenuous efforts to group themselves with people who are basically like themselves.

2   Human beings are capable of drawing amazingly subtle social distinctions and then shaping their lives around them. In the Washington, D.C., area Democratic lawyers tend to live in suburban Maryland, and Republican lawyers tend to live in suburban Virginia. If you asked a Democratic lawyer to move from her $750,000 house in Bethesda, Maryland, to a $750,000 house in Great Falls, Virginia, she'd look at you as if you had just asked her to buy a pickup truck with a gun rack and to shove chewing tobacco in her kid's mouth. In Manhattan the owner of a $3 million SoHo loft would feel out of place moving into a $3 million Fifth Avenue apartment. A West Hollywood interior decorator would feel dislocated if you asked him to move to Orange County. In Georgia, a barista from Athens would probably not fit in serving coffee in Americus.

3   It is a common complaint that every place is starting to look the same. But in the information age, the late writer James Chapin once told me, every place becomes more like itself. People are less often tied down to factories and mills, and they can search for places to live on the basis of cultural affinity. Once they find a town in which people share their values, they flock there, and reinforce whatever was distinctive about the town in the first place. Once Boulder, Colorado, became known as congenial to politically progressive mountain bikers, half the politically progressive mountain bikers in the country (it seems) moved there; they made the place so culturally pure that it has become practically a parody of itself.

4   But people love it. Make no mistake—we are increasing our happiness by segmenting off so rigorously. We are finding places where we are comfortable and where we feel we can flourish. But the choices we make toward that end lead to the very opposite of diversity. The United States might be a diverse nation when considered as a whole, but block by block and institution by institution it is a relatively homogeneous nation.

5   When we use the word "diversity" today we usually mean racial integration. But even here our good intentions seem to have run into the brick wall of human nature. Over the past generation reformers have tried heroically, and in many cases successfully, to end housing discrimination. But recent patterns aren't encouraging: according to an analysis of the 2000 census data, the 1990s saw only a slight increase in the racial integration of neighborhoods in the United States. The number of middle-class and upper-middle-class African American families is rising, but for whatever reasons—racism, psychological comfort—these families tend to congregate in predominantly black neighborhoods.

6   In fact, evidence suggests that some neighborhoods become more segregated over time. New suburbs in Arizona and Nevada, for example, start out reasonably well integrated. These neighborhoods don't yet have reputations, so people choose their houses for other, mostly economic reasons. But as neighborhoods age, they develop personalities (that's where the Asians live, and that's where the Hispanics live), and segmentation occurs. It could be that in a few years the new suburbs in the Southwest will be nearly as segregated as the established ones in the Northeast and the Midwest.

7   Even though race and ethnicity run deep in American society, we should in theory be able to find areas that are at least culturally diverse. But here, too, people show few signs of being truly interested in building diverse communities. If you run a retail company and you're thinking of opening new stores, you can choose among dozens of consulting firms that are quite effective at locating your potential customers. They can do this because people with similar tastes and preferences tend to congregate by ZIP code.

8   The most famous of these precision marketing firms is Claritas, which breaks down the U.S. population into sixty-two psycho-demographic clusters, based on such factors as how much money people make, what they like to read and watch, and what products they have bought in the past. For example, the "suburban sprawl" cluster is composed of young families making about $41,000 a year and living in fast-growing places such as Burnsville, Minnesota, and Bensalem, Pennsylvania. These people are almost twice as likely as other Americans to have three-way calling. They are two and a half times as likely to buy Light n' Lively Kid Yogurt. Members of the "towns & gowns" cluster are recent college graduates in places such as Berkeley, California, and Gainesville, Florida. They are big consumers of Dove Bars and *Saturday Night Live*. They tend to drive small foreign cars and to read *Rolling Stone* and *Scientific American*.

9   Looking through the market research, one can sometimes be amazed by how efficiently people cluster—and by how predictable we all are. If you wanted to sell imported wine, obviously you would have to find places where rich people live. But did you know that the sixteen counties with the greatest proportion of imported-wine drinkers are all in the same three metropolitan areas (New York, San Francisco, and Washington, D.C.)? If you tried to open a motor-home dealership in Montgomery County, Pennsylvania, you'd probably go broke, because people in this ring of the Philadelphia suburbs think RVs are kind of uncool. But if you traveled just a short way north, to Monroe County, Pennsylvania, you would find yourself in the fifth motor-home-friendliest county in America.

10   Geography is not the only way we find ourselves divided from people unlike us. Some of us watch Fox News, while others listen to NPR. Some like David Letterman, and others—typically in less urban neighborhoods—like Jay Leno. Some go to charismatic churches; some go to mainstream churches. Americans tend more and more often to marry people with education levels similar to their own, and to befriend people with backgrounds similar to their own.

11   My favorite illustration of this latter pattern comes from the first, non-controversial chapter of *The Bell Curve*. Think of your twelve closest friends, Richard J. Herrnstein and Charles Murray write. If you had chosen them randomly from the American population, the odds that half of your twelve closest friends would be college graduates would be six in a thousand. The odds that half of the twelve would have advanced degrees would be less than one in a million. Have any of your twelve closest friends graduated from Harvard, Stanford, Yale, Princeton, Caltech, MIT, Duke, Dartmouth, Cornell, Columbia, Chicago, or Brown? If you chose your friends randomly from the American population, the odds against your having four or more friends from those schools would be more than a billion to one.

12   Many of us live in absurdly unlikely groupings, because we have organized our lives that way.

13   It's striking that the institutions that talk the most about diversity often practice it the least. For example, no group of people sings the diversity anthem more frequently and fervently than administrators at just such elite universities. But elite universities are amazingly undiverse in their values, politics, and mores. Professors in particular are drawn from a rather narrow segment of the population. If faculties reflected the general population, 32 percent of professors would be registered Democrats and 31 percent would be registered Republicans. Forty percent would be evangelical Christians. But a recent study of several universities by the conservative Center for the Study of Popular Culture and the American Enterprise Institute found that roughly 90 percent of those professors in the arts and sciences who had registered with a political party had registered Democratic. Fifty-seven professors at Brown were found on the voter-registration rolls. Of those, fifty-four were Democrats. Of the forty-two professors in the English, history, sociology, and political-science departments, all were Democrats. The results at Harvard, Penn State, Maryland, and the University of California at Santa Barbara were similar to the results at Brown.

14   What we are looking at here is human nature. People want to be around others who are roughly like themselves. That's called community. It probably would be psychologically difficult for most Brown professors to share an office with someone who was pro-life, a member of the National Rifle Association, or an evangelical Christian. It's likely that hiring committees would subtly—even unconsciously—screen out any such people they encountered. Republicans and evangelical Christians have sensed that they are not welcome at places like Brown, so they don't even consider working there. In fact, any registered Republican who contemplates a career in academia these days is both a hero and a fool. So, in a semi-self-selective pattern, brainy people with generally liberal social mores flow to academia, and brainy people with generally conservative mores flow elsewhere.

15   The dream of diversity is like the dream of equality. Both are based on ideals we celebrate even as we undermine them daily. (How many times have you seen someone renounce a high-paying job or pull his child from an elite college on the grounds that these things are bad for equality?) On the one hand, the situation is appalling. It is appalling that Americans know so little about one another. It is appalling that many of us are so narrow-minded that we can't tolerate a few people with ideas significantly different from our own. It's appalling that evangelical Christians are practically absent from entire professions, such as academia, the media, and filmmaking. It's appalling that people should be content to cut themselves off from everyone unlike themselves.

16   The segmentation of society means that often we don't even have arguments across the political divide. Within their little validating communities, liberals and conservatives circulate half-truths about the supposed awfulness of the other side. These distortions are believed because it feels good to believe them.

17   On the other hand, there are limits to how diverse any community can or should be. I've come to think that it is not useful to try to hammer diversity into every neighborhood and institution in the United States. Sure, Augusta National should

probably admit women, and university sociology departments should probably hire a conservative or two. It would be nice if all neighborhoods had a good mixture of ethnicities. But human nature being what it is, most places and institutions are going to remain culturally homogeneous.

18 It's probably better to think about diverse lives, not diverse institutions. Human beings, if they are to live well, will have to move through a series of institutions and environments, which may be individually homogeneous but, taken together, will offer diverse experiences. It might also be a good idea to make national service a rite of passage for young people in this country: it would take them out of their narrow neighborhood segment and thrust them in with people unlike themselves. Finally, it's probably important for adults to get out of their own familiar circles. If you live in a coastal, socially liberal neighborhood, maybe you should take out a subscription to *The Door*, the evangelical humor magazine; or maybe you should visit Branson, Missouri. Maybe you should stop in at a megachurch. Sure, it would be superficial familiarity, but it beats the iron curtains that now separate the nation's various cultural zones.

19 Look around at your daily life. Are you really in touch with the broad diversity of American life? Do you care? ◆

FREEWRITING ASSIGNMENT ————————————

If you could live anywhere in the United States, where would you live and why?

CRITICAL READING

1. What does Brooks mean when he says, "Human beings are capable of drawing amazingly subtle social distinctions and then shaping their lives around them" (paragraph 2)? What examples does he give of such distinctions? Can you think of any "subtle distinctions" in your own life that influence where you live and with whom you choose to associate? Explain.
2. What is "cultural affinity"? How does it influence the social and cultural values of a particular area? How is it reinforced, and how can it break down? Explain.
3. When academics and politicians use the word "diversity," what do they mean? What types of diversity are identified by the author? What factors tend to influence people to find others like them?
4. How do marketers use psycho-demographic clusters to sell products? Explain.
5. What is ironic about many institutions that stress diversity (paragraph 13)? Why do they emphasize the need for diversity, and how do they fall short of actually practicing it? Explain.
6. Brooks states that he believes when we live with "people like us" we tend to be happier. Do you agree? If this is true, why do we tend to pay so much lip service to the idea of diversity, but actually fail to achieve it?

CRITICAL WRITING

7. *Personal Narrative*: Describe the neighborhood in which you currently live. How does it connect to the points Brooks makes in his essay? (A dormitory can be considered a "neighborhood.") Consider also in your narrative the reasons why you chose the college you now attend and the social groups with which you associate. Draw connections between your own "cultural cluster" and Brooks's observations on diversity in practice.

8. *Exploratory Writing*: In paragraph 11, Brooks discusses how the first chapter of *The Bell Curve* describes our tendency to collect with "people like us." Apply Herrnstein and Murray's hypothesis to your own life. Write down the names of your twelve closest friends and think about their individual qualities. Then consider them as a group. Write a short essay about what you discover about your own group and how it compares to the observations made in *The Bell Curve*. What do your results reveal about the multicultural face of the nation?

9. Write an essay in which you explain why you believe diversity is, or is not, important to the success of society. Is diversity more critical in certain situations but less important in others? Explain your point of view while also making references to the text.

GROUP PROJECTS

10. In paragraph 5, Brooks observes that many neighborhoods have failed to be truly racially integrated "for whatever reasons." With your group, interview a diverse group of students on where they grew up. Name the region, state, city or town, and even neighborhood, and ask them to describe its demographic (social, intellectual, professional, and economic) profile. Ask the people you interview for their impressions on why their family lived where they did and the cultural influences they experienced. Prepare a report on your findings. What did you discover about demographic clustering? What might it mean for diversity efforts in the next 20 years?

11. Brooks describes in paragraph 8 how some precision marketing firms, including Claritas, break down the population into marketing clusters. Visit the Claritas web site at *www.claritas.com* and find out more about where you live. What marketing cluster traits do they identify for your area? Based on the information you learned about cluster marketing on their web site, identify the best areas in which to sell the following products. Share your guesses with the class. What do marketing clusters tell us about the diversity of the American population?

  • Camel cigarettes
  • Absolut vodka
  • Dodge Dakota trucks
  • Comcast high-speed Internet
  • Apple i-pods

(continued on next page)

- Ann Taylor clothing
- Lugz boots
- Chanel handbags
- Ikea furniture
- Nike golf clubs

When Fair Is Foul

Suzanne Fields

In this essay, Suzanne Fields explains why Thanksgiving is the original multicultural holiday. Overall, most Americans love to celebrate this day dedicated to reflecting with gratitude for the blessings we enjoy. Despite political, social, religious, and intergenerational differences, families still gather for their traditional observance of Thanksgiving. When we celebrate this day, says Fields, we put our differences aside and remember what we have to be thankful for.

Suzanne Fields writes a twice-weekly column for the *Washington Times* and is syndicated nationally by *Tribune Media Services*. She is also the author of *Like Father, Like Daughter: How Father Shapes the Woman His Daughter Becomes* (1983), and *How the Cookie Crumbles* (1996). She is a former editor for *Vogue* magazine and editor of *Innovations*, a magazine for mental health professionals, psychiatrists, psychologists, and social workers. This article first appeared in the November 29, 2002, edition of *Townhall.com*

CRITICAL THINKING   Think about how you celebrate Thanksgiving, (or, if you do not celebrate this American holiday, how you observe a similar day of reflection and thanks.) What is the "meaning" of this day? What does it commemorate?

1   On Thanksgiving, fair is fowl and fowl is fair. Unless you're a vegetarian, of course. The fourth Thursday in November is our original multicultural holiday, commemorating the feast for Indians and colonists celebrating their first harvest together. It's a holiday that unites the spiritual with the material, faith and food, the sacred and secular. Family values crisscross generations.

2   One Web site calls for declaring Thanksgiving a "Day of National Mourning for Native Americans," but the holiday is generally enjoyed without politically correct impositions. Animal-rights advocates may protest the stuffed bird and organic fanatics can insist that the turkey be "free-range" (or, at least, at home on the range), but most of us merely want to gather together to ask the Lord's blessings without arguing whether the mention of God or the president's Thanksgiving proclamation run against the separation of church and state.

3   Gender politics are not so polarized as they used to be. Either a man or a woman can comfortably cook or carve. Not even the transgender advocate will find an argument unless dressing the turkey is misunderstood as a political act, or Uncle Harry arrives in drag. Environmentalists may rail against anyone who drives up in a gas-guzzling SUV, but they're likely to be outnumbered if the families arrive from the suburbs or Thanksgiving is celebrated in corrector-than-thou California (where everybody drives either an SUV or a Lexus, or a Lexus SUV).

4   But conversations around the Thanksgiving table have a way of becoming contentious no matter how much relatives and friends love each other. Different generations examine the nature of the beast through different lenses.

5   The hip grandma who loves Eminem won't win points from the teenybopper no matter how hard she tries. Granny can't possibly dig the rapper's lyrics with authentic cool. If she's faking a fondness for Eminem, that means either the days of the superstar are numbered or Social Security has taken on new meaning. An aging boomer who lacks the long view may want to be trusted past 50, but "the graduate" as played by Dustin Hoffman is already cruising through his sixth decade and Mrs. Robinson is not merely an "older woman" but a senior citizen.

6   So what should we talk about as we pass the cranberries and mashed sweet potatoes with or without the marshmallows? Certain subjects can provoke robust debate, but won't necessarily divide or stereotype generations.

7   The old golf geezers at the table railing against women demanding to join the Augusta National Golf Club, for example, will find allies from young post-feminists who think the elite golf club is an anachronism and could care less whether the club admits one or two rich women. A *New York Times* editorial asks Tiger Woods to carry the burden for feminists and refuse to play there, but we can be pretty sure that the *New York Times* will cover the Masters if there is one. Let the opinions fly. No one's likely to get indigestion over this one.

8   Has *The Sopranos* become too violent? Dismembering one of its members was gory indeed, but what better way to bring home the Sixth Commandment? Even a don knows that thou shalt not kill. The HBO hit has become a melodramatic morality tale as Tony Soprano, the mob boss, gets his own hands bloody and his sensitivity toward "the family" becomes increasingly ironic. He even says goodbye to his therapist. Nietzsche would understand that psychotherapy is dead. The sins of the godfather have turned Christopher, "the hope of the next generation," into a heroin addict. Murder will out.

9   Republicans at the table may feel smug over Election 2002, but the margins are a little slim for open gloating. The Democrats who last year reveled in cracks about George Bush being Dumbo no longer have that card to play, so maybe there can be an earnest discussion over what to do if/when the arms inspectors verify that Saddam Hussein has weapons of mass destruction. We're not talking about Ho Chi Minh here.

10   A Thanksgiving e-mail that floated into my mailbox offers homilies for this holiday that all of us can appreciate:

11   "I am thankful for the wife who says it's hot dogs tonight because she is home with me, not with someone else; for the husband who is on the sofa who is being a

couch potato because he is home with me and not out at the bars; for the teenager who is complaining about doing dishes because that means she is at home, not on the streets; for the taxes I pay, because it means that I am employed; and for the mess to clean after a party because it means that I have been surrounded by friends."

12   Happy Thanksgiving. Even if you're doing the dishes. ◆

FREEWRITING ASSIGNMENT

What does Thanksgiving mean to you? Does it mean travel headaches and hassle? Family? Food? Prayer? Explain.

CRITICAL READING

1. In what ways is Thanksgiving a "multicultural" holiday? In what ways is it a national one? Explain.
2. In paragraph 2, Fields comments that the holiday of Thanksgiving is "generally enjoyed without politically correct impositions." What are the impositions to which she alludes? Why does Fields call objections to Thanksgiving "politically correct impositions"? What does she imply by phrasing her sentence this way? Explain.
3. What assumptions does Fields make concerning her audience for this piece? Identify areas of her essay that reveal who she thinks her audience is likely to be. What is their probable social, political, or ethnic background? Age? Explain.
4. What are the generational aspects of Thanksgiving? Can you identify with any of the ones Fields identifies?
5. Evaluate the topics for dinner discussion Fields describes. If any of these topics were brought up during a Thanksgiving dinner you attended, what would your own personal reaction, if any, be to them? Explain.

CRITICAL WRITING

6. *Research and Opinion*: Fields alludes to the "Day of National Mourning for Native Americans" in her second paragraph. Research this observance, starting with information posted at the Pilgrim Hall museum at *http://www.pilgrimhall.org/daymourn.htm.* Respond to Frank James's points in his speech delivered at Plymouth Rock in 1970 (see *http://home.earthlink.net/~uainendom/wmsuta.htm*) with a short speech of your own expressing your viewpoints on the issues he raised.
7. *Exploratory Writing*: Fields calls Thanksgiving the "original multicultural holiday." Write a paper in which you explore this idea. In what ways is Thanksgiving a multicultural holiday for Americans?

GROUP PROJECTS

8. Many Americans learned about the historical aspects of Thanksgiving in grade school. As a group, discuss your memories of what you learned about Thanksgiving in elementary school, and what social, cultural, and national messages you were taught. How did what you learned then influence your perception of the holiday? What should children learn about Thanksgiving? Should they be taught alternative viewpoints, or focus on national celebration?

9. Read the essay "As American as Pumpkin Pie" by Karin Goldstein, curator of original collections at Plimoth Plantation Museum at *http:// www.plimoth.org/learn/history/thanksgiving/pumpkinpie.asp.* As a group, discuss the "nationalization" of the holiday, why it was introduced, and by whom. Does anything Goldstein discuss surprise you? How would you introduce the concept of Thanksgiving Day to a new immigrant to this country? Explain.

"Please Ask Me 'Who,' Not 'What' I Am"
Jordan Lite

In this piece, Jordan Lite, a young woman who describes herself as "unclassifiable," asks why casual acquaintances seem to think it is permissible to ask about her ethnic background. As she explains, her ethnicity isn't obvious, and Lite wonders why it should matter to people she's just met. The following article appeared in the July 16, 2001, issue of *Newsweek.*

CRITICAL THINKING If America truly is the great "melting pot," why are we so keen on knowing the details of the specific "ingredients"?

1 I've been thinking a lot about that "Seinfeld" episode where Elaine is dating this guy and it's driving her nuts because she doesn't know "what" he is. They ultimately discover that neither is exotic enough for the other and they're so disappointed that they stop seeing each other.

2   It's the story of my life these days. Each new guy I meet, it seems, is fascinated by my ostensible failure to fall into an obvious racial category. Last year we could opt out of defining ourselves to the Census Bureau, but that option doesn't seem to have carried over into real life. I've lost track of how many flirty men have asked me what I am.

3   The first time, I was in Iowa and snobbishly dismissed the inquiry as rural provincialism. Then it happened again while I was on a date in San Francisco, a city that prides itself on its enlightenment.

4   Isn't it rude to ask "what" someone is when you've just met? Common courtesy would suggest so. But many people seem to feel uncomfortable if they can't immediately determine a new person's racial or ethnic background.

5   Of course, I've mused over "what" a stranger might be. But it's never occurred to me that asking "What are you?" of someone I've just met would elicit anything particularly revealing about him. I ask questions, but not that one.

6   So when a potential boyfriend asks me "What are you?" I feel like he wants to instantly categorize me. If he'd only let the answer come out naturally, he'd get a much better sense of what I'm about.

7   Perhaps acknowledging explicitly that race and ethnicity play a role in determining who we are is just being honest. But I'm not sure that such directness is always well intended. After I grouchily retorted "What do you mean, 'What am I?'" to one rather bewildered date, he told me his dad was African American and his mom Japanese, and that he ruminated all the time over how to reconcile such disparate influences. I realized then that he believed my being "different" would magically confer upon me an understanding of what it was like to be like him.

8   If you're looking for your soulmate, maybe it's only natural to want a person who has shared your experience. But for some people, "What are you?" is just a line. "You're exotic-looking," a man at a party explained when I asked him why he wanted to know. In retrospect, I think he probably meant his remark as a compliment. As a Hispanic friend pointed out, when all things Latin became the new craze, it's trendy to be exotic. But if someone wants to get to know me, I wish he would at least pretend it's not because of my looks.

9   Still, this guy's willingness to discuss my discomfort was eye-opening. He told me that he was part Korean, part white. Growing up in the Pacific Northwest, he wasn't the only biracial kid on the block. One could acknowledge race, he said, and still be casual about it.

10   Although I spent my childhood in a town lauded for its racial diversity, discussing race doesn't often feel easy to me. Maybe my Japanese classmate in the first grade could snack on seaweed without being hassled, but I can readily recall being 11 years old and watching a local TV news report about a pack of white boys who beat, then chased a terrified black teen onto a highway, where he was struck by a car and killed. The violence on TV silenced me. It seemed better not to risk asking questions that might offend.

11   Years after we graduated from our private high school, one of my good friends told me how out of place she felt as one of the few black students. Her guardedness had kept me from probing; but there's a part of me that wonders if talking with her then about her unease at school would have made me more comfortable now when people ask me about my place in the world.

12   But as it is, I resent being pressed to explain myself upfront, as if telling a prospective date my ethnicity eliminates his need to participate in a real conversation with me. "What are you?" I am asked, but the background check he's conducting won't show whether we share real interests that would bring us together in a genuine give-and-take.

13   In a way, I enjoy being unclassifiable. Though there are people who try to peg me to a particular ethnic stereotype, I like to think others take my ambiguous ap-

pearance as an opportunity to focus on who I am as a person. So I haven't figured out why being myself should kill any chance of a relationship. Not long ago, a man asked me about my background when we met for a drink.

14   "Just a Jewish girl from New Jersey," I said truthfully.

15   I never heard from him again. ◆

FREEWRITING ASSIGNMENT

The author comments that the men she dates keep trying to find out "what" she is because she looks "exotic." What do you think she means? What is an "exotic" look? Against what standard is it compared?

CRITICAL READING

1. Lite notes that although the Census Bureau no longer requires revealing one's racial background, this latitude is often not afforded in social interaction. Is it important for you to know someone's ethnic background? Is it important to your identity to share your own background with others? Explain.

2. In paragraph 4, Lite asks, "Isn't it rude to ask 'what' someone is when you've just met?" Answer her question, presenting your own perspective.

3. How did the author's experiences as a child influence her "silence"? Is her reaction justifiable considering the circumstances? Is it safer to guard your ethnic background? Explain.

4. How do people react to Lite's hesitancy to answer their questions regarding her ethnicity? How does she interpret their reactions?

5. One reason why Lite resents being asked "what" she is relates to her concern that people want to "instantly categorize" her. How do we categorize people based on "what" they are? How do you think the authors of the preceding section would respond to her concerns?

CRITICAL WRITING

6. *Personal Narrative*: Jordan Lite provides a personal perspective on the ways people identify themselves and the ways others try to identify them. Write an essay about what is important to your own sense of identity. In addition to race, consider other factors such as gender, age, religious background, and education. In your opinion, on what criteria do the people you meet judge you? How does it compare to your personal standards of identity?

7. *Exploratory Writing*: Why is it so important to Americans to know "what" people are? Write an exploratory essay on this subject. If you wish, interview a few people for their perspective and comment in your essay on their response to this question.

GROUP PROJECT

8. Lite wonders why it is so important that the people she meets know "what" she is. As a nation of peoples from many countries and cultures, it is a question many Americans want to ask. Each member of the group should answer this question in their own words, "introducing" themselves to the rest of the group. Then, as a group, discuss what we "do" with this information. How does the answer define us to others? What are others likely to think, and why?

Ending Poem

Aurora Levins Morales

I am what I am.
A child of the Americas.
A light-skinned mestiza of the Caribbean.
A child of many diaspora, born into this continent at a crossroads.
I am Puerto Rican. I am U.S. American.
I am New York Manhattan and the Bronx.
A mountain-born, country-bred, homegrown jíbara child,
up from the shtetl, a California Puerto Rican Jew.
A product of the New York ghettos I have never known.
I am an immigrant
and the daughter and granddaughter of immigrants.
We didn't know our forbears' names with a certainty.
They aren't written anywhere.
First names only, or mija, negra, ne, honey, sugar, dear.

I come from the dirt where the cane was grown.
My people didn't go to dinner parties. They weren't invited.
I am caribeña, island grown.
Spanish is in my flesh, ripples from my tongue, lodges in my hips,
the language of garlic and mangoes.
Boricua. As Boricuas come from the isle or Manhattan.
I am of latinoamerica, rooted in the history of my continent.
I speak from that body. Just brown and pink and full of drums inside.

I am not African.
Africa waters the roots of my tree, but I cannot return.

I am not *Taína*.
I am a late leaf of that ancient tree,
and my roots reach into the soil of two Americas.
Taíno is in me, but there is no way back.

I am not European, though I have dreamt of those cities.
Each plate is different,
wood, clay, papier mâché, metal, basketry, a leaf, a coconut shell.
Europe lives in me but I have no home there.

The table has a cloth woven by one, dyed by another,
embroidered by another still.
I am a child of many mothers.
They have kept it all going
All the civilizations erected on their backs.
All the dinner parties given with their labor

We are new.
They gave us life, kept us going,
brought us to where we are.
Born at a crossroads.
Come, lay that dishcloth down. Eat, dear, eat.
History made us.
We will not eat ourselves up inside anymore.

And we are whole. ◆

VIEWPOINTS

▶ **How to Be a Patriot**
Sam Smith

▶ **What Is Patriotism?**
Charley Reese

Patriotism means different things to different people. For some, it is love of country and national pride. For others, it means serving in the military, making sacrifices, or devoting oneself to public service. It can mean pledging allegiance to the American flag, and reflecting on what the words of the pledge really mean. Or it could be conscientious objection to government policies that seem unfair or unjust. The next two essays take a look at patriotism and what it means to be a patriot in America today.

Sam Smith is editor of the *Progressive Review* and author of several books, including *Why Bother? Getting a Life in a Locked Down Land* (2001), and *Sam Smith's Great American Political Repair Manual* (1997). This essay was first published in the Spring 2003 issue of the quarterly journal, *Yes!*

Conservative Charley Reese is a writer and retired columnist for the *Orlando Sentinel*. Reese joined the *Orlando Sentinel* in 1971 as an assistant metro editor and was later promoted to an assistant to the publisher, then columnist and editorial board member. He still writes occasional columns, which can be viewed on his web site, *http://reese.king-online.com,* where this article was first posted on June 5, 2003.

CRITICAL
THINKING What does patriotism mean to you? Can you define it? Has your perception
of patriotism changed since September 11?

How to Be a Patriot
Sam Smith

1   Before September 11, patriotism wasn't doing all that well. You might have noticed
it at the ballpark, as the "Star Spangled Banner" turned into a novelty number and
the guy next to you continued munching on his hot dog as you stood at attention.
Less obvious, however, was that in the media and the nation's talk it just didn't
seem to matter that much.

2   Yet now, we speak of patriotism again. Why did so many need the Viagra of violence to demonstrate love for their land? Where was this love when NAFTA and
the World Trade Organization (WTO) were being forced down our throats? Where
was it as corporations raped our waters and forests and infected our crops? Where
was it when the young took to the streets to defend old American values against a
new world order?

3   It feels odd to this Vietnam-era vet, whose great-great-great grandfather fought
with his four brothers in the Revolution and whose parents both lost brothers in
World War I, to be lectured on patriotism by those who until the morning of September 11 had evinced so little interest in loyalty to any larger entity than themselves and their careers.

4   To be sure, the rise in patriotic self-branding is not entirely a spontaneous reaction
to the tragedy. It has also been the result of intense government and corporate propaganda capitalizing on these events and on a long-cultivated shift by which Americans
have been reduced to being spectators and consumers, rather than actual citizens, of
their government. We have been taught to cheer rather than act, to wear logos rather
than think, and to purchase rather than control and influence. At a moment calling for
the most rational vision and thought, our leaders—from the White House to CNN—
have instead chosen to turn a disaster into a national policy Super Bowl in which our
only assignment as Americans is to choose the right team and cheer it on.

5   This is a dirty business that does a huge disservice to the country the flag-wavers
purport to honor. Remember that our government, in the months before September
2001, not only assured us that our future lay in giving up our national independence
for the greater good of a corporate-dominated global culture, but arrested young people who dared suggest this was not right, and ridiculed anyone who spoke with feeling of the need to protect America's sovereignty on behalf of its workers, its environment, and its civil liberties. And, until recently, some of the same multinationals that
now bedizen their ads with the flag regarded America mainly as a mail drop.

6   No assault on American sovereignty has been more successful than that carried
out in recent years by corporate globalization, through such mechanisms as NAFTA
and the WTO. Victory, which over the course of our history, had proved impossible

to the British, Mexicans, Confederates, Spanish, Germans, and Japanese, was being accomplished by a handful of lawyers armed only with cell phones, fax machines, and the support of politicians willing to trade their country's nationhood for another campaign contribution. The new agreements not only permit unsafe, polluting foreign trucks on our highways, push down wages for American workers, and ban state and local boycotts against dictatorial governments, but the U.S. Congress was even denied a chance to change them.

7   Today, we justly pledge allegiance to the republic for which America stands, but we do not have to pledge allegiance to the empire or failed policies for which America is now suffering. There are few finer, albeit painful, expressions of loyalty than to tell a friend, a spouse, a child, or a parent that what they are doing may be dangerous or wrong. If our country is about to run into the street without looking, there is absolutely nothing disloyal about crying, "Stop!"

8   True patriotism is an act of love, not of hate. It is debate not salutes, contributions not cheers, participation not prohibition, service not revenge. It's the product of vastly different people with remarkably similar dreams, for it is not a primeval past or cultural similarity that binds us but rather a shared present and future.

9   We need always beware of patriotism's dark side. Like other isms, patriotism is easily driven more by hatred of the other than by positive love of one's own. This is why the KKK and various movements of extreme American nationalism have typically recruited from among society's weakest and most insecure. Further, almost every time our government has sought to decide who qualified as a good American, it added shame to our history.

10   Thus the current hysteria belongs in the same dismal catalog as slavery, the disfranchisement of women and non-property owners, the suspension of habeas corpus during the Civil War, the notorious Palmer raids of the early 20th century, and McCarthyism. It shares absurdity with the FBI's labeling of those fighting in the Spanish Civil War as "premature anti-fascists" and it shares dishonor with the arrest in 1951 of an 82-year-old intellectual because the State Department considered him the "agent of a foreign power," a man better known today for far sounder reasons: W.E.B. Du Bois.

11   But the madness can be far worse than individual injury, for not only is patriotism the last refuge of the scoundrel, it is also the first tool of the tyrant. And while prejudice and hatred have been endemic to the human story, only in the last century have nations developed the technocratic ability to carry them out on a mass scale. Combine primitive patriotic agitprop and the modern technocratic state and you have the essence of fascism, the former drugging the psyche and the latter creating a closed-loop logic impervious to moral inquiry. Was it hard to kill so many Jews? Adolph Eichmann was asked at his trial. No, he said, "To tell you the truth, it was easy. Our language made it easy." It was the language of the technocratic manager, "office talk" they called it.

12   Today, America's discussions are also dominated by manipulative appeals to patriotism on the one hand and the technocratic office talk on the other. Nightly on TV, the military and anti-terrorism experts speak antiseptically of deadly or repressive techniques. Even though this is a struggle framed by religion, moral voices are absent. Even though the solutions often trade the certainty of less liberty for illusions of safety, those speaking on behalf of democracy—our purported cause after all—appear only as an afterthought.

13   One observer has counted six amendments in the Bill of Rights that are currently under attack in the name of freedom. Increased surveillance, searches without
warrants, arrest without habeas corpus, secret and military trials, censorship, restrictions on public information are but a few of the ways the Bush administration has
blasphemously, in the name of patriotism, altered and diminished the nature of
America, its constitution, and its citizens.

14   As Americans, we do not have to accept this. Progressives in particular must
understand that there is nothing to be gained by ducking for cover as so many did
during the McCarthy era. Adopt instead the attitude of Paul Porter of Arnold &
Porter, the only big Washington law firm that represented leftists during those dismal days. Called before a House Committee and asked if it were true that his firm
had represented Communists, Porter replied, "Yes sir, how can I help you?" We
must meet the bullies and charlatans with both resolution and ridicule.

15   Meanwhile, each of us can express our love for America in our own way. The
Green may do so through care of our environment. The libertarian or anarchist may
do so by preserving our faith in liberty. The progressive or socialist may do it by insisting that America's promise of social justice be fulfilled. The conservative may
do it by preserving the good. The deeply religious may do it through personal witness. The oppressed may do it through protest that brings us closer to our ideals. The
cop may do it through upholding the laws of the land—including the most important
one, the Constitution. The artist may paint it, the musician sing about it, the teacher
teach it.

16   And if others don't do it your way, that's America, too. As the cartoonist Walt
Kelly said during the McCarthy era, "We must defend the basic right of every
American to make a damn fool of themselves."

17   At best, our patriotism is still a work in progress, one that, in the end, is defined
by deeds and not words. We are not just fans in the stadium; we are each on the
field. ◆

What Is Patriotism?
Charley Reese

1   What with all the flag-waving, pro-war and anti-war rallies, Memorial Day obser-
vances, and so forth, it seems to be a good time to consider exactly what patriotism
is and what it isn't.

2   The best definition I've run across is "love of the land and its people." Most of
us who live in an urban environment might not have the same feelings about land
that our more agrarian ancestors felt, but we still become attached to places. Familiarity in this case breeds affection. Who doesn't feel affection for the areas where
they were born, grew up and lived?

3   A patriotic love of land, of course, means our own nation—that land within the
borders of the United States. The land immediately on the other side of the bor-

ders—say, in Canada—might look just like our land, but it isn't. I feel more at home on the New York side of the Niagara River than I do on the Canadian side, and I am a Southerner. But Southerner or Yankee or Westerner, we are all Americans. Despite the similarities, the United States and Canada are distinctly different countries with different forms of government, different cultures and different traditions.

4   What makes us unique as a people is certainly not race or ethnicity or religion. We're a hodgepodge of those things. What makes us unique is that we do not take an oath to a politician or to a political party or even to a government. Our oaths in this country are to the Constitution, that written charter of government and basic rights.

5   Teddy Roosevelt, one of the few geniuses to occupy the White House, once said that an American citizen should stand by a public official only so long as and to the extent that the public official stands by the Constitution. This is entirely consistent with America's founding philosophy. If we have to choose between a politician and the Constitution, we must choose the Constitution. To support a politician who doesn't support the Constitution is to be disloyal to the very thing that makes America, America.

6   That being the case, it would be a good idea for all Americans to read their Constitution. It's not a lawyer's document. It was written in plain English by some very intelligent men and was intended for public consumption. There are some ambiguities that could lead to honest disagreement about the meaning, but they are mostly on minor points. Americans should also read *The Federalist papers*, a collection of newspaper articles written during the constitutional ratification debate.

7   There is no room at all for the ridiculous interpretations some judges and others have made of the Constitution. It was intended to be strictly construed, not surrealistically construed, and if changes are needed, they should be amended by the process the Constitution provides. All Americans should object strenuously to "amendment by interpretation." That is as anti-American, as anti-democratic as you can get.

8   Too many Americans, it seems to me, associate patriotism exclusively with war. A constitutional war in defense of our land and our people naturally deserves support. The last war that fits that description ended in 1945. Since then, more than 100,000 Americans have died in battle, but not in defense of our land and our people. Since we are a free people, presumably able to control our government, that is our fault. We must learn not to be so susceptible to demagoguery and propaganda. We were never intended to be a people who would shout "Heil Bush" (or Clinton, Nixon, Reagan or anybody else).

9   The greatest dangers facing us today cannot be solved militarily, yet these civilian concerns are being de-emphasized by unnecessary wars against Third World countries. We had better concentrate on rebuilding the United States rather than Iraq or Afghanistan, and we had better worry more about the health of our people than sending our money to Africa or Asia.

10   Love and concern for our land and our people is the patriotic duty of every American. How about supporting all of the American people for a change instead of just those in uniform? Let us not throw away the very things so many Americans died to protect for some cockamamie scheme to run the whole world. ◆

FREEWRITING ASSIGNMENT

Freewrite a response to one of the titles in this section: "How to Be a Patriot," or "What Is Patriotism?" responding with your own views.

CRITICAL READING

1. In his opening paragraphs, Smith notes that before September 11, many Americans didn't care about patriotism, even to the point of neglecting to stand at baseball games for the national anthem. How did September 11 change this attitude? Did it change yours? Was the feeling sustained? Explain.

2. In paragraph 3, Smith cites his own, and his family's, military background. Why do you think he does this? Explain.

3. What are the authors' opinions of the U.S. Constitution? What positions do they take? If the two of them were in a room together discussing the Constitution, on what points do you think they would be likely to agree or disagree? Explain.

4. What, according to Smith, is the "dark side" of patriotism? How can it be "the first tool of the tyrant"?

5. Smith notes in paragraph 12 that "manipulative appeals to patriotism" are dominating many discussions in the political arena. What does he mean? Can you think of any examples?

6. Smith makes frequent references to the McCarthy era. What was the McCarthy era? Why does he refer to it so much in his essay? In what ways could this period in American history be connected to the present? Explain.

7. What, according to Reese, makes Americans "unique"? Explain.

8. Evaluate Reese's comments in paragraph 7. How does he address the audience? What assumptions does he make? What about his tone?

9. In paragraph 8, Reese states, "We were never intended to be a people who would shout 'Heil Bush' . . ." To what is he referring here? What impact does such a statement make on you as a reader? On his argument? Explain.

CRITICAL WRITING

10. *Exploratory Writing*: Both Reese and Smith are concerned that the Constitution is threatened by lose interpretation or reinterpretation. Review the Constitution at the National Archives web site *http://www.archives.gov/ national_archives_experience/constitution.html.* Do you believe in a strict interpretation of this document? Write an essay presenting your position.

11. Do you consider yourself "patriotic" to your country? How do you demonstrate that patriotism? Why? How are your feelings for your homeland connected to your feelings of patriotism? Or are they? Explain.

12. *Research and Analysis*: Research the background of the McCarthy era and write a short paper drawing parallels between this period in American history and modern political and legal policies designed to protect the U.S. in times of crisis and/or war.

13. Go to *http://www.whitman.edu/commencement/schlesinger03.html* to read Arthur Schlesinger, Jr.'s 2003 commencement speech to graduates of Whitman Collage. In what areas would Reese and Smith agree with Schlesinger, and on what points may they differ? How might the opinions expressed by these three men be different now that some presidential policies have changed.

GROUP PROJECTS

14. As Americans, how do we balance the need for security with our need for freedom? Does one need supercede the other? Discuss as a group the balance between the two, considering the Patriot Act and the protections afforded by the Constitution.
15. Discuss Smith's position on American foreign policy as it relates to war and commerce. As a group, present your own viewpoint on this issue. Where do you stand? Why? Have you expressed this viewpoint in words or actions? Are student groups on your campus expressing any viewpoints? Poll students for their opinions on America's military and international trade policies. As part of a broader class discussion, summarize the results of your poll and its implications.

 How to Turn More Immigrants into Americans
Tamar Jacoby

In 1970, almost two-thirds of all foreigners living in the United States became naturalized citizens. Today, less than half of all immigrants do. Why are fewer immigrants becoming citizens? In this essay, Tamar Jacoby discusses some of the challenges today's immigrants face and poses some solutions to help them become full Americans. Jacoby is a senior fellow at the Manhattan Institute who writes extensively on immigration, citizenship, ethnicity, and race. Her most recent book, a collection of essays, is *Reinventing the Melting Pot* (2004). This article was first printed in the July 3, 2002, edition of the *New York Sun*.

1 The federal marshal overseeing the swearing-in ceremony kept calling them "the citizens"—as in "The citizens should file in first," "Guests and family members, take a seat among the citizens." And though they weren't citizens yet, there was no mistaking how proud this made them.

2 Virtually no one among the 300 or so immigrants being sworn in as new Americans at the Daniel P. Moynihan federal courthouse last Friday was taking it casually. You could tell from the hushed tone in the wood-paneled courtroom. (Someone sitting near me said it felt a little like church.) You could tell from the way they stood up—one man in a turban and a "God Bless America" T-shirt, several women

in traditional African garb, most looking like ordinary, working New Yorkers—to recite the Oath of Allegiance. But most of all, you could tell from the way the citizens talked about what they were going through.

3   "I did it because of the rights," said Sara Medina, 40, a Dominican woman who works in a juvenile detention center. "In my country, we don't get those kinds of freedoms." "I realized how much better it is here," explained Shirley Barth, 29, also from the Dominican Republic, who makes a living cleaning hotel rooms. "Over there, in my country, I could never get what I have here." "I did it to vote," Jose Cappellan, 26, offered in such halting English it was hard to believe him, until he started listing the local officials he was getting ready to vote for.

4   Even those who gave more practical reasons—because it's easier to travel on a U.S. passport, or because they fear an anti-immigrant backlash in the wake of 9/11—couldn't end the conversation without waxing a little patriotic. Virtually no one mentioned the more tangible benefits that dubious Americans sometimes suspect are at work: access to welfare benefits, or the right to bring additional relatives into the country. (Indeed, many heaped scorn on those who did it merely for "convenience.") And even those who couldn't articulate what they felt radiated a kind of quiet commitment: "I just knew it was the right time for me," said one Thai woman who'd been living in the U.S. for 30 years. "I knew it was time to make it official."

5   Of course, not all immigrants feel this way. In fact, despite a surge in applications since 9/11, those who do are a minority, growing smaller all the time. In 1970, nearly two-thirds of the foreigners living in the U.S. had become citizens. By the 2000 census, the figure had dropped to 38%—with only 28% of Latin Americans and 20% of Mexicans doing it. Not surprisingly, this has alarmed many Americans, and it is one of the top reasons anti-immigrant groups cite for restricting the number we allow into the country. After all, the argument goes, if they're not going to assimilate, why do we want them here?

6   In truth, there are many reasons why the foreign-born don't take the trouble to naturalize. It can be a daunting process, especially if your English is less than perfect. There are several tests: in civics and history, and in English. The INS bureaucracy, the one-to-two-year processing time, the $310 fee, even the 10-page form can seem off-putting. And many immigrants, often struggling to get by on two or even three jobs, say they don't feel they need it. "We were fine here," an older couple explained last week. "We had green cards, we worked, we didn't have any problems— and many people already treated us as if we were citizens."

7   For many, it seems, becoming naturalized is like getting married when you've already been living together. The question is what the U.S. could or should be doing to encourage it—an increasingly pressing question in a nation where a tenth of the population is foreign-born.

8   Some people—and some groups—are more likely to take the plunge than others. Where you come from clearly has something to do with it, with those who feel that it wouldn't be hard to go home far less inclined to make a full commitment here. (That's surely one reason why the rate among Asians is more than double the figure for Central Americans.) The more income you make, the more educated you are and—perhaps most important—the longer you've been in the U.S. also increase your chances. (Only 13% of those who arrived since 1990 have gotten around to it – compared to 70% of those who've been here 20 years or more.)

9   All of which might suggest we should just let nature take its course—since most people eventually make the leap anyway. Maybe so, but in a country increasingly fragmented by race and ethnicity, we ought to be doing all we can to encourage a sense of cohesion—and conversations with immigrants suggest that many would welcome more encouragement.

10   Certainly, that was how the nation reacted the last time immigration soared and naturalization rates sank. The Americanization movement of the early 20th century has a bad name these days. But in fact, it aided millions of immigrants, particularly in its early years, before World War I. And both its successes and its failures hold important lessons for today.

11   A broad array of Americans and American institutions participated: from pro-immigrant do-gooders to unabashed racialists who thought the newcomers inferior, from settlement houses and ethnic organizations to business titans like Henry Ford. Almost all the nation's big-city governments were involved. So were the federal bureaucracy and the public school system. Together, this vast, informal public-private network offered a broad array of services—most importantly, English and civics classes.

12   The movement eventually went awry, becoming harshly coercive, even xenophobic. And today, as in the past, some people want to try to force the transition: making English the official language or mandating classes, as some European countries do. (In Germany, for example, new immigrants may soon be required to undergo an astonishing 600 hours of German instruction.) But at its peak—its most effective, early years—the Americanization movement knew better. This was the United States, after all—the land of freedom and opportunity. Far more effective, the early Americanizers understood, to persuade and seduce, even while making classes available to all who wanted them.

13   The movement did this in a variety of ways. Some were showy: big July 4th celebrations, for example, touting the benefits and status that came with citizenship. Others were more prosaic: the Bureau of Naturalization sent the name and address of every immigrant who applied for citizenship to a local institution that could provide English classes. The government published a civics textbook; factory-owners gave time off for learning. Perhaps most important, we as a nation left no doubt: we expected new immigrants to make the leap eventually, becoming full Americans.

14   There's no reason why this shouldn't be possible again today, even in multicultural America. The last thing we need is a new layer of federal bureaucracy—and the government alone is hardly up to the challenge. (New York State currently spends some $2.5 million a year to encourage naturalization. Even so, according to a study by the New York Immigration Coalition, with more than a million immigrants in New York City who would like to take English classes, there are only 50,000 slots available.) But surely the government could do more to encourage others—employers, faith-based organizations, community groups—to provide services, using tax incentives and other inducements to leverage private money.

15   At the very least, the INS could make the naturalization process more efficient. Not easier or less demanding: new citizens are adamant—they don't want that. (On the contrary, out of more than a dozen interviewed last week, only one wanted to make the English test easier, and most thought it should be harder.) But the INS ought to follow through on its promise to reduce the processing time to less than six months. (In New York, the average has been cut to 16 months—an improvement, but hardly enough.)

16   Finally—and arguably most useful—the mainstream can make clear that becoming a citizen is the expected norm. Why not make it a mantra—reinforced by public-service advertising, immigrant-community peer pressure and bully-pulpit politicians, ethnic and otherwise—that every new American be naturalized within 15 years of arriving in the U.S.?

17   The mistakes of the 1920s remind us: you can't strong-arm this. You can't coerce commitment of the kind on display at the Moynihan courthouse last week. But as immigrants themselves often make clear, it helps if the nation expects and demands it. "It only makes sense," one new citizen explained last week. "We're newcomers, and sometimes scared or shy. Why doesn't the country set some standards?" ◆

CRITICAL THINKING

1. Why, according to Jacoby, are fewer immigrants becoming U.S. citizens? Why don't they "bother" to naturalize, and what do they risk by not doing so?
2. What is the author's opinion about naturalization? Why does she feel it is important? Do you agree? Explain.
3. Jacoby suggests that every immigrant to the United States be required to be naturalized within 15 years or face deportation. Do you think this is a good idea? Will it help promote assimilation? What benefits and challenges would such a law create?

RESEARCH PROJECTS

4. In paragraph 15, Jacoby asserts that the INS should make the naturalization process more efficient. Visit the INS web site and research the naturalization process at *http://uscis.gov/graphics/services/natz*. Take the Naturalization Self-Test (under "Eligibility and Testing") and see how you do. Based on your research at the INS web site, describe some of the challenges an immigrant might face in trying to navigate the naturalization process.
5. Research the Americanization movement of the early twentieth century. What agenda did it promote? Who ran it? Why did it go wrong, and how has it influenced public opinion on Americanization programs today? A good place to start your research is at *www.encyclopedia.com* under the keyword "Americanization."

Additional essay topics, writing assignments, research guidelines, and readings for this chapter can be found online at **www.ablongman.com/goshgarian**.

Credits

Image Credits

Text Credits

Index
of **Authors** and **Titles**